The Edinburgh Companion to Anthony Trollope

Edinburgh Companions to Literature and the Humanities

https://edinburghuniversitypress.com/series/ecl

THE EDINBURGH COMPANION TO ANTHONY TROLLOPE

EDITED BY FREDERIK VAN DAM, DAVID SKILTON AND ORTWIN DE GRAEF

EDINBURGH
University Press

Edinburgh University Press is one of the leading university presses in the UK. We publish academic books and journals in our selected subject areas across the humanities and social sciences, combining cutting-edge scholarship with high editorial and production values to produce academic works of lasting importance. For more information visit our website: edinburghuniversitypress.com

Edinburgh University Press Ltd
13 Infirmary Street
Edinburgh, EH1 1LT

First published in hardback by 2019
Edinburgh University Press

Typeset in 10/12 Adobe Sabon by
IDSUK (DataConnection) Ltd

A CIP record for this book is available from the British Library

ISBN 978 1 4744 2440 0 (hardback)
ISBN 978 1 3995 4686 7 (paperback)
ISBN 978 1 4744 2441 7 (webready PDF)
ISBN 978 1 4744 2442 4 (epub)

CONTENTS

Acknowledgements

Unable to pay his debts, Anthony Trollope's father moved his family to Belgium in 1834 to avoid arrest. Although Trollope was soon rescued from his exile by a job offer from the General Post Office in London, the Belgian experience probably remained a bad memory. Yet, by a curious twist of things, he owes the present tribute to his lasting relevance in good measure to a Belgian priest. In 2004, Father Paul Druwé decided to leave his earthly belongings to KU Leuven with the express purpose of furthering the public appreciation and scholarly investigation of the works of Anthony Trollope. We think we have put this generous bequest to good use, first by supporting master's theses and doctoral research on Trollope, then by commissioning a graphic novel adaptation of a Trollope novel (Simon Grennan's *Dispossession*), which was subsequently launched at the Trollope Bicentennial Conference in Leuven in 2015. It is on the basis of this conference that the present *Companion* came about, and we are confident that Paul Druwé would have been proud of it. This book would never have seen the light of day without the kind support of Jackie Jones and Michelle Houston and their team at Edinburgh University Press. We thank Carlijn Cober for her assiduous assistance in the final stages of the editing, and Nigel Starck for going beyond the call of duty in supplying obscure references in an hour of need.

Notes on Contributors

Robert D. Aguirre is Professor of English and Dean of the College of Arts and Letters at James Madison University. He writes about the literary and cultural dimensions of the wider transatlantic world, and is the author of *Informal Empire: Mexico and Central America in Victorian Culture* (2005) and *Mobility and Modernity: Panama in the Nineteenth-Century Anglo American Imagination* (2017).

Steven Amarnick is Professor of English at Kingsborough Community College, City University of New York. He is curator of 'Anthony Trollope: The Art of Modesty', at the Fales Library, New York University, and the editor of *The Duke's Children: The Complete Text*, published by The Folio Society (2015), Everyman's Library (2017), and Oxford University Press's World's Classics series (forthcoming in 2020).

Helen Blythe is a professor of nineteenth-century British literature and director of graduate studies in English at New Mexico Highlands University. She is the author of *The Victorian Colonial Romance with the Antipodes* (2014) and several articles on the works of Anthony Trollope. Her current book project investigates Trollope's last experiments with narrative form, repetition, voice and property, and she is working on a second study of late-Victorian imperial prose romances set in the Americas and the Pacific.

John Bowen is Professor of Nineteenth-Century Literature at the University of York and a Fellow of the English Association. His publications include *Other Dickens: Pickwick to Chuzzlewit* (2000) and *Palgrave Advances in Charles Dickens Studies* (co-edited with Robert L. Patten, 2005) as well as editions of Anthony Trollope's *Phineas Redux* (2011) and *Barchester Towers* (2014). He currently serves as President of the Dickens Fellowship and is editing *Bleak House* for Norton and writing *Reading Charles Dickens* for Cambridge University Press.

Luca Caddia obtained his doctorate in English literature from La Sapienza University of Rome with a dissertation on the relationship between character and career in Anthony Trollope's Palliser Novels (2008). As a scholar of Victorian visual culture he was the recipient of a fellowship at the Yale Center for British Art and a Paul Mellon Grant (both 2010), after which he became the Assistant Curator at the Keats-Shelley House in Rome, a position he has held since 2011. He has also published a number of translations of Trollope's shorter fiction into Italian.

Claire Connolly is Professor of Modern English at University College Cork, a Member of the Royal Irish Academy and a Fellow of the Learned Society of Wales as well as Parnell Fellow in Irish Studies at Magdalene College Cambridge (2018–19). She is author of *A Cultural History of the Irish Novel, 1790–1829* (2011; awarded the Donald J. Murphy Prize by the American Conference for Irish Studies). With Marjorie Howes (Boston College) she is currently Co-General Editor of *Irish Literature in Transition*, a new six-volume series for Cambridge University Press.

Ortwin de Graef is Professor of English Literature at the University of Leuven (Belgium), Vice-Dean of Research at the Faculty of Arts, and director of the Paul Druwé Fund for Trollope Studies. He is the author of two books on Paul de Man and has widely published on Romantic and post-Romantic writing and literary theory. His current research focuses on aesthetic ideologies of sympathy and the State in the post-Romantic condition, on trauma and representations of extremity, and on materialist challenges to models of cultural transmission.

Patrick Fessenbecker is Professor at Bilkent Üniversitesi and postdoctoral researcher at Syddansk Universitet. He received his doctorate from The Johns Hopkins University in 2014. His current book project, entitled *The Ideas in Stories*, uses the reflections on moral deliberation and agency in a series of nineteenth-century British novels as the primary examples for a broader argument about the value intellectual content can give to a work of literary art. He works more generally on issues in philosophy and literature, especially the philosophy of literature.

Kate Flint is Provost Professor of Art History and English at the University of Southern California. She has published *The Woman Reader, 1837–1914* (1993), *The Victorians and The Visual Imagination* (2000), *The Transatlantic Indian 1776–1930* (2008) and *Flash! Photography, Writing, and Surprising Illumination* (2017); edited *The Cambridge History of Victorian Literature* (2012); and written widely on Victorian and modernist fiction, Victorian and early twentieth-century painting and photography, and cultural history.

Sophie Gilmartin is Reader in Nineteenth-Century Literature at Royal Holloway, University of London. She is the author of *Ancestry and Narrative in Nineteenth-Century British Literature* (1999) and, with Rod Mengham, of *Thomas Hardy's Shorter Fiction: A Critical Study* (2007). She has edited Trollope's *The Last Chronicle of Barset* for Penguin Classics (2002). Her main research interests and publications are in the areas of nineteenth-century literature, painting, maritime studies and the Arctic. She is currently writing a book on Victorian women navigators, *The Winter Widows: Cape Horn Voyages, 1856*.

Lauren M. E. Goodlad is Professor of English at Rutgers University. She is the author of books including *The Victorian Geopolitical Aesthetic: Realism, Sovereignty, and Transnational Experience* (2015) and *Victorian Literature and the Victorian State: Character and Governance in a Liberal Society* (2003) as well as the editor or co-editor of special issues such as *Worlding Realisms* (a 2016 special issue of *Novel*), *The Ends of History* (a 2013 special issue of *Victorian Studies*) and *Victorian Internationalisms* (a 2007 special issue of *RaVoN*). Her new book project is tentatively titled 'The Long Afterlives of Nineteenth-Century Genres' and she is simultaneously working on a second project centred on the country house and the world system.

Nancy Henry is the Nancy Moore Goslee Professor of English at the University of Tennessee. She is the author most recently of *Women, Literature and Finance in Victorian Britain: Cultures of Investment* (2018). She is also the author of *George Eliot: A Critical Biography* (2012) and co-editor with George Levine of the new *Cambridge Companion to George Eliot* (2019).

Claire Jarvis is the author of *Exquisite Masochism: Sex, Marriage, and the Novel Form*. She is working on a book about Barbara Pym, Elizabeth Goudge and Dorothy L. Sayers.

Tamara Ketabgian is Professor of English at Beloit College. Her book, *The Lives of Machines: The Industrial Imaginary in Victorian Literature and Culture* (2011), was shortlisted for the annual book prize of the British Society for Literature and Science. She is currently working on a book entitled *Contrivance: Faith, Persuasion, and Technology in Victorian Scientific and Literary Culture*, which explores fantasies of technological design and spiritual intelligence from Charles Babbage to the present.

John McCourt is Professor of English at the University of Macerata. He co-founded the Trieste Joyce School in 1997 and has been running it ever since. He is the author of many books and articles on James Joyce and on nineteenth- and twentieth-century Irish literature including *The Years of Bloom: Joyce in Trieste 1904–1920* (2000). In 2009 his edited collection, *James Joyce in Context*, was published by Cambridge University Press and was followed by *Roll Away the Reel World: James Joyce and Cinema*, with Cork University Press (2010). A Trustee of the International James Joyce Foundation, he is also a member of the academic board of the Yeats Summer school. In 2015 he published *Writing the Frontier: Anthony Trollope between Britain and Ireland*.

Richard Menke, Associate Professor of English at the University of Georgia, is the author of *Telegraphic Realism: Victorian Fiction and Other Information Systems* (2008) and *Literature, Print Culture, and Media Technologies, 1880–1900: Many Inventions* (Cambridge University Press, forthcoming). His essays on nineteenth-century literature, science and media history have appeared in *ELH*, *PMLA*, *Critical Inquiry*, *The Henry James Review*, *Victorian Studies*, *English Language Notes*, *The Victorian Periodicals Review* and elsewhere.

Francis O'Gorman is Saintsbury Professor of English Literature at the University of Edinburgh. Recent publications include editions of Anthony Trollope's *The Way We Live Now* (2016) and *Orley Farm* (2018), and the literary criticism of Edward Thomas (2017).

Clare Pettitt is Professor of Nineteenth Century Literature and Culture at King's College London. She works on the literary and cultural history of the nineteenth century, and is author of *Patent Inventions: Intellectual Property and the Victorian Novel* (2004). *Dr Livingstone, I Presume: Missionaries, Journalists, Explorers and Empire* was published in 2007. She is currently writing a series of three books. *Distant Contemporaries: Seriality, Scale and Print, 1815–1848* will be out by the end of 2019, and *1848: Revolutionary Seriality in Britain, Europe and America* in 2020. The third volume will be entitled *The Digital Switch: Compression and Transmission, 1848–1918*.

Boris M. Proskurnin is Head of the World Literature and Culture Department and Dean of the Modern Languages and Literatures Faculty at Perm State University, Russian Federation. He is the author of more than 200 publications on issues in English, Russian and French Literature from the nineteenth century to the present. His monographs include *Anthony Trollope's Palliser Novels and the English Political Novel* (1993); *English Realists: Dickens, Thackeray, Charlotte Brontë* (1994); *Western European Realistic Prose of the Nineteenth Century* (1998; repr. 2002, 2004, 2008); *The English Political Novel of the Nineteenth Century: Genesis and Development* (2000); *George Eliot's* The Mill on the Floss: *Context, Aesthetics, Poetics* (2004); *Ideas of the Time and Later Novels of George Eliot* (2005); *Foreign Poetry, 1830–1870: Heine, Baudelaire, Whitman* (2010). He is Co-director of the English-Russian Seminar 'Contemporary British Literature in Russian Universities', funded by the 'Oxford-Russia Fund' (from 2005 until the present).

Anat Rosenberg is a cultural legal historian of British capitalism. She is Associate Professor of Law at the Radzyner Law School, the Interdisciplinary Center (IDC) Israel, and a visitor (2017–19) at the Faculty of History and Wolfson College, the University of Cambridge, and the Institute of Advanced Legal Studies, the University of London. She is the author of *Liberalizing Contracts: Nineteenth-Century Promises Through Literature, Law and History* (2018) and has written about Victorian law and literature, liberalism and consumption.

David Skilton, Emeritus Professor in English at Cardiff University, was educated at the Universities of Cambridge and Copenhagen. He has written extensively on Victorian fiction and the Victorian literary system, and on the art and literature of London. As well as editing numerous nineteenth-century novels, he was General Editor of the Trollope Society edition of the collected novels of Anthony Trollope.

Helen Small is Merton Professor of English language and literature at Oxford University. She is the author of *The Long Life* (2007, awarded the Truman Capote Award for Literary Criticism) and the editor of *The Public Intellectual* (2002). Her most recent book is *The Value of the Humanities* (2013), a critical work providing clarification of the strengths and weaknesses of each of the major claims for the Humanities.

Frederik Van Dam is Assistant Professor of European Literature at Radboud University Nijmegen. He is the author of *Anthony Trollope's Late Style: Victorian Liberalism and Literary Form* (Edinburgh University Press, 2016) and has recently edited a special issue on literature and economics in the *European Journal of English Studies* (2017). He is currently working on a literary history of diplomacy from the Congress of Vienna up to the present.

Lydia Wevers is Emeritus Professor at Victoria University of Wellington. A leading literary historian and critic, her books include *Country of Writing: Travel Writing About New Zealand 1809–1900* (2002), *On Reading* (2004) and *Reading on the Farm: Victorian Fiction and the Colonial World* (2010). She is currently engaged on a large Marsden-funded project on the history of reading in New Zealand and Australia, the first part of which is about Dickens and Trollope.

Xiaolan Zuo is Associate Professor of English at the School of Foreign Languages, Shanghai Jiaotong University, China. She is the author of *Trollope: His Later Novels and the Changing Society* (2009), the first full-length critical work on Trollope so far in China. She is currently undertaking a study of fictional ambivalence in Trollope and George Eliot as cultural strategy, focusing on the Victorian Woman Question from the perspective of cultural materialism.

INTRODUCTION

Frederik Van Dam, David Skilton and Ortwin de Graef

SINCE THE TURN of the century, Anthony Trollope has become a central figure in the critical understanding of Victorian literature: his work has proved itself to be a powerful lens for the study of discursive regimes and cultural practices of the long nineteenth century. The ambition of this volume is to test that lens to the full by rereading Trollope's work in new ways. Bringing together eminent Victorianists with various specialties, this is a collection of innovative and challenging perspectives: it presents new ways of understanding this supposedly 'safe' Victorian novelist in his third century, with a particular attention to Trollope's use of language, not least in his manipulation of the reader's responses.

Trollope's emergence as one of the central authors in Victorian studies has coincided with, and perhaps benefited from, the emergence of a new critical climate. Since the turn of the century, after more than three decades of mining literary texts for their hidden depths, scholars have begun to feel that 'critique', as Bruno Latour alleges, has 'run out of steam'.[1] Instead of reading texts 'symptomatically' through the lens of the so-called hermeneutics of suspicion, critics have gained a renewed appreciation for the visible and the concrete. This development within current scholarship is apparent in the affiliation with new disciplinary partners (such as political philosophy) and a host of new methodologies: new formalism, new aestheticism, surface reading, strategic presentism and post-historicism, among many others.[2] Though the means by which scholars within these movements proceed often differ widely, they seem to have the same end in view: they aim to foster an engagement with aspects of literary culture which are easily overlooked as utterly ordinary, but which nonetheless carry important meanings. Their interest lies not so much in the ideological ramifications of the literary text, as in the more tangible aspects of its composition, be these formal or contextual. It is unclear, at this point, if these developments will come to be seen as a distinct 'turn'. According to Joseph North, for one, the new methodologies that we have just listed continue the assumptions behind the historicist and contextualist paradigm that has dominated literary studies since the late 1970s.[3] Even so, this volume hopes to offer a modest contribution to reorient the discipline in general and the study of Anthony Trollope's work in particular. By and large, the contributors to this collection do not treat Anthony Trollope's novels as manifestations of political discourse or social theory; instead they highlight dimensions that have hitherto received only scant attention, and by doing so they aim to cultivate the aesthetic capabilities of Trollope's twenty-first-century readers. The innovative potential in the volume thus lies in the themes it uncovers and the methodologies it displays, more than in its corpus. Our rationale was to present a new Trollope not by looking specifically at neglected works nor by consolidating the state of the art, but by bringing Trollope's work into contact with cutting-edge debates, while tapping into the potential offered by the achievements of the past.

Indeed, the publication of other guides to Trollope in the very recent past has been a decisive factor in the composition of this *Edinburgh Companion*. Our aim was to complement and not to duplicate these guides. Perhaps the best way to capture the features of the present volume, then, is to compare it to the two most recent companions. *The Cambridge Companion to Anthony Trollope* (2010) aims to introduce Trollope's work to undergraduates.[4] It opens with two biographical essays and a survey of Trollope's major works: the Barsetshire novels, the Palliser novels, the later novels and his short fiction. The essays which follow are more argumentative, probing into some of Trollope's thematic concerns: the sensation novel, queerness, the hobbledehoy, masculinity, vulgarity, the law. A third group of essays stresses Trollope's global interests, containing essays on Ireland, the Antipodes, travel and America. The reader is thus given a substantial and lucid overview of Trollope's work, with many insights into Trollope's capacious mind. The pattern of many of the essays and their ambition to cover the whole of Trollope's extensive oeuvre privilege breadth over depth: after the introduction of the topic at hand, chapters generally move to synopses of relevant writings, followed by two or more illustrative readings. *The Edinburgh Companion to Anthony Trollope* does not have the ambition to cover the whole of Trollope's output. Instead, most essays in this collection revolve around issues which at first sight appear of mere passing significance, but which when examined reveal major critical issues for the fiction as a whole.

The *Routledge Research Companion to Anthony Trollope* (2016) offers a very different complement.[5] This collection presents the graduate student and the researcher with a comprehensive overview of the state of the art. It is summative of work to date, giving scholars a solid basis for planning new research projects on the basis of generally accepted common knowledge. Although older arguments are updated and new directions are indicated, the historicist and contextualist paradigm of the last three decades of the twentieth century is markedly present. *The Edinburgh Companion to Anthony Trollope* is more speculative and tentative, creating the lines of investigation yet to be pursued. It refers to and incorporates existing scholarship, but mostly insofar as it points the way to new readings and interpretations. This approach is reflected in the profile of its contributors, who are on the whole eminent Victorianists rather than dedicated Trollopians. Bringing their experience in the study of other authors to bear on Trollope, they open up new lines of investigation. This approach has also resulted in a focus on Trollope's works from the 1870s, which may be taken as a sign of the direction that Trollope studies will be taking in the years to come. Although the many contributions in this volume range across Trollope's work, it appears likely that in the future critics will focus on major texts that have been neglected in favour of the works from the 1860s.

In short, by involving the reader in new readings of Trollope's work, *The Edinburgh Companion to Anthony Trollope* hopes to be a statement of where Trollope studies and Victorian studies might well be the day after tomorrow. We have identified four such lines of investigation and have accordingly divided the essays into four constellations: style, circulation, media networks and economics. As a caveat, we should highlight that this exercise in grouping the essays in such a fashion is an artificial one:

arguably, most essays could easily be brought under other headings. We hope, however, that by assembling the essays together in this fashion we create more interactions between essays within the various different clusters, as well as between the different clusters themselves, thus maximising the *Edinburgh Companion*'s critical purchase. In the remainder of this introduction, we provide a map of this expanse of ideas.

Style

Trollope has often been regarded as a skilled observer of a solid, completely understandable world, which he reproduces, in the words of Nathaniel Hawthorne, as though 'solid, substantial, written on strength of beef and through inspiration of ale'.[6] Trollope cannot resist citing this judgement in *An Autobiography* (1883), to the confusion of multitudes of subsequent commentators. It has been difficult to think about Trollope's writing in terms of common indices of formal power, like precision, complexity and thoughtful revision. Even criticism focussing on Trollope's form often includes caveats about his laxity, his writing's rapidity, and his novels' tendency to include plot holes and vanished characters: 'an incident is ever preferable to an event', as Henry James put it.[7] As a result, the sophistication of Trollope's style has not been awarded the attention it deserves.

Claire Jarvis suggests that Trollope's novels' formal experiments have been read as formal failures because of Trollope's interest in hesitant narration, marked by the narrator's outspoken ambivalence about characters' flaws and failures. This investment can be made clearer if we notice his use of qualifying language as a barrier between narrator and character. By tracking Trollope's use of 'almost' over the course of the Palliser series, she argues that his novels are marked by a hesitancy to enter fully into his characters' minds, in distinction to other nineteenth-century realists. By remaining 'almost' insightful (and as a result only 'almost' in his narrated world), Trollope manages his narrator's nearness to his characters with a model of insight that is asymptotically, rather than proximately, related to narrated thought.

Patrick Fessenbecker examines this hesitant narration from the point of view of moral philosophy. In depicting moral agency, he points out, Trollope's narrator tends to portray the act of believing as itself admitting of moral evaluation: in Trollope's fiction, to believe something is sometimes all on its own a moral success or failure. When describing his characters as having 'taught [themselves] to think' one thing or another, Trollope's narrator marks the ways in which characters are responsible for what they believe, thus rejecting a simpler morality that would limit moral evaluation purely to physical action. At some moments, teaching oneself to think something is part of a crippling self-deception that licenses selfishness; at other moments, it is part of a recognition of one's own weakness, and an integral part of morally praiseworthy self-fashioning.

While Fessenbecker highlights the cognitive aspects of Trollope's narrative method, Sophie Gilmartin draws our attention to the more physical aspects. In her view, free indirect discourse creates a slightly removed, indirect intimacy that underlines the relationship between the physical environment, the body, mind and language. So frequently in Trollope's work, an emotionally revealing free indirect discourse is preceded by seemingly mundane and material details; a character's complex interiority is discovered in the midst of tables, chairs, coffee cups and 'tea things', and a preoccupation with how to navigate these objects. Trollope's fiction involves his characters not only in precise geographical locations (fictional Barchester, the Suffolk seaside, London, the Australian outback) but also in very precise physical spaces within these places: the corner of a room, the fireside, on a rug or balcony, by a mantelpiece or in a stairwell. If others occupy the room, they must be navigated around as well, but they are often brushed against, and skirts and sleeves touch. Because it is so specific about physical details such as these, Trollope's writing can reveal much about the mental pictures that the reader entertains when reading a novel's description of scene.

Just as Sophie Gilmartin's essay echoes the principles of phenomenology, so Helen Blythe's chapter plays with a deconstructive approach. Using as her point of departure Henry James's dismissal of Trollope's late fiction as repetitive, she investigates the way in which Trollope's readers are conscripted: in *An Old Man's Love* (1884), one of the overlooked tales written shortly before he died, Trollope obsessively repeats and alludes to characters and plot-devices from earlier novels, Latin tags, and information from his travel works, as well as the motif of the diamond that is so central *The Eustace Diamonds* (1873). As a result, Trollope's readers are nudged to look for a unity that is actually shaped by their desires and memories.

David Skilton explores readerly conscription in yet another way, examining the function of the figure of the reader in *An Autobiography* while situating this text in the context of contemporary advice literature. This generic context highlights the many rhetorical tricks that Trollope pulls in order to bring his readers alongside and convince them of his professional ethic, a concern that resonates with Patrick Fessenbecker's essay. At the same time, Skilton's observations about Trollope's style can be traced back to the pioneering work of Hugh Sykes Davies in the 1960s. A particularly intriguing topic in this regard is the distinct rhythm of deliberation in Trollope's writing, a Trollopian cadence, which Davies identified and which demands further investigation.[8] Remarkably, Davies's work has not been properly picked up to date, even though technological advances in the field of computational linguistics have made this increasingly feasible, as Claire Jarvis's essay illustrates.

Lauren M. E. Goodlad's contribution looks at genre as well, but from a transtemporal and transnational perspective, in which longitude becomes a narrative dimension. Comparing Victorian novel chronicles to contemporary television series, she detects an underlying similarity, or what one might call a structure of feeling, which is tied to their economic moment: both genres flourished at a time of abstraction, a time when the conditions of global financial speculation were creating a drive for art forms that refused closure and instead kept on growing.

Circulation

The essays in the second constellation bring scholarship to bear on various aspects of Trollope's literary afterlife. The three of us have attempted to make a modest contribution to this afterlife by commissioning graphic novelist Simon Grennan to create an adaptation of Trollope's novel *John Caldigate* (1879). The graphic novel was conceived in two ways: the challenge was to create a new, complete work of visual literature while also introducing readers to the logic of adaptation. One might fruitfully see *Dispossession: A Novel of Few Words* (2016) as a critique of Trollope's original novel. Grennan's graphic novel derives an enigmatic satisfaction in more accurately representing *John*

Caldigate's representation of emigration to Australia than *John Caldigate* itself, in interrogating the novel's plot, and in replacing Trollope's narrative voice, with its attention to internal focalisation, with a distinct visual style that keeps readers at a distance as they 'waltz' through the scene. By developing these historically informed forms of equivalence, *Dispossesion* inquires into the truth buried within Trollope's novel and painstakingly unveils what is missing.[9] Importantly, however, it performs this critical work in a manner dramatically different from the 'symptomatic' or 'suspicious' academic critique we mentioned earlier, and this can be taken quite literally: instead of argumentatively exposing Trollope's putative blind spots, *Dispossession* effectively dramatises the haunting presence of what Trollope left out within the world he has left us.

Trollope himself was not opposed to criticising his contemporaries in such a creative fashion. Critics have long noted Trollope's definition of himself in opposition to Dickens, yet the significance of this for the seemingly minor holiday stories has not been fully appreciated, as Steven Amarnick indicates. Focusing especially on *Harry Heathcote of Gangoil* (1874), Amarnick argues that Trollope found in the genre of the Christmas tale a means with which to define himself against the Dickensian aesthetic. Even in the late part of his career, Trollope continued to nurture his gripe with Dickens to maintain the vibrancy of his own work.

The following two chapters move to the twentieth century. In his reading of 'From Trollope's Journal' (1965), an 'anti-Eisenhower' poem by Elizabeth Bishop, John Bowen shows how Bishop takes a fragment of Trollope's monumental oeuvre to create a distinctly un-monumental work that is profoundly sceptical about men and their monuments. 'From Trollope's Journal' draws directly both from Trollope's letters and *North America* (1862), cutting down Trollope's expansive prose to a succinct dramatic monologue in the form of a double sonnet, voiced by Trollope. It is a poem about disease, both its transmission and its cutting out; about death and infection in war; and about statues and monumental art in Washington, through an international, cross-gendered and cross-century voicing.

Continuing this cluster's exploration of the aesthetics of transmission and creation, Luca Caddia examines the representation of Trollope as a character in works of fiction from the second half of the twentieth century. Novels from Philip Roth's *The Counterlife* (1986) to Alan Hollinghurst's *The Line of Beauty* (2004) present the contemporary reader with a gallery of Trollope's images, in which Caddia detects a concern with issues of solitude and unfitness. At the same time, Trollope's presence also serves as a focal point for self-reflexive debates about the canonical status of contemporary novels.

The following three chapters look at Trollope's reception from a world-historical point of view. Boris M. Proskurnin and Xiaolan Zuo provide insiders' views of Trollope's afterlife in Russia and China, respectively. They provide a detailed overview and periodisation of the various stages of Trollope's reception in both literary criticism and creative writing. Proskurnin thus sketches the history behind (and following) the well-known fact of Lev Tolstoy's interest in Trollope, while Zuo brings a completely novel voice to current debates about Trollope's novels as forms of world literature. Both also pay attention to the commercial, social and political factors that propelled the way in which Trollope was read. These two chapters reveal and describe only the tip of the iceberg, and we hope that they will pave the way for new research and collaboration. Moving even further towards the East, Lydia Wevers's chapter examines Trollope's contemporary reception in New Zealand. By the time Trollope visited New Zealand in 1872, crowds flocked to hear and see him. Tiny local papers all over the country reported his progress from the minute he left Southampton for Australia. Every speech was reported, every sighting noted, and Trollope duly rewarded his audience by publishing *Australia and New Zealand* in 1873. Wevers discusses the traces of Trollope's readers and readership that survive in the print culture of this remote colonial society, and shows how reading may transfer itself into a shared public domain. By examining how Trollope's fiction was read outside England, these chapters prepare the way for what might be the first satisfying geography of a single oeuvre.

Media Networks

The Victorians witnessed a revolution in communications as great as our own, including steam navigation to Australia and the trans-Atlantic telegraph. The chapters in this cluster examine Trollope's interest in various communication technologies. Presiding over many of the following chapters is Bruno Latour, whose actor-network theory has done much in making the cultural impact of technological developments the object of critical scrutiny. Together, these essays highlight how Trollope's experience as a Post Office official and a political journalist made the media networks a formally constitutive element in his fiction, which has previously barely been recognised.

Helen Small examines the figure of the confidential agent as a repository of some of Trollope's most interesting thinking (in his later years) about the nature and the proper limits of political responsibility. Drawing on local records in the East Riding Archive relating to Trollope's failed candidacy for the seat of Beverley in the 1868 parliamentary election, and the subsequent petition and official inquiry into the borough's corruption, she explores the centrality of the managing agent to Trollope's brief and unhappy experience of practical politics, before taking a wider view of how he and certain other mid-Victorian writers came to conceive of the agent, politically, philosophically and dramatically, as indicative of deep, perhaps ineradicable, flaws within a democratic system of election and representative government.

Clare Pettitt explores Trollope's 'ordinariness' both in terms of the media rhythms of the late nineteenth century, and in terms of an emergent liberal consensus in the 1870s, arguing that the two are, in fact, structurally connected. She argues that liberalism performed a distributive function which resists conglomeration or massification by working to separate and relate the increasing numbers of visible and knowable subjects in the modern social world. An extending media network supported the work of connectivity without completion, which came to define the experience of living in a global world in the 1870s. Trollope's literary texts are perhaps best understood as part of this network. If liberalism is always future-directed, open-ended and multi-nodal, so Trollope's literary world also resists closure and replaces judgement with juxtaposition. The chapter suggests that Trollope's work is structured by a model of seriality which has already become not just an important literary form, but also the most important cultural and political form of the nineteenth century.

Approaching Trollope's fiction and career through media archaeology, Richard Menke suggests that Trollope's conceptualisation of authorship was fundamentally shaped by media forms and technologies. In *An Autobiography*, fluent writing is figured as a performance like music, oration, print compositing or telegraphy; daily fictional production is synchronised to the watch – and its material rewards sorted into a notorious table of income. By highlighting the media mechanics of Trollope's authorship, with special attention to the Post, Menke's chapter bridges the gap between his art of representation and the function of the media that helped him practise and understand that art.

In 'Trollope's Living Media: Fox Hunts and Marriage Plots', Tamara Ketabgian explores a very different kind of media network. She addresses the broader social, ecological and narrative aspects of hunting, as a complex network of various human and non-human 'actants', unfolding in the form of a strategic, geographically rooted pursuit. Readers have often dismissed Trollope's sporting scenes, either viewing them as mere action sequences or as naïve idealisations of harmonious class hierarchy. This chapter, however, shows how Trollope unsparingly analyses the role of human and non-human habit, identity, cultivation and character – whether in horses, hounds, foxes, groups or individuals moving through space and time within the marriage plot, a realm that he frequently likens to blood sport. In short, Ketabgian reveals what it means for Trollope to treat 'the system and theory' of hunting as principles of human conduct and character.

Taking the curious conjunction of narrative perspective and knowledge acquired on roads as a starting point, Claire Connolly explores the connections between the narrative strategies of Trollope's Irish novels and the road network along which so many of his plots run. Roads are present in Trollope's Irish fiction in all their various forms: as avenues, paths, cuttings, lanes; and as shaped by grand juries, relief works and mail companies. She argues that Trollope's most compelling imagination of the ironies and instabilities of infrastructure come in the Irish novel that critics find to be his most troubling, *The Landleaguers* (1883).

Robert D. Aguirre's chapter continues the theme of travel. Drawing on recent work in mobility studies, he reads *The West Indies and the Spanish Main* (1859) as an expression of Trollope's own mobility as a travelling subject, as well as a trenchant examination of how travel and mobility were reshaping Central America, and in particular Panama, in the decade prior to Trollope's visit. The question of global transit – of persons, information and commodities – had thrust Central America to the centre of worldwide attention, as travellers demanded swift passage to California, the United States sought to connect the disparate parts of its transcontinental expanse, and the British government fretted about mail delivery to British Columbia and trade with Pacific nations. As a result, the Central American republics became enmeshed in transnational and trans-regional formations. Trollope's mission put him in a privileged position to comment on and, indeed, shape these changes.

Economics

'Of all novelists in any country', W. H. Auden famously wrote, 'Trollope best understands the role of money. Compared with him even Balzac is too romantic.'[10] The essays in the fourth constellation move beyond an analysis of the representation of money in Trollope's fiction and show how the complex economic context in which he was writing can be detected in the very fabric of his writing.

Nancy Henry's chapter situates Trollope's work within the context of recent research on nineteenth-century women investors by historians. Literary critics have paid attention to the financial plots and themes that are so central to Trollope's works, but no one has specifically considered the prevalence of the female investor, a figure who also appears in fiction by his contemporaries. While Miss Dunstable, Lady Laura Kennedy and Lady Glencora had their fortunes invested for them, Mrs Van Siever, Alice Vavasor, Miss Mackenzie, Lizzie Eustace and Madame Max Goesler are investors whose stories explore the profoundly economic nature of human relationships. Trollope's novels suggest that investing was not just something women did; it was a distinctly modern way of thinking about independence, risk, global communities and the future in general.

Opting for a biographical approach, Francis O'Gorman explores the significance of Trollope's move to Montagu Square, both in his life and for his writing. With the ownership of 39 Montagu Square, the novelist could express his pleasure in the success he had made of his life. It was a life that might, after such an unpromising start with a lost paternal inheritance, the disastrous Harrow farm(s) and the lean years in rented rooms at 22 Northumberland Street, have been a failure. The novelist himself, picking up his new house keys sometime in or just before April 1873, had done far, far better than could have been expected; unlike that of many of his speculative investors, his achievement was both real and legal. The property plot of *The Way We Live Now*, the first fiction he wrote in Montagu Square, celebrates it.

John McCourt approaches Trollope's Irish novels with a similar fusion of biography, economics and literary criticism, to which he adds an ethical twist. The major social and ethical issue of hospitality, he argues, provides a useful key for understanding Trollope's relationship with Ireland as staged in his Irish short stories and novels. His chapter examines Trollope's position as a guest of the not-yet-formed Irish nation in a crucial and hugely difficult period in its history. McCourt further draws our attention to Trollope's subsequent hosting of matters Irish (characters, names, political issues) in his more pointedly English fiction, such as *Phineas Finn* and *Phineas Redux*. He concludes with a brief look at how Trollope uses moments of hospitality to enact crucial advances in the plots of his novels.

In 'Power in Numbers: Fetishes and Facts between Trollope and Law', Anat Rosenberg investigates a peculiar occurrence of commodity fetishism in law which gained historical momentum in the late nineteenth century and which can be summarised as a fear of the social basis of economic evaluation. Trollope's writings may illuminate this process. Rosenberg reads *An Autobiography* as a response to the problem of evaluation posed in *The Way We Live Now*. Trollope's obsession with numerical representations of words, pages, hours and finally their corresponding list of prices, is, as critics have noted, a flight from the sociality of the market; it emerges in an almost ridiculously objectified representation of the value of Trollope's (book) commodities. The process in Trollope, in its bluntness, sheds light on similar but less observed processes occurring in areas of consumer credit law. In these areas, numerical representations helped counter the fear of the masses entering markets. Representations of value through balance sheets and budgets were treated as having an asocial objective logic, as an express and overtly willed alternative to a social one.

Kate Flint's chapter makes the *Edinburgh Companion to Anthony Trollope* come full circle. While Claire Jarvis reveals the sophistication behind the alleged shoddiness of Trollope's language, thus understanding shoddiness in a figurative sense, Kate Flint draws a rich skein of meanings from the word 'shoddy' itself – meanings to which a Victorian reader would very likely have been sensible, but that are almost invisible today. On occasion, Trollope employs 'shoddy' in its original meaning, signifying a material made of recycled woollens. The inferior nature of shoddy products gave rise to what is, today, the term's common understanding: something of poor quality and workmanship. Trollope was an author who cared deeply about workmanship, tools and the degree of effort and self-regulation that went into his own writing. He regularly deploys – and relies on his reader to recognise – the web of cultural reference surrounding this particular word in order to link literary production, the importance of maintaining standards within a profession, and probity of character.

Notes

1. Bruno Latour, 'Why Has Critique Run out of Steam? From Matters of Fact to Matters of Concern', *Critical Inquiry*, 30.2 (2004): pp. 225–48.

2. Within the field of Victorian studies, the V21 Manifesto (2015) provides a combative instance of this new direction; see <http://v21collective.org/manifesto-of-the-v21-collective-ten-theses/> (last accessed 28 February 2018). One of the turning points in the history of literary criticism in recent years is arguably Sharon Marcus and Stephen Best (eds), *The Way We Read Now, Representations,* 108.1 (2009). Rita Felski has emerged as the most prominent spokesperson of the turn that the discipline seems to be taking; see *The Limits of Critique* (Chicago: The University of Chicago Press, 2015). For suggestive reflections about and applications of these new methodologies, see 'Theories and Methodologies: On Caroline Levine's *Forms: Whole, Rhythm, Hierarchy, Network*', *PMLA*, 132.5 (2017): pp. 1181–243; and Sarah Copland and Greta Olson (eds), *The Politics of Form* (London and New York: Routledge, 2018).

3. Joseph North, 'The Critical Unconscious', in *Literary Criticism: A Concise Political History* (Cambridge, MA: Harvard University Press, 2017), pp. 124–94. Given North's bleak picture of the impasse that literary criticism on the left finds itself in, as well his solution (a return to the practical criticism of I. A. Richards), it is not surprising that his work has met with criticism; see, for instance, Stefan Collini, 'A Lot to Be Said', *London Review of Books*, 39.21 (2 November 2017): pp. 35–7.

4. Carolyn Dever and Lisa Niles (eds), *The Cambridge Companion to Anthony Trollope*, Cambridge: Cambridge University Press, 2010).

5. Deborah Denenholz Morse, Margeret Markwick and Mark Turner (eds), *The Routledge Research Companion to Anthony Trollope* (London and New York: Routledge, 2016).

6. Anthony Trollope, *An Autobiography and Other Writings*, ed. Nicholas Shrimpton (Oxford: Oxford University Press), ch. 9, p. 93.

7. Henry James, review of *Can You Forgive Her?*, in Donald Smalley (ed.), *Anthony Trollope: The Critical Heritage* (London: Routledge, 1969), p. 252.

8. Hugh Sykes Davies, 'Trollope and His Style', *A Review of English Literature*, 1.4 (1960): pp. 73–85.

9. On *Dispossession*, see Simon Grennan, 'Drawing Dispossession: A New Graphic Adaptation of Anthony Trollope's *John Caldigate*', *European Comic Art*, 7.2 (Autumn 2014): pp. 4–30; Laurence Grove and Simon Grennan (eds), *Transforming Anthony Trollope: Dispossession, Victorianism and Nineteenth-Century Word and Image* (Leuven: Leuven University Press, 2015); and Frederik Van Dam, 'Adapting as a Form of Remediation: A Benjaminian Perspective', in Keith Williams, Chris Murray, Jan Baetens and Sophie Aymes (eds), *Art and Science in Word and Image: Exploration and Discovery*, Word and Image Interactions, vol. 9 (Amsterdam and New York: Brill and Rodopi, 2018).

10. Hugh Wystan Auden, 'A Poet of the Actual', in Edward Mendelson (ed.), *Forewords and Afterwords* (London: Faber and Faber, 1973), p. 266.

Part I
Style

1

ALMOST TROLLOPE

Claire Jarvis

Boring Trollope

THE IDEA FOR this chapter started a year ago, when I was teaching a graduate class on the Palliser series. As always, Trollope's peculiar narrative stance stood out to me, and to my students. Trollope's narrator both understands and sees through his characters, while also maintaining a slight distance from the action. At times, it is almost as though the narrator is making up the stories as he goes along – that he is not quite sure of what it is that has happened, or will happen, to his charges, even though Trollope boasts in his *Autobiography* – stretching the truth a bit – that, unlike many of his comrades in serial writing, he finished each novel before the publishers began bringing out the serials.[1] During that rereading of the Pallisers, I noticed a cluster of words and phrases recurring throughout the novels – 'almost' is one of them, but so are 'something of', 'some kind of', 'such was the', 'nearly', 'quite' and 'rather' – that imply a thin band of distinction between the world the narrator occupies and the world he (securely, often, but always at a remove) narrates. Why does Trollope use these words, most of them syntactical filler, so often? Do other Victorian novelists do the same? My hunch was that Trollope was peculiar in this habit, and that this habit might be an entry point for discussing what, at least in Trollope studies, can be a difficult thing to pin down: his style.

As I was explaining this project to a colleague, I described my excitement upon learning that Trollope used the word 'almost' 285 times in *Phineas Redux*; his moustache bristled, 'We-e-ell', he said, 'he wrote fast.' This essay begins with a word, and, by putting some unseemly pressure on that word, I'll make a leap towards a concept. The theoretical question raised in this paper was prompted by Caroline Levine's recent book *Forms*. Levine makes the case for a capacious definition of form, one that sutures together the political and the aesthetic. To begin with a question: is it possible for a word to constitute a form? Or, if not a single word, a collection of words? How would a critic go about developing a form organised around a set of words?[2]

My aim in these next pages will be to convince you that Trollope's use of 'almost', in itself almost a quintessentially 'empty' word, is a key – one of many – to a central problem in Trollope criticism: how can we go about closely reading this author, who seems in so many ways to resist close reading? He's chock-full of meaningful objects and interactions upon which to hang a close reading, but on the level of the sentence, Trollope eludes us. For a writer who seems to say so much about Victorian social and political mores and habits, and whose plots are so convoluted and compelling, his sentences – his form – leave some doubt as to his work's quality. It is hard not to align oneself with Henry James, who damned Trollope with faint praise a year after his death:

> Trollope, from the first, went in, as they say, for having as little form as possible; it is probably safe to affirm that he had no 'views' whatever on the subject of novel-writing.[3]

There are a variety of reasons given for this critical habit: Trollope's writing is almost ('perceptibly', according to James) mechanically composed, or his narrative world feels ordinary, or the vast (too vast) assembly of characters' speech is strangely static. It is a critical commonplace to say there is something disengaging about Trollope. And although Anthony Trollope's novels have not been consigned to the dust-heap of history, they have suffered more than their fair share of critical derision in comparison to other nineteenth-century realists.

In Henry James's review of *Can You Forgive Her?*, he complains the novel does not fulfil the promise of its plots. Why, James asks, could not Alice Vavasor be made to stay away from John Grey, mulling over her mistakes? Or, why could not Lady Glencora have been driven from her husband and 'vulgarly disposed of'? Finally, James petitions for the rightful death of another character relegated to a life outside the novel's frame:

> As the reader follows George Vavasor deeper into his troubles – all of which are very well described – his excited imagination hankers for – what shall we say? Nothing less positive than Vavasor's death ... But for Mr Trollope anything is preferable to a sensation; an incident is ever preferable to an event. George Vavasor simply takes a ship to America.[4]

By positioning 'incident' against its seeming synonym, 'event', James highlights the difference between the two. An 'incident' is a momentary (scenic) pause in the flow of an action, while an 'event', typified in James's account as Vavasor's 'death', is more final. 'Events' are the kinds of things that typically end novels, or which dramatically alter a plot's course: births, deaths, marriages. If Trollope's novel ends with scenes that appear to be 'events' (birth and marriage), his progress towards these events is made up of a concatenation of 'incidents', scenes that link together in an episodic, but not necessarily linear, plot. Furthermore, in Trollope's world, these end-of-novel events do not signal an 'end' to his characters' lives; Trollope's form is famously the chronicle and not the novel. Instead of sending George Vavasor beyond the novel's margins, James wishes the character's 'life' coterminous with the novel's ending.

This is amusing when we think about how often James himself uses incidents to gesture to events. But, here, one of the complaints he has against Trollope is that he sets up his novels to be full of real plot points – violent deaths, bigamous love plots – but that Trollope always reduces these events to mere incidents, shying away from the volatility he appears to promise. James presciently mimics D. A. Miller's complaint about Trollope's 'moderate schisms'.[5] In Miller's words: 'We begin to see why Trollope's fiction frequently turns on contemporary social, political, and legal "issues", but also why it is at the same time so relatively indifferent to their substance and so little eager to take sides.'[6] Even if we think of the Palliser novels as being 'about' parliamentary life, the actual political content of the novels is relatively minor. This leads to the extremely strange experience of reading through Trollope's accounts of various parliamentary debates only to end up feeling more, and not less, confused about the principles, parties and policies. Do we care what Finn's position on Church disenfranchisement is, or do we care that he has a position? It is the latter, but this points to a mistake many current readers of Trollope make: that reading him, we can learn anything about politics, social mores or even habits of mind. None of these is true.[7]

By respecting incidents as incidents – neither elevating them to the status of an event, nor ignoring them in favour of an event – a neutral form structures Trollope's novels. Both James and Miller agree that Trollope prefers dampening and qualifying his novels' events to sensationalising them, but for them this is a problem. If in James's case, this dampening is a by-product of Trollope's lazy way with a pen, in Miller's case, it's a product of Trollope's collusion with surveillance.

Almostness

Trollope's syntax does not create a stable band of distance: some words, like 'almost', imply a process that is close to completion, whereas others, like 'quite', might imply a world that is close to surpassing its bounds, something that is about to overflow. This language, various as it might seem at first, is a language of degrees, and imagines a world of possible actions, and a narrator who can't quite narrate that world exactly. I call this language 'almostness', and I think Trollope's heavy use of the discourse of almostness is a key to his style. So why would 'almostness' be helpful in understanding the 'aboutness' of Trollope's fiction?[8] Gerard Genette calls attention to this effect in his response to Mieke Bal's criticisms of his discussions of focalisation. Genette writes:

> In internal focalization, the focus coincides with a character, who then becomes the fictive 'subject' of all the perceptions, including those that concern him as object. The narrative in that case *can* tell us everything this character perceives and everything he thinks (it never does, either because it refuses to give irrelevant information or because it deliberately withholds some bit of relevant information [paralepsis], like the moment and the memory of the crime in *Roger Ackroyd*).[9]

'Almostness' shears quite close to paralepsis while maintaining a slightly different stance in relation to a novel's focalisation. If we think of the actions qualified by 'almost' as made barely visible within the novel's diegetic frame, in the form of, perhaps, a shrug or a scarcely perceptible shake of the head, we can see how closely 'almostness' gets to internal narration while still remaining the purview of an omniscient narrator.

I have two pieces of evidence to develop 'almostness' further. The first is a scaled word list drawn from the Chadwyk Healey corpus of British fiction, and presented here with the help of a colleague at Stanford, Mark Algee-Hewitt. This list manages the incidence of 'almost' by taking into account varied novel length, and it offers a comparison of British authors between 1800 and 1900. In the scaled list, Trollope's use of 'almost' is much higher (usually more than twice the number) than all but two writers included in the data set: George Chesney, who wrote the invasion novel *The Battle of Dorking*, and two Romantic period novels by Percy Shelley.[10] After looking at the scaled list, I also perused my bookshelves for books of a similar length, trying to include as many canonical novels as possible, as well as comparing 'almosts' across

Trollope's novelistic corpus: in that list (which is not scaled), the findings are pretty similar: few writers use 'almost' as much as Trollope, Trollope uses 'almost' more during the middle of his career than he does at the end or beginning, and the one person who comes close (but not that close) is Henry James. This is perhaps not entirely surprising, though it would be harder to think of two canonical novelists whose critical afterlives have been more at variance. If, as my colleague suggested, Trollope's use of 'almostness' is a sign of his speed of composition, and a mark of sloppiness, in James's case, the discourse of almostness, a language of qualification, seems like narratorial care, an emblem of James's characteristic meticulousness.

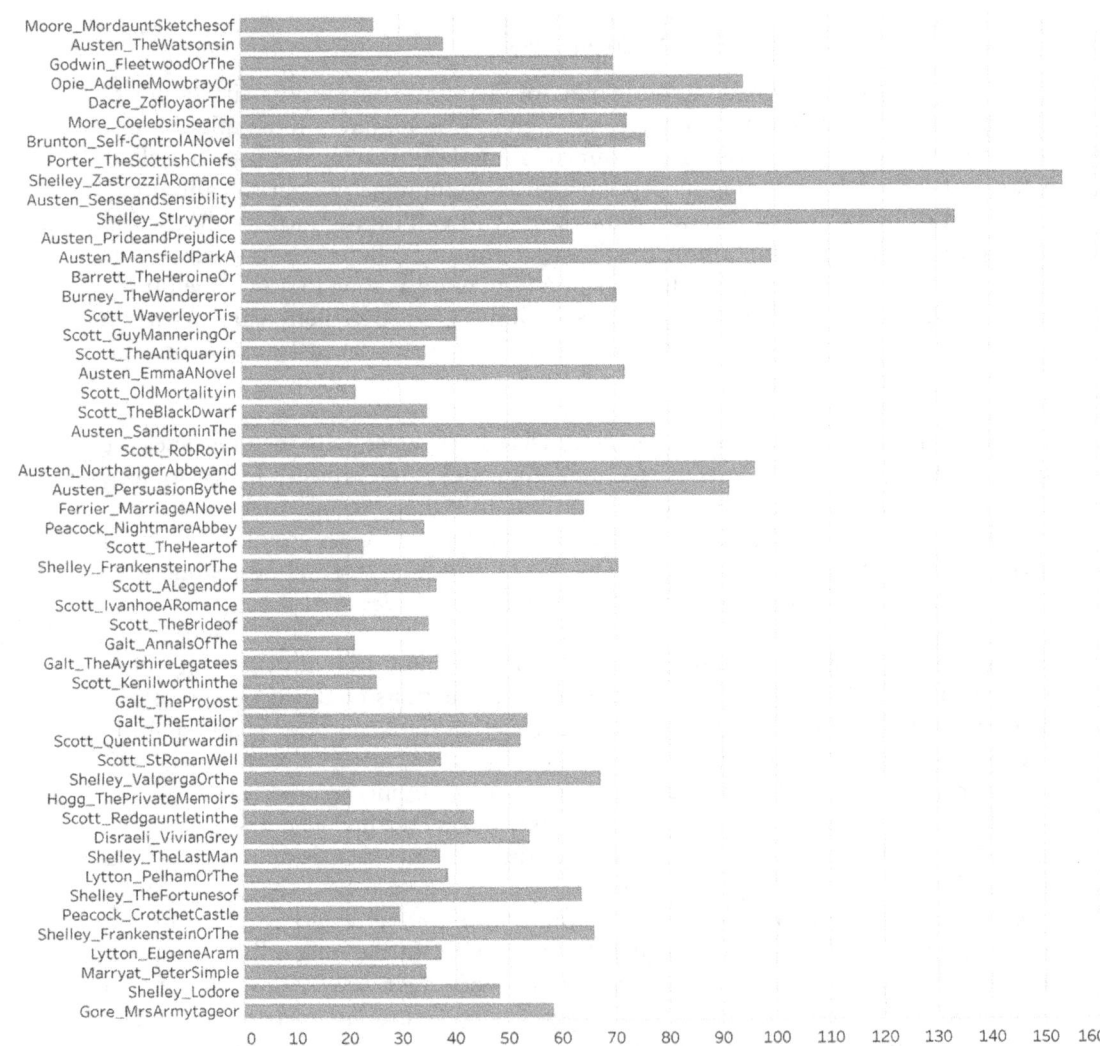

Figure 1.1 – part 1 'Almost', 1800–1836.

We can see this division a bit more clearly if we think about the two novelists' critical reception. James's novels, in a number of critical moments, have been held up as examples of just how precise, just how exact, the novel form can be. In fact, the language of precision and its excess is central to James criticism. Dorothy van Ghent comments that *The Portrait of a Lady* 'is a growing of more delicate and deeper-reaching roots and a nourishment of a more complex, more troubled, more creative personal humanity'.[11] F. R. Leavis called *The Portrait of a Lady* 'an original masterpiece', continuing 'it is one of the great novels in the language'.[12] More recently, Anna Kornbluh calls James 'an exacting critic', linking him to Frederic Jameson,

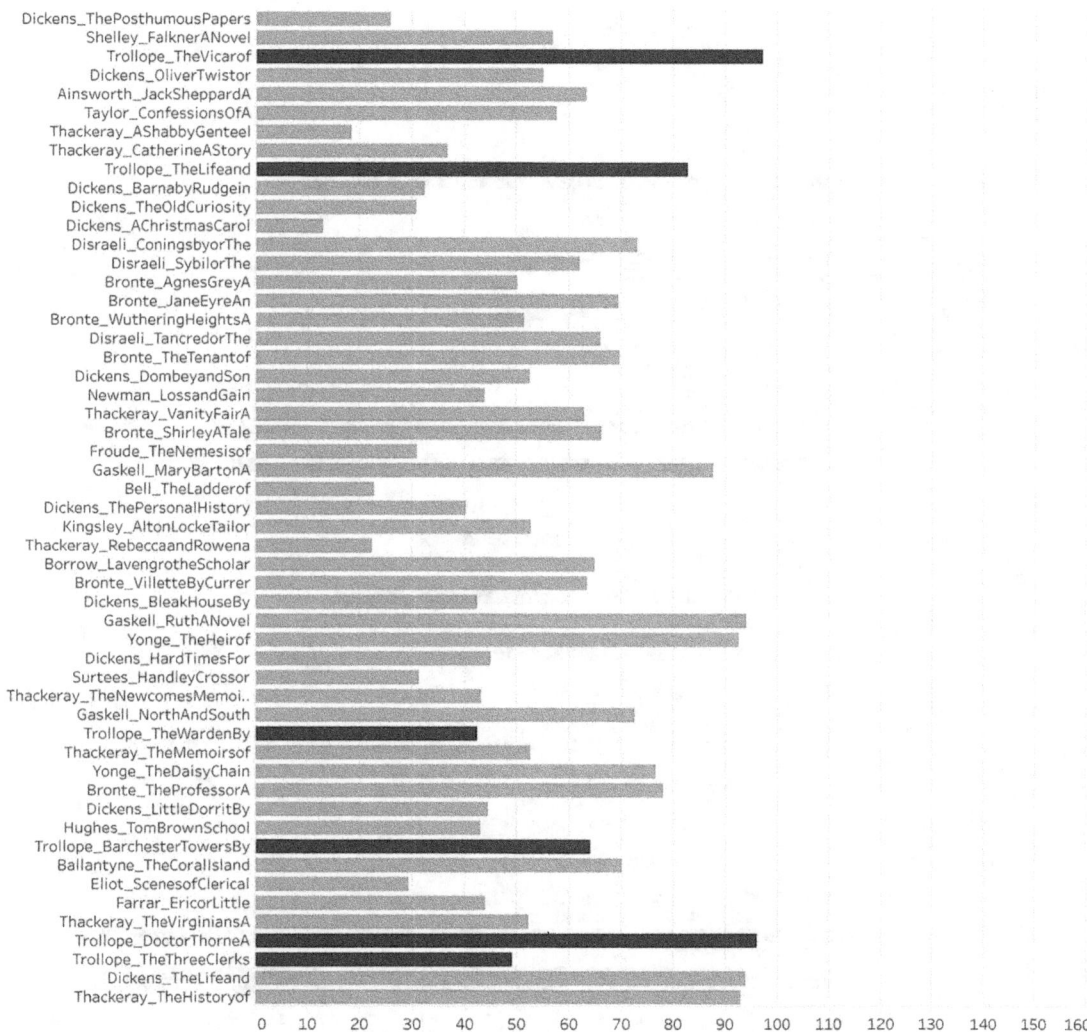

Figure 1.1 – part 2 'Almost', 1837–1857.

and goes on further to describe the way James instantiates his theory of the novel in his 'ambivalent edification' in his corpus: 'every photographic frontispiece James commissioned (twenty-three photos in all) addresses colonnades, arches, bridges, gates, courtyards, grand halls, cathedrals, palaces, plazas, shops, neighboring clusters, houses, and doors, doors, doors – so many forms of open enclosures, of publics spectacular and mundane, of exteriors equally important as his famed interiors', a complex architectural tendency at odds with, for example, the 'decided fictionality of Trollope's Barsetshire'.[13] The assumption of James's novelistic exceptionalism forms the basis of Mark McGurl's *The Novel Art: Elevations of American Fiction*

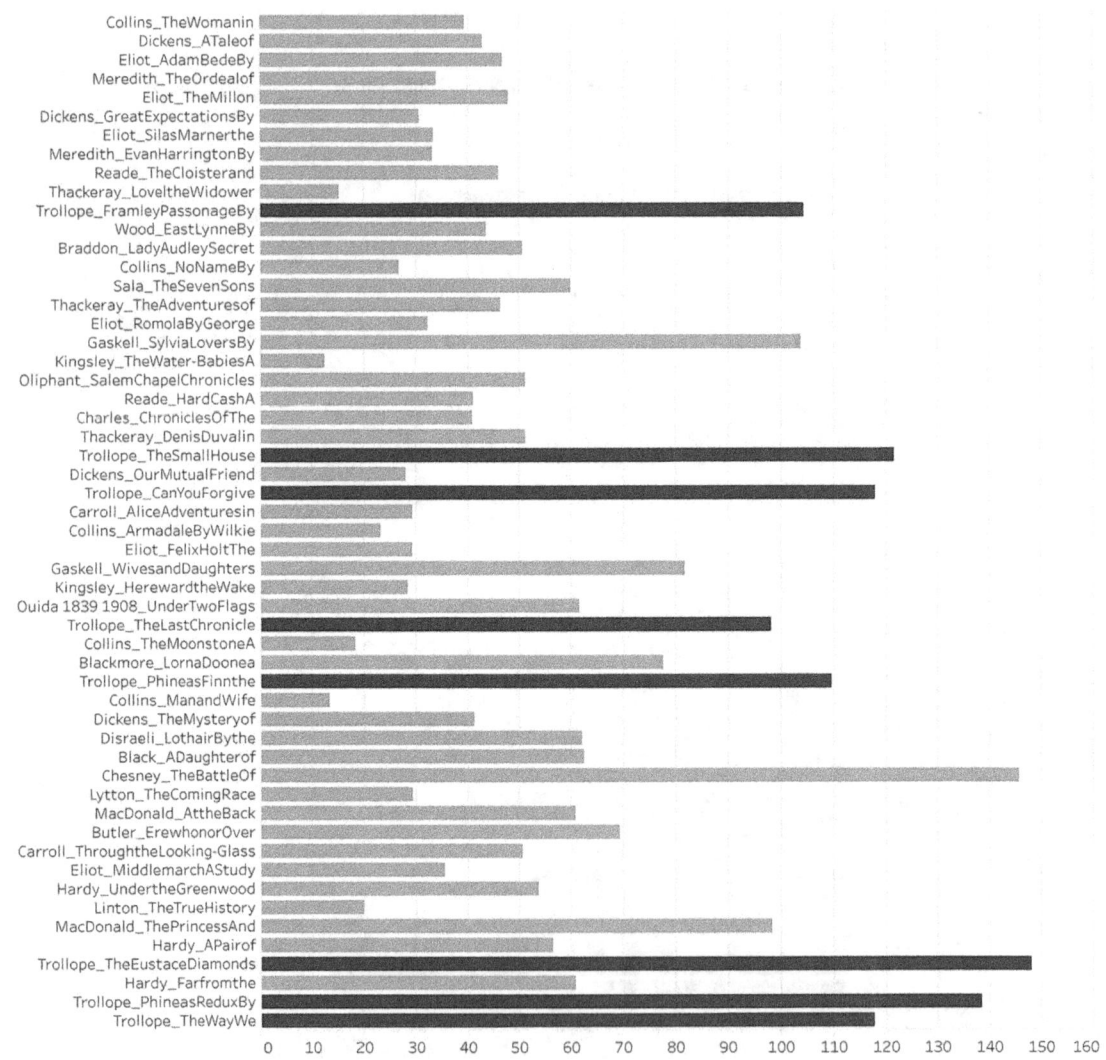

Figure 1.1 – part 3 'Almost', 1858–1875.

after Henry James and, in some ways, *The Program Era: Postwar Fiction and the Rise of Creative Writing*, in which James is credited with prototyping much of the form of the novel in the last century (his copious note-taking, scene-building and his experiments with point of view are all given credit).[14] And Phil Fisher calls *The Ambassadors*, 'perhaps from an academic point of view the most perfect book written by an American'.[15] In each of these cases, James's work as a novelist comes to seem almost like the work the critic ascribes to her own project: James is the most literary critical of novelists.

On the other hand, Trollope's critical reception is rife with takedowns. In one of the most damning, D. A. Miller reminds us of the 'terroristic effects of the banality that Trollope, as a matter of principle and program, relentlessly cultivates'.[16] In Trollope's case, the use of the discourse of 'almostness' is read as a sign of his novels' disorderliness, his too-rapid habits of building a book. This observation, that both

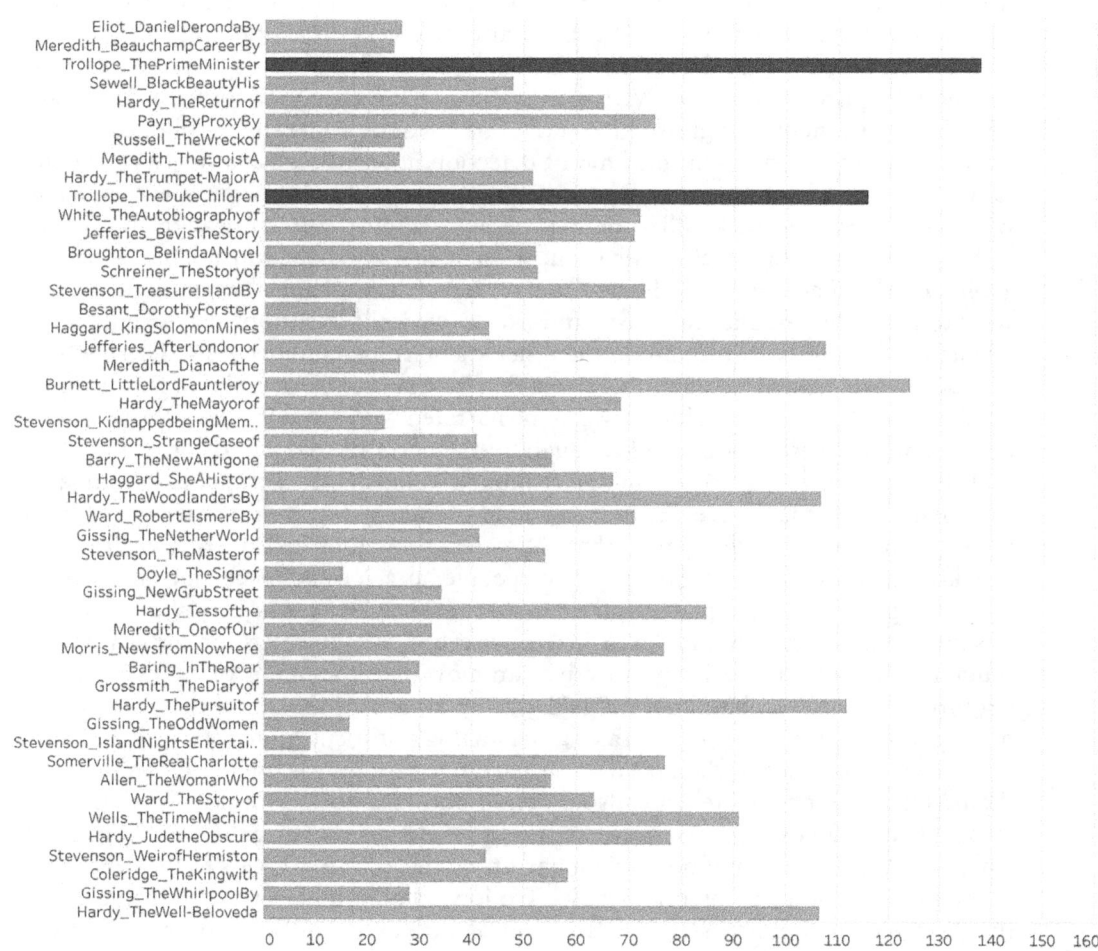

Figure 1.1 – part 4 'Almost', 1876–1897.

authors lean on the discourse of 'almostness' more than other similar realist novelists, aligns Trollope, the novelist most associated with carelessness, with James, the novelist most associated with care, the novelist of banality with the novelist of perfection. The mind-bending precision of Jamesian narration makes him a prime target for critics focused on difficulty, complexity and the fine description of the gradations of human experience. In other words, critics often associate James with just the kind of sensitivity that seems to be missing in Trollope. But in their use of 'almost', we can think of them together. So, why the critical dislocation?

Linguists use word frequency to attribute pieces of writing to specific authors, and also to locate a piece of writing temporally within an author's body of work. What is somewhat surprising – at least it was to me – is that the best words to do this are the least 'syntactically meaningful' words – words like the definite and indefinite articles and personal pronouns.[17] The theory is that these 'function' words, unlike 'key' words (words with author-specific meanings, such as 'shipwreck', which means disaster on the marriage market for Trollope), are difficult to manipulate – writers have specific ways of using these words that make their patterning very difficult to mimic. Jonathan Farina has argued for the importance of seemingly incidental turns of phrase in connecting the epistemic forms of Victorian science to the epistemic forms of Victorian novels; my aim here is slightly different.[18] But I would argue that Trollope's use of 'almost' hovers beyond even this kind of detection in part because it doesn't have the same formulaic charge as does Dickens's 'as if': 'as if' licenses figurative language, whereas 'almost' reads like filler. In fact, because 'almost' and its near relatives tend to be associated with a lack of revision, it might be marshalled instead as a sign of Trollope's sloppiness (his 'shoddiness'), or at least his mechanical rapidity. Instead, I want to make the case that this word and words like it tilt attention away from, on the one hand, the novels' plots, and on the other, the narrative interjections. These words present a world neither here nor there, one that hovers between a realm of fiction and a realm of fact. If the relationship between the narrated world and the narrator is usually quite stable in realist fiction (stable enough for the narrator to dip into consciousnesses and then pop back out, for example) Trollope's 'almostness' disrupts that standard. We might think of narrative distance as a kind of literary focus – if the narrators keep their eyes on a specific character, other characters or actions become fuzzier; if narrators keep their eyes on a specific group of people, at a specific place and time, others groups of people, at other places and times, become harder to see – they slip in and out of sight, or are utterly invisible to the narrative eye. Again, the question of focalisation often imagines that narrative perspective can move into the minds of characters, seeing through their eyes, but 'almostness' lights up a peculiar feature of the all-knowing quality of omniscient narration. Taking the analogy of focus quite seriously, 'almostness' is what happens at the far edges of narrative vision; it is what we barely see at the periphery. If a character intends an action but does not perform it, what (if any) evidence could an external narrative eye perceive? This draws attention, in an indirect way, to the strangest fact of omniscient narration: the narrative access to thoughts and, in the case of actions, to intentions.[19] So, Trollope's hesitation, as typified by his use of the discourse of 'almostness', signals a kind of variable focus in his narrator's attention. The narrator can *almost*, as I'll explain in a moment, see what it is Lady Laura does when she reads Finn's letter.

Conceptually, 'almost' does two things at once: it makes reference to time (when something has 'almost' happened, it may in some future time have happened or it may never happen at all), and it makes reference to an imagined wholeness or filled space (that is, a glass that is 'almost' full, no matter how we experience it, is not, at that moment, either full or empty). We might even divide almostness into two large categories: metaphorical, or conceptual, almostness ('almost' an emotion, for example), and spatial, or literal, almostness ('almost' at a destination). Following from this, almostness's conceptual or spatial qualification comes into play on the level of plot. In fact, one of the key uses of 'almostness' is to manage textual violence. As D. A. Miller has argued, Trollopian worlds are self-policing – Trollope's novels mitigate violence so much that it loses the savour of violence completely, even when moments of extreme violence – a man run over by a train, a man garroted in the street – form the bases of a novel's plot.[20] We can see this effect throughout the discourse I'm describing here. In *Phineas Finn*, for example, characters feel 'almost' anger (*PF*, ch. 11, p. 88; ch. 17, p. 129; ch. 24, p. 175, 'almost' severity (ch. 23, p. 172) and 'almost' annoyance (ch. 12, p. 89).[21] 'Almost' anger and 'almost' severity work along similar lines – if the metaphorical almosts, that is, almosts of concept instead of space, work to draw attention to the way metaphor absolves characters of true shock or worry, by making reactions 'almost' violence ('almost' angry, 'almost' severe . . .). Trollope maintains the condition of gentle fragmentation for which his novels are so famous. On the other hand, 'almost' divine, 'almost' with affection' and 'almost' idolatrous work in the same way to the opposite ends: the positive element is managed by the qualifier so as to soften its attractive potency. 'Almosts' interrupt passages that might rise to a level of intensity at odds with Trollope's soothing narrative pabulum. In these cases, 'almostness' helps to maintain the soft, loosely structured plots for which Trollope's novels are celebrated. But there is another kind of almost which troubles the distinction between narrator and narrated world more significantly. I'll argue in the next section that a more charged 'almost' opens a space in which Trollope's apparently sovereign, but gentle, surveillance gives way.

Bored Narrators

If 'almostness' means something to characters, it means a slightly different thing to a narrator. At times, it's almost as though the narrator is making up his stories as he goes along – that he's not quite sure of what it is that has happened, or will happen, to his charges. Lapsed attention gets us to the problem of 'almostness', that is, the *incapacity* of the narrator to accurately assess actions – or, if to assess accurately, to assess something that is always already partial or which can never reach wholeness. When we land on language that creates this narrative distance ('almost', 'something of', 'some kind of') we see a variety of narrative tactics absorbed under a united group of linguistic signs. When Phineas visits Saulsby about half way through *Phineas Finn*, he is struck by the Earl's confession about the various love plots circulating around Violet Effingham: 'So sudden, indeed, and so confidential was the conversation, that Phineas was almost silenced for a while' (ch. 33, p. 250). What does Trollope mean here? When the qualifying phrase 'for a while' is added, the question of what kind of confused pause

Finn experiences, exactly, becomes hazier. One is silenced, or one is not. Even if Finn is making small, agreeable noises while the Earl speaks, that doesn't count as silence. One could certainly be silenced for a while – shocked into a brief speechlessness – but could one be 'almost' silenced for the small chunk of time that 'for a while' suggests? It seems like this is the sort of 'silence' that Trollope means here – a silence that is not full or true silence, something that is on the way to silence, but not silence itself. This almost slips the narration into something like a metaphor – Finn was so shocked he loses his capacity to respond in words – but that doesn't quite get at the strangeness here. Another example, a little later, when Glencora tries to dissuade Madame Max from entertaining the Duke of Omnium any further, Lady Glencora is seen 'almost hesitating as she spoke, and feeling that the colour was rushing up to her cheeks and covering her brow' (ch. 61, p. 453). How does one 'almost hesitate'? Again, one hesitates or one does not. In this moment, does Glencora's speech betray her in the way that her flush does? Or is it that the flush, noticed after the almost hesitant speech, actually clues the narrator in on the fact of the 'almost hesitation?' In both of these instances, Trollope presents us with a lag or slight time delay in the narration. It isn't that Finn is silenced or that Glencora hesitates, it's that the narration, while close enough to sense Finn's shock and to see Glencora's blood rise, isn't close enough to actually capture these fine gradations of characters' experience. Counter-intuitively, these passages, the small moments when it seems as though Trollope's narrator has a lapse in his attention, come about because the narrator is both attentive and distracted as he does his job. What would it mean for narrators to be so perceptive that they can see a character 'almost' hesitate? Or, if we read slightly differently, what would it mean for a narrator, whose job it is to observe characters' movements, to lose sight of a character at an important emotional juncture? The narrator's see-sawing attention – at once so close to see hesitation, or its close cousin, or perhaps just distracted enough to *not* see that same hesitation – asks that we consider the version of narrator that Trollope develops. Where does he live in relation to the lives he describes? How far is he from the action?

'Narrative distance' is, actually, not a particularly useful way to think about the relationship between Trollope's narrators and his characters. Perhaps something more like 'narrative attention', or 'narrative care' works slightly better – in many of Trollope's novels, the narrator becomes distracted or even bored in the process of narrating his characters, and these lapses in attention occur even when the narrator's in the active process of narrating characters' most intense experiences. To turn to a slightly different form of 'almostness': towards the end of *Phineas Redux*, Lady Laura receives a momentous letter from Finn, one that finally sets down the contours of their relationship. This letter marks the formal end of the possible love plot Lady Laura wants to spur on, so one would expect the narrator to have careful, clear insight into her reception. Trollope writes: 'She did read the letter through, – read it probably more than once, but there was only one sentence in it that had for her any enduring interest. "I will not go to Loughlinter myself."'[22]

Why is it that Trollope's narrator here can't quite see whether or not Lady Laura read the letter more than once? It's a strange lapse in a narration that, on the other hand, often feels incredibly intimate and precise. The narrator perches to the side of Lady Laura, watching her read the letter, but somehow loses his interest, or looks away, just long enough to miss out on whether or not she read the letter again. 'Almostness' calls into question one of the central aspects of Trollope's fiction – the constancy of the narrator's interest in the world his characters occupy. More, perhaps, than most nineteenth-century novelists, Trollope presents us with a continuous world. As Irene Tucker describes this aspect of the realist novel: '[its] particular representational force lies in its capacity to make relatively limited sets of detail appear at once constitutive of an entire, wholly seamless world and of a particular nation. The novel's details gain substantially inasmuch as they bear local, not universal, legibility and weight.'[23] Although Trollope's narrated world is comprehensive, the narrator's relationship to that world is not. If each individual Eliotic or Dickensian novel presents a coherent world, Trollopian novels present a world coherent across the boundaries of the novel itself. And often, this does look like a pattern of precise, local detail. Think about Phineas's hat rolling down the stairs from Kennedy's rooms at MacPherson's Hotel in *Phineas Redux* or of Adelaide Palliser's heart-rending 'banished to – Bou – logne!' in the same novel.[24] These are moments when Trollope captures the energy of experiences in a vivid, seemingly material world. But, in passages like the Lady Laura moment I just discussed, the detail-driven persistence of Trollope's world becomes a little unhinged. And it is that detailed derangement that leads Trollope to consider the difference between certainty and uncertainty in some detail. Narrative hesitation is a useful way of doing things. Certainty makes a mess. In Lady Laura's case, for example, it seals her into a marriage that is a torment. In Lord Fawn's case, it casts a dark cloud over an innocent man. I'll turn now to a short consideration of a dense sequence of passages in *Phineas Redux*, a set of passages that give some shape to the dangers that certainty presents in a Trollopian world.

The Uncanny Passage

In Chapter 47 of *Phineas Redux*, we first get a glimpse of the alley wherein Mr Bonteen meets his doom:

> There is a dark, uncanny-looking passage running from the end of Bolton Row, in May Fair, between the gardens of two great noblemen, coming out among the mews in Berkeley Street, at the corner of Berkeley Square, just opposite the bottom of Hay Hill. It was on the steps leading up from the passage to the level of the ground above that the body was found. The passage was almost as near a way as any from the club to Mr Bonteen's house in St James's Place; but the superintendent declared that gentlemen but seldom used the passage after dark, and he was disposed to think that the unfortunate man must have been forced down the steps by the ruffian who had attacked him from the level above. (ch. 47, p. 335)

Here, Trollope emphasises not only the geographical location of the passage, placing it in clear relation to well-known London landmarks and aristocratic houses, but also to its use: 'gentlemen' don't use the passage after dark. It is 'almost as near a way as any' for Mr Bonteen to return home, but still, the implication remains, he doesn't usually use it. This points to the way that certain spaces, certain experiences in Trollope's novels are excepted from 'gentleman's' (or gentle-lady's) use – this is a way, I think, for Trollope to gesture to the realm of true 'schism' at the heart of his novels. It is no mistake that this passage comes after a murder, an event that severely jeopardises Trollope's habit of moderation. But this passage, which is 'almost as near a way' to get from one place to another as any, ends up being the site of one of Trollope's most sustained engagements with the uncanny, which in turn, is a sustained encounter with 'almostness'. If you'll remember, Lord Fawn's sighting of a Phineas Finn-like character in this passage is what leads to Finn's imprisonment and trial. And after his release, it licenses this amazing passage:

> On a sudden he took his hat, and feeling with a smile for the latchkey which he always carried in his pocket, – thinking of the latchkey which had been made at Prague for the lock of the house in Northumberland Street, New Road, he went down to the front door. (ch. 67, p. 480)

Finn's smile marks his pleasure at freedom after his long confinement, but it also marks the unsettling effect recognition can have on a body. His smile here is rueful, regretting his time in prison, pleased with his newfound freedom, but discomfited by the way his imprisonment and trial have now become part of the fabric of his life. Trollope continues:

> He had taken off the black mourning coat which he had worn during the trial, and had put on the very grey garment by which it had been sought to identify him with the murderer. So clad he crossed Regent Street into Hanover Square, and from thence went a short way down Bond Street, and by Bruton Street into Berkeley Square. He took exactly the reverse of the route by which he had returned home from the club on the night of the murder. Every now and then he trembled as he passed some figure which might be that of a man who would recognise him. But he walked fast, and went on till he came to the spot on which the steps descend from the street into the passage, – the very spot at which the murder had been committed. He looked down it with an awful dread, and stood there as though he were fascinated, thinking of all the details which he had heard throughout the trial. Then he looked around him, and listened whether there were any step approaching through the passage. Hearing none and seeing no one he at last descended, and for the first time in his life passed through that way into Bolton Row. Here it was that the wretch of whom he had heard so much had waited for his enemy, – the wretch for whom during the last six weeks he had been mistaken. Heavens! – that men who had known him should have believed him to have done such a deed as that! He remembered well having shown the life-preserver to Erle and Fitzgibbon at the door of the club; and it had been thought that after having so shown it he had used it for the purpose which in his joke he had alluded! Were men so blind, so ignorant of nature, so little capable of discerning the truth as this? Then he went on till he came to the end of Clarges Street, and looked up the mews opposite to it, – the mews from which the man had been seen to hurry. The place was altogether unknown to him. He had never thought whither it had led when passing it on his way up from Piccadilly to the club. But now he entered the mews so as to test the evidence that had been given, and found that it brought him by a turn close up to the spot at which he had been described as having been last seen by Erle and Fitzgibbon. When there he went on, and crossed the street, and looking back saw the club was lighted up. (ch. 67, p. 480)

'The place was altogether unknown to [Finn]' though he finds himself 'close . . . to the spot at which he had been described as having been last seen'. The perspective here is dizzying; the narrator knows the spot that Erle and Fitzgibbon describe, but of course

Finn does not. And Trollope's narrator is careful to mark out this uncanny moment as partial – limited. Finn does not find himself in precisely the spot that Erle and Fitzgibbon identified, it is 'close up to the spot'. By developing the sense of weird spatial coincidence alongside a narrative recognition that, while it is close to the precise spot, it is not *the* precise spot, Trollope draws attention to the difficult tightrope the narrator walks between entering into Finn's reeling confusion at finding himself in the mews that have so altered his story and the necessity of making this encounter with place wholly new. Not a memory, but a new experience. If the emotional intensity of this moment requires an internal focalisation through Finn, his lack of experience with this place makes a true accounting of the passage's 'uncanny' nature impossible. *Pace* Genette, this passage does, indeed, seem to present something like a doubled focalisation: the narrator requires insight into Finn's consciousness and also a perspective wholly incommensurate with that consciousness.[25]

Remember, too, that Lord Fawn's evidence gets Finn into trouble because it is presented as unimpeachable. It includes a peculiar balancing of coincidence and certainty at odds with the strangely diffuse repetition we see in this passage. To compare:

> At the moment he had not connected the person of the man who passed him with any acquaintance of his own; but he now felt sure, – after what he had heard, – that the man was Mr Finn. As he passed out of the club Finn was putting on his overcoat, and Lord Fawn had observed the peculiarity of the grey colour. It was exactly a similar coat, only with its collar raised, that had passed him in the street. (ch. 47, p. 337)

The coat is 'exactly a similar colour', blending both Fawn's certainty at what he saw and the hesitant possibility – which we come to discover is a fact – that the coats are only similar, not the same.

To return to Finn's late night walk: here, he probes the dangers of such surety himself by mimicking the movements of Bonteen's true murderer, Mr Emilius. This is a sustained encounter with the difficulty of certainty, and as such is full of peculiar switchbacks and confusing qualifications – Finn wears the grey coat that looks 'exactly' like Emilius's 'similar' coat, and Finn takes 'exactly' the reverse of the course he took the night Bonteen was killed, but he also finishes his walk in a 'place altogether unknown to him'. These are the narrator's ways of reassuring us that while Finn walked the same streets that night, it was not Finn that bludgeoned Bonteen in the alley. His walk was the same walk, with a difference. But one sentence in this passage stands out to me over all the others: 'Every now and then he trembled as he passed some figure which might be that of a man who would recognise him.' How do we read the 'mightness' here? A close relative of 'almost', 'might' signals a possibility, something that could happen to Finn as he walks down the street. Does Finn fear he'll be recognised as Emilius, that is, as Mr Bonteen's true murderer? Or does he fear he will be recognised as himself? After all, the Finn who walks through these alleys is, in fact, the Finn that Fawn thought he saw – a tall, muffled, fast-moving figure in a grey coat.

This passage is all about certainty – the same coat, the same passage, the same walk – but it draws attention to the almostness at the core of Finn's story: he *almost* killed Mr Bonteen. And, though my argument shares some DNA with Julian Moynihan's seminal essay on Pip and Orlick, this is not to say that he did kill Bonteen in some psychic way – Finn is not Pip, and Bonteen not Mrs Joe – but there is in the haze that almostness produces, the sense of an unfinished tale, an unfinished murder, one that only loses its charge when Finn walks down this passage – not once, but twice.[26] If you'll recall, this happens, finally, as a purposive revisiting of the site of a trauma that didn't initially, but which has expanded to, include him.

This would be almost enough, but Trollope forces Finn down the alley one more time. He sends Finn, by accident, down this very same passage, a mesmerising coincidence when Finn short-circuits his return to the Universe Club. So, once more, Finn walks down the alley, the one gentlemen don't walk down, the one that 'almost' needn't be there at all:

> Once, and once only, did he break down. On the Wednesday evening he met Barringon Erle, and was asked by him to go to The Universe. At the moment he became very pale, but he at once said that he would go. Had Erle carried him off in a cab the adventure might have been successful; but as they walked, and as they went together through Clarges Street and Bolton Row and Curzon Street, and as the scenes which had been so frequently and so graphically described in Court appeared before him one after another, his heart gave way, and he couldn't do it. 'I know I'm a fool, Barrington; but if you don't mind I'll go home. Don't mind me, but just go on'. Then he turned and walked home, passing through the passage in which the murder had been committed. (ch. 74, p. 522)

If the narrator initially has insight into Finn's perspective when he first enters the uncanny alley, here, he is given no such access. What are we to make of Finn's insistence that he 'couldn't do it', that is, that he couldn't go to the club, when immediately after this, he turns on his heel and walks over the site of the murder? More, the casual tone of this trip down the alley, especially given the exactitude of Finn's earlier movement through that space, strikes an off note. Is this a sign that the trauma has been absorbed into Finn's life? No. This can't be, because he blanches at the thought of going into the Universe Club, the place that connected him to the murder in the first place. But this smooth movement here, 'passing through the passage', slips us into a world where Finn experiences no trauma on walking down this back alley. And it slips us once again into a world, just to the side of the one Trollope narrates, a world almost the same as Finn's, in which Finn is a murderer, and his movement down the alley does not upset him because he has been down the alley before, many times, and not just once. This passage implies a kind of connection between Finn's possible murder of Bonteen – the almostness of his criminality – and his need to turn, once again, down the alley behind Bolton Row. Trollope's narrator tells us, comfortably, that Phineas is not guilty of Bonteen's murder, 'the reader need hardly be told' of this fact, but then why these two uncanny passages? Are we to see Finn as a Pip, his violent feelings towards Bonteen managed and absorbed by Emilius's Orlick? Or is Trollope doing something different? In a world organised by 'almostness', there is the vague sense that Finn *could* have been the murderer, that merely accident keeps him from murdering Bonteen in Emilius's place.

I'll end, here, with a brief return to the idea that a word might count as a form. Word choice, as I've suggested, is most usually recruited to discussions of style. But what shifts if we connect these smallest units of style to the larger-scale concept of form? In *Forms*,

Caroline Levine draws our attention to the centrality of wholeness in many accounts of form.[27] Rather than pushing against this inclination, Levine suggests we 'multiply' rather than destroy formal wholeness: 'an effective strategy', writes Levine, 'for curtailing the power of harmfully totalizing and unifying wholes is nothing other than to introduce *more wholes*'.[28] In Levine's book, 'more wholes' often looks like wholes on a larger scale. And in one sense, what I'm arguing for here is, indeed, form on a grand scale: 285 'almosts' in a novel isn't nothing. But I want to challenge the orthodoxy of largesse; increased attention to excess is not the only way to reassess formalism as a method. In the case I've laid out in these pages, then, we might start to think of a dense, but minute, formalism that accounts for each word in a novel. From the New Critics to new historicism, and into the current moment of 'new formalism', we do a little bit of this each time we produce a close reading that depends on the particular historical and social meanings of a single word. Most often, the words we choose, as readers, are words with a particular conceptual density – as I suggested above, words like Eliot's 'yoke', or Hardy's 'fellow feeling'. Could a less obviously dense word have the same formal power? Digital humanists have argued so: that 'dense' are not the words that most readily identify authors: 'empty' words, particularly articles and pronouns, offer a digital humanist the best chances of identifying an author's particular style. To do this kind of work for each word in a novel? This is impractical. But perhaps if we give ourselves licence to think this way, loosely, we might make ourselves sensitive enough to perceive the gravitational power of a word as seemingly inconsequential as 'almost'. Thinking of form this way encourages us to think of the novel, almost, beyond history, beyond content, beyond character, and beyond story – none of the usual frameworks matter in a reading like this. Or, it doesn't matter at first. My suggestion, in these pages, has been that even this deracinated version of formal reading eventually leads us back into the thicket of history, plot and character that we usually associate with the novel as a literary form. We can, as in other readings, develop reasons for a specific word's density, its gravity. But there is still a surprise when we think of form this way: something that might not be as readily apparent if we searched a novel for a passage of free indirect discourse or a character type. Henry James and Anthony Trollope share a lot: they are both realistic writers, both are primarily read as novelists (though both wrote tales and essays, too), and both are read as novelists particularly attuned to social life, to the complex interpersonal networks that order our social worlds. But Trollope, as I argued above, is often read as slipshod, while James is read as maddeningly precise. When we look at them both through the lens 'almostness' gives us, though, we see something else. We can begin to see how the stories we tell ourselves about novels and novelists – about complexity and precision, and about laziness and repetition – block us from seeing similarity where it might be most evident: in the finest grain of the book – in, almost, a single word.

Notes

1. *An Autobiography* (London: Dodd, Mead, 1912), ch. 8, pp. 103–4.
2. Caroline Levine, *Forms: Whole, Rhythm, Hierarchy, Network* (Princeton: Princeton University Press, 2015).
3. Henry James, 'Anthony Trollope', in *Partial Portraits* (1888), reprinted in Donald Smalley (ed.), *Anthony Trollope: The Critical Heritage* (London: Routledge, 1969),

p. 527. Henry James's 1865 *Nation* review is an example of critical dissatisfaction with *Can You Forgive Her?*; in Smalley (ed.), *The Critical Heritage*, pp. 249–53. The unsigned *Spectator* notice included in the same volume remarks that the novel is 'more than usually loose and straggling' and that 'its central point is far more faint and colourless' than Trollope's other tales (p. 248).

4. James, review of *Can You Forgive Her?*, p. 252.

5. D. A. Miller, *The Novel and the Police* (Berkeley: University of California Press, 1988), pp. 114–15.

6. Ibid. p. 115.

7. In a crystalline version of this claim, which absorbs Trollope's most famous novel into its title, see Adam Gopnik's 'Trollope Trending: Why he's still the novelist of the way we live now' (*The New Yorker*, 4 May 2015), <http://www.newyorker.com/magazine/2015/05/04/trollope-trending> (last accessed 1 November 2016).

8. Digital humanists have developed some tools to describe 'aboutness'. See, for example, Paul Baker's essay about pro-fox hunting writing in the British popular press, which explains how discourse tracking can be used to analyse 'aboutness'; see '"The question is, how cruel is it?" Keywords, Foxhunting and the House of Commons', in Dawn Archer (ed.), *What's in a Word-list?: Investigating Word Frequency and Keyword Extraction* (London: Ashgate, 2009), pp. 125–36. Baker's small corpus drawn from debates around the legality of fox hunting demonstrate how discourse is the key to the 'aboutness' of a piece of writing. By analysing individual words, Baker could predict which side of the fox-hunting debate a speaker was on: pro-hunt speakers used words like 'people', 'Britain', 'freedom', 'fellow' and 'citizen', for example.

9. *Narrative Discourse Revisited* (Ithaca, NY: Cornell University Press, 1988), p. 74.

10. In the Palliser series, *The Duke's Children* has the fewest 'almosts' with 202, while *The Eustace Diamonds* has the most, with 389. To think about this comparatively, *Middlemarch* has 90, *Bleak House* 120, *Jude the Obscure* 91. In the American scene (and these are shorter novels, but the difference is striking), *The House of Mirth* has 62, *The Scarlet Letter* has 48, whereas *The Golden Bowl* has a Trollopian 225.

11. Dorothy van Ghent, *The English Novel: Form and Function* (New York: Harper, 1953), p. 214.

12. F. R. Leavis, *The Great Tradition* (New York: Doubleday, 1954), p. 156.

13. Anna Kornbluh, 'The Realist Blueprint', *The Henry James Review*, 36:3 (2015): p. 199.

14. See *The Novel Art: Elevations of American Fiction after Henry* (Princeton: Princeton University Press, 2001) and *The Program Era: Postwar Fiction and the Rise of Creative Writing* (Cambridge, MA: Harvard University Press, 2011), pp. 98–102.

15. Phil Fisher, *The New American Studies: Essays from* Representations (Berkeley: University of California Press, 1991), p. x.

16. Miller, *The Novel and the Police*, pp. 107–8.

17. Researchers focused on authorship attribution use 'function words' because their functionality makes them 'especially resistant to intentional manipulation by an author'; Dawn Archer, 'Does Frequency Really Matter?', in Dawn Archer (ed.), *What's in a Word-list?*, p. 5. This suggests that '[function word] frequencies should reveal authorial habits which remain relatively constant across a variety of texts' (p. 5). In fact, a given author's use of words that appear high in most used word lists, like pronouns and definite and indefinite articles, offers such researchers the best tools to identify a piece of writing with a specific author because these patterns are hard to manipulate. 'Function words' are chosen 'precisely because the statisticians join in the assumption that the words chosen are unambiguous enough in meaning and stable enough in incidence to admit direct contrasts between the habits of one writer and another or between the large slow phases of a development of style'; J. F. Burrows, *Computation into Criticism: A Study of Jane Austen's Novels and an Experimental Method* (Oxford: Clarendon Press, 1987), pp. 1–2.

18. See Jonathan Farina's 'Dickens "As If"', *Victorian Studies*, 53.3 (2011): pp. 435–6.
19. Books like Ann Banfield's *Unspeakable Sentences* (New York: Routledge, 1982), Dorit Cohn's *Transparent Minds* (Princeton: Princeton University Press, 1984) and, more recently, D. A. Miller's *Jane Austen, or, The Secret of Style* (Princeton: Princeton University Press, 2003) all suggest that free indirect discourse, with its capacity to blur the lines between diegetic and extra-diegetic space, is the central technology of the novel. Although the feature I'm describing might be related to FID, it is distinct. In a more recent formal intervention, David Kurnick draws attention to places where interiority fails to produce an 'alibi' for a character's erotic or scandalous behaviour, and connects those moments of failure to a larger claim about authorial failures in theatrical production; *Empty Houses: Theatrical Failure and the Novel* (Princeton: Princeton University Press, 2012), p. 83. Kurnick's claim, centrally, is that instead of imagining the novel as 'devoted to the all-importance of interiority, the theatrical spaces conjured in [his authors'] novels facilitate a distance from the notion of identitarian consistency' (p. 21). Slightly to the side of Kurnick's assessment, I am interested in the ways that characters can be consistently inconsistent; it is that vital oscillation that exposes the lie of characters' coherent interiors.
20. Miller writes: '[M]oderate schism' in fact structures both the clerical infighting in *Barchester Towers* and the considerable institutional and social coherence accruing to it. 'If there may be such a thing?' There can scarcely be anything else in the novel, where schism reaches neither the rupture nor the healing that are, alternatively, its promised ends. War is total inasmuch as victory never is. The controversies and power struggles that seem to throw such dishonour on the Church are not likely ever to be resolved, and only an outsider and parvenu like Slope is naïve enough to harbour 'a view to putting an end to schism in the diocese'. *The Novel and the Police* (Berkeley: University of California Press, 1988), pp. 114–15.
21. Anthony Trollope, *Phineas Finn* (Oxford: Oxford World's Classics, 2011). All references to *Phineas Finn* are given in the text (*PF*).
22. Ibid. ch. 70, p. 506.
23. Irene Tucker, *A Probable State: The Novel, the Contract, and the Jews* (Chicago: University of Chicago Press, 2000), pp. 5–6.
24. These passages stretch out actions across many chapters through repetition. For example: 'At last the door of the room above was opened, and our hero's hat was sent rolling down the stairs' (ch. 23, p. 168) which eventually returns to the narrator's attention as: 'As soon as the pistol had been fired and Phineas had escaped from the room, the unfortunate man had sunk back in his chair, conscious of what he had done, knowing that he had made himself subject to the law, and expecting every minute that constables would enter the room to seize him. He had seen his enemy's hat lying on the floor, and, when nobody would come to fetch it, had thrown it down the stairs' (ch. 52, p. 368). In a related, but distinct, habit, Trollope repeats phrases or works across multiple chapters to underscore a conceptual fact about a character or plot point. Think of the repetition of the inclusion of both Adelaide Palliser's upset and her very English French accent in repeated sobbing: 'Do you think I will marry the man I love when he tells me that by – marrying – me, he will be – banished to – Bou – logne?' (ch. 42, p. 300).
25. See Genette's discussion of the supposed impossibility of simultaneous focalisation in *Narrative Discourse*, pp. 76–8.
26. See Moynihan's 'The Hero's Guilt', *Essays in Criticism*, 10.1 (1960): pp. 60–79.
27. Levine, *Forms*, pp. 34–9.
28. Ibid. pp. 45–6.

2

HE HAD TAUGHT HIMSELF TO THINK: ANTHONY TROLLOPE ON SELF-CONTROL IN KNOWLEDGE AND BELIEF

Patrick Fessenbecker

IN HIS 1877 ESSAY 'The Ethics of Belief', W. K. Clifford famously argued that our moral responsibility is not limited to our actions, but extends to our beliefs.[1] Our ethical duties entail more than the requirement to act in certain ways; in fact, we have a duty to believe in certain ways as well. It can sound slightly Orwellian to say that one has a duty to believe something – a point I'll come back to – but the initial question is really about what sort of failure it is when one believes something false in the face of obvious evidence to the contrary. In his now-famous phrase, Clifford argues that 'it is wrong always, everywhere, and for anyone, to believe anything upon insufficient evidence'.[2] Anytime I have a belief that is based on 'insufficient evidence', then, I do something wrong.

His key argument for this claims depends, interestingly, upon a narrative:

> A shipowner was about to send to sea an emigrant-ship . . . Doubts had been suggested to him that possibly she was not seaworthy . . . he thought that perhaps he ought to have her thoroughly overhauled and refitted, even though this should put him to great expense. Before the ship sailed, however, he succeeded in overcoming these melancholy reflections. He said to himself that she had gone safely through so many voyages and weathered so many storms that it was idle to suppose she would not come safely home from this trip also. He would put his trust in Providence, which could hardly fail to protect all these unhappy families that were leaving their fatherland to seek for better times elsewhere. He would dismiss from his mind all ungenerous suspicions about the honesty of builders and contractors. In such ways he acquired a sincere and comfortable conviction that his vessel was thoroughly safe and seaworthy; he watched her departure with a light heart . . . and he got his insurance-money when she went down in mid-ocean and told no tales. (*EB*, p. 70)

Clifford concludes such a shipowner would be guilty of murder. And he contends that this is true even if the shipowner is sincere: 'It is admitted that he did sincerely believe in the soundness of his ship; but the sincerity of his conviction can in no wise help him, because he had no right to believe on such evidence as was before him' (*EB*, p. 70). In other words, the epistemological failure of believing the ship to be safe is at one and the same time a moral failure.

It is not hard to imagine a Trollope novel based around a similar story. Perhaps there is a young man on the board of directors of a shipping company; perhaps he is sent to conduct an inspection of a property while simultaneously having the opportunity to buy shares in it; of course, he is in debt, and resents any recognition that expensive repairs are necessary. As Trollope writes of Ferdinand Lopez, 'And so he taught himself to regard . . . himself as a victim. Who among us is there that does not teach himself the same lesson?'[3] Indeed, in that phrase – 'he taught himself' – Trollope marks precisely our epistemological responsibility: to teach oneself is, after all, to exert control over what one believes, and to make something a matter of one's control is also to make it subject to obligation. At the same time, in his rhetorical question – 'Who among us is there that does not teach himself the same lesson?' – Trollope indicates that the problem is by no means unique to villains like Ferdinand Lopez.

As David Skilton has pointed out, the idea of 'teaching oneself' is a characteristic feature in Trollope's fiction.[4] So much so, he observes, that it was in fact a source of criticism: Amy Dillwyn's 1881 review of *Ayala's Angel* faults Trollope 'for making people "tell", "teach", "encourage", or "bring" themselves to think this, that, or the other', when – in her opinion – 'various tenses of the verb "to think" would do equally well'.[5] Skilton argues – to my mind rightly – that Dillwyn here misses a key dimension of Trollope's art; what Skilton calls the 'internal monologue' and 'internal debate' forms a distinct level of action, and purely internal events at this purely internal level often form turning points in Trollope's narratives.[6] Without disagreeing with this characterisation, I want to argue here that Trollope's idea of teaching oneself marks something more specific: a distinctive kind of responsibility, an obligation to be selfless in belief as well as action.

John Kucich contended twenty years ago that 'one of the most important nineteenth-century conflations wrought by preoccupations with honesty . . . is that the relatively clean separation of epistemological and ethical concerns . . . suffered a wholesale collapse'.[7] I think that is right: for Trollope, the duty to be honest pertains to both beliefs and actions, and much of his thought is devoted to understanding how self-deception and irrationality can so pervasively threaten our honesty. My goal in this essay will be to briefly trace Trollope's use of the formula 'he taught himself to think' as a way of tracking his thinking about our responsibility for our beliefs. What that tracking suggests is that while Trollope would agree that Clifford's shipowner does indeed have a moral failing, it is not his dismissal of the evidence; it is rather his failure to be honest. To see this, let me turn to a brief taxonomy of the phrase 'he had taught himself to think'.

Varieties of Teaching Oneself

First and most straightforwardly, Trollope uses the idea of teaching oneself to mark a certain kind of self-deception. I've argued elsewhere that Trollope often depicts what philosophers call motivated reasoning in the use of lay hypothesis formation: that is, when moral agents are assessing evidence in support of beliefs, their desires affect which evidence seems most prominent, and Trollope's references to teaching oneself often indicate this kind of failure.[8] In *The Three Clerks*, for instance, Gertrude wants to believe that her husband Alaric Tudor is not doing anything underhanded; thus, she convinces herself that he is justified in being away from home during the evening – 'she taught herself to believe that his career required him to be among public men'.[9] A more specific type of this kind of self-deception is the motivated reasoning that characters use to justify their own selfishness. This is certainly what Ferdinand Lopez was doing, and *Barchester Towers*' Mr Slope offers a similar example, since, 'with that subtle, selfish, ambiguous sophistry to which the minds of all men are so subject, he had taught himself to think that in doing much for the promotion of his own interests, he was doing much also for the promotion of religion'.[10] Indeed, the analysis of this sort of 'sophistry' is common in Trollope: as Alice Vavasor observes in *Can You Forgive Her?*, Glencora Palliser has 'taught herself to think that she might excuse herself for this sin to her own conscience by the fact that she was childless'.[11] It is in part by describing motivated reasoning of this sort that Trollope's novels point to the psychological impediments constantly interrupting ethical behaviour. It is very difficult to tell, for Trollope's characters, whether they are deceiving themselves in acting as they do.

Yet teaching oneself can sometimes not be a failure but in fact a duty, or at least a praiseworthy action, marking the way a character reinforces his or her decision to act virtuously. For instance, Kate Vavasor, having come to believe that her brother George is not worthy of the support she has given him, attempts to reinforce the belief that she must not 'submit herself to his masterdom' (CY, ch. 55, p. 455). Thus we learn: 'She had gradually so taught herself since he had compelled her to write the first letter in which Alice had been asked to give her money' (CY, ch. 55, p. 455). Here, teaching oneself is an epistemic act at some distance from self-deception: rather than a failure of self-control, in which one's desires influence the process producing beliefs, it marks an act of successful self-control, where a character deliberately changes their beliefs to make sure they act in the way they believe they should. Moreover, when Trollope uses the notion of teaching oneself in the simple past or present tenses – as opposed to the more common past perfect formulation, as in a man who 'had taught himself' – it is often a metaphor for ordinary self-control. Thus we find Henry Norman 'schooling himself' in a praiseworthy attempt to master his jealousy of Alaric Tudor (TC, ch. 13, p. 130).

In its largest sense, then, the notion of teaching oneself in Trollope marks the responsibility agents have for their own character. And perhaps the most complex philosophical issues involved in the notion of teaching oneself occur in this light, when a lesson one teaches oneself conflicts with that character. This conflict is part of what is involved when characters fail to teach themselves something; often, it fails because the lesson violates a core value. A mark of wisdom in Trollope, in fact, is a recognition of what one can and cannot teach oneself; thus, in *The Last Chronicle of Barset*, the narrator tells us that Mr Harding 'could not teach himself to hope that Mr Crawley should be acquitted if Mr Crawley were guilty; – but he could teach himself to believe that Mr Crawley was innocent'.[12] Mr Harding's values will not permit him to sincerely believe that Mr Crawley should escape the penalty for a crime, but they do permit him to believe that the preponderance of the evidence is in this case mistaken and that Mr Crawley is innocent.

Yet often the characters do succeed in teaching themselves such lessons: in a tension between a belief they wish to have and a value at the core of their character, they exert sufficient self-control to instil the belief genuinely. This is perhaps the aspect of self-deception that most fascinates Trollope and forms one of his archetypes for tragedy.

I can only touch on the complexities of the issue here, but perhaps no one in Trollope teaches himself or herself as often as Lady Laura Kennedy does. And for her it is rarely straightforward: as Trollope represents it, it is always that she 'would' teach herself, or perhaps that she 'could not' teach herself, or – most intriguingly – that she 'had almost' taught herself.[13] In one of the instances of lengthy internal monologue that Skilton emphasises, Trollope writes this of Lady Laura:

> She had *schooled herself* about [Phineas Finn] very severely, and had come to various resolutions. She had found out and confessed to herself that she did not, and could not, love her husband. She had found out and confessed to herself that she did love, and could not help loving, Phineas Finn. Then she had resolved to banish him from her presence, and had gone the length of telling him so. After that she had perceived that she had been wrong, and had determined to meet him as she met other men, – and to conquer her love. Then, when this could not be done, when something almost like idolatry grew upon her, she determined that it should be the idolatry of friendship, that she would not sin even in thought, that there should be nothing in her heart of which she need be ashamed; – but that the one great object and purport of her life should be the promotion of this friend's welfare. She had just begun to love after this fashion, *had taught herself to believe* that she might combine something of the pleasure of idolatry towards her friend with a full complement of duty towards her husband, when Phineas came to her with his tale of love for Violet Effingham. The lesson which she got then was a very rough one, – so hard that at first she could not bear it . . . But by sheer force of mind she had conquered that dismay, that feeling of desolation at her heart, and *had almost taught herself to hope* that Phineas might succeed with Violet. (*PF*, ch. 44, p. 332, emphasis added)

Lady Laura presents a revealing contrast to Mr Harding: far from knowing herself well enough to know what she cannot teach herself, she has only come to certain unpleasant realisations through failed attempts at such teaching. In particular, she only sees how thoroughly she loves Phineas Finn when she tries to build a life without him, or with him as something other than her husband. Indeed, this last is striking, insofar as the passage emphasises Lady Laura's attempt to integrate her affection with the life she has made in some reasonably coherent way. After her failure to 'conquer' and erase her love, she then attempts to channel it into a career of advocacy on Phineas's behalf and a corresponding belief that this life can be satisfying, only for this belief to fail when Phineas wants to marry someone else. That she has 'almost' – but not quite – taught herself to accept the new fact of a Phineas married to someone else marks the strength of the conflict in Lady Laura's self. The 'almost' indicates the power of her ability to control her own beliefs, knowing as the reader does how difficult it is for her to abandon her love, yet it also indicates the power of the self that resists attempts at epistemological self-control by marking her failure. It's not surprising, then, that *Phineas Redux* shows Lady Laura on the brink of falling into reclusive insanity: her epistemological and emotional struggles demonstrate the deep fractures in her self.

The Claverings is notable for setting these three kinds of self-education in relation. The story is one common to Trollope's oeuvre: a young man, Harry Clavering, is engaged to one woman but drawn to another; committed to Florence Burton, he cannot help but visit Lady Ongar, who rejected him as a young man but who has now returned to England a rich widow. Like many of Trollope's other heroes, Harry is often self-deceived: he convinces himself that he is justified in flirting with Lady Ongar and can remain committed to Florence while doing so. For example, a key plot point involves whether Lady Ongar knows that Harry is engaged, or whether she thinks he is free. Without telling her that he is engaged, Harry convinces himself both that it would be a good idea for her to know and that she already does know: 'it would be well that she should know of his engagement. Then he thought of the whole interview, and felt sure that she must know it. At any rate he told himself that he was sure.'[14] As with the 'taught himself' formulation, the 'told himself' phrase here marks the extent to which Harry is deceiving himself. At the same time, we suspect he will find his way back to Florence, because he has 'taught himself to think much of the quiet domesticities of life', thus reinforcing his virtuous character (C, ch. 4, p. 31).

One might situate Harry Clavering in the middle of a self-control continuum, with Lady Ongar on the one end and Florence on the other. Lady Ongar's great sin, of course, is that she has married for money without love, while Florence has stayed true to her own affection for Harry. But we can perhaps be more precise: Lady Ongar has controlled her own beliefs. 'She had taught herself that romance could not be allowed to a woman in her position' (C, ch. 3, p. 21) and that, 'for such an one as her, riches were a necessity' (C, ch. 13, p. 105). As with Lady Laura Kennedy, this is a warping of her character; as she thinks of her 'riches' at the end of the novel, 'she came to understand that she was degraded by their acquisition', and thus 'she felt like Judas' (C, ch. 42, pp. 359–60). Florence presents a contrast in this regard, because, as the narrator emphasises, she has not taught herself anything: we learn that she 'had never taught herself to think that she, if she married, would want anything different from that which Providence had given to [her sisters]' (C, ch. 9, p. 70). This suggests that it is not only the mercenary impulse that makes Lady Ongar unworthy of Harry's affection. A more fundamental distinction is between a woman who exerts control over her beliefs, altering her character, and a woman who does not.

What this points towards, of course, is a balancing ideal: where what one teaches oneself accords with and allows for the expression of moral character, without overly repressing it. Trollope's comparison is revealing: 'nor is the heart of any man made so like a weathercock that it needs must turn itself hither and thither, as the wind directs, and be altogether beyond the man's control' (C, ch. 25, p. 209). In expanding upon the kind of control a man should exert, the narrator explains that 'a man, though he may love many, should be devoted only to one'. Much of what a man should do to respect his wife is 'quite independent of love', and 'may be done without love. This is devotion, and it is this which a man owes to the woman who has once promised to be his wife' (C, ch. 25, pp. 239–40). In other words, Harry might not be at fault in being in love with both Lady Ongar and Florence Burton, but he is at fault in devoting himself to both of them. Devotion is within his control, as it is independent of love, and it is his duty to be devoted to Florence that he has violated in flirting with Lady Ongar.

This suggests a tension of the sort characteristic of ideological effects. Trollope argues that it is proper for men to practise devotion: they may fall in love with many people in a morally unimpeachable way, and the only moral requisite is the conscious fostering of one particular relationship to the exclusion of others. However, for women to exert this kind of control is abhorrent: it is somehow a violation of who they really are. If there is anything to say in Trollope's defence, it is perhaps only that he recognises this issue. One of the most striking conversations in the book occurs between Florence's brother and his wife, debating Harry's merits:

> 'Can you believe any good of a man who tells you to your face that he is engaged to two women at once?'
>
> 'I think I can', said Cecilia, hardly venturing to express so dangerous an opinion above her breath.
>
> 'And what would you think of a woman who did so?'
>
> 'Ah, that is so different! I cannot explain it, but you know that it is different.'
>
> 'I know that you would forgive a man anything, and a woman nothing.' (C, ch. 21, p. 265)

In other words, Trollope does not inhabit these conceptions of gender unreflectively. In fact, it is striking that Trollope puts the defence of Harry in the mouth of a woman, and the critique of Harry – and, by extension, the principle that men and women should be held to the same standard – in the mouth of a man.

Dishonesty and Self-Awareness

It is worth acknowledging too that self-deception in Trollope occasionally works precisely by seeming to be an expression of one's real self or fundamental character. In *The Small House at Allington* this is the striking implication of a turning point in the narrative: the moment when Lily Dale, sensing inchoately that Adolphus Crosbie might be regretting their engagement, offers to end the relationship.[15] In one sense this is precisely what Crosbie has hoped for: the amount of money Lily would bring with her upon marriage has disappointed him. But he cannot bring himself to end the relationship: 'Then his heart misgave him, and he lacked the courage to extricate himself from his trouble; or, as he afterwards said to himself, he had not the heart to do it' (*SA*, ch. 15, p. 159). In this moment, Crosbie crucially lies to himself. As the narrator emphasises with the contrast between his initial reaction and subsequent self-reflection, Crosbie's desire to think well of himself – to not be the kind of person who would abandon a girl who loved him because she didn't have enough money – alters his understanding of what has happened. And it does so precisely through a representation of his inner nature. It is more tolerable to believe that his inner core of moral strength refused to let him abandon Lily than to believe that he was too weak to do what he ought to do; thus, he says to himself subsequently that it is his 'heart' that would not let him do it. Taking Crosbie's experience seriously indicates the extent to which one's fundamental character is often inaccessible for Trollope; the mere presence of self-reflection offers no guarantee that characters have succeeded in understanding themselves.

As Skilton notes, *The Small House at Allington* is fascinated more generally with the idea of self-management, and Trollope's depiction of Crosbie offers a sophisticated and extensive example of the failure of epistemological self-control and its relation to one's character.[16] It is important, first of all, that Crosbie refuses at another turning point in the novel to confront what his beliefs actually are. At Courcy Castle following his departure from Lily – a visit of which Trollope's narrator remarks, 'Under such circumstances Mr Crosbie should not have gone to

Courcy Castle' (*SA*, ch. 17, p. 177) – Crosbie's thoughts reveal that he has yet to really reflect on what he wants. Confronted by the public knowledge of his engagement, he finds himself telling John De Courcy, almost without thinking, that he is not in fact engaged – that it is 'all a lie' (*SA*, ch. 17, p. 181). Subsequently reflecting on what exactly to say to others about his engagement, he finds himself torn: on the one hand, he 'had never for a moment entertained a plea of not guilty'; on the other hand, 'he was aware of an aversion on his part to declare himself as engaged to Lilian Dale' (*SA*, ch. 17, p. 181). Importantly, he settles on a strategy that avoids any firm conclusion either way: 'might he not skilfully laugh off the subject?' (*SA*, ch. 17, p. 181). And indeed, he begins to resent the Dales precisely for making him commit: he 'felt for the first time that the Dale family had been almost indelicate in their want of reticence' while talking of his engagement to Lily (*SA*, ch. 17, p. 181). This is of course partly a question of practical deliberation – Crosbie has not yet decided what to do. But it is to a certain extent a question of knowledge as well: Crosbie does not know what to do because he does not yet know what he really wants. The failure to control himself, then, stems from a failure to know himself – a failure in particular to acknowledge his competing desires to marry Lily, to have the social life of an eligible bachelor, and to flirt with Alexandrina De Courcy. In this way, Trollope here, too, marks the close connection between self-control in belief and action.

Crosbie's subsequent deliberations reveal an important dimension of Trollope's representation of the relationship between belief, knowledge and character. As Crosbie engages in the process that will end in the conclusion that he should abandon Lily and marry Alexandrina, he does something besides merely betraying his moral character: he also misunderstands and acts against his own best interests. The moral failure is quite clear: Trollope's narrator writes that '[t]he atmosphere of Courcy Castle had been at work upon him . . . And every word that he had heard, and every word that he had spoken, had tended to destroy all that was good and true within him, and to foster all that was selfish and false' (*SA*, ch. 22, p. 245). This appears most directly in his conviction that in fact a relationship with Alexandrina would be good for Lily:

> What an advantage would such an alliance confer upon that dear little girl; – for, after all, though the dear little girl's attractions were very great, he could not but admit to himself that she wanted a something . . . which some people call style. Lily might certainly learn a great deal from Lady Alexandrina. (*SA*, ch. 17, p. 185)

Needless to say, it takes a particularly blinkered view to think that one should have an affair to further the stylistic education of one's fiancée. The narrator's sarcasm in a subsequent remark drives home the point: 'it was this conviction, no doubt, which made him so sedulous in pleasing that lady on the present occasion' (*SA*, ch. 17, p. 185).

But Crosbie's failure is also a prudential one – both a crime and a mistake, so to speak. This link emerges first when he conclusively decides to break with Lily, on the basis of reasons that Trollope represents as the products of a deep self-deception:

> He had said to himself a dozen times during that week that he never could be happy with Lily Dale, and that he never could make her happy. And then he had used the old sophistry in his endeavour to *teach himself* that it was right to do that

which he wished to do. Would it not be better for Lily that he should desert her, than marry her against the dictates of his own heart? And if he really did not love her, would he not be committing a greater crime in marrying her than in deserting her? He confessed to himself that he had been very wrong in allowing the outer world to get such a hold upon him that the love of a pure girl like Lily could not suffice for his happiness. But *there was the fact*, and he found himself unable to contend against it. If by any absolute self-sacrifice he could secure Lily's well-being, he would not hesitate for a moment. But would it be well to sacrifice her as well as himself? He had discussed the matter in this way within his own breast, till he *had almost taught himself* to believe that it was his duty to break off his engagement with Lily: and *he had also taught himself* to believe that a marriage with a daughter of the house of Courcy would satisfy his ambition and assist him in his battle with the world. (SA, ch. 22, p. 245, emphases mine)

Of course, Trollope's narrator is unsparing here: the overt designation of this chain of reasoning as 'sophistry' drives the moral point home. Noteworthy, though, is the link between two separate acts of self-teaching in the final sentence: it brings together his work on himself to believe that he has a moral duty to break his engagement and his corresponding work to believe that marrying Alexandrina will be the best way to pursue his interests. This is to say that moral and practical beliefs are here combined: in addition to considering what he owes to Lily, Crosbie is considering at the same time what will make him happy. The passage drives home in this moment the extent to which the first act is self-deceived, but what the end of the novel shows is that the second is similar: in other words, Crosbie makes just as significant a mistake in assessing what will make him happy as he does in assessing what he owes to Lily.

This conjunction may seem surprising. After all, on a common-sense view, it is precisely the egoistic emphasis on one's own happiness that leads one to self-deceiving justifications of dismissing obligations to other people. But Trollope touches on a subtle philosophical point – the inadequacy of the simplistic conception of egoism, and the extent to which prudence and morality are in fact expressions of the same capacity for self-mastery. To put it somewhat more precisely, for Trollope there is a link between practical deliberation capable of recognising one's long-term interest over short-term desires and moral deliberation that acknowledges other people, in the sense that an inability to do one is often caused by and causative of a failure to do the other. In her recent work on egoism, Christine Korsgaard has pointed out that the idea of a selfish pursuit of one's happiness is a kind of normativity – after all, it requires the egoistic agent to dismiss those desires that seem to distract from the pursuit of maximum happiness, and prioritise those that contribute most substantively to it.[17] Thus, given a conflict between two incompatible desires, where satisfying one offers more immediate pleasure while satisfying the other offers more happiness overall (that is, over the course of one's life), it is a normative claim to say that is more 'rational' to pursue the second.

If one can imagine taking the perspective of the first, ignored desire, a kind of scepticism about this appeal to rationality seems possible. Why, exactly, is it more rational to prefer greater happiness over the course of one's life to greater satisfaction right now? 'The individual desire whose satisfaction is sacrificed for the sake of overall happiness', Korsgaard points out, 'seems to have some right to protest'.[18]

This scepticism, however, is structurally parallel to scepticism about morality more generally; as Korsgaard writes, '"Why should I be prudent?" is as much in need of an answer as its more famous cousin.'[19] Accordingly, an account of rationality strong enough to answer the question of prudence – in other words, why I ought to care for some broader, long-term fact like my overall happiness more than I care about some powerful desire right now – also justifies an account of moral obligation. Conversely, it shouldn't be surprising – and this is what Trollope depicts with such subtlety – that prudential mistakes and moral failures go together. The sort of selfless-ness that enables one to recognise one's duties is also the sort of broader perspective that enables recognition of what will actually contribute to one's overall happiness. So it's not at all surprising, in this light, for Crosbie to have made both mistakes. In fact, they're really the same mistake: an inability to confront and surmount the desires of the moment.

There is a corresponding epistemological point. Crosbie's failure is not an inad-equate confrontation with the evidence: indeed, in this context there's no relevant evidence other than his own internal psychological data. But his belief formation can nevertheless still be deeply flawed, a fact Trollope highlights – as usual – by explain-ing what Crosbie has 'taught himself' to think. Ironically, the self-deception consists in precisely his conviction that he is not being selfish. Under the guise of an open and honest 'confession' to himself that he has behaved badly, Crosbie licenses his self-ishness. The narrator is not quiet about condemning this sort of dishonesty, asking rhetorically, 'How many a false hound of a man has endeavoured to salve his own conscience by such mock humility?' (*SA*, ch. 22, p. 247). And in treating his desires to live in the 'outer world' as a fact that must be acknowledged rather than overcome, Crosbie's limited sincerity serves to conceal a greater selfishness.

The tragicomic effects of Crosbie's story depend on this self-deception, as he does not achieve clarity until it is too late, when he is irretrievably committed to Alexandrina De Courcy. After he has realised how painful life with Alexandrina will be, the narrator explains that the life will be all the more painful because of his missed opportunity:

> It was in this that Crosbie's failure had been so grievous, – that he had seen and approved the better course, but had chosen for himself to walk in that which was worse. During that week at Courcy Castle, – the week which he passed there imme-diately after his second visit to Allington, – he had deliberately made up his mind that he was more fit for the bad course than for the good one. The course was now before him, and he had no choice but to walk in it. (*SA*, ch. 45, p. 400)

Notably, the passage refuses to excuse Crosbie for his self-deception. Rather than sug-gesting that he was unfortunate in being misled, the narrator here condemns Crosbie for 'deliberately' choosing the 'bad course'. It is a slightly confusing way to describe the scene – after all, in the moment of decision, Crosbie seems to have convinced himself that the bad course was good, rather than reflectively choosing the bad course while recognising its badness – but what the narrator means to emphasise is the extent to which Crosbie is responsible for his own self-deception. Rather than openly con-fronting his unattractive desires for more money, he let himself be deceived both into thinking that abandoning Lily was really the right thing to do, and that what he really required for happiness was a connection to the De Courcy family.

Honesty and Evidence

We saw at the beginning that Clifford thinks our duties to believe something stem from the evidence available to us. As I have suggested, this is not an especially important criterion for Trollope: while he is inclined to agree that we have duties to believe certain things, what and how we should teach ourselves has more to do with our characters than anything to do with the evidence. Now, just at this moment in history, it might seem that Clifford captures a powerful truth. One doesn't have to read too many essays calling climate change a hoax to think that perhaps we do indeed have a duty to follow the evidence.[20] As Clifford puts it,

> no one man's belief is in any case a private matter which concerns himself alone. Our words, our phrases, our forms and processes and modes of thought, are common property . . . An awful privilege, and an awful responsibility, that we should help to create the world in which posterity will live. (*EB*, p. 74)

As the experience of global climate change is demonstrating every day, the refusal of every individual to hold their beliefs to a rigorous standard and the corresponding determination of some to hold onto beliefs not supported by the evidence has real consequences. Much as we might like to think otherwise, we do not hold our beliefs independently of each other. As Simon Blackburn has recently put it, 'Clifford is right. Someone sitting on a completely unreasonable belief is sitting on a time bomb.'[21]

But I mentioned that there was something slightly Orwellian about Clifford's position, and it comes in the implicit ideal of a fully rational society, without disagreement, where all beliefs reflect a shared assessment of the evidence. It's not an accident, I think, that Clifford doesn't imagine the search for evidence will impair the beliefs in moral truths:

> Certain great principles . . . have stood out more and more clearly in proportion to the care and honesty with which they were tested, and have acquired in this way a practical certainty. The beliefs about right and wrong which guide our actions in dealing with men in society . . . these never suffer from investigation; they can take care of themselves. (*EB*, pp. 78–9)

In other words, Clifford's world is one that very explicitly does not allow for substantive moral disagreement: he simply assumes that the 'great principles' of moral life are already known and acted upon, and that the call to base beliefs entirely and only upon evidence will have no effect on these beliefs. As Helen Small has brought out, it's important to remember that Clifford was not in fact aligned with the utilitarian tradition – which offers a view of moral deliberation that fits naturally with an emphasis on evidence – but rather demonstrated significant sympathy with the intuitionist ethics of William Whewell.[22]

And in 'Right and Wrong: The Scientific Ground of their Distinction', the essay Clifford wrote immediately before 'The Ethics of Belief', empirical investigation is limited to considering how best a moral belief might contribute to society; the basic moral assumption – that the 'function' of 'conscience' is 'the preservation of society in the struggle for existence', and that it carries normative force – is unquestioned.[23] Indeed the end of the essay becomes quite declarative on moral truths and feels no need to appeal to evidence: 'I cannot believe', Clifford writes, 'that any falsehood whatever is necessary to morality. It cannot be true of my race and yours that to keep ourselves from becoming scoundrels we must needs believe a lie.'[24] The phrase 'it cannot be true' is striking, since a rigorous attempt to ground all our beliefs on evidence requires admitting precisely that all sorts of fundamental beliefs might be true or false and thus in need of investigation. Thus Clifford only defended his rigorous criterion for belief by separating certain classes of beliefs – in particular our moral beliefs – off from it.

It is to Trollope's credit that he sees this account cannot be quite right: moral disagreement is more fundamental than Clifford would have it. Yet it still seems right to say that people like Clifford's shipowner, not to mention climate-change deniers like Senator James Inhofe, are committing a failure of some sort in believing as they do. If the problem is not their dismissal of evidence, then what is it? For Trollope, the worry about what you might 'teach yourself' wasn't that you might ignore relevant evidence: it was that you might let what you want to be true affect the way you would have assessed the evidence anyway. The self-deception he traces in the moments when his characters 'teach themselves' into a moral failing is one that licenses selfishness, and it is that selfishness that is the problem, not the dismissal of evidence. Clifford's interpreters have often portrayed him as gesturing (somewhat inchoately) towards a special kind of duty: epistemic duties, as opposed to moral or political duties. As Susan Haack puts the point, 'Clifford fails to distinguish "epistemologically wrong" from "morally wrong"', but is correct in thinking that 'it is always epistemologically wrong to believe on inadequate evidence'.[25] Such a distinction is however irrelevant for Trollope: there is no special obligation to believe the truth, whatever that might be. Rather, the obligation in belief is the same as in ordinary action – namely, to not let one's preference for oneself enable the dismissal of other people.

This is to say, in Trollope's preferred terminology, that the shipbuilder is not honest: the problem is not that he dismissed relevant evidence, but that in forming his beliefs about the ship, he did not attain the selflessness he needed. And if he had done so, my own sense is that we would then not hold him necessarily at fault: in a residue of Victorian terminology, we would say he had committed 'an honest mistake'. As regards global climate change, one need only consult the donations from fossil-fuel companies to those politicians who claim it is a hoax to see that Trollope's contention about honesty might have some bearing there as well.[26]

To understand honesty in this way is to see it as an ethics of belief meaningfully different from Clifford's. To take Clifford's test seriously imposes a radical scepticism: genuinely subjecting all our beliefs to the requirement of evidentiary support, after all, will at least at first require a kind of epistemological forest-clearing. As a number of philosophers since Clifford have pointed out – William James perhaps most prominently – many trees we have good reason to care about will get cut down by Clifford's axe.[27] One can see Trollope's recommendation of honesty, then, as a way of preserving the intuitions behind Clifford's view in an account of the ethics of belief that nevertheless permits a space for the many kinds of belief where an insistence on evidence is unhelpful or damaging.

This description of Trollope's conceptualisation of honesty aligns with the view that Amanda Anderson has been developing recently, which portrays Trollope as torn between respect for 'traditional forms of life' and deep liberal commitments.[28] On this view, honesty has a double role: on the one hand, it is a form of 'characterological virtue' exemplified in the silent dignity of Trollope's traditional, 'gentlemanly' characters; on the other hand, it can be an openly articulated form of critique, when the honest moral agent encounters pervasive dishonesty and directly states that it is so.[29] What my account shows is that this double role of honesty is made possible by a re-description of the ethics of belief. To require that all one's virtues and psychological characteristics be assessed on the basis of the best available evidence, after all, would be to let the capacity for critique inherent in honesty overwhelm its characterological dimensions. Limiting epistemic normativity to an aspiration to selflessness, defined as the recognition and dismissal of biasing desire, is a thus a necessary condition for the view that unreflective honesty and indeed the virtues more generally should play a role in moral life.

And though a longer treatment would be necessary to bring this point out, my account of Trollope aligns as well with George Levine's argument in *Dying To Know*, insofar as Levine finds in Trollope's *Autobiography* an interest in the problem of objectivity and the belief that a kind of self-effacement is necessary to attain knowledge.[30] There is however a minor but interesting difference: Levine aligns the pursuit of honesty and the pursuit of objectivity, as if each are versions of the same project.[31] But if the argument given here is correct, honesty does not require the same self-abnegation as the epistemic norms of Cliffordian evidentialism, and is in fact already a compromise between that conception of the objective stance and the limits of the embodied self.

But I want to end by returning briefly to John Kucich. Reading *The Power of Lies* a generation after it was first published, what's striking is how the book feels the need to justify caring about Victorian moral philosophy at all. Kucich can only address the 'bewilderment or indifference' of colleagues who hear he's 'writing about Victorian ethics' by showing that such ethics are not simply 'a philosophical system' but are also a (presumably more interesting) 'reservoir of ideological content'.[32] Without addressing the methodological questions involved here, it seems to me that critics have not exhausted the possibilities that lie in reading Victorian writers philosophically.[33] Much of what makes novels like *The Claverings* or *The Small House at Allington* worth reading is the complexity of their investigations of moral psychology: thinking through their depiction of moral agency is often just what it means to enjoy them.[34] In that sense, to treat Trollope as substantively engaging philosophical questions is to respect the nature of his art.

Notes

1. This article was written with financial support from the Danish National Research Foundation (DNRF127).
2. W. K. Clifford, 'The Ethics of Belief', in *The Ethics of Belief and Other Essays* (New York: Prometheus Books, 1999), pp. 70–96 (p. 77). Further citations are marked *EB* and included parenthetically in the text.
3. Anthony Trollope, *The Prime Minister* (New York: Penguin, 1994), ch. 45, p. 389.
4. David Skilton, *Anthony Trollope and His Contemporaries: A Study in the Theory and Conventions of Mid-Victorian Fiction* (London: Macmillan, 1996), p. 140.
5. Amy Dillwyn, 'Ayala's Angel', *The Spectator* (18 June 1881), pp. 804–5.
6. Skilton, *Anthony Trollope and His Contemporaries*, p. 140.

7. John Kucich, *The Power of Lies: Transgression in Victorian Fiction* (Ithaca, NY: Cornell University Press, 1994), p. 13.

8. Patrick Fessenbecker, 'Anthony Trollope on Akrasia, Self-Deception, and Ethical Confusion', *Victorian Studies*, 56.4 (Summer 2014): pp. 649–74.

9. Anthony Trollope, *The Three Clerks* (London: Bentley, 1867), ch. 33, p. 401. Further citations marked *TC* and included parenthetically in the text.

10. Anthony Trollope, *Barchester Towers* (Oxford: Oxford University Press, 1998), ch. 15, p. 136. Further citations marked *BT* and included parenthetically in the text.

11. Anthony Trollope, *Can You Forgive Her?* (Oxford: Oxford University Press, 2012), ch. 28, p. 235. Further citations marked *CY* and included parenthetically in the text.

12. Anthony Trollope, *The Last Chronicle of Barset* (New York: Penguin, 2002), ch. 42, p. 421. Further citations included parenthetically in the text.

13. This passage, for instance, shows her wavering between several states: 'Having put aside all romance as unfitted to her life, she could, she thought, do her duty as Mr Kennedy's wife. She would teach herself to love him. Nay, – she had taught herself to love him.' Anthony Trollope, *Phineas Finn* (Oxford: Oxford University Press, 2011), ch. 22, p. 164. Further citations marked *PF* and included parenthetically in the text.

14. Anthony Trollope, *The Claverings* (New York: Dover, 1977), ch. 8, p. 63. Further citations marked *C* and included parenthetically in the text.

15. Anthony Trollope, *The Small House at Allington* (New York: Penguin, 1991). Citations marked *SA* and included parenthetically in the text.

16. See Skilton, *Anthony Trollope and His Contemporaries*, p. 140.

17. *The Constitution of Agency: Essays on Practical Reason and Moral Psychology* (Oxford: Oxford University Press, 2008).

18. Ibid. p. 72.

19. Ibid.

20. See, for instance, 'Tens of Thousands of Scientists Declare Climate Change A Hoax', <http://yournewswire.com> (last accessed 11 November 2016). For a more thorough study of climate change denialism, see Naomi Oreskes and Eric M. Conway, *Merchants of Doubt* (London: Bloomsbury, 2010).

21. *Truth: A Guide for the Perplexed* (Oxford: Oxford University Press, 2005), p. 5.

22. Helen Small, 'Science, Liberalism, and the Ethics of Belief: The *Contemporary Review* in 1877', in Geoffrey Cantor and Sally Shuttleworth (eds), *Science Serialized: Representations of the Sciences in Nineteenth-Century Periodicals* (Cambridge, MA: MIT Press, 2004), pp. 239–57, p. 243. She goes on to offer a telling example – Clifford's own inability to maintain a rigorous self-control in the face of the complexity of actual, lived moral dilemmas.

23. 'Right and Wrong: The Scientific Ground of Their Distinction', in *Ethics of Belief and Other Essays*, pp. 28–69 (p. 64).

24. 'Right and Wrong', p. 69.

25. Susan Haack, '"The Ethics of Belief" Reconsidered', in Matthias Steup (ed.), *Knowledge, Truth, and Duty: Essays on Epistemic Justification, Responsibility, and Virtue* (Oxford: Oxford University Press, 2001), pp. 21–33, pp. 27–8. There is a significant and growing literature on the nature of epistemic norms and their relation to other forms of normativity; see, for instance, Nikolaj Nottelmann's *Blameworthy Belief: A Study in Epistemic Deontologism* (New York: Springer, 2007).

26. See *Merchants of Doubt*, or more specifically opensecrets.org's page on Senator James Inhofe's donations, which include $481,450 from the oil and gas industry between 2011 and 2016, <https://www.opensecrets.org/politicians/summary.php?cid=N00005582> (last accessed 11 November 2016).

27. James's famous defence of a pragmatic theory of truth was developed in part against Clifford's insistence on evidence: the analysis of a 'will to believe' in particular saw him

arguing that one could hold certain beliefs even in cases of insufficient or absent evidence. See Timothy Madigan, *W. K. Clifford and the Ethics of Belief* (Cambridge: Cambridge Scholars Press, 2009) for a clear explanation of the various responses to Clifford's argument, including James's.

28. *Bleak Liberalism* (Chicago: University of Chicago Press, 2016), p. 68.
29. Ibid. pp. 64–6.
30. *Dying To Know: Scientific Epistemology and Narrative in Victorian England* (Chicago: University of Chicago Press, 2002), p. 99.
31. Ibid. p. 2.
32. *The Power of Lies* pp. 37–8, p. 2.
33. I have gone somewhat further in addressing these matters at a methodological level in my essay 'In Defense of Paraphrase', *New Literary History*, 44.1 (January 2013): pp. 117–39.
34. Frederik Van Dam has persuasively argued that many of Trollope's works should be read as intentional paraphrases of classical ideas and texts, reflecting his attempt to bring such works to a reading public unable to read easily in Latin or Greek; see *Anthony Trollope's Late Style: Victorian Liberalism and Literary Form* (Edinburgh: Edinburgh University Press, 2016), p. 82. In that sense, to use philosophical paraphrase as our approach to his novels now is only in keeping with Trollope's project.

3

THE PHYSIOLOGY OF THE EVERYDAY: TROLLOPE'S DEFLECTED INTIMACIES OF CLOTHING, TOUCH AND FREE INDIRECT DISCOURSE

Sophie Gilmartin

IN 1871 GEORGE ELIOT wrote in *Middlemarch* of 'the subtle muscular movements which are not taken account of in the consciousness, though they bring about the end that we fix our mind on and desire'.[1] Subtle, almost imperceptible, physical movements come into play in Anthony Trollope's *Can You Forgive Her?* (1864), as the estranged Glencora and Plantagenet Palliser come to a loving understanding with one another: 'Softly, slowly, very gradually, as though he were afraid of what he was doing, he put his arm around her waist . . . She shook her head, touching his breast with her hair as she did so.'[2] Of this scene, the late Stephen Wall wrote that 'Trollope's attentiveness to what each character is thinking is wonderfully unobtrusive, not least in the registration of small but intensely suggestive details of gesture and movement.'[3] George Eliot was conversant with developments in nineteenth-century psychology that posited a materialist concept of the mind, and that argued for the powerful relationship between the body and the unconscious. Her partner, George Henry Lewes, wrote widely on physiology and the mind, notably in his *The Physiology of Common Life* (1859); intellectually alive as they were to each other's work, Eliot was imbued with these ideas. Her novels are interpolated with educative addresses to the reader on new scientific thinking and discoveries, and among these her preoccupation with physiology and the mind is clear. Anthony Trollope also addresses the reader directly, often, but his 'digressions' are rarely concerned with current scientific discoveries or, more specifically, the relationship between body and the unconscious. His familiar, sometimes avuncular narrator proclaims on social matters, fashions and politics, both parliamentary and bedroom. But this seeming lack of gravity or erudition, as compared with his contemporary George Eliot, belies his subtlety and intensive noticing of the reciprocal and constant effects of mind on body, and body on mind. Trollope's writing is not sensational in the same way by which Wilkie Collins's 'woman in white' sent a shock of almost electric impulses through Walter Hartright's body when she gently touched his shoulder in the dusk on Hampstead Heath. Nevertheless, it is very specific, detailed and attentive to how subjectivity, mood and intention may be affected by touch, gesture, one's placement in a room, on a street, or on a fell in Cumbria, or by those 'subtle muscular movements' that lie outside consciousness. Comparing Trollope with sensation writers of the day, and especially Wilkie Collins, Jenny Bourne Taylor writes that 'his multi-plotted stories . . . suggest a multi-faceted reality springing from an intense sense of the significance of detail, in which emotional extremity is often generated through immediate physical response'.[4] This chapter will investigate the subtleties of the superficial in Trollope's writing. The superficies of clothing and how it touches the body; of his characters' physical stances and gestures, and how Trollope places them in a physical space: these aspects of bodily sensation, feeling, movement and spatial awareness often have a strong reciprocal or symbiotic relationship with the subtleties of mind and the unconscious, and of a character's revealed interiority through both direct and indirect discourse.

There are sudden breaks in Trollope's writing from direct speech, direct narration and free indirect discourse, when he turns to a quirky and particular attention to rugs, tables and mantelpieces – the things in a place and his specific deployment of his characters vis-à-vis these things; how we see his characters touch things, touch each other and how their clothes take up space. J. Hillis Miller reflects upon the sensory, spatial images that arise in the mind of the reader of Trollope's novels:

> When I read [*Framley Parsonage*], a vivid imaginary world opens up for me. Just what is that imaginary world like? It is different for each work and no doubt for each reader or for each reading by the same reader. What my inner imaginary world is like when I read *Framley Parsonage* is a complex question. It is also one not much talked about, even in recent research in cognitive science about what happens in reading.[5]

Rather than cognitive science, he considers 'the subjective sensory images as the reader reports them: "Now I am seeing my idea of a long drawing room with many fashionably dressed people standing or sitting in it"'.[6] Even if our mental images of characters and places are influenced by the illustrations of Millais and other artists, by television adaptations, or Victorian daguerreotypes, the pictures in our heads as we read – as Hillis Miller says – 'exceed the data' of what we are given by the author or remember from elsewhere.[7]

To stop oneself, self-consciously, at a moment of reading to ask oneself exactly what is the mental image just formed while reading can feel almost uncanny. The reader mentally seems to remember and repeat a memory that is not their own, but is felt to be, and an elusive image that they only half-created. This readerly act of self-consciousness defamiliarises that which is seemingly intrinsic to the act of reading a novel. And while the pictures in our heads 'exceed the data' given to us, Trollope does make a fascinating case of a writer who provides excessive data – so excessive that the reader might brush it off mentally, if it were not for the fact that Trollope is an idiosyncratic master at stopping the reader in the flow of narrative. He stops the reader in their tracks, forcing upon them an attention to the sensory world that his characters are living in at that moment, and to the surfaces and objects that impinge upon the language of a particular scene. While Trollope rarely describes a landscape – at least not in Romantic or picturesque terms – his description of a room can become very abruptly as particular as Ibsen's meticulous blocking and set descriptions.

Scenes from two early chapters of Trollope's novel *Can You Forgive Her?* (1864) demonstrate this mixture of material detail, physical and spatial awareness, and interiority. Alice Vavasor is on holiday in Switzerland with her cousins Kate and George. Two consecutive chapters deal with the last evening of their holiday, at an inn in Basle: 'The Balcony at Basle', and 'The Bridge Over the Rhine'. The tension of these chapters lies in the fact that Alice was once engaged to her cousin George, but broke it off, and is now engaged to the loving, safe, but perhaps aptly named, John Grey, who is not there. On the last night, George challenges Alice to reconsider her engagement and puts himself forward again. In considering the physical locations of these two chapters, we could say that Alice is deciding between two men and is therefore caught in a liminal space (and indeed engagement itself was viewed as liminal for women, placed as they were between the father's and the husband-to-be's authority). So Alice on the balcony is neither outside nor in, and on the bridge she walks between two shores. In this sense these spaces are 'symbolic', but that is not what really gives the reader pause in this and other scenes that lie in physical spaces brought forward for our attention. The following description is 'symbolic' in many ways, but its sheer actuality and its attention to mere objects are finally more subtle.

> Alice and George were left together sitting on the balcony ... Alice was seated quite at the end of the gallery, and Kate's chair was at her feet in the corner. When Alice and Kate had seated themselves, the waiter had brought a small table for the coffee-cups, and George had placed his chair on the other side of that. So that Alice was, as it were, a prisoner. She could not slip away without some special preparation for going, and Kate had so placed her chair in leaving, that she must actually have asked George to move it before she could escape. But why should she wish to escape? Nothing could be more lovely and enticing than the scene before her.[8]

The description seems – is – prosaic. Why here does Trollope instruct the reader to visualise this small space of tables, chairs and coffee cups? Certainly, calling Alice a 'prisoner' has symbolic cultural and gender resonance, but the data exceeds this point. The very objects in this scene and the way they deflect or demand contact is doing something here in setting up the language that ensues: George's intense direct speech and especially Alice's free indirect discourse (FID).

The mundane and meticulous description of the placement of everyday paraphernalia on the balcony demands that the reader visualise and imaginatively inhabit the space. With his characters and readers among the coffee cups, Trollope's writing suddenly moves from the prosaic to the poetic and a heightened sense of perception: from 'she must actually have asked George to move [the chair] before she could escape' to the FID, 'But why should she wish to escape? Nothing could be more lovely and enticing than the scene before her.' The description of the night over the Rhine goes on at length, using the narratorial voice inflected with Alice's thoughts, then further into Alice's mind through FID. This produces sensory absorption in both character and reader:

> Nothing could be more lovely and enticing than the scene before her. The night had come on ... but there was a rising moon, which just sufficed to give a sheen to the water beneath her. The air was deliciously soft – of that softness which

produces no sensation either of warmth or cold, but which just seems to touch one with loving tenderness, as though the unseen spirits of the air kissed one's forehead as they passed on their wings. The Rhine was running at her feet, so near, that in the soft half-light it seemed as though she might step into its ripple. The Rhine was running by with that delicious sound of rapidly moving waters, that fresh refreshing gurgle of the river, which is so delicious to the ear at all times. If you be talking, it wraps up your speech, keeping it for yourselves, making it difficult neither to her who listens nor to him who speaks. If you would sleep, it is of all lullabies the sweetest. If you are alone and would think, it aids all your thoughts. If you are alone, and, alas! would not think, – if thinking be too painful, – it will dispel your sorrow, and give the comfort which music alone can give. Alice felt that the air kissed her, that the river sang for her its sweetest song, that the moon shone for her with its softest light, – that light which lends the poetry of half-developed beauty to everything that it touches. Why should she leave it?[9]

Trollope admits a few pages earlier in the novel that he has just returned from his holidays in Switzerland, so these or similar perceptions are still fresh to him. In this long descriptive passage, consciousness of the environment is divided between the narrator and Alice's mind revealed in FID. It is not always easy to decide where the narrator leaves off and Alice's consciousness takes over. Trollope is emphasising something here about consciousness itself: we need the narrator to 'say' some things about the scene because Alice cannot verbalise to herself all that is around her: the sound of the river 'wraps up speech'; the river is seen in 'half-light'; its light lends the poetry of 'half-developed' beauty; she experiences a 'half-feeling of danger'.[10] Even an omniscient narrator cannot make us see or sense everything, and in this Trollope makes us aware not only of the tendency of his character's consciousness, but of consciousness generally. Alice's FID here is about what she half-sees, hears as a background, senses on the skin, and these sensory perceptions are half-consciously connected in her mind to a sense of danger that she cannot quite shake off, and her unanswered question of why she should leave the balcony where a man to whom she is half-attracted sits, barring her way: 'There was something that each felt to be sweet, indefinable and dangerous.'[11] We know that if we were fully to perceive the sensory world around us – every drip of the tap, buzz of the lightbulb, we would be if not driven mad, then at least driven to distraction. Equally no reader can perceive everything in the imagined world we inhabit when we read, but Trollope insists nevertheless in placing his characters here firmly among the tables and chairs before he describes the half-descried beauties of the poetic river scene. He raises an awareness in us that we can only half-perceive, but that what our bodies touch and feel subliminally is potent and affecting. Alice, sitting on the balcony, immersed in the beauties of the river and moonlight, remembers somewhere on the edge of her consciousness, in the vibrations of the air and her crinoline, that she may not only smash a coffee cup on trying to leave the balcony, but will brush closely against her ex-lover's body. Like the sweep of a crinoline against another body, or the touch of a hand through a glove, FID is a slightly removed, indirect intimacy. Trollope underlines the relationship between the physical environment, the body, mind and language through the attenuated intimacies of FID.

In his *The Physiology of Common Life* (1859), George Henry Lewes studies how the relationship between physiology and psychology is apparent and demonstrable in the occurrences of everyday life. He gives an example of the sound of a mill wheel in a river (and he wrote this in the same period that his partner George Eliot was writing *The Mill on the Floss*):

> The mill-wheel, at first so obtrusive in its sound, ceases at length to excite any attention. The impressions on our auditory nerves continue; but although we hear them, we cease to think about them: the same reflex feelings are no longer excited. It is held, indeed, that we cease to hear them, in ceasing to be 'conscious' that we hear them; but this is manifestly erroneous. Let the wheel suddenly stop, and there is an immediate corresponding sensational change in us; so much so, that if it occurs during sleep, we awake . . . It afterwards ceased to excite these feelings, and the sensations became *merged* on the general sum of sensations which make up our total Consciousness.[12]

While Alice hears the river 'at her feet', it could be said to have merged with those other sensations making up her consciousness: her mind is absorbed in thoughts and memories, and her sense of sound, touch, light and temperature culminate in the interiority of the FID, 'Why should she leave it?' But Trollope interprets sensation rather differently to Lewes. Lewes writes, 'although a sensation must discharge itself . . . now exciting muscular contractions, and now trains of thought, we are not to suppose the sensation itself is dependent on these effects . . . Sensation is simply the active state of Sensibility, which is the property of ganglionic tissue'[13]. For Trollope however the sound of the river is affected by the interpretive consciousness of the hearer: the river's rush may be lulling, quieting, comforting or inspiring of intimacy. Alice hears it on the edge of her consciousness; the noise carries her mind with the river's drift, a feeling that is voiced by her less restrained cousin Kate a few pages later on the bridge over the Rhine:

> 'I should so like to feel myself going with the stream . . . particularly by this light. I can't fancy in the least that I should be drowned . . . it would be so pleasant to feel the water gliding along one's limbs, and to be carried away headlong.'[14]

Kate fantasises about a freedom by which she is barred from returning home from holiday because the river has carried her away in its drift. She would hardly need to swim; muscular effort would be unnecessary as she could simply glide, feeling the water along her body. Similarly, on the balcony, Alice's muscles relax and she feels no need for movement, her mind and body are made passive by this drift. But Alice's lulled interiority is suddenly interrupted by direct speech when George breaks into the river's sound with an abrupt question, 'When are you to be married, Alice?' The river's sound is violently dispelled: 'Oh George! You ask me a question as though you were putting a pistol to my ear.'[15] What follows is a complete break from sensation and interiority/FID to uncompromising direct speech from George that leaves Alice with little room for anything else in her consciousness. He forces her to listen to reasons why she should not marry John Grey and, as he implies, why she should come together again with him. When George's voice finally stops, she 'sat silent and convicted', and in that silence she becomes again 'aware of the river', and again her thoughts are given at length in free indirect speech, from possibly the second, and certainly by the third sentence in the following passage:

> The music of the river was still in her ears, and there came upon her a struggle as though she were striving to understand its song. Were the waters also telling her of the mistake she had made in in accepting Mr. Grey as her husband? What her cousin was now telling her, – was it not a repetition of words, which she had spoken to herself hundreds of times during the last two months? Was she not telling herself daily, – hourly, – always, – in every thought of her life, that in accepting Mr. Grey she had assumed herself to be mistress of virtues that she did not possess?[16]

Alice is spellbound both by the sound of the river, and what George has said to her; the chapter weaves in and out of the interiority of FID, to thought inflected by the narrator, to George's unrelenting direct speech. George's words are associated with a hard materiality; to Alice they are like 'a pistol to her ear'. George's body, the small table, chairs and the coffee cups, as well as the rough hard surfaces of his speech make a 'prisoner' of Alice on the balcony. But the sensuality of the place and moment have also kept her there more willingly: the last light of the day, the breeze felt on her skin, the river's rush, and it is implied, her erotic attraction to her former lover.

One other item in the category of sensory and material that makes it difficult for Alice to leave the balcony is specifically her crinoline, which was popularly referred to at the time as a 'cage'. Trollope does not mention the crinoline here, although he is much preoccupied with this item of fashion at other times in his writing. As Miss Dunstable proclaims in *Framley Parsonage*: 'I copy everybody that I see, more or less. You did not at first begin to wear big petticoats out of your own head?'[17] A Victorian readership in 1864 would have assumed that Alice would be wearing the fashionable full skirt, supported by a crinoline 'cage' most likely made of linen and sprung steel. It would have been one of the material objects keeping Alice 'prisoner'. This is quite obvious in Hablot Knight Browne's illustration for the scene on the balcony at Basle in the second monthly part of the novel (Figure 3.1).[18]

To get past George she would have to touch him with her skirts, and the crinoline cage was far more able to register touch and vibration of contact than the cumbersome many-layered skirts that preceded the crinoline's invention in 1856. Indeed, the enormous number of comic stereoscopic photographs, and cartoons in *Punch* and other magazines are mostly concerned with the awkwardness of the crinoline, but also with its erotic potential (providing space under the skirts where a secret lover can hide, or showing how mishaps or mismanagement of the crinoline can result in its tipping up to show ankles, undergarments and legs).[19] Trollope has strong opinions about a woman's management of her skirts: two years before the publication of Alice's adventures in underskirts, Trollope wrote his travel volumes *North America* (1862) in which he railed against women in New York City streetcars:

The Balcony at Basle

Figure 3.1 Hablot Knight Browne, 'The Balcony at Basle', frontispiece to *Can You Forgive Her?* Courtesy of the Trollope Society.

as she enters [the streetcar] she drags after her a dirty mass of battered wire-work, which she calls her crinoline ... Of this she takes much heed, not managing it so that it may be conveyed up the carriage with some decency, but striking it about against men's legs, and heaving it with violence over people's knees. The touch of a real woman's dress is in itself delicate; but these blows from a harpy's fins are loathesome.[20]

In describing the crinoline as a fin, Trollope renders it, very negatively, an extension of the woman's body, but for many the lightness and flexibility of the crinoline did indeed render touch and contact, although indirect, sensationally immediate.

Crinolines were large, especially in the 1850s and early 1860s; just their mere surface area made contact difficult to avoid. Because they allowed women's legs to be free of many underskirts they were more hygienic and also allowed more flexibility of movement. The skirts so supported gave a woman a wide circumference, but because her legs were separated from the steel or whalebone 'cage' by mere air and underwear, contact and vibration were felt more readily. As Anita Stamper and Jill Condra argue, 'Lighter overall weight in the below-waist portion of the dress was certainly one result of wearing a crinoline.' Indeed, Amelia Bloomer, 'the woman whose name became associated with women's dress reform, believed the crinoline to be an acceptable alternative to the numerous, heavy petticoats required previously and is reported to have adopted the crinoline and given up the bloomers named for her'.[21] The lightness, and the free circulation of air around the legs, as well as the more awkward fact that the crinoline had to be well managed or it would swing to the side to reveal the legs; these aspects of the fashion all contributed to its sensual charge. Alice, sitting where she is in intimate proximity to George, and in an emotionally charged atmosphere, is half-conscious of the 'danger' and eroticism of where she is placed. Hablot Knight Browne's illustration makes plain to a modern readership what his contemporaries would have understood of the physical and sensual tension in this scene.

Only four years after the publication of *Can You Forgive Her?* the fashion for the crinoline was dead. An article from *Once a Week* in May, 1869, reflects on its former ubiquity and classlessness:

> One never saw any respectable woman without the more or less circular fullness of skirt which told of the hoops within. The dirtiest 'slavey', who went out to scour the bell-handle in the morning, had her octagonal wires pushing out her town dress; the little girls who superintended the apple-barrow had their bits of cane twisted round their petticoats; Sarah the cook had a circumference of petticoat which might have, and sometimes did, put her mistress to shame . . . [22]

When Trollope writes in *North America* that 'the touch of a real woman's dress is in itself delicate' he means a crinolined skirt – as almost all women wore them – but he refers to a woman's sensitivity in the management of her skirts. One of Millais's illustrations for *Framley Parsonage* (1860) demonstrates the 'delicacy of touch' of a woman's clothing, as Millais interprets the scene of an early meeting between Lucy Robarts and Lord Lufton (Figure 3.2). Her eyes are modestly downcast and partly veiled as Lufton takes her hand in kindness and sympathy for her grief at her father's death. Lufton towers over her and his left leg seems to touch her skirts in the shaded background. The combination of the unacknowledged physical contact with the acknowledged and socially appropriate holding of hands is Millais's interpretation of a scene in which a powerful and forbidden attraction lies underneath the social conventions. Both Lufton's kindness and his closeness are on view in this illustration, and the slightest hint of indentation in the airy crinoline indicates a delicacy of touch that is indirect and erotically charged.

Unlike Trollope, Millais seems to have been an enthusiast for the fashionable crinoline. Another of the six illustrations that he produced for *Framley Parsonage* did not

Figure 3.2 John Everett Millais, 'Lord Lufton and Lucy Robarts', from Chapter 11 of *Framley Parsonage*. Courtesy of Special Collections and Archives, Cardiff University.

adhere at all with his author's ideas of women's fashion (Figure 3.3). This illustration, corresponding to the scene in which Lucy Robarts 'threw herself on the bed' in distress after telling Lord Lufton the 'lie' that she could not love him, exhibits Lucy as a tiny face, arm and foot peeping out from an enormous crinolined skirt, covered in flounces. The crinoline is far wider in circumference than the one in the illustration of her meeting with Lord Lufton, discussed above. Trollope wrote to his publisher George Smith that

> the picture is simply ludicrous, and will be thought by most people to have been made so intentionally. It is such a burlesque of such a situation as might do for *Punch*, only that the execution is too bad to have passed muster for that publication.[23]

"WAS IT NOT A LIE?"

Figure 3.3 John Everett Millais, 'Was It Not A Lie?', from Chapter 16 of *Framley Parsonage*. Courtesy of Special Collections and Archives, Cardiff University.

Writing of Trollope's reaction, Simon Cooke has argued that Trollope failed to see how Millais meant this image of Lucy as

> a piece of expressive distortion: the figure is simplified into a monolithic form and the patterns of the crinoline externalize the character's inner turmoil. It acts to deepen the scene's psychological resonance, constructing meaning out of the barest of information and crystallizing Lucy's state of mind in a powerful form. Yet Trollope seems not to understand how his text has been enhanced, and can only complain about the 'very pattern' of the dress, which is so vivid as to create a jarring after-image: 'I saw [it] some time after the picture came out.'[24]

Writing shortly after the June 1861 instalment of *Framley Parsonage* came out, 'J.A.' in *Sharpe's London Magazine* registered something about Millais's picture which may have been intentional, and close to Cooke's interpretation. 'J.A.' wrote that in Millais's interpretation of 'Lucy Robarts in a state of woe' she has become a 'personification of crinoline', and that the glimpses of her body from under it are akin to the 'touches of real human nature' under 'this huge mass of conventionalism'.[25] For this contemporary reviewer, the 'conventionalism' applies to both the crinoline and the novel itself; but this assessment of *Framley Parsonage* aside, Lucy is encircled and constrained by conventions of fashion, society and class in this scene at the end of Chapter 16 and in Millais's illustration. Paul Barlow writes that Millais was 'intrigued' by 'the imagery of entrapment',[26] and one could extend this to his image of Lucy Robarts lying on her bed, her body overwhelmed by an enormous crinoline 'cage'. (And equally, Hablot Knight Browne's illustration of Alice Vavasor, discussed earlier, interprets Trollope's description of her as a 'prisoner' on the balcony, and also as a prisoner in her crinoline 'cage'.) Not only is the 'monolithic' crinolined skirt that Lucy wears indicative of the psychological turmoil that she is going through, as Simon Cooke argues, but its use by Millais here engages with ideas of entrapment, as Lucy is enmeshed in the complexities of family politics and social convention, forced to lie to the man she loves.[27] Once again, Trollope deftly arranges juxtapositions of the material, physical space and the psychological; of intensely felt direct dialogue in this proposal scene with an ending in which Lucy seeks both physical and mental interiority and self-seclusion. As soon as Lord Lufton is dismissed, 'when he was well gone – absolutely out of sight from the window – Lucy walked steadily up to her room, locked the door, and then threw herself on the bed'.[28] This precise physical positioning frames her innermost thoughts and the self-revelation of her feelings for Lufton, given in FID (the FID, 'Was it not a lie?' is chosen as the title for the illustration of this moment). Several chapters later, Lucy reveals that through the intimacy and emotion of this proposal scene, a precise physicality had impinged on her consciousness: she says to her sister-in-law:

> 'Well, it was not a dream. Here, standing here, on this very spot – on that flower of the carpet – he begged me a dozen times to be his wife. I wonder whether you and Mark would let me cut it out and keep it.'[29]

The crinoline also required of a woman that she know how to manage her skirts well, unlike the ladies who infuriated Trollope in the New York streetcars. One woman in Trollope who is more in control of her skirts than any other, who is the most opaque and unapproachable, and who can never be accused of allowing us the intimacy of her free indirect discourse, is Griselda, Lady Dumbello. In Chapter 55 of *The Small House at Allington* (1862), Plantagenet Palliser approaches her at a party, with the intention of suggesting an affair or elopement. She is seated in glorious repose on a sofa. 'It was understood', Trollope writes, 'that Lady Dumbello did not converse – unless it was occasionally with Mr. Palliser.'

> There was room by her on the couch, and once or twice, at Hartlebury, he had ventured so to seat himself. On the present occasion, however, he could not do so without placing himself manifestly on her dress. She would have known how to

fill a larger couch even than that – as she would have known, also, how to make room – had it been her mind to do so. So he stood still over her, and she smiled at him. Such a smile! It was cold as death, flattering no one, saying nothing, hideous in its unmeaning, unreal grace.[30]

In an earlier scene between the two, at Hartlebury, Trollope's narration gives us only physical movement and expression as clues that Griselda may be partial to Plantagenet; she 'raised her head, and the faintest possible gleam of satisfaction might have been discerned upon her features'. She was sitting 'alone, in a large, low chair, made without arms, so as to admit the full expansion of her dress'.[31] She moved her skirts so that Palliser could sit next to her. Presumably the vibrations of Palliser's nearness through the sprung steel ribs of her crinoline carried an erotic charge. But in this later scene of Palliser's dismissal, Griselda expertly uses her skirts to give him a wide berth, and so escapes any taint to her reputation, without, as usual, having to say much or really anything at all. Trollope's narrator gives us only indirect, superficial clues as to her state of mind; she herself repels the intimacy of direct speech with other characters, and, through the narrator, intimacy with the reader by never indulging in free indirect discourse.

The Body and Free Indirect Discourse

Of the novels of Jane Austen, Ann Radcliffe and Walter Scott, Daniel Cottom finds 'a pressure for decorous behavior so immense that it can only eventuate in [a] rebellion of the body'.[32] Those things that the heroine could not express openly are manifested by the rebellious body physically, through blushing, pallor, illness, fainting and breathlessness. Trollope was a great admirer of Austen from a young age, and not everyone was in the Victorian period. She was also one of the first British novelists to employ free indirect discourse, and I would argue, to give the reader a naturalistic sense of how her characters were placed in a room or landscape, and how that impinged on consciousness. A moment – or indeed a few seconds in real time – from *Persuasion* may clarify what it is in Austen's combination of the physical and psychological that I see as influential upon Trollope's writing. This is when Anne Eliot sees Captain Wentworth for the first time in 'almost eight years':

a thousand feelings rushed on Anne, of which this was the most consoling, that it would soon be over. And it was soon over. In two minutes after Charles's preparation, the others appeared; they were in the drawing-room. Her eye half met Captain Wentworth's; a bow, a curtsey passed; she heard his voice – he talked to Mary, said all that was right; said something to the Miss Musgroves, enough to mark an easy footing: the room seemed full – full of persons and voices – but a few minutes ended it. Charles shewed himself at the window, all was ready, their visitor had bowed and was gone; the Miss Musgroves were gone too, suddenly resolving to walk to the end of the village with the sportsmen: the room was cleared, and Anne might finish her breakfast as she could.

'It is over! it is over!' she repeated to herself again, and again, in nervous gratitude. 'The worst is over!'[33]

Anne's perceptions are fragmented: her eye 'half-met' Captain Wentworth's; she half-hears what is said. The half-sentences are in a peculiar type of free indirect style that is so hurried and stressed as to be barely conscious, but conscious she is, of thoughts that are imbedded in her by convention and manners: she knows that Wentworth has said 'all that was right', and that his demeanour shows, 'an easy footing' even if she cannot quite bring to mind exactly what he has said. Her impressions are interspersed with dashes, as if she is out of breath. Rapid eye movement; the rush in her ears from stress; her breathlessness: the connection between body and consciousness are all here in Austen's free indirect discourse, and Trollope both admires and inherits Austen's skill and understanding of this narrative mode.

Both men's and women's bodies betray emotion and psychological stress in Trollope: Phineas Finn for example knows that when he meets Madame Max again he will blush 'as red as a turkey-cock's comb up to the roots of his hair'.[34] Trollope is interested, as Austen was, in the body's responses to social and psychological demands. He demonstrates how the pressures of the unutterable between people, and especially between those who would be intimate, are often displaced onto the body's attenuated contact with mundane materiality.

This is rendered painfully in the scene in which John Eames asks for the hand of Lily Dale for the last time in *The Last Chronicle of Barset*:

> She was now again near the window, and he had not followed her. As she neither turned towards him nor answered him, he moved from the table near which he was standing on to the rug before the fire, and leaned with both his elbows on the mantelpiece. He could still watch her in the mirror over the fireplace, and could see that she was still seeming to gaze out upon the street. And had he not moved her? . . . He had told her now what to him would be green and beautiful, and she did not find herself able to disbelieve him . . . And then – was she in a moment to be talked out of the resolution of years; and was she to give up herself, not because she loved, but because the man who talked to her talked so well that he deserved a reward? Was she now to be as light, as foolish, as easy, as in those former days from which she had learned her wisdom? . . . [B]ut she could not say to herself that he should be her lord and master, the head of her house, the owner of herself, the ruler of her life. The shipwreck to which she had once come, and the fierce regrets which had thence arisen, had forced her to think too much of these things. 'Lily', he said, still facing towards the mirror, 'will you not come to me and speak to me?' She turned round, and stood a moment looking at him, and then, having again resolved that it could not be as he wished, she drew near to him. 'Certainly I will speak to you, John. Here I am.' And she came close to him.[35]

A window, a table, a rug, the fire, mantelpiece, mirror, and Eames speaking to Lily's reflection, elbows on the mantelpiece: it is an extraordinarily specific and prosaic catalogue of objects that they must navigate. The deflected intimacies, lack of eye contact, seem to prepare the reader for the breaking out into intimacy that follows – as was the case in my first example, 'The Balcony at Basle'. The catalogue of furniture sets the scene for Eames's direct and honest tale of his love, and for Lily's free indirect discourse in which she teeters on the edge of accepting him. At first Lily cannot speak to John, and the mundane objects of the room are the backdrop for her refusal to allow herself the poetry of 'tranquil blue waters' with him.[36] But once again, the specific blocking of these characters brings the reader in very close to the scene and the tense proximity of these two. Trollope prepares the reader physically and through his indirect narratorial mode for the failed and deflected intimacies of John and Lily.

A proposal scene in which the forthright and foreign Marie Melmotte is the heroine offers a telling contrast to the frustrated or tenuous contact and speech of so many of Trollope's English lovers. In Chapter 74 of *The Way We Live Now* (1875) Marie finally agrees to marry Lord Nidderdale: 'Oh – I'll have you', she says.[37] She has no time for social subterfuges, painful silences or unacknowledged touch. Marie tells Nidderdale, without rancour, that he has never cared for her:

'You say it now because you think that I shall like it. But it makes no difference now. I don't mind about your arm being there if we are to be married, only it's just as well for both of us to look on it as business.'[38]

When he asks her to name a date for the wedding, she replies:

'You may manage it all just as you like with papa. Oh, yes, – kiss me; of course you may. If I'm to belong to you what does it matter? No; – I won't say that I love you. But if ever I do say it, you may be sure it will be true. That's more than you can say of yourself – John.'[39]

Living in Melmotte's house, Marie is more encumbered by the luxury and superabundance of material things than most. Nidderdale has thrown himself down on the sofa beside her but she can manage herself and her skirts well. Without resort to blushing or fainting, she acknowledges touch and intimacy with Nidderdale. Comically, Trollope's narrator has his character dispense with the narrator, as Marie gives an account of these intimacies herself as they occur – precisely when Nidderdale's arms feel for her waist and when he takes a kiss. Her dismissal of the narrator and her ability to speak openly without the intimacy-at-one-remove of free indirect discourse means that she must take her story to New York City at the close of the novel. She leaves the field to English heroines for whom touch and intimacy are usually left to the narrator to reveal, directly or more intimately in free indirect discourse.

Navigating spaces of threat and violence

Trollope's characters are highly sensitive to touch on skin, the nearness of others, and of the space, objects and sounds around them, and by extension, where they are located in the wider world. He writes against the grain of received ideas and Victorian commonplaces concerning the way in which gender dictates the experience and inhabiting of space both mentally and physically. Writing in 1871, the literary editor of the *Spectator*, R. H. Hutton, provides an example of received ideas about gender and space:

Educated *men's* characters are naturally *in position*, and most vigorous masculine characters of any kind have a defined bearing on the rest of the world, a characteristic attitude, a personal latitude and longitude on the map of human affairs, which an intellectual eye can seize and mark out at once. But it is not usually so with women's characters. They are best expressed not by attitude and outline, but by essence and indefinite tone. As an odour expresses and characterizes a flower even better than its shape and colour, as the note of a bird is in some sense a more personal expression of it than its form and feathers; so there is something of vital essence in a great poet's delineations of women which is far more expressive than any outline or colour.[40]

Although Trollope does describe the 'essence' of his characters – often through descriptions of the eyes or voice – it is *both* men and women who are represented in such a way. Such is the case in his obituary of George Henry Lewes for the *Fortnightly Review* in 1879. Trollope describes his dear friend:

No one could say that he was handsome. The long bushy hair, and the thin cheeks, and the heavy moustache, joined as they were, alas! almost always to a look of sickness, were not attributes of beauty. But there was a brilliance in his eye, which was not to be tamed by any sickness, by any suffering, which overcame all other feeling on looking at him. I have a portrait of him, a finished photograph, which he gave me some years since, in which it would seem as though his face had blazed up suddenly . . . [41]

Women in Trollope may convey an aura or 'essence' at times, and it has to be said that Hablot Knight Browne's and Millais's illustrations (see Figures 3.1 and 3.3) of women in crinolines make them appear as airy and indefinite as clouds. But such illustrations belie the substantiality and the 'latitude and longitude' of his female characters. R. H. Hutton's gendered metaphors are often literally translated, and subverted, in Trollope's writing. This is never more apparent than when women in his novels must respond to stress or fear; these responses are usually the provenance of the sensation novel, but Trollope represents them too, and differently. In times of crisis his heroines do not lose consciousness, as would their Gothic counterparts: instead, their 'rebellion of the body' is to act and even to fight. When threatened by physical violence and possibly murder by her brother, Kate Vavasor's muscular reflexes come into play: 'She set her teeth firmly together, and clenched her little fist.'[42] She gains a heightened consciousness of her location out on the Cumbrian fells:

They were now upon the Fell side, more than three miles away from the Hall; and Kate, as she looked round, saw that they were all alone. Not a cottage, – not a sign of humanity was within sight. Kate saw that it was so, and was aware that the fact pressed itself upon her as being of importance . . . still she would fight him. Her blood was the same as his, and he should know that her courage was, at any rate, as high.[43]

Kate does finally faint, but only after finding her way back to the Hall, walking miles in a storm, pinning her broken arm against her body. She arrives in time for dinner.

Published in the same year as *Framley Parsonage*, Trollope's short story 'Aaron Trow' is set in an isolated house in Bermuda, where a young woman is violently attacked by an escaped convict. Like Kate Vavasor, 'she remembered that there was no human being within sound of her voice but this man'.[44] She stays outwardly calm, with a heightened sense of where she is and what she may be able to do, and gives him food and drink as he commands. But when she has no money to give him, he threatens to rape her. Unusually, Trollope gives a detailed, uncompromising, second-by-second account of the brutal fight between this man and woman, which extends over several pages. The reader is made to focus in on skin, hair, teeth and muscles as she wrestles with Trow with all her strength:

> And then, when one hand was loosed in the struggle, she twisted it through his long hair, and dragged back his head till his eyes were nearly starting from their sockets. Anastasia Bergen had hitherto been sheer woman – all feminine in her nature. But now the foam came to her mouth, and fire sprang from her eyes, and the muscles of her body worked as though she had been trained to deeds of violence.[45]

While this violence is an extreme example of physical and mental engagement, and while it is a fact that the woman fighting is not an English heroine, but a Bermudan colonist, Trollope nevertheless makes us feel sure that Kate Vavasor would fight in such a way if she had to. His women characters are equally conscious of the body and its spatial and muscular uses and limits as are men. Fighting for her man, rather than her life, Hetta Carbury consults a map and becomes one of the first, if not the first, passengers on the London Underground in English literature. She takes it to meet her lover's former mistress in Islington in *The Way We Live Now*:

> That afternoon Hetta trusted herself all alone to the mysteries of the Marylebone underground railway, and emerged with accuracy at King's Cross. She had studied her geography, and she walked from thence to Islington.[46]

In his writings women have, with men, a substantial presence, a 'latitude and longitude' in geographical space.

Trollope was a great admirer of George Henry Lewes's writing, a close personal friend, and a delighted listener to Lewes's stories and discussions of philosophy and science, among other things. He would most probably have heard or read many of Lewes's ideas from his *Physiology of Common Life*. But in so many ways, Trollope's fiction constitutes his own 'physiology of common life'; he attends, unobtrusively yet affectingly, to the movement, touch, clothing, furniture and even the empty air surrounding his characters, and the space that lies between them. He wanted his characters to age and change in real time ('It has been my study that these people, as they grew in years should encounter the changes that come upon us all' and 'On the last day of each month recorded, every person in his novel should be a month older than on the first').[47] And just as he wanted them to be affected and marked by experience in time, so too is he interested in physiological responses to experiences of the moment and how these age and alter his characters.

There is a touching immediacy in a moment of Lewes's composition of his *Physiology of Common Life*, in which he pauses to bring the outside world into conscious focus:

> While I am writing these lines the trees are rustling in the summer wind, the birds are twittering among the leaves, and the muffled sounds of carriages rolling over the Dresden streets reach my ear; but because the mind is occupied with trains of thought these sounds are not perceived, until one of them becomes importunate, or my relaxed attention turns towards them . . . They were not lost; they were not altered in character because their subsequent effects were not manifest in thought; they were not without their influence in adding to the sum of general Consciousness.[48]

With great linguistic skill, Trollope represents the half-perceived, and even the unperceived and unworded, through free indirect style. He juxtaposes this interiority often with direct speech and conversation in a social and physical world that demands something of and influences the consciousness. He depicts those 'subtle muscular movements' that bring us towards a fixed 'desire', in George Eliot's words, and these are important reasons why his characters were so very real to him, and are so still to his readers.[49] But our easy and familiar relationship with his characters and with his particular kind of realism should not lead us to underestimate his brilliant mastery of all those things in everyday life which, almost disregarded, add to the 'sum of general Consciousness'.

Notes

1. George Eliot, *Middlemarch: A Study of Provincial Life* (London: Penguin Books, 2003), pp. 686–7.
2. Anthony Trollope, *Can You Forgive Her?* (Oxford: The World's Classics, 1991), ch. 58, p. 190.
3. Stephen Wall, *Trollope and Character* (London: Faber and Faber, 1988), p. 104.
4. Jenny Bourne Taylor, 'Trollope and the Sensation Novel', in Carolyn Dever and Lisa Niles (eds), *The Cambridge Companion to Anthony Trollope* (Cambridge: Cambridge University Press, 2010) p. 88.
5. J. Hillis Miller, 'Literature and Ethics: Truth and Lie in *Framley Parsonage*', in Ranjan Ghosh and J. Hillis Miller, *Thinking Literature Across Continents* (Durham, NC: Duke University Press, 2016), p. 236.
6. Ibid. p. 236
7. J. Hillis Miller, 'Literature and Ethics', p. 237.
8. Anthony Trollope, *Can You Forgive Her?*, ch. 5, pp. 48–9.
9. Ibid. ch. 5, p. 49.
10. Ibid.
11. Ibid. ch. 5, p. 48.
12. George Henry Lewes, *The Physiology of Common Life*, 2 vols (Edinburgh and London: William Blackwood and Sons, 1859), vol. 2, pp. 59–60.
13. Ibid. p. 88.
14. Anthony Trollope, *Can You Forgive Her?*, ch. 6, p. 58.
15. Ibid. ch. 5, p. 49.

16. Ibid. ch. 5, p. 54.
17. Anthony Trollope, *Framley Parsonage* (London: Penguin Classics, 1984), ch. 29, p. 344.
18. Anthony Trollope's *Can You Forgive Her?* was published originally in monthly parts from January 1864 to August 1865. Hablot Knight Browne's illustration appeared in the second monthly part (February 1864) and illustrates a scene from Chapter 5 of the novel.
19. Denis Pellerin and Brian May, *Crinoline: Fashion's Most Magnificent Disaster* (London: The London Stereoscopic Company, Ltd, 2016).
20. Anthony Trollope, *North America*, 2 vols (Gloucester: Alan Sutton Publishing, 1987), vol. 1, ch. 9, p. 298.
21. Anita Stamper and Jill Londra, *Clothing Through American History: The Civil War through the Gilded Age, 1861–1899* (Santa Barbara, CA: Greenwood, 2011), p. 111.
22. 'Who killed crinoline?', in *Once a Week* 20 (8 May, 1869), p. 370.
23. Quoted in N. John Hall, *Trollope and His Illustrators* (London: Macmillan, 1980), p. 14.
24. Simon Cooke, 'Millais's Illustrations for Trollope', *The Victorian Web*, <www.victorian-web.org/art/illustration/millais> (last accessed 21 March, 2017).
25. 'J.A.', in *Sharpe's London Magazine* 19 (July 1861), quoted in N. John Hall, *Trollope and His Illustrators*, p. 15.
26. Paul Barlow, *Time Present and Time Past: The Art of John Everett Millais* (Abingdon: Routledge, 2016), p. 186.
27. Elaine Schefer provides an extended study of the imagery of birds, cages and imprisonment in Victorian art, including a consideration of women's fashion and the crinoline in her book, *Birds, Cages, and Women in Victorian and Pre-Raphaelite Art*. American University Studies Series xx, vol. 12 (Bern: Peter Lang, 1990).
28. Anthony Trollope, *Framley Parsonage*, ch. 16, p. 213.
29. Ibid. ch. 26, p. 321.
30. Anthony Trollope, *The Small House at Allington* (London: Penguin Books, 1991), ch. 55, p. 611.
31. Ibid. ch. 23, pp. 253 and 252.
32. Daniel Cottom, *The Civilized Imagination: A Study of Ann Radcliffe, Jane Austen and Sir Walter Scott* (Cambridge: Cambridge University Press, 1985), p. 53.
33. Jane Austen, *Persuasion* (Oxford: Oxford University Press, 1817; 1990), p. 60.
34. Anthony Trollope, *Phineas Redux* (Oxford: Oxford World's Classics, 1990), ch. 15, p. 131.
35. Anthony Trollope, *The Last Chronicle of Barset* (London: Penguin Books, 2002), ch. 77, pp. 795–6.
36. Ibid. p. 796.
37. Anthony Trollope, *The Way We Live Now* (Oxford: Oxford University Press, 2016), ch. 74, p. 553.
38. Ibid. ch. 74, p. 554.
39. Ibid. ch. 74, p. 555.
40. Richard Holt Hutton, *Essays Theological and Literary*, 2 vols (London: Strahan and Co., 1871) vol. 2, p. 205. Quoted in David Skilton, '"Depth of Portraiture": What Should Distinguish a Victorian Man from a Victorian Woman?', in Margaret Markwick, Deborah Denenholz Morse and Regenia Gagnier (eds), *The Politics of Gender in Anthony Trollope's Novels* (Abingdon: Routledge, 2016), p. 217.
41. Anthony Trollope, 'George Henry Lewes', *Fortnightly Review*, 1 January 1879.
42. Anthony Trollope, *Can You Forgive Her?*, ch. 56, p. 164.
43. Ibid. ch. 56, pp. 164–5.
44. Anthony Trollope, 'Aaron Trow', originally appeared in *Public Opinion: Literary Supplement*, 14 and 21 December 1861. Reprinted in *Anthony Trollope: The Complete Short Stories*, vol. 3 *Tourists and Colonials* (London: Omnium Publishing for the Trollope Society), p. 220.

45. Ibid. p. 224.
46. Anthony Trollope, *The Way We Live Now*, ch. 91. p. 684.
47. Anthony Trollope, *An Autobiography* (Oxford: Oxford University Press, 1992), ch. 10, p. 184 and p. 233, respectively.
48. George Henry Lewes, *The Physiology of Common Life*, vol. 2, pp. 54–5.
49. As Trollope writes in his autobiography, for example, 'I have wandered alone among the rocks and woods, crying at their grief, laughing at their absurdities, and thoroughly enjoying their joy.' And, of the Pallisers especially, 'They have been as real to me as free trade was to Mr. Cobden.' In *An Autobiography*, ch. 10, pp. 176 and 180 respectively.

4

'RUBBISH AND PASTE': READING AND RECURRENCE IN *AN OLD MAN'S LOVE*

Helen Blythe

Diamonds, indeed! I'd diamond him! I don't believe, not in a single diamond. They're all rubbish and paste.[1]

WRITING IN THE YEAR following Anthony Trollope's death in December 1882, Henry James stated of Trollope's later work that it was 'strong wine too copiously watered . . . too little of a new story and too much of an old one'.[2] Subsequent scholars have challenged this view, treating Trollope's final novels as complex innovations; but few have concentrated on Trollope's last completed novel, *An Old Man's Love*, published posthumously in 1884.[3] I suggest that the novel deserves our attention because its metafictional elaboration of recurrence challenges the conclusion that some texts are merely diluted repetitions of previous masterpieces. Trollope structures his exploration of return by revisiting the diamond metaphor dealt with in *The Eustace Diamonds* (1869) to imply that originality and transparency are always compromised, and that rather than genuine diamonds, literary works are 'rubbish and paste' (*OML*, ch. 11, p. 114), each one a conglomeration of previous texts and so bits of glass, not 'precious stone' (ch. 14, p. 147). Nonetheless, as with each shake of the kaleidoscope, readers determine the pattern of meaning into which the glass pieces fall, highlighting the difference that resides within repetition.

Trollope's last novels have received little or mixed attention during the various resurgences of interest in his corpus, but they have intrigued scholars interested in form. Michael Sadleir, for instance, describes them as a 'transformation in kind', yet Robert Polhemus labels them mostly 'repetitive and flabby'.[4] James Kincaid agrees that 'The Late Experimental Novels' are 'particularly lame', yet observes their attention to structure, even drawing from *An Old Man's Love* to demonstrate how 'each seems to challenge in very different ways the bases of the forms it operates in'.[5] Some contemporary reviewers admired the novel's style and structure and others its realistic protagonist, Mr Whittlestaff, but those expecting a complex plot were less impressed.[6] While the *Saturday Review* admiringly called the novel 'original in design', *The Academy* concluded that Trollope's 'stream was getting dry'.[7] The divergent responses continued in the following decades with R. C. Terry deciding that *An Old Man's Love* exemplified Trollope's exhaustion.[8] And in their respective editions of the novel published in the 1990s, David Skilton called it 'a forward-looking work', while John Sutherland wrote that Trollope's failing imagination had created improbable scenes.[9]

An Old Man's Love has surfaced occasionally in discussions on Trollope's style, repetitions, and intertextuality because of its classical allusions. Such references are thought to create what Hugh Osbourne calls a 'male preserve' of gentleman readers, and signal the reader that Trollope's narrators are, as Skilton puts it, 'like the novelist, "one of us"'.[10] Looking more at Trollope's tags as 'markers within as well as the substance of large, resonant texts', Elizabeth Epperly goes so far as to declare Trollope a 'master of repetition'.[11] More recently, Frederik Van Dam observes in *An Old Man's Love* Trollope's 'sophisticated, self-reflexive play with citations and paraphrases' and 'operations of paraphrasis at the meta-level'.[12] And John Bowen and Matthew Sussman agree that across his works, Trollope's seemingly unimportant repetitions produce an interesting indeterminacy, one that according to Van Dam challenges the assumption in individualism that 'subjects can really penetrate the remotest corners of their inner minds'.[13]

Adding to the conversation, I concur that the recurrence elaborated in *An Old Man's Love* functions to emphasise uncertainty, but through a dissolving of distinctions between repetition and originality in reading and writing, anticipating Roland Barthes's description of a text as a 'stereophony of echoes, citations, and references'.[14] Trollope draws attention to the literary marketplace of readers examining, classifying and judging texts as dealers might appraise diamonds. Stitching together literary works and authentic gems or their paste-glass counterfeits to construct his own story, Trollope not only merges copies and genuine forms, he implies that readers cannot unequivocally determine a text's meaning or value as art. Centred on a character's pockets supposedly full of diamonds, the narrative on one hand undermines the believability or authenticity of the stones because no one ever sees them. On the other, diamonds simultaneously call to mind the materiality and transparency of realism, leading Patrick Brantlinger to label them 'the ultimate metaphor for the real' in his study of *The Eustace Diamonds*.[15] In this respect, the sharp visible contours of the cut diamond are analogous to James Kincaid's 'typically realistic world' that 'is very sharply *seen* . . . a world of things, a visual world'.[16] Elucidating the tension between 'real' diamonds and their insubstantiality or invisibility, Trollope interweaves the authentic and counterfeit in recurrences at the plot and meta-narrative levels, opening up the text to multifaceted inferences.

Diamonds and Horace: The Recurrence of the Pocket

The triangular love plot centred on the heroine, Mary Lawrie, introduces the novel's key repetitions: two marriage proposals and the pairing of diamonds with literary works. As a young man, the presumed hero Mr Whittlestaff turned to reading poetry for solace after being jilted by Catherine Bailey. Now over fifty, he repeats the loss after taking in Mary, a penniless young woman to whom he subsequently proposes marriage. But Mary still loves an impoverished young man, John Gordon, who disappeared into the diamond fields to make his fortune. On the day that Mary dutifully accepts Whittlestaff's proposal, Gordon unexpectedly reappears also ready to propose and with 'pockets full of diamonds' (ch. 12, p. 125). The ensuing chapters elaborate their inward agonising until Whittlestaff finally releases Mary to Gordon.[17] At the outset, however, Whittlestaff and his housekeeper do not believe in Gordon or his diamonds. Mrs Baggett indicates that both are 'rubbish and paste'; and Whittlestaff wonders whether Gordon is 'glass', not 'precious stone' (ch. 11, p. 147). Their views introduce doubt over whether Gordon's character is genuine or fake, though Mrs Baggett later appears to believe in his diamonds, asking why Whittlestaff is 'not to get a wife just because a man's come home with his pockets full of diamonds?' (ch. 19, p. 215). While Gordon's pockets are purportedly packed with diamonds, Whittlestaff's pocket contains a book of Horace's poems that he reads daily, 'always having the volume in his pocket' (ch. 16, p. 178). Devoted to reading, Whittlestaff tries to understand his own existence, 'thinking of himself in all his readings; and as years had gone by, he had told himself that for him there was to be nothing better than reading' (ch. 20, p. 220). The contents of Whittlestaff and Gordon's pockets thus distinguish their rival identities and viability as romantic heroes; but equally significantly, they suture diamonds to literary works and highlight the pocket as a metaphor of possession.[18]

The contents of the men's pockets in *An Old Man's Love* and their corresponding right to possess the heroine foreground classifications of literary and diamond forms – either as precious originals or cheap imitations. The analogy was not unusual in Victorian literature, according to Stefanie Markovits, who claims that in nineteenth-century texts, 'thinking about diamonds means thinking about forms of genre'.[19] She observes diamonds surfacing in literary works 'at moments and as signs of extreme generic self-consciousness', and calls them 'generic touchstones', containing both narrative and lyric value.[20] The male characters' analysis and evaluation of diamonds and literary works in *An Old Man's Love* indicate this concern with interpretation and judgements of value, but suture them also to forms of women. John Gordon's acquaintance, Montagu Blake, loves to compare women, measuring their qualities against those of his fiancée, Kattie Forrester, whose manner, music, language, wit and hair colour crystallise into a priceless possession (*OML*, ch. 13, p. 142), while Gordon declares of women that 'comparisons are odious' (ch. 13, p. 142). Nonetheless, he imagines giving Whittlestaff multifarious diamonds, 'polished, and diamonds in the rough, diamonds pure and white, and diamonds pink-tinted' (ch. 7, p. 72), demonstrating his familiarity as a diamond-miner with dealing in and classifying precious stones. For their part, the narrator and Whittlestaff dwell on literary classifications of romantic heroines. Taken together, the men's preferences illustrate how forms of property, whether women, diamonds or texts, are valued in relation to others of their kind.

Recurrence in Scenes of Reading

Trollope uses scenes of reading to illuminate, however, that often readers fail to determine the value or meaning of such forms. He introduces the subject with the narrator's direct address, which propels the reader to acknowledge the difficulty of describing heroines in novel-writing. Trollope evidently envisages a reader knowledgeable of the British novel since his narrator inserts Mary Lawrie in a list of well-known fictional heroines, while insisting on the impossibility of giving 'a true idea' of her and that comprehension comes only 'from the reading of the whole book' (ch. 3, p. 25). The narrator at this juncture indicates Mary's centrality to the plot, though studies on the novel diminish her importance, focusing more on Whittlestaff despite the absence of a single man in the inventory. Commencing his classifications with Clarissa in Samuel Richardson's *Clarissa* (1748) and Amelia in Henry Fielding's *Amelia* (1751), the narrator then moves to Di Vernon in Walter Scott's historical romance, *Rob Roy* (1817), before ending with female protagonists in Victorian novels: Beatrix in William Thackeray's *The History of Henry Esmond* (1852) and Maggie Tulliver in George Eliot's *The Mill on the Floss* (1860). Based on novels with and without illustrations, the narrator's catalogue exemplifies how authors guide readers, who nonetheless form pictures of characters in their imaginations through inference rather than description.

Trollope focuses here on the operations of fiction rather than the triangular love plot, on writers writing and readers reading literature. James Kincaid calls this narrative occasion a noteworthy departure from realism, arguing that the narrator's introduction of Mary moves the reader 'away from the illusion of real life to a sense of artificiality so extreme it finally has no visual shape'.[21] He considers the example a more significant shift from realism than Trollope's commonly noted 'aural' approach and 'reminders of artifice'.[22] Moreover, in drawing on a literary community of writers and readers familiar with the genre of the British novel, and positioning Mary beside the heroines in esteemed masterpieces, Trollope demands that the reader consider Mary's right to be included in the list. And likewise, therefore, his readers are encouraged to appraise the novel that they are reading, *An Old Man's Love,* alongside the others in the inventory. The result is a metafictional discourse on the novel genre, and on how writers write novels and readers read and judge them in relation to others. However, the reader's ensuing comparisons create a disorienting dissonance that is never resolved because in being pushed to compare the slight figure of Mary to the heroines in Trollope's more respected works, and *An Old Man's Love* to his earlier masterpieces, the reader is jarred out of the social reality depicted within the story and into the literary marketplace outside it that classifies and judges the value of the texts, including the one being read.

Rather than resolving the disunity, Trollope extends it in moving to Whittlestaff's recursive reading habits. Originally a poet, Whittlestaff gave up writing poems not only because his fiancée jilted him, but because he missed out on a poetry fellowship. Having retreated decades before to his rural property, Croker's Hall, Whittlestaff reads and analyses literary texts, particularly by Horace, whose pocketbook of poetry he regularly takes to his 'favourite haunt', where 'he was wont to sit and read his Horace, and think of the affairs of the world as Horace depicted them' (ch. 16, p. 177). Whittlestaff interprets Horace through the lens of his personal experiences and desires; he 'would take a few lines and then digest them thoroughly, wailing over them or rejoicing, as the case might be' (ch. 17, p. 181). The words 'wailing' and 'rejoicing' exemplify his intimate attachment to Horace's poetry and characters, his life led through them, and his incapacity for judging them objectively. Wayne Booth draws on Trollope's statements about this effect of reading in relation to Thackeray's 'vicious protagonist' in *Barry Lyndon*, whom Trollope likes in spite of himself, to argue 'how strongly a prolonged intimate view of a character works against our capacity for judgement'.[23] In *An Old Man's Love*, Trollope explores the same effect through the character of Whittlestaff, who reads and rereads literary works, reiterating and repeating his loss over the decades, thinking 'much of love, reading about it in all the poets with whose lines he was conversant. He was one who, in all that he read, would take the gist of it home to himself, and ask himself how it was with him in that matter' (*OML*, ch. 20, p. 220). The narrative thus implies that in stemming from his emotions, desires and memories, and his habitual and intimate association with Horace through his poetry, the hero's interpretations lack objectivity and accuracy. Illuminating Trollope's concern with the limitations of reading, they also point to the instrumental role of the reader, anticipating Barthes's insistence that 'a text's unity lies not in its origin but in its destination, . . . that *someone* who holds together in a single field all the traces by which the written text is constituted'.[24]

The implications that a text's unity only forms when it is read and that authors incorporate other texts in writing their own further undermine the possibility of achieving authorial originality, a point reinforced with a second catalogue of women that also affirms how authors and readers alike construct paste-glass diamond texts in respectively assembling their own partly from others, or interpreting literature through the lens of subjective memories and experiences. Whittlestaff crafts his genealogy of women from works by Horace, Petrarch, Shakespeare and possibly Tennyson, providing additional scaffolding for the ideas that recurrence is inevitable in reading and writing, and accurate judgements of value are almost impossible. Replicating the narrator in cataloguing literary heroines, Whittlestaff substitutes the genres of poetry and drama for fiction to compare their versions of love with his own. Much of the plot concerns Whittlestaff's and Mary's feelings towards each other after Gordon's arrival, and so Whittlestaff's list prompts readers to copy him in comparing Mary to the women in his inventory of literary love affairs. But such scrutiny extends the disorientating dissonance, confirming Robert Tracy's conclusion that a 'failure of understanding is a pattern throughout the book'.[25]

Whittlestaff rejects Horace's articulation because his 'fresh love for every day' proves that the poet 'knew nothing of love' (*OML*, ch. 20, p. 220). Fancying himself a more ardent lover, Whittlestaff also dispenses with Petrarch, whose love for Laura is 'expression', not 'passion', though readers here recall his passionless engagement to Mary, who is relieved that Whittlestaff had 'not asked for her love', because 'she certainly had not given it' (ch. 4, p. 43). Whittlestaff later admits that Mary 'could hardly be brought to love passionately' (ch. 14, p. 153) an old man like himself; but for considerable time, he ignores her love for Gordon because it conflicts with his own imagined position as romantic hero.[26] After dismissing Petrarch, Whittlestaff extends his list more precisely, concluding that 'Prince Arthur in his love for Guinevere, went nearer the mark which he had fancied for himself' (ch. 20, p. 220), since Guinevere loves Launcelot first before meeting Arthur – like Mary, who saw and loved Gordon first.[27] But then Whittlestaff settles on Shakespeare's faithful Imogen in *Cymbeline*, because her 'love for Posthumus draws a picture of all that love should be' (ch. 20, p. 220). Here, Whittlestaff misunderstands either the play or his situation because Imogen's love mirrors Mary's devotion to Gordon, who in turn is a more fitting Posthumous, the commoner-turned-prince and first lover of Imogen. Trollope never untangles the allusions seemingly inserted as ambiguous clues for readers familiar with literary history and analysis, while simultaneously foregrounding the replications and divergences that structure acts of reading.

Readerly Disorientations

The classifications of the narrator and characters are likewise linked to possession since readers 'pocket' an author's work upon reading it as one might pocket a diamond in stealing it. Readers can miss or dismiss an author's intended meaning when they interpret and so possess a text, and they may be shaped by or live out what they read as when Whittlestaff's imagination sutures the memories of his first love, Catherine Bailey, to his present dilemma with Mary Lawrie, and to the heroines he encounters in verse. Conversely, authors wish to retain possession of a work upon its publication, hoping that the public will praise it in a further merging of the author's and reader's minds. Trollope lectured on the fluidity between writers and readers in 'Prose Fiction as a Rational Amusement', noting the importance of the reader and how 'the taste of the community forms the writer, while the power of the writer . . . reacts upon the public taste'.[28] Dwelling on novel-reading, the lecture foregrounds that readers merge fiction with their experiences as 'our memories are laden with the stories which we read, with the plots which are unraveled for us, and with the characters which are drawn for us'.[29] According to Debra Gettelman, the recognition that the tastes and minds of writers and readers blend together was a nineteenth-century 'cultural phenomenon', which developed as readers increasingly saw the novel providing liberating 'intellectual freedom'.[30]

Gettelman discusses how the idea of reading 'as an expression of individuality and mental liberty' gradually eclipsed the older view that novels corrupted impressionable readers into desiring experience of what they read, or interpreting texts to fit their own memories and desires.[31] She asserts that increased literacy and availability of literary works produced 'less knowable' readers, which generated anxiety among Victorian novelists 'not knowing how their books would be read', and fear that readers would 'respond in less than desirable ways'.[32] Composed twenty years after Trollope's lecture, *An Old Man's Love* registers these diverging functions of reading and their effect on the public. Its scenes of reading invite readers – and presumably Trollope's critics – to reflect on the limitations and inaccuracies of their interpretations and judgements of value. According to N. John Hall, Trollope was very interested in the reception of his works and generally responded good-naturedly to reviews, though some 'must have been troublesome'.[33]

In this respect, Trollope's work investigates a common problem for nineteenth-century authors. According to Garrett Stewart, the apprehensions of Victorian writers led them to 'conscript' their reader while they wrote, acknowledging the reader as collaborator partly writing the text in reading it.[34] His term, the 'conscripted reader', refers to those moments when the reader is 'deliberately drafted by the text, written *with*', when:

> through the direct address or a structural parallel . . . your private reading – along with that of every other reader – is actually convoked and restaged, put in service to the text. Either as an identifying notation or as a narrative event, this reading in of your reading – or of you reading – is what I mean by the notion of a conscripted response.[35]

Reiterating Barthes's focus on the importance of a text's destination, Stewart quotes Joseph Conrad's remark that 'one writes only half the book: the other half is with the reader'.[36] If *An Old Man's Love* is Trollope's response to the reception of his last works, it affirms Stewart's contention that Victorian novelists made a 'concerted structural effort to extend the marked interpenetration of form and substance beyond even the narrative confines of a given novel into the space between text and reception'.[37] But for some readers of *An Old Man's Love,* this in-between space is the origin of a disorientation, which reveals that texts conscript diverse readers differently. Indeed, the subjectivity of interpretation enables a reader to achieve a degree of originality denied to authors, who cannot control how readers will receive their works.

'Difference Inhabits Repetition'

As a foray into blurring the distinctions between the minds of writers and readers, *An Old Man's Love* obliges the reader to acknowledge also the merging that occurs of originality and repetition, or difference and repetition, as Gilles Deleuze puts it.[38] Deleuze points to the contradictory nature of repetition in asking: 'Does not the paradox of repetition lie in the fact that one can speak of repetition only by virtue of the change or difference that it introduces into the mind which contemplates it? By virtue of a difference that the mind *draws from* repetition?'[39] Thus the answer to his question is that 'difference inhabits repetition'.[40] Writing some years on in *The World, the Text, and the Critic* (1984), Edward Said focuses less on the difference within repetition than on how, in criticism, the critic's potentially '*mediated* reshaping and redisposition' of an original text can enhance rather than debase its meaning, because the repetition leads to 'consciousness of two where there had been repose in one'.[41] Such repetitions engender further questions, more difficulties, but also the possibility of more complex truths. The operation of recurrence in *An Old Man's Love* indeed highlights the complicated divergences in acts of reading and criticism. Whittlestaff repeatedly reads and analyses literature; and the author conscripts readers to contemplate themselves in the act of reading, thereby producing a mediated reshaping and redisposition of the text each time it is read. Trollope's recurrences evoke further questions, comparisons and judgements of value that coalesce into features of metafiction; that is, they challenge 'realism and foreground the role of the author in inventing the fiction and of the reader receiving the fiction'.[42]

Reflecting on themselves as readers while reading *An Old Man's Love,* readers are led to compare themselves to other readers of the text as well as those within it. The implied reader of *An Old Man's Love* is usually identified as a scholarly gentleman familiar with classical literature because of the text's untranslated Latin tags.[43] In this view, Whittlestaff is sympathetic, flawed but noble and self-sacrificing, and somewhat like Trollope.[44] Accordingly, the novel's title is thought to refer to Whittlestaff's love for Mary, prompting descriptions of the text as 'an old man's book', and 'an older man's novel'.[45] This interpretive lens treats the young lovers as inconsequential; Tracy, for instance, concludes that 'Trollope is not really interested in Mary Lawrie, nor in John Gordon'.[46] However, Trollope provides other clues that connote Mary's larger importance; and Stewart's conscripted reader, who collaborates with the writer, points to how diverse readers participate differently in the collaboration, receiving the text in accord with their unique experiences, memories and desires. So it is reasonable to envisage a woman or a young man drawing alternative connotations from the repetitions in *An Old Man's Love.*[47] Indeed, the new questions and difficulties regarding the possession of diamonds, women and literary works that arise from the novel's recurrences indicate a subject broader than that of an older man's love and self-sacrifice.

In particular, the repetitions lead to greater consideration of the acts of reading, interpretation and possession in relation to Mary Lawrie and John Gordon. The unexpected return of Gordon introduces two ideas where initially there was one, destabilising the authority of Whittlestaff's love story in which he had reposed as hero, and forcing his replacement by the novel's end. This recurrence produces difficult questions as to which man is the counterfeit or genuine hero, and whether Mary should marry Gordon, her first love, or Whittlestaff, who first proposes to her. Trollope has Gordon directly request that Whittlestaff address the 'burning questions' of whether Mary 'loved John Gordon the longest? Did she love him the best?' (*OML*, ch. 14, pp. 146–7). And he gives Mary another key question that challenges the dominant narrative, when even before Gordon's arrival, she silently asks: 'Were there to be no questions raised as to her own life, her own contentment, her own ideas of what was proper?' (ch. 3, p. 32). Overlooked in criticism because Whittlestaff's perspective dominates the narrative space, and because Mary never voices the question, she nonetheless guides this reader at least to acknowledge her significance and ponder whether she had viable options beyond the 'poor shrunken death' (ch. 5, p. 55) of governess work, or gift of herself in marriage to Whittlestaff as settlement of her debt.

The novel's various classifications merge, therefore, into a narrative about men's reading habits, and their possession, interpretation and judgement of women, particularly Mary Lawrie. After all, Trollope lists 'Mary Lawrie' and not Whittlestaff as one of three possible titles in his notes to the manuscript.[48] Mary has surfaced in Trollope studies on gender as a minor derivation of women in his previous texts; her 'exquisite scruple' is thought to repeat that depicted in *Sir Harry Hotspur* (1871), *Cousin Henry* (1879) and *Kept in the Dark* (1882).[49] She is also perceived as a copy of Mary Lowther in *The Vicar of Bullhampton* (1870), sharing her first name, initials and internal strife before marriage to a young lover.[50] Margaret Markwick likewise lists Mary Lawrie as a Coventry Patmore 'Angel of the House' inserted after Mary Lowther, Lily Dale and other heroines in a list of 'Trollope's Virgins'.[51] Reviews and criticism join Trollope, or he joins them, therefore, in exemplifying how readers recall previous heroes and heroines when encountering new ones and search for patterns of repetition within and across novels, forming necklaces of heroines as paste-glass derivations or genuine jewels.

Conglomerations of Bits of Glass

Given the central role of diamonds in *An Old Man's Love*, Mary's character immediately recalls Trollope's heroines in *The Eustace Diamonds*. In several ways, the later novel's pairing of women and jewels repeats the earlier masterpiece, whose titular jewels continue to inspire studies.[52] Readers might conclude that Mary Lawrie mirrors Lucy Morris, the 'treasure' in whose eye, a 'diamond of a tear was lurking', or Lizzie Eustace, who 'knew that she was paste . . . that Lucy was real stone'.[53] While *An Old Man's Love* departs from *The Eustace Diamonds* in linking a male character to diamonds, it still associates Mary obliquely to jewels in highlighting the transience of possession visible in her remark: 'A woman has a little gleam of prettiness about her . . . something soft, which will soon pass away' (*OML*, ch. 19, p. 208). Trollope also deploys the language of possession to highlight Mary's sense of imprisonment after voluntarily gifting herself like an object to Whittlestaff. Mary accepts his proposal certain that 'all the longings of her very soul were fixed' (ch. 5, p. 49) on Gordon; and even before Gordon's arrival, she becomes horrified at Whittlestaff's statement: 'your regard to me is worth now more than any other possession' (p. 53). She tries to break the engagement, but cannot speak her mind because Whittlestaff had 'taken complete possession of her, by right of the deed of gift which she had made of herself that morning' (p. 56). When he refuses to release her, Mary's horror becomes 'absolute hatred' (ch. 16, p. 170), especially in Gordon's presence, because Whittlestaff casts 'over her the deadly mantle of his ownership', and she is 'debarred from all right over her own words and action' (p. 170). Mary is left despairing 'how sad and miserable, must her future days be' (p. 170), having reduced herself to an ornament.

That Mary is correct in assuming she is Whittlestaff's property is evident in his reading, though his reading habits also provide hope that she can slip out of his grasp. Whittlestaff sutures Latin tags from Horace's odes and epistles in another scene of reading that exemplifies the author's assemblage of a text from other ones and the convergence of multiple texts in the reader's mind. Along with emphasising men's reduction of women to a piece of property, Trollope merges lines from two distinct works, dissolving their discrete boundaries to create the third that constitutes his novel. Horace's nineteenth ode in the third book concerns wine, music and love, and refers to a young woman 'ill-yoked to an old man', which corresponds to Mary's engagement to Whittlestaff.[54] The second epistle in the second book philosophises on the value of poetry, the false passions for money and materialism, and the transience of possession. These allusions further illuminate Mary's centrality, while conveying Trollope's expectation that his readers know Latin, and particularly Horace's works.

Pondering whether he should renounce his claim so that Mary can marry Gordon, Whittlestaff first meditates on lines from Horace's epistle: 'Gemmas, marmor, ebur', and 'Sunt qui non habeant; est qui non curat habere' (ch. 16, p. 177), which translate as 'Jewels, marble, ivory . . . there are those who do not have them, and there is the man who does not want them.'[55] Whittlestaff decides that he does care for jewels, etc., before quoting from Horace's ode: 'Me lentus Glycerae torret amor mææ' (p. 178), or 'tenacious love for Glycera consumes me'.[56] The passage obliquely links Mary with jewels, affirming that Whittlestaff sees her as a material possession, albeit a temporary item, since the epistle concerns not just 'the nature of possession', but 'how . . . transient it is, at the best'.[57] The resulting composite text of *An Old Man's Love* implies that to understand the function of Mary's character within the narrative, readers should not just complete the novel as the narrator first recommended, they should read beyond it to Horace's full epistle and ode. Trollope's reading effect thus dismantles the discrete form of the novel and singular reading act, foregrounding instead the merging of texts read across time, forming a conglomeration of bits of glass, and not the unique diamond of a text with a single interpretation.

The Rubbish and Paste of Novels and Novelists

Reading beyond the confines of the text into the space of reception is also useful for understanding the function of Gordon's character and his diamonds in *An Old Man's Love* in relation to Whittlestaff and also the author. The potency of the diamond metaphor springs from its paradoxical qualities of concreteness, transparency and hardness that suggest singularity and totality, and, conversely, from its indeterminacy, elusiveness, multifacetedness and portability. Discussing *The Eustace Diamonds*, Andrew Miller asserts that 'the most remarkable thing about the titular diamonds themselves is how rarely we see them'.[58] He treats the elusive necklace as a symbol of 'the futility of possession', writing that in the novel, 'like the diamonds themselves, the self becomes fugitive'.[59] *An Old Man's Love* expands on the idea of diamonds representing the transitory nature of possession and identity since people talk and think repeatedly about Gordon's pockets of diamonds, but never lay eyes on a single one. Despite their distinct forms and men's desire to possess them, diamonds are represented as potentially fleeting, insubstantial things that slip away from their owners like the literary text that disappears from the author's control upon its publication.

The analogy of diamonds and literary texts that Trollope reinforces by placing them in Gordon's and Whittlestaff's pockets, respectively, points to both items not merely slipping out of one's possession, but being revealed as counterfeit imitations or fictitious symbols of the real. For instance, in speaking with Gordon, Whittlestaff declares of diamonds, 'I trust them not at all – and I do not trust you, because you deal in them' (ch. 21, p. 234). Elsewhere he dismisses diamonds as insubstantial, 'volatile – not trustworthy' (ch. 11, p. 119), or declares that they easily 'melt and become as nothing', and are 'things which a man can carry in his pocket, and lose or give away' (ch. 14, p. 147). Given the coupling of Gordon's pocketed diamonds and Whittlestaff's pocketbook of Horace's poetry, the mistrust expressed towards diamonds and diamond dealers extends indirectly to characters, readers, literary works and their authors.

Readers potentially steal the text in purchasing or borrowing and then reading it, and Whittlestaff fears that Gordon has greater right to Mary, or that the younger man will steal her away. Equally significant is that Trollope's pairing of jewels and literary works conveys an untrustworthiness, criminality or trickery associated with the act of writing literature.[60] Suzanne Daly elucidates how 'jewels are the locus of an extraordinary amount of criminal activity' in Victorian novels; and an indication that Trollope's novel playfully associates diamonds, dealers, literary works and writers with mistrust, fraudulence and thievery is evident if we accept the narrative's invitation to read beyond the text to Trollope's travel account *South Africa* (1879) just as we read beyond the novel to Horace's *Odes* and *Epistles*. After the South African diamond rush began in the early 1870s, Trollope visited the region and composed the travel account on which he draws directly in voicing Gordon's experiences as a diamond miner at Kimberley (*OML*, ch. 15, pp. 159–61). In Chapter 6, the narrator likewise becomes a mouthpiece for Trollope in describing the diamond fields and calling Kimberley 'odious' (ch. 6, p. 68), and later chapters represent the South African subplot of Mr and Mrs Tookey (ch. 18, pp. 190–205). These allusions lead John Sutherland to conclude that the ailing author 'dragged in' his travel account after he 'dried up in the middle sections' of *An Old Man's Love*.[61] But the references in *South Africa* to diamonds unearthed, possessed, valued and stolen (like the land itself) resonate in *An Old Man's Love* in the substitution of Mary for the diamondiferous lands, and emphasis on counterfeit or untrustworthy characters, readers and authors who pretend, plunder and plagiarise.

The excerpts from the travel account function in the novel like the Latin tags that Trollope takes from Horace to increase the reader's understanding of Mary, introducing a repetition that also names a difference, leads to new questions and produces a greater complexity in accord with Said's view of criticism. Both *An Old Man's Love* and *South Africa* connect diamonds to mistrust, thievery and transient possession, 'easy come and easy gone', illustrating how Africans were denied 'possession of the diamonds they dug from the earth' (*OML*, ch. 15, p. 159), and Trollope's view that men like to take things not rightfully theirs.[62] The ambivalent narrator of the travel account rejects the 'accusation against the Colonial Office of having stolen the Diamond Fields' in 1871, yet entitles the Kimberley section: 'Why we took it', emphasising taking rather than purchasing the diamondiferous lands. He also notes that fair dealing is impossible (*SA*, ch. 7, p. 153), that the English stole African and Dutch lands, and purchased communally owned land from individuals who had no right to sell it (p. 145). Trollope does not ignore the uncomfortable questions of to whom 'did the land belong', and 'what were the rights of the owners either to the stones beneath the surface or to the use of the surface for the purpose of searching?' (p. 153). The same questions recur – with a difference – in *An Old Man's Love*, principally, what are the rights of Gordon and Whittlestaff to Mary, and which would be the more suitable husband? Trollope's explicit incorporation of sections from *South Africa* in *An Old Man's Love* thus generates additional complexity, providing ballast for the argument that recurrence is intrinsic to reading and writing, and enabling the reader to infer that authors cannot be trusted to create genuine diamonds. Instead, they are thieves stealing other writings in composing their own. But neither can readers be trusted in their reading, half-writing a text into a unity shaped by their desires and memories.

As with the allusions to Horace, by incorporating material from *South Africa*, Trollope invites readers to read beyond the discrete leaves of *An Old Man's Love* to his travel account in contemplating the significance of Gordon's character; and within it, we find a direct link between the novelist and the diamond thief – and a return to diamonds residing in pockets. Gazing at the diamonds in the Kimberley diamond-dealer's shop, the respectable Trollope confesses his desire to steal one: 'I could not but think how easy it would be to put just one big one into my pocket!' (*SA*, ch. 9, p. 195). He further identifies with untrustworthy thieves in imagining robbing the mail carts transporting the diamonds, stating that 'a great robbery might be effected by two persons, and the goods which would be so stolen are of all property the most portable . . . and diamonds in the rough cannot be traced' (p. 196). Identifying with a diamond thief plotting the heist, Trollope connects himself to people taking what is not rightfully theirs, and also to Gordon, the actual diamond miner in *An Old Man's Love*. Despite Gordon's association with believability, and therefore 'the real', the travel account that readers are led to read reminds them that Gordon's fortune results from the theft of precious stones and land belonging to Africans. Moreover, when Gordon returns to claim the disputed jewel of Mary, she is the official fiancée of another man. The mistrust applies to everyone, however, including Whittlestaff, who in relinquishing Mary confesses to taking what was not rightfully his: 'To shame myself by taking that which belongs to another, as though it were my own property' (*OML*, ch. 21, p. 236). As in *The Eustace Diamonds*, about which Patrick Brantlinger remarks the text of 'reality' and the characters appear to be 'counterfeit', *An Old Man's Love* undermines each character's claim to authenticity and trustworthiness.[63] Even Mary knows that she is counterfeit paste because she loves Gordon but fraudulently acts the part of genuine jewel when gifting herself to Whittlestaff.

Trollope highlights the transience of possession and determinacy even in the final pages, pushing readers to accept ambiguity and recognise the difficulty of transcending the habit of misreading people and texts. A last disorientating dissonance complicates the happy ending when rather than feeling freed by Whittlestaff's grand relinquishment of her, Mary is re-enslaved by a further insidious 'debt of gratitude' that keeps her unhappy because of the 'tragedy connected with her matrimonial circumstances' (ch. 24, p. 261). Indeed, she wonders whether she now loves Whittlestaff more than Gordon, which frustrates the reader relieved that the young lovers finally can marry. And though Whittlestaff's last-minute acceptance of Gordon alleviates Mary's misery, the reader remains mistrustful to the end because of Whittlestaff's last words: 'I shall never cease to regret all that I have lost' (p. 265). They indicate that instead of embracing Mary as his new daughter, Whittlestaff has returned to viewing her as a lost lover – like Catherine Bailey and his favourite heroines in literature, a recurrence that unequivocally destabilises the traditional tidy ending.

Trollope's conscription of the reader into contemplating multiple endings, and his own connection with thievery or mistrust, find further affirmation in another tag from Horace surfacing in *An Old Man's Love*. Irritated by Mr Blake's hints that Gordon has more right to Mary, Whittlestaff says to her: '*Per contatorem fugito nam garrulus idem est*' (ch. 14, p. 155), which Sutherland translates as: 'Flee from the storyteller for such a person cannot hold his tongue', and other translations include 'talkative', 'questioner', 'tattler' or 'inquisitive person'.[64] Taken together, and considering also Kenneth Haynes's assertion that Trollope deployed classical allusions for 'deception and delusion', the translations invite the conjecture that Trollope was having the last word, so to speak, humorously highlighting the untrustworthiness of writers like himself, whose innumerable publications were a form of talkativeness.[65]

Robert Scholes and Robert Kellogg describe Trollope as the 'maker of a purely fictitious narrative', not the '*histor*' who 'can only seek the truth'; and assert that, as a result, he endured 'harsh criticism', because like the magician, the novelist 'is not supposed to let the audience see how he does his tricks'.[66] But, they conclude, 'no one really believes . . . that a magician creates an egg or a rabbit from nothing. We know it is a trick. Some magicians acknowledge this as part of their performance and some do not, but such acknowledgement is not the basis on which we judge or enjoy them.'[67] Trollope's habit of conjuring through inference rather than description in his fiction leads the classical scholar Edward P. Morris to note the proximity of Trollope's stylistic approach to Horace's, asserting that both powerfully picture characters through 'suggestion', not 'description', encouraging readers 'to analyse and classify', activities that form the foundation of *An Old Man's Love*. Prodded to search within and beyond the text for traces of its meaning, the reader is conscripted into examining not only Horace's odes and epistles, but Trollope's own previous writings, and all merge with the narrator and Whittlestaff's lists of texts to create a paste diamond that is, nonetheless, a repetition with a difference, and so, paradoxically, an original gem.[68]

Notes

1. Anthony Trollope, *An Old Man's Love*, ed. John Sutherland (Oxford: Oxford University Press, 1991), ch. 11, p. 114. Further citations are given parenthetically (*OML*).

2. Henry James, 'Anthony Trollope', *The Century: A Popular Quarterly*, 26.3 (July 1883): pp. 384–95.

3. Notably, Robert Tracy, *Trollope's Later Novels* (Berkeley: University of California Press, 1978); John Sutherland, 'Introduction', pp. vii–xxii; David Skilton, 'Introduction', in Anthony Trollope, *An Old Man's Love* (London: The Trollope Society, 1998), pp. vii–xv; and Frederik Van Dam's *Anthony Trollope's Late Style: Victorian Liberalism and Literary Form* (Edinburgh: Edinburgh University Press, 2016).

4. Michael Sadleir, *Trollope: A Commentary* (New York: Farrar, Straus and Company, 1947) pp. 538, 40; Robert Polhemus, *The Changing World of Anthony Trollope* (Berkeley and Los Angeles: University of California Press, 1968), p. 219.

5. James Kincaid, *The Novels of Anthony Trollope* (Oxford: Clarendon Press, 1997), p. 64.

6. See A. S. Shand [anon.], *The Times* (14 April 1884), p. 3, in Smalley (ed.), *Trollope*, p. 523; attribution from *The Times* Editorial Diaries. See David Skilton, *Anthony Trollope and His Contemporaries: A Study in the Theory and Conventions of Mid-Victorian Fiction* (London: Longman, 1972), p. 163.

7. C. E. Dawkins, *Academy* xxv. 220 (29 March 1884), in Donald Smalley (ed.), *Trollope: The Critical Heritage* (London: Routledge and Kegan Paul, 1969), p. 520. Unsigned notice, *Saturday Review* lvii (29 March 1884), pp. 414–15, in Smalley (ed.), *Trollope*, p. 521. See also Skilton, *Anthony Trollope*, p. 163.

8. R. C. Terry, *Anthony Trollope: The Artist in Hiding* (London and Basingstoke: Macmillan Press, 1977) pp. 169–70.

9. David Skilton, 'Introduction', p. xiii, and John Sutherland, 'Introduction', pp. xi–xii.

10. Hugh Osborne, 'Hooked on Classics: Discourses of Allusion in the Mid-Victorian Novel', in Roger Ellis and Lis Oakley-Brown (eds), *Translations and Nation: Towards a Cultural Politics of Englishness* (Clevedon: Multilingual Matters, 2001), p. 149, and David Skilton, 'Schoolboy Latin and the Mid-Victorian Novelist: A Study in Reader Competence', *Browning Institute Studies*, 16 (1988): p. 49. See also Van Dam, *Trollope's Late Style*, pp. 81–99; Robert Tracy, '*Lana Medicata Fuco*: Trollope's Classicism', in John Halperin (ed.), *Trollope Centenary Essays* (London and Basingstoke: Macmillan, 1982), pp. 1–23; and Margaret Markwick, *New Men in Trollope's Fiction: Rewriting the Victorian Male* (Aldershot: Ashgate, 2007), pp. 192–3.

11. Elizabeth Epperly, *Patterns of Repetition in Trollope* (Washington, DC: The Catholic University of America Press, 1989), pp. 1–2.

12. Van Dam, *Trollope's Late Style*, p. 87.

13. Ibid. p. 3. See John Bowen, 'Introduction', in Anthony Trollope, *Phineas Redux*, (Oxford: Oxford University Press, 2011), p. xix, p. xxv; and Matthew Sussman, 'Trollope's Honesty', *Studies in Literature*, 53.4 (Autumn 2013): p. 890.

14. Roland Barthes, *Image-Music-Text*, trans. Stephen Heath (New York: Hill and Wang 1977), p. 160.

15. See Patrick Brantlinger, *The Reading Lesson: The Threat of Mass Literacy in Nineteenth-Century British Fiction* (Bloomington: Indiana University Press, 1998), p. 134.

16. Kincaid, *The Novels*, p. 50. Kincaid sees Trollope 'both tied to and separated from the realist tradition' (p. 51).

17. The subplot concerning Mr Whittlestaff's housekeeper, Mrs Baggett, and her wayward husband is sufficiently important to deserve a separate discussion.

18. Christopher Todd Matthews discusses how pockets distinguish men's identity in terms of class and masculinity in 'Form and Deformity: The Trouble with Victorian Pockets', *Victorian Studies*, 52.4 (Summer 2010): pp. 562–90.

19. Stefanie Markovits, 'Form Things: Looking at Genre through Victorian Diamonds', *Victorian Studies*, 52.4 (Summer 2010): pp. 591–619. Markovits asserts that 'diamonds focus authors' reflections on form because they are invariably discussed *in terms of* form. Despite their material density, diamonds are, in some ways, *all* form: a shape as well as a thing. Indeed, diamonds' crystalline structure limits the shapes in which they occur, setting them apart from most other substances (including translucent glass)' (p. 599). They are, therefore, 'an obvious lens through which to consider the kinds of literary form we call *genres*' (p. 599).

20. Ibid. p. 595.

21. Kincaid, *The Novels*, p. 50.

22. Ibid. pp. 50–1.

23. Wayne Booth, *The Rhetoric of Fiction* (Chicago: University of Chicago Press, 1961), p. 322. Trollope writes that 'it is almost impossible not to entertain something of a friendly feeling for him' (as quoted in Booth, p. 323).

24. Barthes, *Image-Music-Text*, pp. 142, 148.

25. Tracy, *Trollope's Later Novels,* p. 318.

26. Patricia Waugh would view Trollope's depiction of Whittlestaff a 'minimal form of metafiction', in that his 'inauthentic role and personal dissatisfaction' lead to 'obsessive . . . practices of self-fictionalization' (pp. 117–18) in *Metafiction: The Theory and Practice of Self-Consciousness Fiction* (London: Routledge, 1988).

27. Alfred Lord Tennyson, 'Guinevere', ll. 375–8, in *Idylls of the King*, in *Poems of Tennyson*, ed. Jerome Buckley (Boston: Houghton Mifflin Co., 1958), p. 452.

28. Anthony Trollope, 'On English Prose Fiction as a Rational Amusement', *Anthony Trollope: An Autobiography and Other Writings* (Oxford: Oxford University Press, 2014), p. 235.

29. Ibid. p. 244.

30. Debra Gettelman, 'The Victorian Novel and its Readers', in Lisa Rodensky (ed.), *The Oxford Handbook of the Victorian Novel* (Oxford: Oxford University Press, 2013), pp. 112–13, p. 120.

31. See the anonymous essay, 'Novels, Past, and Present', in *Saturday Review* (14 April 1866), p. 440, which declares of the woman reader: 'She has a dangerous habit of identifying situations of a novel with the circumstances of her own life' (as quoted in Gettelman, p. 121).

32. Ibid. p. 119.

33. N. John Hall, *Trollope: A Biography* (Oxford: Oxford University Press, 1993), p. 454. Trollope 'closely followed the reviews', and was particularly 'dismayed' by the criticism of *Thackeray* (1879) (p. 453), writing in reference to his next book, *An Eye for an Eye* (1879): 'I look forward with some grim pleasantry to its publication . . . and to the declaration of the critics that it has been the work of a period of life at which the power of writing novels had passed from me' (as quoted in Hall, p. 455). Trollope 'felt that critics were by and large good to him', but not when they thought he was 'meddling with things too high for him' (Hall, p. 474).

34. Garrett Stewart, *Dear Reader: The Conscripted Audience in Nineteenth-Century British Fiction* (Baltimore and London: Johns Hopkins University Press, 1996, p. 395).

35. Ibid. p. 8.

36. Ibid. p. 393.
37. Ibid. p. 395.
38. Gilles Deleuze, *Difference and Repetition*, trans. Paul Patton (New York: Columbia University Press, 1994).
39. Ibid. p. 70.
40. Ibid. p. 76. See also Roland Barthes, *S/Z: An Essay*, trans. Richard Miller (New York: Hill and Wang, 1974), which concludes that 'infinitude . . . results from repetition: repetition is, very precisely, the fact that there is no reason to stop' (p. 177).
41. Edward Said, *The World, the Text, and the Critic* (London: Faber and Faber, 1984), p. 125.
42. See M. H. Abrams's definition of 'metafiction' in *Glossary of Literary Terms* (Boston, MA: Thomson Wadsworth, 2005), p. 203.
43. See Tracy, '*Lana Medicata Fuco*', pp. 1–23; Skilton, 'Schoolboy Latin', pp. 39–55; Osborne, 'Hooked on Classics', pp. 120–66.
44. Tracy, Sutherland and Michael Sadleir conclude that Trollope saw himself in Whittlestaff, and perhaps was exploring his relationships with Kate Field and Florence Bland. See Sadleir, *Trollope*, p. 220; Sutherland, 'Introduction', p. xv; and Tracy, *Trollope's Later Novels*, p. 318. David Skilton, by contrast, underscores their differences, writing that 'quiet seclusion' and 'pained withdrawal' were not Trollope's style. See 'Introduction', p. viii.
45. Tracy, *Trollope's Later Novels*, p. 311; and Sutherland, 'Introduction', p. vii.
46. Tracy, *Trollope's Later Novels*, p. 312.
47. See Barthes's argument that 'the connotative signified is literally an *index*: it points but does not tell', whereas in denotation, the truth 'is immediately revealed' (*S/Z*, p. 62). Trollope designs *An Old Man's Love* enigmatically, relying more on connotation.
48. The titles listed are 'An Old Man's Love', 'Crocus Hall' and 'Mary Lawrie'. See Sutherland, 'Introduction', p. xxiii.
49. Terry, *Anthony Trollope*, pp. 101–2.
50. Shirley Robin Letwin, *The Gentleman in Trollope: Individuality and Moral Conduct* (Hong Kong: Macmillan Press, 1982) pp. 140–1.
51. Margaret Markwick, *Trollope and Women* (London and Rio Grande: The Hambledon Press, 1997), pp. 26–7.
52. Representative examples include Andrew Miller, *Novels behind Glass: Commodity Culture and Victorian Narrative* (Cambridge University Press, 1995); John Plotz, *Portable Property: Victorian Culture on the Move* (Princeton: Princeton University Press, 2009); Jen Sattaur, 'Commodities, Ownership, and *The Eustace Diamonds*: The Value of Femininity', *Victorian Literature and Culture*, 38.1 (2010): pp. 39–52; Markovits, 'Form Things' pp. 607–10; and Brantlinger, *The Reading Lesson*, pp. 121–41.
53. Anthony Trollope, *The Eustace Diamonds* (Oxford: Oxford University Press, 2011), ch. 3, p. 21; ch. 3, pp. 24–5; ch. 65, p. 474.
54. Horace, *Ode* 3.19, l. 24, in *The Complete Odes and Epodes*, trans. David West (Oxford: Oxford University Press, 1997) p. 97.
55. Horace, *Epistles* 2.2, ll. 180–2, in Trollope, *OML*, trans. note, p. 283.
56. Horace, *Odes* 3.19, l. 28, in Trollope, *OML*, trans. note, p. 283.
57. Horace, *Epistles* 2.2, in Edward Morris (ed.), *Satires and Epistles* (Norman: University of Oklahoma Press, 1968), pp. 181–8.
58. Miller, *Novels*, p. 160.
59. Ibid. p. 162.
60. Suzanne Daly, *The Empire Inside: Indian Commodities in Victorian Domestic Novels* (Ann Arbor: University of Michigan Press, 2011), p. 71.
61. Sutherland, 'Introduction', p. xi.
62. Anthony Trollope, *South Africa*, 2 vols (London: Chapman and Hall, 1878), vol. 2, ch. 11, p. 202. Further citations are given parenthetically (*SA*).

63. Brantlinger, *The Reading Lesson*, pp. 140–1.
64. Horace, *Epistles* 1.18, l. 69, quoted in *OML*, ed. John Sutherland, p. 282, note 155. See also 'avoid a questioner, for he is also a tattler' quoted in Osborne, 'Hooked', p. 166, note 12. The 1828 edition of the *Eton Latin Grammar* includes: 'Avoid an inquisitive person', quoted in Van Dam, p. 85; while Tracy translates the line: 'I flee the questioner, for he is talkative', in 'Lana', p. 23.
65. Kenneth Haynes, 'Gentleman's Latin, Lady's Greek', in Lisa Rodensky (ed.), *The Oxford Handbook of the Victorian Novel* (Oxford: Oxford University Press, 2013), p. 426.
66. Robert Scholes and Robert Kellogg, *The Nature of Narrative* (New York: Oxford University Press, 1966), pp. 267–8.
67. Ibid. p. 268.
68. Morris, 'Introduction', p. 20.

5

READING *An Autobiography* AS
ADVICE LITERATURE

David Skilton

Trollope's *An Autobiography* is a mine of information about his professional life, about the Victorian literary system and the History of the Book. It is cited in many works claiming autobiography is a genre, and many critics have found it an irresistible source of speculation about his psychology, whether that may be simple or complex. Yet the work has yet to be located clearly in another important context, that of advice literature. Everyone knows that it offers advice to new writers, but few commentators take Trollope's first sentence seriously enough to bear it in mind at all times. To do so is not to simplify, but to keep more meanings simultaneously in play. In the following pages I shall concentrate on this single aspect, because it seems to me to be only partially understood. In the process I hope to show how renewed application of traditional reading can be as successful in bringing new meanings to light in Trollope as radically innovative methodologies.

The opening sentence will illustrate how easy it is to miss much of what Trollope is saying:

> In writing these pages, which, for the want of a better name, I shall be fain to call the autobiography of so insignificant a person as myself, it will not be so much my intention to speak of the little details of my private life, as to what I, and perhaps others round me, have done in literature, of my failures and successes such as they have been, and their causes, and of the opening which a literary career offers to men and women for the earning of their bread.[1]

Nothing, it seems, could be simpler, and we rarely ever pause for long over this sentence. It is, however, carefully rhetorical, containing a disclaimer of the importance of the author as an object of attention, and, after that concession, suggesting, possibly with mock modesty, that nevertheless as a writer he may have something significant to express. This sort of opening gambit is a rhetorical commonplace, and in the mid-Victorian period is becoming familiar in accounts of a writer's own life, establishing a convention for the literary form which is increasingly being called an 'autobiography', although the word is strange enough for Trollope to include a second apology, this time for being 'fain' to use it because he is unable to find a more apposite alternative.

In the years before Trollope began to write his life in 1875, a dozen or more other 'autobiographies' appeared, a small number of which were published by acquaintances of his, including John Stuart Mill's in 1873 and Sir Henry Taylor's in 1874.[2] Mill's, for example, begins, 'I do not for a moment imagine that any part of what I have to relate can be interesting to the public as a narrative or as being connected with myself.'[3] This age-old tactic effectively disables the criticism that the subject is not worthy of treatment. Trollope and Mill in this particular remind us of the rather less modest opening of Dickens's novel, *David Copperfield* (1849–50): 'Whether I shall turn out to be the hero of my own life, or whether that station will be held by anybody else, these pages must show.'[4] The reader has been 'brought alongside', as the naval metaphor has it, and having been thus made a familiar of the author, may be inclined to proceed apace, taking the rest of Trollope's first sentence as a mere elaboration or intensification of the disclaimer of the importance of the narrating self. To take it so simply is to miss the fact that Trollope may actually mean that a principal subject of his work will be 'what I, and perhaps others round me, have done in literature, of my failures and successes such as they have been, and their causes, and of the opening which a literary career offers to men and women for the earning of their bread'. With a touch of false modesty, Trollope is saying that his literary career is to be of interest as a source of guidance to others intending to earn a living from their pens.

Mill's equivalent statement runs as follows:

I do not for a moment imagine that any part of what I have to relate, can be interesting to the public as a narrative, or as being connected with myself. But I have thought that in an age in which education, and its improvement, are the subject of more . . . study than at any former period . . . it may be useful that there should be some record of an education which was unusual and remarkable, and which . . . has proved how much more than is commonly supposed may be taught . . . in those early years which, in the common modes of what is called instruction, are little better than wasted.[5]

Mill's life is 'uneventful' in the sense of having few dramatic adventures worth narrating, just as Trollope as a 'person' is 'insignificant' upon the national or international stage of history. These lives will not centre on private and domestic matters, which it would in any case be bad manners to put on public display. As Sir Henry Taylor explains at the end of the second and final volume of his *Autobiography*, 'With whatever measure of unreserve I may seem to have written about myself, it has been no part of my design to speak the whole truth. A man may tell the truth of himself somewhat largely without disclosing either the inward offences or the weaknesses and littlenesses of his life and nature.'[6] Trollope's parallel passage at the end of his *Autobiography* reads:

It will not, I trust, be supposed by any reader that I have intended in this so-called autobiography to give a record of my inner life. No man ever did so truly, – and no man ever will. Rousseau probably attempted it, but who doubts but that Rousseau has confessed in much the thoughts and convictions rather than the facts of his life? If the rustle of a woman's petticoat has ever stirred my blood, if a cup of wine has been a joy to me, if I have thought tobacco at midnight in pleasant company to be one of the elements of an earthly Paradise, if now and again I have somewhat recklessly fluttered a £5 note over a card table, of what matter is that to any reader?

I have betrayed no woman. Wine has brought me to no sorrow. It has been the companionship of smoking that I have loved rather than the habit. I have never desired to win money and I have lost none. To enjoy the excitement of pleasure, but to be free from its vices and ill effects; to have the sweet and to leave the bitter untasted, – that has been my study. (*A*, ch. 20, p. 232)

The autobiographers of the 1870s, that is, are demanding not to be reproached for omitting or concealing the intimate and domestic facts of their lives. Both Mill and Trollope are clearly distancing themselves from Rousseau in particular, Trollope from his life-writing and Mill from his theories of education, at which Trollope also had an earlier shy in *Orley Farm*, in which Felix Graham fails to groom the daughter of a drunken engraver as a suitable wife for himself, following Rousseau's prescription as famously put into practice by Thomas Day of the Birmingham Lunar Society in the previous century.[7] Although we shall not have space to pursue all the game that this quick sweep has started, we note in passing the contrast between Mill's intensively controlled education and Trollope's upbringing, which, by the novelist's own account, was exactly described by Mill as 'those early years which, in the common modes of what is called instruction, are little better than wasted'.[8] Trollope, then, is generally in accord on questions of the proper content of an autobiography with his friend and fellow advanced Liberal, Mill, and with his more conservative fellow civil servant and favourite living dramatist, Sir Henry Taylor, poet of the 'closet' play, *Philip Van Artevelde* (1834). But he is uneasy about the standards of what might almost be called another 'camp' of fiction and life-writing, the Dickens–Forster circle.

Many of Trollope's statements about the novel and novelists in *An Autobiography* are also in part a commentary on one of the most important literary lives of the period, John Forster's *Life of Charles Dickens* (1872–4), to which it makes both explicit and implicit reference. Yet because of the number of years separating the publication of the two, little attention has been paid to the immediacy of the intertextual links between them. I shall concentrate on the professional conduct of authors, advice to new novelists and some social aspects of the debate on 'the dignity of literature'.

Trollope started his work on *An Autobiography* in late October 1875 on a voyage home from New York, then set it aside until the New Year and finished it on 11 April 1876, returning to it to make a number of detailed changes a few years later. The manuscript, which is in the British Library, is in a wrapper labelled, 'An Autobiography – / Begun 1 January 1876 / Finished 11 April 1876'.[9] John Forster's *The Life of Charles Dickens* appeared in three volumes, separately published in December 1871 (dated 1872), November 1872 and February 1874. In *An Autobiography* Trollope makes two explicit references to Forster's biography which occur in Chapters 5 ('My First Success') and 13 ('On English Novelists of the Present Day'). The context of the first is his dealings as a literary newcomer with the very well-established Forster over letters on Ireland that Trollope had written for the radical weekly, the *Examiner*, which Forster edited, and Trollope uses a well-known illustration to help his reader visualise the scene and register the gulf between the powerful editor on the one hand and himself, the outsider, on the other. The illustration in question is a sketch by Daniel Maclise, which became sufficiently well known to grace domestic walls well into the next century, and which shows Dickens reading

The Chimes to an admiring circle of friends and devotees. By the time Trollope was writing his own life, the image had been popularised as a plate in Forster's *Life*. As Trollope recalls, he had the worst of the encounter, having his letters printed but no payment for them. Forster, though ever, as a cabman famously said of him, 'an arbitrary cove',[10] later became 'an intimate and valued friend' (*A*, ch. 5, p. 57).

The second mention of Forster's *Life* occurs in a passage in which Trollope presents evidence of Dickens's overwhelming and unequalled popularity:

> The certainty with which his novels are found in every house, the familiarity of his name in all English-speaking countries, the popularity of such characters as Mrs Gamp, Micawber, Pecksniff and many others whose names have entered into the English language and become well-known words, the grief of the country at his death, and the honours paid to him at his funeral, all testify to his popularity. Since the last book he wrote himself I doubt whether any book has been so popular as his biography by John Forster. There is no withstanding such testimony as this. (*A*, ch. 13, pp. 158–9)

For our purposes it is important to note that this approbation rests on the judgement of the market, on sales, and on popular and critical acclaim. These are Trollope's criteria for what he calls 'success', and his estimate of other elements in a writer's achievement and character may be quite independent of these factors. It is noteworthy that in the case of *Lady Anna* he takes public rejection of the work as 'the strongest testimony I could receive of the merits of the story' (*A*, ch. 19, p. 220).

So great was Dickens's 'success' that the intending writer should not seek to emulate him. He was, after all, given the soubriquet 'the Inimitable'. His practice of composition in particular left much to be desired. Trollope was constant at his task, writing for a set time each day, and producing a standard number of words every fifteen minutes, ready to go to the press when wanted. Admittedly Charles Dickens's art earned its author a fine living, but Dickens was frequently rescuing himself from difficult situations by a combination of brilliance and violent exertion neither of which the tyro could expect to equal. Most writers required more disciplined procedures. The dominance in the Victorian mind of the notion of literature as example – and moral example at that – could not be better demonstrated than by Trollope's assumption that descriptions of Dickens at work were potentially dangerous for inexperienced writers. In holding up his own practice as an example to follow, Trollope implicitly warns these aspirants away from the misleading example of Dickens in three further respects: the completion of a work before the start of serial or part issue; rigid adherence to the length of text agreed with a publisher and reliance on the literary help of others in process of rewriting, or cutting or adding matter. The picture of Dickens as in some degree less businesslike than Trollope leads the latter into a certain exaggeration of his own perfection – a quite unnecessary exaggeration, given the extraordinary powers he displayed. Whereas Dickens is frequently seen in Forster's *Life* labouring under some strain to produce the next month's part of a current novel, and on one occasion actually failing to supply a month's quota because of overwhelming grief, Trollope claimed always to write his novels to the end before publication commenced, with the single exception of *Framley Parsonage*, which was commissioned in the eleventh hour for the launch of the new *Cornhill Magazine* when the editor, Thackeray, failed to deliver:

[I]t had always been a principle with me in my art that no part of a novel should be published till the entire story was completed. I knew, from what I read from month to month, that his hurried publication of uncompleted work was frequently, I might say, always adopted by the leading novelists of the day. That such has been the case is proved by the fact that Dickens, Thackeray, and Mrs Gaskell died with unfinished novels of which portions had already been published. I had not yet entered upon the system of publishing novels in parts, and therefore had never been tempted. But I was aware that an artist should keep in his hand the power of fitting the beginning of his work to the end. (*A*, ch. 8, p. 92)

We must allow our author a little latitude, and admit that he rarely offended against his own rule, but though *An Autobiography* is silent on the subject, *The Belton Estate* was written between 30 January and 4 September 1865, and serialised from 15 May of the same year to 1 January 1866. This, however, was another case of a rush to find a suitable serial for a new journal, in this case the *Fortnightly Review*, of which Trollope was one of the founders. The journal was founded to promote radical liberal principles, and its first issue contained the opening of a work by another of the founders, George Henry Lewes, *The Principles of Success in Literature*.[11] This being a cause close to Trollope's heart, he supplied a novel intended to illustrate Lewes's 'Principles'. We shall return to this case later. He overstates his case throughout, and should perhaps have written that he would not commence publication until nearly all of the work was complete. When he suffered his fatal stroke on 3 November 1882, the first instalment of *The Landleaguers* was about to appear on the sixteenth of the month, and only forty-eight of the planned total of sixty chapters were written – substantially more than in the case of any one of the three delinquent colleagues he names.

Dickens's sins, however, are deeper than this, as can be seen from an anecdote in *An Autobiography* which must be quoted at length:

Some years since a critic of the day . . . showed me the manuscript of a book recently published, – the work of a popular author of the day. It was handsomely bound and was a valuable and desirable possession. It had been just given to him by the author as an acknowledgment for a laudatory review in one of the leading journals of the day. As I was expressly asked whether I did not regard such a token as a sign of grace both in the giver and in the receiver, I said that I thought it should neither have been given nor have been taken. My theory was repudiated with scorn, and I was told that I was strait-laced, visionary and impracticable! In all that, the damage did not lie in the fact of that one present, but in the feeling on the part of the critic that his office was not debased by the acceptance of presents from those whom he criticised. This man was a professional critic, – bound by his contract with certain employers to review such books as were sent to him. How could he, when he had received a valuable present for praising one book, censure another by the same author? (ch. 14, pp. 169–70)[12]

This is where the anecdote ends in the first edition of *An Autobiography*. The manuscript, however, shows that Trollope intended to round it off with the following *coup de grâce*: 'He knew indeed that there was no question of censure, – that with an author so popular it was his duty to praise. All which makes the whole matter very much the worse' (*A*, ch. 14, p. 170).

The critic in question was Eneas Sweetland Dallas, the 'popular author of the day' was Dickens, and the 'book recently published' was *Our Mutual Friend*. Cross-reference to an earlier appearance of Dallas in *An Autobiography* in relation to Trollope's *The West Indies and the Spanish Main* may suggest that Trollope's irritability on the subject was simply ad hominem:

> [T]here appeared three articles in [*The Times*], one closely after another, which made the fortune of the book. Had it been very bad I suppose its fortune could not have been made for it, even by the Times newspaper. I afterwards became acquainted with the writer of those articles, – the contributor himself informing me that he had written them. I told him that he had done me a greater service than can often be done by one man to another, but that I was under no obligation to him. I do not think that he saw the matter quite in the same light. (*A*, ch. 7, p. 87)

The subjects under discussion here are the moral and practical aspects of book-reviewing, and not the actual substance of the review, the favourable nature of which is summed up simply in the statement, 'The view I took of the relative position in the West Indies of black men and white men was the view of the *Times* newspaper at the period.' Were the views of author and reviewer the focus, it might be relevant to mention that Dallas was a planter's son, born in Jamaica, thus possessing relevant information and prejudice, but Trollope is intent on inculcating proper standards for the relation of author and reviewer, while not underestimating the advance in a literary career that can be produced by influential criticism:

> I am aware that by that criticism I was much raised in my position as an author. Whether such lifting up by such means is good or bad for literature is a question which I hope to discuss in a future chapter. But the result was immediate to me for I at once went to Chapman & Hall and successfully demanded £600 for my next novel. (*A*, ch. 7, p. 87)

While claiming the moral high ground here, Trollope elsewhere acknowledges that Dallas was one of the best critics of the day. Making matters worse is Forster's enthusiastic reporting of what Trollope considered Dickens's improper relations with his critics. Here is one instance:

> [Dickens] had pleasant communication with Lockhart, dining with him at Cruik-shank's a little later, and this was the prelude to a *Quarterly* review of *Oliver* by Mr Ford, written at the instance of Lockhart but without the raciness he would have put in it, in which amende was made for previous less favourable notice in that review. Dickens had not however waited for this to express publicly his hearty sympathy with Lockhart's handling of some passages in his admirable *Life of Scott* that had drawn down upon him the wrath of the Ballantynes. This he did in the *Examiner* . . .[13]

This exchange of favours was anathema to Trollope.

Anyone in the London literary scene would know that Forster commonly regarded reviewers as potential collaborators in the business of promoting a promising book or career. Happy the literary agent (a role Forster invented and adopted on behalf of a number of his contemporaries) whose clients are of such quality that good reviews appear a natural right! Three further examples will suffice, showing Forster acting as he thought quite correctly. Robert Browning gave Forster the manuscript of *Paracelsus* inscribed in gratitude for services which included a very favourable review, and requests to his friends W. J. Fox and Leigh Hunt that they should receive the book in the same spirit. Forster's review predates the first meeting between the two men, which occurred on New Year's Eve 1835, when the critic greeted the poet with the words, 'Did you see a little notice I wrote of you in the *Examiner*?'[14] This was in all probability merely socially improper by the standards of the time, but two instances from the 1860s cannot escape so lightly. To oblige Edward Bulwer-Lytton, Forster arranged for a favourable review in the *Examiner* of *Poems and Ballads* by Swinburne, of whose work Forster – by now the model for Dickens's Mr Podsnap – morally disapproved. His twentieth-century biographer, whose theme is that Forster was an honest practitioner amongst rogues, remarks, 'In the interests of friendship literary principles could now be compromised.'[15] Just so. The third example must have been known to Trollope, since it concerned pressure brought to bear on Chapman and Hall, the publishers of the *Fortnightly Review*. Hearing that George Meredith had written an unfavourable review of Robert Lytton's *Chronicles and Characters* for the *Fortnightly*, Forster threatened to take the author, his protégé 'Owen Meredith' (Bulwer Lytton's son), away from the publisher.[16] Clearly Dickens and Forster were models to avoid.

In private, Trollope revealed further objections to Dickens and to Forster's *Life*, this time concerning his private life, which, as we have observed, was unmentionable to Trollope, and should have been to Dickens and Forster too. On 27 February 1872, having been reading the first volume of Forster's *Life*, Trollope writes to his friends George Eliot and George Henry Lewes as follows:

> Forsters [sic] first volume is distasteful to me, – as I was sure it would be. Dickens was no hero; he was a powerful, clever, humorous, and, in many respects, wise man; – very ignorant, thick-skinned, who had taught himself to be his own God, and to believe himself to be a sufficient God for all who came near him; – not a hero at all. Forster tells of him things which should disgrace him, – as the picture he drew of his own father, & the hard words he intended to have published of his own mother; but Forster himself is too coarse-grained, (though also a very powerful man) to know what is and is not disgraceful; what is or is not heroic. (*Letters*, pp. 557–8)

The forthright judgement predates Forster's account of the final breakdown of Dickens's marriage in 1858, and the very public way Dickens announced it in the press. It is irresistible to read Trollope's own very careful references to his own wife as a quiet reproach to Foster for revealing Dickens's behaviour towards his. There have been suggestions that Trollope's animus against Dickens arose from the latter's affair with Ellen Ternan, the sister of Frances Eleanor Ternan, who married Trollope's elder brother, Thomas Adolphus. There is no trace of this motive in or at the time of the writing of *An Autobiography*, and the family certainly retained no memory of a rift when in 1883 Trollope's grandson Frank was sent from Australia to the school which Ellen, now rehabilitated, with a new identity and a more recent date of birth, ran in Margate with her husband, the Reverend George Wharton Robinson.[17]

It is strange to today's reader to see fiction discussed without attention to many of its features we regard as necessary and intrinsic. In fact, many matters now incorporated into narratology and discourse analysis are present in the writings of the most interesting mid-Victorian critics, but no new, agreed terminology had yet been developed to speak of things other than character and story, and no forum for discussion existed. Fiction was however prominent in the world as a commodity, and as many people then sent the manuscripts of novels to publishers as today hope to develop careers in television or online services. Guides on how to make a living by writing and publishing novels were therefore commonplace. In addition to Trollope, whose *Autobiography* must be included in this category, and George Henry Lewes, both Walter Besant and James Payn wrote works of guidance for would-be novelists, while H. Byerley Thomson included writing as a possible career for any educated person in his *Choice of a Profession* in 1857, and in 1887–8 Robert Louis Stevenson wrote a humorous essay, 'On the Choice of a Profession', satirising bourgeois horror at the choice of a literary career, which remained unpublished until after his death.[18] The relentless surge of recruits was noted by George Eliot who pointed out that there were 'no barriers for incapacity to stumble against, no external criteria to prevent a writer from mistaking foolish facility for mastery', and by W. R. Greg who complained, 'Every educated lady can handle a pen *tant bien que mal*: all such, therefore, take to writing – and to novel-writing, both as the kind which requires the least special qualifications and the least severe study, and also as the only kind which will sell.'[19] John Sutherland estimates the number of fictional titles in the Victorian period at 60,000, and the number of novelists at 'around 7,000'.[20] These facts point to the existence of a class of would-be writers in need of practical advice, and, whatever its title and whatever else its purposes, Trollope's *Autobiography* is aimed in part at such a readership, and we should believe him when he says as much in the first sentence of the work.

Nine months after his letter to the Leweses, Trollope writes to his close Australian friend, George William Rusden:

> Have you read Macreadys [*sic*] Memoirs. These books do not make one pleased with humanity. It is disgusting to see the self-consciousness and irritated craving for applause which such men as Macready & Dickens have exhibited; – & which dear old Thackeray did exhibit also. It astonishes me not that men should feel it, but that they shew it. I am sure of myself that whenever such a disease has been oppressing me I have been able to tread it out. (*Letters*, p. 671)

The editor of the *Letters*, N. John Hall, notes, 'It is possible that the publication of *Macready's Reminiscences* . . . and Forster's *Life of Charles Dickens* . . . strengthened Trollope's resolve to write an autobiography' (*Letters*, p. 671, note 2). The closer the matter is examined, the greater that possibility becomes. Passages in which Trollope mentions his wife, for example, are in marked contrast to mentions of Catherine Dickens in Forster's *Life*. Trollope names his wedding-day 'that happy day . . . the commencement of my better life' (*A* 48). That is as personal as he becomes. 'My marriage was like the marriage of other people and of no special interest to any one except my wife and me' (*A*, 50), in contrast to Dickens's, which was spread across the press. It is difficult to believe that readers are not intended to draw the contrast for themselves. An even more pointed omission of the name of Dickens is the following:

> No one had read it but my wife; nor, as far as I am aware, has any other friend of mine ever read a word of my writing before it was printed. She, I think, has so read almost everything – to my very great advantage in matters of taste. I am sure I have never asked a friend to read a line; nor have I ever read a word of my own writing aloud, – even to her. (*A*, ch. 4, p. 51)

This makes it clear that, unlike Dickens, he has a marriage properly based in mutual respect and loyalty, and that he has kept his wife's name out of the press. When his play, *The Noble Jilt*, was rejected by a theatre manager, 'I accepted the judgment loyally, and said not a word on the subject to any one. I merely showed the letter to my wife declaring my conviction, that it must be taken as gospel' (*A*, ch. 5, p. 59). At one stage in his career, when he was travelling nearly every day, 'I worked with a pencil and what I wrote my wife copied afterwards. In this way was composed the greater part of *Barchester Towers* and of the novel which succeeded it, and much also of others subsequent to them' (*A*, ch. 6, p. 70). A principled objection can be made from a later point of view to a man's having a wife as his unpaid amenuensis, but the Trollopes had a more equal relationship than the Dickenses. Trollope makes this clear while not even mentioning Catherine Dickens. He retired from the Post Office in 1867, 'after due consultation with my wife' (*A*, ch. 14, p. 178).[21] And of course he travelled with his wife on the Continent and to Australia.

There have been rather unconvincing suggestions that Trollope deliberately enters into a competition with Dickens on rival accounts of dreadful nineteenth-century childhoods, but Trollope's account of his childhood and youth stands perfectly well on its own, and the reviewer of his *Autobiography* in the *Atlantic Monthly* sums it up aptly in the following words:

> Trollope's boyhood was a miserable existence, haunted by indigent gentility, and cursed with more than ordinary boyish awkwardness and isolation. The distinctness with which he remembers all his wretchedness induces a mingled sense of pity and shame. Poor little Trollope! he says to himself. You were kicked and cuffed about; but oh, how generally unattractive you must have been![22]

This is accurate, and is the opposite of Dickens's (perfectly justified) self-pity and self-admiration for his early rise to fame.

Trollope's working life as a civil servant and author interests us more. His method of composition is carefully explained as an example which is to be followed or adapted to need. It involves meticulous preparation, during which he allocated speech and action to his characters in imagined scenes, and, it appears, ran them (as we should say of film 'takes') in his head, memorising much of the language, especially the dialogue, which was carefully fitted to each character. He obviously had a large stock of ready-made fragments of narrative and dialogue, adaptable to a variety of characters and situations, along with a rich collection of quotations, rhetorical turns of phrase and so on. Without these well-ordered in his mind he could not have written at his celebrated speed of 250 words every quarter of an hour. Scholarly investigation of this matter is long overdue, having been proposed by Hugh Sykes Davies as long ago as the late 1960s.[23] The process can be analysed as a period of composition followed by controlled but extraordinarily rapid transcription of a mental 'text' which was already engendered and largely completed and memorised.[24]

Admitting that he was perhaps unusually able to perform at such intensity, he nevertheless advises that comparable dedication and unremitting application are essential for literary work. The work must be judged to be good work, according to a set of criteria in which the moral and the technical are interconnected to a degree to which we are unaccustomed today. The story must be told and the characters must be individualised and must age as fictional or narrated time passes.

Trollope ends the narrative of his autobiography with a list of earnings, and while most of his contemporaries see nothing inappropriate about this, having from the first believed him when he said he was writing a book which at least in part partook of the nature of advice literature, some later critics find it boastful, but to me it is self-satisfied in a carefully balanced way. Complex works generate numerous meanings, and to see Trollope's *Autobiography* as an example of advice literature for the intending writer does not deny it the power to create other meanings, other narratives and other readerships. His letter to George William Rusden quoted above goes on to throw a different light on to his record of achievement, making it not only a worldly tally but a far loftier memorial. Trollope seems to have been at ease with the idea of a deity who rewards people for how well they have occupied their place in the world, or how well they have fulfilled their promise in the Church of England catechism, to 'do my duty in that state of life, unto which it shall please God to call me'. He seems to interpret this to mean that in his case he promised to be a good civil servant and a good writer of fiction. Presumably he also undertook to be a good son, husband, father and so on, but does not expatiate on this in a life story which, unlike Dickens's, seeks to exclude the personal, the intimate and the domestic. Trollope's list of books completed, all of them guaranteed to be healthy for their readers, is an example to the tyro novelist and a guarantee of a life well spent, and in the letter to George William Rusden already quoted from, he even seems to claim that his 'honest' literary achievements qualify him for redemption. He is going to show his accounts to the deity and expects them to be received and feels he should get his quittance. Here is the letter, contrasting his own view of justification by works with Macready's reliance on justification by faith:

> . . . (in defending Macready) you tell me of his beautiful humility before God! I do not prize humility before God. I can understand that a man should be humble before his brother men the smallness of whose vision requires self-abasement in others – but not that any one should be humble before God. To my God I can be true, and if I think myself to have done well I cannot but say so. To you, if I speak of my own work, I must belittle myself. I must say that it is naught. But if I speak of it to my God, I say, 'Thou knowest that it is honest; – that I strove to do good; – that if ever there came to me the choice between success and truth, I stuck to truth. And I own that I feel it impossible that the Lord should damn me, and how can I be humble before God when I tell him that I expect from him eternal bliss as the reward of my life on earth. (*Letters*, p. 691)

It seems that his list of earnings near the end of *An Autobiography* is far more than a demonstration of worldly success. If we sometimes puzzle at the book, we must realise among other things it is a faithful servant's report to the Head Office in the sky. His readers are of paramount importance in this document, for they have been the purchasers of his wares in this commodity market. In the matter of 'success' in writing, vox populi has indeed been vox dei – the voice of the people, the voice of God. In this view, his list of earnings is the final word in proving his 'success' as a writer and as part of a divine creation.

Notes

1. Anthony Trollope, *An Autobiography*, ed. David Skilton (London: Penguin, 1996), p. 7. Subsequent references are in the main text (*A*).
2. J. S. Mill, *Autobiography* (London: Longmans, Green, Reader, and Dyer, 1873); *Autobiography of Henry Taylor 1800–1875* was first published in two volumes in 1874 and 1877, and a second edition in two volumes in 1885 (London: Longmans, Green & Co., now the standard edition).
3. Mill, *Autobiography*, p. 1.
4. The opening words of Charles Dickens, *The Personal History and Experience of David Copperfield the Younger* (London: Bradbury and Evans, 1850), p. 1.
5. Mill, *Autobiography*, p. 1.
6. *Autobiography of Henry Taylor*, 2 vols (London: Longmans, Green, 1885), vol. 2, p. 345.
7. See Brycchan Carey, 'Thomas Day (1748–1789)', <www.brycchancarey.com/abolition/day.htm> (last accessed 14 March 2016).
8. This is not the place to discuss what was lacking in Mill's Utilitarian childhood, and the consequences for him of that lack.
9. British Library ADDITIONAL MS 42856. For the chronology of Trollope's life see *The Letters of Anthony Trollope*, ed. N. J. Hall, 2 vols (Stanford: Stanford University Press, 1983). Subsequent references are in the main text (*Letters*).
10. There was a very well circulated anecdote about Forster which alleged that he had once been summoned before a magistrate by a cabman ostensibly because of a supposed irregularity in the payment of his fare. The cabman, when pressed, admitted that he had little grounds for bringing the case, but did so because the customer 'were such a harbitrary cove'. The Dickens circle was well aware of the story, as was Forster himself. The phrase got into more general circulation. I am grateful to Michael Slater and Bill Long for this information.
11. The six chapters of *The Principles of Success in Literature* appeared irregularly in the first two volumes of the *Fortnightly Review* from 15 May to 1 November 1865; it was published in volume form in the 1890s (Boston, MA: Allyn and Bacon, 1891; London: Scott, n.d. [1892?, 1898?]).
12. See also F. X. Roellinger, 'E. S. Dallas in Trollope's *Autobiography*', *MLN*, 55 (1940): pp. 422–4; and Kate Field, '*Our Mutual Friend* in Manuscript', *Scribner's Monthly*, 8 (1874): p. 472.
13. John Forster, *The Life of Charles Dickens* (London: Chapman and Hall, 1872–4), vol. 1, p. 161.
14. James A. Davies, *John Forster: A Literary Life* (Leicester: Leicester University Press, 1983), pp. 131–2 and 138.
15. Ibid. p. 122.
16. Ibid. p. 43.

17. See Nigel Starck, *The First Celebrity. Anthony Trollope's Australasian Odyssey* (Tusmore, SA: Writes of Passage, 2014; and Bath: Lansdown Media, 2014), p. 150.

18. Walter Besant, *The Art of Fiction* (London: Chatto & Windus, 1884); James Payn, 'The Literary Calling and its Future', *Nineteenth Century*, 6 (December 1879); H. Byerley Thomson, *The Choice of a Profession: a Concise Account and Comparative Review of the English Professions* (London: Chapman and Hall, 1857) and Robert Louis Stevenson, *On the Choice of a Profession* (London: Chatto & Windus, 1916). See also 'The Office of Novelist' in my *The Early and Mid-Victorian Novel* (London: Routledge, 1993), pp. 161–80.

19. See George Eliot (anon.), 'Silly Novels by Lady Novelists', *Westminster Review*, 66 (October 1856): pp. 442–61 (p. 461), and 'Authorship', in 'Leaves from a Notebook', in Thomas Pinney (ed.), *Essays of George Eliot* (London: Routledge and Kegan Paul, 1963), pp. 437–9; and W. R. Greg (anon.), 'False Morality of Lady Novelists', *National Review*, 1 (1859): pp. 147–9.

20. John Sutherland, *The Longman Companion to Victorian Fiction* (London: Longman, 1988), p. 1.

21. The first edition and the Oxford University Press 1950 edition both read 'consideration'. To the present writer, the MS reads 'consultation'.

22. (Anon.), 'Mr Trollopes [*sic*] Latest Character', *Atlantic Monthly*, 53 (February 1884): pp. 267–71 (p. 268).

23. In a number of conversations with the present writer.

24. See also the discussion of Trollope's description of his writing practice in Richard Menke, 'Mimesis, Media Archaeology and the Postage Stamp in *John Caldigate*' in this volume.

6

Trollope, Seriality, Series

Lauren M. E. Goodlad

To a greater extent than any short-form medium, serialised narratives create a real-life experience of inhabiting worlds whose uncertain storylines thwart our longings for knowledge and plenitude. As they do so, long-form serials generate multiple plots that 'divide the fictional world' and 'disperse the reader's attention'.[1] In place of formal unity as it is typically conceived, multiplot narratives generalise by crossing discrete storyworlds to ramify particular thematic, stylistic and spatial perceptions. Serialisation also entails the capacity to choreograph 'what bodies do in time and space',[2] producing opportunities for shared aesthetic, affective and intellectual engagement. The Victorian practice of publishing new part issues on 'Magazine Day', for example, created 'numerous and large communities' of simultaneous readers.[3] As Linda Hughes and Michael Lund have observed, 'We need to see the serial taking place amidst many different texts, and many different voices.'[4]

With decades of research into nineteenth-century print cultures to build upon, scholars of serialisation have begun to explore their object from transtemporal, transnational and transmedia perspectives. Their inspiration is partly the new TV 'golden age' that HBO's *The Sopranos* (1999–2007) helped to usher in at the turn of the millennium.[5] In the decades since, serial television has become a global phenomenon, as digital technologies multiply the modes of production, delivery, circulation and consumption first innovated in the cable era. Thus, even prior to the advent of streaming, scholars began to conceive seriality as a lens on past and present: for example, the comparisons between Charles Dickens's *Bleak House* (1852–3) and HBO's *The Wire* (2002–8) which migrated from classrooms and conferences to water coolers and *The Atlantic Monthly*.[6] This transtemporal perspective reminds us that the format of twenty monthly parts which came into being when a series of illustrated sketches morphed into *The Pickwick Papers* (1836–7) was not only a formidable profit-making machine. It was also a means of turning periodicals into vehicles for 'quality fiction'.[7]

That said, it is not Dickens, but Anthony Trollope who, according to the *New Yorker*, is the 'trending' Victorian whose works most befit the way we live now.[8] Though Trollope's prominence as an 'advanced, Conservative Liberal' may also explain his resonance in a neo-liberal era,[9] the author's exceptional popularity during a new serial 'golden age' is telling. Indeed, it is only when we turn to Trollope that we notice how the generative analogies between *The Wire* and *Bleak House* overlook the fact that HBO's series encompassed five discrete seasons over six years of programming, while Dickens's novel had no sequel beyond the original nineteenth-month sequence of parts. Thus, whereas the seriality of *Bleak House* worked through a structure of parts and whole, that of Trollope's series overran the boundaries of individual novels. As described by Lynette Felber, one of the few Victorianist scholars to discuss the series novel or *roman-fleuve*, the format expresses a desire for 'continuing relationship' which is absent in narrative poetics that stress climax and unity.[10]

To be sure, the nineteenth century's most influential 'novel-river' is Balzac's *La Comédie humaine* which, at more than ninety works, far exceeds the seven or eight seasons of the longest-running television serials. Émile Zola's naturalistic Rougon Macquart cycle of twenty novels (1871–93) is closer to the scale of series television but appeared after the peak impact of seriality on novel form. William Makepeace Thackeray, whose *History of Pendennis* (1848–50) echoes Balzac's *Bildungsromane*, may perhaps have had the French author in mind when he injected characters from *Vanity Fair* (1847–8) into later works such as *The Newcomes* (1855). But given Thackeray's limited success with what many contemporaries regarded as a sign of declining creativity, it is Trollope's Barsetshire and Palliser series, each composed of six inter-linked works published over twelve- or fifteen-year spans respectively, which offer the strongest Victorian parallels to millennial serials.[11] That is so even though the still-budding author had not serialised *any* novel before *Framley Parsonage* (1860–1). Thus, the work that turned Trollope into a literary celebrity and helped to establish the *Cornhill* as a leading venue for new fiction was the fourth of the series that came to be known as the Chronicles of Barsetshire. Could it be that the *Cornhill*'s ambitious publisher, George Murray Smith, and its editor, Thackeray, purposely sought out the only British author who was successfully extending storylines and characters from one novel to another? What we know for certain is that Smith's request for 'an English tale . . . with a clerical flavour' called for a fourth Barsetshire novel in spirit if not in letter.[12]

In this chapter, I explore Trollope's transformation into a series novelist and self-styled chronicler by way of highlighting his importance to a fertile period in Victorian print culture which I call 'the long 1860s'. My goal is partly to advance the new Victorianist interest in transtemporal and comparative approaches to nineteenth-century archives. By building on the *longue durée* analysis that Giovanni Arrighi set forth in *The Long Twentieth Century: Money, Power, and the Origins of Our Times* (1999, 2010), I make the case for a structure of recurrent seriality called 'Bigger Love' (a nod to Mark V. Olsen and Will Scheffer's HBO show, *Big Love* (2006–11)).[13] As we will see, both 'the long 1860s' and its millennial counterpart, 'the long 2000s', witnessed an intensification of audience engagement with multiplot serials which coincided with shifts in the flow of capital from production to speculation. If the archetypal televisual expressions of this structure of feeling were multi-season cable shows such as *The Wire* and *Big Love*, their print correlatives were novels like Trollope's *The Small House at Allington* (1862–4) and *The Last Chronicle of Barset* (1866–7). In these doubly serial works, publication in parts helped to consummate the shape of the Trollopian *roman-fleuve* while marking concomitant transitions in the world economy. 'Bigger Love' thus conceived provides another instance of what, in *The Victorian Geopolitical Aesthetic* (2015), I described as the after-echoes of mid-Victorian-era realist forms in television serials from the recent past.[14]

From Serialisation to 'Bigger Love'

The nineteenth-century boom for serialised fiction has been attributed to technological advances (in paper, print and transportation), demographic shifts (toward larger audiences for narrative fiction), serendipitous accident (wherein two 'lucky booksellers' happened on the one literary aspirant 'who could write letterpress for *all* the people'), as well as a maturing capitalist economy (transforming 'petty' book production into a full-blown 'commodity-form' that created a mass audience for new fiction).[15] Cutting across these enabling conditions is the simple fact that serialised narratives were longer and more multiplotted than those of the past. The success of *The Pickwick Papers* thus closely coincided with the new *roman-feuilletons* that Honoré de Balzac and Alexandre Dumas were popularising in the daily pages of *La Presse* and *Le Siècle*.[16]

In an economy fed by 'growth', writes Robert L. Patten, 'huge' increases in the sale of print spurred the production of ever 'bigger editions' supplied through ever 'larger, faster' technologies.[17] The serial print culture that emerged mobilised long-form fiction to heighten the profits from this boosted capacity. Publishers could multiply their investment in a novelist's labour through diversified formats that targeted particular demographics such as shilling parts for budget-conscious readers, multi-volume editions for circulating libraries and special editions for export or individual sale. At the same time, the long duration of serial fiction enabled reader discussions and reviewer commentaries to circulate inside and beyond national borders. The pleasure of reading them was partly collective anticipation for the newest instalment – along with the spates of page-turning, dialogue, letter-writing and reviewing which followed. Through energetic relays of print and conversation, favourite characters, scenes, or suspenseful storylines might percolate public consciousness on an international scale.

To be sure, Dickens's acclaim could only go so far in authorising the artistic merits of what *Times* critic E. S. Dallas disparaged as novels 'sold in minute doses'.[18] A literature consumed in monthly or (worse still) weekly parts, Dallas believed, conduced towards banality. Writing on the cusp of a decade-long craze for sensation fiction, Dallas did not imagine that 'a monthly dole' of fiction, snatched in 'little half-hours' of leisure, could yield genuine aesthetic pleasure. Yet, by 1861, when his article appeared, a very different sensibility had begun to prize seriality for its own sake – imagining vehicles for delivery that were not so much cheaper and faster as more elevated and capacious. Crucial to this zeitgeist was the new kind of periodical envisioned by Smith, the young scion of Smith, Elder & Co., whose career would establish him as an 'epoch-making' publisher.[19] Launched in 1860, the *Cornhill* set out to proffer 'first-class fiction' and edifying content under Thackeray's editorship – all for the same shilling that had once purchased a stint of fiction alone.[20]

Smith's 'lavish' bids to coveted novelists such as George Eliot suggests a business model that sought to corner the market on literary prestige.[21] But according to George Henry Lewes, what prompted Eliot to publish *Romola* (1862–3) in the *Cornhill*'s pages was not munificent payment but the advantage to the work 'of being read slowly and deliberately, instead of being galloped through in three volumes'.[22] Thus, whereas Dallas saw serialisation as a kind of Victorian 'boob tube', Lewes reversed this transtemporal comparison, depicting the patrons of circulating libraries as, in effect, Victorian bingers 'galloping through' chapters with thoughtless abandon.[23] The same desire for a committed readership prompted William Blackwood, a decade later, to consider a pause of *two* months between the parts of *Daniel Deronda* (1874–6) because, as he wrote, the serialisation of *Middlemarch* (1871–2) had taught him that 'it takes the public a long time to digest and fully appreciate the value of such food' as Eliot offers, and to 'talk to their neighbours about it'.[24] In this way, even as sensation novels pushed the envelope on what 'good' editors might publish, the launch of new magazines such as *Macmillan's* in 1859 (edited by the esteemed literary critic David Masson), the *Cornhill* under Thackeray the following year, and the *Fortnightly Review* in 1865 (edited by Lewes), conferred the stamp of selectivity on the new serial content. A kind of mid-Victorian 'slow print', the 'Bigger Love' that emerged marks the aspirational (if all too elusive) dimensions of a cultural phenomenon born of prized aesthetic experiences, intervals of reflection and the communities of conversation they spark.[25]

Of course, discourses of 'quality', then and now, can underwrite self-serving gambits for market share as well as dubious distinctions of class or gender.[26] As Michael Szalay has shown, HBO's aggressive branding – 'It's not TV. It's HBO' – bespeaks a highly capitalised network's desire to maintain managerial control in 'an era of downsizing'. The *Cornhill's* positioning of itself as a pioneering platform, willing to spare no expense to deliver 'quality' to an exacting audience, thus anticipated the model of the premiere cable subscription.[27] Indeed, when Smith's first issue sold more than 100,000 copies, it prompted one trade publication to pronounce 'the great fact of there being a very large and hitherto overlooked mass of readers for literature of high class'.[28] No doubt HBO identified an analogous opportunity when it morphed from a 'home box office' for movies into a producer of original serial content.

According to Sean O'Sullivan, the thirteen-episode season that HBO introduced with *The Sopranos* is a 'distinct narrative form', comparable to a sonnet, which became the template for the millennial era's 'most ambitious serials'. This rhythmic sequence transformed the television season from the pre-cable era's 'vague sprawl' of episodes into a carefully choreographed poetics of meaning.[29] In a similar vein, Thomas Doherty has described a novel-like 'Arc TV', a term 'underscor[ing] the dramatic curvature' of 'finely crafted' serials 'built around arcs of interconnected action'.[30] In my own take on the new seriality, long-form TV dramas offer narratively layered, intellectually provocative and richly aestheticised performances of a Braudelian 'dialectic of temporalities'.[31] Whatever their intra-diegetic treatment *of* time, these writerly serials enunciate their duration *in* time by creating dialectical movement both within and between the distinct frames of the episode, multi-episode season, and multi-season series. Thus, like the nineteenth-century novels they often resemble, these layered narrative arcs proffer quotidian pictures of 'real life' which capture the real-life experience of inhabiting the structures of a long-evolving, fast-changing global economy. In doing so, they have the potential to spark 'Bigger Love'.

A recurrent structure and structure of feeling, Bigger Love materialises through continuing storylines, returning character, and familiar locations as they traverse the boundaries of episodes, chapters, seasons and volumes. In doing so, such series ignite the desire for 'continuing relationship' beyond a particular endpoint or climax. The resulting 'slow print' or 'slow TV' interrupts the torrent of information and commerce, cultivating narrative rhythms of elaboration, repetition, duration and pause and – as they do so – intensifying habits of reader/viewer engagement. Nonetheless, it is here we must note the distinctly Trollopian features of the Bigger Love that evolved in the long 1860s. In *Writing By Numbers* (1987), Mary Hamer shows how Trollope's transition from the three-volume works favoured by circulating libraries, to monthly serialisation, conduced toward novels that were not only longer but also richer, more 'ambiguous' and more 'complex'.[32] Nonetheless, in modelling her study on Dickens's example, Hamer downplays the impact of Trollope's simultaneous transition into a series novelist – one, moreover, whose cultivation of the *roman-fleuve* took place in a climate that was hostile to what one review called 'the *repetita crambe*' (re-stewed cabbage) of 'second-hand characters'.[33] To grasp Trollope's eventual triumph over this critical reflex we must return to our *longue durée* approach.

The Long 1860s

According to Arrighi, the long nineteenth century's British hegemony combined industrial production with far-flung commercial networks and an expanding territorial empire that provided military power, raw materials and a market for British goods. By contrast, the long twentieth century's United States hegemony was enabled by vertically integrated capitalist structures, domestic natural resources, Pacific as well as Atlantic spheres of influence, and post-war geopolitical power. It is important to recognise, however, that each of these world-systems is built on substantial overlap with predecessors and successors; thus, the long 'twentieth' century begins in 1870, while the long 'nineteenth' century closes at the end of World War II. What nonetheless distinguishes each is the gradual rise and decline of the distinct technological, commercial, imperial and geopolitical logics fostered throughout the 'world' at large.[34] The result is a recurring pattern that visibilises the opening, peak and eventual close of each long century's systemic effects.

This works through a kind of feedback loop: as profits from the productive economy accumulate beyond what can be fruitfully reinvested, liquidity is diverted to lucrative speculation and lending. When trade and production slow in response, the retracting economy produces 'massive, systemwide redistributions of income and wealth' *from* society at large (i.e. those whose earnings derive from production and commerce) and *to* the 'agencies that control mobile capital' (i.e. the much smaller group who profit from speculation and lending).[35] This 'financial' phase continues until a new order of profitable production emerges. The story of rising inequality as economies shift from the relative prosperity of production and toward financialisation's hyper-enrichment of elites is familiar to Victorianists who know how novels by Dickens, Trollope and others vivify the speculative economy. But it is also familiar to anyone living today. For like Britons after the 1860s, we today are living through the financial phase of transition toward a new economy: a long twenty-first century that, in fact, has yet to materialise.[36]

As *longue durée* scholars of serialisation, we can identify the emergent speculation of 'the long 1860s' as a subset of the long nineteenth century's financial phase which can be compared to its long twentieth century counterpart in 'the long 2000s' – the period of financialisation which ushered in HBO's 'sonnet season' and the golden age of cable TV so-called. Such an analysis bears comparison to Leigh Claire La Berge's recent study of financial fiction in the long 1980s – an earlier subset of twentieth-century financialisation dominated by the Savings & Loan crisis. Asking 'what happens to narrative form when too much money circulates at once', La Berge points to 'capitalist realism' – a fictional mode that narrativises the abstractions of financialisation.[37]

Of course, neither financialisation nor the realist visibilisation of capitalist abstractions is new to the twentieth century. Both are latent in Dickens's *Dombey and Son* (1846–8), a novel written in the climate of loosened trade regulations which sparked what Karl Marx described as 'the first great railway swindle'.[38] In *Bleak House*, according to Gordon Bigelow, 'the accelerated motion and increasing abstraction of [market] value' is a 'fundamental motive force', a 'circulation without end or essence'.[39] A few years later, the Limited Liability Act of 1855 made it possible for speculators to gamble with borrowed capital, triggering 'the first world-wide commercial crisis in the history of modern capitalism' soon after.[40] Hence, from the railway juggernaut of *Dombey* and the fraudulent speculation of *Little Dorrit*, to the hypostatised 'Shares' of *Our Mutual Friend* (1864–6), Dickens's fiction reckons with 'too much money circulat[ing] at once'. These dark Dickensian works anticipated Victorian Britain's most astute financial journalist, Walter Bagehot, who wrote in 1873, 'There never was so much borrowed money collected in the world as is now collected in London.' Shortly afterwards, the panic of that year triggered the so-called Long Depression.[41]

Unsurprisingly, the 1860s became 'a watershed' in the rise of the 'stock-market villain': not only Dickens's Merdle, but also sensational variants including George Godolphin in Ellen Wood's *The Shadow of Ashlydyat* (1861–3) in which Gothic motifs express the 'growing fascination with the magicality of finance capitalism'.[42] By the end of the decade, Trollope's own stock-market narratives coincided with a heightened naturalism and a new habit of villainising perceived outsiders: e.g., Joseph Emilius in *The Eustace Diamonds* (1871–3), Augustus Melmotte and Hamilton K. Fisker in *The Way We Live Now* (1874–5) and Ferdinand Lopez in *The Prime Minister* (1875–6). In contrast to the comic irony of the Barsetshire novels, these works from the 1870s were 'instigated by the commercial profligacy of the age'.[43] The thoroughgoing disenchantment they evoke pictures Hobbesian combatants as they struggle to wrest wealth and power from the all-but-substanceless flow of exchange.

Thus defined, the long 1860s is the gateway to the long nineteenth century's financial phase: a new periodisation that, from a literary standpoint, is both a hotbed of capitalist realism and a catalyst for Bigger Love. Broadly speaking, if *Dombey and Son* foreshadows it in the time of Chartism, Continental revolutions, and railway booms and busts, the period's true coming of age might be *Little Dorrit* – the mid-50s novel that George Bernard Shaw thought 'more seditious than *Das Kapital*'.[44] A suitable endpoint would be 1879, encompassing the 1873 panic; the early years of the Long Depression; the rise of the New Imperialism; the emergence of Zola's naturalism; and – in line with his own naturalistic turn – the close of Trollope's Palliser series. A kind of *echt*-novelist for this period, Trollope was at the peak of his fame in the 1860s; indeed, between January 1860, when page 1 of *Framley Parsonage* became the first page of the *Cornhill*, and July 1867, when the final Barsetshire novel concluded, readers could anticipate a new instalment of at least one current Trollope serial without pause.[45] The ideal mid-point for the long 1860s thus falls between 1862 and 1867, corresponding to the serialisation of the last two Barsetshire novels. As they mark Trollope's transition to a consummate *fleuviste*, *The Small House at Allington* and *The Last Chronicle of Barset* are also *about* the transition from production to finance.

It is therefore worth noting that the *Cornhill Magazine* was as openly financial as it was opportunistically highbrow: the name Cornhill, a street in the City of London, derives from the address of Smith, Elder, & Co's lucrative side-concern supplying banking services to officers of the East India Company.[46] The magazine's cover, by placing images of seasonal labour such as ploughing atop a title that hails London's financial centre, bridges the temporalities of 'the past and the future'.[47] As we will see, Trollope's final Barsetshire novels stage a comparable dialectics between country and city, use and exchange value, through an updating of the kind of country-house novel which Trollope had admired in Jane Austen (a favourite author and one to whom his works are sometimes compared).[48]

Love, Trollopian Style

In emphasising Trollope's last two Barsetshire novels, my point is not to single out their 'quality', but to demonstrate their importance as literary cornerstones of the long 1860s. Trollope himself makes a key point about series writing when he attributes the longevity of *Barchester Towers* at least partly to successors that enhanced the earlier work's 'vitality' and renown.[49] That the author's popularity rests in large part on series readers can hardly surprise us. For Ruth apRoberts, this 'infinitely variable' fiction speaks to the modern need to test institutions and meet 'ambiguous and demanding situations'.[50] Felber likens the 'patterns' of the Palliser sequence to a kind of history, while Laurie Langbauer tells us that Barsetshire 'performs the everyday' as though it were everything.[51] These diverse critical outlooks illuminate the formal terrain that Trollope shares with Balzac, whose 1842 introduction to *La Comédie humaine* described 'a plan which includes both a history and criticism of society'.[52] Equally telling are Trollope's autobiographical reflections on the 'new shire' he had 'added to the English counties' – the space of 'its roads and railroads', 'towns and parishes', 'castles', 'hunts', 'parks' and 'churches', as vividly concretised as if he 'had lived and wandered there'.[53]

Although there is much to suggest that Trollope's contemporaries shared this interest in a storyworld that outlived the close of each novel, the critical reception shows that such Bigger Love could be years in the making. Reviewing *Barchester Towers* (1857), the *Athenaeum* typified the reigning scepticism when it expressed surprise that the new novel had shown *The Warden* (1855) to be 'an uncompleted story'. Implying that Trollope had thus sought to spare himself the 'difficulty' of attracting readers to new material, the review points out the even 'worse difficulty' of sustaining interest in a recycled plot. The conclusion that *Barchester Towers* is the better of the two works, does not dispel these misgivings.[54] As we turn to *Doctor Thorne* (1858), published in the same year as *The Three Clerks*, the critical conversation shifts to worrisome 'fecundity'. Though Trollope's 'progeny' are 'very much above the average', wrote the *Saturday Review*, the production of three novels in less than two years provokes 'uneasiness'.[55] Nor did Trollope's popular success in the *Cornhill* deter the *Dublin University Magazine* from opening its review of *Framley Parsonage* with a withering swipe at Thomas Hughes: 'How many admirers' of *Tom Brown's Schooldays* (1857) 'have managed to wade through' the 'tedious' serialisation of *Tom Brown at Oxford*, the writer ponders. Such 'inducements' to impose on a 'willing public', had, in Trollope's case, resulted in a 'dreary tale' premised on the 'merciless reintroduction of old friends'. Declaring a clear preference for characters with 'the redeeming merit of being new', the essay queried, 'When are we to see the last of Bishop and Mrs Proudie, of the Grantlys, of Tom Towers, of Dr. Thorne?'[56] The question echoed the *Saturday Review*'s critique of the new 'fashion' for reappearing heroes: the next time Trollope's work 'comes before the public', it concluded, 'we trust' that 'Barchester and its Bishop' may be 'sleeping in a common grave'.[57]

It is little wonder, then, that Trollope was tentative and even contrite about his penchant for series writing. When Chapman and Hall issued a complete edition of the 'Chronicles of Barsetshire' in 1879, the author's introduction stressed a separation that did not obligate readers to follow a 'sequence'. Although the sequence existed, Trollope explained, it did so 'only in the Author's mind'. That neither Walter Scott nor Thackeray had managed to interest the public in 'novels written in continuation' was unpropitious – so much so that, on publishing *Doctor Thorne*, Trollope hoped its Barsetshirean 'locality might not be recognized'.[58] Here Trollope relates a years-long effort to conceal the signs that his novels were evolving into a series: the 'records' of a 'dear county' that the author, its chronicler, imaginatively inhabited for more than a decade.[59]

Nonetheless, as the series continued, its new 'seasons' began to call forth a receptive critical idiom. This could take the form of hyperbole, as when the *National Review* erroneously claimed that 'the *Cornhill* counts its readers by millions'.[60] More interesting is a piece on *Doctor Thorne* which playfully validated Barsetshire's expanding space in a mode like the author's: 'Mr Trollope in his new story quits his old cathedral town only to pass into its county, and to make acquaintance with some of the county families.'[61] A notice of *Framley Parsonage* brought would-be series readers up to date: '*Barchester Towers* is a sequel to the *Warden*', and '*Framley Parsonage* is an appendix to . . . both'.[62] The *London Review*, noting the 'many hundreds [that] have read' *Framley Parsonage* evoked delightful familiarity: 'We know all the characters . . . as well as if we had been introduced to them at Miss Dunstable's grand party, had sat with them in Lady Lufton's state drawing-room, or had driven over to Barchester in the little basket-phaeton.'[63] Even the *Saturday Review* wondered at this intimacy: 'It is a difficult thing to estimate' the 'merit of a book' that 'has been an inmate of the drawing-room', 'has travelled with us in the train', 'has lain on the breakfast-table', and 'with which we are all so familiar'.[64] What stands out in this commentary, beyond the felt authenticity of characters and scenes, is the keen perception of how serial experience penetrates readers' lived time and space.

To be sure, Trollope's critics remained (laudably) suspicious of commercial gimmicks and author shortcuts and never spoke of a 'series' as such. (We might say that though Trollope published a successful *roman-fleuve*, he did not quite turn that form into a 'thing'.) What is, nonetheless, legible in the critics' discourse, despite the author's denial, is the cumulative concretion of a fictional world as its characters and geography unfold through successive works – an impact that, after *Framley Parsonage*, was amplified through the duration and rhythms of serialisation. Yet, while Trollope admits that he became 'bolder' in *Framley Parsonage* 'in going back to the society of [his] old friends',[65] he overlooks another dimension of his developing *fleuvisme* which may have been equally determinative; that is to say, Trollope's narrator begins to speak in the voice of a chronicler.

While previous Trollope novels speak of 'chronicles' to denote passing references to newspapers or memoirs, *Framley Parsonage* is the first to refer to earlier works in the series *as if they were chronicles*. Hence, when Mr Arabin is introduced, the narrator recounts 'that quick and great promotion' from Fellow of Lazarus to Dean of Barchester, adding that these events *'may be read [of] in the diocesan and county chronicles'.*[66] In thus styling earlier works as 'chronicles', *Framley* seizes on a device that is both characteristically British (as in the ninth-century *Anglo-Saxon Chronicle* or the sixteenth-century *Holinshed's Chronicles of England, Scotlande, and Irelande*) and characteristically modern (as in the fictitious *County Chronicle* that relates the details of Bell Dale's marriage in *The Small House at Allington*). In this way, the quasi-closeted chronicler foreshadowed that fuller outing that came in *The Last Chronicle of Barset* and the collected edition of 1879. Accordingly, in calling attention to pre-cursors in the series, the narrator of *Framley Parsonage* contrasts the hyper-modern fixation on the 'merit of being new' to the chronicle's cumulative modern temporality. Like the serialised novel that is its constituent part, the Trollopian chronicle stages a dialectic of old and new through a format that substitutes 'the sense of an ending', with its own illusion of never ending at all.[67] Elizabeth Gaskell epitomised this serial sensibility when she wrote, 'I wish Mr Trollope would go on writing Framley Parsonage forever. I don't see any reason why it should ever come to an end.'[68]

No wonder that when *The Small House at Allington* was serialised two years after *Framley Parsonage*, critics addressed it in terms of its serial effects. As the once-sceptical *Athenaeum* put it:

> It is characteristic of this story, that the characters are all living, human beings; and there has been as much speculation whether Lily Dale would marry Johnny Eames as about any [courtship] . . . in any town or village in Great Britain. Readers have made it a personal question, and there have been vehement discussions as to the probability of her forgiving Adolphus Crosbie . . .[69]

As the 'speculations' and 'discussions' of Trollope's readers come to the fore, the role of the critic visibly changes. No longer primarily an arbiter of 'quality' or originality, advising readers on whether to take up a novel, the critic facilitates a collective experience that is already in progress – that is to say, a Bigger Love.

As Hamer's invaluable study shows, the 'problem with three-volume form' for Trollope was the limits it imposed on the ironising effects of multiple narratives.[70] Publication in parts, by contrast, provided greater space for multiplots and a built-in structure – the multi-chapter instalment – through which to accentuate parallels, juxtapositions and tensions. Through careful chapter groupings and the use of chapter- and number-endings to emphasise key tensions, Trollope's fiction drew strength from the same complex format that had nurtured Dickens's maturity. Nonetheless, such a focus leaves open the distinctly Trollopian question of how the novel *series* – defined by Langbauer as 'successive novels . . . linked together . . . by recurrent characters or settings'[71] – both echoes and amplifies the very features of serialisation which electrified Trollope's novel poetics.

The Chronicles of Barsetshire

To begin with, however, we should emphasise that all six Barsetshire novels share a provincial storyworld in which the hallowed ideal of sovereign English history is subjected to modern pressures. *The Warden* (1855) introduces readers to the series-wide motif of the *heirloom*, a crucial form of property that, like the temporality of the chronicle, accumulates ethico-cultural worth in excess of abstract exchange value. In doing so, what I have called *heirloom sovereignty* helps to bind what might otherwise dissolve into an atomised assemblage of possessive individuals. Because the cultural value of heirlooms accumulates through time, to figure it, this single-volume novel envisions a resonant heirloom space of enchantment (Barchester Cathedral), an exemplary social relation through which to diffuse its effects (the Warden's pastoral care), and a venerable character to perform that relation (the Warden himself).[72]

In *Barchester Towers*, the same ideal finds more sceptical treatment. From the opening chapter, in which the uncertain timing of a father's death competes with an imminent change of ministry, Trollope's sequel ironises the attunement of past and present which John Bold's marriage to the Warden's daughter had seemed to presage. With Eleanor's widowhood dissolving this synthesis, the ensuing courtship plot becomes enmeshed in a war of clerical factions. Archdeacon Grantly, ever-volatile in his obstinacy, joins a raft of newly minted live wires including the guileful Slope, the domineering Mrs Proudie and the seductive Signora Neroni. This abundance of character-driven plotting and plot-driven characters threatens to burst open the three-volume novel at its seams. Nonetheless, the resulting workarounds, torques and compressions are formally astute. Indeed, *Barchester Towers* seems to stage its rending of the three-decker in the high-comic tableau of the Signora's sofa catching 'there is no saying how much' of Mrs Proudie's 'garniture'. In a symphony of cracked stitches, falling flounces and exposed breadths which leaves 'a long ruin of rent lace' in its wake (*BT*, ch. 11, p. 76), the first volume defamiliarises that 'highly developed system of familiarizations' which D. A. Miller, too hastily perhaps, assumes it is not Trollope's business to trouble.[73] As R. H. Hutton observed, 'Everybody in Mr Trollope' is 'under pressure, swayed hither and thither . . . assailed on this side and on that by the strategy of rivals . . . Everywhere time is short.'[74] In *Barchester Towers*, this predicament finds its keenest expression in Mr Arabin, with whose introduction the second volume opens. Though neither as exemplary as Harding, nor as worldly as Grantly, Eleanor's future husband leaves Oxford to put the 'day-dream of his youth' behind him (*BT*, ch. 20, p. 196). The would-be apostle's embrace of ordinary vocation and conjugal pleasure thus captures the mood of this sequel, making Barchester's 'everyday' the sign of a series that ironises, humanises and domesticates the forces of change, but does not arrest them or wish them away.[75]

Scholars have noticed how the formal challenge of managing Barchester's bedlam led Trollope to a long hiatus spent writing non-fiction as well as a work that inadvertently packed six months of events into a three-month time frame.[76] Moreover, midway through Volume 2, the novel's hitherto unremarkable pace (in which chapters mark the passage of hours, days or weeks), slows to an almost surreal sequence of eight chapters to describe the events of a single garden party. The result is a striking experiment in figuring simultaneity through a kind of narrative slow motion. Not incidentally, the location for this exceptional duration is a country house. Ullathorne Court, seat of the eccentric Thorne siblings, is 'a perfect gem . . . of English architecture', notable for a 'tawny yellow colour' cultivated through 300 years of plant growth – a topos that figures the heirloom's accretive temporality while setting the stage for Trollope's slow print (*BT*, ch. 22, p. 220). Indeed, we might think of the garden party sequence, like the sequel to *The Warden*, as an attempt to achieve serialisation's effects by other means.

In matters of real estate, location is everything. *Barchester Towers'* long excursion to Ullathorne foreshadows the series' turn from town to county. The country house, as Richard Gill notes, is British fiction's 'outstanding' social symbol; from Austen to Henry James and beyond, it provides 'a means of embodying the qualities and values of community, whether in a state of decay, transformation, or renewal'.[77] In *The Country and the City* (1973), Raymond Williams studies a variety of country-house genres, showing how the pastoral rendering of estates entailed an aestheticisation of enclosure and, thus, agrarian capitalism.[78] During a 300-year-long period that culminated in the Austen-era emergence of the long nineteenth century's productive phase, enclosure dispossessed England's peasantry of their common-use rights. The same process of primitive accumulation that turned these farmers into wage labourers turned the largest tenants into a class of producers who were compelled to maximise returns on rising rents. Landowners also might 'improve' their estates, just as wealthy industrialists (like Roger Scatcherd in *Doctor Thorne*) might purchase country houses of their own. Thus, as George Eliot wrote in an 1856 essay, on the Continent, 'a vital connection with the past is much more vividly felt' than in England, where 'commerce' has 'modernized the face of the land'.[79]

Whereas the antiquarian Thorne siblings stave off such modernity with medieval sports and eighteenth-century periodicals, Archdeacon Grantly, 'a thoroughly practical man of the world', demonstrates partial accommodation (*BT*, ch. 20, p. 191).[80] Pausing from clerical scrimmage to visit St Ewold's parsonage, Grantly insists that the new vicar, Arabin, 'must positively . . . remodel' an out-of-date dining room (*BT*, ch. 21, pp. 208). Such positioning of Grantly as both unbending guardian of ecclesiastic privilege and avid home improver, illustrates comic irony at work. We are reminded of Austen who also used modernising schemes to situate characters in light of fast-changing milieus.

While the first two Barset novels illustrate the clergy's modest power to uphold the sovereignty of heirloom traditions, *Doctor Thorne* pronounces the new turn to land in its opening chapter. Musing on Greshamsbury, a 'fine old' estate, the narrator proclaims that while commerce is 'good and necessary', it is not yet 'esteemed the noblest work of an Englishman'.[81] But rubbing against this declaration is the fact that Squire Gresham has squandered his fortune on political adventures. As the heir to a mortgaged property, Frank Gresham 'must marry money': an imperative the novel repeats no less than thirty-six times. The arrival of Martha Dunstable, an affable heiress whose 'fabulous wealth' issues from a patented ointment (*DT*, ch. 18, p. 257), stimulates marital overtures from a sheepish Frank, his cousin George (son of the cash-strapped Earl De Courcy), as well as Gustavus Moffat (an arriviste who jilts Augusta Gresham in the effort to land a bigger dowry). In the end, Frank's beloved Mary – the illegitimate daughter of a working woman – turns out to be a 'great heiress' (*DT*, ch. 11, p. 151).[82] Hence, while Mary's worth is affirmed, Frank *does* marry money – derived, moreover, from a working-class uncle's genius for railroads. Nor is the novel's high demand for wealthy brides the only sign of pervasive modern-day mammon. The most unprepossessing estate in this 'purely agricultural' county (*DT*, ch. 1, p. 1) belongs to the Duke of Omnium. His Gatherum Castle, an 'immense pile', 'lately erected at an enormous cost', 'destroy[s]' ordinary comfort so thoroughly that the Duke prefers to inhabit the house he inherited from his grandfather (*DT*, ch. 19, p. 254).[83]

The narrator of *Framley Parsonage*, now writing as a newly pronounced chronicler in a framework of sixteen monthly parts, finds space to elaborate the divisions between East and West Barsetshire. The Duke's (Western) set of 'gamblers, Whigs, atheists, men of loose pleasure, and Proudieites', as a disapprovingly Eastern and Tory Lady Lufton describes them, nearly ruins Framley's parson, Mark Robarts (*FP*, ch. 14, p. 180). Symptomatic of the West's depravity is Chaldicotes, seat of Nathaniel Sowerby, who ensnares Robarts in his gambling debts. Trollope's wider, longer multiplot web thus contrasts a parson's perilous social climbing both to his cautious sister's ascent to rank and to Miss Dunstable's acquisition of Chaldicotes as the new Mrs Thorne.[84] But the struggle of Josiah Crawley foreshadows stories that lie beyond such vitalising progress. The curate's impoverishment, the chronicler soberly avers, is 'neither picturesque, nor time-honoured, nor feudal' (*FP*, ch. 14, p. 187) – that is, most unlike that heirloom social relations enshrined in *The Warden*.

It is, however, *The Small House at Allington* that is frequently singled out as the 'darkest' of the Barset novels. In a plot that replays the jilting of Augusta in a minor key, Adolphus Crosbie, who deserts Lily Dale for an unhappy marriage to Alexandrina De Courcy, is a 'powerful invader from London' before whom the 'pastoral world seems to collapse'.[85] From this view, Trollope pits the heirloom qualities of the Allington estate, just outside Barsetshire, against a fallen London. Nonetheless, as readers of an ongoing series perceive, the novel's entanglement of country and city stands apart from the earlier affirmations of heirloom continuity, clerical bounty and a providence stocked with heiresses. Hence, while *Framley Parsonage* points to the demand for capital through a comic plot that turns on gambling debts, *The Small House at Allington* –the first Barsetshire novel to appear in twenty parts – is also the first to figure capital's increasing migration into finance.

Already in an 1861 short story, Trollope had introduced his readers to an English traveller so anxious about paper currencies that he travels abroad with a chest of gold sovereigns.[86] Conversely, the ambitious tradesman-narrator of *The Struggles of Brown, Jones, and Robinson* (1860–1) extols the transformative powers of credit and advertising – two simulated modes of value. The story opens by proclaiming the narrator's failed efforts to enrich himself while 'further[ing] British commerce'. Whereas 'Capital is a crumbling old tower . . . pretty nigh brought to its last ruin', he explains, 'Credit is the polished shaft . . . on which the new world of trade will be content to lean.' 'Get credit, and capital will follow', he declares, so long as one makes certain to 'Advertise, advertise, advertise!'[87] In this way, the author who had upheld commerce as the 'good and necessary' complement to land in *Doctor Thorne*, now satirises it as the mere manipulation of exchange-value.

The Small House at Allington likewise depicts a credit economy but, unlike Trollope's critically neglected satire,[88] it does so by altering the patterns laid down in earlier Barset narratives. The chronicler returns to Courcy Castle, seat of the pompous aristocrats whose determination to 'marry money' reverberated throughout *Doctor Thorne*. By contrast, Guestwick Manor is home to Lord De Guest, a 'very poor' earl who admirably focuses on breeding cattle, knowing 'every acre of his . . . estate', and living within his means (*SHA*, ch. 12, p. 109). Perhaps the most distinguishing feature of this more naturalistic Barset novel is its intense visualisation of London spaces including the 'cold' and 'comfortless' De Courcy townhouse in Portman Square (*SHA*, ch. 40, p. 365), the rental in St John's Wood which Crosbie inhabits during his brief married life (a dwelling so new that it reeks of mortar), and, in more comic vein, the down-market boarding house in which Johnny Eames flirts with his landlady's daughter.

Nonetheless, in pages that hark back to *Doctor Thorne*'s opening claim for the nobility of land, *The Small House* begins by describing the Dales' exemplary relation to their estate. Under Dale stewardship, Allington's

> acres had remained intact, growing in value and not decreasing in number, though guarded by no entail . . . There had been with them so much of adherence to a sacred law, that no acre of the property had ever been parted from the [Dale] hands . . . Some futile attempts had been made to increase the territory . . . Old Kit Dale, who had married money, had bought outlying farms . . . But these farms and bits of ground had gone again before our time. To them had been attached no religion. (*SHA*, ch. 1, p. 5)

Remarkable here is the careful distinction between two species of landed property: heirloom and commodified. The difference between the 'sacred' land one inherits and the secular land one buys (for example, by 'marrying money') complements the familiar Barset tension between a revered repository of living history and a mere liquefiable asset. One is non-alienable and (as far as the Dales are concerned) subject to a higher law than entail; the other is nearly commensurate with exchange value. Thus, whereas the Dale 'religion' requires stewarding one's 'real' property, it is at best indifferent to ownership for the sake of aggrandisement or fungible wealth. These distinctions, I contend, ground an even more substantial difference between the exchange value that dominates a financial economy and a kind of 'use' that mattered to Bigger Love in the long 1860s – and perhaps also has since.

In his *Contribution to the Critique of Political Economy* (1859), Marx wrote that 'use-value' is 'realized only in the process of consumption' – as distinct from exchange.[89] But because heirlooms, by definition, are forms of property that cannot be consumed (in the sense of 'used up') and cannot be sold (or they become commodities), Trollope's narrativisation of this non-capitalist abstraction gives rise to a different idea of use-value. Simply put, heirloom value is the kind of 'use' that must be held in perpetuity on behalf of a collectivity. Though we might imagine such 'use' consisting in the enjoyment of natural beauty or public art, for the purposes of Trollope's chronicles, a more salient case is the common-use rights in land accessible to Britain's agricultural population prior to enclosure. In this sense, the exceptional status of the Dale family land derives from a 'use-value' that – at least in theory – is held on behalf of the common.[90] While these estates are useful in an ordinary way (exemplified by De Guest's cattle and Dale's kitchen garden), they are simultaneously envisioned as the stewarded repositories of an (heirloom) use that stands for common resources including common experience.

Here, then, is the special importance of the multiplot contrast between these still-dignified country houses and London counterparts like Crosbie's rental in St John's Wood (the kind of suburb invented to bring a simulated style of country living within commuting distance of the metropole).[91] Whereas the Dale gardens are lovingly maintained with 'no pretensions . . . to the grandeur of a domain', the De Courcy mode of living is pretentious but not very grand (*SHA*, ch. 1, p. 9). Thus, having jilted Lily to cash in on the symbolic capital of Alexandrina's title, Crosbie learns soon enough that he has sacrificed the chance for modest happiness ('a small house, full of babies') for what proves to be the mere appearance of fashionable life (*SHA*, ch. 7, p. 63) Crosbie is instructed in the 'little family economies' that are 'vitally essential' to men who must 'maintain a decorous outward face towards the fashionable world' with 'limited means' (*SHA*, ch. 40, p. 362). Clothes must be dirtier and home meals cheaper to afford the leasing of an ostentatious carriage. Servants are hired when guests visit but reduced to a minimum for everyday comfort (a kind of social equivalent of the commercial imperative to 'advertise'). What is more, Alexandrina's lawyer brother-in-law has tied up Crosbie's assets in settlements, leaving Crosbie to borrow for his needs and pay interest. In effect, he becomes a 'revolver' – one whose labour is consumed by the servicing of debt.[92] Trollope's most complex Barsetshire novel so far thus includes a dark vein of plotting, premised on the interplay of country and city, which anticipates the even starker naturalism of his 1870s novels.

In a comic complement to this sombre narrative, the novel concludes with a demand for common use. This surprising turn comes about when Hopkins, the estate's gardener, refuses to desist from a long-standing habit of 'pretend[ing] to the right of taking' his share of stable manure. When Dale intervenes in the 'feud' between Allington's bailiff and a retainer who has husbanded the estate's produce for 'nigh seventy years', the squire explains that no modern landlord permits such unrestricted use (*SHA*, ch. 60, pp. 537–8). Hopkins's refusal to accept his wages reaffirms the principle of property held in common, implying, in effect, that payment in cash is no just recompense for his labour. This avowal of common use, if partly a comic device to reverse Lily's plans to leave Allington, is a striking rejoinder to a narrative that has idealised the Dales' stewardship of land.[93]

The Small House at Allington has been called an 'ambiguous . . . critique of the domestic ideal'.[94] Crosbie's marriage to Alexandrina proves so unendurable that the pair separate. According to the *Saturday Review*, Crosbie is 'so exactly the sort of man who would court and deserve the fate that overtakes him' that the character is one of Trollope's 'masterpieces'.[95] The childless Earl De Guest befriends Johnny, who loves Lily and wants to marry her. By offering some of his own income to help the pair wed, the Earl persuades Squire Dale, another bachelor, to dower both of his nieces. But the older generation's plan founders because Lily believes that, having given her heart to Crosbie, she cannot marry anyone else. Meanwhile Dale's plan to marry Lily's sister to his heir, Bernard, also fails when she prefers the local doctor. The novel ends with Lily committed to a spinster's life, Johnny pining for Lily, Bernard off travelling and Alexandrina living in Baden Baden with her mother. With the future stewards of the Allington and De Guest estates uncertain, one can hardly speak of these country houses in light of 'transformation, or renewal'.

Indeed, there is a sense in which this formally transitional novel projects a lack of certainty about the future which borders on stasis – like that emerging productive economy for the twenty-first century which has yet to materialise.[96] Whereas *Doctor Thorne* made Mary the surprise possessor of £300,000, this much longer story withholds on manure and a 'small house, full of babies'. This is a crisis of productivity if it is anything at all. At the level of reception, however, we can hardly be surprised that Trollope's readers 'continually' wrote him letters 'beg[ging him] to marry Lily Dale to Johnny Eames'. Trollope refused to grant them their wish on the grounds that, as he saw it, it 'was because she could not get over her troubles that they loved her'.[97] Trollope, that is to say, denies his readers their wish for the sake of a Bigger Love. Instead of fulfilling desire, in the manner of a financial economy, through the magicality of a happiness on paper, *The Small House at Allington* chronicles a capitalist realism fit for the times. The vision of use-value held for the common remains the aspiration of Bigger Love even as Trollope's country houses visibly become retreats for old bachelors and corrupt arrivistes.

'Capital Lying Dead'

By the time he returned to Barsetshire almost four years later, Trollope had laid the ground for a second *roman-fleuve*, this time built around political ambitions and centred in London.[98] Moreover, at the request of a publisher ever keen for commercial experiments, *The Last Chronicle of Barset* was published in weekly part-issues.[99] More than a decade after *The Warden*, the cumulative form and temporality of the series, and the reappearance of 'old friends', were now objects of warm public discussion – the anticipation of each new 'season' now subject to a subsuming desire for 'continuing relationship'. The Barchester novels, according to *The Literary Examiner*, are both 'the best set of "sequels" in our literature' and a new phenomenon; whereas Homer's epics and Aeschylus' tragedies were 'complete stories', Trollope's 'chain of novels' is 'essentially a birth of our own time'.[100] The advantage of this mode of seriality, wrote *The Athenaeum*, is its 'remarkable substance and vitality'.[101]

It is, perhaps, paradoxical that the consummation of this timely Bigger Love is a narrative of deepening financialisation – its focal point no needy heir, worthy miss or well-to-do clergyman wrestling with reformers but, rather, the perpetual curate of Hogglestock, Josiah Crawley. Harrowed to the point of derangement despite matchless devotion to his cure, this modern Job is tormented by the inability to meet the demands of his position without falling into debt. So maddened by the need to accept charity from fellow clergy, Crawley cannot adequately explain how he came to possess a £20 cheque. The novel's first page presents him as an abject figure who cannot 'show his face in the High Street'. For Mrs Proudie, he is 'a disgrace to the diocese'. 'Think what it would be to have all the Crawleys in our house' and 'all their debts', cries Archdeacon Grantly upon learning that his son loves Josiah's daughter, Grace.[102] Ironically, Crawley's double in this abjection is Adolphus Crosbie, now a widower, whose own 'load of debt' was foisted on him by the rapacious De Courcys. This once ambitious man of the world inhabits a condition of chronic uncertainty, unsure 'what would happen to him if his bill should be dishonoured'. Trollope's narrator, ever compassionate toward such scoundrels, draws the debtor's 'melancholy' steps as he vainly searches for money in the face of a 'killing . . . shame' (*LCB*, ch. 43, pp. 446–7). Then too, the same novel that subjects Crawley and Crosbie to these agonies makes the moneylender himself, Dobbs Broughton, a Merdle-like fraud who shoots himself in the City of London.[103]

Such dour capitalist realism cannot but provide meagre soil for houses full of babies. Though the passing of Mr Harding and Mrs Proudie is movingly memorable, in this summative chronicle, significant deaths outnumber the weddings. Thus, while Grace eventually wins over the Archdeacon, Lily, determined to style herself 'Old Maid', rejects both Crosbie's renewed proposal and the repeated offers of Eames (*LCB*, ch. 35, p. 361). If such persistent 'troubles' were sure to disappoint the readers who had longed for Lily's marriage, *The Last Chronicle* makes clear that Johnny, despite good intentions, has internalised the ambiguous futurity of the long 1860s. The man who had earlier perpetuated a risky romance with a working woman (who rightly called out his hypocrisy and class privilege) is no longer a 'hobbledehoy' (*SHA*, ch. 5, p. 45). But the 'unfortunate slips' to which he is prone continue to mark him as one who, if hardly so blighted as Crosbie, has never fully matured and perhaps never will (*LCB*, ch. 70, p. 755). Tellingly, then, though the Earl's favourite prides himself on solvency, he is the novel's conduit to the sordid City people who surround Dobbs Broughton – creatures of the financial economy who fulfil his telling desire for purposeless flirtation and vicarious disrepute.

In *The Eustace Diamonds,* the most naturalistic of Trollope's financial narratives, the legal status of an heirloom is defined in opposition to commodified repositories of exchange-value.[104] One way to understand Eames's restiveness is, thus, to mark his inability to develop the kind of 'heirloom' use which inheres in well-stewarded land, dutifully performed pastorship, ancient cathedrals, great works of literature (like the Greek epics Crawley reads to his daughter) and, not least of all, living histories (including the Chronicles of Barsetshire). The refusal to accept the finality of Lily's decision encourages Johnny to defer *Bildung*, positioning him, in effect, as an investment of capital which has yet to mature. Hence, while much is made of Johnny's spontaneous heroics (saving an earl from a bull, thrashing Crosbie, finding Mrs Arabin), we perceive the symptoms of malaise. To be sure, we would not mistake Johnny for a Crosbie-like 'personification of the cleverish, good-looking, shallow, popular man' of which London 'presents so very many examples', to quote the *Saturday Review*.[105] Yet, while the depiction of Eames is far from a 'masterpiece', it foreshadows the mode of characterisation which Henry James would perfect: the focalising character who, in filtering our access to the material world, shows its penetration of consciousness through every pore.

Perhaps the presence that looms the largest in this Eames-filtered social world is the 'ghastly' Mrs Van Siever, who, as the 'widow of a Dutch merchant' and a silent partner in Broughton's moneylending operation, evokes the long seventeenth century's financial hegemony in spectral form.[106] The fact that this elderly lady's 'false front' and 'false curls' are so unmistakably faux, suggests that, for Mrs Van Siever, the falseless of one's fronts is precisely the point. At a dinner party at Broughton's rented mansion, 'Mother Van' objects to the claim that 'silver forks' leave 'a lot of capital lying dead'. 'Capital', she counters, 'isn't lying dead so long as people know that you've got it', rather, 'the appearance of the thing goes for a great deal' (*LCB*, ch. 24, pp. 245–6). In this way, *The Last Chronicle* anticipates *The Eustace Diamonds* in distinguishing such fungible commodities from either dead capital or use-value of any credible kind. By marking one's access to ready money, silver plate functions both to store capital in easily exchanged bullion, and to advertise one's ability to perform the financial economy's trick of turning capital into more capital without producing a thing.

Of course, the game of turning the collective need for credit into a speculative bid for the highest return, is always precarious. As the flirtatious Madalina Demolines tells Johnny, the Broughtons live 'in the crater of a volcano' and there 'is no saying what day a smash may come' (*LCB*, ch. 39, p. 399). Though her own risky business is a profitless romance with Eames, in matters of investment Madalina prefers a sure thing: the great benefit of land, she tells Johnny, as if predicting what *he* will soon do, is that it 'can't run away' (*LCB*, ch. 25, p. 259). Though Mrs Van Siever more daringly seeks out the higher returns that a financial economy offers to capital, her hedge is knowing how the game is played by those who keep their names off 'the dirty door' (*LCB*, ch. 37, p. 375). Told that 'in the City' there 'is no doubt' as to Broughton's wealth, she replies that she wouldn't ask about him 'in the City' and wouldn't 'believe what people told' her if she did. None of this is news to Johnny, who knows fully well that his new acquaintances are the sort of people who 'stink of money' that they may not even have (*LCB*, ch. 24, p. 252).

*   *   *

If at such moments we could imagine ourselves reading *The Way We Live Now*, the fact remains that most readers looked to *The Last Chronicle of Barset* for the very different kinds of affect which Trollope's long-evolving chronicles could claim as their own heirloom invention. The 'last news from the Cathedral-close . . . has now reached us', declared *The British Quarterly Review*, as though beckoning aficionados to join the discussion of a popular finale.[107] By populating the abstractions, erasures and ruptures of financial modernity with 'endeared' scenes, situations and characters, such series, in the words of the *London Review*, 'inspire . . . gentle melancholy' on their closing.[108] Elongating the effects of those long-form serialisations which, since Dickens, had been marking time's passage through purposeful pauses, 'The Chronicles of Barsetshire' created a Bigger Love. As the *London Review* put it, 'Barset has long been a real country': the 'voices of the people . . . known to our ears, and the pavements . . . familiar to our footsteps.' 'If this really be . . . the last chronicle of Barset', 'we cannot but feel grieved . . . to say farewell.'[109]

For comparative nineteenth-centuryists working across the *longue durée*, the study of seriality, and especially the Trollopian series, invites continued exploration of untapped archives and new ways of understanding familiar works in light of dialogues with our own fast-transforming material culture. We might ask ourselves what Trollope chronicles for today's audiences at a time when a market-driven cult of bingeing, alongside financialisation with no end in sight, suggests that our own Bigger Loves are already behind us.[110] Of course, the bingeing phenomenon is overhyped to the extent that multiplot stories resist hyper-acceleration – their length and complexity persist unchanged no matter what the tempo of reading or viewing. The diminishing returns of 'Peak TV' may mean that the real question is not how fast or how much people watch, but, rather, what serials get made with the bingeing viewer in mind.[111] If this takes us back to Dallas's apprehensions at the beginning of the long 1860s, we might remember that Dallas himself did not foresee the new social relation through which Bigger Stories like Trollope's would spark forms of commonality that resisted the reign of exchange value. Whether slowly savoured in parts, or wolfed down by three-volume bingers with hardly a pause, Bigger Stories interrupt the 'circulation without end or essence'. The potential they bear to hold value in common in a time of financialisation may yet continue to call upon us to pay a different kind of interest.

Notes

I thank Kailana Durden for her help with research; for advice on early drafts I am indebted to Gordon Bigelow, Herbert Tucker and Frederik Van Dam; and for speedy and much-needed help with a final draft, I am grateful to Nick Birns, Rachel Buurma, Ayelet Ben-Yishai and Nancy Blake.

1. Peter Garrett, *The Victorian Multiplot Novel: Studies in Dialogical Form* (New Haven: Yale University Press, 1980), p. 2.

2. Robyn R. Warhol, *Having a Good Cry: Effeminate Feelings and Pop-Culture Forms* (Columbus: Ohio State University Press, 2003), p. 72.

3. Laurel Brake, *Print in Transition, 1850–1910: Studies in Media and Book History* (New York: Palgrave, 2001), p. 11.

4. Linda K. Hughes and Michael Lund, *The Victorian Serial* (Charlottesville: University Press of Virginia, 1991), p. 11.

5. Mohsin Hamid with Adam Kirsch, 'Are the New "Golden Age" TV Shows the New Novels?' *New York Times Sunday Book Review* (25 February 2014).

6. On Dickens and serial television, see, e.g., Sean O'Sullivan, 'Old, New, Borrowed, Blue: *Deadwood* and Serial Fiction', in David Lavery (ed.), *Reading 'Deadwood'* (London: Tauris, 2006), pp. 115–29. For a popular spoof that suggests *The Wire*'s Victorian provenance, see Joy DeLyria and Michael Sean Robinson, '"When It's Not Your Turn": The Quintessentially Victorian Vision of Ogden's *The Wire*', part of an online round-table on *The Wire* on the weblog, *The Hooded Utilitarian* (23 March 2011), as well as Noah Berlasky, 'Was *The Wire* Really a Victorian Novel?', *The Atlantic Monthly* (10 September 2012).

7. Mary Hamer, *Writing By Numbers: Trollope's Serial Fiction* (New York: Cambridge University Press, 1987), p. 9. On Dickens's innovation see Robert L. Patten, *Charles Dickens and His Publishers* (Oxford: Clarendon, 1978) as well as N. N. Feltes, *Modes of Production of Victorian Novels* (Chicago: University of Chicago Press, 1986), pp. 1–15. For a rich discussion of the problematic discourse of quality television so-called, see Jason Mittell, *Complex TV: The Poetics of Contemporary Television Storytelling* (New York: New York University Press, 2015), esp. ch. 6.

8. Adam Gopnik, 'Trollope Trending', *The New Yorker* (24 May 2014), <https://www.newyorker.com/ magazine/2015/05/04/trollope-trending> (last accessed 28 February 2018).

9. Trollope's self-description appears in *An Autobiography*, ed. David Skilton (London: Penguin, 1996), p. 188. For more on Trollope as Liberal see, for example, Lauren M. E. Goodlad and Frederik Van Dam, 'Trollope and Politics', in Deborah Denenholz Morse et al. (eds), *The Routledge Research Companion to Anthony Trollope* (New York: Routledge, 2017), pp. 15–34.

10. Lynette Felber, *Gender and Genre in Novels without End: The British 'Roman-Fleuve'* (Gainesville: University Press of Florida, 1995), pp. ix ff.

11. For the complaint that 'Trollope and Thackeray are exceedingly prone' to 'serving up the same characters in successive novels', see Christopher Grim, 'My Club-Table', *Dublin University Magazine*, 55.326 (February 1860): p. 236. See also the *Saturday Review*'s unsigned review of *Framley Parsonage*, which portrays the latter novel as a '*réchauffé*' of *Barchester Towers* much as Thackeray's *The Newcomes* is of *Vanity Fair*, 'Framley Parsonage', *Saturday Review*, 11.288 (4 May 1861): p. 452.

12. Trollope, *An Autobiography*, p. 94.

13. For the argument that Fernand Braudel's call for new periodisations and temporalities, like Arrighi's *longue durée* analysis, offer compelling bigger methods to Victorianist scholarship, see Lauren M. E. Goodlad, 'Bigger Love', *New Literary History* 48.4 (Autumn 2017), especially pp. 703–7. In 'History and the Social Sciences', Braudel argued that the work of *longue*

durée historians is, above all, to recognise temporal plurality and to study the 'dialectic of temporalities' which puts forward any particular material condition as 'the conjoining of movements with different rhythms', in Peter Burke (ed.), *Economy and Society in Early Modern Europe: Essays from Annales* (New York: Harper, 1972), pp. 258, 254.

14. Lauren M. E. Goodlad, *The Victorian Geopolitical Aesthetic: Realism, Sovereignty, and Transnational Experience* (Oxford: Oxford University Press, 2015).

15. On the lucky booksellers see Patten, *Charles Dickens and His Publishers*, p. 46, as well as his more recent 'Publishing in Parts' in Patten and John Bowen (eds), *Palgrave Advances in Charles Dickens Studies* (Basingstoke and New York: Palgrave 2006), pp. 11–47. On the commodification of the literary text, see Feltes, *Modes of Production of Victorian Novels*, especially pp. 1–15.

16. See Toni Johnson-Woods's entry, *'Roman-Feuilleton'*, in Paul Schellinger (ed.), *Encyclopedia of the Novel* (London: Routledge, 1999), vol. 2: pp. 1108–10.

17. Robert L. Patten, 'The New Cultural Marketplace: Victorian Publishing and Reading Practices', in Juliet John (ed.), *The Oxford Handbook of Victorian Literary Culture* (Oxford, Oxford University Press), p. 483.

18. E. S. Dallas, unsigned review of *'Great Expectations'*, *The Times* (17 October 1861), p. 6.

19. (Anon.), 'George Murray Smith', *Publishers Weekly* (27 April 1901), p. 1059.

20. Smith as quoted in Andrew Blake, *Reading Victorian Fiction: The Cultural Context and Ideological Content of the Nineteenth-Century* (New York, Palgrave Macmillan, 1989), p. 88.

21. Ibid. p. 88.

22. Lewes's letter of 5 July 1862 is cited in 'George Eliot: Her Life and Writings', an unsigned essay published a year after the author's death in *The Westminster Review*, 116 (July/October 1881): p. 176 (pp. 154–98).

23. On the discourse of the 'boob tube', evoking mass entertainment that 'makes people stupid', see Michael Z. Newman and Elana Levine, *Legitimating Television: Media Convergence and Cultural Studies* (London: Routledge, 2012), pp. 16–17.

24. Blackwood as quoted in Carol A Martin, *George Eliot's Serial Fiction* (Columbus: Ohio State University Press, 1994), p. 216.

25. As Hughes and Lund put it, the Victorians favoured 'slow, steady development in installments over time', *The Victorian Serial*, p. 257. I borrow 'slow print' from Elizabeth Carolyn Miller whose develops the term to describe the print culture *fin-de-siècle* radicals used to counter the onslaught of commercial fare; *Slow Print: Literary Radicalism and Late Victorian Print Culture* (Standford: Stanford Univeristy Press, 2013). For an earlier version of this argument, which emphasises the Victorianist interest in 'bigger' methodologies, see Goodlad, 'Bigger Love'.

26. For example, Newman and Levine, *Legitimating Television*.

27. On HBO see Szalay, 'Pimps and Pied Pipers: Quality Television in the Age of Its Direct Delivery', *Journal of American Studies*, 49.4 (October 2015): p. 3. The station's puffed-up claims to 'aesthetic autonomy', Szalay argues, percolate HBO's content, showing up in hypermasculine storyworlds. For the *Cornhill*'s gender strategies, emphasising the masculinisation of editorial work, see Mark W. Turner, 'Gendered Issues: Intertextuality and The Small House at Allington in Cornhill Magazine', *Victorian Periodicals Review*, 26.4 (1993): p. 228.

28. Quoted in John Sutherland, *Victorian Novelists and Publishers* (London: Athlone, 1976), p. 43.

29. Sean O'Sullivan, 'Broken on Purpose: Poetry, Serial Television, and the Season', *StoryWorlds: A Journal of Narrative Studies*, 2.1 (2010): p. 68 (pp. 59–77).

30. Thomas Doherty, 'Storied TV: Cable is the New Novel', *The Chronicle of Higher Education* (17 September 2012), <http://www.chronicle.com/article/Cable-Is-the-New-Novel/134420> (last accessed 28 February 2018). See also Mittell for the argument that complex serial television derives from novels and comics, not from soap opera, *Complex TV*, Chapter 7.

31. Braudel, 'History and the Social Sciences', p. 258.

32. Hamer, *Writing by Numbers*, p. 59 and *passim*.

33. '*Framley Parsonage*', *Saturday Review*, pp. 451–2.

34. As Immanuel Wallerstein writes, 'A world-system is not the system of *the* world, but a system *that is a* world and that . . . most often has been, located in an area less than the entire globe', *World-Systems Analysis: An Introduction* (Durham, NC: Duke University Press, 2004), p. 98. On Trollope in this 'worlded' context, see Goodlad, *The Victorian Geopolitical Aesthetic*, esp. chs 2, 3 and 8 and for an Arrighian perspective on Trollope's modernity in *The Way We Live Now*, see Frederik Van Dam, *Anthony Trollope's Late Style: Victorian Liberalism and Literary Form* (Edinburgh: Edinburgh University Press, 2016), esp. ch. 1.

35. Giovanni Arrighi and Beverly J. Silver, *Chaos and Governance in the Modern World System* (Minneapolis: University of Minnesota Press, 1999), p. 32.

36. On the decline of US hegemony and the stalled twenty-first-century emergence of a new territorial hegemon, see Arrighi, 'Hegemony Unravelling', *New Left Review*, 32 (2005): pp. 23–80; for Arrighi's speculations about the future, see *Adam Smith in Beijing: Lineages of the Twenty-First Century* (London: Verso, 2007).

37. Leigh Claire La Berge, *Scandals and Abstraction: Financial Fiction of the Long 1980s* (Oxford: Oxford University Press, 2013), pp. 3, 10. For a fuller discussion of the long 2000s see Goodlad, 'Bigger Love'. Since the financialisation of the long twentieth century continues in force, surviving even the subprime collapse, Arrighi's framing of the phase is open to many such sub-periodisations as capital finds new ways to accumulate profit, sometimes creating temporary booms or bubbles which collapse with the next shock.

38. Marx quoted in R. A. Bryer, 'Accounting for the 'Railway Mania' of 1845 – A Great Railway Swindle?', *Accounting, Organizations and Society*, 15.5 (1991): p. 441 (pp. 439–86).

39. Gordon Bigelow, *Fiction, Famine, and the Rise of Economics in Victorian Britain and Ireland* (Cambridge: Cambridge University Press, 2003), p. 79.

40. J. R. T. Hughes, 'The Commercial Crisis of 1857', *Oxford Economic Papers*, 8.2 (1956): p. 194. On limited liability, see also Mary Poovey, *Making a Social Body: British Cultural Formation, 1830–1864* (Chicago: University of Chicago Press, 1995), Chapter 8.

41. Walter Bagehot, *Lombard Street: A Description of the Money Mark* [1873] (New York: Wiley, 1999), p. 17. Economic historians vary on whether the Long Depression or Great Depression of this period ended at the close of the 1870s or lingered well into the 1890s culminating in the peak financialisation of the long nineteenth century.

42. Tamara S. Wagner, 'Speculators at Home in the Victorian Novel: Making Stock-Market Villains and New Paper Fictions', *Victorian Literature and Culture*, 36.1 (2008): pp. 21–40. See also Gail Turley Houston, *From Dickens to Dracula: Gothic, Economics, and Victorian Fiction* (Cambridge: Cambridge University Press, 2005). On Trollope's The Three Clerks (1857), which addressed the theme of fraud through a style somewhat like that of *Little Dorrit*, see Goodlad, *Victorian Literature and the Victorian State: Character and Governance in a Liberal Society* (Baltimore: Johns Hopkins University Press, 2003), Chapter 5.

43. Trollope, *An Autobiography*, 224.

44. Dan H. Laurence and Martin Quinn (eds), *Shaw on Dickens* (Toronto: Maxwell Macmillan, 1985), p. 51.

45. See Hamer, *Writing By Numbers*.

46. Leslie Howsam, *Kegan Paul – A Victorian Imprint: Publishers, Books, and Cultural History* (London: Kegan Paul International, 1999), p. 19. See also Hamer, *Writing by Numbers*, p. 19.

47. Mark W. Turner, '"Telling of My Weekly Doings": The Material Culture of the Victorian Novel', in Francis O'Gorman (ed.), *A Concise Companion to the Victorian Novel* (Oxford: Blackwell, 2005), p. 132 (pp. 113–33).

48. For example, Richard Holt Hutton's unsigned 'From Miss Austen and Mr Trollope', *Spectator*, 55 (16 December 1882): pp. 1609–11.

49. Trollope, *An Autobiography*, p. 55.

50. Ruth apRoberts, 'Trollope and the Zeitgeist', *Nineteenth-Century Fiction*, 37.3 (1982): p. 271 (pp. 259–71).

51. Felber, *Gender and Genre in Novels without End: The British 'Roman-Fleuve'* (Gainesville: University Press of Florida, 1995), p. 34; Laurie Langbauer, *Novels of Everyday Life: The Series in English Fiction, 1850–1930*, p. 93.

52. Balzac, 'Author's Introduction', *The Human Comedy*, Project Gutenberg Ebook, n.p. <http://www.gutenberg.org/files/1968/1968-h/1968-h.htm> (last accessed 6 June 2018).

53. Trollope, *An Autobiography*, p. 101.

54. Unsigned notice, *Athenaeum*, 1544 (30 May 1857): p. 689.

55. 'Unsigned notice, *Saturday Review* (12 June 1858)', excerpted in Donald Smalley, *Anthony Trollope: The Critical Heritage* (London: Routledge, 1969), p. 73. Smalley attributes the review to Henry Maine.

56. Unsigned, 'A Batch of Last Year's Novels', *Dublin University Magazine*, 59.352 (April 1862): p. 405. According to the *Wellesley Index to Victorian Periodicals*, the essay was penned by Lionel James Trotter, an Anglo-Indian writer of Irish descent. <https://login. ezproxy.wellesley.edu/login?qurl=http://gateway.proquest.com%2fopenurl%3furl_ ver%3dZ39.88> (last accessed 28 February 2018).

57. '*Framley Parsonage*', *Saturday Review*, p. 452.

58. Trollope, 'Introduction to the Chronicles of Barsetshire (1878)', Appendix to Trollope, *The Small House at Allington*, ed. Dinah Birch (Oxford: Oxford University Press, 2014), p. 547. On Trollope's payment for copyrights to various publishers see Nicholas Shrimpton, 'Note on the Text', in Trollope, *The Last Chronicle of Barset*, ed. Helen Small (Oxford: Oxford University Press, 2015), pp. xxx–xxxii.

59. Trollope, 'Introduction to Chronicles of Barsetshire (1878)', p. 425; Trollope, *An Autobiography*, 79.

60. Unsigned notice, '*Orley Farm*', *The National Review*, 16, no. 31 (January 1863): p. 28. Though occasionally attributed to R. H. Hutton, one of the editors of the *National*, the likely author, according to the *Wellesley Periodical Index* is Henry Stewart Cunningham.

61. 'Unsigned notice, *Examiner* (29 May 1858)', in Smalley, *Anthony Trollope*, p. 68.

62. 'Unsigned review, *Examiner* (20 April 1861)', in Smalley, *Anthony Trollope*, p. 118. Note the reviewer's apparent oversight of *Doctor Thorne*.

63. 'Unsigned notice, *London Review* (11 May 1861)', in Smalley, *Anthony Trollope*, p. 126.

64. '*Framley Parsonage*', *Saturday Review*, p. 451.

65. Trollope, 'Introduction to Chronicles of Barsetshire (1878)', p. 425.

66. Anthony Trollope, *Framley Parsonage*, ed. David Skilton and Peter Willis (London: Penguin, 2004), ch. 15, p. 192, emphasis added. See also Chapter 38 and Chapter 39 for similar references to 'chronicles' with respect to *Doctor Thorne*.

67. Frank Kermode, *The Sense of an Ending: Studies in the Theory of Fiction* [1967] (New York: Oxford University Press, 2000), p. 45. I discuss this aspect of seriality in Goodlad, *The Victorian Geopolitical Aesthetic*, Coda; but see also Felber's earlier discussion in *Gender and Genre in Novels Without End*.

68. 'Elizabeth Gaskell to George Smith (1 March 1860)', in *The Letters of Mrs Gaskell*, ed. J. A. V. Chapple and Arthur Pollard (Manchester: Manchester University Press, 1997), p. 602. The point reminds us that Gaskell's *Cranford* (published in eight parts 1851 and 1853) is itself a notable case of a serialised narrative dominated by its fictional locale.

69. 'Unsigned review, *Athenaneum* (26 March 1864)', in Smalley, *Anthony Trollope*, p. 194.

70. Hamer, *Writing By Numbers*, p. 57.

71. Langbauer, *Novels of Everyday Life*, p. 8.

72. See Goodlad, *The Victorian Geopolitical Aesthetic*, esp. ch. 3 which discusses *The Warden*'s evocation of an ethico-culturally intact heirloom sovereignty that evolves over time – a Trollopian variation on the holistic social world of Scott's historical novels.

73. D. A. Miller, *The Novel and the Police* (Berkeley: University of California Press, 1988), p. 107.

74. [Hutton], 'From Miss Austen and Mr Trollope', p. 1610. It should be noted, however, that Hutton underestimates the signs of modernity at work in Austen's fiction, just as later critics have underestimated it in Trollope's.

75. For more on these aspects of *Barchester Towers*, see Goodlad and Van Dam, 'Trollope and Politics'.

76. See Sutherland, 'Notes on the Text', in Trollope, *Barchester Towers*, ed. Michael Sadleir and Frederick Page (Oxford: Oxford University Press), p. xxxi. See also Chapter 51, in which the narrator addresses the reader on the difficulties of completing a three-volume novel.

77. Richard Gill, *Happy Rural Seat: The English Country House and the Literary Imagination* (New Haven: Yale University Press, 1972), p. 14.

78. Raymond Williams, *The Country and the City* (Oxford: Oxford University Press, 1973).

79. George Eliot, 'The Natural History of German Life', in *Selected Critical Writings*, ed. Rosemary Ashton (Oxford: Oxford University Press, 2000), pp. 283–4 (pp. 260–96).

80. Though the quotation directly applies to Dr Gwynne, it is equally applicable to Grantly.

81. Trollope, *Doctor Thorne*, ed. David Skilton (Oxford: Oxford University Press, 2000), ch. 1, p. 12.

82. For a useful reading, see Tess O'Toole, 'Adoption and the "Improvement of the Estate" in Trollope and Craik', *Nineteenth-Century Literature*, 52.1 (1997): especially pp. 69–70 (pp. 59–79).

83. That the referent turns out to be Matching Priory, the Yorkshire estate that appears throughout the Palliser novels, indicates that the author of *Doctor Thorne* had already begun to anticipate the second of his *romans-fleuves*. It is worth noting also that neither the Palliser novels, nor the more chronologically proximate *Orley Farm*, also set in Yorkshire, has much to say about this real-life county. That is to say, Trollope's first series is *about* Barsetshire and the ontology of place in ways that neither his London-centric Palliser series nor other Trollope works tend to reprise. For an interesting exception, see the description of Devon in *Rachel Ray* (1863) and, for a discussion, Nicholas Birns, 'Place and Topicality: *La Vendée* and Trollope's Novels of 'Regional Change' in Deborah Denenholz Morse, Margaret Markwick and Mark W. Turner (eds), *The Routledge Research Companion to Anthony Trollope* (New York: Routledge, 2017), pp. 378–87.

84. See Hamer on how the novel's eleventh number (Chapters 31–3) concentrates overlapping crises including Lucy's refusal to marry Lord Lufton without his mother's consent, Sowerby's loss of the Duke's support and Mark's financial disgrace; '*Framley Parsonage*: Trollope's First Serial', *The Review of English Studies*, 26.102 (May 1975): p. 159 (pp. 154–70).

85. James R. Kincaid, *The Novels of Anthony Trollope* (Oxford: Clarendon, 1977), pp. 96 and 126. See also Deborah Denenholz Morse, who observes an interrogation or breakage of ostensibly pastoral innocence: *Reforming Trollope: Race, Gender, and Englishness in the Novels of Anthony Trollope* (New York: Routledge, 2013), Chapter 1.

86. Originally published in two parts in *Public Opinion*, 'The Man Who Kept His Money in a Box', was reprinted in the second series of Trollope's *Tales for All Countries* (London: Chapman and Hall, 1863), pp. 321–71.

87. Trollope, *The Struggles of Brown, Jones, and Robinson* (London: Smith, Elder, 1870), ch. 1, pp. 3–4. Notably, the narrator's surname in both the short story and the eight-part novel is Robinson. The point is not to suggest kinship but, rather, to establish both narrators (as well as the titular Brown and Jones) as archetypal Englishmen of their respective classes. Parts of the work were drafted in 1857 at a time when Trollope's fiction at times showed the influence of Dickens's *Little Dorrit*.

88. See Matthew Titolo for a nuanced appreciation of Trollope's satire, which, as the author's second serial for the *Cornhill*, is usually understood as a critical failure, 'Sincerity and Reflexive Satire in Anthony Trollope's *The Struggles of Brown, Jones, and Robinson*', *Victorian Literature and Culture*, 43, no. 1 (2015): pp. 23–39.

89. Karl Marx, *A Contribution to the Critique of Political Economy*, trans. N. I. Stone (Chicago: Kerr, 1913), p. 20.

90. The notion of the 'heirloom' estate thus compares to the juridically explicit idea of land as the possession of society at large that John Stuart Mill (though not Trollope) formulated in defence of land reform in Ireland. See Mill, *England and Ireland* (London: Longmans, Green, Reader, and Dyer, 1868) and, for a discussion, E. D. Steele, *Irish Land and British Politics: Tenant-Right and Nationality, 1865–1870* (Cambridge: Cambridge University Press, 1974). For comparison of Mill and Trollope on the issue, see also Goodlad and Van Dam, 'Trollope and Politics'. On Trollope's Irish politics more generally, see Bigelow, 'Irish Questions: Ireland and the Trollope Novels', in *The Routledge Research Companion*, pp. 363–77.

91. See Donald J. Olsen, 'Victorian London: Specialization, Segregation, and Privacy', *Victorian Studies*, 17.3 (1974): pp. 265–78.

92. See Andrew Ross, *Creditocracy and the Case for Debt Refusal* (New York: OR Books, 2014).

93. On the cottage economy that enabled peasants and landless commoners to benefit from access to useful agricultural by-products (such as manure, wood, reeds and furze) see, for example, J. M. Neeson, *Commoners: Common Right, Enclosure and Social Change in England, 1700–1820* (Cambridge: Cambridge University Press, 1996).

94. Mark W. Turner, *Trollope and the Magazines: Gendered Issues in Mid-Victorian Britain* (New York: St. Martin's, 2000), p. 21.

95. 'Unsigned notice, *Saturday Review* (14 May 1864)', in Smalley (ed.), *Anthony Trollope*, p. 205 (pp. 205–10).

96. Compare to the 'virtually stagnant' population of Europe between 1990 and 2012 – that is, during the long 2000s; see Thomas Piketty, *Capital in the Twenty-First Century*, trans. Arthur Goldhammer, (Cambridge, MA: Harvard University Press, 2014), p. 104.

97. Trollope, *Autobiography*, p. 92.

98. Plantagenet's first appearance is in Chapter 23 of *The Small House at Allington* whereupon his dangerous flirtation with the married Lady Dumbello complements the themes of late-blooming manhood (Eames) and restless ambition (Crosbie).

99. On the formal particularities of this format, including details of Smith's negotiations with Trollope, see Hamer, *Writing By Numbers*, Chapter 6.

100. (Anon.), *The London Examiner* (20 July 1867), p. 452.

101. (Anon.), *The Athenaeum* (3 August 1867), p. 141.

102. Trollope, *Last Chronicle of Barset*, ed. Stephen Gill (Oxford: Oxford University Press, 1980), ch. 1, p. 1; ch. 5, p. 43; ch. 2, p. 19.

103. In her very different reading, Mary Poovey argues that *The Last Chronicle of Barset* 'is virtually, if not completely, self-contained', *Genres of the Credit Economy: Mediating Value in Eighteenth- and Nineteenth-Century Britain* (Chicago: University of Chicago Press, 2008), pp. 384–5. Her conception of novels as vehicles of literary value which acclimate readers to fictitious credit underwrites her understanding of the cheque (a 'credit instrument whose value' is highly 'mediated' and 'deferred') as 'an objective correlative for Mr Crawley himself' (p. 390). More complementary for my reading is J. Jeffrey Franklin's Bourdieuvian interpretation which, if somewhat literal in taxonomising the novel's modes of economic exchange, nonetheless accounts for the social expectations that readers bring to the novel: 'The contradiction between the code of the gentleman and receiving charity', Franklin writes, 'generates a sort of amnesia in the

text' which leads Arabin and Crawley to forget details that could exonerate the curate; 'Anthony Trollope Meets Pierre Bourdieu: The Conversion of Capital as Plot in the Mid-Victorian British Novel', *Victorian Literature and Culture*, 31.2 (2003), p. 506. Of course, what Arabin forgets concerns Mrs Arabin's decision to add a cheque to the envelope for Crawley, a situation that both highlights Eleanor's confusion about finance (she does not recognise the difference between a cheque and a bank note) and takes us back to Arabin's own limited means prior to his marrying a well-endowed widow. On Trollope's financial narratives see also Nancy Henry, '"Rushing into Eternity": Suicide and Finance in Victorian Fiction', in Nancy Henry and Cannon Schmitt (eds), *Victorian Investments: New Perspectives on Finance and Culture* (Indiana: Indiana University Press, 2008), Chapter 8 (pp. 161–81).

104. According to Turtle Dove's expert legal opinion, the diamonds at stake in this novel, 'as mere "trinkets", reducible to a "dirty question of money"', are 'the ultimate *non-heirlooms*, incapable of signifying extra-economic value in any concrete or permanent way', Goodlad, *The Victorian Geopolitical Aesthetic,* p. 92; see also, Kathy Alexis Psomiades, 'Heterosexual Exchange and Other Victorian Fictions: *The Eustace Diamonds* and Victorian Anthropology', *NOVEL*, 33.1 (1999): pp. 93–118; and, more recently, Ayelet en-Yishai, 'The Fact of a Rumor: Anthony Trollope's *The Eustace Diamonds*', *Nineteenth-Century Literature*, 62, no. 1 (2007): pp. 88–120.

105. 'Unsigned notice, *Saturday Review* (14 May 1864)', in Smalley (ed.), *Anthony Trollope,* p. 205.

106. See Arrighi, *The Long Twentieth Century*, Chapter 2.

107. (Anon.), *British Quarterly Review*, 92 (October 1867): p. 557.

108. (Anon.), *The London Review*, 20 July 1867, p. 81

109. Ibid. p. 81.

110. For this comparative case for *longue durée* study see Goodlad, *The Victorian Geopolitical Aesthetic*, especially Coda.

111. Jonathan Bernstein, 'TV OD: Have we Reached Peak Televison?' *The Guardian*, 24 July 2017, <https://www.theguardian.com/tv-and-radio/2017/jul/24/tv-od-peak-the-get-downsense8-girlboss> (last accessed 6 June 2018). In a market flooded by too much content, 'Peak TV' conduces towards small 'communities of viewers, perpetually thirsting' for originality even as many of the bolder (and most expensive) shows fail to capture an audience.

Part II

Circulation

7

A Christmas Cavil: Trollope Re-Writes Dickens in the Outback

Steven Amarnick

A n *Autobiography* is perhaps Anthony Trollope's most elusive narrative. Take, for instance, his account of how Mrs Proudie's death came about as he was writing *The Last Chronicle of Barset*. It defies belief – though some have believed it – that a self-respecting novelist would impulsively eliminate a character from his popular series just because he eavesdrops on two clergymen complaining at their club. 'I will go home and kill her before the week is over', he tells the perplexed men, and does not reverse his decision even after 'one of them begged me to forget his frivolous observations'.[1] If, however, we scrutinise the passage, we can infer that Trollope had already been planning Mrs Proudie's demise before he walked into the Athenaeum; what he needed was to put aside any 'misgivings' (*A*, ch. 15, p. 275) and accomplish the deed. By saying out loud to witnesses what he had in mind, he could not renege so easily.[2]

As Trollope states in the opening paragraph of *An Autobiography*, 'But this I protest; – that nothing that I say shall be untrue' (*A*, ch. 1, pp. 1–2). Given his propensity, throughout his career, to cite and quote Shakespeare, Trollope may well be winking at us here, as his 'protest' reminds us of a certain lady who doth too much of it. Yet the wink, if it exists, is both playful and pointed; Trollope may be deeply aware that telling the truth is a complicated matter, yet he will not knowingly lie. He may get little things wrong – as he explains when declaring himself a man of 'vision' rather than a man of 'facts' ('But the man who writes *currente calamo*, who works with a rapidity which will not admit of accuracy, may be as true, and in one sense as trustworthy, as he who bases every word upon a rock of facts') (*A*, ch. 7, p. 130). He may leave out plenty of details – and so we hear nearly nothing about his apparently happy marriage of over three decades ('That I, or any man, should tell everything of himself, I hold to be impossible') (*A* ch. 1, p. 1). He may even go as far as to craftily mislead those who read too quickly, as we see in the Mrs Proudie passage. However, from start to finish he invites us to peruse his autobiography – and his many works that he comments on – attentively. Few may do so, as Trollope acknowledges when he mentions his minute 'delineation' of character through several books in the Palliser series, 'each of which will be forgotten even by the most zealous reader almost as soon as read' (*A*, ch. 20, p. 360). But the invitation is there.

It is with this in mind that I turn to *Harry Heathcote of Gangoil: A Tale of Australian Bushlife*, the shortest of Trollope's forty-seven novels. He tells us, accurately, that he wrote it for the *Graphic* in 1873 as a Christmas commission, and that the story is heavily based on his own son's problems – 'the mingled accidents of heat and bad neighbours' (*A*, ch. 20, p. 357) – in Australia. He also says that he was 'not loth' (*A*, ch. 20, p. 357) to do it – after first making it clear how much he despised producing such tales for the annual market. The opportunity to turn his son into a sympathetic fictional hero partially accounts for the sunnier attitude – as does the sun itself, for Trollope makes a point of mentioning the mid-summer setting in the brief paragraph that he devotes to his account of the novel; to depict the holidays in a land far from chilly England was in itself no doubt liberating. Yet if we look closely at his complaints about Christmas fare – and about the man who had become so deeply associated with the holiday – and then at *Harry Heathcote of Gangoil* itself, we can also see the scope of Trollope's ambition, his delight in subverting reader expectations. Harry is a version of Fred Trollope – and of Ebenezer Scrooge. Or, rather, Harry is Scrooge-like enough for us to consider how his author embedded the character in a narrative that takes bold aim at Charles Dickens's aesthetic. This slim novel, which has received scant critical attention,[3] shows what so many of his works do: that Trollope's realist aim of supplying a 'faithful portrayal of recognizable characters'[4] coexists with his desire to set fresh challenges for himself, to experiment in surprising ways.

Nearly forty years of age, Trollope was still finding his way as a writer when he tasked himself with skewering Dickens in *The Warden* (1855), his first novel which takes place in contemporary England. Whereas his style was unformed, his tastes were well-ingrained, certainly regarding Dickens – here known as Mr Popular Sentiment – about whom he did not waver through the rest of his career. Mr Sentiment is a simplistic rabble-rouser, author of a coarse novel, *The Almshouse*, that is inspired by the scandal engulfing the warden. Though the 'glaring colours'[5] that Mr Sentiment uses in his books have positive real-world effects, making reform possible by stirring the outrage of 'the million',[6] they do not belong on a first-rate literary canvas. By contrast, Trollope touts his more muted palette. His warden, the gentle Mr Harding, is a decent man caught up in a complicated situation. Once he is accused of taking his comfortable salary from funds that should rightfully go elsewhere, he enters a protracted battle with his own conscience – and with his very determined son-in-law, Archdeacon Grantly – before finally resigning. It is the kind of nuanced portrayal, we are urged to believe, that Mr Sentiment would never bother to attempt.

While Trollope did write an affectionate obituary article for *Saint Pauls Magazine* after Dickens's death in 1870, nothing in it refutes the substantive critique he had made fifteen years earlier. Rather, he devotes a great deal of space to the 'vitality' of the man.[7] And though he notes that 'no other writer of [the] English language except Shakespeare has left so many types of character',[8] he implicitly aligns himself with those critics who see a 'want of nature'[9] in such creations. What is different now is his unwillingness to mock Dickens's fans; as he puts it, 'It is fatuous to condemn that as deficient in art which has been so full of art as to captivate all men.'[10] He may well be looking in the mirror at his own earlier fatuous self, given how the name Mr Popular Sentiment connotes scorn for both the audience and the writer who panders to it. Trollope will now grant that anyone so beloved for so long must have done something right as an artist – even if, personally, he has no more regard for Dickens's work than he ever did.

Understandably, Trollope was at his most respectful when penning his tribute in 1870. Six years later, when he wrote most of *An Autobiography* – which would be published posthumously, as he intended – he was no longer so guarded. 'I do acknowledge', he writes, that Mrs Gamp, Micawber, Pecksniff, and others have become household words in every house, as though they were human beings; but to my judgement they are not human beings, nor are any of the characters human which Dickens has portrayed. It has been the peculiarity and the marvel of this man's power, that he has invested his puppets with a charm that has enabled him to dispense with human nature. (*A*, ch. 13, p. 248)

Trollope still refrains from maligning readers for their poor taste. Instead, it is as if they are under a spell, with those charming puppets mesmerising them in ways both peculiar and marvellous to behold. He continues: 'Nor is the pathos of Dickens human. It is stagey and melodramatic' (*A*, ch. 13, pp. 248–9). And also: 'Of Dickens's style it is impossible to speak in praise. It is jerky, ungrammatical, and created by himself in defiance of rules' (*A*, ch. 13, p. 249). The manner of attack has changed; gone is the almost bombastic declaration of independence from Trollope's early novel. Yet if anything, the criticism is more thorough-going, exuding the confidence of a man reaching out to his own considerable, and loyal, audience.

The attack is extended several chapters later in *An Autobiography*. 'Nothing can be more distasteful to me', he declares, 'than to have to give a relish of Christmas to what I write. I feel the humbug implied by the nature of the order' (*A*, ch. 20, p. 356). He then goes on to accuse Dickens of humbug, saying that the only palatable Christmas stories he wrote were the first two, *A Christmas Carol* (1843) and, presumably, *The Chimes* (1844), though the latter more specifically is about the new year.[11] Thereafter, 'the things written annually – all of which have been fixed to Christmas like children's toys to a Christmas tree – have had no real savour of Christmas about them' (*A*, ch. 20, p. 357). Dickens had published *The Cricket on the Hearth* in 1845, *The Battle of Life* in 1846 and *The Haunted Man* in 1848; he skipped 1847 to finish *Dombey and Son* and 1849 to finish *David Copperfield*. In 1850, he began editing *Household Words*, and found that its pre-Christmas edition, stuffed with articles (one by himself) about the season, sold extremely well. In 1851 he put out a special Christmas edition of the weekly, 'and so began a tradition which continued for the next sixteen years, being carried over from *Household Words* to its successor, *All the Year Round*'.[12] Trollope's passive construction – 'the things written annually' – allows him to indict Dickens as both author and editor. At the least, Dickens and his fellow contributors had been guilty of mechanically droning on, becoming writers whose work was 'one piece of stiff mechanism' (*A*, ch. 12, p. 232) when they no longer had anything new to say. At worst, he had cynically turned Christmas into a cash cow.[13]

Yet regardless of Dickens's sins, Trollope knew that it was a fool's errand to try to compete with him. Perhaps in the 1850s, as he was writing *The Warden*, he hoped that Dickens could one day be dethroned, becoming far less popular as tastes and sentiments changed. (Indeed, the object of his other satirical attack, Thomas Carlyle – Dr Pessimist Anticant in the novel – has for decades suffered a decline in reputation that is unlikely to be reversed.) By the time of the obituary article, however, and into the 1870s, it was apparent that Dickens was an institution, that he was not going away. An obvious parody, or any other kind of full assault, would only seem petty and pointless.

Why not, though, continue to demonstrate how Dickens – even the 'good' Dickens, as represented by a landmark work like *A Christmas Carol* – was alien to Trollope's own sensibilities? *A Christmas Carol* would make an especially appealing target, so central was it to Dickens's godlike status. It had been an immediate sensation when it came out in December 1843, with pirated versions appearing soon after, and eight theatrical productions in London by February. And when Dickens himself had, ten years later, begun acting out scenes from his work in public, he drew heavily on *A Christmas Carol*, even developing a complete ninety-minute performance text of the story that he tinkered with continually. As Paul Davis writes, '[N]othing did more for Dickens' popular image than his public readings. From the first reading in 1853 to the last shortly before he died . . . Dickens made the *Carol* the pièce de résistance in his repertoire.'[14] Even many people who had never read a word of his writing 'looked upon Dickens as the spirit of Christmas incarnate: as being, in a word, Father Christmas itself'.[15] Such novels as *The Pickwick Papers*, *Oliver Twist* and *Nicholas Nickleby* had made Dickens a literary wunderkind, but *A Christmas Carol* catapulted him to another level. And by the time he died, 'the *Carol* had become the first gospel in the Dickensian scripture'.[16]

A Christmas Carol is so well known that it would be pointless to summarise the plot. It is as famous now as it ever was, with countless stage adaptations and community readings dotting the land – many lands – and sundry film adaptations shown on television. Late in every year, the Morgan Library in New York brings out the manuscript of *A Christmas Carol* for visitors to gaze at reverentially, and now has published a new facsimile edition of that manuscript. As Colm Tóibín writes in the foreword, Scrooge's redemption 'has come to mean an opening of the self, a way of reimagining the world. And so, with that change, from nightmare to sweet reality, from miserliness to giving, from misery to merriness, Christmas came into being. Courtesy of Dickens, we live in its shadow still.'[17] That shadow is a long one; Dickens may not quite be 'the man who invented Christmas',[18] but it is impossible for many people to think of the holiday today without soon invoking his name or that of Ebenezer Scrooge.

Harry Heathcote of Gangoil, on the other hand, is barely known at all. It emerged from the same 1871–2 trip around the colonies that produced *Australia and New Zealand*, but unlike the latter, it is a quick read. Harry, an Englishman in his twenties, is a sheep farmer in Queensland who, in the days leading up to Christmas, faces imminent ruin, as his enemies wish to burn down and destroy his pastures. Harry alienates the one man, Giles Medlicot, who would be most useful in thwarting those enemies. In the end, though, the bad guys are put down, as Giles comes round and even gets to marry the pretty and amiable sister of Harry's wife. Everyone sits down to Christmas dinner, and in the final paragraph, with the meal now over, Harry proclaims: 'That's what I call a happy Christmas' (*HHG*, ch. 12, p. 125).

From what I've just said, *Harry Heathcote of Gangoil* sounds heart-warming, and harmless, enough. Yet from the start of the novel, Harry is a dark and complicated figure – and, significantly, he barely changes by the end. Unlike Scrooge, who is so very bad until he almost immediately becomes so very good, Harry has many redeeming features that we do not have to strain to see: a wife and sister-in-law who, in a sense, vouch for him through their adoration, a strong work ethic and a strong sense of integrity.[19] 'I s'pose the poor must live somewheres' (*HHG*, ch. 1, p. 7), Harry's maidservant, Mrs Growler, says to him early in the novel after he has spoken harshly. But Harry is quick to defend himself, telling her she has 'jump[ed] to conclusions' and that she has 'rebuked me under the impression that I was grudging something to the poor' (*HHG*, ch. 1, p. 7). Harry is no Scrooge – even if Mrs Growler and some others tend to see him that way. Yet he does share with Scrooge certain tendencies.

Like Scrooge he is pathetically alone. He is friendless and unwilling to make friends, saying, 'I want to see no one from year's end to year's end but my own family and my own people' (*HHG*, ch. 3, p. 28). Neighbours, he says, are 'humbug' (*HHG*, ch. 3, p. 26). His wife begs him to confide in her, but he refuses, and when she later suggests to him that Giles might be an ally, he scoffs and feels even more isolated, with 'a terrible feeling of loneliness' (*HHG* ch. 5, p. 46) to the point where 'He sometimes felt, when alone in the bush, that he would fain get off his horse and lie upon the ground and weep till he slept' (*HHG*, ch. 5, p. 46). Like Scrooge, all he does is work and sleep; 'as for pleasure, it had come to be altogether beyond the purpose of his life to go in quest of that' (*HHG*, ch. 1, p. 6).

Like Scrooge too Harry is deeply paranoid and partakes of 'urgent watchfulness' (*HHG*, ch. 3, p. 25) over men who he fears will destroy him. When his wife urges him 'to forgive your neighbours' because '[i]t's Christmas time', Harry silences her, saying, 'What sort of a Christmas will it be if . . . [we] are all burned out of Gangoil'? (*HHG*, ch. 7, p. 67). While he is right to be paranoid – he really does have enemies out to get him – he is incapable of making distinctions; everybody is suspicious. And Harry has no consciousness of his own role in creating his enemies; like Scrooge he is clueless about his self-destruction. He is nasty to his loyal worker Jacko, calling him a 'young monkey' (*HHG*, ch. 2, p. 21) among other things, until at one point Jacko lights a match and throws it to the ground after getting insulted. Jacko has no intention of letting the fire burn, but he wants to show how easily he could cause trouble if he wanted to. Harry creates one enemy, Boscobel, by directly telling the man to his face that he's a liar; he creates another enemy, Bill Nokes, by throwing him over a fence; and he treats a whole family, the Brownbies, 'as though they were dirt beneath his feet' (*HHG*, ch. 6, p. 57). The Brownbies feel that Harry 'was a proud, stuck-up, unsocial young cub, whom to rob was a pleasure, and to ruin would be a delight' (*HHG*, ch. 6, p. 57). These men are all bad guys who do try to ruin Harry – but they are bad guys with feelings, and bad guys who under other circumstances might have behaved differently; and ultimately Trollope is explicit about how they could have been on Harry's side had he treated them with some diplomacy. He writes, 'It is a small and narrow point that turns the rushing train to the right or to the left. The rushing man is often turned off by a point as small and narrow' (*HHG*, ch. 9, p. 92). One such 'rushing man', Karl Bender, is loyal to Harry, but only after he 'had made his way through the crust of his master's character' (*HHG*, ch. 2, p. 21). In his case too, though, he 'could have quarrelled, and have avenged himself, had it not chanced that he had come to the point of loving instead of hating his employer' (*HHG*, ch. 2, p. 21).

From Harry's perspective, he is merely being honest, unwilling to indulge in flattery. Though his behaviour is self-destructive, it is partially noble too – for his fault is telling too much of the truth. In his dealings with Giles Medlicot, however, Harry is merely foolish. He rejects Giles's overtures of friendship, in part because of his prejudices against Johnny-come-lately 'free-selectors', or landowners.[20] And when Giles employs Bill Nokes, who ends up being the ringleader of the efforts to burn him out of business, Harry demands that Giles fire the man, without bothering to think about the best way to make his case. The narrator tells us that Giles has hired and retained Nokes because he had 'unconsciously made up his mind to commence hostilities' (*HHG*, ch. 3, pp. 27–8) – hostilities that we are meant to see as entirely avoidable. It is only because of Giles's own good sense that he comes to see on his own what Nokes and the others are up to; and in the climactic battle he joins with Harry to save the day. Without Giles, Harry would indeed have been ruined – and though, again, the enemies were real, he would still have had himself to blame.

In *A Christmas Carol* Scrooge suffers through a terrifying night and emerges transformed, spreading joy and taking pleasure in the most minute things. His crust gets scraped away rather easily – already in the Ghost of Christmas Past section his essential goodness emerges as he sees his childhood mates. In *Harry Heathcote of Gangoil*, Harry suffers through a series of terrifying nights – for that is when his lands are in danger – and emerges after the long battle on Christmas Eve as at best only a bit transformed. His crust gets scraped away, and his essential goodness comes through – but there is still plenty of crust that remains. Right after his victory, he remains entirely befuddled that a man like Boscobel could so turn against him. Karl Bender replies, 'You told him of it too plain' (*HHG*, ch. 10, p. 99) – 'it' being Harry's legitimate grievance that Boscobel was not earning his pay. Harry responds exactly the way he did earlier in the novel, saying *of course* he should tell a man who's cheating him that he's a dirty low-down cheater – to which Karl responds by shrugging his shoulders. As Harry continues his tirade, Karl and Giles and Jacko and two others who had fought alongside Harry 'all understood him very well; . . . and, though, no doubt, there was a feeling within the hearts of the men that Harry Heathcote was imperious, still they respected him – and they believed him' (*HHG*, ch. 10, p. 100). If there is any hope that the 'imperious' Harry might change, it comes a few minutes later, when he is alone and 'had begun to perceive that life would be very hard to him in his present position, or perhaps altogether impossible, as long as he was at enmity with all those around him' (*HHG*, ch. 10, p. 101). He is still explicitly disdainful of 'soft-sawder' (*HHG*, ch. 10, p. 101) – a term that Trollope uses in other novels too; here, it means a willingness to not express all the truth all the time, and even to engage in just a wee bit of buttering up – but he is at least able to admit to himself that 'his own plan had hardly answered' (*HHG*, ch. 10, p. 101). Perhaps with the help of his future brother-in-law and others Harry over time will in fact change – but it won't happen in one night or one week or one month, no matter how treacherous his experiences.

In presenting Harry, and even the minor characters, this way, Trollope takes great pains to portray 'human nature' and avoid Dickens's 'puppets', and in the ending especially he avoids the 'pathos' as well. It isn't only that Trollope leaves out almost all of that 'savour of Christmas' that suffuses Dickens's text – the songs, the games, the foods, the talk of good cheer and charity, even the children (Harry is the father of a toddler and an infant, who are almost entirely invisible at the novel's climax). Trollope's other Christmas writing also goes very light on the holiday details.[21] For instance, though Christmas is the excuse for the family gathering in 'Christmas at Thompson Hall', that gathering could just as well have occurred at any other time of the year. What the story is about is a woman going into the wrong hotel room and spreading mustard over the wrong man while he sleeps.[22] Or in 'Christmas Day at Kirkby Cottage', the misunderstanding between the two lovers is set in motion when the man proclaims that 'Christmas Day is a bore'.[23] Once the two are united, Trollope does nothing to show how Christmas isn't, or even is, a bore; it doesn't really matter.[24] What distinguishes the ending of *Harry Heathcote of Gangoil* is how only marginally happy it is. Harry's own behaviour could cause him trouble in the future; moreover,

Trollope goes out of his way to catalogue all the troubles that could still await him, including 'fires' and 'rebellious servants' and 'floods' and 'droughts' and 'wild dogs to worry the lambs' (*HHG*, ch. 12, p. 117).[25] Trollope certainly was not going to deliver a tragic Christmas story to the *Graphic* magazine, but he makes his happy ending as muted as he can.[26]

And from the beginning of the novel he has promised us something unusual. At first Trollope includes a brief scene, taking place two weeks before Christmas, in which a young man, soon revealed to be Harry, comes home after working all morning, all afternoon, and into the evening, and is greeted by his wife and sister-in-law and two silent babies. It's a heart-warming scene and one that would not be out of place in Dickens. Except that Harry has complained about the heat – which causes the narrator to make this declaration:

> From all this I trust the reader will understand that the Christmas to which he is introduced is not the Christmas with which he is intimate on this side of the Equator – a Christmas of blazing fires indoors, and of sleet and snow and frost outside – but the Christmas of Australia, in which happy land the Christmas fires are apt to be lighted, or to light themselves, when they are by no means needed. (*HHG*, ch. 1, pp. 3–4)

And with this, Trollope is off and running. Instead of frost, his tale will contain oppressive, even unprecedented, heat. Instead of sleet and snow, his tale will contain oppressive, even unprecedented, drought. Instead of happy blazing fires inside, his tale will contain Christmas fires that destroy.[27]

Whatever Trollope might have privately thought about the value of his own oeuvre compared to Dickens's, it is difficult to imagine that he believed *Harry Heathcote of Gangoil* was superior to *A Christmas Carol* as a work of art. Even if one considers Scrooge to be a prime example of Dickens's puppetry, few sane readers would wish him otherwise. And even if one believes that Scrooge's nephew's view of Christmas is idealised – he calls the season 'a kind, forgiving, charitable, pleasant time . . . when men and women seem by one consent to open their shut-up hearts, freely, and to think of people below them as if they really were fellow-passengers to the grave, and not another race of creatures bound on other journeys'[28] – few would consider it an improvement if Dickens presented a more measured view of what adults think and feel during the holiday. We can understand why Trollope found it such a chore – *Harry Heathcote of Gangoil* excepted – to write uplifting Christmas stories. Unwilling as he was to sacrifice his notions of human behaviour, and how it should be depicted in fiction, he was deeply unsuited for the task.

Why then did he bother? Once again it is necessary to look closely at what Trollope says and doesn't say in *An Autobiography*. In the paragraph preceding the one where he discusses *Harry Heathcote of Gangoil*, he is especially dramatic in his choice of metaphor as he tells about his Christmas woes. He states, 'I feel, with regard to literature, somewhat as I suppose an upholsterer and undertaker feels when he is called upon to supply a funeral. He has to supply it, however distasteful it may be. It is his business, and he will starve if he neglect it' (*A*, ch. 20, p. 356). On one hand, this is a variation of a central point in *An Autobiography*: the successful writer will keep regular hours and go to his desk every day, no matter what mood he's in, no matter how enthusiastic or unenthusiastic he happens to be. Whether he is an undertaker, a shoemaker, or a novelist, it is his job to show up and do the work. On the other hand, even if it is his 'business' to write, Trollope is not driven by necessity to write about Christmas specifically; he can turn down those commissions, and not miss a meal.[29] Might Trollope then be as guilty as Dickens and others who crave their Christmas payday? His extension of the funeral metaphor, right after denouncing Dickens, may give an impression that he finds this work to be deplorable and remunerative and nothing more. 'Alas!' he exclaims,

> at this very moment I have one to write, which I have promised to supply within three weeks of this time, – the picture-makers always require a long interval, – as to which I have in vain been cudgelling my brain for the last month. I can't send away the order to another shop, but I do not know how I shall ever get the coffin made. (*A*, ch. 20, p. 357)

Yet if we take the view, as with the Mrs Proudie anecdote, that Trollope is willing to omit much, so as not to be explicit about what he is really thinking; that he is even willing to playfully mislead, though not to lie, we may come away with a different interpretation of the passage. Trollope's brain cudgelling is necessary because he takes the task seriously – or, more precisely, the task he has set for himself to write about Christmas in a way that does not offend his own sensibilities yet still satisfies his publishers and readers. Trollope is truthful about his hostility toward those sentimental stories, written seemingly by rote, that lacked the 'real savour of Christmas'; he is truthful, too, about how difficult and even unpleasant it can be to write a Christmas story that he can endorse. But his metaphors obscure the reason why his struggles are worthwhile. Whether for a three-volume novel or a seasonal short story, the challenge meant everything to Trollope, as he cultivated habits that would keep his writing fresh and help him avoid the stultification of so many other authors with long careers. The shoemaker and the undertaker can thrive more or less doing the same thing year after year, as long as he stays alert to any new trends that might affect his customers; once he has gained proficiency, the work need not be particularly difficult in order for it to be good. For a serious writer, though, to get into any sort of automatic groove – other than in the actual work habits of sitting down to work and aiming for a certain number of words every day – would mean the death of his art. It may well have been onerous for Trollope to do these Christmas stories – but it was also entirely useful. And regardless of what everyone else thought about Dickens, it was useful for Trollope to keep reminding himself of just how much his own work differed. That he succeeded in keeping himself fresh is evident by the work he published late in his career: long novels like *The Duke's Children*, *John Caldigate*, *Ayala's Angel* and *Mr Scarborough's Family* can plausibly be counted among his best books, and there is much shorter fascinating work: *Cousin Henry*, *Dr Wortle's School*, *An Old Man's Love* and the stories 'The Telegraph Girl', 'Alice Dugdale', 'Catherine Carmichael; or Three Years Running', and the Christmas tale 'The Two Heroines of Plumplington', among others. It is staggering that Trollope was able to create at such a high level so late in his career, but it didn't happen by accident.[30] He was a man with an ambitious plan, and Dickens, and Christmas, played a part in it.

Notes

1. *An Autobiography*, ed. Michael Sadleir and Frederick Page (Oxford: Oxford University Press, 1999), p. 275. Subsequent references are in the main text (*A*).

2. The title of *The Last Chronicle of Barset* itself acts as such a declaration; with such a title (and the elegiac farewell of the final pages), it would be near impossible for Trollope in the future to succumb to temptation and write another (lucrative) Barsetshire novel. For more about the craftiness of the Mrs Proudie anecdote, see my article, 'Killing Mrs Proudie', *Trollopiana*, 94 (2012–13): pp. 2–6.

3. For a fine, detailed overview, see P. D. Edwards's introduction to the Oxford Classics edition. Edwards, though, sees Trollope as largely compliant with Dickens's guidelines for Christmas stories. He writes, 'The essential requirement of the species, as established by Dickens in the 1840s, was a spectacular resolution of class-conflicts and a patching up of personal differences, preferably consummated over Christmas dinner at the end of the tale. Christmas, which ushered in the restoration of hope for all mankind, had to be shown doing the same for beleaguered individuals, ensuring their worldly if not eternal salvation and answering their most fervent prayers. In Trollope's novel this is effected by the formation of an alliance between the young hero and the representative of the class which poses the greatest threat to his livelihood and perhaps even his personal safety.' *Harry Heathcote of Gangoil: A Tale of Australian Bushlife*, ed. P. D. Edwards (Oxford: Oxford University Press, 1992), p. ix. Subsequent references are in the main text (*HHG*).

4. George Levine, *The Realistic Imagination: English Fiction from Frankenstein to Lady Chatterley* (Chicago: University of Chicago Press, 1981), p. 183.

5. Anthony Trollope, *The Warden*, ed. David Skilton (Oxford: Oxford University Press, 2008), p. 208.

6. Ibid. p. 208.

7. Anthony Trollope, *The Saint Pauls Magazine*, vol. 6, April to September (London: Strahan & Co., 1870), p. 371.

8. Ibid. p. 372.

9. Ibid. p. 373.

10. Ibid. p. 374.

11. It is possible, too, that Trollope is referring to 'The Story of the Goblins Who Stole a Sexton', which was incorporated into *The Pickwick Papers*, in which case *A Christmas Carol* would count as the second of his tales. The main character of 'Goblins', Gabriel Grub, is in many ways similar to, and thus an earlier version of, Ebenezer Scrooge.

12. Michael Slater, 'Introduction', in *A Christmas Carol and Other Christmas Writings* (London: Penguin Books, 2003), p. xxiv.

13. Deborah A. Thomas writes that '*A Christmas Carol* is a brief masterpiece, and Dickens' holiday excursions into the world of fancy in *The Chimes* and *The Haunted Man* well repay artistic examination'. And though she tells us, in a detailed chapter, that 'some of Dickens' other Christmas writings are undeniably little more than potboilers – created to make the most of the Christmas market – or perfunctory holiday tributes', she makes a case that several of the later works deserve attention too. *Dickens and the Short Story* (Philadelphia: University of Pennsylvania Press, 1982), p. 62.

14. Paul Davis, *The Life and Times of Ebenezer Scrooge* (New Haven: Yale University Press, 1990), p. 53.

15. Ibid. p. 53. Davis quotes here from a 1907 article titled 'Dickens and Father Christmas', in *Nineteenth Century*.

16. Ibid. p. 58.

17. Colm Tóibín, 'Foreword', in *A Christmas Carol: The Original Manuscript Edition* (New York: W. W. Norton & Company, 2017), p. xi.

18. As David Parker explains, Dickens was first called 'the man who invented Christmas' in a 1903 magazine article, and it's a characterisation that has had surprising durability. More properly, he argues, Dickens can be credited with an 'intensification' of feeling about the holiday; it is pure myth to say that 'before *A Christmas Carol* there was widespread indifference to Christmas, after it almost universal enthusiasm'. *Christmas and Charles Dickens* (New York: AMS Press, 2005), p. 17, p. x. See also Kathryn Harrison's review of Les Standiford's *The Man Who Invented Christmas: How Charles Dickens's* A Christmas Carol *Rescued His Career and Revived Our Holiday Spirits*, in *The New York Times Book Review*, December 5, 2008, p. BR14.

19. Parker astutely observes that 'we are made to admire [Scrooge] from the start, despite ourselves. In the opening pages, the narrative denounces him as "a squeezing, wrenching, grasping, scraping, clutching, covetous old sinner", but it is clear that he engages vitally with those about him, however perversely. He is witty, nimble-minded, and mischievous.' Parker, *Christmas and Charles Dickens*, p. 202. Yet it is apparent that even if we do admire the life-force in Scrooge, he is still a thoroughgoing ogre – until he's not.

20. By contrast, squatters like Harry – and Fred Trollope – leased the land from the Crown. In his travel book about Australia, Trollope writes about the competing claims and attitudes of squatters and free-selectors, stating: 'Personally, I love a squatter . . . But on principle I take the part of the free-selector.' *Australia and New Zealand* (London: Dawsons of Pall Mall, 1968), p. 177.

21. See Lisa Niles's discussion of 'the persistent secularity of Trollope's holiday tales' in her chapter on 'Trollope's Short Fiction', in Carolyn Dever and Lisa Niles (eds), *The Cambridge Companion to Anthony Trollope* (Cambridge: Cambridge University Press, 2010), pp. 76–7.

22. In his appreciation of *A Christmas Carol*, Adam Gopnik mentions this story in an aside about Dickens's 'single greatest contemporary'. As Gopnik notes, 'In Trollope's Christmas stories, the Dickensian apparatus is spoofed and treated sardonically.' *Winter: Five Windows on the Season* (Toronto: House of Anansi Press, 2011), p. 113.

23. Anthony Trollope, *The Complete Shorter Fiction*, ed. Julian Thompson (New York: Carroll & Graf, 1992), p. 658.

24. For a Christmas filled with food and games, see the chapter entitled 'Christmas at Noningsby' in Trollope, *Orley Farm*, ed. David Skilton (Oxford: Oxford University Press, 1991). However, even here, Christmas mostly falls away in the latter part of the chapter. There is a certain amount of eating and drinking and game-playing and flirtation, but ultimately few reminders that it is indeed Christmas.

25. Though it is highly unlikely that he would have read an obscure novel by Anthony Trollope, James Baldwin captures this same feeling in the ending of his classic short story 'Sonny's Blues'. Sonny, a drug addict who has gone clean for a while, makes profound music at the piano as his previously estranged brother watches, and listens, and understands. Yes, Sonny is triumphant, and the siblings are united, but how long will it last? As the brother (and narrator) tells us, 'I was yet aware that this was only a moment, that the world waited outside, as hungry as a tiger, and that trouble stretched above us, longer than the sky.' *The Norton Introduction to Literature, Shorter 12th Edition*, ed. Kelly J. Mays (New York: W. W. Norton & Company, 2017), pp. 114–15.

26. In focusing on the female characters in her chapter on Trollope and Australia, Diana C. Archibald writes about the ending: 'The "angels" in the bush, then, can achieve limited success in creating a "home" in the wilderness. They supposedly bring order, propriety, and beauty to an untamed land, and do, in fact, demonstrate their power to alter the course of events by creating communal ties. Ultimately, however, their "home" in the bush is never safe and never permanent. It is no honest man's Arcady . . . Even the narrator of the story's happy ending can claim that Harry has been "triumphant" only "so far". This "home"

that the ladies of Gangoil have striven to establish is clearly a temporary one whether Harry succeeds or fails, since even if his neighbors never have the courage to renew their attempts to ruin him, Harry's livelihood is still open to the legal threat of free-selectors and the harsh natural environment. He may lose Gangoil, and thus his independence, at any time.' *Domesticity, Imperialism, and Emigration in the Victorian Novel* (Columbia: University of Missouri Press, 2002), pp. 91–2.

27. As Nicholas Birns notes, Trollope did not set the novel in 'temperate' New South Wales, where his son was, but Queensland instead, so as to create a complete contrast with the weather of an English Christmas. He writes too that 'Christmas, customarily the site of home and hearth, becomes instead a symbol of exile and displacement' and that critics have wrongly tended 'to regard the surface disjunction of Australia and Christmas as concealing a far less surprising conservatism. Trollope, on this view, sets his novel so far away only in order to emphasize values near-at-hand and close to home.' 'The Empire Turned Upside Down: The Colonial Fictions of Anthony Trollope', *Ariel: A Review of International English*, 27 (1996): p. 9, p. 10.

28. Charles Dickens, *A Christmas Carol: The Original Manuscript Edition* (New York: W. W. Norton & Company, 2016), p. 11.

29. P. D. Edwards, in his Oxford Classics introduction, suggests that because 'the demand for new novels by Trollope began to slacken' (*HHG*, Introduction, p. vii) by the 1870s, Trollope was more willing to write for the Christmas market even though he hated doing so. However, the more significant slackening occurred later in the 1870s, after Trollope had written *An Autobiography*, accounting for the footnote he added when revising lightly in 1879 about the 'diminution in price' *(A*, ch. 9, p. 161) he had received from his publishers. Even if one grants that Trollope had passed the peak of his popularity by the time he wrote *Harry Heathcote of Gangoil*, and thus was more eager to find new ways to reach readers, his claim that he was forced to write for Christmas cannot be taken at face value.

30. Even more puzzling than Trollope's decision to try his hand at Christmas stories is his investment in *North America*, written in the midst of the Civil War. Trollope interrupted his burgeoning career as a novelist for nine months – and took a leave from his Post Office job – to produce a long travel book that is aggressively, purposely dull. His decision to do so makes little sense – except that he was writing in response to his mother's aggressively lively bestseller from three decades earlier, *Domestic Manners of the Americans*. If the need to write a book so strikingly different from his mother's freed him to return to novel-writing with renewed zest, the nine-month interruption was worthwhile. Moreover, any kind of travelling was useful in providing new stimuli, 'to that work of observation and reception from which has come [the novelist's] power, without which work his power cannot be continued' (*A*, ch. 12, pp. 230–1). One could imagine a long critical work on Trollope focusing on dozens of such decisions throughout his career – decisions that allowed his writing to remain vital to the very end.

8

CREATION AS CRITICISM: ANTHONY TROLLOPE, ANTHONY POWELL AND ELIZABETH BISHOP

John Bowen

The real and durable form that criticism takes, then, is *the next job*, creation at once subsequent and consequent. Creation is itself the highest, widest, and deepest form of criticism. This, whether or not the artistic medium or the literary kind happen to stay the same.[1]

General Liddament's Explosion

CHRISTOPHER RICKS'S CLAIM makes a radical inversion of our customary sense of what matters in criticism, and in literature. For him, it is the response of creative artists in their literary work, rather than that of critics, reviewers and scholars, that is 'the highest, widest, and deepest form of criticism'. Yet critical accounts of Anthony Trollope, histories of his changing reputation and collections of critical essays rarely foreground, and sometimes do not even register, such work. There are lengthy entries in the invaluable *Oxford Reader's Companion to Trollope* on 'Critical Opinions of Trollope', for example, but nothing on creative writers' responses, other than when, as with Henry James, they write criticism.[2] There are of course substantial conceptual problems lurking behind any attempt firmly to separate the 'creative' from the 'critical' but even if one does not share Ricks's sense of the supreme importance of 'creative' work in understanding past authors, his remark should at least remind us not to neglect it. It would seem a foolish and self-defeating gesture for those seeking to understand Trollope not to learn from some of his most inventive and knowledgeable readers. Indeed, through the surprise occasioned by authentic literary creativity, it may well prove an invaluable way to understand him in new and better ways.

Such creative work may appear in unexpected places. One of the most influential poets of the twentieth century, Elizabeth Bishop, for example, wrote an important poem that is not just about Trollope but deeply Trollopian in its voice and subject matter, and yet it is a text that rarely registers in criticism – or indeed biography – of the novelist's work. This impoverishes our understanding both of Bishop and Trollope, and of potential creative dialogues between their writing. For Bishop's creative response, even in a relatively short poem, is able to release a very different critical understanding of Trollope's work and sense of self. Trollope himself wrote on a monumental scale and this may have skewed scholarship and criticism towards larger forms, such as editions, biographies and substantial critical works. But a short poem may matter as much, or more. In this chapter, I want to explore the figuring of Trollope and his writing in two exemplary creative responses: that of Anthony

Powell's *roman-fleuve*, *A Dance to the Music of Time* (1951–75), and of Elizabeth Bishop's 1965 poem 'From Trollope's Journal'. In the twentieth century, Trollope's fiction was often wrongly seen as a shelter in times of trouble, a means of escape into a peaceful world of small-beer quarrels. V. S. Pritchett, for example, writing in the *New Statesman* in 1946 thought that Trollope 'since 1918 . . . has become one of the great air raid shelters. He presides over the "eternal Munich of the heart".'[3] The two examples that I discuss see Trollope's work in a very different relationship to the disorder and sufferings of war. In both, his writing has a deeply discomforting presence.

Trollope erupts violently into the wartime section of Anthony Powell's mid-century *A Dance to the Music of Time*. In *The Soldier's Art* (1966), the eighth novel of the series, set in the early years of World War II, Major General Liddament asks the more junior Nick Jenkins, the narrator of the novel:

'What do you think of Trollope?'
'Never found him easy to read, sir'.
My answer had an incisive effect. He kicked the chair away from him, with such violence that it fell to the ground with a great clatter. Then he put his feet to the floor, screwing round his own chair so that he faced me.
'*You've never found Trollope easy to read?*'
'No, sir'.
He was clearly unable to credit my words. This was an unhappy situation. There was a long pause while he glared at me.
'Why not?' he asked at last.
He spoke very sternly. I tried to think of an answer. From the past, a few shreds of long forgotten literary criticism were just pliant enough to be patched hurriedly together in substitute for a more suitable garment to cover the dialectical nakedness of the statement just made.
'. . . the style . . . certain repetitive tricks of phrasing . . . psychology often unconvincing . . . sometimes downright dishonest in the treatment of individual relationships . . . women don't analyse their own predicaments as there represented . . . in fact, the author does more thinking than feeling . . . of course, possessor of enormous narrative gifts . . . marshalling material . . . all that amounting to genius . . . certain sense of character even if stylised . . . and naturally as a picture of the times . . . '.
'Rubbish', said General Liddament.
He sounded very angry indeed. All the good humour . . . had been dissipated by a thoughtless expression of literary prejudice on my own part. It might have been wiser to have passed some noncommittal judgement. Possibly I should be put under arrest for holding such mutinous views.[4]

It is a very funny scene, in which the amiable if slightly uneasy exchanges of the two characters are suddenly punctuated by the explosive wrath of the General. The violence of war suddenly bursts into an apparently trivial conversation, comically disrupting the *politesse* of civilised life. Liddament seems to find in Trollope's work a comfort in a time of conflict, whereas the younger Jenkins shares his generation's modernist contempt for Victorians such as Trollope. Once committed to the 'dialectical nakedness' of his rejection, Jenkins does his best to salvage the situation through producing a 'few shreds' of criticism. It is done in his characteristically self-deprecating mode but nevertheless packs a good number of serious and distinctive objections to Trollope into five or six lines of text, including repetitive phrasing, unconvincing psychology and dishonesty.

Such a judgement is of a piece with many early and mid-twentieth-century reactions to Trollope's work, which was often disparaged or only grudgingly praised in the period. This is the case even for novelists who, one might think, would share or be sympathetic to Trollope's characteristic interests and ambition. In *A Dance*, Powell himself, for example, created one of the most ambitious and successful twentieth-century *romans-fleuves*, which has some similar ambitions to Trollope's two great novel sequences. Powell's twelve-novel series provides a similarly satisfying experience of wide social range and complex character development over time to the 'Barchester' and parliamentary (or 'Palliser') series. The time frames of each sequence stretch over more than one generation and in both sequences everyday middle- and upper-class life is counterpointed by the public world of the political and social life of high society. Trollope's range was considerable – from the Duke of Omnium down at least as far as Quintus Slide, the sleazy editor of the *People's Banner* newspaper – as indeed was Powell's. Trollope's bulk is greater, of course, and his novels more quickly written but, like Powell's, each novel in the sequence can be read as a single coherent volume but is strengthened and deepened by its part in the wider whole. There are other parallels between the two authors: both went to public school, had slightly rackety phases as young men and had to make a living from their pens, remaining socially within and yet at a certain distance from 'high society'. As well as being writers of fiction and biography, both men had careers as literary journalists: Trollope as editor of *Saint Pauls*, Powell as literary editor of the *Daily Telegraph* and the *TLS*. Their major works are multi-novel sequences concerned with a group of interlocking characters, drawn mainly from the English upper- and middle-class literary, political and professional worlds, whom we see over lengthy periods of time, some of whom survive and flourish, some of whom die or drop away, many of whom reappear later in the sequence, as minor characters turn out to have major significance, or vice versa, in subsequent volumes.

Despite these many similarities, Trollope in *The Soldier's Art* seems to epitomise everything that Jenkins and indeed Powell dislike in fiction. It is, we infer, the antithesis – in style, phrasing, psychology and understanding of women – of the kind of fiction that Jenkins and Powell admire, the work of an author who does 'more thinking than feeling'. We might call the passage, then, an *apotropaic* one that seeks to ward off a powerful fictional precursor, whose presence is both threatening ('possibly I should be put under arrest') and absurd.[5] A novelist who in many ways seems one of the closest twentieth-century successors to Trollope – an English novelist of the middle and upper classes who writes a sequence of linked novels about contemporary life – declares himself his 'dialectical' opposite, allowing his presence briefly to appear in the novel, only to be immediately rejected as repetitive, unconvincing and dishonest.

Trollope's *North America*

Such disparagement of Trollope's work was begun early, not least by Trollope himself in his posthumous *Autobiography*. The plot of *The Bertrams*, for example, he described as 'more than ordinarily bad', *Castle Richmond* 'as a whole . . . a failure' and *Ralph the Heir* 'one of the worst novels I have written'.[6] Perhaps the most brutal self-dismissal, though, is of his 1862 travel book *North America* which he describes as:

> not well done. It is tedious and confused, and will hardly, I think, be of future value to those who wish to make themselves acquainted with the United States . . . [M]y book . . . was not a good book. I can recommend no one to read it now in order that he may be either instructed or amused.[7]

The strangeness of this judgement is worth emphasising. Authors, we imagine, write in order to remember things and to be remembered, to create something of value to be sent into an unknown future. Trollope here will have none of that. Unlike, say, a typical politician, whose memoir is characteristically full of self-regard and self-justification, Trollope is happy to let his labours go. Its damning tone is remarkable: it is not a matter of modest self-deprecation but more like that of a frank contemporary, an editor or headmaster perhaps. The book, Trollope knows, will continue to exist but he can recommend it to no one. Such a brusque dismissal leaves admiring readers of his work in something of a double bind. If such readers wished to know Trollope's work well, they would need to know this book, but to be faithful to his autobiographical injunction, they should not read it. But the reader is not quite forbidden to read the book, simply warned off, as Trollope did not withdraw *North America* or forbid republication. If for no other reason, this should make it interesting to us. It is not the only text that Trollope dismisses in his *Autobiography* (although this is one of the most hostile judgements) but the strangeness of permitting yet so powerfully discouraging its reading seems to have been little registered by his critics or admirers.

Apart from its marginal, disavowed position in Trollope's oeuvre, there is an even stronger reason to take *North America* seriously; for we know that at least one important admirer of the book defied his discouragement. A very different twentieth-century writer from either Powell or Pritchett, the poet Elizabeth Bishop had a much more creative relationship to Trollope's writing than they, and an attitude to the book a good deal less dismissive than that of the writer himself. Whereas Jenkins sought to salvage some good qualities in Trollope through praising his characterisation and narrative scope in creating a 'portrait of the times', Bishop takes a different and more subtle route. Her reading of *North America* finds its significance not as a Victorian period piece, but as a text of a strangely doubled temporality, existing simultaneously in Trollope's time in the 1860s and in Bishop's, a century later. What Bishop finds to admire in Trollope is not amplitude or range, has little to do with characterisation and is barely a matter of narrative. Instead she created a poem from a very short passage from the book that is concerned with one foggy day in Washington, DC, a broken monument, a sick man and some cattle. Bishop's poem, 'From Trollope's Journal', does not try either to emulate or to resist Trollope's major fiction but finds poetic significance in a marginal, non-fictional text that the author himself rejected. It should make us think again and differently about Trollope's work, but not in order to show that *North America* is an important but neglected masterpiece, or to argue that it contains a subtext that makes it peculiarly revelatory about Trollope's life or work. Rather, Bishop's creative response to Trollope matters because it created an important poem and because it helps us see a strangeness and subtlety to Trollope's art that is often lost in critical accounts focused on the larger structures and developments of his narratives.

Bishop's most celebrated poem, the villanelle 'One Art', is about 'the art of losing', an art, the poem tells us, that 'isn't hard to master':

> so many things seem filled with the intent
> to be lost that their loss is no disaster.[8]

The subject matter of 'One Art', which it also models in its form, is an anti-monumental art; it is one that she also practises on Trollope's *North America*, a book that seems, to use Bishop's words from the poem, 'filled with the intent / to be lost'. In 'From Trollope's Journal', she transforms this near-lost book by Trollope into something that is very faithful to its precursor-text, indeed partly voiced in Trollope's own words, and radically different from it. Like Powell and Pritchett, she too thinks about war when she thinks about Trollope; not as an escape, irrelevance, air-raid shelter or capitulation, however, but as a strangely prescient augur of modern America, and the pervasiveness of war within it.

Unlike Bishop, most of posterity has followed Trollope's advice. There have thus been relatively few readers of the book and fewer admirers, and it has not loomed large in modern criticism and scholarship. Although Amanda Claybaugh has described Trollope as 'one of the most discerning' of nineteenth-century travel writers who wrote about British–American relations, hers is an isolated voice.[9] *North America* is taken for granted in the main as yet one more nineteenth-century travel book about the United States, an unnecessary latecomer behind Frances Trollope's *Domestic Manners of the Americans* (1832), Charles Dickens's *American Notes* (1842) and many, many more, its content seemingly as dull as its title. It has usually been abridged when reprinted, as in Bradford Booth's 1951 edition and the even shorter Penguin edition of 1969.[10] The *Oxford Reader's Companion to Trollope* reports that 'We fret over its flatness and turn with relief to the rounded world of his imagination.'[11] Yet there are striking and important things within *North America*, not least its description of Washington in the winter of 1861, that turning point in the history of the modern United States when Lincoln was in the White House and the country in the midst of Civil War. It was a difficult time to be in the capital, and for Trollope particularly so as war between the United States and Great Britain over the 'Trent' affair seemed likely.[12] The city was full of more than 200,000 Union soldiers, with sentries on each street corner and great herds of cattle ready to be slaughtered to feed them. To Trollope, it seemed folly to have built (or half-built) a new capital in such an unlikely place and he found the whole experience a deeply dismal one, made worse by his suffering from a painful anthrax on his face.

The chapter he wrote about his time in Washington is particularly significant because a century later it inspired Bishop's double sonnet 'From Trollope's Journal (Winter, 1861)', which drew directly not from a 'Journal' (for there is none) but from *North America* and Trollope's letters. Instead of seeking to capture Trollope's narrative breadth or fictional invention, Bishop selects a short passage of reportage, from one of his least-known books. Despite the formal contrast – short poem, long book – the verbal closeness of the two works is striking. Bishop herself wrote to Robert Lowell to say that 'It's almost word for word out of *North America*' and that 'The whole thing should really be in quotation marks, I suppose; the reason it doesn't sound like me is because it sounds like Trollope . . . Have you read his *North America*? I just copied out some of the Washington chapter.'[13] This account of the poem's relation to its precursor text has broadly been accepted by critics of Bishop. Few seem to have looked at the relevant Trollope passages, wrongly describing Trollope's account as a 'cynical' one, for example.[14] But it is an unnecessarily self-deprecating, indeed misleading, account of the poem, whose creative relationship with its precursor is both a significant achievement in itself and markedly different from our usual sense of what twentieth-century readers found either to admire or dislike in Trollope's work. His bulk has usually been answered with yet more bulk, his Stakhanovite fictional labours by a matching or competing scholarly productivity whose dominant genres have been large-scale biographies, editions and criticism. Bishop's poetic concision could not be more different. John Ruskin praised Robert Browning's poem 'The Bishop orders his Tomb in Saint Praxed's Church' as containing 'nearly all that I said of the central Renaissance in thirty pages of The Stones of Venice put into as many lines' and Bishop seems to have had a similar epitomising or condensing ambition with Trollope's work, in even briefer compass.[15] Two of Bishop's most celebrated poems, 'Casabianca' and 'The Gentleman of Shalott', draw on and revise influential nineteenth-century poems: Felicia Hemans's 'Casabianca' ('The boy stood on the burning deck', 1826) and Tennyson's 'The Lady of Shalott' (1832). Bishop is able to release a disconcerting conceptual or erotic energy from these familiar anthology pieces, in 'Casabianca' through unsettlingly selective quotation and repetition:

Love's the boy stood on the burning deck
trying to recite 'The boy stood on
the burning deck'.[16]

She does something similar, if less radical, to Trollope's more unlikely precursor text.

Bishop read widely in Victorian prose as well as poetry, including the works of Trollope, Charles Dickens and Thomas Carlyle. 'Our century', her friend Robert Lowell wrote to her, 'really can't match the best Victorians for nonfictional prose' and Bishop seemed to concur.[17] This at first may seem surprising, as it would be hard to imagine a sharper contrast between these authors' writing methods and bodies of work, and her own. She published fewer than one hundred short lyric poems; Trollope, by contrast, almost as many lengthy prose volumes (forty-seven novels, many in three volumes, as well as several travel books and biographies). She was the serial non-completer, he an unstoppable writing machine. In their writings, an art of economy and concision meets an art of accumulation and expansion; an oeuvre of monumental size is met by a non-monumental art; and in her poem, formal perfection is wrought from a loose baggy monster. Bishop, like her friend Marianne Moore, admired Trollope greatly, reading much of his work and, perhaps anticipating Mark Turner's revelation of 'queer Trollope' by half a century, commended his 'queer travel stories' to Lowell.[18] She was not just an attentive but also a creative reader, driven by a desire to rework and re-voice the Victorian authors she so admired: 'I am also reading at bedtime all of Dickens, volume by volume, with the strange ambition of writing, or rather finishing, one sonnet about him.'[19] She never completed the Dickens sonnet nor finished 'Mr and Mrs Carlyle', a poem that tries to condense the Carlyles' lifetime of marital strife into a pocket-size poem that culminates in the remarkable detached quatrain;

> One flesh and two heads
>   engaged in kisses or in pecks
> Oh white seething marriage!
>   Oh Swan with two necks![20]

The Carlyles in five stanzas, Dickens in a sonnet, Trollope in two. Victorian literary elephants give birth to powerful modern poetic mice.

'From Trollope's Journal'

'From Trollope's Journal (1861)' is the penultimate poem in Bishop's 1965 collection *Questions of Travel*, forming a concluding pair or diptych with 'Visits to St Elizabeth's', her celebrated poem about her post-war visits to Ezra Pound in the asylum near Washington which begins:

> This is the house of Bedlam.
> This is the man
> that lies in the house of Bedlam.[21]

The only two poems in the collection with dates in their titles ('1951' for 'St Elizabeth's', 'Winter 1861' for 'From Trollope's Journal'), both poems are about visits to Washington; both about remarkable, prolific male authors, one 'mad', one robustly sane, who have come there from abroad: Trollope from England, Pound from Italy; both are about illness of different sorts; and both are compact poems that refract a good deal of thought about the politics of the United States in the mid-twentieth century through their literary prisms; both are about powerful men who find themselves in the American capital under treatment and at a loss.

The immediate origins of the Trollope poem can be traced to a visit that Bishop made to the newly built Brasilia in 1958 with Aldous Huxley, about which she wrote her longest piece of non-fictional prose, an article which was intended for the *New Yorker* but rejected by it – as indeed was 'From Trollope's Journal'.[22] After some critical remarks about Brasilia, Bishop makes a striking parallel, quoting loosely from Trollope:

> Another English author [i.e. Trollope], more outspoken than Huxley, wrote 'I have a strong idea . . . that no man can ordain that on such a spot shall be built a great and thriving city . . . There is much desolate land within the country, but I think that none is so desolate as three-fourths of the ground on which is supposed to stand the city . . . [T]he land is wild, trackless, unabridged, uninhabited, and desolate. . . .
>
> For myself, I do not believe in cities made after this fashion. Commerce, I think, must elect the site of all large congregations of mankind'. . . .

These are a few of Anthony Trollope's gentler comments on the city of Washington in 1861. The United States of the nineteenth century and the Brazil of the twentieth are not, perhaps, really very comparable; however, Trollope, and his mother, and all the many other prophets of failure were wrong about Washington, and it behooves Americans to be particularly careful in predictions about Brasilia.[23]

Thinking about Brasilia, Bishop thinks of Washington a century earlier, another raw, unfinished capital with an unsympathetic climate, and asks herself how it might appear to a visitor from outside. Bishop here sees Trollope as essentially wrong in the judgement that he made a century before. Brasilia might look raw, but so too did Washington a century ago and Bishop's fellow Americans should learn from this, and not dismiss the prospect of Brasilia flourishing in the future, as Washington does now. The desolate nature of 1860s Washington gave no sense of what it would become a century later, and so contemporary citizens of the USA should not rush to patronise or condemn Brasilia. The point is deftly made but when Bishop later comes to write her poem about the very same passage from Trollope's book, the valency changes. In 'From Trollope's Journal', there is no comparison made with Brasilia, and no prospect held out of future improvement. The relationship between past and present is not one, as in the article, of contrast but of analogy; Washington was unpleasant then, and it is unclear that it is any better now. We are led to see Trollope not as wrongly condemnatory but strangely prescient. In the article, Bishop suggests that Trollope got it wrong; in her poem, he gets it substantially right. It is a work, perhaps unsurprisingly, of deep ambivalence: Robert Lowell, the great friend and admirer of Bishop and her work, initially misunderstood its intent. Ironically, given that Bishop told him it was 'probably very much influenced by you', Lowell radically misinterpreted the poem, at first taking it 'as a spoof at the superficial condescending English'.[24] Bishop's target was not Trollope, though, but the Washington he saw and which she felt had deep continuities with its 1950s incarnation. Lowell eventually came to agree, writing to her that 'Trollope, the more I read it the more I think he was right about Washington.'[25]

'From Trollope's Journal' is a dramatic monologue, that nineteenth-century form reinvigorated for Bishop's generation by Lowell's 1951 *Mills of the Kavanaghs*, and a poem about many things: about the nature of monumentality and public commemoration in the art of statuary; about the ubiquitous disease and infection that Trollope finds; about unfinished things in uncertain states and what might be cut out or cut away; and about war. It presents a marshy, melancholy capital and an unnamed and decidedly unheroic Lincoln, the 'present President', the diminishing phrase (and diminished, the second word shrinking back into the first) both cutting down Lincoln and pointing to Eisenhower, Bishop's present President and another soldier who poisons the air. A poem from civilian life in the midst of a terrible modern war, in a place full of soldiers and cattle about to die, 'From Trollope's Journal' begins with a strange repetition of 'far':

As far as statues go, so far there's not
much choice: they're either Washingtons
or Indians, a whitewashed, stubby lot,
His country's Father or His foster sons.[26]

The poem seems to ask at its very beginning how far it can go – or Washington has come – since Trollope's visit. A statue, of course, is fixed and can't go at all, let alone go far. The poem swiftly draws a Washington going nowhere; only so far as a statue might go, on heavy ground in which Trollope

> wandered, – rather,
> I floundered, . . . (ll. 9–10)

Surrounded by standing, 'wond'ring' cattle, their legs seemingly caked in blood, Trollope finds himself at a loss, overcome by pity for the

> Poor, starving, dumb
> or lowing creatures . . . (ll. 20–1)

Characteristically for Bishop, it is a landscape from which the human is excluded, as the sociability and proliferation of characters we naturally identify with Trollope's fiction have disappeared to leave a solitary man surrounded by 'numberless' cattle standing in mud.[27] Everything is unfinished and between states: 'half-ice, half-mud' or 'wreathed with fog', sick or about to die. The president has 'ague or fever'; the capital city is inhabited by animals and statues; the author is lost and alone. Forms of centrality – presidential, capital, authorial, human – become peripheral.

'The Strangeness of his Undertaking'

Perhaps the most famous judgement on Trollope by one of his contemporaries was also by an American, his fellow novelist, Nathaniel Hawthorne, who asked in a letter to the American publisher James T. Fields:

> Have you ever read the novels of Anthony Trollope? They precisely suit my taste; solid, substantial, written on strength of beef and through inspiration of ale, and just as real as if some giant had hewn a great lump out of the earth and put it under a glass case, with all its inhabitants going about their daily business, and not suspecting that they were made a show of.[28]

Trollope approvingly quotes this judgement in his *Autobiography* and adds that

> the criticism, whether just or unjust, describes with wonderful accuracy the purport that I have ever had in view in my writing. I have always desired 'to hew out some lump of the earth' and to make men and women walk upon it just as they do walk here among us.[29]

Trollope, for Hawthorne and for the novelist himself, is a writer the virtues of whose fiction lie in transparency ('under a glass jar'), dense materiality and specificity ('some lump of the earth') and which has human beings as its central concern ('to make men and women walk upon it'). Trollope in this view is a novelist of strength and Englishness, a man of beef and ale. But the poem draws our attention to a very different relationship between Trollope and a 'lump of the earth', which he here finds intractable, heavy going, impossible to be lifted up or easily seen, lost as it is in fog. Statues and animals matter as much as humans to the passage as the poem presents a Trollope who is not a giant of confidence and beefy self-belief, but a sick man, lost in heavy ground.

Bishop, who had lived in Washington when she was Poet Laureate to the Library of Congress from 1949 to 1950, wrote a number of poems about the city, including 'View of the Capitol from the Library of Congress', which – like 'From Trollope's Journal' – have a complex relationship to their 'Cold War' context.[30] And in this poem, as in the USA in the depths of the Cold War, temporary thaws are followed by freezes. Washington in the 1860s, like Washington in the 1950s, is a place and time in which 'everyone's sick' or unhealthy: the White House is built 'in a sad, unhealthy spot'; the President 'has got / ague or fever in each backwoods limb'; the soldiers 'poison the air'; Trollope himself has a 'damned anthrax on [his] forehead', even the surgeon who treats him has 'a sore throat himself'. Voice is emptied or edited out: the cattle are 'dumb / or lowing', the doctor croaks, Bishop's voice is lost in Trollope's, Trollope's in Bishop's. Indeed, in a letter to Robert Lowell, she calls it an 'anti-Eisenhower poem' but does so in a decidedly equivocal way. It is, she writes, 'actually an anti-Eisenhower poem, I think', with a phrasing that like the poem itself both asserts – 'actually an anti-Eisenhower poem' – and withdraws from that assertion – 'I think'. Seemingly uncertain how far it wants to go in its criticism or its politics, it seems stuck like the cattle as it works across the heavy ground of what we could call its political melancholy.[31]

The sole surviving draft of the poem consists for the most part of verbatim extracts from the book.[32] In her poetic appropriation of Victorian prose into poetry, Bishop has an important precursor in W. B. Yeats who famously versified Walter Pater's description of Leonardo's 'Mona Lisa' in *The Renaissance* ('She is older than the rocks among which she sits; like the vampire she has been dead many times') as the opening item in his *Oxford Book of Modern Verse 1892–1935*, although the more prosaic Trollope would seem to be a much less likely candidate for such treatment. Whereas Yeats selected a highly wrought, evocative purple passage of Pater's prose, Bishop chooses a more quotidian and workmanlike author and passage to transform. Here, for example, is Trollope on the cattle that he sees in the centre of Washington, ready to be slaughtered to feed the Union army, then in the middle of fighting the American Civil War:

> A sad and saddening spot was that marsh, as I wandered down on it all alone one Sunday afternoon. The ground was frozen and I could walk dry-shod, but there was not a blade of grass. Around me on all sides were cattle in great numbers – steers and big oxen – lowing in their hunger for a meal. They were beef for the army, and never again I suppose would it be allowed to them to fill their big maws and chew the patient cud.[33]

This is a clear origin for the first quatrain of the second sonnet, where Bishop takes Trollope's cattle, 'maw' and 'cud' in her description of the

> Poor, starving, dumb
> or lowing creatures, never to chew the cud
> or fill their maws again! (ll. 20–2)

Elsewhere she both revises and subtracts, cutting down Trollope's two volumes to two sonnets, with admiring if ruthless poetic economy. The poem begins, for example, with a description of the many statues in the city:

> As far as statues go, so far there's not
> much choice: they're either Washingtons
> or Indians, a whitewashed, stubby lot,
> His country's Father or His foster sons. (ll. 1–4)

This is taken from Trollope's more robustly satirical observations:

> Statuary at Washington runs too much on two subjects, who are repeated perhaps almost ad nauseam; one is that of a stiff, steady-looking, healthy, but ugly individual, with a square jaw and big jowl, which represents the great General [Washington]; he does not prepossess the beholder, because he appears to be thoroughly ill-natured. And the other represents a melancholy, weak figure without any hair, but often covered with feathers, and is intended to typify the red Indian. The red Indian is generally supposed to be receiving comfort; but it is manifest that he never enjoys the comfort ministered to him.[34]

Sometimes the rather pedestrian phrasing of the poem – 'wreathed with fog', 'caked in mud' – is, perhaps surprisingly, Bishop's own rather than Trollope's but she adds here, for example, the telling and racially inflected 'whitewashed' and 'foster-sons' to describe the statues of Native Americans.

One of the most striking omissions in Bishop's use of Trollope is of the object at the centre of Trollope's chapter, his 'type of the city', the Washington monument, whose construction was begun in 1848 but halted for more than twenty years due to a lack of funding, political conflict and the Civil War. As Trollope puts it:

> It is unfinished, – not a third of it having as yet been erected, – and in all human probability ever will remain so. If finished it would be the highest monument of its kind standing on the face of the globe, – and yet, after all, what would it be even then as compared with one of the great pyramids? . . . No one has a word to say for it. No one thinks that money will ever again be subscribed for its completion. I saw somewhere a box of plate-glass kept for contributions for this purpose, and looking in perceived that two half-dollar pieces had been given; – but both of them were bad. I was told also that the absolute foundation of the edifice is bad; – that the ground, which is near the river and swampy, would not bear the weight intended to be imposed on it. . . . It was as though I were looking on the genius of the city. It was vast, pretentious, bold, boastful with a loud voice, already taller by many heads than other obelisks, but nevertheless still in its infancy, – ugly, unpromising, and false.[35]

Pretentious, unfinished, unnecessary and impossible to complete – the 'genius of the city' for Trollope, unmentioned in Bishop; the passage is included in the draft but absent from the poem itself.

In rewriting Trollope's travel book as a double sonnet and calling it 'From Trollope's Journal', Bishop simultaneously makes it more intimate, informal and self-communing (like a journal), and more formally elaborated and 'literary': a double striction within and through which the poem works. It has on the whole a rather flat diction and two of the more 'Victorian' and suggestive terms – 'effluvium' (an overflowing of minute particles, an exhalation, or disgusting odour) and 'anthrax' – are not taken from Trollope's book at all. The latter term is added from one of his letters of the period and forms the most striking addition to the poem.[36] Although Trollope says that he was 'hardly out of the doctor's hands' when in Washington, and quotes the doctor's view that the air was 'poisoned by the soldiers . . . and everybody is ill', the word 'anthrax' does not appear at all. An acute and often fatal disease that killed thousands of people and animals before vaccines were developed in the late nineteenth century and mid-twentieth century, its progressive elimination was accompanied by its industrial weaponisation. Both superpowers were stockpiling large quantities of anthrax weapons throughout the 1950s and 60s and it is hard not to think of this context for Bishop's poem, so close together does it put the soldiers, the anthrax and the poisoned air. Earlier in the decade the USA had been accused of deploying anthrax in the Korean War; nuclear fallout seemed an equally present possibility. The doctor would have meant the words literally, in a period when miasma theory was still dominant; the phrase is allowed to resonate more widely, the spores of the anthrax to stick to our face and clothing too.

As Bishop's concern with America's wars of the nineteenth and twentieth centuries become apparent in the poem, it is hard not to be reminded of another double sonnet concerned with war, which became probably the best-known war poem of the twentieth century. Bishop's poem is a good deal less polemical than Wilfred Owen's 'Dulce et Decorum est', is the work of a civilian in time of peace and a much more implicit, understated and reticent poem, but nevertheless owes an intelligently revisionary debt to this precursor. Bishop's poem does not simply have the same double-sonnet form as Owen's but is also concerned, albeit indirectly, with chemical warfare. She does not mention 'Dulce et Decorum est' in her letters or other writings but her knowledge of Owen's work is clear, writing in 1943 to tell her friend Lloyd Frankenberg that 'I've just re-read all of [poet Wilfred] Owen' this morning.'[37] Indeed, she borrows the rhyming in 'Dulce et Decorum est' of 'cud' and 'blood' and ends 'From Trollope's Journal', as Owen does his poem, with a quotation: his 'old lie' becomes in Bishop's poem the damning words of the doctor who treats Trollope's anthrax:

'Sir, I do declare
everyone's sick! The soldiers poison the air'. (ll. 27–8)

The soldiers, of course, poison (and are poisoned by) the air in 'Dulce et Decorum est' too, and both poems present a world in which 'everyone's sick!' The cattle in Bishop's poem are 'caked the colour of dried blood', just as the soldiers in 'Dulce et Decorum est' are 'blood-shod'.

What Bishop seems to most admire in Trollope's work is his literal-mindedness, his ability to allow observed reality to suggest but not pass too quickly into symbol or figure. He seems to share the plain-spokenness, the 'daylight clarity' that Seamus Heaney has noted in her work, of 'justice being done to the facts of the situation'.[38] It was a quality that Bishop also found in the work of Charles Darwin, about whom she wrote a celebrated letter praising the beautiful solid case . . . built up out of his endless, heroic observations, almost unconscious or automatic – and then comes a sudden relaxation, a forgetful phrase, and one feels the strangeness of his undertaking, sees the lonely young man, his eyes fixed on facts and minute details, sinking or sliding giddily off into the unknown. What one seems to want in art, in experiencing it, is the same thing that is necessary for its creation, a self-forgetful, perfectly useless concentration.[39]

That quality of heroic observation and of a 'self-forgetful, perfectly useless concentration' that is suddenly punctuated by a relaxation that intimates the vulnerability of the observer and the strangeness of the scene might well describe Trollope in Washington too, as he seems not the over-confident, opinionated blusterer of many biographical accounts or the monumental author of the library shelves, but lost, vulnerable and different.

Trollope takes the fragments of the Washington monument as the type and genius of the city; Bishop takes fragments from his monumental oeuvre as a fair type and genius of its author. At first the poem may seem politically to muffle itself, or to muffle Trollope's critique, satire or disgust at the Washington he saw, in omitting the half-built monument so central to his understanding of its pretentious boastfulness. Lowell's initial misreading of the poem is revealing, and it might seem as if Bishop's is part of the failure of much post-war American lyric to rise to its political occasions. But in substituting the unmentioned anthrax for the unfinished monument, the invisible particles for the all too visible stones, she sharpens the poem's edge. 'From Trollope's Journal' does not try to build a monument to Trollope's work, as many scholars, critics and editors have done, but cuts it down, as it also cuts down the stubby statues of Washingtons and 'Indians', and the polity, then and now, that made them. Seamus Heaney described Bishop's poem 'Sestina' as 'a Victorian genre piece, almost'; the same term, with the same qualification, could be used also of 'From Trollope's Journal'.[40] Bishop takes a fragment of Trollope's monumental oeuvre to create a distinctly un-monumental work that is profoundly sceptical about men and their monuments, simultaneously a guerrilla raid and posthumous possession, which winnows his messy bulk into a meditative tightness. It returns us to Trollope as a different kind of reader, aware of, to quote the Darwin letter, 'the strangeness of his undertaking', that of a hunting man who is most insightful when he finds the ground heavy going, like Darwin a 'lonely . . . man . . . sinking or sliding into the unknown'. It is a very different Trollope from the hard-working modern professional of contemporary criticism.[41] The poem cuts Trollope down without cutting him down to size, allowing his words (which are also her words) to resonate or infect us through their minute particles or particulars across, between and beyond the two authors, genders, centuries, continents, texts, volumes and sonnets that are at play. Bishop's is an art of salvage as much as an art of losing, although she has to lose most of Trollope to do that necessary work. There may have been few admirers of this book, but that one, and her one art, may suffice.

Notes

1. Christopher Ricks, 'The Novelist as Critic', in Lisa Rodensky (ed.), *The Oxford Handbook of the Victorian Novel* (Oxford: Oxford University Press, 2013), p. 635.
2. R. C. Terry (ed.), *Oxford Reader's Companion to Trollope* (Oxford: Oxford University Press, 1999), pp. 129–39.

3. *New Statesman* 8 June 1946, p. 415, as quoted in Terry (ed.), *Oxford Reader's Companion to Trollope*, p. 130.

4. Anthony Powell, *The Soldier's Art* (London: Fontana, 1979), pp. 47–8.

5. On the apotropaic, see, for example, J. Hillis Miller, 'The Critic as Host', *Critical Inquiry*, 3.3 (1977), p. 446.

6. Anthony Trollope, *An Autobiography and Other Writings*, ed. Nicholas Shrimpton (Oxford: Oxford University Press, 2014), p. 83, p. 100, p. 212.

7. Trollope, *An Autobiography*, pp. 104–6. By contrast, Trollope calls his travel book *The West Indies and the Spanish Main* (London: Chapman and Hall, 1859) 'the best book that has come from my pen': Trollope, *An Autobiography*, p. 84.

8. Bishop, *The Complete Poems 1926–1979* (London: Chatto and Windus, 1983), p. 178.

9. Amanda Claybaugh, 'Trollope and America', in Carolyn Dever and Lisa Niles (eds), *The Cambridge Companion to Anthony Trollope*, (Cambridge: Cambridge University Press, 2011), p. 211. See also Lauren M. E. Goodlad, *The Victorian Geopolitical Aesthetic: Realism, Sovereignty, and Transnational Experience* (Oxford: Oxford University Press, 2015), pp. 77–80.

10. Anthony Trollope, *North America*, ed. Donald Smalley and Bradford Allen Booth (New York: Knopf, 1951). Anthony Trollope, *North America*, ed. Robert Mason (Harmondsworth: Penguin, 1968).

11. *Oxford Reader's Companion to Trollope*, p. 394.

12. On the Trent affair, see N. John Hall, *Trollope: A Biography* (Oxford: Oxford University Press, 1993), p. 233.

13. Bishop to Lowell, 29 June 1960, *Words in Air: The Complete Correspondence between Elizabeth Bishop and Robert Lowell*, ed. Thomas Travisano with Saskia Hamilton (New York: Farrar, Straus and Giroux, 2008), p. 330; Bishop to Lowell, 27 July 1960, in *Words in Air*, p. 332. Five years later, Bishop made the same point, describing the poem as 'really almost all Trollope – phrase after phrase'; Bishop to Lowell, 18 November 1965, in *Words in Air*, p. 594. Lowell replied 'Why isn't it yours if you rimed and metered it so beautifully?'; Lowell to Bishop, 24 November 1965, in *Words in Air*, p. 597.

14. Jay Prosser, *Light in the Dark Room: Poetry and Loss* (Minneapolis: University of Minnesota Press, 2004), p. 151. It is closer to what Colm Tóibín characterises as Bishop's tone 'of mild, distracted, solitary unease'; see Colm Tóibín, *On Elizabeth Bishop* (Princeton: Princeton University Press, 2015), p. 5.

15. John Ruskin, *Modern Painters*, vol. 4 (London: George Allen, 1892), p. 379.

16. Elizabeth Bishop, 'Casabianca', in *Complete Poems* (London: Chatto and Windus, 1991), p. 5. On Bishop's attunement to Hemans's poem's 'status as the preeminent choice for memorization and recitation by children of the British Empire', see Catherine Robson, 'Standing on the Burning Deck: Poetry, Performance, History', *PMLA*, 120.1 (2005): p. 148.

17. Lowell to Bishop, 1 January 1954, in *Words in Air*, p. 151; Bishop to Lowell, 30 November 30 1954, in *Words in Air*, p. 154.

18. Bishop to Lowell, 5 December 1953, in *Words in Air*, p. 147. Mark Turner, *Trollope and the Magazines: Gendered Issues in Mid-Victorian Britain* (London: Palgrave, 2000). Marianne Moore compiled a list of the greatest literary works for the book *Pour une bibliothèque idéale*, edited by Raymond Queneau. In a short list she included both Trollope's *Autobiography* and *Phineas Finn*, but no Dickens, George Eliot or Brontës. Moore also wrote an unpublished novel entitled, after Trollope, *The Way We Live Now*.

19. Bishop to Kit and Ilse Barker, 29 August 1953, in Elizabeth Bishop, *One Art: Letters*, ed. Robert Giroux (New York: Farrar, Straus and Giroux, 1994), p. 270. See also Bishop's letter to Joseph and U. T. Summers, 9 December 1953, in *One Art*, p. 283: 'I also read all of Dickens, Trollope, Freud', and letter of 30 November 1954 to Lowell, in *Words in Air*, p. 154: 'I've been reading Dickens too, volume by volume, and having a wonderful time. That abundance and playfulness and slopping all over the place is so wonderful.'

20. Elizabeth Bishop, 'Mr and Mrs Carlyle', in *Poems, Prose, and Letters*, ed. Robert Giroux and Lloyd Schwartz (New York: Library of America, 2008), p. 264. The Dickens sonnet 'does not survive'; *Words in Air*, p. 149n.
21. Bishop, *Complete Poems*, p. 133, ll. 1–3.
22. Elizabeth Bishop, 'A New Capital, Aldous Huxley, and Some Indians' (1958), in *Poems, Prose, and Letters*, pp. 365–401.
23. Ibid. pp. 400–1.
24. Lowell to Bishop, 28 October 1965, in *Words in Air*, p. 591.
25. Bishop to Lowell 19 May 1960, in *One Art* 327. Lowell to Bishop, 28 October 1965, in *One Art*, p. 591.
26. Bishop, *Complete Poems*, p. 132, ll. 1–4. Further references to the poem have line numbers in the text.
27. On landscapes 'from which we are excluded' in Bishop's work, see David Kalstone, *Five Temperaments* (New York: Oxford University Press, 1977), p. 24.
28. Hawthorne's letter to the American publisher James T. Fields (11 February 1860) is quoted in Trollope, *Autobiography*, p. 93.
29. Trollope, *Autobiography*, p. 94.
30. Camille Roman, *Elizabeth Bishop's World War II–Cold War View* (New York: Palgrave, 2001). On Bishop's politics, see also Steven Gould Axelrod, 'Bishop, History, Politics', in Angus Cleghorn and Jonathan Ellis (eds), *The Cambridge Companion to Elizabeth Bishop* (Cambridge: Cambridge University Press, 2014), pp. 35–48; Steven Gould Axelrod, 'Between Modernism and Postmodernism: The Cold War Poetics of Bishop, Lowell, and Ginsberg', *Pacific Coast Philology*, 42.1 (2007): pp. 1–23; and Steven Gould Axelrod, 'Elizabeth Bishop and Containment Policy', *American Literature*, 75.4 (2003): pp. 843–67.
31. Bishop to Lowell, 18 November 1965, in *Words in Air*, p. 594. Tóibín notes her 'characteristically self-correcting' idiom; *On Elizabeth Bishop*, p. 7.
32. Now in Vassar College. Possible titles were 'Trollope Looks At Washington' and 'Trollope in Washington'.
33. Anthony Trollope, *North America*, vol. 2 (Philadelphia: Lippincott, 1863), ch. 1, p. 20.
34. Ibid. vol. 2 , ch. 1, p. 12.
35. Ibid. vol. 2 , ch. 1, p. 19.
36. Anthony Trollope to Kate Field, 17 December 1861: 'I am in a lamentable position. I have an anthrax on my forehead & can not get out of the house . . . A doctor has chopped it across twice . . . But the chops will keep healing and the thing which has collected inside will not come out. Tomorrow it is to be chopped again and the chops cauterised to prevent their healing'; *The Letters of Anthony Trollope*, ed. N. John Hall (Stanford: Stanford University Press, 1983), pp. 164–5. Bishop will presumably have known the letter from its appearance in Bradford A. Booth, *The Letters of Anthony Trollope* (Oxford: Oxford University Press, 1951).
37. Bishop to Lloyd Frankenburg, 29 June 1943, in *One Art*, p. 112.
38. Seamus Heaney, *The Redress of Poetry: Oxford Lectures* (London: Faber and Faber, 1995), p. 168.
39. Bishop to Ann Stevenson, 8–20 January 1964, in *Poems, Prose, and Letters*, p. 861.
40. Heaney, *The Redress of Poetry*, pp. 168–9.
41. Nicholas Dames, 'Trollope and the Career: Vocational Trajectories and the Management of Ambition', *Victorian Studies*, 45.2 (2003): pp. 247–78; Amanda Anderson, 'Trollope's Modernity', *ELH*, 74.3 (2007): pp. 509–34.

9

THE WAY WE COUNTERLIVE NOW: TROLLOPE'S FICTIONAL HERITAGE

Luca Caddia

TROLLOPE'S READERS AND CRITICS will be familiar with major writers' picturesque views of him, from Nathaniel Hawthorne's panoptical giant to Henry James's 'novelist who hunted the fox'.[1] But what if one were to examine the image of Trollope in works of fiction in lieu of articles and letters? Hardly a writer's writer, the mid-Victorian novelist has some claim to be recognised as a '*characters*' writer' since his conspicuous appearance in other authors' stories is often expressed through the medium of their fictional creatures. This chapter argues that these appearances are part of what one may call 'Trollope's fictional heritage'. A complete inventory of Trollope's fictional heritage would of course also have to include sequels, adaptations or original stories set in the places that Trollope himself had conceived.[2] The present chapter has a critical purpose more than an encyclopaedic one, however, and therefore leaves the long list of fiction that aims to compete with Trollope on the same ground out of its focus. Instead, it examines a number of original works from the twentieth and the twenty-first centuries in which references to Trollope not only inform the economy of single narratives, but may be read analytically as whole pieces of Trollope criticism. In particular, the following pages aim to demonstrate that these works make a substantial, if not always coherent, use of Trollope to express concerns with the interior life of the self-conscious character, a subject that in this article will be generally referred to as a 'counterlife'. This word has been borrowed from Philip Roth's eponymous novel from 1986, in which a conversation on and an original reconstruction of a section of *The Way We Live Now*, so far unacknowledged, provides some deep insight into Trollope's fiction. I will adapt and develop this idea to accommodate the way in which Trollope figures in later works, convinced as I am that it is possible to identify the issue at stake as a common denominator.

The Counterlife (1986) is a novel that takes an antagonistic attitude towards the literary tradition that it informally comments upon: in a way, one could even say that it expresses reverence for it through its paradoxical breakdown; this act of empowerment is meant, among other things, to affirm the role of the author within a revitalised canon. While any sort of realistic narration may be considered as a counterlife, insofar as it reflects on real life itself, in this novel the 'counterlives' represent alternatives to the main story: the volume's five parts offer different possibilities of narrative development for Nathan Zuckerman, a character who stars quite often in Roth's oeuvre and who has been perceived as the author's alter ego by virtue of his successful literary career.

One of the main subjects of the story is the protagonist's Jewishness which, as a cosmopolitan New Yorker, he never takes into account except when geographic reasons compel him to do so. When Zuckerman travels to Israel, for instance, he clashes with his brother's fanatical clique, who have made Zionism the quintessence of their identity. More importantly, when he is introduced to his wife Maria's family in England, he discovers that her relatives, members of the decadent gentry, are profoundly anti-Semitic. For the 45-year-old Zuckerman, who had met his 28-year-old wife in New York where a relationship between individuals as individuals is a real possibility, this English experience proves challenging because his Jewishness is treated prejudicially. The episode that matters the most here has to do with a conversation he has with Maria's abrasive sister Sarah, who suggests that Nathan read *The Way We Live Now* in order to realise that his 'pathetic yearning to partake of English civility' is incompatible with the British anti-Semitism so realistically portrayed in Trollope's novel.

> 'I do think Maria should have told you that she is from the sort of people who, if you knew anything about English society, you would have expected to be anti-Semitic . . . I recommend beginning your education with . . . Trollope. . . . It may knock some of the stuffing from your pathetic yearning to partake of English civility. It will tell you all about people like us. Read *The Way We Live Now*. It may help to explode those myths that fuel the pathetic Jewish Anglophilia Maria's cashing in on. The book is rather like a soap opera, but the main meat of it from your point of view is a little subplot, an account of Miss Longestaffe, an English young lady from an upper-class home, sort of country gentry, a bit over the hill, and she's furious that nobody's married her, . . . and because she's determined to have a rich social life in London, she's going to demean herself by marrying a middle-aged Jew'. . . .
>   'How does the family take on the Jew?' . . .
>   'They're thunderstruck. . . . She's so upset by their reaction that her defiance turns to doubt, and she has a correspondence with him. . . . What will be particularly instructive to you is their correspondence, what it reveals about the attitudes of a large number of people to Jews, attitudes that only *appear* to be one hundred years old.'[3]

This lengthy section taken from the fifth part of the novel ('Christendom') is far from representing the isolated delirium of an unsympathetic character. Sarah's double stress on 'the Breghert Correspondence', or Chapter 79 of *The Way We Live Now*, which Amanda Anderson has interpreted as a 'counterposing' ideal to the system of communication employed by Paul Montague towards Hetta Carbury, will have direct consequences on the construction of *The Counterlife*'s conclusion.[4] Beginning with Mr Breghert's 'My Dear Georgiana' and ending with 'My Dear Miss Longestaffe', the Breghert correspondence is a masterly 'Dear John' case study showing, among other things, that a Jew can be more of a gentleman than his Christian counterparts. In the first letter, the earnest banker clarifies to his fiancée that her family's three objections to his marrying her (his trade, family, Jewishness) are actually limited to the last. Sensing Georgiana's worldly motives, he anticipates that he will be unable to offer her a residence in London for three years because of a large loss of invested money. Since Georgiana's only reason for getting married to him was to be able to live in London during the season, her reply insists on the clarification of this point, whereupon Mr Breghert graciously releases her from the engagement. Sandwiched between his determination to appear transparent to her prejudiced family and his resistance to accept an interested wife, Georgiana will not, to employ Sarah's words in *The Counterlife*, 'cash in on [his] pathetic Jewish Anglophilia', but will end up herself as the pathetic one.

Roth exploits the chapter's potential by offering a variation of it at the very end of the novel, when Nathan and Maria, who are pretty much the same age as Breghert and Georgiana, undertake a correspondence whose first letter begins with 'Dear Nathan' and the last has 'My Dear Maria', thus inverting Trollope's narrative situation. The Zuckerman correspondence is meant to represent a new possibility for the couple who, following the failure of the English experience and Maria's own discovery of *The Counterlife*'s draft, split up since Maria is aghast at having been turned into a fictional character; in his reply to her, however, the writer clarifies tenderly but unremorsefully that the only possible happiness for a couple like them is to be found in the non-real quality of a fictional world. The very last words of the novel insist that, far from being the opposite of life, the counterlife is in fact the closest thing to it, reality being infected by those limitations and divergences that could only result in the couple's disbandment.

By choosing a very specific Trollope episode as the text against which the novel's achievement will be realised, Roth is far from dismissing the Victorian writer as a philistine advocate of the way of the world; on the contrary, he is acknowledging Trollope's genetic function in the solution of his own problem, which he thinks he may face by capitalising on the originally unprofitable outcome of the Breghert/Longestaffe subplot. I just used the word *genetic* because it represents both the discourse on ethnicity which is at stake here and, above all, the relationship between the different forms of subjectivity described in this novel.[5] Rejecting both the type (someone whose identity is socially subsumed, that of the Jew) and the self (those whose characteristics make them unique, i.e. Zuckerman the successful American writer), the subjectivity Zuckerman aspires to in *The Counterlife* is made possible thanks to his belief that 'the burden isn't either / or, consciously choosing between possibilities equally difficult or regrettable – it's and / and / and / and / and as well'.[6] This is why the Trollope episode matters so much to a reading of *The Counterlife*: Mr Breghert provides an excellent instance of assimilated Other whose inability to start a counterlife together with Georgiana has nothing to do with either authorial limits or character flaws, but with the fact that he lives in a prototypically realistic novel. By creating a figure of similar moral value in a postmodern context, where characters know they are fictional, Roth can imagine his 'mixed' couple succeeding as his novel, unlike Trollope's, is not meant to represent the way they lived then, but only its own truth.[7] Even the title of Roth's novel seems to be a backhanded homage to Trollope, and considering that it was originally meant to be *The Metamorphosis*, one wonders whether Roth only made up his mind after completing this very last section.[8]

Furthermore, while the identities Zuckerman progressively goes through in *The Counterlife* are as many as the book's parts, there are no instances of internal changes within the single parts themselves; so even though it is true that the character undergoes many changes throughout the novel, it does not necessarily follow that these indicate a fluid personality. In this regard, Roth is also echoing Trollope's interest in character change. Trollope's typical male hero is someone who, when faced with the necessity of change, will accept the challenge only if this will not have consequences for his integrity. More often than not, however, especially in later productions such as *The Way We Live Now*, characters' integrity *is* eventually compromised by circumstances. In *The Counterlife*, Roth has an interesting word to describe this situation: Sarah, again the abrasive sister, explains to Nathan that unlike the works of John Buchan, whose blasé anti-Semitism is expressed in the form of a 'shared consciousness', what Trollope is interested in depicting is 'the predicament'.[9] Like other contemporary novelists with an interest in Trollope, Roth seems to suggest that, far from providing 'a picture of common life enlivened by humour and sweetened by pathos',[10] Trollope's oeuvre provides a vantage point for the representation of individual struggle – a fact that Leavisite critics had been particularly unwilling to recognise. That said, in *The Counterlife* Roth sees change as a possibility related to the factual inexistence of the self the way the self is traditionally conceived, while Trollope finds change to be more and more an attack on one's character: whereas in an early novel such as *The Warden* the struggle created by external pressure is more narrowly framed in ethical terms, in the novels of the 1870s, the same struggles are less a question of honesty than a problem of adaptation. In other words, it may be fine for postmodern fiction to apply a dice-throwing principle to character development, but Trollope's artistic practice is informed by different concerns.

These concerns are developed in a somewhat sneering way in Alan Hollinghurst's *The Line of Beauty* (2004), in which the protagonist, a middle-class gay Oxonian named Nick Guest, cannot reconcile his professional interest in Henry James with the novels of Anthony Trollope. Nick is a literary outsider whose experience as a long-term guest in a Conservative MP's household provides a glimpse into the life of the 1980s British ruling classes. Unlike him, these people *do* like Trollope; this is not surprising, of course, when one considers how many Conservative British politicians, from Harold Macmillan to John Major, publicly expressed their interest in him over the years. In the first part of the novel Nick is taken to a Buckinghamshire mansion, where he admires the family collection of artefacts and books. At some point he finds a copy of *The Way We Live Now* and begins a conversation on Trollope with his host, one Lord Kessler:

> Nick found a set of Trollope which had a relatively modest and approachable look among the rest, and took down *The Way We Live Now*, with an armorial bookplate, the pages uncut. 'What have you found there?' said Lord Kessler, in a genially possessive tone. 'Ah, you're a Trollope man, are you'. 'I am not sure I am, really', said Nick. 'I always think he wrote too fast. What was it Henry James said, about Trollope and his "great heavy shovelfuls of testimony to constituted English matters"?' Lord Kessler paid a moment's wry respect to this bit of showing-off, but said, 'Oh, Trollope's good. He's very good on money'. 'Oh . . . yes . . .' said Nick, feeling doubly disqualified by his complete ignorance on money and by the aesthetic prejudice which had stopped him from ever reading Trollope. 'To be honest, there's a lot of him I haven't yet read'. 'You must know that one, though', said Lord Kessler. 'No, this one is pretty good', Nick said, gazing at the spine with an air of judicious concession.[11]

The gratuitous offences implied in the expressions 'modest and approachable look' (Trollope is cheap) and 'heavy shovelfuls of testimony' (Trollope is trash) apart, the considerations here articulated (praise for the writer's understanding of things pecuniary and aesthetic admonition for writing too fast) are connected, as readers of *An Autobiography* will know: scholars have argued that Trollope's production anxiety is related to his determination to be taken seriously as a male writer in an age of industrial progress.[12] The sentence on Trollope writing too fast, moreover, is also significant in that it highlights Trollope's peculiar interest in a progressive movement aimed at completion, a disposition that will be acknowledged more significantly by other works of fiction considered here and therefore analysed in more detail in the following pages.

Hollinghurst is not the first author to oppose Trollope and Henry James in a dialectical fashion: Edith Wharton also does so in 'Xingu' (1911), a short satire on people's literary pretensions. In this story, a woman called Mrs Roby disgraces herself in the eyes of the other lady members of a book club when she reveals she has been reading Trollope instead of the latest novel by the Jamesian author Osric Dane, who is all the rage:

> 'I can understand that, with all your other pursuits, you should not find much time for reading; but I should have thought you might at least have got up *The Wings of Death* before Osric Dane's arrival'. Mrs Roby took this rebuke good-humouredly. She had meant, she owned to glance through the book; but she had been so absorbed in a novel of Trollope's that that – 'No one reads Trollope now', Mrs Ballinger interrupted impatiently. Mrs Roby looked pained. 'I'm only just beginning', she confessed. 'And does he interest you?' Mrs Plinth inquired. 'He amuses me'. 'Amusement', said Mrs Plinth sententiously, 'is hardly what I look for in my choice of books'.[13]

The split between in-depth analysis ('does he interest you?') and entertainment ('He amuses me') appears unbridgeable after 1910, the year Virginia Woolf considered a watershed moment in cultural history. Before World War I the battle between modernists and their Victorian predecessors could not admit of neutrality, and therefore the character reading Trollope for fun is not fit to purpose. Wharton details Mrs Roby's reasons for not reading Osric Dane by explaining that she was 'absorbed' in a Trollope novel. Absorption, which is in fact a powerful form of interest, is strongly related to openness to experience and may lead to dissociative states. A person absorbed in something does, technically, take flight towards a different form of life. Fully equipped to experience a 'counterlife' with Trollope, Mrs Roby could hardly find a reason to fly on *The Wings of Death*.

Compared to the original use in Roth's novel, the idea of the counterlife as an alternate reality here takes on different contours: it is conceptualised, in a less metafictional way, as a distraction from real life. Such a distraction may be motivated by boredom, as for Mrs Roby, but also by fear, which is the case in the next novel, where a Trollope reader is treated inquisitorially.

The novel in question is *The Inheritance of Loss* (2006), Kiran Desai's second work of fiction and winner of the Man Booker Prize. Set in the hill resort of Kalimpong, West Bengal, at the time of the insurrection of the Gorkha National Liberation Front in the second half of the 1980s,[14] the novel features Lola, the Anglophile widow of an Indian gentleman who lives with her unmarried sister Noni and takes pride in a daughter who has a 'pucca' English accent. Lola is characterised not unlike a Dickensian automaton and her sheer rejection of change (involving a branded British identity sustained by After Eights and M&S underwear) prepares the reader for the fact that Trollope is one of her favourite writers. Later in the novel, when the GNLF is about to take over the area, Lola and other characters are kept at a police checkpoint following a jeep trip to the circulating library in Darjeeling.

> The checkpoint guards now began to examine the pile of books, regarding them with wrinkled noses.
>
> 'What is this?' They hoped for literature of an antinational and inflammatory nature.
>
> 'Trollope', Lola said brightly, excited and aroused by the turn of events. 'I always said', she turned to the others in a frivolous fashion, 'that I would save Trollope for my dotage; I knew it would be a perfect slow indulgence when I had nothing much to do and, well, here I am. Old-fashioned books is what I like. Not the new kind of thing, no beginning, no middle, no end, just a thread of . . . free floating plasma . . .
>
> 'English writer', she told the guard. He flipped through: *The Last Chronicle of Barset: The Archdeacon goes to Framley, Mrs Dobbs Broughton Piles her Fagots* [sic].
>
> 'Did you know', Lola asked the others, 'that he also invented the post box?' 'Why are you reading it?'
>
> 'To take my mind off all of this'. She gestured vaguely and rudely at the scene in general and the guard himself. Who had his pride. Knew he was something. Knew his mother knew he was something. Not even an hour ago she had fed her belief and her son with pari aloo accompanied by a lemony-limy-luscious Limca, the fizz from which had made a mini excitement about his nose. Angry at Lola's insolence, his face still awake from the soda spray, he gave orders for the book to be placed in the police jeep.[15]

There is more than meets the eye in this comic scene. Because the police are looking for evidence of anti-nationalistic literature, Lola thinks that she is safe with Trollope, and rightly so, but this is only revealed in the next chapter, when the books are returned by the police, 'having been declared harmless'.[16] In this specific passage, she derides the guard because he cannot see that Trollope is politically inoffensive, but this results in the exposure of the irregular legal status of one of Lola's friends, a Swiss alcoholic called Father Booty who has long forgotten to update his visa and is therefore expelled from the country. This sneering attitude is strangely shared by the narrator, as the free indirect speech starting with 'knew he was something' indicates. After this event, the characters' personal safety and property begin to be compromised by the impending Nepali insurgence, a condition shown gradually and climactically during the second half of the novel.

For a book in which the influence of Western culture is presented as self-deluding at best and a major cause for social inequality at worst,[17] this part of the novel paradoxically focuses mainly on the drama lived by the educated characters, that is, those whose station had been theretofore guaranteed by their connection, direct or indirect, to Britain. In contrast, the Nepali rioters, whose reasons are clarified only in a paragraph in Chapter 26, where a non-character referred to as 'the man' urges the participants to react to the status quo, end up appearing more like twenty-first-century terrorists than they need be.[18] The consequence of this treatment is that readers are led to sympathise with the characters they rationally know to be 'wrong' (the one-sided upper-class characters like Lola), while they are compelled to be appalled by the behaviour of the rioters.[19] In the passage quoted, the paradox is formulated through Lola's expression 'no beginning, no middle, no end, just a thread of . . . free floating plasma' to refer to contemporary literature, which implies that Trollope's work, on the contrary, *does* have a starting point, a development and an end. Since this progressive movement is used to exemplify the immobility a character such as Lola has been prey to for decades, it follows that the linear progression identified with the structure of Trollope's novels is regarded by the narrator as a vicious cycle and not as a real evolution.

While the novel is fully awake to its split nature,[20] it remains to be determined whether the author is aware that the situation she presents to the readers is also one that Trollope fell back on time and again. In the Barsetshire series, for instance, the necessity of change is accepted only after it is made clear that the characters who are doomed to adjust their ways are also those with whom one is supposed to sympathise.[21] Trollope, however, is here represented as the epitome of stasis instead of one who presented the idiosyncrasies of his changing world and who, no matter which side he was on officially, pressured his characters to go through what Roth has called 'the predicament'. In this sense, *The Inheritance of Loss* seems to be the only one among the novels presented in this chapter that, while still employing Trollope astutely to express some sort of concern with reality, ends up betraying an oblivious Trollopian perspective.

Peter Cameron's *Someday This Pain Will Be Useful to You* (2007) develops the issue of how characters resist change through the story of a twenty-first-century teenager from downtown Manhattan. A fine example of Post-Gay *Bildungsroman*,[22] in which the protagonist's gay identity is taken as read, the novel charts the protagonist's social struggle and relates it to his reading of Trollope. James Sveck lives with his mother, a woman who, at the beginning of the novel, has just left her third husband during their honeymoon in Las Vegas, and his sister Gillian, who has now established that her name should be pronounced with a hard 'G' since her new date, a Language Theory Professor from Columbia, persuaded her that 'mispronouncing [a] name is a subtle and insidious form of child abuse'.[23] James's father is a lawyer who is about to have 'elective cosmetic surgery' applied to his eye bags but still instructs his son not to order pasta when eating out as 'it isn't manly' (a word charged with Trollopian overtones, which he is obviously unaware of). No wonder, then, that James has developed an anti-social attitude which makes him question every single thing other people say. So much so, in fact, that he makes up his mind to stop talking to people altogether and not to go to college. When his father asks him what he intends to do with his life, he defiantly says: 'I think I can learn all I need and want to know by reading Shakespeare and Trollope.'[24] He even plans to buy a house in Kansas so that he does not have to meet people and may read Trollope in isolation. This is also what he would have been happy to do during the American Classroom seminar, an experience that represents 'the predicament' in this novel. During that episode, James wishes he could stay in his hotel room reading *Can You Forgive Her?* instead of spending time with people he does not like, and the impossibility of achieving this leads him to practise light self-mutilation and, in the end, to disappear for two days. This incident reminds one of a famous Trollope review by Richard Holt Hutton who, comparing Trollope's characters to Jane Austen's, wrote that while 'Miss Austen's characters are what they are by the natural force of their own nature and taste, . . . Mr Trollope's people are themselves as far as the circumstances of the day will allow them to be themselves, but very often are much distorted from their most natural selves'.[25] With this comment in mind, it is not difficult to understand why the inability to be himself leads such an obstinate character as James to desire to 'disappear without effect'.[26] The fact that, of all Trollope's books, the boy would like to read *Can You Forgive Her?* but is not in a position to do so is meaningful: *Can You Forgive Her?* is arguably the last major novel written by Trollope in which adjustment to social prescriptions proves successful to the characters involved. It is for this reason that I interpret James's reiterated inability to read *Can You Forgive Her?* as a symptom of his resistance to 'move forward', an issue he admits having.[27] The fact that he cannot adjust to the way of the world imposes a reflection on the argument that Trollope's 'stories turn on a named progression of professional stations, how quickly those stations are traversed, and how that progression veers from suddenly fluid to insuperably blocked'.[28] What emerges from a comparison between this ultimately blocked linear path and the utter inability of a Trollope fan to make his way up to it, is that those 'disruptive energies' – identified by Nicholas Dames as the forces that the career is supposed to channel in the ordered sequence of the series – appear, in this twenty-first-century novel, more powerful than the career itself. To put it differently, Trollope seems to be cherished here less for his normative role than for his focus on what Amanda Anderson has defined as 'recalcitrant psychology'.[29] This would confirm that James's reluctance to make his way through the straight path of career is not related to his being gay, but to the fact that what he is really after is walking back – in the literal as well as the metaphorical sense of this idea. James desires to find the origin of his struggle, and is eventually persuaded to go and see a psychiatrist. Among the several instances the novel employs to describe this concern,[30] there is an interesting reference to Marcel Proust,[31] a writer who gradually takes the rôle that had been Trollope's in the novel and with whom the Victorian novelist seems to stand in a sort of specular relationship.

Trollope and Proust are also compared in Alan Bennett's novella *The Uncommon Reader* (2007), where Queen Elizabeth II asks a room full of politicians whether they had ever read the French author, to which a former foreign secretary naïvely replies, '"I have read Trollope". "One is glad to hear it", said the Queen, "but Trollope is not Proust"'.[32] I would like to push this statement a bit further and add that Trollope's fiction actually turns out to be the literal (if not the literary) opposite of Proust's. Whereas Trollope's working ethic is invested heavily in the kind of progressive movement that is thematised in *The Line of Beauty*, Proust's ultimate goal is a quest for meaning that can be achieved only by retreating into the memory of one's lifetime. In this sense, one could even say that Trollope is a 'counter Proust'. Be that as it may, James from *Someday This Pain Will Be Useful to You* has not read Proust yet (he was discouraged to do so until he had fallen in and out of love); at the same time, having failed to read *Can You Forgive Her?*, too, he is still unfit to pursue the kind of adjustment to the way of the world that Trollope's novel would teach him. This means that his research for lost time with a non-read Trollope novel as a torch makes him incapable to cure his own distress. As such, it is only the optimistic title of the novel that makes one hope that someday, no longer torn between moving forward and walking back, he will just come round.

The obliteration of memory is also a theme in Jacques Roubaud's *The Great Fire of London* (1989), first published in French, which will allow us to develop a second variation on the idea of the counterlife, that is, as the interior life of the self-conscious reader. Part novel and part autobiography, *The Great Fire of London* was originally conceived as an attempt to come to terms with the death of the author's young wife, but instead of recounting the circumstances that led to the tragedy or his reactions to it, proceeds, through sets of digressions called interpolations and bifurcations, to deal with the subject only obliquely. Roubaud thus applies the principles established by fellow-Oulipian writers such as Georges Perec and Italo Calvino, who sought to construct fiction by imposing certain technical constraints upon themselves. Far from telling anything about the 1666 fire that destroyed central London, the book's title is an allegory of the narrator's mnemonic process which, instead of developing or unleashing as in the modernist tradition, he chooses to eradicate, thus providing a sort of counter-account of what happened. Curiously, but perhaps not so much considering the implicitly anti-modernist statement of intent of this postmodern novel, the protagonist makes a significant use of Trollope in the text, which indeed includes several 'Trollopian anecdotes', as they are called in the book. One of these is related to a time when, as a widower living in Rue d'Amsterdam in Paris, he would spend every morning having breakfast at the same bar, always sitting at the same table, reading Trollope's 'novels one by one, in their proper order, chapter by chapter, in small morning rations . . . before returning home to resume the dull monotony . . . of my daily activities'. He then writes that on the following day he would

> leave on my table the same, always exactly calculated sum, and absorb myself again as quickly as possible into my book, the almost twenty-four hours having elapsed since the day before instantly abolished in thought. But, as a true Trollopian, I didn't realise that changing urban customs and passing time . . . were gradually going to turn my innocent habit into an anachronism. For, one by one, the cafés of the square shifted their opening times ever later into the day. And, one morning, the owner of the establishment I patronised came to me and explained . . . that for a month I had been their only customer, . . . [so] they really couldn't keep this any longer, and to please accept his apology. I had reached the end of *Orley Farm*. I had been oblivious to everything. All Trollopians will understand me.[33]

The narrator's methodical absorption into Trollope's fiction, which he shares with other Trollopian characters mentioned in this article and which is described in terms clearly resembling those for which the Victorian novelist is notorious, speaks volumes about the role reading takes for Roubaud's character. Trollope's orderly production is not meant to contain the undomesticated flame of the widower's sorrow; in other words, the narrator is not reading his novels because their light contents will distract him from the thought of his wife's death. It thus transpires that whereas Trollope is unfit to enter the literary canon of the aesthetically conscious modernists, the Victorian writer is given a different role by next-generation writers such as Roubaud, who no longer believe that life can really be given meaning. The protagonist of *The Great Fire of London* is someone whose reluctance to share sorrow and, above all, to think that by thus doing he may accept and therefore liquidate the tragic death of his wife, seems to imply that any effort in that sense is tantamount to self-indulgence. And in a sense, his recovery of a pre-modernist writer – in fact, the non-modernist writer par excellence – to reject his own generation's predecessors (the modernists) appears as dialectical and as necessary as the efforts made by Henry James and the early 1900s writers against their own literary fathers, such as Trollope. To put it differently, Trollope may well be Henry James's Alan Bennett, but in the hands of Roubaud the modernists only appear as different shades of Mrs Brown.

It remains to be determined whether the counter-reading of Trollope provided by twentieth- and twenty-first-century fiction is only a modern projection, or whether it stands in some sort of concrete relationship to the Victorian writer himself. In other words, are there instances in Trollope's oeuvre where a counterlife may be found? *The Duke's Children*, and especially the recently published unabridged edition by the Folio Society, affords a number of examples. In Chapter 25, the ex-Prime Minister is having breakfast with his sons and says that

> 'as far as my experience goes, the happiest man is he who . . . has his hands the fullest of work'. . . .
> 'Isn't that a great grind, sir?' asked Silverbridge.
> 'A very great grind, as you call it. . . . But it is the grind that makes the happiness.'[34]

In light of what I have argued about Trollope's role in *The Great Fire of London*, it might be useful to remember that the character who is pronouncing these words is also a widower. If it is true that many instances may be found showing that in practice Plantagenet Palliser did support this apology of the grind even when Lady Glencora was alive, the implications of this speech in its proper context are, however, that the Duke cannot be happy again. The gap between others and himself, which his wife could, if awkwardly, reduce by virtue of her natural sociability, is exposed in this novel as unbridgeable, and the reference to the specific word 'grind' appears illuminating if one considers that the literal meaning of it is that of reducing to powder or small fragments. The fire in Roubaud's novel is an allegory of a similar principle, that is, the transformation of too heavy a memory and the conviction that happiness with others is, de facto, no longer possible. If it is possible for this interpretation to be credible from a critical point of view, then one might have to recognise that a sentence such as the one quoted above from the Duke may not be saying the whole truth. Something is being omitted, not in the sense of being hidden intentionally, but expressed *in absentia*, not unlike Lady Glencora's influence in this specific novel. If it is possible to conceive this, that is, to consider that what a Trollope character says may need a counter-reading to be fully unfurled, then this identification might give the expression 'read between the lines' new vigour, let alone help re-establish the importance of close reading with regard to Trollope's own fiction.

The Duke's trajectory of loss anticipates a motif that is reflected in the works that this chapter has analysed, works which all express different and yet consistent forms of movement that lend themselves to a symbolical interpretation. *The Line of Beauty* is serpentine and its gratuitous shape (beauty is an end in itself in both Hollinghurst's novel and for most of Henry James's protagonists, as opposed to interested characters).[35] It stands in contrast to the straight path that James Sveck is supposed to but cannot teach himself to go through in *Someday This Pain Will Be Useful to You*, and which represents the channelled energies of the career, that is, a progressive movement with a clear goal (that of reaching the top). Nathan Zuckerman in *The Counterlife* is in a position to elude the problem of a reality whose prejudices are hard to stomach by breaking his identity into different parts and thus following different directions, safe in the knowledge that he is in a novel. In *The Great Fire of London*, the refusal to get over sorrow by means of the mnemonic process so dear to the modernists is tantamount to sheer rejection of change which ends up breaking through different levels of experience (bifurcations and interpolations). In the absence of some connection between reality and thought, life becomes something similar to that absorption in one's world which Edith Wharton expresses, if comically, with Mrs Roby in 'Xingu' and Kiran Desai with Lola in *The Inheritance of Loss*. The fact that all of these works employ Trollope to express a concern with issues of solitude and unfitness appears to me to represent a solid contribution in the exciting task of reforming Trollope in which we are all involved. Future research might want to analyse whether this issue informs his oeuvre so much so as to demand a new shift in his role within the literary canon.

Notes

I would like to thank those friends and colleagues who, knowing of my professional interest in the works of Anthony Trollope, drew my attention to some of these novels over the years. These include Robert L. Caserio, Giulio Maria Corbelli, Ortwin de Graef and Kristoffer O. Jacobsson.

1. Hawthorne's enthusiastic comment on Trollope's novels, originally written in a letter to Joseph M. Field (11 February 1860), fascinated Trollope, who later recorded it in *An Autobiography*; James's more dynamic image, which he set in an unusual favourable comparison to what he called 'the sedentary school' of French Naturalism, is taken from his *Partial Portraits* (1888). Both appear in Donald Smalley (ed.), *Anthony Trollope: The Critical Heritage* (London and New York: Routledge, [1969] 1995), p. 110 and p. 540.
2. 'Sequels' of Trollope's novels include Angela Thirkell's *The Duke's Daughter* (1951) and John F. Wirenius's *Phineas at Bay* (2014), the former being part of a bunch, if not exactly a series, of novels set in Barsetshire (not really rendered justice by Thirkell's hand, if it were not for a handful of Firbankian sparks thrown here and there), the latter a manly effort in ventriloquism I personally regard highly. Such sequels written by non-original authors are also known as 'post-texts'. See Amanda Gilroy, 'Our Austen: Fan Fiction in the Classroom', *Persuasions On-Line* 31.1 (2010), <http://www.jasna.org/persuasions/on-line/vol31no1/gilroy.html> (last accessed 22 September 2016). For Simon Grennan's critically acclaimed graphic adaptation of *John Caldigate*, *Dispossession: A Novel of Few Words* (London: Jonathan Cape, 2015), see Sophie Ratcliffe, 'Drawing "Perhaps"', *Times Literary Supplement*, 16 March 2016, p. 21. Last, I should mention the existence of two crime or Gothic stories set in Barchester: *The Stalls of Barchester Cathedral* (1911) by M. R. James and *The Barchester Murders* (2015) by G. M. Best.
3. Philip Roth, *The Counterlife* (London: Vintage Books, [1986] 2005), pp. 284–5.
4. Amanda Anderson, 'Trollope's Modernity', *ELH*, 74.3 (Fall 2007): pp. 531 and 534.
5. For a solid discussion on the historical development of subjectivity in fiction, see Amélie Oksenberg Rorty, 'Characters, Selves, Persons, Individuals', in Michael McKeon (ed.), *Theory of the Novel: A Historical Approach* (Baltimore and London: Johns Hopkins University Press, 2000), pp. 537–53.
6. *The Counterlife*, p. 310.

7. Trollope may have agreed on this point since it was he who wrote that 'there is no happiness in love, except at the end of an English novel'. This fortunate quote from Chapter 27 of *Barchester Towers*, articulated by Madeline Neroni and also mentioned in Jeffrey Eugenides's *The Marriage Plot* (2011), is meant to show that, ultimately, Roth does not really provide a solution to the issues dealt with by the same Trollope, persuaded as he seems that anti-Semitic sentiments 'only *appear* to be one hundred years old'.

8. See Claudia Roth Pierpont, *Roth Unbound: A Writer and His Books* (New York: Jonathan Cape, 2013), p. 140.

9. *The Counterlife*, p. 285.

10. Trollope's own definition of a novel. See *An Autobiography* (Oxford and New York: Oxford University Press, 1999), p. 126.

11. Alan Hollinghurst, *The Line of Beauty* (London, Basingstoke and Oxford: Picador, 2004), pp. 52–3.

12. See Walter Kendrick, *The Novel-Machine: The Theory and Fiction of Anthony Trollope* (Baltimore: Johns Hopkins University Press, 1980); Andrew Dowling, *Manliness and the Male Novelist in Victorian Literature* (Aldershot: Ashgate, 2001); and Kate Thomas, *Postal Pleasures: Sex, Scandal, and Victorian Letters* (Oxford and New York: Oxford University Press, 2012), esp. ch. 2, which acknowledges, among other things, J. Hillis Miller's and Richard Dellamora's contributions on the subject of Trollope's production anxiety in moral and sexual terms.

13. Edith Wharton, 'Xingu', in *Collected Stories 1911–1937* (New York: Library of America, 2001), p. 3.

14. Unsatisfied with the life conditions of the Nepali citizens of West Bengal following the Indo-Nepal treaty of 1950, the GNLF brought forward an aggressive independence campaign which reached its first acme on Sunday, 27 July 1986, when a violent repression by the police resulted in the killing of thirteen people (including children) in a public square.

15. Kiran Desai, *The Inheritance of Loss* (London: Hamish Hamilton, 2006), pp. 217–18.

16. *The Inheritance of Loss*, p. 220.

17. For a development of the argument according to which globalisation is a new form of imperial coercion, see Adriana Elena Stoican, 'Competing Western Hegemonies in Kiran Desai's *The Inheritance of Loss*', *Humanicus* 7 (2012), <http://www.humanicus.org/global/issues/humanicus-7-2012/humanicus-7–2012–1.pdf> (last accessed 20 September 2016).

18. The opinion I have just expressed is part of a wider concern that was also formulated in *The Guardian*, where it was reported that among the local people of Kalimpong, the world-acclaimed *The Inheritance of Loss* was received with dismay. See Randeep Ramesh, 'Book-burning threat over town's portrayal in Booker-winning novel', *The Guardian*, 2 November 2006, <https://www.theguardian.com/world/2006/nov/02/books.india> (last accessed 5 October 2016).

19. When Lola is finally humiliated by the GNLF following a major attack to her property by some of their supporters, she begins to question her values: 'Just when Lola had thought it would continue, a hundred years like the one past – Trollope, BBC, a burst of hilarity at Christmas – all of a sudden, all that they had claimed innocent, fun, funny, not really to matter, was proven wrong.' *The Inheritance of Loss*, pp. 241–2.

20. There are several other scenes in which the narration reflects on this situation. One of the more powerful instances is described in Chapter 8, where the judge, remembering his departure from India in the 1930s in order to study at Cambridge, is about to leave the harbour and his father shrieks from the platform that he must remember to throw a coconut in the sea as a good omen: 'Jemubhai looked at his father, a barely educated man venturing where he should not be, and the love in Jemubhai's heart mingled with pity, the pity with shame. . . . Jemu watched his father disappear. He didn't throw the coconut and he didn't cry. Never again would he know love for a human being that wasn't adulterated by another, contradictory emotion.' *The Inheritance of Loss*, p. 37.

21. This is certainly the case in *The Warden*, where one feels for Mr Harding but not for John Bold, notwithstanding the acknowledgement that the reform undertaken by the latter is necessary. In the hands of, say, George Eliot, the sympathy would have been with the reformer and not with the character perpetuating the anachronism (Lydgate in *Middlemarch*), which is why I am referring to this situation as typically Trollopian in the Victorian canon.

22. For a definition of 'Post-Gay' literature, see Guy Davidson, 'The Time of AIDS and the Rise of Post-Gay', in Scott Herring (ed.), *The Cambridge Companion to American Gay and Lesbian Literature* (Cambridge and New York: Cambridge University Press, 2015), pp. 139–54: 'post-gay [applies] to a broad set of disparate, and even contradictory, trends that nevertheless share a rhetorical abandonment of defining features of 1970s gay and lesbian identity, culture and politics.' Referring to 'an assimilationist discourse . . . post-gay indexes a historical moment in which . . . gay and lesbians are accorded an unprecedented level of acceptance and representation' (p. 140).

23. Peter Cameron, *Someday This Pain Will Be Useful to You* (New York: Farrar, Straus and Giroux, 2007), p. 8.

24. *Someday This Pain*, p. 35.

25. Cited in David Skilton, *Anthony Trollope and His Contemporaries: A Study in the Theory and Conventions of Mid-Victorian Fiction* (London: Longman, 1972), pp. 116–17.

26. *Someday This Pain*, p. 175.

27. Ibid. p. 80.

28. Nicholas Dames, 'Trollope and the Career: Vocational Trajectories and the Management of Ambition', *Victorian Studies*, 45.2 (2003): p. 248.

29. 'Trollope's Modernity', p. 510 ff. 'Recalcitrance' is a word employed by the same James Sveck to define his way. See *Some Day This Pain*, p. 97.

30. These instances, that focus on a paradoxical eagerness to get old as opposed to grow up, include a visit to the National Gallery in Washington, DC, where James is spellbound by Thomas Cole's 'Old Age' from the *Voyage of Life* series (1842), and a privileged relationship with his grandmother. See *Someday This Pain*, Chapter 10.

31. See *Someday This Pain*, pp. 86–7.

32. Alan Bennett, *The Uncommon Reader* (London: Faber and Faber and Profile Books, 2007), p. 117.

33. Jacques Roubaud, *The Great Fire of London: a story with interpolations and bifurcations* [Le Grand Incendie de Londres, récit avec incises et bifurcations], translated with an afterword by Dominic Di Bernardi (Elmwood Park: Dalkey Archive Press, [1989] 1992), pp. 274–5.

34. Anthony Trollope, *The Duke's Children*, ed. Steven Amarnick, Robert F. Wiseman and Susan Lowell Humphreys (London: The Folio Society, 2015), ch. 25, p. 213.

35. See William Hogarth, *The Analysis of Beauty: Written with a View of Fixing the Fluctuating Ideas of Taste* (London: T. Davidson, Lombard Street, Whitefriars, [1753] 1810), Chapter VII ('Of Lines').

10

TROLLOPE IN CHINA: TROLLOPE'S TRANSCULTURATION FROM THE LATE QING DYNASTY TO THE PRESENT

Xiaolan Zuo

THIS CHAPTER EXAMINES the evolving process of the relation between Anthony Trollope and his readers in China. Over the course of the past two centuries, Chinese contact with Trollope has been conditioned by various social, cultural, ideological and aesthetic factors. To examine Trollope's transculturation in China is to look closely at the various ways in which Trollope, as a novelist and as a man, has been received, reviewed and studied by Chinese readers and scholars, and to understand the causes for an up-and-down trend of Trollopian studies in the context of the general cultural convergence in China.[1] I will address the issues regarding Chinese readers' access to and estimation of Trollope's works at different time periods. I will also analyse the reasons behind some special phenomena that pertain to the introduction, translation and study of Trollope under particular circumstances, along with a discussion about the extent and significance of Trollope's transculturation in the context of globalisation.

Initial Contact and Acceptance amidst Swirling Eddies of Dynastic Change and Nationalist Cultural Awakening

The introduction and translation of Western literary works in China in modern times gathered steam in the 1870s during the late Qing Dynasty (1840–1911). It was marked by the translations of 'A Voyage to Lilliput' from Jonathan Swift's *Gulliver's Travels* (*Tan ying xiao lu*, 《谈瀛小录》) in 1872, 'Rip Van Winkle' ('Yi shui qishi nian', 一睡七十年) from Washington Irving's *The Sketchbook of Geoffrey Crayon, Gent* in 1872 and Edward Bulwer Lytton's *Night and Morning* (*Xin xi xian tan*, 《昕夕闲谈》) in 1873.[2] Over the first three decades of the twentieth century, this process developed more conspicuously as an active response to the influx of Western ideas. China's intellectuals felt it was necessary to learn from the West in order to reform the Chinese feudal social system, root out social evils and, above all, strengthen national prowess. Under the influence of Western concepts of democracy, human rights and individual freedom, leading liberal intellectuals, such as Kang Youwei (1858–1927), Liang Qichao (1873–1929) and Yan Fu (1854–1921) were bent on undertaking political and cultural reforms in order to turn a problem-ridden China into an advanced modern country.

Under such circumstances, Western fiction was believed to be a kind of faith-cure for social problems and endowed with a new social and didactic status, hence its mission of reform and cultural enlightenment. Liang Qichao, a leading late-Qing reformist, considered fiction as 'the greatest vehicle of all literature' for its 'astonishing potentiality to affect the ways of man'.[3]

The first half of the twentieth century witnessed profound changes in the political, economic and intellectual aspects of national life. The New Cultural Movement (1917–23) accentuated the cultural and political functions of literature, the novel in particular, to a higher degree.[4] Guided by the strong ideological and aesthetic conviction that fiction could be utilised for the purpose of 'enlightening the people and thus contributing substantially to the impending radical changes in the fate of the Chinese nation', many modern Chinese cultural pioneers and reformists began to dedicate themselves to translating Western literary works and made great contributions to the introduction of Western literature and the modernisation of traditional Chinese literature.[5]

During the ensuing three decades before 1949, literary realism in China gradually gained momentum, accompanied by a growing awareness about 'literary masterpieces'. This marked the beginning of translation as a conscious cultural act.

The boom in translation and the introduction of Western fiction thus became one of the vital factors for speeding up the dynamic interaction between Chinese culture and other cultures despite (and because of) dissonances and even conflicts in the process of cultural convergence. The concurrent upsurge of literary journals, modern newspapers and magazines helped spread modern theoretical beliefs and boosted a large amount of paraphrased or translated foreign literature, nurturing a potential readership of Western fiction in China. Ideology, poetics, publishing institutions and a book market that contributed to transculturation were undergoing gradual maturation, making possible the reception of Western literature and cross-transfer of literary resources in China.

Anthony Trollope was among the earliest Victorian novelists to be introduced for Chinese readers. Metaphorically speaking, Trollope first set foot upon the soil of China around 1858 and was visibly present until 1938 through English newspaper articles, reviews, editorials and display advertisements.[6] Although the intended readers of these newspapers were mainly Western diplomats, missionaries and businessmen in China, two noteworthy facts, among others, may give us some clue as to how Trollope came to be known to well-educated local people.

First, on 13 March 1858, *The North-China Herald* (1850–67) published a list of twenty books which the Shanghai Library (1851–1913) had received from England, almost all being literary works. Among them was Trollope's *The Three Clerks*, which was presumably one of the earliest of Trollope's novels ever put on a library bookshelf in China.[7] The recently published novel, *The Three Clerks*, was only the beginning of Trollope's promotion and ensuing circulation in China. By 1860, three of Trollope's other novels had been made accessible to Western residents in Shanghai: *Barchester Towers*, *Doctor Thorne* and *Castle Richmond*. Later, in 1913, when the Shanghai Library was turned into the Public Library of Shanghai Municipal Council, these resources became available to local Shanghai citizens. Such accessibility to both Western and local readers through the Shanghai Library was not only indicative of

Trollope's established success as a popular Victorian novelist and the eager demand for Trollope's novels among native English readers, but also suggestive of the latent chance of initial Chinese contact with Trollope.

Secondly, in addition to newspaper articles and comments and reviews about his works, there were also reports about Trollope's travel accounts (of Australia and South Africa), and about his novels, both published and forthcoming. Meanwhile, there were several references to Trollope in English sermons, literary commentaries and reviews during the 1920s and 1930s. Editorials on the 'revised estimate' from Sir George Saintsbury in 1921 were clear evidence of Trollope's rising star. Excerpts from *An Autobiography* and other novels were as common as appraising comments of Michael Sadleir's *Trollope: A Commentary*. Given the low level of literacy of the general Chinese populace at that time, the Chinese readership of English newspapers was limited to the Chinese literati or interested intellectual elite with personal exposure to the English language and Western culture. The publicity about Trollope in English newspapers circulated in China was transculturally significant in that it reflected his fluctuating literary reputation in England over time and it helped to make it possible for enlightened Chinese literati to have initial contact with Trollope.

The actual extent and nature of the relationship between Trollope and his distant overseas audience upon their very first contact in the mid-nineteenth century are hard to fathom. But it is clear that it was not until after his literary comeback in the 1920s that Trollope began to receive wider publicity in China and Trollope's transculturation made its debut with deeper cross-cultural implications, which manifested themselves over time.

While the late Qing Period was one of drastic changes, characterised by fundamental socio-economic and intellectual transformation, the Nationalist Period (1912–49) before the founding of the People's Republic of China was one of ideological awakening and of domestic squabbles accompanied by the Chinese people's hard struggle to drive off imperialist invaders. As a result, for a long time the nation was deeply troubled with violent social upheaval, constant political dissension and ideological chaos. Chinese society was in an 'indescribable' condition in terms of social and ideological orientations.[8] Despite such an unstable social condition, intellectual and literary activities never stopped during the major part of the Nationalist Period. 'Literary masterpieces' and 'literariness' gradually became more widely accepted standards for Western literature translation, which had its first flowering period between the 1920s and mid-1930s. Literary realism in China gradually gained momentum, making possible the prioritised choice of works of a realistic nature in foreign literature transfer.

Trollope's image was presented for the first time before the eyes of common Chinese readers through a portrait published in the *English Magazine*, a publication addressed at middle-school learners of English in 1923, together with the portraits of five near contemporaries.[9] However, the introductory remarks about Trollope were scanty and far from accurate. After this introduction, Trollope did not receive adequate attention and due evaluation in China for almost three decades, until 1949. Trollope could be found mainly in mediated histories of English literature compiled by either Western or Chinese scholars. And even in these books, Trollope received only perfunctory attention, and the assessment was, to some extent, biased or underrated. Nevertheless, some of these books do deserve our attention, because, however uncertain or contradictory the basic tone might be, they introduced some typical features of Trollope's novels, which were to present an enduring appeal to Chinese readers and pave the way for deeper cultural transfer and convergence in the long run.

The earliest introduction to Chinese readers of Anthony Trollope as an English novelist appeared in *The Outline of Literature* (1927), the first foreign literary history book ever compiled in China, by Zheng Zhenduo (1898–1958), an enlightened scholar and pre-eminent man of letters during the Nationalist Period. Zheng's pioneering book was remarkable for its open-mindedness shared by those enlightened leading Chinese literati at that time in their wish to embrace the eye-opening world literature. Nineteenth-century fiction, in particular, as Zheng believed, 'reached a stage of brilliant exuberance' which he metaphorically referred to as 'a rose garden in springtime and a golden field of rape in March'.[10] The cultural awareness shown in the *Outline* accidentally coincided with the gradual revival of Trollope's reputation in his homeland, which was marked by Michael Sadleir's monumental biography of Trollope published in the same year of 1927. As Zheng wrote, 'All [Trollope's] novels depict English middle-class people and society, and this is a newly opened area for literary portrayal. With a marvellous imagination, he captures faithfully and delineates truthfully the mentality, feelings, manners and customs of middle-class society.'[11] Though far from comprehensive, Zheng's general introduction to Trollope's subject matter and social range as a novelist was pertinent, even though he judged that Trollope 'was not a great novelist'. Zheng's underestimation was a reflection of the status quo of Trollope's literary reputation among Western scholars in England and elsewhere at that time. Undeniably, what first drew the attention of Chinese literary elite of the time were the various aspects of English social life, for which Trollope is reputedly acclaimed. The realistic point of view tied in well with the standing Chinese literary tradition of realism. However, the acceptance of Trollope in modern China was affected by many factors that existed in the complex historical conditions during the Nationalist Period.

During the 1930s, judgements by those compilers were still tinged with underestimation and contradiction. The common literary image of Trollope as sketched in these books was, at best, an admirer of Thackeray in technical skills and narrative stance – literally, a 'lesser Thackeray'. Often introduced with scanty words, he was regarded as either 'a literary hack'[12] or a minor writer 'whose works were empty of literary values'.[13] In *The Outline of English Literature* (1937) compiled by Jin Donglei, Trollope was placed in the 'Other Writers' category and labelled as 'a follower of Thackeray in style' with all the Barsetshire series being 'second-rate production', except for *Barchester Towers*.[14] Introductions such as these often seemed somehow self-contradictory. In a journal article, Trollope was considered as a 'most prolific' and 'great novelist', but one definitely without any special artistic talents, though 'his works sold well'.[15]

In the 1940s, signs of significant change appeared as a result of the rising importance of Trollope in England, which lent a new push to Trollope's introduction to and acceptance among Chinese readers. The most noteworthy was a growing recognition of the exceptional success of the Barchester Chronicles. In Wilbur L. Cross's book *The Development of the English Novel* (1936), co-translated by three Chinese scholars, there was a detailed analysis of *The Warden* and *Barchester Towers* as sequels. Special attention was given to their plot development, with a favourable critical comment on Trollope's faithful, minute character portrayal and psychological subtleties – despite at places a somewhat disparaging tone. This was not an isolated judgement. In his 1946 book adapted from J. B. Priestley, *The English*

Novel, Li Rumian regarded Trollope as 'a remarkable man', a novelist of 'exceptional artistic feat', outstanding in realistic depiction of social life.[16] Li drew readers' attention to, among other things, Trollope's convincing realism, well-crafted plots and his well-knit structure in the Barchester Chronicles. Through these new introductions, the realistic and truthful psychological qualities of Trollope's works were more clearly recognised and accentuated.[17] The year 1942 saw the appearance in the magazine *China Traveler* of the first Chinese translation ever of a work by Trollope, 'A Journey to Panama' by Shen Si.[18] It was translated in smooth and easy-reading modern vernacular Chinese, which is a clear pointer to the fact that ordinary Chinese readers somehow became acquainted with Trollope. An English literary master was gradually on his way to receiving recognition.

In 1947, a critical article on Trollope by a Western scholar, whose name was transliterated as 衛斯特亨 (*Wei si te heng*), was translated by Huai Jie and published in the magazine *Progress*.[19] It offered the Chinese reading public brand new aspects of Trollope that surely helped in deepening their overall understanding. The article reported the renewed enthusiasm for reading Trollope in the West, explained the causes for the chequered history of Trollope's literary reputation before World War II and, equally importantly, introduced *An Autobiography* (1883) for the first time in China.[20] Apart from gaining a fairly large amount of important biographical information and learning the news about Oxford University Press's projected complete collection of Trollope's works, Chinese readers were also informed through this article that a revised edition of Michael Sadleir's *Trollope: A Commentary* was published in New York in 1947. All this certainly had very important implications for Chinese scholars' budding research interest in Trollope. In the same year, Trollope was introduced in an English literature coursebook designed by the National Ministry of Education. Whereas in 1927 Trollope's literary reputation had just resurfaced, now Trollope was practically 'due for a come-back' in the West. While Trollope's increasing acceptance in China corresponded with his literary revival worldwide, his appearance in the magazine *Progress* also seems symbolic. It not only signified a progressive leap in the revival of Trollope's reputation in England, but also anticipated a period of further development in Trollope's transculturation in China after 1949. By then, more dimensions of affinity between Trollope and Chinese readers were established through cultural contact in the continuing merging process.

By and large, during the Nationalist Period, Chinese literary circles had a comparatively belated reaction and lukewarm attitude towards Trollope. Trollope missed the first golden period of translation of Western literature between the 1920s and mid-1930s. Compared with other great Victorian novelists, Trollope was not accepted readily or widely in China in terms of either introduction or translation – even when his novels had been available in the Shanghai Library and other public libraries for several decades, and even though 'critical esteem for Trollope did indeed take an abrupt rise',[21] as he became 'one of the Great Air-Raid Shelters' in the 1940s.[22] How should we explain this phenomenon? Generally speaking, as translating in itself is a cultural act involving complex factors, the reasons for the neglect or marginalisation of a Western writer can be manifold. Conditioned by the interplay between the dominant ideological thinking and literary values before 1949, translated literature, like Chinese modern literature in general, was endowed with an enlightening and didactic mission beyond its intrinsic entertaining role, and '[o]nly those that reflected topical thematic concerns were likely to be accepted by the mainstream culture and literature'.[23] Such an ideological and topical demand had got the upper hand since the Literary Movement of 1917, culminating in the predominance of leftist literature (as represented by Lu Xün (1881–1936), a well-known modern writer and translator), Soviet literature and the spread of new literary theories after the outbreak of the Anti-Japanese War (1937–45). During this period, when many Chinese writers and translators were involved in a protest against the existing social order, Chinese literary works of social realism, which could carry out a didactic social mission in the fight against feudalism and imperialism, were thought to be much more relevant and inspiring to Chinese readers than Western realistic novels of middle-class life. Consequently, due to the topical need for such a national theme and spiritual appeal, Trollope, with his typical Englishness in mentality as well as fictional subject matter and stance, was met with misunderstanding, reluctance, or even suspicion, more than other Western writers, such as Jonathan Swift, Charles Dickens and Thomas Hardy, among others. Moreover, as Trollope was introduced often with the badge of 'a second-rate' novelist in books on literary history, his artistic qualities had been lamentably underrated, which made him almost unworthy of translation. Furthermore, to quote Shen Zhiyuan, the one-time general director of the Compilation Bureau, 'translation of foreign works [at that time] was on the whole not a well-regulated activity and remained practically a personal matter as the choice of source work was determined by translators' own preference.'[24] These are some of the reasons why the literary value of Trollope's works remained rather vague to Chinese literary scholars and translators, and why literary activities such as the translation of Trollope's fiction and scholarly research remained virtually a vacuum. Trollope's transculturation failed to progress any further.

New Critical Dimensions through Fruitful Transcultural Endeavours in More Recent Times

After the founding of the People's Republic of China in 1949, all aspects of China's social, political and cultural life underwent a fundamental change. In the Chinese cultural context, developments in ideology and poetics, as well as the book market and publishing industry, often make their influence felt in introductions to foreign literature, translations and literary criticism.[25] In the 1950s, following the adoption of the Soviet model of ideology, activities in literary circles in China were largely oriented towards the political conception of class struggle, and a clear distinction between 'progressive' socialist values and the 'dark and corrupt' Western capitalist social values became a yardstick for evaluating Western literature. A noticeable instance is the understanding of 'socialist realism'.[26]

Regarding Trollope's transculturation in the form of introduction, translation and critical research, two historical periods deserve our special attention. 'The period before 1957 was a booming period for translated literature over the seventeen years after the founding of New China [i.e. between 1949 and 1966]', and the second flowering period for translation came about in the 1980s and 1990s.[27]

The year 1949 inaugurated a new period of cultural development. With the implementation of national Five-Year Plans, the systematic and organised programme of Western literary studies began to take shape. During the 1950s, 'meeting the political needs became the primary principle for the choice of foreign works for translation' as priority was given to works of European critical realism in choosing translating sources. Rather than being a stimulus and reference for new norms of literary practice, foreign literature translation was made subordinate to political and ideological monism and thus became a means of consolidating the ideological system.[28] In a historical context where the cultural tides made literary transfer possible through translation, the situation of lukewarm acceptance of Trollope changed significantly during this period. There was groundbreaking progress in translation for Trollope's transculturation through the New Literature and Art Press's 1957 publication of Chinese versions of Trollope's *The Warden* and *Nina Balatka*, translated by Zhu Wan (主万) and Wu Renshan (吴人珊) respectively. The choice for these two novels was largely topical. Those involved were led by the ideological urge to criticise Western bourgeois society in order to prove that socialist proletarian values were superior. In the case of these two novels, the criticism and exposure of social and religious prejudice in England (and the capitalist world) was a main consideration. This can be clearly seen in the synopsis of the translations:

> Through this amusing story [*The Warden*], the author exposed the hypocritical and shameful nature and the fake benevolence on the part of the Church. And meanwhile, through the scenes of romance, he revealed a variety of comic social phenomena commonly seen among the British bourgeoisie.[29]

In the Preface to the 1986 revised version of *The Warden*, Zhu Wan provided a deeper analysis of both *The Warden* and *Barchester Towers* as 'political novels' of topical relevance, the corruptions and malpractices shown in the ecclesiastical circles being reflections of those commonly seen in mid-nineteenth-century English officialdom:

> What Trollope wrote about in the Chronicles of Barsetshire, particularly *The Warden* and *Barchester Towers* was mainly topical. Therefore, broadly understood, the various forms of dark corruption of the church he satirized, such as the sinecure, the absenteeism, the lavish way of life, the struggle for power among clergymen and also the 'petticoat' politics, are these not the common phenomena of English officialdom at that time? Although the author wrote about the diocese of Barchester, what was exactly sketched is the contours of contemporary social life of the English middle and upper-middle classes.[30]

In fact, to find a subtle balance between ideology and aestheticism, translators often had to give priority to the consideration of ideology over aesthetics, and very often they had to resort to some expedient, covert, yet effective way as a 'self-protective translation strategy'.[31] Similarly, as its synopsis suggested, *Nina Balatka* could be regarded as a window to the life of Western society with its problems of social prejudice and religious dogmatism and persecution. Such topical preference fitted in well with the mainstream realistic tradition in modern China and contemporaneous ideological orientation of the period before 1978.[32]

Although overtones of class ideology still lingered, by and large the political climate had gradually turned mild. Trollope's novels, like those of many other Victorian novelists, began to find a place in the assets of translated foreign literature in China. Apparently, given the promising condition of Trollope's introduction and translation, this new development could have become a tremendous stimulus to Trollope's transculturation in the following years had it not been for the Great Proletarian Cultural Revolution (1966–76). For a whole decade, almost all forms of Western literary study came to a standstill. All the non-proletarian cultures, Chinese or Western, which were thought to promote bourgeois or capitalist values, were repudiated and rejected. Trollope was certainly no exception.

This situation took a dramatic turn when the implementation of Reform and Opening-up in 1978 created an unprecedentedly buoyant social and cultural atmosphere favourable to the development of foreign literary studies. As a result of the significant change in the overall cultural climate, the door was opened wider and wider to academic and cultural exchange between Chinese literary scholars and their Western counterparts. There was an evident need to pay due recognition to some Western writers and literary trends in order to broaden the intellectual and literary horizon while discarding narrow-minded ways of critical judgement misled by rigid leftist political principles. Literariness, rather than political or ideological correctness, became a major criterion for literary criticism and translation, despite a lingering influence of political ideology.

Trollope's transculturation grew noticeably with the impetus from both the first Trollope Centenary worldwide and the changing domestic academic climate. The year 1982 witnessed the publication of two essays by Mei Shaowu and Zhu Hong respectively, marking the inception of Trollopian studies in China.[33] And, during the next two decades, substantial work of revaluation through newly compiled English literary history books, well-regulated translations and intensive research upgraded Trollope's transculturation in China to a higher level. The cultural affinity between Trollope and Chinese readers became more prominent along with the impetus from Western critical inspiration.

To begin with, in the mid-1980s and 1990s, numerous books of the history of English literature were published to meet the demands of university education in the humanities. The compilers, mostly professors teaching English literature or comparative literature, made efforts to define or redefine the fundamental characteristics of Trollope and his art. For all the remaining doubtful and conflicting voices, signs of growing consensus came into sight, leading to the acceptance of Trollope as an acclaimed literary master. *The Way We Live Now* and the Palliser novels, among others, were introduced and received due critical attention.[34] Liang Shiqiu, an eminent Chinese literary scholar, writer and translator, critically responded to Henry James's famous view about Trollope's great and inestimable capacity for 'a complete appreciation of the usual'. He pointed out that 'What is considered his greatest merit can be perhaps exactly his demerit',[35] thus echoing the issue of the 'Trollope problem' as regards the undefined intrinsic qualities of Trollope's art that had been studied by such contemporary Western Trollopians as David Skilton (1972), James R. Kincaid (1977), John Halperin (1977), Juliet McMaster (1978), Robert Tracy (1978), Geoffrey Harvey (1980) and later Deborah Denenholz Morse (1987).[36] In their noteworthy book (1985), Niu Yongmao and Jiang Lianjie, two professors of Chinese literature, argued for Trollope's realistic portrayal of clerical life 'pregnant with ironical overtones' 'without any breach upon their truthful reality'.[37] Written with a well-balanced standpoint between the general framework of Marxist ideology and a kind of discriminating scholarship, this book was ahead of its time in its width of concern and depth of insight. By emphasising that '[Trollope's] works are charged with considerable enlightening educational significance and they are also treasured for their high artistic value', the book did help to set right the unsettled and wavering attitude previously taken by many scholars.[38]

More sustained views and wider critical dimensions of Trollope's art were put forth by Qian Qing, a professor of English and American literature and a leading Chinese Trollopian scholar, and Jiang Chengyong, a professor of Comparative Literature and World Literature, in their 2006 books on English literature. In Qian's book, major artistic aspects of Trollope were analysed in both personal and cultural contexts, such as characterisation, psychological depiction, social depth and innovation in modes of novel-writing. 'Trollope was one of the most popular and best Victorian novelists of his time. He produced profusely, but never shallowly.'[39] With reputed urbanity and tolerance, and never susceptible to extreme feelings of pathos or anger, Trollope, as Qian astutely observed, was most accurate in capturing both the changing social and historical tempers and emerging problems of mid-Victorian English society with the mental and psychological subtleties on the part of both characters and their creator alike. In his book, Jiang responded to and clarified some scholars' uninformed and misleading comments on Trollope's style, theme and plot construction. Jiang's book was also evident of a crucial and significant turn in critical methodology in China from a relatively exclusive concern for a novel's intrinsic value to a multidisciplinary perspective with contemporary cultural awareness. Jiang pointed out that Trollope's depth of thought and the dimensions of his art still awaited clearer definition or redefinition.[40] Qian's astute judgement about Trollope's profundity and accuracy as a Victorian novelist in understanding all aspects of Victorian life and, ultimately, human nature, together with Jiang's emphasis on the novelist's 'rational social critique' of contemporary changing social manners and cultural values without 'stale didacticism' and 'affected sentimentalism', may serve as good evidence for Chinese scholars' aesthetic insights and their awareness of Trollope's complexity as a novelist and as a man. More such insights can be found in Chinese scholars' research on Trollope. These invaluable books effectively brought Trollope's transculturation in China in closer contact with contemporary global scholarship, while contributing to the critical activity with distinctive Chinese perception.

The second vital area worth examining is the greater impact of translations, which are essential in bringing a foreign writer into deeper and wider cultural contact and convergence with a local readership. An early Trollope readership was fostered by the assorted articles and introductions that appeared in books, newspapers, magazines and academic journals around the first Trollope Centenary in 1982. The leading expert translators aside, some sixteen scholars also contributed their various translated works by Trollope, even some rare pieces. These included such miscellaneous subjects as Trollope's theory of novel-writing, Trollope's short stories, Trollope's family, Frances Trollope, Trollope and stamps, letters, Trollope's sketching skill, and Kate Field. In addition to the 1957 translation of two novels, the majority of the existing Chinese versions appeared during the 1980s and 1990s. Specifically, they include *The Warden*

(《巴徹斯养老院》(1957), 《巴彻斯特养老院》(1986)), *Nina Balatka* (《尼娜·巴拉特伽》(1957)), *Barchester Towers* (《巴彻斯特大教堂》(1987)), *An Autobiography* (《特罗洛普自传》 (1987)), *The Prime Minister* (《首相》 (1988, revised 2014)), *Mr Scarborough's Family* (《斯卡伯勒的婚约》(1992)), *Doctor Thorne* (《索恩医生》(1994)), *The Way We Live Now* (《如今世道》(1995, revised 2008 and 2014)), *Framley Parsonage* (《弗莱姆利教区》(2001)), *North America* (《北美游记》 (2006)), *The Last Chronicle of Barset* (《巴赛特的最后纪事》(2007)) and the two collections of short stories, *Katchein's Caprices* (《任性的卡琴》(1988), 《特罗洛普中短篇小说精选》(reprinted 2006)) and *Katchein's Caprices: Selected Short Fiction by Trollope* (《任性的凯琴姑娘 – 特罗洛普中短篇小说选》(1992)).

Most of the translated novels were published by prestigious publishing houses in either 'The World's Literary Masterpiece Library' by the People's Literature Publishing House, 'The Foreign Literary Masterpiece Series' by the Shanghai Translation Publishing House, or 'The World's Famous Biography Series' by the Hunan People's Publishing House. With these publications, the artistic merits and worth of Trollope came to be more clearly recognised and intensively studied in China, particularly in the hands of his Chinese translators at different periods. Thus, Trollope, together with some other long-neglected English writers, began to occupy a place as an established English novelist in the Chinese canon of Western literature, and became part of a dynamic world literature repertoire.

The Trollope translators deserve our great respect because their translating expertise, together with their research into the original works, qualifies them as Trollope translator-researchers. They wrote analytical and critical commentaries in the form of prefaces, postscripts or translator's notes in order to illuminate some central issues concerned in the works in question and provided readers with detailed notes and illustrations, reliable background information as well as their own critical viewpoints. Apart from the excellent quality of translation, in their scholarly comments we can see both their perceptive understanding as translators and their originality as sophisticated critics. Much of Chinese scholars' critical reaction to Trollope should be accredited to the illuminating views of these translators. In the 'Preface to the Translated Version' for *The Warden*, Zhu Wan made two keen observations about Trollope's greatness: Trollope's strong English national characteristics epitomised by his realism and the 'universality and profundity of his works . . . deeply rooted in his perceptive understanding of human nature'.[41] Moreover, the detailed annotated notes of both a contextual and cultural nature made Zhu Wan's two translations especially helpful to scholars and common readers alike in their understanding of the cultures of both England and other Western countries. Similarly, interested readers of Trollope were able to learn Trollope's established literary status in Western countries through Mei Shaowu's introductory essay to Trollope in *Biographies of Famous Foreign Writers*[42] which was perhaps the earliest ever of Mei's long and devoted efforts to Trollope introduction and translation. In his 'Preface by the Translator' to the Chinese version of *Mr Scarborough's Family*, the translator Wu Xinqiang persuasively critiqued Trollope's serious moral concerns and worldview in connection with his dual social and political stance. Wu also pointed out that the plain, straightforward style of writing, dull and flat as it might seem, together with authorial asides, very effectively served Trollope's ultimate purpose of sincere communication with readers about a certain thematic moral issue, without the obstacles of suspension and mystery in plot development.[43] Its frequent reference to Western Trollopian scholarship over a long period of critical history manifested a more mature literary approach coupled with academic independence.

In his 'Foreword' to *The Last Chronicle of Barset*, Su Fuzhong, a Trollopian dev-otee and an early translator of Trollope's novels,[44] incisively pointed out the novel's relevance to some contemporary cultural issues at times of social transformation and regarded Trollope's liberal concern with individuals' values and psychology as the main reason for his success as a social critic. 'Trollope has shown through his pen individuals' values, individuals' sense of being and individuals' psychology at times of social transformation.' He concluded that 'it is exactly this quality of the-matic concern that makes his works close to the level of modern novel-writing and stand the test of ever-fresh critical judgement and analysis of modern critics'.[45] Here much was suggested about the novel's relevance to contemporary cultural issues and this inevitably attracted the attention of researchers. The fact that Trollope's rationalism, dialectic attitude, liberal thinking and thematic subtleties and com-plexities, together with his social and psychological realism, were among his defin-ing qualities was frequently mentioned and reiterated by Zhu Hong, Zhu Wan, Su Fuzhong and Zhang Yujiu, translator of *An Autobiography* (1987). What appealed to these scholars, above all, was Trollope's sincerity and honesty, which made him 'a Victorian writer with the least Victorianism'.[46] The cultural implications and transcultural relevance of Trollope's works as literary texts came to be manifested and duly recognised.

Generally speaking, then, the translation of Trollope's works has developed gradually yet noticeably. The changing tides of Trollope's literary reputation over time aside, this gradual development has been largely influenced by the ideological and aesthetic factors at work in China's history. As the construction of the world literature canon in China has been based not so much on principles of 'literariness' and 'canonical repertoire status' as on the 'educational value' of a work, the liter-ary status of Trollope in China has been hampered considerably, which definitely accounts for the chequered state of translation of Trollope's works. Specifically, for a long time before 1978 and for a period of time afterwards, the literary pendu-lum was still determined to a certain extent by leftist political orientations, which accounted for the overemphasis on Chinese national conditions as well as topicality and choice regarding Western literature. With the advent of the new century, Chi-na's development towards a market economy has brought significant repercussions upon publishing institutions, resulting in the complications in the choice of source work, readership profile and translation quantity and quality.[47] Consequently, Trol-lope may have also been 'thrown into the market' under the changing circumstances of the book market in similar ways as he benefited from cultural prosperity of the 1980s.[48] As things stand, to further promote Trollope's transculturation to a higher level, we still have a long way to go. Currently, the demand for more translations to satisfy both the general readership and academic scholarship remains urgent.[49] Most urgent of all is the task to find ways to fill up the shortage of well-trained and enthu-siastic young translators of sufficient literary and translating expertise. Here there is a bottleneck in Trollope translation, which applies to a great extent to high-quality foreign literary translation in general in China.

The third notable area worth special scrutiny is research. It is in this area that we find the transcultural process of Trollope in China most promising. In fact, in the critical study of Trollope undertaken by Chinese scholars, there has been a constant respect, whether conscious or subconscious, for Western critical scholarship, which is definitely a positive factor in upgrading the overall critical standard of Trollope criticism in China. More importantly, the progress made in Trollopian studies should be amply accredited to the pioneering and original work done by Chinese Trollopian scholars since the 1980s. Scholars from the Foreign Literature Research Institute of Chinese Academy of Social Sciences (CASS) were the first to respond critically to Trollope's literary theory and works. Their pioneering work helped inform Chinese literary circles of Western Trollope scholarship, legitimise Trollopian studies in China's Western literary studies and ultimately lay a solid foundation for later growth. And the younger generation of scholars is also indispensable in consolidating the acculturation of Trollope through cultural convergence in the new century.

Mei Shaowu, Zhu Hong and Lu Jiande, eminent Trollopian critics from CASS, deserve special respect. Around 1980, Mei began to write articles to introduce Trollope and his art through various forms of publication, and also made devoted exertions on translation and research. In his noted 1982 critical essay, Mei not only expounded the complexity of Trollope's personal political and social stance and his artistic principles, but also presented before the Chinese reader a multifaceted image of Trollope who could be viewed from a variety of perspectives, such as a realistic artist, political novelist, psychologist, social historian, moralist and social ameliorator. Attention was paid to Trollope's ambivalent world view and resilient moral consciousness, alongside the critical opinions of many renowned Western Trollopians of the time. Thus Trollopian studies in China was launched with a global vision and altitude. Most notably, Mei provided inspiration for the study of the deeper transcultural connection between Trollope's works and some traditional Chinese moral and aesthetical concepts, of which, as Mei pointed out, the literary practice of Ba Jin (1904–2005) could be a cogent example.[50] Mei also translated seven of Trollope's short stories, categorised them into four major groups and praised some of them as 'outstanding works among all Victorian short fiction', and as most noteworthy for Trollope's 'humorous self-portraiture, his deep exploration into human nature and his original views about writing' – aspects of his art 'less found in his long fiction'.[51]

Zhu Hong, a renowned early Trollopian critic, is best known for her 1982 essay 'Trollope and Other Related Thoughts'. In this essay, Zhu dwelt upon the pressing issue of critical reassessment with regard to a number of long-neglected eminent English and European writers, such as Trollope, George Eliot, Kafka, Joyce and others during earlier literary periods. She astutely pointed out that arbitrary and wilful neglect had actually led to the unsatisfactory condition of foreign literature translation and hampered the critical acceptance of many outstanding writers. She argued that without the overall vision of the representative writers at each period of literary history, there would have been neither complete understanding of the literary development of other countries, nor profound critical observations through comparison about the so-called 'literary summit'.[52] In literary criticism, as Zhu maintained, there should be a fundamental shift from the rigid and stereotyped political standards to aesthetic standards so as to accept broader literary classes of realism, including those truly great works of thematic complexities and multifacetedness, 'deeply rooted in the life and going deeply into the hearts of the people'.[53] Zhu's timely and candid insistence upon a new turn in critical criteria definitely proved to be a crucial step forward in Trollope's transculturation in China, and even in Trollope's eventual canonisation in Chinese foreign literature study. In another important essay, Zhu made a critical assessment of the thematic, stylistic and other aspects of Trollope's novels and short fiction.[54] Like Mei, back in 1980, Zhu began strongly to commend Trollope's 'exceptional attainment' as a short-story writer.[55] As a sign of active reaction and renewed interest in Trollope as a literary master, several publications came out consecutively in the early 1980s which collected Trollope's thoughts and reflections on many aspects of fiction.[56]

Lu Jiande, an eminent Victorianist and leading Trollopian scholar, published his essay 'Trollope and Politics' in the journal *Book Town* to address the issue of English politics, an academic area where to Chinese scholars misunderstanding might arise owing to cultural differences.[57] Lu made a point of understanding Trollope's political stand against the historical background of interplay of Victorian liberalism, conservatism and radicalism, thus drawing critics' attention to a wide range of social and cultural issues contextualised in Victorian society and culture in general. An erudite, liberal-minded scholar steeped in traditional Chinese culture and with a solid Cambridge background, Lu is insistent upon undertaking foreign literary studies with a cross-cultural awareness, a liberal stand as well as a commitment to cultural enrichment in the Chinese social context. Lu represents the kind of critical perspicuity and intellectual liberal humanism that Chinese critical circles of foreign literary studies need urgently for further promotion of Trollope's transculturation.

At the turn of the century, Trollopian studies in China received fresh incentives from the growing tendency of opening up to the outside world and the ensuing frequent academic exchange with scholars abroad. The support of funds from various organisations, mostly at the national and the provincial levels, has led to serious academic achievements in Trollopian studies. Meanwhile, the introduction of Trollope's works in postgraduate literature courses signified a step forward in Trollope's transculturation. Notably, the fruitful teaching and impressive research work on Trollope by Qian Qing, Professor of literature at Beijing Foreign Studies University, and Yin Qiping, Professor of literature at Zhejiang University,[58] brought penetrating critical insights and fresh theoretical perspectives to Trollope's Palliser novels and other works of social criticism. The cultural values of Trollope's semi-political novels were further studied and tapped into by Chinese researchers. Fruitful results, among others, could also be evidenced by the scholarly undertakings by myself and Yang Yingjun under Qian's guidance. In my book-length monograph *Trollope: His Later Novels and the Changing Society* (2009), I made a study of the 'Trollope problem' by addressing Trollope's ambivalent attitudes toward major social and moral issues of his day and arguing for Trollope's liberal and humanistic perception and understanding of the changing Victorian political, social and moral life. This book continued other Chinese scholars' efforts to carry on a cross-cultural dialogue with Western Trollopian scholarship.[59] Yang Yingjun scrutinised the underlying causes of such ambivalence and duality in the light of Trollope's theoretical Liberalism and instinctive conservative tendency in general. The biographical and critical value of *The New Zealander* (1857) was explored in Yang's research.[60] These critical attempts represented worthy contributions by Chinese scholars in merging Trollope's literary assets with Chinese critical resources. Yang and I have also done our bit in promoting Trollope teaching and research at the postgraduate level.

Over the past fifteen years in the new century, the enduring appeal of Trollope and his works has continued to ferment and take root in Chinese academic circles of foreign literature studies, bringing in its wake more concentrated research endeavours and achievements. The fruitful scholarship of both devoted translators and foreign literature researchers has helped to broaden and deepen the understanding of Trollope from various perspectives as a varied, subtle artist 'who helps the heart of man to know itself' (Nathaniel Hawthorne). The image of Anthony Trollope as an acclaimed Victorian novelist, deep, complex and multifaceted, has begun to evolve and find ever-fresh assonance with its Chinese critical perception and inspiration. Emerging younger Trollopian scholars and enthusiasts majoring in world literature, Chinese and history have turned out praiseworthy research achievements that have definitely given a forceful impetus to Trollopian studies. New critical approaches have been adopted to explore issues of cultural concerns that may have a bearing upon both Trollope's time and the contemporary social life. More recently, the theories of Cultural Materialism, neo-Marxism, narratology and media are creatively applied much to the critical advantage in exploring Trollope's Victorian world and its values. And much of what is typical of Trollope as a Victorian realistic novelist has been subjected to new exploration and interpretation through informed critiques regarding Trollope's modernity and universality in the contemporary cross-cultural context. Recent years have witnessed an increasing number of critiques pertaining to gender issues (women's role and independence, and masculinity), the ethics of capitalism and commercialism, social justices, and Trollope's liberal humanism, all explored in the Victorian cultural context and some of them studied with contemporary interpretations. Such critical visions may point to the universality of Trollope's works in our times, and thus consolidate the cultural value of Trollope's transculturation in China.

Admittedly, research on Trollope and his works is far from exhaustive. Nearly two-thirds of Trollope's works, including most of his short fiction, travel writings, hunting sketches, literary biographies and criticism, still remain under-explored territories, while some oft-studied works still deserve more creative endeavours. Some areas of research interest such as the international theme, anti-Semitism, modernity and the law still await further delving and tapping.

Since the first Chinese contact with Trollope through the Shanghai Library resources nearly 160 years ago, Trollope's transculturation in China has gradually developed against the background of the broad ideological, cultural and literary changes. Accepting and studying Trollope, we are in contact with a Victorian writer whose novels examine complex social issues from a variety of highly nuanced perspectives. We treasure our contact with such a great English novelist, because we have found in this literary master a rare talent with an enduring art, unexcelled literary percipience, humanistic vision and cultural universality. In the third Trollope centenary, Trollope's transculturation in China will certainly promise new landscapes and meaning when we place Trollopian studies in diversified cultural and interdisciplinary contexts where the rich resources of Chinese traditional and modern literary theory and practice are explored transculturally. The universal significance and value of Trollope and his works will surely be more clearly recognised when Chinese culture and Western culture come into a closer contact and convergence.

Notes

1. In this chapter, the concept of transculturation is used to refer to the complex process of cultural interaction through literary introduction and study. As a means of global cultural convergence, transculturation has become indispensable for a deeper understanding between different cultures in our times.

2. The translation of Western works into Chinese began in the late Ming Dynasty (1368–1644). The translation of Western literature, in particular, began in earnest during the second wave of 'New Learning', a movement that was characterised by the intellectual reorientation of China's modernisation programme. Yan Fu (1854–1921) and Lin Shu (1851–1924) were 'twin luminaries' among the earliest translators. Yan's contributions lie in acquainting Chinese readers with translations of Western works such as T. H. Huxley's *Evolution and Ethics* and J. Stuart Mill's *On Liberty* and *Logic*, while Lin did the same with translations of Western fiction such as Alexandre Dumas's *La Dame aux camellias*, Harriet Beecher Stowe's *Uncle Tom's Cabin*, and many novels by Charles Dickens and Sir Walter Scott. See Immanuel C. Y. Hsü, *The Rise of Modern China*, 3rd edn (New York: Oxford University Press, 1983), pp. 419–26.

3. Liang Qichao [梁启超], 'Fiction Seen in Relation to the Guidance of Society' ['论小说与群治之关系', 'Lun xiaoshuo yu qunzhizhi guanxi'] (1902), as quoted in A. Ying [阿英] (ed.), *Anthology of Late Qing Literature: Research Materials on Fiction and Drama* [《晚清文学丛钞：小说戏曲研究卷》, *Wan Qing wenxue congchao: xiaoshuo xiqu yanjiu juan*] (Beijing: Zhonghua Book Company, 1960), pp. 14–15. Liang's radical theory of fiction was first expounded in 'Foreword to Our Series of Political Novels in Translation' ['译印政治小说序', 'Yiyin zhengzhi xiaoshuo xu'], *The China Discussion* [《清议报》, *Qingyi bao*] 1 (1898), in A. Ying [阿英](ed.), *Anthology of Late Qing Literature: Research Materials on Fiction and Drama* [《晚清文学丛钞：小说戏曲研究卷》, *Wan Qing wenxue congchao: xiaoshuo xiqu yanjiu juan*] (Beijing: Zhonghua Book Company, 1960), pp. 13–14. With deep admiration for the political novel then in vogue in Japan, Liang strongly, yet somewhat fancifully, emphasised the role of the political novel as 'the most instrumental in making the governments of America, England, Germany, France, Austria, Italy, and Japan daily more progressive or enlightened'. See C. T. Hsia, 'Yen Fu and Liang Ch'i-ch'ao as Advocates of New Fiction' in Adele Austin Rickett (ed.), *Chinese Approaches to Literature from Confucius to Liang Ch'i-Ch'ao* (Princeton: Princeton University Press, 1978), pp. 221–57.

4. Starting with the Literary Revolution of 1917, this movement marked a new stage in the Chinese response to Western influence and opened the door for China's modernisation and national regeneration. It advocated human rights, democracy and freedom, and repudiated traditionalism, Confucianism in particular. Also called the New Thought Movement or the New Tide, it was hailed by Hu Shi [胡适] (1891–1962), a leader of the movement, as a 'Chinese Renaissance'. With the ensuing May Fourth Movement of 1919, it gradually took a radical turn to become a patriotic movement in stimulating nationalism, with literature assuming a shift 'from literary revolution to revolutionary literature'. See Immanuel C. Y. Hsü, *The Rise of Modern China*, 3rd edn (New York: Oxford University Press, 1983), pp. 493–511.

5. Milena Doleželová-Velingerová, *The Chinese Novel at the Turn of the Century* (Toronto: University of Toronto Press, 1980), 'Introduction', p. 7.

6. A fact inferred from the retrieved database material in ProQuest Historical Newspapers: Chinese Newspapers Collection, 1832–1953' ['近现代中国英文报纸库, 1832–1953', 'Jinxiandai Zhongguo yingwen baozhiku, 1832–1953'], which yields seventy-three results from four English-language newspapers run by English or American businessmen between 1850 and 1950: *The North-China Herald* [《北华捷报》, *Bei Hua jiebao*, later known as

《字林西报》, Zilin xibao] (1850–67; seven notices), *The North-China Herald and Supreme Court & Consular Gazette* [《北华捷报和最高法庭与领事公报》, *Bei Hua jiebao he zuigao fating yu lingshi gongbao*] (1870–1941; forty-eight notices), *The China Press* [《大陆报》 *Dalu Bao*] (1925–38; sixteen notices), *The China Weekly Review* or *Millard's Review* [《密勒氏评论报》 *Mileshi pinglun bao*] (1923–50; one notice). The first two of these were the earliest in Shanghai while the second and the third were the most influential ones for quite a long time.

7. The Shanghai Library began as the Shanghai Book Club, which had been set up in 1849 by some Western residents to cater to the needs of Western readership in Shanghai concessions (1843–1943).

8. A situation designating diverse ideological orientations and changing topical themes. See Zha Mingjian [查明建] and Xie Tianzhen [谢天振] (eds), *A History of the 20th-Century Foreign Literary Translation in China* [中国20世纪外国文学翻译史, *Zhongguo ershi shiji waiguo wenxue fanyishi*] (Wuhan: Hubei Education Press, 2007), p. 562.

9. Yingwen zazhi [《英文杂志》], *English Magazine*, 9.10 (1923): p. 2. The other five English authors were John Henry Newman, Charles Dickens, William Makepeace Thackeray, Charles Reade and George Eliot.

10. Zheng Zhenduo [郑振铎], *The Outline of Literature* [《文学大纲》, *Wenxue dagang*] (Shanghai: The Commercial Press, 1927), p. 73.

11. Ibid. p. 108.

12. Zhang Yuerui [张越瑞] (trans., ed.), *A Survey of English and American Literature* [《英美文学概观》, *Yingmei wenxue gaiguan*] Wang Yunwu [王云五] (ed.) (Shanghai: The Commercial Press, 1934), p. 67.

13. Lafcadio Hearn [小泉八云], *A Study in English Literature* [《英国文学研究》, *Yingguo wenxue yanjiu*], trans. Sun Xizhen [孙席珍] (Shanghai: Modern Book Bureau, 1932), p. 216.

14. Jin Donglei [金东雷], *The Outline of English Literature* [《英国文学史纲》, *Yingguo wenxue shigang*] (Shanghai: The Commercial Press, 1937), p. 413.

15. Yi Mei [一梅], 'On English Novelists of the Nineteenth Century' ['十九世纪的英国小说家', *Shijiu shijide yingguo xiaoshuojia*], *Journal of Youth Monthly* 3.3 [《青年月刊》, *Qingnian yuekan*] (1936), p. 43.

16. Li Rumian [李儒勉] (trans.), *The English Novel* [《英国小说概论》, *Yinguo xiaoshuo gailun*] (Shanghai: The Commercial Press, 1946), p. 53.

17. Ibid. pp. 53–4.

18. Shen Si [沈思] (trans.), 'A Journey to Panama' ['返棹记', 'Fan zhuo ji'], *China Traveler* [《旅行杂志》, *Lüxing zazhi*], 6.2 (1942): pp. 73–86.

19. 衛斯特亨, Huai Jie [怀杰] (trans.), 'Trollope: A Nineteenth-Century Novelist Who Has Come Back Into Favour' ['杜羅拉伯 – 重投时好的十九世纪英国小说家', *Te luo la bo – chongtou shihaode shijiu shiji yingguo xiaoshuojia*], *Progress* [《進步》, *Jinbu*], 1.5 (1947): p. 14.

20. The possession of *An Autobiography* by individuals, especially professional writers and scholars, is apparent from the donation of their copies of the book to China's National Library and Beijing University Library by, respectively, Ba Jin [巴金] (1904–2005), an eminent and prolific modern Chinese writer, and Achilles Fang [方志彤] (1910–95), a 1932 Tsinghua graduate and a Harvard research fellow.

21. Donald Smalley (ed.), 'Introduction', in: *Trollope: The Critical Heritage* (London: Routledge & Kegan Paul, 1969), p. 12.

22. V. S. Pritchett, quoted by Markwick et al., in Margaret Markwick, Deborah Denenholz Morse and Regenia Gagnier (eds), *The Politics of Gender in Anthony Trollope's Novels: New Readings for the Twenty-First Century* (Aldershot: Ashgate, 2009), p. 2.

23. Zha and Xie (eds), *A History*, p. 1448.

24. Shen Zhiyuan [沈志远], 'An Address on the Planning and Improving the Quality of Translation' ['为翻译工作的计划化和提高质量而奋斗', Wei fanyi gongzuode jihuahua he tigao zhiliang er fendou] *Bulletin of Translation* [《翻译通报》, *Fanyi tongbao*], 3.5 (1951): p. 10. Research shows that some ambitious projects of translation of the world's literary classics which had been launched earlier by many publishing houses and literary societies were aborted during the wartime period. See Zou Zhenhuan [邹振环], *Twentieth-Century Publication of Translated Works in Shanghai and the Cultural Changes* [《二十世纪上海翻译出版与文化变迁》, *Ershi shiji Shanghai fanyi chuban yu wenhua bianqian*] (Nanning: Guangxi Education Publishing House, 2001), pp. 172–82.

25. Zha and Xie (eds), *A History*, pp. 1443–4.

26. The concept of realism was linked with the idea that 'a good piece of literature has to be both true to life and ideologically correct'. See Li Tien-yi, 'Continuity and Change in Modern Chinese Literature', *The Annals of the American Academy of Political and Social Science*, 321.1 (January 1959): pp. 90–9, Sage Publications, Inc.

27. Zha and Xie (eds), *A History*, pp. 1450–1.

28. Ibid. pp. 1449–50.

29. See 'Synopsis' ['内容提要' 'Neirong tiyao'], in Zhu Wan [主万] (trans.), *The Warden* [《巴徹斯养老院》 *Ba Che Si yanglaoyuan*] (Shanghai: New Literature and Art Press, 1957).

30. Zhu Wan [主万], 'Preface to the Translated Version' ['译本序', 'Yiben xu'], in Zhu Wan [主万] (trans.), *The Warden* [《巴彻斯特养老院》, *Ba che si te yanglaoyuan*] (Shanghai: Shanghai Translation Publishing House 1986), p. 18.

31. Zha and Xie (eds), *A History*, pp. 768–9.

32. In 1978, two years after the Great Proletarian Cultural Revolution ended, China began to adopt a policy of Reform and Opening-up to re-embark upon the road towards modernisation via a market economy through ideological and intellectual readjustment and structural reorganisation.

33. These are Mei's essay 'A Tentative Study of the "Trollope Problem" – Upon Trollope's Centenary Memorial' ['"特罗洛普问题"初探 – 纪念安东尼·特罗洛普逝世百周年', 'Te luo luo pu wenti' chutan – jinian An dong ni·Te luo luo pu shishi baizhounian], *The World's Literature*, 6 (1982): pp. 211–29, and Zhu's essay 'Trollope and Other Related Thoughts' ['从特罗洛普想到的', 'Cong Te luo luo pu xiangdaode'], *Reading Magazine* [《读书》, *Dushu*], 11 (1982): pp. 84–98.

34. Mei Shaowu [梅绍武] introduced with critical analysis *The Way We Live Now* around 1980 with the Chinese version [《我们现在的生活方式》, *Women xianzaide shengshuo fangshi*]. His critical introduction to the Palliser novels was also among the earliest, regarding *The Prime Minister* 'the best' in the series. See Mei Shaowu, 'A Tentative Study of the "Trollope Problem"', pp. 216–17. In his book on English literature, Chen Jia [陈嘉], Professor of English at Nanjing University, opened a new dimension of Trollope as 'a prolific writer of many novels' with his introduction of 'the novels of parliamentary life', *Phineas Finn* and *Phineas Redux* in particular, though mainly leaning on the political line of class struggle. See Chen Jia, [《英国文学史》 *A History of English Literature* [*Yingguo wenxueshi*] (Beijing: The Commercial Press, 1986), vol. 3, pp. 379–80.

35. Liang Shiqiu [梁实秋], *A History of English Literature*, vol. 3 [《英国文学史》(第三卷), *Yingguo wenxueshi* (disan juan)] (Taibei: Xiezhi Industry Series Publishing Company Ltd, 1985), vol. 3, p. 1695.

36. Among noteworthy book-length studies and collections in the 1970s and 1980s, these Western Trollopian scholars stood out with their sophisticated criticism, despite unanimity in viewpoints, regarding 'the challenge of Trollope studies . . . to define the very qualities of the man, both as writer and as personality' (N. John Hall) and drew Chinese scholars' attention to the complexity of Trollope's art. In his *Anthony Trollope and his Contemporaries* (1972), David Skilton argues for 'the cause of [Trollope's] uncompromising realism' which

'at different times obeys, defies or gently stretches'. (Quoted in Zuo Xiaolan [左晓岚], *Trollope: His Later Novels and the Changing Society* (Shanghai: Shanghai Jiao Tong University Press, 2009), p. 83.) James R. Kincaid provides his astute insights into Trollope's formal strategies in drawing upon traditions of Jacobean drama and the comedy of manners 'for exploring human life with delicacy and profundity' (Ibid. p. 2), 'brilliantly extend[ing] our sense of diversity and intricacy' (R. C. Terry, ed. *Oxford Reader's Companion to Trollope* (Oxford University Press, 1999), p. 132). While John Halperin bases his critical analysis of the Palliser series mainly on his argument about Trollope's extreme conservatism in political standpoint (1977), Deborah Denenholz Morse considers 'Trollope's duality and conflict in Trollope's vision of Victorian womanhood' (1987), a fruitful work in depth and focus following Juliet McMaster's study of Trollope's unifying principles in *Trollope's Palliser Novels: Theme and Pattern* (London: Macmillan, 1978). Robert Tracy's claim of Trollope's social conventionality in *Trollope's Later Novels* (Berkeley: University of California Press, 1978) is challenged by Geoffrey Harvey's critical viewpoint about Trollope's radical attitude towards the society he lived in, a judgement antithetical to many general critical observations.

37. Niu Yongmao and Jiang Lianjie [牛庸懋, 蒋连杰] (eds), *Nineteenth-Century English Literature* [《十九世纪英国文学》, *Shijiu shiji Yingguo wenxue*] (Zhengzhou: Yellow River Literature and Art Publishing House, 1985), p. 267.

38. Ibid. p. 257.

39. Qian Qing [钱青], 'Trollope' ['特罗洛普', Te luo luo pu], in Qian Qing (ed.), *A History of Nineteenth-Century English Literature* [《英国19世纪文学史》, *Yingguo shijiu shiji wenxueshi*] (Beijing: Foreign Language Teaching and Research Press, 2006), p. 311.

40. See Jiang Chengyong [蒋承勇], *A History of British Fiction* [《英国小说发展史》, *Yingguo xiaoshuo fazhanshi*] (Hangzhou: Zhejiang University Press, 2006), pp. 185–8.

41. Zhu Wan [主万], 'Preface to the Translated Version' ['译本序', Yiben xu], in Zhu Wan (trans.), *The Warden* [《巴彻斯特养老院》, *Ba che si te yanglaoyuan*] (Shanghai: Shanghai Translation Publishing House, 1986), p. 19.

42. Mei Shaowu [梅绍武], 'Trollope' ['特罗洛普'Te luo luo pu], in Zhang Yinglun [张英伦] (ed.), *Biographies of Famous Foreign Writers* [《外国名作家传》, *Waiguo ming zuojia zhuan*] (Beijing: CASS Press, 1980), pp. 533–7.

43. Wu Xinqiang [吴信强], 'Preface by the Translator' ['译者序'Yizhe xu in Wu Xinqiang] (trans.), *Mr Scarborough's Family* [《斯卡伯勒的婚约》, *Si ka bo le de hunyue*] (Shanghai: Shanghai Translation Publishing House, 1992), p. 12 and p. 15.

44. Su's translations include *Doctor Thorne* [《索恩医生》 , *Suo en yisheng*] (Shanghai: Shanghai Translation Publishing House, 1994), *The Last Chronicle of Barset* [《巴赛特的最后纪事 》, *Ba sai te de zuihou jishi*] (Beijing: People's Literature Publishing House, 2007) and 'The Lady of Launay' [《终成眷属 》, *Zhong cheng juanshu*] (*Appreciation of Literary Masterpieces*) [《名作欣赏》, *Mingzuo xinshang*], 5 (1985): pp. 119–31, with different pen names, Wen Xin [文心], Zhou Zhihuai [周治淮], Zang Shulin [臧树林], Fang Huimin [方慧敏], and Su Fuzhong [苏福衷], for the above translations respectively.

45. Su Fuzhong [苏福忠], 'Foreword' ['前言', 'Qianyan'], in Zhou Zhihuai, Zang Shulin and Fang Huimin [周治淮，臧树林，方慧敏] (trans.), *The Last Chronicle of Barset* [《巴赛特的最后纪事》, *Ba sai te de zuihou jishi*] (Beijing: People's Literature Publishing House, 2007), p. 13.

46. Zhu Hong, 'Anthony Trollope and the Artistic Accomplishments of His Fiction' [朱虹, '安东尼·特罗洛普和他的小说成就', An dong ni·Te luo luo pu he tade xiaoshuo chengjiu], in Zhu Hong [朱虹,] *Golden Time of English Fiction: 1813–1873* [《英国小说的黄金时代：1813–1873》, *Yingguo xiaoshuo de huangjin shidai: 1813–1873*].

47. For the existing problems of translating market of the 1980s and 1990s, see Zha and Xie, *A History*, pp. 808–13.

48. The question must be more complicated when it comes to the individual translators and the publishers they worked with, a typical case in point being Mei Shaowu's giving up his translation of *The Way We Live Now* halfway through the 1980s 'owing to the wavering attitude of the publisher'. See Hei Ma [黑马], 'A Clear Light in the Midst of a Bustling World' ['喧哗躁动中的一盏清灯', Xuanhua zaodong zhongde yizhan qingdeng], *China Reading Weekly* [《中华读书报》, *Zhonghua dushubao*], 23 March (2005). But curiously enough, the opposite cases can also be found. For example, the translated version by Zi Pei [秭佩] of this novel was published consecutively by three different publishing houses in 1995, 2008 and 2014, with Dunhuang Literature and Art Press, The Chongqing Publishing House and Lanzhou University Press: *Studies on English Fiction* [《英国小说研究》] (Beijing: CASS Press, 1997), p. 251.

49. Encouragingly, the year 2004 saw the publication by Foreign Language Teaching and Research Press of an adapted version of *The Warden*《养老院院长》 from the UK edition by J. Y. K. Kerr (1995) as classified audio reading material for senior high-school students, and thus Trollope readership got expanded. A more recent English–Chinese version of the novel adapted from Clare West's simplified version 《巴彻斯特教堂尖塔》 was published by the same press in 2014, the intended readers being senior high-school students and university freshmen and sophomores as well.

50. See Mei, 'A Tentative Study of the "Trollope Problem"', p. 224.

51. Mei Shaowu [梅绍武], *Katchein's Caprices: Selected Short Fiction by Trollope* [《任性的凯琴姑娘 – 特罗洛普中短篇小说选》, *Renxingde Kai qin guniang – Te luo luo pu zhongduanpian xiaoshuo xuan*] (Shanghai: Shanghai Translation Publishing House, 1992), pp. 4–9. Also, in his brief critical review of 'La Mère Bauche', Mei pointed out the 'considerable realistic moral significance of the tragedy that may still have its modern version in some countries, including here in ours' (pp. 10–11). Thus, a link was struck, quite foreseeably, between Trollope's works and related aspects of contemporary Chinese society. One of his earliest Trollope translations, 'La Mère Bauche' ['鲍什妈妈', Bao shen mama] first appeared in *The World's Literature* [《世界文学》, *Shijie wenxue*], 6 (1982): pp. 177–210.

52. Zhu, 'Trollope and Other Related Thoughts', p. 95.

53. Ibid. p. 94.

54. See Zhu, 'Anthony Trollope and the Artistic Accomplishments of His Fiction', in Zhu Hong, *Golden Time*, pp. 214–53.

55. Zhu, 'On the Development of English Short Story' ['浅谈英国短篇小说的发展', Qiantan yingguo duanpian xiaoshuode fazhan], in Zhu Hong (ed.), *A Collection of English Short Stories* [《英国短篇小说选》 *Yingguo duanpian xiaoshuo xuan*] (Beijing: People's Literature Publishing House, 1980), p. 4. Mei's translation of Trollope's 'The Journey to Panama' ['巴拿马之行', Banama zhi xing] was collected in it. His translation of 'Malachi's Cove' ['马拉凯海峡', Ma la kai haixia] appeared in another book edited by Zhu in 1981.

56. See Luo Wanhua [罗婉华], 'On the Creation of the Novel' by Trollope ['谈小说创作', Tan xiaoshuo chuangzuo], *Theoretical Studies in Literature and Art* [《文艺理论研究》, *Wenyi lilun yanjiu*], 1 (1982): pp. 139–44. See Liu Ruoduan [刘若端], 'On the Novel and Writing Techniques' by Trollope ['论小说及其写作技巧', 'Lun xiaoshuo jiqi xiezuo jiqiao'], *Translation Series in Theories of Literature and Art 2* [《文艺理论译丛》, *Wenyi lilun yicong*] 2 (China's Literature Association Press, 1984), pp. 270–89. See Wang Peiji [汪培基], 'On the Novel and the Art of Novel-Writing' ['论小说和小说的写作艺术', Lun xiaoshuo he xiaoshuo d xiezuo yishu], Wang Yuanchun [王元春] (ed.), *English Writers on Literature*) [《英国作家论文学》, *Yingguo zuojia lun wenxue*] (Beijing: SDX Joint Publishing Company, 1985), pp. 173–83.

57. This essay first appeared as 'Preface' ['序', Xu] my *Trollope: His Later Novels and the Changing Society* [《特罗洛普：动态社会与小说世界》] (Shanghai: Shanghai Jiao Tong University Press, 2009).

58. See Yin Qiping [殷企平], 'The Causes for Melmotte's Downfall: With a Comment on the Changing Social Values under Trollope's Pen', ['麦尔墨特的败因 – 兼论特罗洛普笔下的社会价值观变迁', Mai er mo te de baiyin – jianlun Te luo luo pu bixiade shehui jiazhiguan bianqian] (*Foreign Languages*) [《外国语》, *Waiguoyu*], 5 (2002): pp. 62–6, and '"The Diamond Incident" on the Road to "Success": Warnings from *The Eustace Diamonds*' ['"成功"道路上的"钻石风波" – 《尤斯蒂斯钻石》的警示'), 《解放军外国语学院学报》, *Jiefangjun waiguoyu xueyuan xuebao*] *Academic Journal of PLA Foreign Languages Institute*, 1 (2006): pp. 69–75.

59. I would like to repeat my acknowledgement for the warm encouragement and generous help from Donald D. Stone and Mary Jacobus. See 'Preface', in Zuo Xiaolan [左晓岚, 《特罗洛普：动态社会与小说世界》] (*Trollope: His Later Novels and the Changing Society*) (Shanghai: Shanghai Jiao Tong University Press, 2009), pp. iii–iv.

60. In a state-funded key research project 'Foreign Literature in the Process of Modernisation' ['现代化进程中的外国文学', Xiandaihua jincheng zhongde waiguowenxue] of which Lu Jiande [陆建德] is the chief researcher, Yang has contributed an exclusive chapter on Trollope's politics.

11

TROLLOPE AND RUSSIA

Boris M. Proskurnin

In CONTEMPORARY RUSSIA, specialists in English literature call Anthony Trollope 'a forgotten classic'. This phrase helps us to understand some of the peculiarities of Trollope's Russian reception, from 1863, the moment that the Russian reading public was first acquainted with Trollope's work, up until 1991, the last year in which one of his novels was translated and published. More particularly, we can distinguish three periods in the history of Trollope's reception in Russia: his rise to prominence in the pre-1917 period, his fall into obscurity in the period from 1917 to 1991, and his return in the academy in the period from 1991 until the present (the so-called 'new Russian' period).

Pre-Soviet Russia

The first period is characterised by Trollope's widespread popularity among translators, publishers and literary critics, for which there were commercial, sociocultural and even political reasons. Between 1863 (when the first translation appeared) and 1898 (when the last pre-1917 translation of Trollope's novels was published), twenty-two novels were translated, some of them several times: *The Claverings* (in 1867 and in 1871), *The Prime Minister* (in 1877 and in 1882) and *The Way We Live Now* (in 1875 and in 1876). Since the publishing business in pre-1917 Russia was based on market laws, the very fact that Trollope's novels were so frequently published implies that it was quite profitable to do so. In this period, Russian translations were often published almost immediately after the first English publication. *The Eustace Diamonds* was one of several novels that were being read in Russian in the same year as they were first read in English. The earliest of Trollope's novels to be translated into Russian were *The Small House at Allington* (in 1863) and *Rachel Ray* (in 1864). In the 1870s, twelve of Trollope's novels were published in several thousand copies each, in addition to their serial publication in the Russian literary journals, which in the second half of the nineteenth century had a dominant influence over the social thought of the time. As such, Trollope's popularity in the Russia of the 1870s and 1880s was greater than that of many other English novelists of the mid-nineteenth century. It was, for example, greater than that of Thackeray (who always was – and is now – more popular in Russia than in England itself), and even rivalled that of Dickens; the overwhelming Dickens-centrism of the Russian literary canon of the nineteenth century misrepresents the history of the English literature of that period.

Judging by the list of the works that were translated and published in Russia in the late 1860s and 1870s, we notice that publishers, literary critics and the reading public were interested mainly in the Palliser novels, as well as in those novels that are socially critical and psychologically more profound, such as *He Knew He Was Right* (published twice, in 1871 and in 1876), *The Way We Live Now* and *Is He Popenjoy?* (published in 1878). Conversely, Trollope's novels of the 1850s and early 1860s were largely ignored. Readers knew about such masterpieces as *The Warden, Barchester Towers, Dr Thorne* and *Framley Parsonage* only through essays and reviews by Russian literary critics. We may say that for pre-1917 Russian readers the majority of the Barsetshire novels were definitely unknown. A likely reason for this lacuna is that Russian publishers probably considered the internal problems of the Anglican Church to be confusing for their readers. Although Trollope's mastery of social irony and the grotesque was absolute, the confrontation between Low and High Church, quite familiar to English readers, did not generate any appeal for a Russian audience. Even the publication in 1872 of Nikolai Leskov's famous *Clergy* [*Соборяне, Soboriane*] (a book depicting the everyday life of Russian Orthodox clergy) did not spark interest in similar works by the best interpreter of Church issues in English literature. However, to say that Russian readers of that time knew nothing about Trollope's attitude towards the Anglican Church would be unjust. In many novels, one or two representatives of the established Church are present: one of Trollope's main intentions was to give as wide a panorama as possible of English social life in the mid-nineteenth century, and the clergy was a very important sector of this social landscape. Some Russian interest in these social strata of English society is signalled by the fact that *The Vicar of Bullhampton* was published three times (in 1870, 1871 and 1873, and in two different translations). Even so, it is not the Church and religious problems that are at the centre of this novel's plot, but intense psychological questions; one may therefore safely assume that publishers and readers would have been attracted as much by the psychological depth and idealism of the protagonist, Frank Fenwick, whose drama of disillusion is couched in a sophisticated plot structure, as by religious issues.

The fact that the Barsetshire novels with their everyday drama of the clergy and gentry did not captivate Russian translators and publishers can be explained by the political and social situation of Russia itself, which had become more explosive after the reforms of 1861 (the abolition of serfdom) and other liberal measures of Alexander II. New sociopolitical forces had come to the foreground of Russian social and political life – the so-called 'raznochintsy': mostly intellectuals, and other social strata that opposed aristocracy and gentry. This phenomenon marked the emergence of the third estate as a leading sociocultural force. The politicisation of Russian social thought in the 1860s and 1870s explains why novels with political themes like George Eliot's *Felix Holt, the Radical* and George Meredith's *Beauchamp's Career* were popular in Russia, and why a comparable interest was shown in Trollope's political series, the Palliser novels. The greater popularity of the Palliser novels and the context in which Trollope is mentioned in Russian literary journals suggest that the writer's political views and his special interest in the human component of any political activity fitted many Russian intellectuals' ideas of the political and parliamentary structure of a future Russia. Only *Can You Forgive Her?* was not translated into Russian. Russian readers were introduced to Plantagenet Palliser and Lady Glencora as early as in 1863, the same year as English readers, when *The Small House at Allington* was translated and published. No doubt the satirical and ironic attitudes of English writer towards British political life and leading political figures could not but impress Russians, especially after the events of the Crimean War.

Other reasons for Trollope's popularity can be found in contemporary Russian journals and Russian encyclopedias. The very fact that articles on him appeared in the encyclopedias is a mark of how highly valued he was among readers. The encyclopedia was a compulsory display in the house of any educated Russian. 'Mr Trollope', we are told by Granat's encyclopedia, 'shows a talent as a fine narrator, very lively and always interesting'; he is 'a writer who is at his best depicting the rural gentry with all sorts of fascinating details'.[1] In Brokgaus's encyclopedia we are told that 'falsity, artificiality prevailed in popular fiction of Trollope's time, whereas he, moving mainstream, gave true and honest portrayals of the life of middle-class people'. His writing was 'photo-graphically accurate, and at the same time, artistic and full of life'.[2] These observations would have appealed to many Russian readers, in particular those who came from the rural gentry, the middle classes, the clergy and intellectuals. They read Trollope's works to satisfy a hunger for details about the life of their English contemporaries, a life very different from their own. This must be understood against another cultural phenomenon of this period: the Gallomania that had dominated the life of the higher levels of Russian society since the eighteenth century just in the decades mentioned was being replaced by Anglomania: in *War and Peace* by Leo Tolstoy (1863–9), which depicts the Russia of the early nineteenth century, the reader encounters characters such as Pierre, Anatole, Helene, Julie; in *Anna Karenina* (1873–6), in which Russian life of the current time is presented, the reader encounters Betsy, Dolly, Kitty, Steve – which is quite a remarkable change.

When we admire the number of Trollope's novels translated into Russian in the second half of the nineteenth century (leaving aside the quality of these translations and the number of readers: in many cases translations were too literal, and illiteracy in Russia was huge in the second half of the nineteenth century), we should remember that the Russian reading public's interest in Trollope's novels was a part of a greater attraction to European and American literature. All major journals and solid publishing houses dealt with publications of foreign writers' works, from the classical writers of the early modern period up to the present time.

The famous critic Piotr Tkachiov provides one key to understand the considerable interest in foreign novels in his essay 'People of the Future and Heroes of Philistinism', published in the journal *Affair* [*Delo*] in 1868:

> Recently, our lifeless and insipid fiction, which is offered to our reading public as the latest and the most effective means to put its mental capacities to sleep, all of a sudden was brightened by some novels in translation that make us think. In these novels, some aspects of contemporary life are touched upon, and, together with some everyday life scenes, quite another picture of family and social life is presented; these novels help us to see in the heroes and heroines not only some familiar types with whom we deal every day and every hour, but some new ones, whom we do not know at all; in a word, we see in these novels not only a contemporary man as he is, but a man as he should be according to the ideas of the thinking majority of our time.[3]

Though Tkachiov penned this observation in 1868 and he was referring to the translations of the foreign novels published in the 1860s (Zola, Hugo, Sand, Spielhagen, George Eliot and others), his thoughts about novels that made Russian readers look for ideals in the present and think about the future by and large hold for other authors such as Trollope; by 1868, three of Trollope's novels had been already translated.

In this respect it is worth quoting Dmitrii Pisarev, another famous Russian literary critic of the second half of the nineteenth century, who wrote in his essay 'Realists':

> That is why any consistent realist sees in Dickens, Thackeray, Trollope, George Sand, Hugo remarkable poets and extraordinary useful workers of our age. These writers with the help of their works bridge progressive thinkers and semi-educated crowd of both sexes, various ages and means.[4]

Including the name of Trollope in this list and speaking of him as a writer who supports and develops progressive ideas is striking, as it absolutely contradicts the Soviet interpretation of him as a minor conservative bourgeois writer.

Russians of that time saw Trollope's characters as representatives of the English national character, and the plots of his novels as examples of changes taking place within the English middle classes, which Russians understood to be the most powerful class. For example, the publication of *The Way We Live Now* produced a number of reviews assuming that it was an exact description of 'the new times' in England, and of definite changes in social and moral life. Leonid Polonskii, a prominent liberal literary critic who was also a passionate advocate of English literature, asked readers to believe that Trollope was the 'the most true-to-life writer of morals and manners'.[5]

At the same time, Russian readers did not fail to notice the aesthetic pleasure of Trollope's art, as is apparent from reviews appear in such well-known literary journals as *The Herald of Europe* [Вестник Европы, *Vestnik Evropy*], *Affair* [Дело; *Delo*] and *Fatherland Notes [Отечественные записки, Otechestvennye zapiski*). We can find a characteristic Russian approach to Trollope in the judgement of Leonid Polonskii: 'Dickens is too poetic, Thackeray – too bitter, but Trollope and his world perfectly mirror reality.'[6] In several Russian essays and reviews of the time, Trollope's name was associated with Balzac's: 'Trollope, like Balzac, created a whole fictitious and quite complete English world.'[7] Their fictional worlds were felt to be similar, not only because both used re-appearing characters and recurring plot-patterns, but mostly because they used similar structural principles to create their worlds: a unity of time and space, and a socio-psychological continuity that enabled them to depict a variety of activities in a unified world. Russian critics thought that Balzac and Trollope, while depicting everyday life, were at their best in finding the necessary dramatic tension for an interesting narrative. Zinaida Vengerova (probably the first Russian to create a systematic history of foreign literature at the turn of the nineteenth century) felt that the French novelist's interest in everyday life had become an obsession, as a consequence of his unbridled enthusiasm for explaining and categorising everything. Of Trollope, she said in her essay for Brokgaus's encyclopedia that 'he did not explain anything; he only narrated and registered everyday speech'.[8] Even when Trollope was writing about the higher levels of society, she thought of him as predominantly the author of the everyday life of ordinary people. It is obvious now that Vengerova did not take into account *The Way We Live Now* and some other novels of Trollope written by him in the later years of his life in quite a different manner from his Barsetshire novels.

Russian readers and literary critics of the nineteenth century were impressed by Trollope's skill at creating characters that did not seem puppets but living beings. For example, Leonid Polonskii, Daniil Mordovtsev and Zinaida Vengerova, among many others, considered Trollope to be the most exact of Western writers to understand and depict a woman's character and inner world.[9] As Polonskii stresses, 'Any female individual whom he is depicting becomes remarkably alive, because in every word, in each gesture noticed by the author she is absolutely true to a reality which we are capable of comprehending at once.'[10] The critic contrasts Trollope with George Eliot who, he says, concentrates on extreme tensions and contrasts in depicting the inner life of her female characters, and who uses them as an instrument to explore her own ideas and beliefs (Polonskii was referring, no doubt, to Dorothea Brook, Maggie Tulliver or Romola). Trollope has no such a programme: he was interested in everyday reality, and Russian readers were urged to admire his portrayal of Lady Glencora, Clara Belton, Rachel Ray and Lucy Robarts.[11]

One of the striking moments in the Russian reception of Trollope in the 1870s–80s was that his novels about political life, as he saw, understood and interpreted it, were in the centre of the Russian reading (and intelligent) public of the time when some serious political reforms in Russia were very much on the agenda. No doubt, Russian liberal and democratic critics had their own country's political situation in mind (especially before the assassination of Alexander II) when writing about Trollope's treatment of power, parties and an individual's social rights and duties. In Trollope's treatment of politics they saw an alternative to the autocracy and despotism that determined the whole structure of Russian life in the second half of the nineteenth century. The novels of Trollope as well as Charles Dickens, Elizabeth Gaskell, George Eliot, George Meredith and others, were of help to the liberals, known at that time as 'Westerners', in their arguments against so-called 'Slavophiles'. Even more, Trollope's novels and the works of many other English writers were of help to many educated Russian readers (the number of whom increased every year) to understand 'the way they lived then', to think deeply about general human rights and about the necessity of social and moral improvement of life. Leonid Polonskii, for instance, in one essay analyses a political episode from *Framley Parsonage* (the struggle between De Terrier and Brock, a Tory and a Whig, wittily depicted as a fight of the Gods and Titans), which he interprets in progressive terms: 'In a free country, any individual, group or party, while fighting for its own interests, inevitably acts as high and absolute force for the benefit of society as a whole.'[12] Elsewhere, in his analysis of the two Phineas novels and *Can You Forgive Her?*, his observations reveal much about the Russian understanding of Trollope's novels on the whole. He emphasises Trollope's fictionalisation of politics, that is, his invention of scenes in which his prominent politicians are shown not only in the Houses of Parliament or in Whitehall, but also as ordinary people, at their homes, at dinner parties, at private talks and rendezvous when they have conversations with non-political people, with women of their acquaintance. Thus Trollope avoided turning a novel into a political treatise and instead wrote a novel that blends politics and private life, political analysis and psychology. The Russian critic rightly supposed that the new nineteenth-century genre of the English political novel was being reinvested with fresh artistic strength.

Trollope's political novels captivated advanced circles of Russian society of this period, then, because they organically presented the individual with his or her peculiarities, internal torments, and his or her search for a place in a changing social life. In addition, Russians of that time were naturally intrigued by foreign manners, traditions, everyday life and culture. Another literary critic and a writer, Piotr Boborykin, when writing about George Eliot and Anthony Trollope, emphasises that owing to these two novelists 'the English literature of the time gave more and more attention to the experience of the intellectually richly furnished and receptive individual who has so few illusions'.[13] The emerging Russian intelligentsia's aspirations were close to Trollope's ideas, distinctly expressed by him at the end of *Phineas Finn*, when the protagonist, after some hard inner struggle, finds his comfort in honest execution of his human and social duties for the sake of his homeland.

Russians of that time were not, however, uncritical admirers of Trollope's work. Some people thought he lacked great social ideas, and that his works were famous 'not for their originality, but for their meticulousness'.[14] Their author was 'a keen observer' but not a 'reformer'.[15] He was 'subtly analytic, very much talented and true at its highest degree, though sometimes too slow a narrator'.[16] They also thought it was rather vulgar to have a foreigner as the main villain (something which also occurs in Dickens and Thackeray) and pointed at Neroni, Lopez and Melmotte.[17]

Nevertheless, it is noteworthy that Trollope's great satire *The Way We Live Now* was translated and published as a separate book twice by the Moscow publishing house of Katkov in 1875 and in 1876, and some episodes of the novel were translated and introduced by Leonid Polonskii in the December issue of *The Herald of Europe* [Вестник Европы, *Vestnik Evropy*] in 1875. To a certain extent, the translators and publishers saw a degree of similarity between the picture of life made by Trollope in the novel and current Russian life of the 1870s. When Polonskii stresses how different this novel is in comparison with Trollope's previous ones, and locates the bitterness of Trollope's satire in his depiction of a society in which 'the former structure of life, social views, tastes and mores' were radically changed not at all for the better, he is referring to England as well as to Russia.[18] Polonskii pays particular attention to this idea in the later essay 'The Contemporary English Novel' in the November issue of the journal.[19]

One of the most interesting judgements of Trollope is Leo Tolstoy's, who was reading Trollope's novels while writing both *War and Peace* and *Anna Karenina*. In September and October 1865, he records his reading progress in various diary entries:

> I am reading Trollope. If it were not so diffuse it would be a pleasure. . . .
> Read some Trollope. Good. . . .
> I am reading 'The Bertrams'. It is delightful. . . .[20]

No doubt English lovers of Trollope know Tolstoy's famous judgement: 'Trollope kills me with his sheer skill.' But elsewhere he also noted: 'Trollope overwhelms me with his sheer tediousness.'[21] Interviews further show that Trollope and his works occupied a not unimportant place. William Thomas Stead, the British journalist, recounts in his book *Truth about Russia* (1888) how during a meeting with Tolstoy in May 1888 he asked whom Tolstoy thought to be the best English writers: 'Three best English novelists, – he said, – are (in the descending line) Dickens, Thackeray, Trollope; and after Trollope whom else have you?'[22] When Tolstoy had a conversation with the French translator and traveller Jules Legras in Moscow on 20 December 1893, he mentioned the name of Trollope along with the names of Dickens and Thackeray as those 'who led English literature and English novel not long ago'[23]. Another British journalist, Robert Edward Long, recounts how he and Tolstoy met in Yasnaia Poliana in the spring of 1899, when Tolstoy said of Trollope that '[h]e was one of the most talented contemporary English writers. But his novels are entirely based on random incidents.'[24] Although there is no direct evidence of a direct link, it seems likely that Tolstoy, a very emotional reader, was influenced by the impressive scene of Lopez's death in *The Prime Minister* when he wrote his *Anna Karenina*. Even more, it is tempting to suggest that the English novel that Anna is reading on her way from Moscow to Saint Petersburg was Trollope's *The Prime Minister*.

Soviet Russia

From 1917 until 1991, Trollope's creative works were neglected under the pretext of being too defensively bourgeois and too bright an example of 'the crisis of the social novel of the 1850s and 1860s'.[25] The attitude to Trollope from 1930 onwards was based on the words of Maxim Gorky, who proclaimed at the first Congress of Soviet Writers in 1934:

> In the bourgeois literature of the West we should see two groups of authors: one group lauds and amuses its social class – Trollope, Wilkie Collins, Braddon, Marryat, Jerome, Paul de Kock, Paul Fevale, Octave Feuillet, Gregor Samarov, Julius Stinde – hundreds of the like. They all are typical 'good bourgeois', with little talent, quite cunning and trivial, as their readers are. Another group is of just a few tens, and they are outstanding representatives of critical realism and revolutionary romanticism.[26]

In accordance with these approaches, Boris Kuzmin, the author of a small chapter on Trollope in 'The History of English Literature' [*История английской литературы*], published in 1955 by the Soviet Academy of Sciences, admits that 'Trollope's works were quite popular', but then he qualifies his evaluation: 'Not raising serious ideas, Trollope meets the tastes of bourgeois Philistines.'[27] What is more, he writes about 'the naïve and good-humoured cynicism' of which the writer's works and especially *An Autobiography* are full.[28] One of the things that seperates Trollope from Thackeray is 'the principle of moderate tones, with neither heroism and villainy'. The critic sees in it the basic principle of realism, which Trollope defended in his novels, in *An Autobiography* and in *Thackeray*.[29] Kuzmin writes that 'Trollope's scope of the reality depicted is very much narrow' and that the Balzacian principle of recurring characters and social strata does not produce the desired effect.[30] He stresses that the strong points of Trollope's art are 'the deliberate, careful depicting of little nothings of life, the portrayal of individual peculiarities of characters' manner, speech, and behaviour'.[31] He also indicates that even when 'Trollope depicts various aspects of his characters, he does not look for any general feature'.[32] Kuzmin is so profoundly preoccupied with the idea of the crisis of critical realism in the English literature of the second half of the nineteenth century, and with the lack of anti-bourgeois enthusiasm, that he undermines or misses the core feature of Trollope's art: his deep and nuanced psychological approach to reconstructing characters.

This idea prevailed in Soviet literary criticism and even influenced a good critic such as Alexandre Anikst, the author of the first Soviet textbook on the *History of English Literature* [*История английской литературы*], published in 1956 and aimed at the students of higher education institutions. In this book, the name of Trollope is not even mentioned. In his introduction to the chapter on the realist novel from the 1860s until 1890s, however, having paid tribute to the policy of the crisis of the social realism in English literature of those decades, he begins to speak – probably for the first time in the Soviet reception of English literature – about 'writer-realists of the period as good keepers of the progressive traditions of English literature'.[33] He writes:

> Having no such breadth and depth in depicting social reality and its contradictions as Walter Scott, Dickens and Thackeray, the English writers of the second half of the nineteenth century developed realism in one essential aspect – in depth, precision, and diversity of characters' psychology. The development of psychological analysis was the main gain of the realism of that time in England.[34]

Anikst's revisionist understanding of the role of the English novel of the second half of the nineteenth century paved the way for one extraordinary publication. If we take into account that for forty years the author had been considered to be 'the apologist of the petty bourgeoisie and Philistines',[35] in 1970 a book appeared, almost out of nowhere, that upset this status quo: *Barchester Towers*, in a brilliant translation by Irina Gurova, and with a profound *Foreword* written by Anna Elistratova, a prominent Soviet literary critic of the mid-twentieth century. This signalled the start of new approaches both to Trollope's novels and to the English novel of the second half of the nineteenth century more generally. Anna Elistratova perceptively observes in her 'Foreword' that 'the aliveness of characters and details of everyday life, good-natured humour and witty irony . . . have made *Barchester Towers* a classic masterpiece of English literature'.[36] There is no mention of any lack of social criticism or of petit-bourgeois themes in the novel, the staples of talks about Trollope from the 1940s up until the 1960s. This was the first attempt to give a serious analysis of Trollope's novel as a work of art, free from ideological considerations.

Despite the high figure of 100,000 copies, the 1970 edition of *Barchester Towers* sold out quickly. Even so, since then this translation has been the only recent translation in Russia. It was reprinted in 1990 in a print run of 300,000 copies, and in 2010 in a print run of only 3,000 copies (in the series under the remarkable title – unthinkable in the preceding decades – *A Book for All Times*). I think that the 1970 publication of *Barchester Towers* can be seen as an echo of 'the Thaw'. In the late 1960s and 1970s, many books were translated and published in a hundred thousand copies which in earlier times one could not even mention without attracting serious criticism – Franz Kafka and Knut Hamsun, to name but a few. Russian literary academics began to write about the nineteenth-century English authors of the 'second row' – George Eliot, George Meredith, Emily Brontë, Wilkie Collins and some others. Anthony Trollope was among them. His name was mentioned in a new edition of *Great Soviet Encyclopedia* [Большая советская энциклопедия] in the 1960s and some PhD dissertations on his work were written and defended in the USSR in the 1970s and 1980s: Yurii Sotkis's *Peculiarities of the Generation of the Paragraph in Various Styles of Speech (on the basis of Anthony Trollope's works)* [Особенности организации и вычленения абзаца в разных стилях речи (на материале произведений А.Троллопа]] (Moscow, 1975); Maina Petrova's *Realism and its Peculiarity in the 'Barsetshire Chronicles' of Anthony Trollope* [Особенности реализма в «Барсетширских хрониках» Энтони Троллопа] (Moscow, 1981); my own dissertation – *'The Palliser Novels' of Anthony Trollope: Issues of Method and Genre* [«Паллизеровские романы» Энтони Троллопа: метод и жанр] (Moscow, 1982); Tatiana Cherezova's *On Comparative Studies of Vertical Contexts of Artistic Texts (on the basis of Anthony Trollope's and C. P. Snow's*

Works) [*Сравнительное изучение вертикальных контекстов художественных текстов (на примере произведений Энтони Троллопа и Ч.П.Сноу)*] (Moscow, 1985); and Galina Lisovaia's *Peculiarities of Anthony Trollope's Realism in his Later Novels (The end of the 1860s and the 1870s)* [*Особенности реализма Энтони Троллопа в поздних романах (конец 1860-х – 1870-е гг)*](Moscow, 1989).

There were two more turning points in (Soviet) Russian Trollopiana in the two final decades of this epoch: the first was a book by the Moscow State University Professor Valentina Ivasheva, *The English Realist Novel of the Nineteenth Century in the Contemporary Context* [*Английский реалистический роман XIX века в его современном звучании*] (1974), with a substantial chapter on Trollope, and the essay of her colleague Albert Karelskii, *From a Hero to a Man*, published in September 1983 in the leading contemporary Soviet (now Russian) journal of literary criticism *Issues of Literature* [*Вопросы литературы, Voprosy literatury*], and in 1990 expanded into a large book of the same title.

Valentina Ivasheva was not utterly free from caution in her appraisal of Trollope's contribution to English literature in her semi-ironically titled chapter, 'The Epos of Everyday Life'. Nevertheless, this chapter was one of the first serious investigations into Trollope's art in twentieth-century Russia. She begins with the assertion that, for her, there is no doubt that Trollope 'should be read and understood afresh today', which leads her to a survey of the majority of Trollope's novels.[37] A traditional Soviet aspect is evident in her chapter: she prefers the Barsetshire chronicles, not thinking highly of the political series or other works of the writer. Interestingly enough, she moves more and more away from the one-sided (i.e. sociological and ideological) approach to the art of the writer. It is not by chance that she finishes her essay by agreeing with Kate and Geoffrey Tillotson that Trollope 'is a giant among the novelists and not only due to the quantity of the novels written but due to the quality of them'.[38]

The essay of Professor Albert Karelskii builds on the assumption that the second half of the nineteenth century in the history of English literature is to be understood on its own terms and on the basis of its own aesthetics, rather than in endless comparison with the literature of the 1840s ('hungry forties') and with the works of Dickens in particular. Trollope is important for him as a writer who turned literature into the complex and many-levelled depiction of the inner life of a human being who lives through everyday life, who lives 'here and now', who is not 'a hero' but just 'a man'.[39] Karelskii's essay and book betray an obvious wish to be free of the old-fashioned and rigid approach to the foreign literature that characterised literary studies in Soviet times; he ignores the axiom that the English novel in the second half of the nineteenth century experienced a crisis just because it lacked anti-bourgeois criticism. He thus to a significant extent opened a new stage in the reception of Trollope's novels in Russia.

At the end of this period, practically any serious manual and textbook on foreign (and English) literature of the nineteenth century, written for the students of Russian universities, has either a chapter or at least several pages devoted to Trollope. The ideas of Karelskii were picked up by a new generation of Trollopians in Russia after 'perestroika'. My own *The 'Parliamentary Novels' of Anthony Trollope and the Development of the English Political Novel* [*«Парламентские романы» Энтони Троллопа и проблемы развития английского политического романа*] (1992) coincides with some ideas of Albert Karelskii, especially in its attention to Trollope's mastery in character-making and to his psychologically intense narration (see the chapter 'Peculiarities of Psychological Analysis and Narration in "Can You Forgive Her?" and "The Eustace Diamonds" ').[40]

New Russia

The interest in Trollope since the 1990s has been purely academic, with an adequate understanding of his role in the history of English realism and with a more limited output: only one PhD dissertation, *A Reader in the Artistic System of the Novels of Anthony Trollope in the 1860s* [*Читатель в художественной системе романов Энтони Троллопа 1860-х годов*] (Perm, 2009), by Varvara Biachkova, in addition to several essays written by her and by the young academics Natalia Sarkisova from Saint Petersburg State University and Irina Gniusova from Tomsk State University. These young authors are continuing an attempt to discredit some of the stereotypes and clichés that dominated in Soviet Trollopiana. In their articles we see new readings of Trollope's novels as works that are interesting not only from the point of view of subtle psychoanalytical writing, not only due to 'the simplicity and truthfulness of the characters and types depicted', but also because of their 'affinity to the creative search of the novelists of the twentieth century'.[41] Irina Gniusova and Varvara Biachkova have actually launched a new trend in Russian Trollopiana – a comparative study of Trollope's novels and the works of Russian writers.[42]

Unfortunately, publishing policies in present-day Russia have not found room for the works of Anthony Trollope. In the twenty-first century, the writer has been noticed only by the reprint of *Barchester Towers* in 2010 and by the translation of his novella *Christmas at Thompson Hall* in a collection of detective tales of the nineteenth century published in 2011. I think the reason for this is not the quality of Trollope's art, but market laws: because of many years of neglect, Trollope's real role in the development of English literature has been forgotten. The disregard of his merits as a brilliant connoisseur of human psychology and of everyday life ensured that he did not become 'a brand name' for publishers like those of Dickens, Brontë, Gaskell and Thackeray.

It was therefore a real pity that Trollope's bicentenary was practically unnoticed in Russia. I hope that some kind of tribute to it was the publication of two essays on Trollope in *Voprosy Literatury* [Вопросы литературы; *Issues of Literature*] in December 2015. One essay is the Russian translation of the work written by Karen Hewitt, in which she tries to show the place and the role of Trollope in the development of English literature and in English novel, and to which I provided a response.

Bibliography of Russian translations of Anthony Trollope's novels

(1863), *The Small House at Allington* [*Домик в Оллингтоне*, *Ollingtonskii malyi dom*], Saint Petersburg: K. Wulf Publishing House.

(1864), *Rachel Ray* [*Рэйчел Рэй*, *Reichel Rei*], Saint Petersburg: K. Wulf Publishing House.

(1867), *The Claverings* [*Клеверинги*, *Kleveringi*], Saint Petersburg: I. I. Glazunov Publishing House.

(1869) *The Vicar of Bullhampton* [*Булхэмптонский викарий*, *Bulgamptonskii vikarii*], Moscow: University Publishing House.

(1870), *The Vicar of Bullhampton* [*Булхэмптонский викарий*, *Belgamptonskii vikarii*], Saint Petersburg: E. N. Akhmatova Publishing House.

(1871), *The Belton Estate* [*Поместье Белтон, Beltonskoe pomestie*], Saint Petersburg: E. N. Akhmatova Publishing House.

(1871), *The Claverings* [*Клеверинги, Kleveringi*], Saint Petersburg: E. N. Akhmatova Publishing House.

(1871), *He Knew He Was Right* [*Он так и знал, On znal, chto on prav*], Saint Petersburg: Maikov Publishing House.

(1871), *Ralph the Heir* [*Ральф наследник, Naslednik Ralf*], Saint Petersburg: E. N. Akhmatova Publishing House.

(1871), *Sir Harry Hotspur of Humblethwaite* [*Сэр Гарри Хатспур из Гумблетвэйта, Ser Gerri Gotspur*] Saint Petersburg: E. N. Akhmatova Publishing House.

(1873), *The Eustace Diamonds* [*Бриллианты Юстаса, Brillianty Yustesov*], Saint Petersburg: E. N. Akhmatova Publishing House.

(1873), *The Golden Lion of Granpère* [*Золотой лев в Гроппере, Zolotoi lev v Gropperei*], Saint Petersburg: V. Ashin Publishing House.

(1873), *He Knew He Was Right* [*Он так и знал, On znal, chto on prav*], Saint Petersburg: E. N. Akhmatova Publishing House.

(1873), *Phineas Finn, the Irish Member* [*Финеас Финн, Finias Finn, irlandskii chlen parlamenta*], Saint Petersburg: E. N. Akhmatova Publishing House.

(1873), *Ralph the Heir* [*Ральф наследник, Naslednik Ralf*], Saint Petersburg: E. N. Akhmatova Publishing House.

(1873), *The Vicar of Bullhampton* [*Булхэмптонский викарий, Belgamptonskii vikarii*], Saint Petersburg: E. N. Akhmatova Publishing House.

(1874), *Lady Anna* [*Леди Анна, Ledi Anna*], Moscow: University Publishing House and Katkov i Company Publishing House.

(1875), *Harry Heathcote of Gangoil* [*Гарри Хиткоут из Гэнгула, Genrikh Gitkot iz Gengualia: Iz zhizni avstraliiskikh pereselentsev*] Saint Petersburg: F. S. Sushinskii Publishing House.

(1875), *Phineas Redux* [*Финеас возвращается!, Finias Finn, vozvrativshiisia nazad*], Saint Petersburg: E. N. Akhmatova Publishing House.

(1875), *The Way We Live Now* [*Как мы теперь живем, Kak my teper zhiviom*], Moscow: University Publishing House and Katkov i Company Publishing House.

(1876), *The Way We Live Now* [*Как мы теперь живем, Kak my teper zhiviom*], Moscow: University Publishing House and Katkov i Company Publishing House.

(1877), *The Prime Minister* [*Премьер-министр, Pervyi ministr*], Saint Petersburg: E. N. Akhmatova Publishing House.

(1878), *Is He Popenjoy?* [*Попенджой ли он?, Popenjoi li on?*], Saint Petersburg: E. N. Akhmatova Publishing House.

(1880), *Cousin Henry* [*Кузен Генри, Dvoiurodnyi brat*], Moscow: M. N . Lavrov Publishing House.

(1882), *Doctor Wortle's School* [*Школа доктора Уортла, Oko za oko: shkola doktora Vortlia*], Saint Petersburg: E. N. Akhmatova Publishing House.

(1882), *The Duke's Children* [*Дети герцога, Deti gertsoga*], Saint Petersburg: E. N. Akhmatova Publishing House.

(1882), *The Prime Minister* [*Премьер-министр, Pervyi ministr*], Saint Petersburg, A. A. Kraevskii Publishing House.

(1898), *Ayala's Angel* [*Ангел Айалы, Eialin Angel*], trans. O. M. Soloviiov, Saint Petersburg: Novyi zhurnal inostrannoi literatury.

(1970), *Barchester Towers* [*Барчестерские башни, Barchesterskie bashni*], trans. I. Gurova, reprinted in 1990 and 2010, Moscow: Khudozhestvennaia literatura Publishing House.

Notes

1. 'Trollope, Anthony' ['Троллоп, Антони', 'Trollop, 'Antoni'], in *Encyclopedian Dictionary Granat* [*Энциклопедический словарь Гранат*, *Entsiklopedicheskii slovar Granat*] (Moscow: Granat, 1901), vol. 41.9, p. 302.

2. Zinaida Vengerova, 'Trollope, Anthony' ['Троллоп, Антони', 'Trollop, 'Antoni'], in *Brokgaus-Efron Encyclopedian Dictionary* [*Энциклопедический словарь Брокгауз*, *Entsiklopedicheskii slovar Brokgauza-Efrona*] (Moscow: Brokgauz-Efron, 1901), vol. 33a, p. 890.

3. Piotr Tkachiov, 'People of the Future and Heroes of Philistinism' ['Люди будущего и герои филистерства', 'Liudi buduschego i geroi filisterstva'], *Affair* [*Дело, Delo*], 4 (1868): p. 77.

4. Dmitrii Pisarev, *Realists* [*Реалисты, Realisty*], in *Works* [*Сочинения, Sochinenia*] (Saint Petersburg: A. Golovachiov Publishing House, 1866), p. 208.

5. Leonid Polonskii, 'Sketches of English Society in the Novels of Anthony Trollope' ['Очерки английского общества в романах А. Троллопа', 'Ocherki angliiskogo obschestva v romanakh A. Trollopa'], *Herald of Europe* [*Вестник Европы, Vestnik Evropy*], 8 (1870): p. 625.

6. Ibid. p. 620.

7. Ibid. p. 627.

8. Vengerova, 'Trollope', p. 890.

9. See Leonid Polonskii, 'Sketches', p. 628; Leonid Polonskii, 'Female Types in the Novels of Trollope' ['Женские типы в романах Троллопа', 'Zhenskie tipy v romanakh Trollopa'], *Herald of Europe* [*Вестник Европы, Vestnik Evropy*], 8 (1871): p. 513.

10. Ibid. p. 514.

11. Ibid. p. 515.

12. Leonid Polonskii, 'Sketches', pp. 667–8. For Polonskii, the 'absolute force' was social justice.

13. Piotr Boborykin, *The European Novel in the Nineteenth Century: The Novel in the West in the Second Third of the Century* [*Европейский роман в девятнадцатом веке: роман на Западе во второй трети века*; *Evropeiskii roman v XIX stoletii: Roman na Zapade za dve treti veka*] (Saint Petersburg: M. M. Stasiulevich Publishing House, 1890), p. 532.

14. Zinaida Vengerova, 'Trollope, Anthony', p. 890.

15. Ibid. p. 890.

16. Leonid Polonskii, 'Sketches', p. 626.

17. Leonid Polonskii, 'An Episode from the Life of a Minister' ['Эпизод из жизни министра', 'Epizod iz zhizni ministra'], *Herald of Europe* [*Вестник Европы, Vestnik Evropy*], 6 (1877): pp. 500–26.

18. Leonid Polonskii, '*The Way We Live Now*: Episodes from the Novel of A. Trollope' ['*Как мы теперь живем*: Эпизоды из романа А.Троллопа', '*Kak my teper zhiviom*: Ocherki iz romana A. Trollopa'], *Herald of Europe* [*Вестник Европы, Vestnik Evropy*], 12 (1875): p. 726.

19. See Leonid Polonskii, 'The Contemporary Novel in England' ['Современный роман в Англии', 'Sovremennyi roman v Anglii'], *Herald of Europe* [*Вестник Европы, Vestnik Evropy*], 10 (1875): pp. 245–81.

20. Leo Tolstoy, *Diaries and Entries* [*Дневники и дневниковые записи, Dnevniki i dnevnikovye zapisi*], in *Complete Works* [*Полное собрание сочинений, Polnoe sobranie sochinenii*], reprinted edition of 1928–58, 90 vols (Moscow: Terra, 1992), vols 48–9, p. 63, p. 64.

21. Ibid. p. 62.

22. A. S. Makashin (ed.), *Literary Legacy: Tolstoy and the Foreign World* [*Литературное наследство: Толстой и зарубежный мир, Literaturnoe nasledstvo: Tolstoy i zarubezhnyi mir*] (Moscow: Nauka, 1965), vol. 75.2, p. 108.

23. Ibid. p. 12.

24. Ibid. p. 114.

25. Boris Kuzmin, 'The Crisis of the English Social Novel in the 50s–60s of the Nineteenth Century: Eliot, Trollope, Reed, Collins [Кризис английского социального романа в 50-е – 60-е годы XIX века: Элиот, Троллоп, Рид, Коллинз, Krizis angliiskogo sotsialnogo romana v 50kh–60kh godakh XIX veka: Eliot, Trollop, Rid, Kollinz'], in I. I. Anisimov, A. A. Elistrtova, A. F. Ivaschenko and Iu. M. Kondratiev (eds), *History of English Literature* [*История английской литературы*] (Moscow: Academy of Sciences, 1955), vol. 2.2, p. 395.

26. Maxim Gorky, 'Speech at the First Congress of the Soviet Writers' ['Речь на Первом съезде советских писателей', 'Rech na Pervom siezde sovetskih pisatelei'], in *Complete Works* [*Полное собрание сочинений*, *Polnoe sobranie sochinenii*] (Moscow: Goslitizdat, 1947), vol. 27, p. 310.

27. Kuzmin, 'Crisis', p. 420.

28. Ibid.

29. Ibid. p. 421.

30. Ibid.

31. Ibid.

32. Ibid. p. 422.

33. Aleksandr Anikst, *History of English Literature* [*История английской литературы*, *Istoriia angliiskoi literatury*] (Moscow: Uchpedgiz Publishing House, 1956), p. 338.

34. Ibid. p. 338.

35. Kuzmin, 'Crisis', p. 422.

36. Anna Elistratova, 'Foreword' ['Предисловие', 'Predislovie'], in Antony Trollope, *Barchester Towers* [*Барчестреские башни*, *Barchesterskie bashni*], trans. I. Gurova (Moscow: Pravda Publishing House, 1990), p. 18.

37. Valentina Ivasheva, 'Epics of Everyday Life' ['Эпос обыденной жизни', 'Epos obydennoi zhizni'], in *The English Realist Novel in Contemporary Context* [*Английский реалистический роман XIX века в его современном звучании*, *Angliiskii realisticheskii roman XIX veka v ego sovremennom zvuchanii*] (Moscow: Khudozhestvennaia literatura Publishing House, 1974), p. 414.

38. Ibid. p. 448.

39. Albert Karelskii, 'From a Hero to a Man: The Development of Realist Psychology in the European Novel of the 30s–60s of the Nineteenth Century' ['От героя к человеку: Развитие реалистической психологии в европейском романе 30-х – 60 –х годов девятнадцатого века', 'Ot geroia k cheloveku. Razvitie realisticheskogo realizma v evropeiskom romane 30s–60s godov XIX veka'], *Issues of Literature* [*Вопросы литературы*, *Voprosy literatury*], 3 (1983): p. 110.

40. See Boris Proskurnin, *The 'Parliamentary Novels' of Anthony Trollope and the Problems of English Political Novel's Development* [*«Парламентские романы» Энтони Троллопа и проблемы развития английского политического романа*, *Parlamentskie romany' Entony Trollopa i problemy razvitiia angliiskogo politicheskogo romana*] (Perm: Perm University Publishing House, 1992).

41. Nataliia Sarkisova, 'Anthony Trollope' ['Энтони Троллоп', 'Entoni Trollop'], in L. V. Sidorchenko and I. I. Burova (eds), *History of Western European Literature: Nineteenth-Century England* [*История западноевропейской литературы: девятнадцатый век. Англия*, *Istoriia zapadnoevropeiskoi literatury: XIX vek. Angliia*] (Moscow: Academia, 2004), p. 337.

42. See Varvara Biachkova, 'Thoughts on Female Fate in the Russian and English Realist Novel of the Second Half of the Nineteenth Century (on the Material of the Works of A. Trollope and L. N. Tolstoy)' ['Размышления о женской судьбе в русском и английском реалистическом романе второй половины XIX века (на материале произведений Э.Троллопа и Л.Н.Толстого', 'Razmyshleniia o zhenskoi sudbe v russkom i angliiskom realisticheskom romane vtoroi poloviny XIX veka (na materiale proizvedenii E. Trollopa

i L. N. Tolstogo)'], in O. I. Polovinkina (ed.), *Genre and its Metamorphoses in the Literature of Russia and England* [*Жанр и его метаморфозы в литературе России и Англии, Zhanr i ego metamorphozy v literature Rossii i Anglii*] (Vladimir: Vladimirskii pedagogicheskii universitet, 2010), pp. 34–9; Varvara Biachkova, 'Thoughts on Unhappy Families in the Russian and English Novel of the Second Half of the Nineteenth century (on the Material of the Novels of L. N. Tolstoy and A. Trollope)' [Размышления о несчастливых семьях в русском и английском романе второй половины девятнадцатого века (уа материале романов Л.Н.Толстого и Э.Троллопа, 'Razmyshleniia o neschastlivykh semiakh v russkom i angliiskom romane vtoroi poloviny XIX veka (na materiale romanov L. N.Tolstogo i E. Trollopa)'], in N. S. Bochkareva, V. A. Biachkova, and B. M. Proskurnin (eds), *World Literature in the Context of Culture* [*Mirovaia literatura v kontekste kultury*] (Perm: Perm University Publishing House, 2010), pp. 97–100; Varvara Biachkova, 'The Image of the Clergyman in the Novels of the Barchester Series of A. Trollope and "Soboriane" of N. S. Leskov' ['Образ священнослужителя в романах Барчестерской серии Э.Троллопа и "Соборяне" Н.С.Лескова', 'Obraz sviaschennosluzhitelia v romanakh Barchesterskogo tsikla E. Trollopa i "Soboriane" N. S. Leskova'], *Philology and Culture* [*Филология и культура, Filologiia i kultura*], 3.32 (2013): pp. 80–4; Irina Gniusova, '"I console myself that he has own, and I have mine": Leo Tolstoy's Creative Dialogue with Anthony Trollope' ['Я утешаюсь, что у него свое, а у меня свое': творческий диалог Л.Н.Толстого и Энтони Троллопа, '"Ia uteshaius, chto u nego svoio, a u menia svoio": tvorcheskii dialog L. N. Tolstogo i Entoni Trollopa'], *Tomsk University Journal* [*Вестник Томского университета, Vestnik Tomskogo universiteta*], 389 (2014): pp. 15–21; Irina Gniusova, 'Trivia of Episcopal Life by N. S. Leskov in the Context of English Prose about the Clergy (George Eliot and A.Trollope)' ['"Мелочи архиерейской жизни" Н. С. Лескова в контексте английской прозы о священнослужителях', '"Melochi arkhiereiskoi zhizni" N. S. Leskova v kontekste angliiskoi prozy o zhizni sviaschennosluzhitelei (Dzh. Eliot i E. Trollop)'], *Perm University Journal* [*Вестник Пермского университета, Vestnik Permskogo universiteta*], 1.29 (2015): pp. 98–107.

12

READING TROLLOPE IN NEW ZEALAND

Lydia Wevers

Robert Darnton has suggested the majority of readers are beyond histori-cal reach and for the most part that is the case. It is, however, possible to have glimpses of readers and reading life through an investigation of newspapers of the small British colony of New Zealand in the early 1870s. At this time the colony was only thirty years old and very strongly affiliated to British print culture and intellectual life. Rumours about Anthony Trollope's projected visit to Australia and New Zealand in 1871–2 were reported in newspaper columns, and once he had actually embarked for Australia there were regular updates across both countries about his appearances, engagements and movements. The attention paid to Trollope throws some aspects of his readership and reception into relief.

First and most obviously, the newspapers make readers of Trollope become visible as readers and as buyers of books. The health of the print economy is written all over nineteenth-century newspapers, both in the proliferation of local and regional news-papers and in the print news they carry – such as advertisements for books, literary notices and general allusions to reading. Secondly, readers appear as participants in the literary field. Individual readers establish themselves as opinionated, self-registered stakeholders by sending in letters and articles to the paper about their reading, thus illustrating the cultural and social capital reading represents. Reading functions as a cultural shorthand, what Didier Eribon has called a 'vector of distinction', facilitating a form of intervention in the world republic of letters.[1] Some of these active individuals leave their trace, in letters, diaries and books. This chapter will discuss how Trollope's readership in New Zealand becomes markedly visible during his visit to New Zealand and Australia in 1871–2, and will discuss one individual reader in particular.

Book-Buying

The first mention of Trollope's novels in New Zealand was in 1862, when Varty's book-seller in Auckland advertised 'New Books' in the *Daily Southern Cross*.[2] They included five novels by Trollope: *The Three Clerks*, *The Bertrams*, *Doctor Thorne*, *The Kellys and the O'Kellys* and *The Macdermots of Ballycloran*. In the same year, the *Otago Daily Times* was serialising extracts from *The Warden*. In Australia, as one might expect from a bigger and more developed colony, references to Trollope started earlier, with a review reprinted from *The Times* of 'Mr Trollope's new novel', *Barchester Towers* in 1857, described as a 'contamination of *The Warden*'.[3] The reprinted review of *Barchester Tow-ers* suggests the existence of a well-established readership by the later 1850s, which was probably due to the growth of circulating libraries in Australia and New Zealand. These notices of course do not mark the advent of Trollope's novels to either colony, but they do suggest the existence of a reading and book-buying public by these dates. *Orley Farm*, Trollope's tenth novel, for instance, was reviewed in Australia immediately in the year of its publication, 1862. Furthermore, Trollope's appearance in Australia and New Zealand in 1871–2 caused a substantive increase in the visibility of his readership in the public domain of the newspaper. This suggests not only the powerful draw of celebrity, but also the role and value of reading as a means of participating in the parent culture.

Trollope's Visit to Australia in 1871

An unusual set of newspaper references to the novelist's work in 1870–1 was probably related to Trollope's impending visit. There had been considerable interest in the New Zealand papers in 1869 in the possibilities of making clothing from paper, described by the *Taranaki Herald* in a syndicated article as a 'new branch of industry':

We have for some time been familiar with various novel applications of *paper*. We had good *paper* shirt collars and wristbands, *paper* shirt fronts or dickeys (just as ill-looking) and we have seen bonnets, which, however, no female denizen of Whitechapel would think of putting upon her head. But now the uses of *paper* are very much extended by a patent process of M. Pavy.[4]

Among the uses of this new kind of felted paper were day covers for beds, curtains, quilts, tablecloths and petticoats. The following January the 'Miscellaneous' column of the *Southland Times* featured an item with the subheading 'Paper Petticoats':

Paper Petticoats have come into fashion. The following advertisement thereof appears in an English paper: 'Madame Percale begs leave to call the attention of ladies about to visit the seaside to her new and richly embroidered paper petticoats at one shilling each. Each petticoat contains an instalment of a new novel of great domestic interest by Anthony Trollope entitled Tucks or Frills. The story will be completed in fifty weekly petticoats'.[5]

This titbit of news, which appeared in American provincial newspapers in 1869 and in a number of regional Australian papers such as the *Bendigo Advertiser*, also appealed to New Zealand provincial newspapers. It was reprinted in ten papers through 1870–1: the *Tuapeka Times*, the *Cromwell Argus*, the *West Coast Times*, the *Bruce Herald*, the *New Zealand Herald*, the *Wairarapa Mercury*, the *Otago Witness* and the *Evening Post*. It is not clear if this item is news or advertising. It is not inconceivable that Trollope would supply a novel syndicated on petticoats, but there is no record in his bibliography of anything called *Tucks or Frills* and it seems more likely to be a spoof. But it shows among other things, like the voracious appetite for news of any kind in colonial papers, that Trollope was a marketable and widely recognised name across the colonial world by the 1860s.

If we place this quirky item in the larger context of Trollope's presence in periodicals, previously confined mostly to advertisements of books for sale, it becomes clear that Trollope's impending visit made any items about him newsworthy, and represents a distinct historical moment in the reading history of the colony. The numbers of articles mentioning Trollope show a very clear pattern of peak and decline, a pattern

Table 12.1 Articles about Trollope in Australian and New Zealand newspapers.

Australia	Number of articles	New Zealand	Number of articles
1870	50	1863	3
1871	305	1871	209
1872	203	1872	156
1873	403	1873	313
1874	107	1874	27
1882	183	1882	37

which corresponds to the dates of Trollope's visit to Australia and New Zealand and reflects what Nigel Starck has called the 'first celebrity' in popular culture.[6]

Trollope remarks in his *Autobiography*: 'In the spring of 1871 we – I and my wife – had decided that we would go to Australia to visit our shepherd son. Of course before doing so I made a contract with a publisher for a book about the Colonies.'[7] The novelist and his wife arrived in Melbourne on 27 July 1871 and in New Zealand on 3 August 1872. Once he was in Australia every tiny New Zealand newspaper recorded his internal travels, his speeches and who received him. When he made it across the Tasman Sea his every move was observed and described, not always favourably.

Whether interest in a celebrity author is a reflection of the size of his or her readership is a debatable question, but there is no doubt that the two are connected, and it is reasonable to suppose that Trollope's readership materially increased during his visit. It is certainly notable that the peak of references to Trollope in both countries is in 1873, the year he published *Australia and New Zealand*, a book that came in for a great deal of indignant rebuttal. Australians particularly hated Trollope's characterisations of them as 'blowers', and his views of their country, which they thought were underinformed and made on the fly. The *Gympie Times* objected to his references to 'rickety public buildings' and 'an atmosphere in which everything seems to be rowdy and have about it a flavour of brandy and water'.[8] Presumably, there was little comfort in Trollope's assertion that New Zealanders were even worse, surpassing their 'Australian rivals' in getting drunk and being 'more English than any Englishman'.[9] Trollope was aware that his travelogue would provoke comment, writing to George William Rusden, the Australian historian with whom he had become friends, that:

Your letter about my book has given me very great satisfaction as you say what I hoped you might be able to say in its praise and with great warmth, and what I know you would have to say in its dispraise with the mildest voice. I knew that I had to be inaccurate – and that I could write a better book by allowing myself to be so than I could have done by studying to be absolutely correct. The very nature of such a book required that it should be written 'currente calamo'. Had I waited to verify every statement I made it would have become tedious and would not have been accepted and read by large numbers. Ordinary readers will not understand this but you know enough of literature to be aware that a book of the sort which I undertook had to be done at a dash . . .[10]

Rusden has written across the top: 'From Anthony Trollope the describer of English life and manners and himself one of the best of Englishmen.'[11] Any inaccuracies in *Australia and New Zealand* were of course pounced on by the local press, to such an extent that Trollope's name became proverbial. In 1874 a review of H. A. Merewether's *By Sea and By Land; Being a Trip through Egypt, India, Ceylon, Australia New Zealand and America* was described as having 'out Anthonied Anthony' in its carelessness with spelling proper nouns —'not a chapter, not a page, hardly a line' is free of them.[12] Mistakes regardless, it seems clear that the peak of references to Trollope in 1873 has a lot to do with the captive market for the travel book: readers longed to read and be infuriated by Trollope's account of them. But it was because he was a writer of novels read and loved across the two colonies that people wanted to read what he had to say about them. In an address to the citizens of Rockhampton in Queensland in September 1871, Trollope had declared that he was not there as a writer of novels (even though, as reported that same month, he was writing a serial story in the *Fortnightly* called *The Eustace Diamonds*). Instead, his aim was to give a 'fair, just and true account of what I have seen here'.[13]

Trollope's narratives of love and money, in which class and financial ambitions are entangled with romance, were perhaps too tame for some colonial readers, but they did form part of the colonial mindset. His popularity among readers, like Dickens's before him, has a great deal to do with the way his novels show the structures of feeling which complicate, but more importantly naturalise, the pursuit of material and social gain. And for colonial readers they could also be vessels of experience. Like Dickens's, his plots inevitably feature characters looking for a fortune or men led astray, usually by money, who emigrate to the colonies, like Alaric Tudor in *The Three Clerks*.

Trollope himself was never one to miss a financial opportunity, and one of the things colonial readers admired was his reputed business success. Ironically, a much reprinted article published after Trollope's death, 'The Gains of Authors', showed he earned less through his novels than some of his contemporaries.[14] The *Evening Star* commented:

> One thing, however, is certain: Trollope received comparatively small honorariums for his later works, and at no time can he have been at all well off, for his personalty (as proved by will) is under £25,000. This is very different to the £100,000 first talked of. Charles Dickens left £90,000, and Thackeray about £40,000. Many people can't manage to read Trollope at all – colonists especially, who like their fiction (like their whisky and water) hot and strong, finding his tales deadly dull. To an Englishman of the middle class, however, they are most interesting pictures of contemporary life and manners.[15]

The extent of Trollope's colonial readership became clear when the novelist appeared among them. The chairman of the Caxton Commemoration Fund in Melbourne, introducing Trollope to his audience in late 1871, said he was a 'casual visitor to our shores but not a stranger, for he was well known to us by his works'.[16] Trollope was speaking on 'Modern Fiction as Rational Amusement'. The *West Coast Times* of New Zealand, a paper that served a widely distributed population of just over 15,000 people, mentioned this lecture as well, albeit in the briefest of terms: 'Mr Anthony Trollope's lecture, in aid of the Caxton Fund, has been eminently successful. The attendance was very large, and the net result to the fund is something considerable.'[17] Readers of his novels would have been perhaps a third of that number – generously estimated – yet these proportions show the scale of Trollope's reading public, who subscribed to his view of the 'modern novel' as bound to be both 'sensational and lifelike': 'Stories charmed not simply because they were tragic, but because we felt men and women, creatures with who we could sympathise, were struggling amidst their woe.'[18] These qualities of his fiction of course struck a chord with colonial readers, but the other great attraction of Trollope was, as Rusden put it, as the describer of English life and manners. Trollope's obituary in the *Wairarapa Daily Times* declares:

> We believe that Mr Trollope exercised a wider influence over the minds of the dwellers in Great Britain than even the high and illustrious personage who passed away almost simultaneously with him [i.e. the Archbishop of Canterbury]. Wherever the English tongue is spoken and read ANTHONY TROLLOPE the novelist is better known and loved than almost any living Englishman. He was not a man of high genius or of any position. He was simply the best delineator we have had since THACKERAY died, of social life in England. In every country and colony there are thousands of men and women to whom Trollope's heroes and heroines are living breathing beings to whom the late Archibishop was a stranger and a myth. In a colony like New Zealand we specially depended on a writer of this character for faithful and honest photographs of life as it now is in England. With ANTHONY TROLLOPE as a guide, we are at Home in St. Stephens, in the City Clubs, and drawing rooms, as well as in the country homes of England. No purer or fresher pictures of English home life can be found than those painted by this novelist . . . they are more powerful than the voice of the most eloquent preacher.[19]

The devotion of Trollope's readers evoked by the *Wairarapa Daily Times* speaks for the potent mix of nostalgia and cultural maintenance that colonial reading more generally expresses – the most potent way perhaps of remaining British while also becoming colonial. In 1867 the London Correspondent for the *Nelson Examiner*, reporting Trollope's retirement from the Civil Service, remarks that '[a] farewell dinner was given two nights since to Mr Anthony Trollope, on his retirement from the Civil Service. I assume that your readers are interested in the fact; as I know at least one Nelsonian who used to have his 'Orley Farm' sent out to him by each mail, to relieve the monotony of a sheep farmer's life.'[20]

What surfaces in colonial newspapers is what I think of as a reading shadow. It is given more materiality by what we know about the infrastructure, especially the numbers of booksellers and public libraries which developed in New Zealand in the second half of the nineteenth century. J. E. Traue has referred to a public library explosion: 263 in the first thirty-four years of settlement (1840–74) and another 506 by 1914. Traue notes that remote country areas were particularly well served and that the number of libraries to total population in New Zealand within fifty years of settlement was the highest density ever reached in any country or state in the world.[21] Trollope commented on the reading habits of the New Zealand population when he visited the tiny town of Tuapeka in a snowstorm.

In spite of the weather I went round the town, and visited the Atheneum or reading-room. In all these towns there are libraries, and the books are strongly bound and well thumbed. Carlyle, Macaulay and Dickens are certainly better known to small communities in New Zealand than they are to similar congregations of men and women at home. I should have liked Tuapika had it not snowed so bitterly on me when I was there.[22]

However, some degree of swotty preparation may have lain behind Trollope's impressions of the Tuapeka settlers. On 15 August the following letter appeared in the *Tuapeka Times*.

SIR – Can you tell me the reason why there was such a rush to the Atheneum last week? Amongst those most frequently at the institution recently, I noticed several who set themselves up as great authorities in literature, and who are in the habit of claiming familiarity with the writings of every author that wrote since the expulsion of Adam from the Garden of Eden. Is the explanation suggested by a friend of mine, viz., that many who intended to be present at the dinner proposed to be given to Mr Trollope, wanted to find out the titles of the books that gentleman has written, is [sic] order that they might not be considered ignorant cusses, correct? Yours truly
IGNORAMOUS
[We don't know. – Ed][23]

Trollope's visit to the far south generated other kinds of comment, suggesting that the author's celebrity tour was regarded with mixed feelings by a not always impressed populace. The same snowstorm caused a small flurry about Trollope in the local papers. The *Lake Wakatip Mail* reported that the conveyance carrying the celebrated author had got caught in a snowdrift. A dispute arose between the driver and a commercial traveller who were shovelling out the snow, and Trollope 'rather sharply demanded' of the traveller if he knew who he was. 'No! Who are you?' 'I am Anthony Trollope Sir!' 'I thought it was some d———fool', replies the traveller.[24] A week or two later a letter from the 'Commercial Traveller' was printed in the Christchurch *Press*. The writer denied the snow-shovelling story but said that after six hours driving on bad roads he had met an 'elderly and stout man on foot'. After an ill-tempered exchange about the state of the roads, the commercial traveller called after him '"Are you Mr Trollope?" "Yes sir, that's my name sir" in a voice as uncivil as it was gruff'.

No dispute of any kind occurred between Mr Trollope and myself, and the only oaths I heard were those of Mr Trollope as he walked away anathematizing the state of our beautiful roads, and what he called the impertinent inquisitiveness of those he met on them.[25]

The reported speech of this encounter offers a tantalising glimpse of two grumpy men in the snow. The commercial traveller was sufficiently offended to ask rhetorically:

Why we should bow down to a man like this, who is no more than a 'commercial' himself, as he was travelling to gather what printers call 'matter' for a book . . . I know not and care less, but this I do know, that he was sufficiently rude and uncouth himself to create a very unfavourable impression wherever he went.[26]

Perhaps it was these experiences in the back settlements of New Zealand in 1872 that provoked a scene in *Phineas Redux,* serialised in 1873. Phineas Finn, reflecting gloomily on his chances of being invited to join Mr Gresham's government, worries that poverty would force him to 'go to some New Zealand or back Canadian settlement to look for his bread'.[27]

Reading Trollope

How does reading Trollope transfer into other domains of public life? I have suggested above that one of the ways is through the discourse and practice of capitalism: money is the driving force of most of his plots, and it also happens to be the driving force of colonialism. As James Belich has said, the desire to 'better oneself', which usually involved the acquisition of land, is the primary motive for emigration, in New Zealand as elsewhere.[28] It is not surprising then that the novel which seems to have the highest profile by name in the New Zealand papers is *Orley Farm.* If wear and tear and annotations are a good guide, *Orley Farm* is also the most heavily read of Trollope's novels held in the Brancepeth Library, a collection formed and read on a sheep station from 1880 to 1910. While the Nelsonian mentioned earlier is said to have ordered it to relieve the monotony of his sheep station, *Orley Farm* is a signal example of nineteenth-century fiction's obsessive preoccupation with property – desire for it, possession of it, litigation over it – which reflects and is reflected in the grand narrative of imperialism. *Orley Farm,* it might be said, is what colonists wanted to own, and the legal, moral and emotional entanglements that surround it, the painful education of those who wish to possess it, transfer with some acuteness to colonial life, where hope of the acquisition of property and improvements in status and standards of living are the primary motivations for being there at all.

In September 1872, the *Auckland Star* published an essay by its columnist 'Bee', on Anthony Trollope – the 'illustrious visitor to our shores' – which gives a potted biography and booklist. *Orley Farm* and *Doctor Thorne* are singled out as 'among the best of Trollope's fictions', but it is *Orley Farm* which gives Trollope his name recognition:

> The welcome that the author of 'Orley Farm' received in Auckland was of that unostentatious nature as it should ever be, which disturbs not the equilibrium of the feelings, and which will enable him when again on Albion's shores to tell to his countrymen the 'plain unvarnished tale' of his *colonial* experiences.[29]

Bee obviously also expected readers to pick up the reference to Paul Montague's letter breaking it off with Mrs Hurtle, the 'plain unvarnished tale' in *The Way We Live Now. Orley Farm* appeared again in a news item, widely copied in the local papers, about a law suit in 1877.

> An Equity suit was opened in the Supreme Court on Monday which, according to the counsel for the plaintiff, leads to the question of perjury, and possesses features as romantic as those celebrated cases recorded in Warren's 'Ten thousand a year', and Anthony Trollope's 'Orley Farm'. The plaintiff is Thomas Robertson, an old settler living at Anderson's Bay, and he seeks to set aside a deed of conveyance to

his son-in-law and daughter, Mr and Mrs D. McRoss of Timaru, on the ground that the deed in question was procured by fraud. The case promises to last for several days. The plaintiff was giving evidence nearly the whole of Tuesday, and for a man nearly eighty years of age displayed great powers of endurance.[30]

And after Trollope's death, 'Novels and Novelists' in the Auckland *New Zealand Observer* of 1888 singled *Orley Farm* out as the high point in what was by then Trollope's defunct career:

Time was when Anthony Trollope was the rage, and when the appearance of a new work by the author of 'Orley Farm' was the literary event of the season. Who reads Trollope now?

Popularity is influential of course, and *Orley Farm*'s high profile with the New Zealand readership is no doubt partly transferred from its popular reception in the British market, but it also has some acute resonances with the colonial situation. Both *Barchester Towers* and *The Eustace Diamonds* make brief appearances as points of reference in local newspapers, illustrating, as does *Orley Farm*, the way reading underlies people's apprehension of daily events and provides linking structures for memory imagination and feelings. Reading also indicates the existence of what could be called, to borrow Benedict Anderson's phrase, a 'horizontal comradeship'[31] – in this case disputes transferred across the British world. A letter from Montreal reported in Wellington in 1866 describes the volunteer army assembled against the Fenian uprising, to 'teach them a lesson'.[32] The writer of the letter declares that though the Fenians here and at home 'feel quite sure the blow must be struck', like 'Mr Trollope's Bishop of Barchester Towers, they also feel it cannot be now'. For cognisant readers this reference brings up the undue influence of Mrs Proudie over the weak-willed bishop and associates the Fenians with his inability to act, sentiments which perhaps had some purchase in Wellington.

The Eustace Diamonds made the Wellington papers in a more sensational way in 1872, while being serialised in *The Australasian*. The writer alludes to the novel's plot, in which the reported burglary of Lady Eustace's diamonds was fabricated by their owner, and hints that local criticism of police incompetence might be similarly misplaced. Like many references to fiction in nineteenth-century newspapers, the writer invokes the reader's capacity to link the turns of fiction to local events, and in this covertly suggests, while denying, that the Wellington burglaries (or perhaps just one of them) might mirror Trollope's plot device.

Apropos of a suggestion that the efficiency of our police force should be increased by the addition of detectives, the occasion for such being a couple of mysterious and still undetected robberies – a gentleman's jewellery and £100 from a butcher's shop – Mr Anthony Trollope has written a tale called 'The Eustace Diamonds', which is now in the course of publication in the 'Australasian' and the following remarks which are taken from it have considerable bearing on the suggestion referred to: '. . . Two or three of the leading newspapers had first hinted at and then openly condemned the incompetence and slowness of the police. Such censure as we know is very common, and in nine cases out of ten it is unjust . . .' Of course we do not mean to say that the story of the 'Eustace Diamonds' has been paralleled in Wellington; but it is still very apropos in order to show that censure should not be passed too swiftly. There are mysterious robberies sometimes that are far too simple to be unravelled by all the trained craft of Bow Street.[33]

Perhaps *The Eustace Diamonds* was slower than *Orley Farm* or *Barchester Towers* to disseminate around the colony, but like all of Trollope's novels it had a later life in colonial editions. In 1883 it was announced in the *Akaroa Mail* as 'Good News For Readers' when it arrived among the new books from Mudie's Circulating Library.[34] Though references to Trollope decline sharply after his death, colonial editions kept most of his fiction in circulation.

Readers Found on the Page

These glimpses in the print media illustrate the elusiveness of reading history, which is like tracking a fish underwater. Occasionally it shows its back and one can see the paths it has taken and the ripples of its track. Because reading is both private terrain and a culturally loaded activity, because reading references show you something of what someone has in their heads while thinking of other things but mostly does not show the individual reader, the history of reading is always partial and skewed to those whose visibility is important to them. As this chapter has shown, newspapers make a Trollopian readership visible and occasionally give it a voice, but the majority of the people who bought the books and visited the Atheneum in Tuapeka remains largely submerged.

In the Brancepeth Library, a private subscription library on a large sheep station in New Zealand, some individuals are visible.[35] The library, a collection of some 2,000 books begun sometime in the 1870s, is 80 per cent fiction, and was borrowed and read by the subscribing workers and family members living on the station. Books were sent out to men working in remote areas (the sheep station at its maximum was about 76,000 acres) and show the evidence of their travelling lives. If damage and dirt are an indication of reader use, the most heavily read of Trollope's fourteen novels is *Orley Farm*. Most of the books are cheap colonial editions brought out after Trollope's death. *Orley Farm* also has the most anonymous marginalia. Crosses, corrections and lines mark the pages. Crosses seem to mark what has struck a reader: at one point, a cross appears at this line 'I wish there were no such things as young men at all' (p. 377). The following page there is a cross at 'It seems to me that she prefers mind to matter which is a great deal to say for a young lady.' Crosses perhaps also mark crossings – where what a reader sees on the page crosses into their life, as experience, or insight, or truism. For instance, 'was he not a gentleman by birth, education and tastes? What more should a man want for a son-in-law?' (p. 382) seems to reflect one of the persistent colonial anxieties: were people really who they said they were and how did colonials maintain their class status? There is an indecipherable name and date confidently written on the last page of *Orley Farm*: R. Hells or Helb, 6/7/82. Is the date recording when he finished the novel or is it a date of purchase? I haven't been able to decipher this name and know nothing about who it might be. Another reader's name appears twice in the Brancepeth copy of *Doctor Thorne*: M. E. Parsons. Mary

Elizabeth Parsons was the wife of George Parsons, a bullock driver and rabbiter who worked on the sheep station. He held the library subscription and would very probably have borrowed books for the family to read. But M. E. Parsons appears on page 1 over a bookseller's stamp. Were these books donated by Mary Elizabeth Parsons, or did she simply write her name in them? And then there is John Vaughan Miller, the station clerk and former Admiralty clerk, who annotated several hundred of the books in the collection and who read everything, including Trollope.

Miller was a performative reader, leaving corrections (especially of Latin or Greek phrases and quotations), glosses, annotations, scholia, translations (often from or in Greek) and sharp opinionated comments in many of the library books. In Trollope he confines himself to correcting the text, but on the final page of *Ralph the Heir*, where Miller very characteristically corrects the Latin phrase magnum opus (rendered in the text as 'magnus opus') another reader, extremely faintly, chimes in with a scrawl of the novel's concluding words 'may yet be written', as it were in response to Miller's correction, and as if echoing the generally proposed view, ten years after Trollope died, which relegated him to minor status as a novelist, well after Thackeray and Dickens. Or not? Perhaps someone was just doodling an idle moment away. It is these tantalising scraps of possible dialogue, or flashes of literary memory, or sparks of literary emotions that enliven the history of reading, and allow Trollope's readers to become briefly visible in the disseminations of his work and his work to become visible in other moments of history.

Notes

1. Darnton, Robert. 'First Steps Toward a History of Reading', in *The Kiss of Lamourette: Reflections in Cultural History* (New York: W. W. Norton, 1990). Didier Eribon, *Returning to Reims*, trans. Michael Lucey, Los Angeles: Semiotext(e), 2013.
2. *Daily Southern Cross* (21 February 1862), p. 3. This information has been retrieved by means of the webtool QueryPic, a tool which allows one to graph historical newspaper searches. It was developed for use in the Australian online newspaper archive, *Trove*. See <http://dhistory.org/querypic/> (last accessed 22 February 2018).
3. *Empire* (23 December 1857), p. 3.
4. *Taranaki Herald* (31 July 1869), p. 4.
5. *Southland Times* (7 January 1870), p. 3.
6. Nigel Starck, *The First Celebrity Anthony Trollope's Australasian Odyssey* (Tusmore, South Australia: Writes of Passage, 2014).
7. Anthony Trollope, *An Autobiography* (Edinburgh: Blackwood, 1883), vol. 2, ch. 19, p. 193.
8. *Gympie Times* (2 March 1872) cited Starck, pp. 33–4.
9. Anthony Trollope, *Australia and New Zealand*, 2 vols (London: Chapman and Hall, 1873), vol. 2, ch. 20, pp. 457–8.
10. Trollope, *The Letters of Anthony Trollope*, ed. N. John Hall, 2 vols (Stanford: Stanford University Press, 1983), vol. 1, p. 594.
11. National Library of New Zealand, Alexander Turnbull Library, Manuscript Papers 1706.
12. *Otago Witness* (18 July 1874,) p. 6.
13. 'Mr Anthony Trollope at Rockhampton', *Argus* (9 September 1871), p. 6.
14. *Marlborough Express* (16 February 1883), p. 2.
15. *Evening Star* (7 April 1883), p. 2.
16. *Argus* (19 December 1871), p. 6.
17. *West Coast Times* (27 December 1871), p. 2.

18. Anthony Trollope, 'On English Prose Fiction as a Rational Amusement' (1870), in *Four Lectures*, ed. Morris L. Parrish (London: Constable, [1870] 1938), p. 124.
19. *Wairarapa Daily Times* (13 December 1882), p. 2.
20. *Nelson Examiner* (31 December 1867), p. 3.
21. J. E. Traue 'The Public Library Explosion in Colonial New Zealand', *Libraries & the Cultural Record*, 42.2 (2007): pp. 151–2.
22. Anthony Trollope, *Australia and New Zealand*, 2 vols (London: Chapman and Hall, 1873), vol. 2, ch. 20, pp. 336–7.
23. *Tuapeka Times* (5 August 1872), p. 7.
24. *Lake Wakatip Mail* (27 August, 1873), p. 2.
25. *Christchurch Press* (11 September 1873), p. 2.
26. Ibid.
27. Anthony Trollope, *Phineas Redux*, ed. John Bowen (Oxford: Oxford University Press, 2014), ch. 37, p. 261.
28. James Belich, *Making Peoples: A History of the New Zealanders From Polynesian Settlement to the End of the Nineteenth Century* (Auckland: Penguin Books, 1996), p. 328.
29. *Auckland Star* (28 September 1872), p. 2.
30. *Colonist* (25 January 1877), p. 3.
31. Benedict Anderson, *Imagined Communities* (London and New York: Verso, 1991), p. 7.
32. Anonymous letter cited in 'Canada', *Evening Post* (23 June 1866), p. 2.
33. *Wellington Independent* (13 September 1872), p. 2.
34. 'Peninsula News', *Akaroa Mail and Banks Peninsula Advertiser* (3 August 1883), p. 2.
35. Lydia Wevers, *Reading on the Farm: Victorian Fiction and the Colonial World* (Wellington: Victoria University Press, 2010).

Part III

Media Networks

13

Realism v. Realpolitik: Trollope and the Parliamentary Career Manqué

Helen Small

If the tell-tale tic of Trollope's style and signature preoccupation of his narratives is, as Nicholas Dames has proposed, the concern with 'making one's way' or, 'in plainer words, with career',[1] unsuccessful parliamentary candidacy is the most psychologically charged form of career frustration in the fiction and the life. In the 1868 general election, Trollope stood for the East Riding borough of Beverley. Defeat was all but inevitable: he was standing in a notoriously corrupt constituency, in the expectation that he would fail and Beverley would be disfranchised. Still, the losing hurt – to such an extent that Trollope never again pursued '[what] should be the highest object of ambition to every educated Englishman': a seat in Parliament.[2] Impurity of motive – willingness to do a public service mixing with political aspiration and a hunger for self-vindication[3] – is one sign of the excessive desire distinguishing Trollope's attitude to his parliamentary career manqué from his career at the Post Office and in literature. Another is the disruption of narrative *Bildung*.

'Beverley' is the title given to Chapter 16 of the *Autobiography*, which covers Trollope's early political ambitions, his political theory, a lost opportunity to stand for the county of Essex in 1867 (close to his home at Waltham Cross), the Beverley campaign (almost 200 miles away), its result, and Trollope's embittered retrospection on 'the most wretched fortnight of my manhood' (*A*, ch. 16, p. 186). This separated story of political aspiration, political opportunity and political experience interrupts the otherwise steady plotting of his achieved careers. The effect is that of a late false start – opening up and subsequently closing down the possibility of a third, in his estimation more important, public life.[4] Although Trollope's political *Bildung* falters at 'Beverley', the political theory he articulates in this chapter is firm-footed to the point of intransigence. Labelling himself 'an advanced but still a conservative Liberal',[5] Trollope presents his Liberal convictions as advanced (after John Stuart Mill) and looking to assist the historical tendency toward greater equality between men, though gladly keeping company with his Conservative opponent, who takes equality to be in the divine long-term plan, but is careful to apply the brakes lest the coach run out of control (*A*, ch. 16, p. 183).[6] The most striking aspect of Trollope's political theory, read in context, is its touted immunity to experience: 'my political feelings and convictions have never undergone any change. They are what they became when I first began to have political feelings and convictions. Nor do I find in myself any tendency to modify them' (*A*, ch. 16, pp. 181–2).

I take Chapter 16 to be a defensive account of what happens when a flexible but tenaciously held theory of gradualist liberal progressivism runs up hard against modern realpolitik and declines, in theory, to yield. The difficulty for Trollope was that his brief and bruising experience on the ground conformed neither to the Millite Liberal strand in his political thinking nor to the touches of older Burkean Whiggery in his make-up. However, it is a pre-emptively moral reading of the field of political debate on Trollope's part, and on the part of subsequent historians, that would have us understand the Beverley election simply as evidence of corrupt influences, liable (if left unchallenged) to scupper the trajectory of modern reformism. This is the dominant story Trollope tells in the *Autobiography* and in the political fiction written in the wake of the 1868 election, during and just after the petition and Royal Commission that resulted in the constituency's disfranchisement. Depicting himself and the fictional protagonists of *Ralph the Heir* (1870–1) and *Phineas Redux* (1873–4) who replay his hustings experiences as unhappy sacrifices to an incomplete process of political modernisation, Trollope does not fully register the nature of the opposition he met within the constituency. Enraged by overt practices of vote-buying and treating, and by the humiliation of his own public ambitions, he is too scarred by defeat, perhaps also too romantic in his view of parliamentary election, to turn a realist's eye on a regionally based Tory politics supported by trade and equipped with an organisational structure as cogently articulated to itself as the professional organisations he was more at home with – the law, the Post Office and (to a degree) literature.

What Trollope cannot willingly acknowledge at the level of narrative agencies nevertheless makes itself felt at the level of literary form. 'Beverley' and its fictional counterparts Percycross and Tankerville have a distortive effect on the style and narrative structure of Trollope's fiction and *Autobiography*. Hustings scenes put pressure on realism, producing a distortive gear-shift into angry satire on the bruising interest-group manoeuvring and overt cynicism (as it seemed to him) of an unreformed electoral system. The result is a localised but significant destabilisation of tone and purpose: a flaring up of political *ressentiment* of a piece with but qualitatively unlike those other 'formal variations' that Lauren M. E. Goodlad and Frederik Van Dam describe as the Palliser series' versatile stylistic response to social and political changes instituted by 'an expanding democracy, commercial power, and empire'.[7]

This local destabilisation has consequences for the novels' practice in the domain of provincial realism. The 'semi-detached provincial novel', as John Plotz and others have described it, mediates between the provincial and the national, treating provincialism's local attachments and intrigues as a 'template' for the more detached mode of contemplation brought to the idea of a national political culture.[8] The 'fully realised' texture of the local experience models, or gives 'formal congruence', to the vaguer texture of the 'general' experience. In Plotz's and others' revisions of Bakhtin, provincialism betokens 'compactness, familiarity, distinctiveness (usually from the metropole), nostalgia-inducing comparative backwardness, and negative definition' (ruling out plots and possibilities that a metropolitan or more varied setting would make possible), though the 'world beyond' is continually disclosing itself within or alongside this compact world, reminding us that the local culture is imbricated in national, and indeed global, cultures.[9] This is neither the logic nor the temper of *Ralph the Heir* and *Phineas Redux,* as they respond to Trollope's experience of electoral politics. Offending against his understanding of what Conservatism is and what function it should perform within a wider system of representative government, Beverley realpolitik casts doubt on the core rationale of the semi-detached provincial novel, the assumption of

> *magnum in parvo,* whereby provincial life is desirable for its capacity to locate its inhabitants at once in a trivial (but chartable) Nowheresville and in a universal (but strangely ephemeral) everywhere.[10]

Beverley is all too particular, known by name and persistent news reports in the period between 1868 and 1871, plainly visible behind its pseudonyms. In so far as the case admits of generalisation, it does so under the paradoxical sign of Tory localism.

Beverley realpolitik has consequences also for Trollope's development of the political *Bildungsroman,* as he had undertaken it in *Phineas Finn,* the first of his novels to treat the parliamentary career as a viable aspiration for an educated man 'with no vestige of property' and 'without a penny in his purse' (*A,* ch. 1, p. 10). The non-meritocratic nature of access to parliament and unpredictability of politics are significant pressures on the political career. Ultimately, they are less salient here than the degree to which exposure to the constituency – the people who vote one into office, the party agents and party members – brings into momentarily sharp focus the priority of the local culture and local concerns over any political theories or convictions the candidate brings to the place. When Trollope stood 'for Beverley' in 1868 he argued that what the party needed at this juncture was disciplined loyalty: 'the chief duty of a Liberal member in the next House of Commons will be to give a firm and continued support to the Leader of the Liberal party', as he expressed it.[11] He had strong views also about disestablishment of the Irish Church, and about the relation of Church and State more generally: 'but my political ideas were all leather and prunella to the men whose votes I was soliciting. They cared nothing for my doctrines, and could not be made to understand that I should have any' (*A,* ch. 16, p. 187). The pragmatic accent on loyalty to party, and the importance (to himself) of making his own convictions known, brought him into quick conflict with the electorate's interests and priorities – not least, local support for the secret ballot.[12]

Trollope's subsequent fiction plays out a recurrent narrative predicament in which the parliamentary protagonist must, in order to be true to his own convictions, cast a vote contrary to his pledges to his constituency and/or against his own party line. As Trollope presents them, these are moral dilemmas more than political dilemmas. Their political content remains under-articulated and secondary to questions of good conscience and civic virtue as they affect the decisions of the political actor. If this often-remarked personalisation of conflict is indicative of the strong strain of civic republicanism in Trollope's make-up ('emphasiz[ing] public participation and the positive freedom to develop citizen character'[13]) it is also, especially post '68, symptomatic of a difficulty in confronting dilemmas posed by Beverley as they do and do not fall within the scope of 'that classic Trollopean move', by which 'major issues in [a] novel are almost always referable to the law but are not actually resolved by it, being left instead to characters' and readers' own moral judgement'.[14] The law pronounces on electoral corruption, in the novels as in reality, but not on legitimate differences of political outlook. The conflicted and conflictual views left behind in the Trollopean constituency raise basic and in some degree intractable questions for representative democracy. What are the conditions under which strong local interests can legitimately overrule national interests as conceived at the metropolitan centre of politics? What is the extent of a representative's obligation to represent the constituency, even at the expense of giving 'firm and continued support' to party, or articulating his own views as a (more or less) conscientious parliamentarian?

Realpolitik

It is an irony of Trollope's one attempt on Parliament that (like John Stuart Mill, standing for re-election in Westminster) he failed as a Liberal candidate in an election that saw a landslide victory for Gladstonian Liberalism over Disraelian Conservatism. The 1868 general election was the first after the Second Reform Act, the last before the Ballot Act of 1872. It was, notoriously, defaced by allegations of misconduct, there being a direct link between expansion in the number of seats contested and increases in bribery. The passing of the Parliamentary Elections Act (1868) marks the point at which historical case law burgeons, as litigants sought to test common law before judges who heard electoral petitions around the country, Beverley's included. But if the state was energetic in seeking to reform and standardise political behaviour across Great Britain, local practice often resisted the aspirations of the political centre.[15]

The bribery of voters, Graeme Orr observes, only came to be widely deplored once old paternalistic patterns of relation between landholders and tenants gave way in the mid-Victorian period to 'the republican ideal of the autonomous, independent voter'.[16] Changes in the nature of land-holding and property ownership, expansion of the franchise, and the emergence of new social classes seeking parliamentary power directly (as representatives) or at one remove (as agents of representatives) all contributed to a gradual denaturalisation of the old system of voter inducements. The 'customary displays' of the past – vote-buying, bribing under cover of donations to charity, 'colourable employment' (paying canvassers and runners for little or no work), treating with alcohol, conveyancing, and many more elaborate briberies practised by electoral agents – only ceased to seem 'legitimate concomitants of natural interest' with the emergence of professional party organisations bringing local activities under the control of central party bureaucracies.[17]

That process had a tendency to look tardier the further one went from Westminster. The geographical map of electoral corruption built up in the course of O'Malley and Hardcastle's seven-volume collection of the *Decisions of the Judges for the Trial of Election Petitions* (1870–1929) is not confined to constituencies remote from London,[18] but the patterns of distribution suggest entrenched 'traditionalism' in the north of England and in Ireland. Yet, then as now, the central party depended on some of these regions for economic and administrative support. As Mill observed in the 1860s, no party had to date seriously opposed the determination of rich men to keep Parliament as their special preserve. There is 'a rooted feeling among our legislators of both political parties', he wrote, adding that it was almost the only point on which I believe them to be really ill-intentioned. They care comparatively little who votes, as long as they feel assured that none but persons of their own class can be voted for . . . [T]he subservience of *nouveaux enrichis* who are knocking at the door of the class is a still surer reliance.[19]

Trollope's principal rival might or might not have counted as a *nouveau enrichi*, depending on the degree of one's snobbery. Sir Henry Edwards, Bart., was the incumbent MP for Beverley having held the seat since 1857. The baronetcy was just two years old, one of many honours handed out by the Conservative Prime Minister Lord Derby in late 1866, outraging some quarters of the independent and radical press.[20] Previously MP for Halifax from 1847 to 1852, currently Beverley Justice of the Peace, a freemason[21] and, since 1863, Lieutenant-Colonel Commandant of the 2nd West Yorkshire Yeomanry Cavalry,[22] Edwards was reputedly the largest landowner in the Halifax district and a major figure in the mercantile, social, political and Established Church life of the Ridings.[23] His grandfather, John Edwards, had come to Yorkshire from

Figure 13.1 Stephen Pearce, *Sir Henry Edwards, 1st Baronet (1812–86), High Sheriff of Yorkshire, here shown as Lieutenant-Colonel Commandant of the 2nd West York Yeomanry Cavalry*, 1873. Engraving by Alex Scott (proof mezzotint). Photograph by Nick Cistone, The Bodleian Libraries, The University of Oxford.
Courtesy of Helen Small.

Birmingham 100 years earlier, founding a woollen manufacturing firm that exported 'goods, such as blankets and Baizes', chiefly to South America.[24] From the 1820s the headquarters of 'John Edwards and Sons' were the Canal Mills, near Sowerby Bridge; a vast six-storey edifice on both sides of the Calder & Hebble Navigation canal. Henry Edwards assumed the senior partnership in 1848 on the death of his father, becoming resident proprietor of the family estate, Pye Nest: 134 acres, surrounding a flamboyant Italianate pile designed by John Carr and built *c*.1777.[25] Around twenty of Sir Henry's horses were buried in the grounds.[26]

Pye Nest's location in the West Riding, sixty-seven miles from Beverley, exposed Edwards to objections that he had 'bought' his parliamentary interest in the East Riding,[27] but his investments in the constituency were vital to the local economy and more than tokenism. In 1864 he purchased the Beverley Iron and Wagon Co., formerly Crosskill and Co. Iron Works, manufacturers of carts, wagons, engines and farm machinery, the largest employer in mid nineteenth-century Beverley.[28] During the Crimean War the firm had produced 'over 3,000 army carts and wagons and some ordnance', but the post-war collapse of its mortgage holder, the East Riding Bank, imperilled its survival.[29] Edwards's intervention prevented bankruptcy. One part of the electoral corruption charge sheet against him was that the works manager, Richard Norfolk, committed 'wholesale bribery with funds advanced by a local Bank at

A. Butler. lith   Stannard & Dixon 7 Poland St.

PYE NEST, HALIFAX,
THE SEAT OF HENRY EDWARDS ESQ

Figure 13.2 Augustus Butler, *Pye Nest, Halifax*, illustration lithographed by Messrs. Stannard & Dixon, from Burke, *A Visitation*, II, facing p. 210. Courtesy of the Bodleian Libraries, The University of Oxford, 6 Theta 60.

which neither Mr Norfolk nor the Company banked' – that he had, in other words, been given an election 'pot'.[30] In Edwards's defence, his attorney (Sergeant Ballantyne) argued unblushingly that his client had taken over the company purely as an act of charity to keep 300–400 men in work.[31]

Edwards frankly told the electors in 1868 that he and any running mate he approved should be returned by reason of his substantial financial investments in the region – investments that made the Liberal interest in the region look paltry:

TO THE BURGESSES OF THE BOROUGH OF BEVERLEY.

GENTLEMEN,

The very unexpected retirement of my colleague, Mr [Christopher] Sykes [MP for Beverley, 1865–8], in consequence of his intention to stand for the [West] Riding, has overwhelmed me with grief and alarm, as it may cause a . . . contest for the Borough, and I may be called upon to pay some election expenses, which, however, I shall avoid if possible, and I hope I shall find as good a colleague as Mr Sykes, and one who will be as 'liberal' with his purse as he has been. You know my expenditure at my first election was sufficient for a life time.

. . . Allow me to add that I do not wish needlessly and prematurely to disturb the Borough by political agitation. The Borough is mine, and I have told my patrons you will elect any nominee they choose to send to be my colleague.

I remain with the deepest regard and gratitude to you and my Government patrons,
        Your obliged and faithful servant,
        HENRY EDWARDS.
        Pyment, near Halifax, July 25th, 1868.[32]

If we are to shorthand this as 'paternalism' (after Orr), it is paternalism of a bracingly pragmatic kind: not a quasi-feudalistic assertion of propriety, but a blustering get-my-money's worth, 'buggered if I'm going to fork out any more than I already have' form of entitlement. Toryism of this variety is consciously commercial, provocatively vulgarian – cheerfully twisting the term 'liberal' away from its party-political meaning to connote fiscal openhandedness.

Sir Henry's political views were straightforward: 'A conservative and strenuous supporter of the Church of England as established at the Reformation', opposed to recent rises in income tax,[33] a moderate protectionist,[34] vehemently anti-Catholic (he was responsible for spreading rumours in 1868 that Gladstone was a closet papist)[35] and, more attractively, a campaigner for clean air and water in an age of almost unchecked industrial pollution.[36] His recorded contributions to debates in the House are few, brief and confined to factory legislation and matters concerning the yeomanry.[37] His hustings speeches have some blustering appeal, but he was no 'charismatic leader' in Max Weber's sense of the term.[38]

Edwards knew the importance of political ties between the regions and the metropolitan centre. His Toryism was conceived and executed on the basis of local attachments: both ideologically and practically, he was a committed Disraelian Conservative – Disraeli's success in this period resting very largely on his recognition that to lose sight of local interests and local cultures is a political mistake. England, as Disraeli

described it, was the 'only important European community . . . still governed by tradi-
tionary influences'.[39] Her political exceptionalism, in this durable Conservative view,
rested on the fact that 'society has always been more powerful than the State'.[40] For
Edwards, as for Disraeli, most people's political affiliations (except in times of emer-
gency) arise out of local interests and commitments. The provincial bases, however,
must be harnessed to an efficient party machine.[41]

As a local business leader Edwards had the support of highly effective local
agents. Both Trollope and the Victorian press concentrated on one man: William
Smales Wreghitt, the original of *Ralph the Heir*'s Mr Trigger (the name almost an
anagram of 'Wreghitt'). Sneeringly referred to by the barrister for the petitioners as
Sir Henry's 'recognised confidant',[42] Wreghitt was a linen draper who found a profitable addition to his trade in working to 'consolidate the [mill owner's] position . . .
as member for the borough',[43] intervening aggressively in the management of local
charities and the distribution of common pasturage to ensure Tory control of benefits. A significant problem for Trollope was that he could not be certain that his own
agent was not operating in like manner (though he could be sure the man had shal-
lower pockets): Trollope testified that he had no idea what was done with the £400
he sent to the Liberal party agent in Beverley to cover 'expenses' (*A*, 188).[44] Like
the fictional Trigger, Wreghitt was boldfaced under hostile questioning: 'He believed
that the last Parliamentary Election for Beverley was the purest in England.'[45] He
was serviceable to Sir Henry in large part because the candidate could turn a blind
eye to what was done in his name and with his purse. A man who cared little for his
own reputation, Wreghitt used his own initiative and left no legally compromising
paper trail.

Of more interest to historians should have been another man, who makes no
appearance in Trollope's writings and scant appearance in most of the newspaper
coverage. Frederick William Cronhelm (1787–1871) was, like his father before him,
financial overseer of the Edwards family businesses, described in his *Halifax Courier*
obituary as the Edwards's 'confidential friend and adviser'.[46] A thoroughgoing Tory in
his own right, honoured by the local party in 1871 for many years of service, he was
far cleverer than the man he helped keep in parliamentary office,[47] and possessed a different order of competence to the loose cannon, Wreghitt. When the Royal Commission of 1869 re-examined the allegations of bribery he was belatedly required to testify
on the basis of his knowledge as a '"trusted cashier" who kept the locked private
ledger and oversaw the work of ten or twelve bookkeepers' responsible for the general
and other ledgers.[48] In his eighty-third year and not in good health, he was lucid in his
testimony, and decisive with regard to the trial outcome:

> [he] admitted that he had destroyed all letters and accounts pertaining to elec-
> tion expenditure documents while acting as manager for Sir Henry Edwards . . .
> [I]t seems that his motive . . . was the protection of his colleagues. He explained
> to the Chief Commissioner, 'I felt it a duty to my friends to destroy every letter.'[49]

Sir Henry was duly committed for trial, and the trial faltered for lack of evidence.

With hindsight we can see William Wreghitt and, more credibly, Frederick Cronhelm as early runners in the creation of the system Weber observed in 1919, whereby
professionalised English election agents were operating '*outside* the parliaments' in

the manner of entrepreneurs'[50] – privately financed forerunners of the more systematic local party organisations to come. Beverley was not Britain *in parvo* (neither Trollope nor the legal system was mistaken in identifying gross electoral abuses), but it was in critical ways forward-looking, financing a quasi-professional system for leveraging local commercial influences with a view to advancing regional interests in Westminster.

Trollope underestimated the organisational sophistication of Edwards's campaigns. He seems to have known very little about how far Edwards made himself serviceable in the management of Disraeli's party in the House of Commons. Edwards's surviving letters to Disraeli,[51] written between 1859 (when Edwards was MP for Halifax) and 1871 (after the termination of his parliamentary career), show him energetic in his efforts at rebuilding Conservatism in the 'manufacturing boroughs' of the West Riding and active in his role as President of the local Conservative Registration Association, and committed to functioning, in effect, as a party whip in Westminster.[52] Whips, as Angus Hawkins explains, were vital components of the party system from the early 1840s. They worked behind the scenes to inform party leaders of the levels of support and dissent attaching to parliamentary measures: 'shadowy presence[s]', with 'no official status', whose 'efforts at persuasion tended to rest . . . on appeals to "the welfare of the country" rather than the success of the party'.[53] In Gladstone's nice phrase, they were 'the medium everybody knows, but nobody names'.[54]

Sir Henry spent a great deal of money and time strengthening Disraeli's hold over the party. Letters from the early 1860s show him acting as his party chief's eyes and ears at the Carlton Club (the oldest and most important of the London Conservative clubs), reporting back on reactions to Disraeli's speeches, canvassing support for motions, giving advance notice of rumoured resignations, chivvying Tory MPs to attend sittings of the House, and urging Disraeli's attendance at 'political dinners' held at Edwards's home at 14 Bruton Street, later in Beverley Square and then Dover Street, where the party leader might make himself better known to those Tory MPs for whom he was a distant figurehead.[55] (Trollope had heard of the dinners.) How far Disraeli valued these exertions is a matter for guesswork.[56] '[A]s a rule you make a point of declining all gentlemen's parties', Edwards complains in one letter.[57] A pressing invitation to visit Pye Nest in 1859 seems to have met with refusal,[58] but annual gifts of grouse from Sir Henry's moors were accepted,[59] and Disraeli wrote offering personal sympathies when Edwards was unseated in March 1869.[60]

He could hardly have claimed to be ignorant of what Edwards was doing in Beverley, having been thoroughly informed on almost every point, including the strategic purchase of the Beverley Iron and Wagon Company[61] and the process by which Edwards had taken control of the mayoralty, the wardens, the corporation and the Pasture Masters ('the key to the Parliamentary Representation').[62] 'The Augean Stable has been thoroughly cleaned & purified from liberal corruption', Edwards had crowed to Disraeli in November 1862; it was a sadly exiled Sir Henry, then, who wrote in June 1871 complaining that his last letter had gone unanswered, and begging tickets for the Queen's Ball. In the Ridings his stature was little diminished by his trial. When the Royal Commission delivered its verdict that corruption in Beverley was manifest but there was no proof of Sir Henry's involvement, he was welcomed back to the constituency with fanfare and trumpets (a lone protester on the town council unable to check the jubilant mood in the borough).[63] A full-length subscription portrait was commissioned (see p. 207 above) and a public banquet was held in his honour at the

Assembly Rooms on 4 February with the mayor and most of the local dignitaries in attendance. The bells of the Minster and St Mary's Church were rung, and Sir Henry entered the town in a four-horse carriage led by a band playing 'See the Conquering Hero Comes'.[64] As the taxi driver who took me from Beverley railway station into the centre of town on my last trip to the East Riding archives put the point robustly: 'at least he did something for the place'.

Excessive Realism

Henry Edwards presents a version of constituency politics that Trollope is barely willing to acknowledge in his political theory, even when he comes to write the *Autobiography*. Beverley was notoriously corrupt – an outlier even by the uneven standards of the day – but other, less roguish features of Edwards's Westminster career are (on a long view) more interesting than the corruption. His vested regionalism was by no means exceptional: it was entirely of a piece not only with Disraeli's position on localism but with that of many Liberals, the great challenge of Gladstone's 'regionalism' being to connect the metropolitan political centre to the 'periphery' through direct representation, 'astute use of the press' and 'control and demonstration of executive power'.[65]

What Trollope sees, from his Liberal-gradualist perspective, is an extreme case of uneven development between regional and Westminster political cultures: one that attracts the full force of his satiric castigation. The disconnect between modern metropole and unreformed constituency is the gist of the scene of mutual condolence in *Ralph the Heir* between Old Pile – 'a sort of father of the [Percycross] borough in the way of Conservatives'[66] – and Mr Trigger, the local Tory electoral agent assigned to Sir Thomas. Both agents are disgusted by the new breed of candidate coming up from London, looking to Percycross to enable their metropolitan political careers. 'What's the meaning of it all?', complains Old Pile:

> It's just this, – that folks wants what they wants without paying for it . . . When I see the chaps as come here and talk of Purity, I know they mean that nothing ain't to be as it used to be. Nobody is to trust no one. There ain't to be nothing warm, nor friendly, nor comfortable any more. This Sir Thomas you've brought down is just as bad as that shoemaking chap [the radical candidate]; – worse if anything . . . Why isn't a poor man, as can't hardly live, to have his three half-crowns or fifteen shillings, as things may go, for voting for a stranger such as him? (*RH*, ch. 26, pp. 226–7)

Trollope's use of his own Liberal candidacy as the model for Sir Thomas's Tory candidacy looks, as it is, a superficial change in this context. The pressure for transparency is resented across the constituency party spectrum, the radical London bootmaker, Ontario Moggs, being as offensive to the agents as the London toff. Trollope's narrative affords little respect to their outlook. Rendered comic by the gesturally regional dialogue, heavy-handed names and the hyper-aggressive parochialism that perversely appropriates radical catchphrases (as in the final term of the chapter title: 'Moggs, Purity and the Rights of Labour'), the party agents' protest occupies an oddly indeterminate position between realism and satiric deformation of the real. This is at once a caricature and a description of what happened at Beverley, the implication being that reality has outstripped the satirist's power of invention.

It is a weakness of Trollope's satire on the constituency that it fails to take localism seriously. Old Pile is not irrational after all (though he is corrupt) when he objects to the incursion of London metropolitan interests into a regional politics strongly connected to the local economy: why *should* a man expect to come 'down' from London and ask for the support of the constituency while giving nothing up front in return? Why trust a stranger to be an accurate representative? One excuse made for bribing even after 1867 was that men 'as can't hardly live' may feel they have insufficient reason to relinquish an hour or more's paid labour to vote unless there be some immediate making good of their economic loss or compensatory appeal to their self-interest. This Henry Edwards understood.

The portraits of 'old Griffenbottom' in *Ralph the Heir* and Mr Browborough in *Phineas Redux* are caricatures of Trollope's real-life opponent. We are told that Browborough owed his current seat purely to his willingness to 'spen[d] a fortune' in the constituency.[67] No great asset to his party on the hustings platform, his preferred style is to 'stand up with unabashed brow and repeat with enduring audacity the same words a dozen times over – "The prosperity of England depends on the Church of her people"' (*PR*, ch. 4, p. 32). Once seated in the House of Commons he 'never spoke' but wanted nothing, had plenty of money and gave dinners (*PR*, ch. 44, p. 311). Corrupt and self-serving, the best to be said of him is that he has stamina: he 'had evil things said of him, and had gone through the very heat of the fire of political warfare' without stumbling; and, having secured his seat, he had 'voted like a man with his party' (*PR*, ch. 13, p. 98). The 'Browborough Trial' (Chapter 44 of *Phineas Redux*) precedes Phineas's own trial for murder, and is close enough to it to unsettle any expectation that the law will resolve the novel's other major political and ethical dilemma. Mr Browborough is 'the hero of the piece':

> The idea of putting [him] into prison for conduct . . . second nature to a large proportion of the House was distressing to Members of Parliament generally . . . [T]here could be no reason why [Mr Daubeny's] Attorney-General should prosecute his own ally . . . – a poor, faithful creature, who had never in his life voted against his party. (*PR*, ch. 44, pp. 311–13)

Where the local commission of inquiry (reported on but not represented) is characterised by too much seriousness ('an indignant and sometimes an indiscreet zeal' [p. 315]), the trial (closely depicted) is non-serious, having a 'general flavour . . . of good humoured raillery' [p. 315]).

The modern reader who sets Trollope's hustings and election trial scenes alongside the *Autobiography*, like the Victorian reader encountering Trollope's post-1868 accounts of electioneering amid extensive local and national newspaper coverage of the corruption investigations into Beverley, knows that satire, after all, rides weakly in the wake of political events. Trollope's election scenes have had their admirers over the years,[68] but the genre was near exhaustion by 1868: so familiar a set piece of English comic fiction since 1815 that Trollope's efforts in the genre inevitably suggest sub-Dickens, or sub-Samuel Warren, or sub-Bulwer-Lytton.[69] The chief interest of later Victorian hustings satire for readers today, Albert Pionke suggests, may lie in what the genre says about novelists' efforts to counterpoint their professional integrity as writers, serving the public good, to the manifest want of public integrity on display in such ritualised scenes of electoral politics. The exaggerated realism of hustings satire induces, he argues (after Catherine Gallagher), 'ironic credulity': a form of 'believability that does not solicit belief'.[70] Readers of these scenes are 'encouraged to anticipate problems, make suppositional predictions' rather than naïvely immerse themselves in the proffered reality. The appeal is to their 'pleasure as much as to their reformist sensibilities of moral outrage' – encouraging them 'to recognise the possibility of corruption and thereby to invest the imaginary corporate figure of the Victorian novelist' with a professional authority that his or her parliamentary equivalents have signally failed to earn.[71] Yet in Trollope's case it is unclear either that irony can be the right word for such palpable anger, or that the motive of shoring up literature's professional credentials had much traction in relation to Beverley. Having attempted without success to leverage his writerly reputation on the hustings,[72] he was unlikely to seek self-legitimation by such a route, though the principle might have appealed. Recycling an old form, his hustings satires and their near relation, satire on the electoral bribery laws, bespeak savage indignation evidently compromised by personal grievance.

Realism: The Parliamentarian as Man of Conscience without a Constituency

All the more striking, then, that Trollope's realist attention to the 'ethical ambivalence' generated in the individual MP by contrary commitments to near interests and scrupulous disinterestedness[73] is accompanied by so little consideration of the electoral constituency as a political entity. The constituency, as we meet it in *Phineas Finn*, is peripheral to the novel's vision. A conversation between the radical Mr Turnbull and the Conservative Mr Kennedy alerts the reader to a changing national picture: Mr Turnbull comments that the major 'commercial constituencies' now operate on a scale more conducive to democracy than towns (like Beverley) capable of domination by a single rich individual – but though we hear of such constituencies working well (Mr Monk represents one), we do not encounter them at first hand.[74] The primary reason why Phineas Finn is so loathed by the venomous radical journalist, Quintus Slide, is that he is the willing beneficiary of more than one remaining stronghold of 'aristocratic influence', though of a Whig/Liberal rather than Tory variety. He is a political placeman, gifted the Irish seat of Loughshane, by the resident Liberal earl, on the grounds that he satisfies the local desire for an Irish Catholic and the Westminster desire for 'one who would support "the party"' (*PF*, ch. 1, p. 11). Turfed out of Loughshane in favour of the earl's son, he is next granted the English seat of Saulsby under the patronage of Lady Laura Kennedy and her father Lord Brentford. Trollope describes neither electorate in any detail: both locations have no narrative presence other than at election time.[75]

Of much greater interest to Trollope than Phineas's relationship to his constituencies (which is merely expedient: they are routes into the House of Commons) is his relation to party. As many critics have observed, *Phineas Finn* charts its protagonist's development to the point where he realises that on one matter he cannot with integrity take the party line. The debate over Irish tenant-right provokes in him something singularly lacking in his political engagements hitherto: 'conviction'. It establishes his liberalism, in short, at the expense of his alignment with other Liberals.[76] This is the moment at which Phineas steps, as Trollope rather archly puts it, out of 'the decorum of Government ways' and discovers the 'delights of . . . wild irresponsible oratory' (ch. 66, p. 493). Strikingly, the novel does not ask the reader to share in, or with any great depth to understand, the political issue that so suddenly goads Finn into action:

> He had been told, he said, that it was a misfortune in itself for one so young as he to have convictions. But his Irish birth and Irish connection had brought this misfortune of his country so closely home to him that he had found the task of extricating himself from it to be impossible. Of what further he said, speaking on that terribly unintelligible subject, a tenant-right proposed for Irish farmers, no English reader will desire to know much . . . For us now it is enough to know that to our hero was accorded that attention which orators love, – which will almost make an orator if it can be assured. A full House with a promise of big type on the next morning would wake to eloquence the propounder of a Canadian grievance, or the mover of an Indian budget. (*PF*, ch. 75, p. 555)

Elaine Hadley rightly observes that the crisis of conscience that here defines Phineas at 'his most liberal' has a distinctively 'Irish brogue'.[77] That is, the question of the Irish tenant's right to a property in the land he farms prompts, and is a fitting synecdoche for, the Irish-English parliamentarian's declaration of a property in himself that cannot be subsumed in party, or, one might add, in constituency, and indeed only finds its true articulation when he steps aside from party and from representational politics altogether.

Fleetingly attractive compensations for loss of representative power become available to Finn in this moment: the pleasure of the orator, whose exceptional eloquence may make even the dullest of political subjects (this novel has no interest in them[78]) momentarily appetising to the listener ('a Canadian grievance, or . . . an Indian budget'); relatedly, the gratification of making the front page of the morning papers. This is cynicism, at least as it pertains to motive in parliamentary voting (on the pleasures of oratory, it is relatively forgiving) – but the cynicism attaches more to the implied author than to Finn, who only borrows the cynic's idiom when he alludes to those jaded parliamentary men who think it 'a misfortune in itself for one so young as he to have convictions' (the misfortune belongs to the Irish). Irish though he is, Finn has no elected authority to speak on reform of Irish tenant law. Having given up on the possibility of an Irish seat for want of funds, and having accepted patronage in the securing of an English seat, he knows himself to be without a constituency warrant when he speaks. From one angle this is a prerequisite for liberal 'abstraction': formally detached from the question, he can give it more dispassionate rational appraisal. But an absolute requirement for detachment would threaten the very logic of regional parliamentary representation and of the political novel as a form that might function in some sort analogously with constituency representation (mediating between the regions and the centre).

Finn loses his seat, and opts for a safer path with career security: a romantic marriage and 'a permanent Government appointment' as a poor-law inspector for Ireland with £1,000 a year (*PF*, ch. 76, p. 567). Both Patrick Lonergan and Cathrine O. Frank have persuasively read this turn of events as evidence of the pressure Finn's Irishness puts upon *Phineas Finn*:

> Trollope wants to represent a realistic Irish MP, but his personal resistance to Home Rule meant that if he wanted to keep it out of his novels he would have to deemphasise Phineas's Irishness or change his politics, thereby rendering him unrealistic.[79]

Allowing Finn to speak for tenant-right, and against party, preserves his Irishness, but at the expense of his ability to function in the British House. This foregrounding of Finn's national character delivers a powerful reading of Trollope's Unionism – but at some risk of accenting nation over those local ties that remain lost to realism when Finn's Irishness comes under preferential scrutiny: responsibilities to those constituency men and women who would only find direct representation were Finn not swayed by 'what is so closely home to him'.

In sharp contrast, Trollope's immediately post-election novel, *Ralph the Heir*, gives the constituency an importance that all but derails the novel, unable as it is to balance the aggression of its satire on regional political culture with an account of regional interests sufficiently in good faith to support 'provincial realism'. The story of Sir Thomas's failed bid to represent Percycross cuts across the stories of the two Ralphs (the legitimate but spendthrift London heir of Squire Newton, and the illegitimate but responsible son, raised on the country estate). The plot progresses largely through the protagonists' movements between metropole and the provinces, but the narrative resolution is rather a redistribution of lots than a reconciliation of conflicting interests. The squire's plan to buy out the legitimate son is prevented by death on the hunting field; the legitimate nephew takes over the estate and marries the daughter of a baronet from a neighbouring county; the illegitimate son purchases his own land in Norfolk and marries the ward of Sir Thomas; Sir Thomas retires from public life. These individual plot turns substantially disturb the stabilities of geographic, communal and hereditary stability associated with the Barchester series: indeed, the novel might be said to turn on the unhappy subordination of personal merit and personal expectations to the law (the illegitimate son's predicament serving to expose a merely formal distinction in rights). The election plot undermines localism at least as fundamentally. Percycross (as we saw) puts forward no candidate of its own. There is no more allotted space than there was in *Phineas Finn* for taking account of the interests of the locality, nor does the novel find any more compelling means to bring together the impulses of realism, satire and romance than in Ralph the Heir's pragmatic marriage settlement – he and the baronet's daughter being 'incapable of what men and women call love when they speak of love as a passion linked with romance' (*RH*, ch. 56, p. 485).

Ralph the Heir having created serious strain around the relationship of regional constituency to metropole, *Phineas Redux* re-enters the arena of representational politics with requisite caution. Phineas, as presented at the start of the novel, has no very clear motivation for returning to Parliament beyond being, once again, a free man entitled to risk his own neck. He is politically pliable, agreeing to adopt a strong anti-establishment stance on the hustings because it will help temper his Catholicism for the Tankerville electors (Tankerville lying within the Anglican diocese of Durham), not because he really cares. This makes his emergence halfway through the novel as, once again, a spokesman for political conviction over and above party loyalty all the more striking. The problem with Mr Daubeny's bill to disestablish the Church of England, as Finn sees it, is that it confirms a mode of Tory-party operation in which retention of power has become the only driver. That Conservatives are pushing through Liberal measures is the great political problem of *Phineas Redux*, as it was in reality the great political issue of 1867 (with respect to the Reform Bill) and 1868 (with respect to Disestablishment). By appealing to the more honest on the Tory benches to vote with 'their hearts', Finn calls out the cynicism of Daubeny's and his own party's nascent disciplinary machines, urging a restoration of an ethos of civic responsibility rooted in the virtue of individual members of the House:

> He repeated his assertion that it would be an evil thing for the country that the measure should be carried by men who in their hearts condemned it, and was vehemently called to order for this assertion about the hearts of gentlemen. But a speaker who can certainly be made amenable to authority for vilipending in debate the heart of any specified opponent, may with safety attribute all manner of ill to the agglomerated hearts of a party. To have told any individual Conservative, – Sir Orlando Drought for instance, – that he was abandoning all the convictions of his life, because he was a creature at the command of Mr Daubeny, would have been an insult that would have moved even the Speaker from his serenity; but you can hardly be personal to a whole bench of Conservatives, – to bench above bench of Conservatives. The charge had been made and repeated over and over again, till all the Orlando Droughts were ready to cut some man's throat, – whether their own, or Mr Daubeny's, or Mr Gresham's, they hardly knew. It might probably have been Mr Daubeny's for choice, had any real cutting of a throat been possible. (*PR*, ch. 36, p. 257)

In Lauren M. E. Goodlad's nice phrasing, 'Finn's political honesty punches through the party system' – and does so in the context of a novelistic series that gives eloquent expression to the 'fear that swaggering *realpolitik* may [be] modernity's very mode'.[80] That is right. But it matters not a little that the conflict between ethical idealism and a tougher realism[81] competent to confront brute 'realpolitik' can only be articulated at the point where Finn (once again) believes himself to have no career worth saving in the house. Only at that point can opposition to one's party and one's constituency be a charismatic act strong enough to threaten a political strategist of the order of Daubeny/Disraeli and his party machine. The crash in register, from the orotund, 'amenable to authority for vilipending in debate', to cut-throat violence pays testimony (again) to Finn's rhetorical prowess. It also, of course, registers a warning that the man of conscience is a danger not just to party but to that tacit code of conduct by which party binds individual political representatives into impersonal units of action.

It is critical to *Phineas Finn*'s depiction of the relationship between parliamentarian and party that the immediate (apparent) casualty of his resistance to party is

Mr Bonteen ('Bonteen and Co'. in Phineas's bitter sneer [*PR*, ch. 37, p. 261]: com-mercial analogue of the party careerist). The plot turns on the murder (rhetoric yielding to brute reality) of this devotee of party order, slated to become Chancellor of the Exchequer upon the elevation of the incumbent, Plantagenet Palliser, to the House of Lords:

> His hopes had been raised or abased among the places of £1,000, £1,200, or £1,500 a year. He had hitherto culminated at £2,000, and had been supposed with diligence to have worked himself up to the top of the ladder, . . . And now he was spoken of in connection with one of the highest offices of the State! (*PR*, ch. 32, p. 227)

Cynicism again, through the narrative device of free indirect style: this time measur-ing political motive in the careerist currency of salary increments, and inviting the reader to identify (and eschew identification) with an *épatissant* establishment shock that a mere diligent hack is poised at the door of 11 Downing Street. *Ressentiment*, in this heavily ironised scenario, is not the possession only of Bonteen's competitors for office; it attaches diffusely to all those 'rich men' (as Mill put it) presumed to be above the petty motives of salary, and, in Trollope's novels most effectively portrayed by the drawing-room manoeuvring of their wives. (Lady Glencora is characteristically skewering on the subject of Mrs Bonteen's arrivism: 'Next to myself, she is the most talkative and political woman we have' [*PR*, ch. 31, p. 222].)

Should we associate the unease of a Bonteen-enabling, Bonteen-resenting establish-ment with the personal resentment felt by Finn, chafing under this man's suspicion that his loyalty to party is not what it should be? Although the establishment's disap-proval is ironised, Finn's anger against Bonteen is not condoned. It is characteristic of Trollope's realist predilection for putting his hero in the wrong that the party man, unpleasant though he is, has better arguments on his side than Finn does (Mr Monk tells Finn as much). You must either vote against us 'as usual', Bonteen charges Finn, or 'break every promise that you made at Tankerville': 'independence . . . grand as it may be on the part of men who avowedly abstain from office, is a little dangerous when it is now and again adopted by men who have taken place.' Painfully deficient in Finn's gift of the gab, Bonteen finds one metaphor that hits hard: 'I like to be sure that the men who are in the same boat with me won't take it into their heads that their duty requires them to scuttle the ship' (*PR*, ch. 34, pp. 246–7). It is a metaphor calculated to conflate the vessel of party with the ship of state.

Finn's position is indeed ironic, if not perverse: having taken an anti-Church of England stance to woo his Durham electors, he now finds himself on the verge *both* of breaking faith with his constituency *and* defying his party. He makes a sincere appeal for his Tory colleagues to vote with their individual consciences, rather than follow Daubeny in voting for a measure they must loathe in their hearts. Yet Finn himself backed Disestablishment at the hustings without conviction, and his speech to the house now is galvanised by ill-concealed personal vexation that a Tory challenge to Mr Bonteen's appointment was seen off the day before. The oddity of *Finn*'s position is that he defies his own party whip and declines to vote as a Liberal ought to vote on this issue in order to contest *Tory* party dishonesty. The oddity of *Trollope*'s position, by extension, is that he makes us feel that Finn is right, even though (or perhaps because) his being right after this manner spells the end of his being a major political player in the Palliser series.

In truth there is very little political distance between Finn and Mr Bonteen: both have sought to make their way up through the party ranks by merit and hard work; both are known to be 'seeker[s] after office' (as Quintus Slide sneeringly puts it) (*PR*, ch. 28, p. 199); both fear that the other is actively blocking their ambitions; both have a large measure of Trollopean romanticism in their attachment to the idea of 'parliamentary renown' (*PR*, ch. 1, p. 13); both loathe the dishonesty of Daubeny's manoeuvring for party advantage. We hear of Mr Bonteen's disgust at the Disestablishment ruse well before we hear of it as a matter of special concern for Phineas.

The murder of Mr Bonteen looks to be a political killing by Finn. It is, as the daunt-less Madame Max Goesler will prove, in truth a desperate attempt by Mr Emilius to conceal the bigamous status of his marriage to Lizzie Eustace. As the novel shifts into sensation mode – Finn languishing in jail, Marie Max Goesler racing to Prague in search of the evidence of Emilius's motive – parliamentary *Bildung* is put on hold. And yet, in so determinedly pursuing Emilius, she retraces steps that Bonteen himself took just a few months earlier – at the height of his attempt on the Chancellorship of the Exchequer – when he visited Prague and found the woman 'believed to be Mrs Emilius' (*PR*, ch. 45, p. 322). Though Bonteen's friendly aid to Lady Eustace mobilises the same 'energy for which he was so conspicuous' (322) in Westminster the novel denies him heroic status. He is not corrupt, he never abuses his office, but 'Bonteens', like 'Ratlers', are a type (ch. 1, p. 15; ch. 40, p. 284; ch. 51, p. 361). The distinction between Bonteen and Finn is made to rest finally on the fact that Finn chooses, in the House of Commons, publicly to 'entertain [a] high political theory' (ch. 37, p. 260), where Mr Bonteen keeps his unhappiness with the Disestablishment vote closer to his chest, 'lest, when the house door should at last be opened, he might not be invited to enter with the others' (ch. 8, p. 64). A great deal – too much – rests at this point on the 'height' attributed to that 'high political theory', which sounds more rhetorical than not, and at risk of special pleading.

Trollope, plainly, does not wish to be anti-meritocratic in the sense of resist-ing the rising new men. Elsewhere keen to stabilise distinctions between good new political blood and corrupt careerism (*The Prime Minister* is largely focused on that problem), in Bonteen's case he insists to the point of prejudice on thin distinctions. In doing so, he rules out a version of the parliamentary career that might have seen individual conscience given some of the institutional supports of party organisa-tion. Alert to the structural similarities between Finn and Bonteen's careerism and their advocacy for other men's wives, Cathrine O. Frank again sees the differences primarily in national terms: 'Bonteen's vitriol against Finn nearly always emphasises his Irish-ness', she observes, 'and imputes an Irish separatist agenda to him', calling forth exactly the hot-headed, hyper-masculine image of Phineas that he has 'worked to distance himself [from] in order better to assimilate into the House of Com-mons'.[82] As Frank extends that reading, Finn's characterological complexity emerges in the course of his false accusation for the other man's murder, which would have him behaving as the violent masculine Irishman Bonteen charged him with being – forcing Finn to ask himself what resources of private self-assurance he possesses that are not 'contingent upon the public construction of identity'.[83] Frank points out, with justice, that Finn's perception, on his release, that he has been left 'unfit for public utility' rests on a perception that '[l]iving for public utility is a heightened order of being in the world',[84] requiring the 'freedom from self-consciousness' (*PR*, ch. 57, p. 479) that would enable him to 'think of others, especially the constituents he represents in Parliament'.[85] All the more reason to recall that the constituents Finn represents are not the angry Irish but the angry Tankervillians of the North of England, who have so little interest in the Irish question, and whose interest now in Finn he signally fails to reciprocate. If Bonteen sees in Finn a dangerous Irishman, he also sees in him a bad constituency MP ('impossible that . . . the Tankervillians would . . . replace him in his seat after manifest apostasy to his pledge' [ch. 20, p. 146]). Tankerville does re-elect Finn, in the face of his reluctance, warming to the idea of being represented by a man who has publicly suffered a great wrong. Finn's psychological realism may well be established in part through his efforts to repel the stereotype of the Irishman, but there is a vital element of his political career (so ambivalently resumed at the end of the novel) that depends on the attraction he now holds for contrarian 'political spirits' (ch. 71, p. 508) back in the constituency who choose for their representative a man who thanks them for their friendship but flatly refuses to visit.

* * *

Trollope's unwillingness to look hard at the nature and sources of constituency power in the form in which Henry Edwards mobilised it – commercial, regionalist, unapologetically masculine, uninterested in high culture and aware of the polemical power of offending against its representatives (Trollope himself included) – marks a limitation in his political reading of what happened in 1868. It would be wrong to claim that it mars the political novels. He was under no obligation to interest himself in Henry Edwards further than political and legal events obliged him to. It is a matter for critical judgement, indeed, how far his satire is weakened by its lack of interest in Edwards's relationship to his constituency, or what kind of political career the man carved out for himself in Westminster (not all readers have thought it as compromised as this essay has suggested). The more sustained, and for the admirer of Trollope's realism the more rewarding, legacy of that 'miserable fortnight' in 1868 is the additional intensity it lends to Finn's self-consciousness: that bolstering of the individualist, civic republican character of the politician who makes his own political way, with or without regard for the constituency he represents.

This facet of Trollope's politics was not the creation of 1868: he had already committed himself to a model of the politician as, primarily, a moral actor in his non-fictional writing about the history of politics from the 1870s.[86] And with electoral reform constantly under debate in the 1860s, he was certainly not alone in worrying that democracy, in the imperfect form in which it existed in Britain, was ill-served by a system in which, as Mill put it, 'electors are almost always obliged . . . to select their representative from persons of a station in life widely different from theirs, and having a different class interest, who will affirm that they ought to abandon themselves to his discretion'.[87] But before 1868, Trollope had been inclined to take the constituency for granted: to acknowledge its claims only at the point where access to a parliamentary career demands that they be given some attention. After 1868, however disinclined he remained to allow 'demos' a major voice in the politician's story, it was much less easy for him simply to close the door on the electoral locality. What we are left with, in the late political novels, is a version of representative politics in which uncertainty about the grounds of the representative's authority – How far does it actually reside in himself? How far in party? How far in his role as representative? – becomes part of the realist construction of the politician as man of conscience.

Notes

I am grateful to Lauren M. E. Goodlad, Stefan Collini and Nicholas Shrimpton for their astute comments on draft versions of this essay.

1. 'Trollope and the Career: Vocational Trajectories and the Management of Ambition', *Victorian Studies*, 45.2 (2003): pp. 247–78.
2. Anthony Trollope, *An Autobiography and Other Writings*, ed. Nicholas Shrimpton (Oxford: Oxford University Press, 2014), p. 181. Subsequent references are in the main text (*A*).
3. With some bitterness the *Autobiography* recalls the uncle (long dead) who once met his youthful confession of parliamentary ambitions with a jeer that 'few clerks in the Post Office . . . become Members of Parliament' (p. 181).
4. Trollope must then backtrack in Chapter 17 to report on unfinished business with the Post Office (Chapter 15 ended with his resignation at pensionable age), and resume the plotting of his literary career (held in suspension at the conclusion of the Barsetshire Chronicles and founding of *Saint Pauls Magazine* (October 1867)).
5. I revert, at this point, to Trollope's manuscript text, rather than the modification 'Advanced Conservative-Liberal' (*A*, ch. 16, p. 183) introduced by his son Henry Trollope when he copied the work for the printer. For discussion, see 'Note on the Text', in *Anthony Trollope: An Autobiography*, ed. David Skilton (London: Penguin, 1996), pp. xxvi–xxvii.
6. Plantagenet Palliser articulates the preferential accent on Liberalism when he applies the same metaphor to his son's early flirtation with Conservatism: 'every carriage should have a drag to its wheels, but . . . an ambitious soul would choose to be the coachman rather than the drag'. Anthony Trollope, *The Duke's Children*, eds Katherine Mullin and Francis O'Gorman (Oxford: Oxford University Press, 2011), p. 359.
7. Lauren M. E. Goodlad and Frederik Van Dam, 'Trollope and Politics', in Deborah Denenholz Morse, Margaret Markwick and Mark W. Turner (eds), *The Routledge Research Companion to Trollope* (London: Routledge, 2016), p. 20. The comparison is with the stabilising historical mode of the Barchester series. See also Lauren M. E. Goodlad, *The Victorian Geopolitical Aesthetic: Realism, Sovereignty, and Transnational Experience* (Oxford: Oxford University Press, 2015). Of special importance is Chapter 3 on Trollope's 'two-part foreign policy discourse', whereby the comic-ironic novels of the 1850s and 1860s 'exert "centripetal force" against the imperial dispersion of English identity', simulating, by the dialectical play between global ranginess and English regionalism, something close to 'the liberal-humanist ideal of a genuinely "negotiated" rooted cosmopolitanism' (p. 68).
8. John Plotz, 'The Semi-Detached Provincial Novel', *Victorian Studies*, 53.3 (2011): pp. 405–16, p. 405.
9. Ibid. p. 409, drawing on Mikhail Baktin, 'Forms and Time of the Chronotope in the Novel: Towards a Historical Poetics', in *The Dialogic Imagination: Four Essays*, ed. Michael

Holquist, trans. Caryl Emerson and Michael Holquist (Austin: University of Texas Press, 1981), pp. 84–258; and Ian Duncan, 'Provincial or Regional Novel', *A Companion to the Victorian Novel*, ed. Patrick Brantlinger and William Thesing (Oxford: Blackwell, 2002), pp. 318–35.

10. Plotz, 'Semi-Detached', p. 407.

11. Anthony Trollope, hustings poster, 'To the Freemen and Other Electors of the Borough of Beverley', 28 October 1868. East Riding Archives, DDBC/11/106.

12. He considered it 'unEnglish' and 'unmanly', and thought the electoral reforms underway should be a sufficient protection for the honest voter. *Autobiography*, p. 187; and see Elaine Hadley, *Living Liberalism: Practical Citizenship in Mid-Victorian Britain* (Chicago: University of Chicago Press, 2010), p. 197.

13. Goodlad and Van Dam, 'Trollope and Politics', p. 28.

14. Cathrine O. Frank, 'Trial Separations: Divorce, Disestablishment, and Home Rule in *Phineas Redux*', *College Literature*, 35.3 (2008): pp. 30–56, p. 44.

15. Graeme Orr, 'Suppressing Vote-Buying: The "War" on Electoral Bribery from 1868', *The Journal of Legal History*, 27.3 (2006): pp. 289–314; Frank O'Gorman, *Voters, Patrons, and Parties: The Unreformed Electoral System of Hanoverian England, 1734–1832* (Oxford: Clarendon Press, 1989), p. 46, p. 142; Ivor Jennings, *Party Politics*, 3 vols (Cambridge: Cambridge University Press, 1960–2), vol. 1, *Appeal to the People*, pp. 86–9.

16. Orr, 'Suppressing Vote-Buying: pp. 289–314, p. 301 and *passim*.

17. O'Gorman, *Voters, Patrons, and Parties*, p. 142.

18. Edward Loughlin O'Malley and Henry Hardcastle, *Reports on the Decisions of the Judges for the Trial of Electoral Petitions in England and Ireland*, 7 vols (London: Stevens and Haynes, 1870–1929).

19. J. S. Mill, 'Considerations on Representative Government' (1861), in *Essays on Politics and Society Part 2*, ed. J. M. Robson (Toronto: University of Toronto Press, 1977), pp. 371–577, p. 497.

20. 'Six Months of Patronage', *The Spectator* (19 January 1867), pp. 67–8.

21. In 1874 the Prince of Wales appointed him Grand Master of the Freemasons in West Yorkshire. 'Death of Sir H. Edwards', *Manchester Guardian* (24 April 1886), p. 8a.

22. Details provided in the course of a description of a painting of Edwards's son, Lieutenant-Colonel Charles Grove Edwards, in the collections of the National Army Museum. Available at <http://www.nam.ac.uk/online-collection, NAM. 1961-10-90-2> (last accessed 9 September 2015).

23. Henry Edwards's father and grandfather had considerably expanded the estates inherited from Joseph Edwards, 'buying Hope Hall in 1850 and creating the new estate of Castle Carr in 1852–53'. Elyze Agnes Charles Smeets, *Landscape and Society in Twente & Utrecht: A Geography of Dutch Country Estates, Circa 1800–1950*, unpublished PhD dissertation, University of Leeds (2005), p. 212. J. T. Ward's *East Yorkshire Landed Estates in the Nineteenth Century* (East Yorkshire Local History Society, 1967) documents the scale of the major East Riding estates, the richest in this period being Sir Tatton Skye's Sledmere estate, Lord Londesborough's estate, the increasingly sub-divided Strickland estates, and the Wenlock estate (pp. 13–20). See especially pp. 13–14 on Sir Tatton's younger brother, Christopher (1831–98), who represented Beverley alongside Sir Henry from 1865 to 1868.

24. Michael E. Scorgie and Therese A. Joiner, 'Frederick William Cronhelm (1787–1871), *Abacus*, 31/2 (1995): pp. 229–43, p. 238.

25. John Bernard Burke, A Visitation of the Seats and Arms of the Noblemen and Gentlemen of Great Britain, 2 vols (London: Hurst and Blackett Publishers, 1854–5), vol. 2, p. 210.

26. Brian Wragg, *The Life and Works of John Carr of York*, ed. Giles Worsley (York: Oblong Creative, 2000), p. 193.

27. 'Beverley Election Petition. Proceedings Yesterday. Before Mr Baron Martin', unsourced newspaper report in 'Scrapbook C' ('Beverley Newspaper and Local "Titbits"' volume), presented by John A. Hudson, Esq., Nov. 1910, East Riding of Yorkshire Archives and Local Studies Centre collection, DDX 1314/11 [hereafter Scrapbook C], p. 13v: 'Sir Henry Edwards, [Mr Sarsgood] believed, was at the time when he first entered into a Parliamentary career, in regard to Beverley, an absolute stranger to the town, so far as any connection with its mercantile interest or political status was concerned. He was a person carrying on an extensive manufacturing business at Halifax, the manufacture of agricultural implements. (Laughter.) Well, at any rate, he (Mr Sargood) was told that was the occupation he carried on in that town.'

28. Pamela Hopkins, *The History of Beverley East Yorkshire from Earliest Times to the Year 2000*, 2nd edn (Pickering: Blackthorn Press, 2011), p. 299. In the wake of Edwards's purchase of their family firm, Alfred and Edmund Crosskill set up a rival firm in Beverley, William Crosskill and Sons (p. 300).

29. A. P. Baggs, L. M. Brown, G. C. F. Forster, I. Hall, R. E. Horrox, G. H. R. Kent and D. Neave, 'Modern Beverley: Economy, 1835–1918', in K. J. Allison (ed.), *A History of the County of York: East Riding*, vol. 6: *The Borough and Liberties of Beverley* (London: Oxford University Press for the Institute of Historical Research, 1989), pp. 138–9. The Beverley Iron and Wagon Co. survived until the Depression of the late 1870s, closing in 1879 with debts on a scale that suggest Edwards had ceased for some time to subsidise it (139).

30. *The Times* (5 April 1869), p. 9. See also O'Malley and Hardcastle, *Electoral Petitions*, vol. 1, pp. 147–9.

31. 'Proceedings Yesterday. Before Mr Baron Martin', unsourced and undated extract in Scrapbook C, p. 15r. As a gauge of the scale of this investment: the primary Edwards family business at Canal Mills was employing, in 1868, 'between 400 and 500 hands'. *Third Report of the Commissioners Appointed in 1868 to Inquire into the Best Means of Preventing the Pollution of Rivers. Pollution Arising from the Woollen Manufacture, and Processes Connected Therewith*, vol. 2: *Evidence* (London: Her Majesty's Stationery Office, 1871), p. 153.

32. Scrapbook C, p. 4v.

33. 'An advocate for the reduction of those taxes which press unduly upon the working classes'. *Handbook of the Court and Peerage and the House of Commons 1862* (London: P. S. King, 1862), p. 157. On the political importance of income tax as 'one of the very few points at which central government directly affected a law-abiding middle-class mid-Victorian', and the broad split between Conservatives who either sought the abolition of Peel's 'temporary' income tax or favoured an undifferentiated band of taxation, and more liberal or radical voices calling for increased direct taxation, see H. C. G. Matthew, 'Disraeli, Gladstone, and the Politics of Mid-Victorian Budgets', *Historical Journal*, 22.3 (1979): pp. 615–43, pp. 617–18.

34. For his desire to 'give [free trade] a fair trial' while retaining 'moderate' protectionism, see his speech seconding a motion to amend the hours and mode of work under the Factory Act, HC Deb, 14 March 1850, vol. 109, cc883–933. Available at <http://hansard.millbanksystems. com/commons/1850/mar/14/factories#S3V0109P0_18500314_HOC_10> (last accessed 20 September 2016). He spoke repeatedly against the proposed two-hour increase in the limit to daily labour by children and women.

35. See the *Manchester Guardian*'s coverage of an Edwards hustings speech at Beverley: 'I don't want to say that Mr Gladstone is a Roman Catholic but he looks deuced like it. (Great uproar, howling and yelling.)'. 'Sir H. Edwards on Mr Gladstone', *Manchester Guardian* (7 November 1868), p. 5f. Also extracts from the press quoted in 'Beverley

Borough Election . . . Opinions of the Press': '[T]he scatter-brained baronet . . . eagerly takes a discussion of the Irish Church question as the best channel through which he can get rid of his superfluous bile, and denounces the leader of the Opposition [as a] "thorough Roman Catholic, and of the worst description, because he is a Jesuit"' (attrib. *The Sportsman*); 'If, when Sir Henry Edwards tells the electors of Beverley, that Mr Gladstone is a Roman Catholic and a Jesuit, he believes what he says, he simply proves his own utter incapacity for a seat in the House of Commons' (attrib. *Manchester Guardian*). Michael John Wickham points out that anti-Catholicism was a minority position by the late 1860s, 'the exception rather than the rule'. *Electoral Politics in Berwick-Upon-Tweed, 1832–1885*, Master's Thesis, Durham University (2002), p. 221 (Durham Theses Online). Available at <http://etheses.dur.ac.uk/4098/1/4098/> (last accessed 9 September 2015).

36. On his long-running feud with John Edward Wainhouse, over the smoke nuisance of the Washer Lane Dye works, see *The Yorkshire Journal*, 3 (2012): pp. 22–5. Available at <https://theyorkshirejournal.files.wordpress.com/2014/11/the-yorkshire-journal-autumn-2012.pdf> (last accessed 20 September 2016).

37. See, for example, his contribution to the debate on 'Supply – Army Estimates', HC Deb 26 July 1850 vol. 113 cc360–91. Available at <http://hansard.millbanksystems.com/commons/1850/jul/26/supply-army-estimates#S3V0113P0_18500726_HOC_149> (last accessed 20 September 2016).

38. Max Weber, 'Politics as a Vocation', in H. H. Gerth and C. Wright Mills (eds), *From Max Weber: Essays in Sociology* (London: Kegan Paul, Trench, Trubner & Co. Ltd, 1947), p. 80.

39. B[enjamin] Disraeli, *Lord George Bentinck: A Political Biography*, 4th rev. edn (London: Colburn and Co., 1852), p. 555.

40. Disraeli, Speech for the Merchant Taylors' Company, Banquet to the Ministers, *The Times* (18 June 1868), 9b. Quoted and discussed in Jonathan Parry, 'Benjamin Disraeli', *Oxford Dictionary of National Biography*, online edition, accessed 26 January 2016.

41. A critical proviso is that, in Disraeli's one nationism, but not as certainly in Edwards's thinking, the strategic brilliance of the party leader counts for more, finally, than the party machine.

42. 'Beverley Election Petition. Proceedings Yesterday. Before Mr Baron Martin', Scrapbook C, p. 13v. Also 'The Beverley Election Petition', *The Hull Packet and East Riding Times* (12 March 1869), p. 7a.

43. 'Beverley Election Petition. Proceedings Yesterday. Before Mr Baron Martin', Scrapbook C, p. 13v.

44. *An Autobiography*, p. 188. The electoral advisor to the Liberal Party in the East Riding is identified in press reports as Mr Lehman. See, for example, the hostile report in *The Standard* (19 March 1870). Scrapbook C, 25r.

45. 'Beverley Election Petition. Proceedings Yesterday. Before Mr Baron Martin', Scrapbook C, p. 15v.

46. 10 June 1871; quoted in Scorgie and Joiner, 'Frederick William Cronhelm', p. 237.

47. Cronhelm was bilingual in English and German, a gifted mathematician and logician, a poet, a part-time newspaper editor, and author of religious treatises. He is remembered to history as the author of *Double Entry by Single, A New Method of Book-Keeping* (London: Longman, Hurst, Rees, Orme, and Brown, 1818), dedicated to Henry Lees Edwards (H. E.'s father). This treatise identified 'the algebraic basis of double entry' some 130 years in advance of modern computer-processing of accounting data. See Scorgie and Joiner, 'Frederick William Cronhelm', p. 232.

48. *Reports from Commissioners* 1870, vol. 18, pp. viii, 504, as quoted in Scorgie and Joiner, 'Frederick William Cronhelm', p. 238. Reported in, inter alia, *The Scotsman* (21 September 1869), p. 3a.

49. Scorgie and Joiner, 'Frederick William Cronhelm', p. 241, quoting *The Times* (21 September 1869), p. 10d. See also report in *The Daily Telegraph* (8 August 1870), excerpted in Scrapbook C, p. 30r.

50. Weber, 'Politics as a Vocation', p. 80.

51. Fifty-five letters survive from Edwards and his wife (only three from her). Bodleian MSS, Hughenden Dep Box 126/1, fols. 100–211.

52. Edwards is fairly clearly referring to himself when he employs this title in a letter to Disraeli of 11 April 186[2?]: 'My dear Mr D – . / I am sorry if you felt annoyed last night at my observation respecting the abuse of your Whips.' Hughenden Dep Box 126/1, fols. 118–19 (118r).

53. Angus Hawkins, *Victorian Political Culture: 'Habits of Heart and Mind'* (Oxford: Oxford University Press, 2015), p. 115.

54. 'The Declining Efficiency of Parliament', *Quarterly Review*, 99 (1856): p. 551; quoted and discussed in Hawkins, *Victorian Political Culture*, p. 115.

55. See especially letters of 20 June 1860, 6 June 186[2?]; 6 May 186[4?]; 1 March 186[6?]; Hughenden Dep Box 126/1, fols. 108–9, 124–6, 144–5, 163–4.

56. See Ivor Bulmer-Thomas, *The Growth of the British Party System*, 2nd edn, 2 vols (London: Baker, 1967), vol. 1, pp. 109–14 on Disraeli's transformation of the relations between the Conservative party organisation across the country and the parliamentary leadership. Though Edwards was intimately involved in that process the scandal attached to his behaviour in Beverley has generally prevented any attention to his wider party involvements. See, for example, H. J. Hanham, *Elections and Party Management: Politics in the Time of Disraeli and Gladstone* (London: Longmans, 1959), p. 215, pp. 265–6, p. 276.

57. 6 May 186[4?], Hughenden Dep Box 126/1, fols. 144–5 (144r-v). And see Disraeli, letter to Henry Edwards, 20 June 1860, declining an open invitation to an arranged political dinner: 'I am sorry to say I am engaged every Wednesday, & Saturday, until / we leave town.' *Benjamin Disraeli Letters*, ed. J. A. W. Gunn et al., 10 vols (Toronto: University of Toronto Press, 1982–2013), VIII, p. 41.

58. 1 November 1859, Hughenden Dep Box 126/1, fols. 102–3 (102v).

59. For example, 8 December 1859 and 11 December 1861, Hughenden Dep Box 126/1, (fols. 104–5 [105v], 114–15 [114r]). Disraeli himself seems to have preserved and underlined a newspaper report from the *Halifax Guardian* describing a shooting party at Sir Henry's lodge, Castle Carr, where 713 grouse were bagged over a few days. Hughenden Dep Box 126/1, fol. 129.

60. Henry Edwards to Disraeli, 22 March 1869: 'I feel quite ashamed not to have thanked you sooner for your kind sympathy in my cruel disappointment, but I could not find words to express my feelings and Lady Edwards's on your most friendly letter, which I shall preserve as an heirloom in the archives of our family, that any descendants may see this testimonial from the first statesman of his age, to my faithful services during near a quarter of a century.' Hughenden Dep Box 126/1, fol. 186.

61. 27 November 1864, Hughenden Dep Box 126/1 fols. 155–7 (fol. 156r-v): 'To secure our preponderating political influence in Beverley, I have been induced to become chairman of the great Iron & Wagon Co. limited which will for a long time to come – be the key to the Boro'–'.

62. Letter to Disraeli, 4 November 1862, Hughenden Dep Box 126/1, fols. 131–2; see also letter of 1 November 1862, Hughenden Dep Box 126/1 fols. 133–4.

63. At a lively meeting of the town council in September 1870 the councillor was unable to prevent a formal vote of thanks to Sir Henry (most of his supporters, Wreghitt included, still retaining their seats on the council). 'The Beverley Town Council and Sir Henry Edwards', *The York Herald* (17 September 1870), p. 7.

64. Extract from the *Halifax Guardian*, Scrapbook C, p. 31v; 'Presentation and Dinner to Sir Henry Edwards, Bart., at Beverley', *The York Herald* (4 February 1871), p. 5.

65. H. C. G. Matthew, *Gladstone, 1809–1898* (Oxford: Oxford University Press, 1997), p. 130.

66. Anthony Trollope, *Ralph the Heir*, introduction by John Letts (London: Folio Society, 1996), p. 174. Subsequent references are in the main text (*RH*).

67. Anthony Trollope, *Phineas Redux*, ed. John Bowen (Oxford: Oxford University Press, 2011), p. 12. Subsequent references are in the main text (*PR*).

68. Michael Sadleir, *Trollope: A Commentary* (London: Constable & Co. Ltd, 1927), pp. 294–5; H. G. Nicholas, *To the Hustings: Election Scenes from English Fiction* (London: Cassell & Co. Ltd, 1956), pp. ix–xi.

69. For a critical overview of the genre, see Nicholas, *To the Hustings*; and Joseph Grego, *A History of Parliamentary Elections and Electioneering in the Old Days* (London: Chatto and Windus, 1886), esp. ch. 14.

70. Gallagher derives the term 'ironic credulity' from Felix Martinez-Bonati. See 'The Rise of Fictionality', in Franco Moretti (ed.), *The Novel*, 2 vols (Princeton: Princeton University Press, 2006), I, p. 346, p. 340.

71. Albert D. Pionke, *The Ritual Culture of Victorian Professionals: Competing for Ceremonial Status, 1838–1877* (Farnham: Ashgate, 2013), p. 128.

72. On the Liberal side, see, e.g., 'Beverley Borough Election . . . Opinions of the Press', Liberal Party pamphlet (quotation attributed to *The Sportsman*), in Scrapbook C, between pp. 4 and 5: 'the "free and independent" electors of Beverley will, when the election day comes . . . prefer even the rival candidate and popular writer of fiction, Mr Anthony Trollope, to the wrong-headed baronet'. And on the Tory side, satiric verses published in the *Beverley Gazette*, 14 November 1868: 'Just fancy him stuck on a Draining Committee, / Or bored like his own Phineas Finn!' Quoted in Lance O. Tingay, *Anthony Trollope Politician: His Parliamentary Candidature at Beverley 1868* (London: The Silverbridge Press, 1988), p. 25.

73. See Hadley, *Living Liberalism*, esp. chs 2 and 5.

74. Anthony Trollope, *Phineas Finn*, ed. Simon Dentith (Oxford: Oxford University Press, 2011), p. 136. All subsequent references are given in the text (*PF*).

75. The attention given to the borough of Silverbridge in *The Prime Minister* might be an exception to this pattern, were it not that the constituency is in effect synonymous with the ducal estate. The willingness of the electors to continue the local tradition of electing the duke's chosen candidate, in spite of Palliser's efforts to persuade them of their individual democratic responsibilities, is the nub of his conflict with Glencora Palliser in that novel.

76. In pursuing this line of thought I am extending readings proposed by Hadley, *Living Liberalism*, 229–90: and Goodlad, *Victorian Geopolitical Aesthetic*, esp. ch. 3. I am also responding, more obliquely, to Fredric Jameson's claim that Trollope's political fiction shows mid nineteenth-century realism losing its capacity to represent capacious histories as politics devolves, under the pressure of too many competing points of view, parties, factions, into the 'specialized' subject matter of 'those institutionalized genres which deal with parliament or representational dramas and characters'. *Antinomies of Realism* (London: Verso Press, 2013), p. 272.

77. Hadley, *Living Liberalism*, p. 261.

78. See Lauren M. E. Goodlad's persuasive account of *The Eustace Diamonds* as an exception to Trollope's surprising lack of interest in India, given the exceptional geopolitical reach of his writing. In her reading, this 'the most naturalistic [anti-idealist] of the Palliser novels, captures the governmentality of "liberal imperialism" in crisis alongside the emergence of a new mode of Tory imperialism'. Goodlad, *The Victorian Geopolitical Aesthetic*, p. 88.

79. Patrick Lonergan, 'The Representation of Phineas Finn: Anthony Trollope's Palliser Series and Victorian Ireland', *Victorian Literature and Culture*, 32/1 (2004): pp. 147–58; quoted and discussed by Frank, 'Trial Separations', pp. 34–5.
80. Goodlad, *Victorian Geopolitical Aesthetic*, p. 109.
81. 'Unflinching naturalism', in Goodlad's reading. *Victorian Geopolitical* Aesthetic, p. 109.
82. Frank, 'Trial Separations', p. 46.
83. Ibid. p. 45.
84. Ibid. p. 46.
85. Ibid.
86. Goodlad and van Dam, 'Trollope and Politics', p. 20.
87. J. S. Mill, 'Considerations on Representative Government', p. 507.

14

IN-BETWEEN TIMES: TROLLOPE'S ORDINAL NUMBERS

Clare Pettitt

T ROLLOPE'S NOVELS WORK very hard at being ordinary. And it is their exquisite ordinariness that keeps them perpetually popular. Christina Crosby has gone so far as to suggest that Trollope's readers are 'addicted' to the ordinary, and that his novels 'enthral with the charm of the obvious, but obviousness itself must be continually renewed'.[1] This chapter explores Trollope's 'ordinariness' both in terms of the media rhythms of the late nineteenth century, and in terms of an emergent liberal consensus in the 1870s, arguing that the two are structurally connected. With particular attention to what Amanda Claybaugh has called 'Trollope's most important novel', *The Way We Live Now* (1874–5), this chapter tracks Trollopian time as it unspools across the novel, beating out the rhythm of the ordinary from the *Morning Breakfast Table* to the *Evening Pulpit*.[2] The chapter is particularly interested in Trollope's attention to the ordinariness of the time and space between events, and how mapping these spaces becomes important for the wider liberal project of the 1870s. It argues that liberalism performs a distributive function which resists conglomeration or massification by working to separate and relate the increasing numbers of visible and knowable subjects in the modern social world. Trollope's literary texts are best understood as part of an extending media network which supports this work of connectivity without completion which is coming to define the experience of living in a global world in the 1870s. Connectivity without closure is also the emergent mode of liberalism, developing alongside and through capitalism in the same period. If liberalism is always future-directed, open-ended and multi-nodal, so Trollope's late work also resists closure and replaces judgement with juxtaposition. This chapter argues that Trollope's novels of the 1870s are structured by a model of multiplying seriality which has already become not just an important nineteenth-century literary form, but also the most important cultural and political form of the age.[3] I argue that seriality has a distributive function as well as a sequential one: to order information it creates spaces between significant values. The conclusion draws a link between Trollope's distribution of one 'meanwhile' over multiple narrative strands in *The Way We Live Now* and the politico-technological distributions of wealth, attention and information attendant upon the 'new liberalism'.[4]

The Clock and the Calendar

The precision of timing in Trollope's longest novel, *The Way We Live Now*, has long been noted. Bert G. Hornback noticed back in 1963 that 'the novel is . . . closely governed by a sense of time' and suggested that Trollope must have used a desk diary for the year 1872 to plot its chronology so closely.[5] And more recently, Francis O'Gorman has given us a more nuanced account of the workings of time in the novel, suggesting that 'Trollope's narration is interested in psychological chronology' and that

> [t]he novel asks its reader to think – but also vicariously to experience – time's simultaneity, too. Across its different plots, so dynamically in conversation with each other, *The Way We Live Now* depicts events that are concurrent . . . Taking us backwards and forwards through time, this carefully plotted, day-by-day, hour-by-hour novel proposes a remarkable awareness of the psychological changefulness, as well as of literal physical locomotion, of men and women going on their way, through time, all at once.[6]

It is absolutely true that this is a novel that is always glancing at the clock and at the calendar, and this is one of the means by which it produces its sense of 'ordinariness' – when 'ordinary' takes its meaning of orderly, in order and customary. For example (and there are many examples), 'It was now between nine and ten in the evening'; 'At about nine that evening John Crumb called at Mrs Pipkin's'; 'It was now Wednesday'; 'On that Thursday afternoon'; 'That was on the day after Lady Monogram's party'; or, 'Ten days had passed since the meeting narrated in the last chapter.'[7] Daily routines are carefully established: '[h]e, Melmotte, always left the house at ten and never returned till six' (*WWLN*, ch. 63, p. 482); as are weekly routines, so that Lady Carbury has 'a few friends every Tuesday evening'(*WWLN* ch.1, p. 14). Precise dates are given in the text, so that when Georgiana Longestaffe writes to her mother about her engagement to Brehgert she 'dat[es] her letter for the following morning: – Hill Street, 9th July, 187–' (*WWLN*, ch. 65, p. 498). Train and boat times are also supplied straight from the timetable; Georgiana, for example, takes 'the 2.30 train from London' (*WWLN*, ch. 65, p. 499) back to Caversham, and Marie Melmotte plans to book a passage to America on 'The "Adriatic", – that's a White Star boat, [which] goes on Thursday week at noon' (*WWLN*, ch. 41, p. 316).

Such precision also allows for a careful mapping of event against event, and many of them overlap in time. 'In the meantime' is both structural and metonymic to this novel's seriality. Just as lots of things presumably happened to its first readers between its twenty monthly parts, lots of things happen to its characters in those twenty monthly parts while something else is going on elsewhere. Trollope is interested in the 'concurrency' of events in this novel. 'In the meantime another scene was being acted in the room below' (*WWLN*, ch. 77, p. 593) or '[i]n the meantime a scene of a different kind was going on in the House of Commons' (*WWLN*, ch. 69, p. 529). Sometimes chapters open with 'in the meantime': Chapter 94 starts, 'In the meantime great preparations were going on down in Suffolk' (*WWLN*, ch. 94, p. 717) and Chapter 98, 'In the meantime Marie Melmotte was living with Madame Melmotte in their lodgings up at Hampstead' (*WWLN*, ch. 98, p. 746).[8] The reader is constantly pulled back from the onward momentum of the scene at hand and obliged to return to an alternative past. Although the novel's 'meantime' might signal the concurrency of events, the order of narration means that simultaneous events can never be experienced by the reader in parallel. The novel layers its multiple plots over one another in a complex pattern, mapping the movement of its characters through time and space, from Suffolk, to Islington, to the House of Commons, to Liverpool, to San Francisco and so on.

Of course, this 'meanwhile-ness' is a common and oft-noted feature of what Peter K. Garrett famously called 'The Victorian Multiplot Novel'. In his chapter on Trollope, Garrett suggests that 'Trollope repeatedly multiplied narrative lines to enlarge and diversify his novels' – that odd near-tautology of 'repeatedly multiplied' suggesting an excess which Garrett explains as a result of Trollope's 'lesser artistic ambitions'; which mean that his novels are 'not animated by such powerful impulses toward unity' as Dickens's *Bleak House*; Thackeray's *Vanity Fair*; or George Eliot's *Middlemarch*.[9] 'Trollope's narrator', Garrett adds, 'is as prominent an authorial persona as George Eliot's, but he "knows" less.'[10] But surely this 'tendency toward dispersion', as Garrett later calls it, has little to do with Trollope's supposedly 'lesser artistic ambitions' and is rather the result of a wide *distribution* of knowledge in the novel which is *spread* across its many plots.[11] 'Spread' is a word borrowed from Mark W. Turner, who has written about Trollope's 'model [of global modernity] based on continual spread', asking '[c]an the centre, even an imagined or constructed one, "hold"?' Turner points out that in Trollope's work, '[t]he rhythm of global modernity . . . is arrival and departure rather than extended connection, and the movement is imagined as spread and diffusion rather than cohesion'.[12] I argue that in the place of 'a powerful impulse towards unity' in Trollope's multiplot novel, there stands the complexity of a distributive network of narrative attention. *The Way We Live Now* models in its very form the distribution of information, of distributive communications networks; the post, the telegraph, the print media, and also, and importantly, a model of political liberalism which struggles both to link and to hold separate different social groups. If we read it this way, *The Way We Live Now* is less ordinary than it looks. Indeed, on such a reading it reveals itself to be less concerned with order and orderliness and more concerned with the collective strain of maintaining the spaces between, of 'holding the line' on the separations which create and perform distinctions in a fast-moving world. In its restless proliferating spread, the novel produces multiple holding patterns rather than the 'unified form' which was once so eagerly sought by literary critics.

In the 1870s, the state was waking up to the power of the media in achieving spread and distribution. Government was beginning to understand that the ways in which knowledge moved and was diffused were changing, and that new information could come back to the centre from almost anywhere. Trollope opens his 1861 short story, 'The Journey to Panama', with an embarkation scene at Southampton: '[t]here are several of these great ocean routes', he tells us, 'of which by the common consent, as it seems, of the world, England is the centre'. But there is a hint of the undercutting to come in his description of 'the great West–Indian route':

> . . . great, not on account of our poor West Indian Islands, which cannot at the present moment make anything great, but because it spreads itself out from thence to Mexico and Cuba, to Guiana and the republics of Grenada and Venezuela, to Central America, the Isthmus of Panama, and from thence to California, Vancouver's Island, Peru and Chili.[13]

The story decentres England as 'it spreads itself out', ultimately leaving the reader stranded in a travellers' hotel in Panama. The narrative is interrupted by the arrival of a letter from Peru which has travelled along the 'news' routes on the Pacific steamer from South America to Panama. This letter cuts the 'English' plot dead, decouples the protagonists of this curious quasi-love story, and abruptly ends the tale. Once information networks are fully international, England cannot hold the centre, and consequently the imaginative pull of England's centrality becomes even more intense. Laurie Langbauer, in an excellent chapter on Trollope, says that 'Trollope recognised that English culture was not the limit of his fiction; it was interdependent on its often occluded relation with other cultures.'[14] Trollope wrote *The Way We Live Now* having spent eighteen months in the Australian Colonies and in New Zealand. He returned to England via San Francisco, Salt Lake City and New York, arriving back in London in December 1872. Commerce in the novel is transatlantic: the South Central Pacific and Mexican Railway scheme extends its imagined tracks right into the centre of London. The liberalisation of the market, global commerce and imperial expansion were the clear trajectories of the liberalism of the 1870s. Horkheimer and Adorno would later describe the void of a capitalist culture in which, 'everything has to run incessantly, to keep moving', and *The Way We Live Now* is a novel of speed, jostle and movement.[15] Information becomes loose and multiple in Trollope; letters, newspapers and print, advertisements, gossip: all combine and circulate along different but sometimes overlapping routes. And inevitably as information moves faster and spreads further it becomes harder to track and harder to control.[16]

The state is also urgently concerned with the problems of spread in this period, as telegraph, postal and transport networks extended nationally and internationally, superimposing themselves upon one another. State control of communications became an urgent issue for debate. Liberalism itself performs a distributive function by working to identify, separate, but relate the increasing numbers of visible and knowable subjects in the modern social world. Trollope reproduces this incomplete and open connectivity across whole series of novels, and not only in *The Way We Live Now*. The six-novel series of the 1870s, known collectively as the 'Palliser novels', sometimes called the 'Parliamentary novels', uses recurring characters and linked storylines not to create an orderly series, but to evoke a muddled, circumstantial and contingent network that meets and touches only to disconnect and detach. The novels' interest in parliamentary politics generates a recursive system of representation, by which liberalism is repeatedly defined in terms of itself and replicates its forms across different narrative fields. Parliamentary liberalism turns out to be only one of the intersecting and colliding versions of the liberal. In two novels that precede *The Way We Live Now*, and which form part of the Palliser series, *The Eustace Diamonds* (1871) and *Phineas Redux* (1873), Trollope creates one of his most explicitly 'Liberal' characters, Plantagenet Palliser. As Chancellor of the Exchequer, Plantagenet Palliser attempts to introduce a decimal currency to better manage massive numbers and to expedite distributive fiscal systems on a global scale: 'he sat all alone, and meditated how he might best reconcile the forty-eight farthings which go to a shilling with that thorough-going useful decimal, fifty'.[17] But the sums are difficult. One of the challenges of the decimalisation project is how to describe the new fractional coins that would fall between the new units:

By what denomination should the fifth part of a penny be hereafter known? Someone had, ill-naturedly, whispered to Mr Palliser that a farthing meant a fourth, and at once there arose a new trouble, which for a time bore very heavily on him. Should he boldly disregard the original meaning of the useful old word; or should he venture on the dangers of new nomenclature? October, as he said to himself, is still the tenth month of the year, November the eleventh, and so on, though by these names they are so plainly called the eighth and ninth. All France tried to rid itself of this absurdity, and failed. Should he stick by the farthing; or should he call it a fifthing, a quint, or a semitenth? 'There's the "Fortnightly Review" comes out but once a month', he said to his friend Mr Bonteen, 'and I'm told that it does very well'. Mr Bonteen, who was a rational man, thought the 'Review' would do better if it were called by a more rational name, and was very much in favour of 'a quint'.[18]

The challenge of such standardisation is in maintaining the proper order of parts and finding a solution for those that fall in between named categories. Trollope enjoys ironising the difficulties of categorising and including everything in the right order here, but the problem remains an intractable and fundamental one not just for Plantagenet's decimalisation plan, but also for Trollope's narrative within this novel. The problem of maintaining sequence is only compounded when the fractal relationship of all the Palliser novels in the series is also taken into account. Ultimately this problem of ordering within and across different units of activity is one for the wider liberal project, too. The recursive referentiality of Trollope's series always operates on several different scales at once.

The spread structure of the plot of *The Way We Live Now* is rhymed against the time of the media. Media time is both regular and also unruly, and multiple media rhythms beat through the novel. Trollope's media landscape is both cacophonous *and* carefully segmented, '[t]he new farthing newspaper, "The Mob"' (*WWLN*, ch. 69, p. 524), for example, is clearly a very different publication to Mr Booker's *Literary Chronicle*. The *Morning Breakfast Table*, which was originally (in Trollope's outlines for the novel) going to be a 'Weekly Chronicle' or a 'Gazette', and the *Evening Pulpit* mark out in print the multiple daily rhythms of the media which are further augmented by the appearance of late editions, the 'second editions of the evening papers' (*WWLN*, ch. 64, p. 492).[19] Some of the characters themselves appear in the newspapers in the course of the novel: Marie Melmotte's failed elopement is discussed in the society gossip pages, as is her father's election campaign, of course, in the parliamentary reporting.[20] Newspapers reach every social level in the novel, from the Marquis of Auld Reekie, 'lighting a cigar as he took up the newspaper' (*WWLN*, ch. 85, p. 653), to the financier, Melmotte, who 'always breakfasted alone with a heap of newspapers around him' (*WWLN*, ch. 63, p. 482), to Mrs Pipkin telling Ruby Ruggles that she must go out as a nursemaid, and 'You must put a 'vertisement into the paper' (*WWLN* ch. 80, p. 614).[21] The newspaper, like Trollope's novel, both orders and connects the social world, mediating its encounters while reaffirming permeable divides.

Media Spread – State Spread

The paper and electronic media technologies of the 1870s were, of course, structurally connected to an emergent state bureaucracy. Liberal political ideology saw national networks not as centralising but as connective and progressive, linking the countryside and the city, and improving the condition of the people. The state enthusiastically took up the opportunity to spread its operative functions through communications and information technologies: indeed, Patrick Joyce even defines liberalism as 'the systematic technomanagement of freedom'.[22] Joyce claims that the first ever 'Large-scale Technological System' (LTS) was the British Post Office, which 'combin[ed] . . . the reproduction of the state *and* capitalism. Industrial capitalism and the state both seem to have arrived as "systems" at about the same time, or at least to have become more system-like than hitherto'.[23] Bernhard Siegert has pointed out that with the advent of a large-scale postal service, the address was delivered by the letter, rather than the letter being delivered to the address.[24] In other words, the rapidly growing postal service demanded postal addresses for more and more correspondents, and it therefore 'situated' people, creating a form of individualism that was networked into a collective while also allowing for new possibilities of state control and surveillance. Trollope uses the disciplinary potential of the network in one of the key scenes in *The Way We Live Now*.

In Chapter 50 of *The Way We Live Now*, when a telegraph message leads to Marie Melmotte and her maid, Elise Didon, being apprehended at Liverpool Station, so that Marie's plan to elope to America with Felix Carbury is foiled, Trollope's narrator is slyly ironic:

> It may be well doubted whether upon the whole the telegraph has not added more to the annoyances than to the comforts of life, and whether the gentlemen who spent all the public money without authority ought not to have been punished with special severity in that they had injured humanity, rather than pardoned because of the good they had produced. Who is benefited by telegrams? The newspapers are robbed of all their old interest, and the very soul of intrigue is destroyed. Poor Marie, when she heard her fate, would certainly have gladly hanged Mr Scudamore. (*WWLN*, ch. 50, p. 384)

This most topical of allusions may now require some explanation. When Trollope was planning and starting to write his novel in May 1873, a financial scandal which would have particularly engaged his attention was breaking noisily in Whitehall. Trollope had resigned from the Post Office in 1867 when a younger man, Frank Ives Scudamore, had been promoted over him. Scudamore went on to become the 'director of the first significant experiment in nationalization undertaken in modern British history', when he energetically undertook to buy up all the private telegraph companies operating in England on behalf of the Post Office and then to network them into one massively extended national telegraphic system.[25] '[W]hat has been the public cry?' wrote Scudamore, 'Has it not been continually? [*sic*] Give us more wires on existing lines! Give us extensions of wires to outlying places! Bring the offices of transmission and delivery closer to our doors!'[26] This plan to massively extend the network was a very ambitious undertaking. As one of Scudamore's team at the Post Office explained:

> Under the private companies comparatively few places, and those only towns of a fair size, had telegraphic intercommunication; but now the affair had been acquired by the Post Office it was intended that every place of sufficient importance to be a money-order office should also be made a centre for the receipt and despatch of telegrams.[27]

By making sub-post offices which were already operated by the Post Office all over the country double up as telegraph offices, Scudamore was able to extend the network with 40,000 new miles of wire.[28] The cost of sending messages dropped significantly and over the next two years the number of messages sent doubled.[29] But in the spring of 1873, it emerged through the Parliamentary Committee of Public Accounts that Scudamore had paid over the odds for the individual companies and had refinanced the project without asking permission from the government by using Post Office Savings Bank deposits to the sum of £812,000. This is the history of that sideways glance in *The Way We Live Now* at 'the gentlemen who spent all the public money without authority' (*WWLN*, ch. 50, p. 384). For Trollope's first readers, Scudamore's name was associated with what economic historian Charles Perry has described as 'a major scandal in 1873 which had lasting results'.[30] The scandal hit Gladstone's Liberal government hard in the wake of the defeat of the Irish University Bill and was to slow down further government interventions into private industry for years to come. Some of this commercial-governmental scandal clearly percolates into *The Way We Live Now* through the Melmotte plot, but I am more interested in the fact that Trollope is careful to add that Scudamore and his colleagues were 'pardoned because of the good they had produced' (*WWLN*, ch. 50, p. 384). Readings of *The Way We Live Now* as a critique of capitalism seem to me to miss some of Trollope's understanding of the complexities of the relationship between the state and the market under the Liberal administration of the 1870s.[31]

Edmund Yates, one of Dickens's 'young men', was employed by Scudamore to negotiate contracts to run telegraph poles and wires across private land. He later recalled a particularly prickly landowner's vociferous objections: 'Why the etcetera had the Government meddled in the matter? The private companies did the thing well, and in a gentlemanly manner, without interfering with the rights of property; but this etcetera Liberal Government wanted to grab everything.'[32] And in a sense this incensed proprietor was right: the Liberal government did want to 'grab everything'. As Patrick Joyce has argued, '[t]he most significant feature of the Post Office [during the nineteenth century] is the way in which the service begins not only to deliver letters, but to become a *universal* communications system'.[33] Trollope's work registers the spread of the state under Gladstone's Liberal administration through technological infrastructures such as the nationalised telegraph system. His work dramatises the way in which the state, by its constant extension of coverage, is becoming naturalised into all of his characters' lives. Trollope's work thus helps to answer Oleg Kharkhordin's question about the formation of the modern state in Europe: 'What made it possible to think of an almost mystic entity – "the state" – that nobody sees but that everybody presumes to exist and to act, frequently in an overwhelming manner, on our lives?'[34] Patrick Joyce suggests that the state is embedding itself as 'part of our "common sense" and common knowledge' in the last quarter of the nineteenth century, and so, in that sense, the state becomes *ordinary*.[35] But at the same time, Trollope is also conveying the limits of this attempt, as in fact it proves impossible to 'grab everything' and information remains inherently volatile. Think of Melmotte's impromptu speech in Covent Garden which unexpectedly turns around the public mood vis-à-vis his election.

Switchback and Fast Forward

'Trollope, according to his own account, wrote *The Way We Live Now* sequentially, from chapter 1 to 100.'[36] But the action of the novel is never entirely sequential, or even merely 'concurrent'. Consider a few examples: 'A few days before that period in our story which we have now reached' (*WWLN*, ch. 60, p. 457); 'This took place on the day after the balloting at Westminster, when the result was not yet known' (*WWLN*, ch. 67, p. 511); 'But now we must go back to the adventures of John Crumb after he had left the house' (*WWLN*, ch. 71, p. 543); 'But this departure had not as yet taken place at the time at which we have now arrived' (*WWLN*, ch. 83, p. 636); 'But in all this the details necessary for the telling of our story are anticipated. Mr Longestaffe had remained in London actually over the 1st of September . . . before the letter was written to which allusion has been made' (*WWLN*, ch. 88, p. 675); 'When Hetta Carbury received that letter from her lover which was given to the reader some chapters back' (*WWLN*, ch. 90, p. 687); 'We must now go back a little in our story, – about three weeks' (*WWLN*, ch. 96, p. 731); 'A few days before . . . Miss Longestaffe was seated in Lady Monogram's back drawing-room' (*WWLN*, ch. 60, p. 457). In fact, the novel uses switchback and fast-forward techniques more than it uses the more juxtapositional 'meanwhile'. The grammatical awkwardness of these sentences and phrases such as 'before [the time] we have now reached' (*WWLN*, ch. 60, p. 457) and 'had not as yet taken place' (*WWLN*, ch. 83, p. 636) draws deliberate attention to Trollope's capricious treatment of linear time. *The Way We Live Now* is ultimately a book about reading *out of order*: a self-consciously disrupted serial which draws quite deliberate attention to the political and social risks suggested by its own damaged seriality.[37]

The effect on the reader of these switchbacks and fast-forward moments in the text is complicated. Readers are pulled forcibly out of the particular narrative 'present' that they have been inhabiting, and propelled back to experience that present again in a different space and from a different perspective. 'Trollope also encourages us', Francis O'Gorman says, 'in the very experience of reading, to comprehend what it might be like to be able to read more than one chapter, more than one narrative strand, at once.'[38] Or even what it might be like to read them in a different order? Concurrency implies seriality, so that events run parallel in time, while Trollope neatly alternates his narration of them in order to maintain the illusion of an isomorphic relationship to linear time. But Trollope's time frames in *The Way We Live Now* sometimes seem to be complexifying out of control. It is worth examining more closely a particular scene in the novel that seems to be drawing attention to the dangers of disrupted sequencing in the delivery of information.

Switching: Mrs Hurtle's Letters

When Mrs Hurtle summons Paul Montague to her for their penultimate interview, it is by letter. A very short letter, which reads, 'Yes. Come. W. H' (*WWLN*, ch. 51, p. 392).[39] The reader knows this is in fact the third of three letters that she has written to Paul, but the only one she has posted. When he arrives she shows him the two others, explaining that 'I could not send them all by post, together. But you may see them all now' (*WWLN*, ch. 51, p. 394). By delivering them herself, in the order she chooses, Mrs Hurtle makes her letters into a linear sequence under her control – a sequence they would obviously have lost if she had posted them all at once.

'There is one. You may read that first. While I was writing it, I was determined that that should go' (*WWLN*, ch. 51, p. 394). 'There is one', she says, not – 'there is the first', but 'there is one', for in fact the letter she now hands him is 'the sheet of paper which contained the threat of the horsewhip' (*WWLN*, ch. 51, p. 394), which was not the first letter she wrote, but rather the second. She avoids ordinal numbers, which would reveal the sequence of writing. The very first letter she wrote she presents to Paul last, explaining that '"[t]he charm of womanly weakness presented itself to my mind in a soft moment, – and then I wrote this other letter. You may as well see them all". And so she handed him the scrap which had been written at Lowestoft' (*WWLN*, ch. 51, p. 395). She deliberately muddles the sequence of the letters, and, without exactly lying, strongly implies that the softer letter was written *after* the angry one, and so reduces Paul to tears so that he throws 'himself on his knees at her feet, sobbing' (*WWLN*, ch. 51, p. 395).

This all occurs in Chapter 51, a chapter entitled, 'Which Shall it Be?', a title which returns the reader emphatically to a future-directed present. Mrs Hurtle, having written the self-sacrificing and loving note at Lowestoft, turns over the sheet of paper she has written on and 'gave play to all her strongest feelings on the other side, – being in truth torn in two directions' (*WWLN*, ch. 51, p. 392). 'On the other side' refers of course to both of the sheet of paper and the other side of the question. In an interesting moment of meta-plot-switching (Which Shall it Be?), Trollope's novel draws his readers' attention to the control of information. Mrs Hurtle controls Paul's reactions by re-sequencing her letters. He is controlled, as we are both as readers of this novel, by his access to information and the order in which it is dispatched. The part-issue monthly serial form that he uses for *The Way We Live Now* was already out of date and unusual by 1874. But Trollope creates something new of it in this novel, by making it switchback and fast forward, thereby stylistically compressing and distorting the regular narrative distances between characters and stories. When we switch back three weeks, or are told something has not yet happened, the effect is of a kind of time-collision. Too much is happening in too many different places to be controlled by the narrative, so that the timeline has consequently overloaded, and any model of linear seriality has buckled and broken. In its stead we are offered a stretchy network of multiple serialities.

And the risk of losing any sense of indexicality to a linear serial system is that we lose the order. The ordinal numbers: what happened first, second, third, are confounded by late delivery, and for Trollope this represents a political risk, as much as a narratological one. In social terms, too much compression of distance, too much muddling of the order, could lead to 'equality', to a society where there is no first, second or third at all, but rather what Trollope himself described as 'communism . . . ruin . . . insane democracy'.[40] The 'Liberal', explains Trollope in his *Autobiography* (and he had of course himself stood as a Liberal parliamentary candidate at Beverley in 1868), 'is alive to the fact that these distances [between people of different classes] are day by day becoming less,' and while he applauds the prevailing 'tendency towards equality' he stops short of advocating total 'equality', a word which he claims is 'offensive'.[41] His own description of himself as 'an advanced, but still a conservative Liberal' (*Autobiography* ch. 16, p. 183) has something of a switchback quality to it, looking forwards and backwards at the same time. The fact that it is the acceleratively named Mrs Hurtle, the not-quite-respectable American with 'a bit of the wild cat in her breeding' (*WWLN*, ch. 38, p. 292), who muddles the texts in this scene further suggests a connection between the disruption of narrative, and democracy and social risk.

So what does it really mean to read Trollope as a Liberal writer? Amanda Anderson returns us to Lionel Trilling's *The Liberal Imagination* (1950) because she says that Trilling reminds us that the liberal ideology was not so straightforward, progressive and uncomplicated as its critics have often suggested. Trollope's interest in the disrupted serial then perhaps speaks to the obstacles and finitudes which stand in the path of any liberal progressive narrative. Anderson asks us to consider 'how compellingly the aesthetic features of a work or author seem . . . to dovetail with the philosophical and political terrain of liberalism'.[42] But this is still a juxtapositional approach: the 'dovetailing' of a text and a political philosophy. I would suggest that the boundary between the aesthetic and political is a false one. Literary critics have long worried about the ephemerality and dailiness of Trollope's serial novels. The *Saturday Review* warned in 1869 that the isomorphism of Trollope's novel series to newspapers threatened their aesthetic integrity and detracted from an ideal of the novel as 'a simple and harmonious whole':

> The multiplication of figures is the chief thing, and the system of extending the story indefinitely to a certain extent baffles criticism. You can never say that the whole displeases you, because you can never be sure that you have got the whole. If the plan is pushed much further, clever novels bid fair to become as ephemeral as the daily papers.[43]

Trollope's novels of the 1870s are perhaps best understood as an integral part of the extending media network. The media is performing the work of connectivity without completion which is coming to define the experience of living in a global world. The unspooling serial is the emergent mode of liberalism developing alongside and through capitalism in the same period. Trollope's serials are not 'simple', 'harmonious', nor, crucially, 'whole', but always incomplete, as modern techno-culture spreads itself out into polycentric and multi-layered networks. Trollope's texts feel 'ordinary' because they are plugged into this edgeless media world, and the experience of reading them is also the daily experience of living in media-time as it unspools towards an uncertain future.[44]

Notes

1. Christina Crosby, '"A taste for more": Trollope's Addictive Realism', in Mark Osteen and Martha Woodmansee (eds), *The New Economic Criticism: Studies at the Interface of Literature and Economics* (London: Routledge, 1999), pp. 293–306 (p. 304). See also Jonathan Farina's discussion of Trollope's repeated use of the phrase 'of course' in his fiction. Jonathan Farina, '"As a matter of course": Trollope's Ordinary Realism', in Deborah Denenholz Morse, Margaret Markwick and Mark W. Turner (eds), *The Routledge Research Companion to Anthony Trollope* (Abingdon and New York: Routledge, 2016), pp. 142–53.
2. Amanda Claybaugh, 'Trollope in America', in Carolyn Dever and Lisa Niles (eds), *The Cambridge Companion to Anthony Trollope* (Cambridge: Cambridge University Press, 2011), pp. 210–23 (p. 220).
3. For a more sustained analysis of the political and aesthetic importance of seriality in the nineteenth century, see my forthcoming series of three monographs with Oxford University

Press, *Distant Contemporaries: Revolution, Seriality and Print 1815–1848*; *Serial Revolutions: 1848 in Britain, Europe and America*; and *The Digital Switch: Literature, Compression and Transmission, 1848–1918*.

4. For recent discussion of the 'forms' of liberalism in the nineteenth century, see Amanda Anderson, *Bleak Liberalism* (Chicago: University of Chicago Press, 2016), Elaine Hadley, *Living Liberalism: Practical Citizenship in Mid-Victorian Britain* (Chicago: University of Chicago Press, 2010), Domenico Losurdo, *Liberalism: A Counter-History* (London: Verso, 2014), and Patrick Joyce, *The State of Freedom: A Social History of the British State Since 1800* (Cambridge: Cambridge University Press, 2013).

5. Bert G. Hornback, 'Anthony Trollope and the Calendar of 1872: The Chronology of *The Way We Live Now*', *Notes and Queries*, 208 (1963): p. 455. P. D. Edwards disagreed and suggested instead that Trollope wrote his own working chronology for the novel; see P. D. Edwards, 'The Chronology of *The Way We Live Now*', *Notes and Queries*, 214 (1969): pp. 214–16. John Sutherland reviews their positions thus: 'The time-scheme of *The Way We Live Now* is very close and somewhat controversial. As Bert Hornback points out, 98 of the novel's 100 chapters occupy February–September 1872 and "forty-five days account for sixty-six of the novel's chapters". Hornback goes on to argue that Trollope must have guided himself through the tangle of his multiplot novel by constant reference to an 1872 calendar. In an answering article, P. D. Edwards refuted this alleged recourse to a mechanical aid. Trollope, he pointed out, made up his own calendar for the novel's main events and incorporated it into his list of chapter titles for the novel.' John Sutherland, 'Trollope at Work on *The Way We Live Now*', *Nineteenth-Century Fiction*, 37.3 (1982): pp. 472–93 (p. 491).

6. Francis O'Gorman, 'Introduction', in Anthony Trollope, *The Way We Live Now* (Oxford: Oxford University Press, 2016), p. xxviii. This edition clearly signals the novel's interest in timekeeping by using an image of clocks and watches on its cover. See also Francis O'Gorman, 'Is Trollope's *The Way We Live Now* (1875) about the "commercial profligacy of the age"?', *Review of English Studies*, 67.281 (2016): pp. 751–63.

7. Anthony Trollope, *The Way We Live Now*, ed. Frank Kermode (London: Penguin, 1994), ch. 84, p. 647; ch. 70, p. 540; ch. 81, p. 623; ch. 83, p. 635; ch. 65, p. 502; and ch. 92, p. 701. All subsequent references to *The Way We Live Now* are to this edition and given in the text. I would like to thank Marina Ristuccia for her help with footnotes and page references.

8. Helena Michie, in a suggestive article about the intertwining of simultaneous personal and public histories in the nineteenth-century novel, has noticed that '[h]istoricist sentences in realist novels are often, although not exclusively, found at moments of transition, or at the beginning of chapters'. She also calls attention to the 'predictable awkwardnesses' of grammar in these sentences, which she attributes 'to the challenges of suturing literature and history through words and to describing an embodying in linear form the idea of simultaneity on which many of these sentences are based'. Helena Michie, 'Victorian(ist) "Whiles" and the Tenses of Historicism', *Narrative*, 17:3 (2009): pp. 274–90 (p. 276 and p. 275).

9. Peter K. Garrett, 'Trollope: Eccentricities', in *The Victorian Multiplot Novel: Studies in Dialogic Form* (New Haven and London: Yale University Press, 1980), pp. 180–200 (p. 180). More recent criticism has since moved away from the idea of 'unity' in nineteenth-century novels, but Garrett's reading was powerful and his differentiation of Trollopian plotting from that of Dickens, Eliot and Thackeray remains intriguing.

10. Garrett, 'Trollope: Eccentricities', p. 183.

11. Ibid. p. 185. Garrett concedes that the impulse towards dispersal never completely dominates a Trollope novel, but he gives no adequate explanation of why not.

12. Mark W. Turner, 'Trollope and Global Modernity', in Deborah Denenholz Morse, Margaret Markwick and Mark W. Turner (eds), *The Routledge Research Companion to Anthony Trollope* (Abingdon and New York: Routledge, 2016), pp. 423–34, all quotations p. 426.

13. Anthony Trollope, 'The Journey to Panama', in Adelaide A. Procter (ed.), *The Victoria Regia: A Volume of Original Contributions in Poetry and Prose* (London: Emily Faithfull and Co., The Victoria Press, 1861), pp. 187–214 (p. 189).

14. Laurie Langbauer, 'The Everyday as Everything: Pushing the Limits of Culture in Trollope's Series Fiction', in *Novels of Everyday Life: The Series in English Fiction, 1850–1930* (Ithaca, NY and London: Cornell University Press, 1999), pp. 85–127 (p. 108).

15. Horkheimer and Adorno, 'The Culture Industry: Enlightenment as Mass Deception', in *The Dialectic of Enlightenment*, trans. John Cumming (New York: Herder and Herder, 1944), pp. 120–67 (p. 134).

16. I am grateful to my colleague, Mark W. Turner, for his suggestions here. Jonathan Grossman touches on this idea too when he briefly discusses the 'sustaining "Meanwhile . . ." correlation between novel and nation that [Benedict] Anderson explains' in *Imagined Communities*. Anderson's idea, he says, 'fully applies . . . to Dickens's novels through *Bleak House*'. But he argues that the growth of international transport networks into the 1860s undermines the national in 'Dickens's later tales, developing his insights into the public transport revolution, [and] help expose an unsustainable slippage in Anderson's argument that the meanwhile structure enables the imagining of national community'. Jonathan H. Grossman, *Charles Dickens's Networks: Public Transport and the Novel* (Oxford: Oxford University Press, 2012), p. 187. Frederik Van Dam thinks about the return of 'occluded information' from the colonies in 'A Bond of Discord: Colonialism and Allegory', in *Anthony Trollope's Late Style: Victorian Liberalism and Literary Form* (Edinburgh: Edinburgh University Press, 2016), pp. 26–37.

17. Anthony Trollope, *Phineas Redux*, ed. John Bowen, (Oxford: Oxford University Press, 2011), ch. 26, p. 186. I would like to thank Nicola Kirkby for pointing to Trollope's use of decimalisation. For more on the history of decimalisation attempts in the nineteenth century, see note 346 in Anthony Trollope, *The Eustace Diamonds*, ed. Helen Small (Oxford: Oxford University Press, 2011), p. 628.

18. Anthony Trollope, *The Eustace Diamonds*, ed. W. J. McCormack (Oxford: Oxford University Press, 1998), ch. 55, pp. 140–1.

19. John Sutherland reminds us of Trollope's plan for Mr Broune: 'Editor of the ~~weekly Literary Chronicle Gazette~~ Morning Break-fast Table. Pall Mall-office in Trafalgar Square'; 'Trollope at Work', p. 480. The number of newspaper editions was increasing from the 1840s onwards. *The News of the World*, for example, was quick to exploit the possibilities of special and late editions: 'from Friday evening to Sunday morning, there is a perpetual succession of editions'. See Laurel Brake and Mark W. Turner, 'Rebranding the *News of the World* 1856–90', in Laurel Brake, Chandrika Kaul, Mark W. Turner (eds), *The News of the World and the British Press, 1843–2011: 'Journalism for the Rich, Journalism for the Poor'* (Basingstoke: Palgrave, 2016), pp. 27–42, note 25, p. 40. Also Laurel Brake, *Print in Transition, 1850–1910* (London: Palgrave, 2001) and Mark W. Turner, 'Periodical Time in the Nineteenth Century', *Media History*, 8.2 (2002): pp. 183–96.

20. Celebrity gossip was a relatively new addition to the newspaper in the 1870s and became more popular in the 1880s. See Alexis Easley, *Literary Celebrity, Gender, and Victorian Authorship, 1850–1914* (Newark: University of Delaware Press, 2011).

21. Leah Price has noticed that in Trollope often 'the book offers disconnection from a known person', and newspapers and books can become separators or defensive screens. Leah Price, 'Anthony Trollope and the Repellent Book', in *How to Do Things with Books in Victorian Britain* (Princeton: Princeton University Press, 2012), pp. 45–71 (p. 60).

22. Joyce, *The State of Freedom*, p. 83.

23. Ibid. pp. 37–8.

24. Bernhard Seigert, *Relays: Literature as an Epoch of the Postal System*, trans. Kevin Repp, (Stanford: Stanford University Press, 1999), p. 116.

25. Charles R. Perry, 'Frank Ives Scudamore and the Post Office Telegraph', *Albion: A Quarterly Journal Concerned with British Studies*, 12.4 (1980): pp. 350–67 (p. 350).

26. Scudamore to Monsell, 27 March 1873, Post 30/290, E1075/1876. Quoted in Perry, 'Scudamore', p. 360.

27. Edmund Yates, *Edmund Yates: His Recollections and Experiences* (London: Richard Bentley and Son, 1884), 2 vols, vol. 2, pp. 201–2.

28. See W. S. Jevons, 'On the Analogy between the Post Office, Telegraph, and other systems of conveyance of the United Kingdom, as regards Government Control', in *Methods of Social Reform* (London: Macmillan & Co., 1883), pp. 277–92. Read at the Manchester Statistical Society, 10 April 1867. 'Instead of two or three companies with parallel coterminous wires, and different sets of costly city stations, we shall have a single set of stations; and the very same wires, when aggregated into one body, will admit of more convenient arrangements, and more economical employment. The greater the number of messages sent through a given office, the more regularly and economically may the work of transmission and delivery be performed in general' (pp. 281–2).

29. See Roland Wenzlheumer, *Connecting the Nineteenth-Century World: The Telegraph and Globalization* (Cambridge: Cambridge University Press, 2013), p. 175.

30. Perry, 'Scudamore', p. 351.

31. See for example, Tamara S. Wagner, 'Speculators at Home in the Victorian Novel: Making Stock-Market Villains and New Paper Fictions', *Victorian Literature and Culture*, 36.1 (2008): pp. 21–40 and Denise Lovett, 'The Socially-Embedded Market and the Future of English Capitalism in Anthony Trollope's *The Way We Live Now*', *Victorian Literature and Culture*, 42.4 (2014): pp. 691–707. A posthumous essay on Trollope remarked that in Trollope's novels 'you see a good deal of the machinery of Parliament and of the greater administrative offices of the State . . . [Society] is [in Trollope] a great web of which London is the centre, and some kind of London life for the most part the motive-power. The change from Miss Austen to Mr Trollope is the change from social home-rule to social centralization.' Unsigned Essay, *Spectator* 55 (9 December 1882), pp. 1573–4. Quoted in Donald Smalley (ed.), *Trollope: The Critical Heritage* (London: Routledge & Kegan Paul, 1969), pp. 504–8, p. 511.

32. Yates, p. 209.

33. Joyce, *The State of Freedom*, p. 83. Emphasis original.

34. Oleg Kharkhordin, 'What is the State? The Russian Concept of *Gosudarvstvo* in the European Context', *History and Theory*, 40 (May 2001): p. 209. Quoted in Patrick Joyce, *The State of Freedom*, p. 14.

35. Ibid. p. 310.

36. Sutherland, 'Trollope at Work', p. 476.

37. All serials are, of course, always already disrupted by reading out of order, and by recaps, returns and proleptic moments in narrative, but I am suggesting that something more extreme and more deliberate is at play in *The Way We Live Now*.

38. Francis O'Gorman, 'Introduction', in Anthony Trollope, *The Way We Live Now* (Oxford: Oxford University Press, 2016), p. xxviii.

39. Susan Zieger has described Mrs Hurtle's summons as 'powerfully minimalist' and describes this scene as performing 'a new kind of interpersonal bureaucracy'. Susan Zieger, 'Affect and Logistics: Trollope's Postal Work', *Victorians: A Journal of Culture and Literature*, 128 (Fall 2015): pp. 226–44 (p. 234).

40. Anthony Trollope, *An Autobiography and Other Writings*, ed. Nicholas Shrimpton (Oxford: Oxford University Press, 2014), ch. 16, p. 183. Trollope writes, 'I will not say equality, for the word is offensive, and presents to the imaginations of men ideas of communism, of ruin, and insane democracy.'

41. Ibid. ch. 16, p. 182.

42. Amanda Anderson, 'Liberal Aesthetics', in Jane Elliott and Derek Attridge (eds), *Theory after Theory* (Abingdon: Routledge, 2011), pp. 249–61 (p. 259).

43. Anon., '*Phineas Finn*', *Saturday Review* (27 March 1869): pp. 431–2 (p. 432).

44. As Laurie Langbauer points out, '[i]n presenting the everyday as everything, and that everything as more than we can ever take in, Trollope's series shows us the site and mode of our engagement with the social system – its performance, not its end.' Langbauer, 'The Everyday as Everything', p. 127.

15

MIMESIS, MEDIA ARCHAEOLOGY AND THE POSTAGE STAMP IN *JOHN CALDIGATE*

Richard Menke

ANTHONY TROLLOPE NOT only began his professional life as a clerk in the bureaucracy of the General Post Office but also combined the careers of postal official and novelist for years. His travels to Ireland and elsewhere as a postal surveyor inform the settings of many of his novels, and his fiction often incidentally reveals 'his pride in the Post Office, his knowledge of its practices, [and] his amusement at the eccentricities of its patrons', sometimes as a sort of knowing joke shared with readers.[1] Noting Trollope's 'fondness for transcribing the letters of his love-lorn maidens and other embarrassed persons', Henry James claimed that 'no contemporary story-teller deals so much in letters'. 'The modern English epistle (very happily imitated, for the most part), is his unfailing resource', declared James, and several more recent critics have echoed this praise.[2]

James somewhat vaguely suggests that a career at the Post-Office is uniquely 'fitted to impress a man with the diversity of human relations'.[3] Or perhaps Trollope's equable, matter-of-fact prose style and efficient, regimented writing habits owe something to his training as a writer of memos and reports.[4] Still, the deeper relationships between Trollope's work as postal official and as novelist have proved harder to define. One source of connections between Trollope's postal work and his fiction is their relationship to the histories of media and information at a time of rapid technological and conceptual change. His bureaucratic fictions from *The Three Clerks* (1857) to 'The Telegraph Girl' (1877) suggest some of the affiliations between office work, institutional and technical change, and the narratives of work, courtship and daily life that justified Trollope's self-description as 'realistic'.[5] Moreover, from the implementation of Rowland Hill's Penny Postage reforms to the nationalisation of Britain's electric telegraph systems, Trollope's Post Office was at the centre of some of the century's most critical developments in media and information.

A medium is a means of recording or transmitting content, a means for communication, inscription, or both. But at the same time, media comprise concrete objects working within layered systems of physical function and social meaning. Before Hill's reforms, the postage for every letter was calculated according to its individual trajectory from origin to destination, with the fee to be collected from the letter's recipient. Since postage also depended on how many sheets of paper the letter included, thick or heavy letters also had to be 'candled' (examined in front of a strong light) to ascertain their contents – which might allow an unscrupulous clerk to detect and remove a banknote or other valuable item he happened to notice hidden there. Hill's great insight was to recognise that a system of cheap, uniform prepaid postage for light letters would soon pay for itself, especially since the lower fees would dramatically increase use of the post. At the Post Office, Trollope's most celebrated and enduring contribution to British media history was his suggestion to add public letter boxes to the postal network.[6] Although Trollope initially made this recommendation to help accommodate the vagaries of maritime postal collections on the Channel Islands, his pillar boxes were soon adopted across Great Britain and Ireland, becoming a familiar feature of the built environment and a signifier of the coherence and ubiquity of the entire postal system. Trollope helped complete Hill's system by ensuring that a letter prepaid by the sender with a postage stamp (Hill's own most famous legacy) could be posted at any time in a pillar box before being received just as impersonally through a mail slot in a door. A letter's transit now became less a sequence of personal interactions than an everyday flow in an information network.

The example of Trollope's pillar box helps suggest the possibilities for a media-oriented analysis that considers a particular media object's physical make-up and use against its place in larger media, social and institutional systems. Such an investigation can analyse the local conditions in which a media device arises and has meaning as well as the broader structures in which it functions: the General Post Office, say – or Trollopian realism. In Victorian fiction, media often come to mediate not merely between characters but also between the local and the general, and between fiction and the real world. Consider the text of an inset letter in a Trollope novel, a medium within that medium: how it runs between mimesis and diegesis, between composition by one fictitious personage, reception by another one, and interpretation by readers. A moment of high realism that momentarily merges the perceptions of a fictional character and a real reader, the incorporation of a letter's text within a nineteenth-century novel also constitutes a self-conscious glance at the epistolary heritage of English fiction.

In the context of a novel, interpolated textual media such as letters and telegrams often simultaneously highlight both the effort to represent the real world and the sheer machinery of telling a fictitious story, the dual nature of realistic fiction.[7] Yet the relationships between reality and fiction's mechanics shift when a letter appears not simply as a text in a novel but as a media object, as evidence of the workings of an information system. Media that appear as physical objects and evidence solicit an investigation beyond narrative analysis. The rest of this chapter will examine Trollope's *Autobiography* (posthumously published in 1883) and *John Caldigate* (1879), one of Trollope's most informatically focused novels, through media archaeology, a loose-knit approach to media that has so far been more closely associated with European thought than with anglophone intellectual traditions, as well as with scholars reacting against literary or humanistic approaches to media.

The term *media archaeology* covers a variety of approaches to media partly inspired by the work of the late media theorist and historian Friedrich Kittler as well as by creative work in art, technology and media curation.[8] The history of media might seem unitary, a tale of improvement, supersession and obsolescence, but media archaeology challenges such simplistic accounts. Its practitioners often draw attention to forgotten, ignored or 'weird' media – and to the weirdness of our own media – rather than celebrating a triumphant march of invention that leads smoothly and inevitably to the present media environment. Even the story of postal reform includes divagations, failures and dead ends. Hill's plan envisaged prepayment via special envelopes; the idea of the postage stamp only arose as an afterthought, a provision for customers with minimal literacy who showed up at the post office wanting to send a letter that someone else had addressed.[9] In the end, however, postal customers turned to stamps, and Hill's envelopes proved so unpopular that a special furnace had to be built in order to burn them.[10]

Media archaeology counters a version of media history from the viewpoint of technologies that became familiar or dominant, emphasising blind ends and gaps – as well as unexpected continuities. It also suggests that more conventional analyses of media have been hasty to oversimplify or ignore their actual mechanics. In the work of some practitioners, media archaeology tends to foreground the physics of media over their philosophy or social significance. It draws attention to particular media, to the material difference that divergent media technologies can make: prepaid letters versus letters payable on delivery, post-paid envelopes versus adhesive postage stamps. At its most stringent, media archaeology poses its emphasis on the material properties of technological artefacts against the phenomenological or cultural bias of media history, against humanistic approaches based on analysing discourses and 'telling media stories'.[11] Scholars such as Wolfgang Ernst have contrasted the 'literary' and 'narrative' leanings of Anglo-American media studies to media archaeology, with its focus on devices and technics rather than on ideas and ideologies. It's hardly surprising, then, that media archaeology has as yet seldom been brought to bear on literature – either on literature's media mechanics (a focus traditionally shunted off as part of book history) or literature's imagination and incorporation of the functions of media.[12]

Still, media archaeology has much to offer media historians and literary scholars: its alignment of scholarship with the study, use, curation and repair of actual devices, and of new artistic creation with forays into old media archives; its alertness to technical processes and materials; the attention it pays to untimely and even imaginary media, as well as to famous or successful ones; its emphasis on gaps and temporal breaks rather than on step-by-step historical development. Against 'the idea of inexorable, quasi-natural, technical progress', media archaeology proposes 'a variantology' of the conjunction of aesthetics, communication and technology that we've come to call *media*.[13]

Trollope exemplifies the challenge of approaching literary representation through media archaeology but also the possibilities of combining a technically oriented archaeology of media with attention to the mechanics of representation. Here is an author noted for his quasi-anthropological fascination with the ways in which characters negotiate institutions and social systems (the government, church, law, marriage market and family) – and perhaps notable for the paradoxical slipperiness of his calculatedly forthright style. But thinking of Trollope medially can help highlight the relationships between realism, media mechanics and media systems. Trollope may typify the need to think of mimetic art not simply in terms of one medium or another, but in terms of systems that link social formations with varied media-forms and formats. Trollope meets media archaeology – at least halfway. His art suggests that telling media stories might help us attend to the differences made by technical details and divergences in media.

In a well-known passage from his *Autobiography*, Trollope explicitly treats authorship in terms of media forms and technologies. Here Trollope considers 'the vehicle which a writer uses for conveying his thoughts to the public':

His language must come from him as music comes from the rapid touch of the great performer's fingers; as words come from the mouth of the indignant orator; as letters fly from the fingers of the trained compositor; as the syllables tinkled out by little bells form themselves to the ear of the telegraphist. A man who thinks much of his words as he writes them will generally leave behind him work that smells of oil. I speak here, of course, of prose; for in poetry we know what care is necessary . . .[14]

In his sequence of similes for fluent prose production, Trollope offers a miniature media history that takes us from musical performance to public oration, alphabetic print and acoustic telegraphy. These intermedial analogies also move full circle, from the non-verbal sound patterns of instrumental music, to vocalisation, to movable type, and then finally to a modern electric textuality that uses sound patterns once again. As part of Trollope's attempt to downplay thought and deliberation in this process, his collection of media modalities represents fluency by conflating the production of meaning with performance (the musician), with transcription (the compositor), and ultimately with something that resembles reception (the telegraph operator hearing a real-time transmission from a long way off). We might almost fail to notice that one of these similes quietly describes a critical stage in the process by which Trollope trusts that his words will come to us; the letters that compose this passage will themselves have flown from the hands of the expert printer.

This string of technical comparisons flattens out medial distinctions in order to conceptualise the production of a fluid and immersive prose. Trollope aligns multiple media to illustrate the idea of textual production that overcomes the signs of mediation altogether; the passage's rhetorical strategy and content come together to explain and enact the deliberate production of clarity, directness and the impression of effortlessness – another example of Trollope's wily forthrightness. Both as individual images and as a suite of different media operations, then, these similes appear as a representation of producing media-'work' in which the mechanics of communication disappears into its content. Trollope's complaint against over-thought, self-conscious prose is not simply that it will 'smell of the lamp' – the usual classical expression for laboriously wrought writing – but that it will smell of 'oil':[15] the residue of the scholar's lamplight labour slides over into the physical trace of the machinery involved in producing it. Smell, the impingement of material traces into our olfactory consciousness, is a particularly apt figure for that intrusion. But even as the passage turns away from the scent of midnight elucubrations, it rhetorically lubricates the seamless transitions from one medium to the next and the next.

Trollope's *Autobiography* links his fiction to a suite of practical media work, even as it also places his writing process in a workaday technical substrate of its own: the 'diary, divided into weeks', in which he enters his daily production of pages (at 250 words per page, with 'every word counted as I went'), and the timepiece.[16]

[I]t still is my custom, though of late I have become a little lenient to myself, – to write with my watch before me, and to require from myself 250 words every quarter of an hour. I have found that the 250 words have been forthcoming as regularly as my watch went . . . This division of time allowed me to produce over ten pages of an ordinary novel volume a day, and if kept up through ten months, would have given as its results three novels of three volumes each in the year . . .[17]

Writing a novel calls for a fluency that minimises the intrusion of technical processes, but this smooth flow of prose is also stimulated, regulated and recorded by the watch ticking out the quarter hours and the diary that records the number of words produced; authorship approaches 'the predictable regularity of a machine'.[18] Novels are matters of characters and plots but also matters of the time it takes to write a page, and of the amount of script needed to fill the volumes, numbers or journal instalments that constituted the mid-Victorian publishing system's formats for long prose fiction.

As it lays out Trollope's procedures for imagining and efficiently producing the 'vehicle' of prose representation, the *Autobiography* presents the technical details of a medium for realistic representation in relation to systems of multiple media. Mimesis meets media archaeology. Written shortly after Trollope drafted his *Autobiography* – it would be the final novel included in the *Autobiography*'s notorious tally of books written and payments received (the pecuniary cousin of the writing diary) – *John Caldigate* reiterates the movement from attending to a medium in its material specificity to placing these material details within the larger systems of recording, transmission, representation and control.

The vehicles and formats of the novel itself are meaningful but standard for the late 1870s, confirming *John Caldigate*'s enmeshment in Victorian systems for producing and distributing fiction: fifteen parts serialised in *Blackwood's Magazine* beginning in April 1878, and a three-volume novel largely intended in the first instance for the private circulating libraries. As the novel opens, Caldigate returns home from university in debt and prepares to exchange his prospective inheritance for a financial settlement from his disappointed father, which will pay his bills and allow him to sail to New South Wales to look for gold. Felicitously, he strikes it rich. Cashing out his mining investments in order to repatriate his colonial wealth, Caldigate soon returns to England to reconcile with his father, reclaim his patrimony and marry the young woman close to home who has filled his Antipodean dreams. The novel's first volume ends with the wedding of its main characters, John Caldigate and Hester Bolton – a signal that the novel is experimenting with the marriage plot and the triple-decker form rather than simply turning to marriage as a form of third-volume closure.

Via a set of vivid scenes set in Cambridgeshire, on shipboard and in Australia, Trollope has already rushed us through what could have been the main plot of another novel to reach the kernel of *John Caldigate*. When the Australian gold unexpectedly runs out, Caldigate's former mining partner returns to England to reclaim some of the money he has just paid – by blackmail, if necessary. As it turns out, during much of John Caldigate's time in Australia, he was living with a mysterious actress whom he had met on his voyage from England to Melbourne: Mrs Smith, sometimes known as Mademoiselle Cettini. An anonymous letter about her has already prompted Caldigate to confess his romantic history to Hester before they married. But now *John Caldigate* approaches the great question of its young protagonist's seedy past in 'the wilds of Australia': was it merely an unsanctioned romance as John Caldigate openly cohabited with Euphemia Smith-Cettini – or was it a clandestine marriage?[19]

An extended love affair on a far-off continent would be one thing, bigamy quite another. In addition to its unusual scenes of the jerry-rigged lives of miners in a state of semi-civilisation at the frontier of settler colonialism, the novel suggests that the ordinary code of sexual respectability might be acceptably more flexible at the peripheries of empire, at least when it comes to young European men – quite an extension of the sense of anthropological equanimity with which Trollope often approaches his characters' psychologies and mores. 'It was a wild kind of life up there', notes John to Hester's stepbrother, admitting that he had even once promised to marry Mrs Smith, and that in Australia she sometimes called herself 'Mrs Caldigate'.[20] Trollope offers a twist on the mid-Victorian bigamy plot: if the sexual relationship of John Caldigate and Euphemia Smith in Australia was strictly illicit, then things in England should be fine; John, Hester, and their baby are a legitimate family and in the clear. But what if back in Australia the two lovers had indeed tried to make things respectable with the help of an itinerant Wesleyan minister? Having followed John back to England, Caldigate's former business partner stands united with his former sexual partner to threaten to charge him with bigamy, unless he pays them a share of the money he has received for the depleted mine.

In *George Eliot and Blackmail*, Alexander Welsh reads the blackmail plot as a device through which Victorian fiction could treat the transition from a culture of shared knowledge into a rising world of fungible information. As Welsh points out, information is a kind of 'knowledge in the abstract'.[21] In Victorian novels, information often appears as knowledge-at-a-distance or as 'hidden' or 'latent knowledge' that must be retrieved before it can attain value by coming into circulation and use.[22] *John Caldigate* supports these insights, treating the gap between shared knowledge and commodified information as not simply a definitional difference but a structural source of narrative tension and energy. In a wet and dreary patch of Cambridgeshire, the Caldigate family and their ancestors have lived in the same house and owned most of the parish 'for three hundred years'.[23] Since Cambridge lies only ten miles away, there is never a prospect that news of John's undergraduate debts won't reach his father, for instance. Perhaps the paradigm of shared knowledge through proximity has even shaped Trollope's placement of the Caldigate family seat so close to the scene of John's college dissipations in the first place; in this novel, secrets and revelations are largely a colonial affair. Hester Bolton, who marries John Caldigate in England, is also part of this local world; the daughter of old Caldigate's banker and his puritanical wife, she has grown up in another village near Cambridge. In contrast, the blackmail threat imports information about John's life in Australia, news about scenes that the novel has pointedly neglected to include in its regular narrative.

The conventional blackmail plot doesn't last long in *John Caldigate*. In an inversion of the normal blackmail sequence, when John indignantly refuses to pay the conspirators, they carry out their threat to have him charged with bigamy – after which he eventually pays them anyway, since apart from any questions of blackmail, it does seem unfair to him that the mine should have run dry so soon after he sold his shares in it. But the questions of his possible Australian marriage and the evidence that might be proffered for it in an English courtroom remain unresolved. The ceremony is supposed to have been performed on the peripheries of British settlement, with few witnesses. In the absence of a wedding registry, or of the Wesleyan bush minister who is supposed to have presided (he is said to have died on Fiji), the bigamy charge depends on the testimony of the claimants and on the documents they can offer as evidence. The novel's second volume culminates in the trial of John Caldigate for bigamy; at the beginning of the third, he is found guilty.

Leaving the extortion plot behind, the novel proceeds from abstract information to the physical media that might convey or confirm it. Narrative attention quickly shifts from blackmail to imperial mail. During and after John Caldigate's bigamy trial, one document receives disproportionate forensic and narrative attention: an envelope, addressed in what John Caldigate admits is his own handwriting, to 'Mrs Caldigate, Ahalala, Nobble' – the rough (and fictional) colonial outpost where the marriage is supposed to have taken place – and postmarked from Sydney, the real-life capital of New South Wales.[24] In terms of the letter as a physical medium, we could call the envelope and its markings *paratexts*, material outside the content of the main text that nevertheless may profoundly shape its meaning and interpretation.[25] In informatic terms, we can think of the envelope as offering *metadata*, data about other data: its origin, structure, disposition, or status, for example (as with Trollope's daily record-keeping about his writing).

Postally speaking, metadata is 'not the content of the letter, it's what is on the envelope'. At least that's how it has been explained by a more recent Australian, Prime Minister Tony Abbott, trying in 2014 to describe what would be covered by the controversial data retention law that his government was introducing.[26] As critics of the bill pointed out, Abbott's analogy between postal mail and electronic media is fuzzy at best. An email address and subject line might distantly resemble the address written on the envelope of a paper letter, but what about the URL identifying a website, or a device's IP address, or satellite location data that lies embedded within an image file? Many electronic media – and, for that matter, a heavily marked-up postal envelope or a postcard – blur the line between metadata and content. In the United States, similar issues arose in the wake of Edward Snowden's 2013 revelation of the National Security Administration's secret programme to harvest massive amounts of metadata that tracked domestic telephone calls and internet communication.

The plot of Trollope's novel confirms exactly what some of Abbott's critics also noted: just how much information can reside on an envelope. Indeed, in the novel, the envelope carefully preserved and presented by the woman who would be Mrs Caldigate comes to be considered 'more damning' than any other evidence. 'The letter itself she also produced, but it told less than the envelope', notes Trollope's narrator, since the letter deals mostly with mining shares and their various prices, mere 'money matters, though perhaps hardly . . . such as a man generally discusses with his wife'. There can be only one Mrs John Caldigate; the envelope itself, or at least the man who admits that he inscribed it, seems to bestow that name on one woman and take it away from another. In the letter's salutation, a man greets a woman by a nickname ('Dearest Feemy'), but the intimacy of this personal address means less than the formal address written on this envelope to be read and processed by the public postal system.[27]

The crucial question becomes whether that information was ever used, whether the envelope and the address were ever recognised and processed by the postal system. If metadata gains power when it is also content (as with the location data in an image file), it might lose that power when it becomes merely external metadata (say, an arbitrary filename that encodes nothing in particular about the data to which it is attached). This is something like the explanation John Caldigate offers for the name written on the envelope. At trial, his barrister Sir John Joram concedes that the writing is John Caldigate's but denies that it was ever metadata for any item in the postal network, including the letter now enclosed in the envelope:

I acknowledge, that if a man could make a woman his wife by so describing her on a morsel of paper, this man would have made this woman his wife. I acknowledge so much, though I do not acknowledge, though I deny, that any letter was ever sent to this woman in the envelope which I hold in my hand. His own story is that he wrote those words at a moment of soft and foolish confidence, when they two together were talking of a future marriage, – a marriage which no doubt was contemplated, and which probably had been promised. Then he wrote the address, showing the woman the name which would be hers should they ever be married; – and she has craftily kept the document.[28]

That is, Sir John asserts, the inscription on the envelope is not actually metadata for a letter at all but a fiction, plausible but counterfactual mimesis, a work of realism. What's even odder, perhaps, is all the fuss about an envelope in the first place – as various characters including the barrister point out, nevertheless dwelling on the envelope all the while. Since the post office does not ask recipients of letters to confirm their legal names, the mere delivery of a letter to a recipient would be no confirmation of status or personal identity.

At the frontier of colonialism, settler life could be provisional and anarchic, as the question of the first Mrs Caldigate confirms. The post conveys not only letters but also the sense of a functional everyday system with aspirations to cover even Ahalala. For the long-distance British Empire, the post office had the practical and ideological function of linking metropole to colonies via daily communication. Trollope helped sustain this function in his early postal work in Ireland and witnessed its extension during his later trips to Australia and New Zealand to visit his son Frederic, whose emigration helped inspire the Australian scenes of *John Caldigate*. By the 1870s, that connective function ran along two lines, postal and telegraphic. Telegrams between Britain and Australia transacted urgent business and brought news: Australia's famous Overland Telegraph opened in 1872, running north–south through the heart of the continent from Port Darwin to Port Augusta and linking the cities on the southern and eastern coasts to the international telegraph system via the island of Java. 'If the gentle reader will think only of the amount of wire required for 1,800 miles of telegraph communication, and of the circumstances of its carriage, he will, I think, recognise the magnitude of the enterprise', writes Trollope in his non-fictional *Australia and New Zealand* (1873); the great telegraph line had been completed shortly after his own first visit to the colonies.[29] A literal timestamp, the postmark on the Caldigate envelope – Sydney, '10th May 1873' – places the letter and the main action of the novel in the era of this new system, which began to operate between the two trips Trollope made to Australia in the 1870s.[30]

The arrival of international telegraphy connected British settlements in Australia to a growing worldwide grid for lightning-fast communication. But it also highlighted the physical disparity between disembodied electrical information and the stubborn, evidentiary materiality of the circulating paper documents – letters in the mail – that imperial telegraphy so dramatically outpaced. In *John Caldigate*, the general preoccupation with the envelope and its physical markings suggests that the contrast between the post's transportation of objects and the telegraph's transmission of data patterns emphasises the material nature of communication via letter. As the novel's bankruptcy, blackmail and bigamy plot starts to unfold, 'a multiplicity of telegrams' from Australia, 'very costly', bear the first ill news of the goldmine John has just sold, to be followed by 'very long letters, long and loud' – and finally, by a threatening letter signed 'EUPHEMIA CALDIGATE' (the novel's typography foregrounds the fictitious identity-proclaiming signature) and urgently demanding a reply 'back by wire'.[31] Imperial distances exaggerate the trade-off between fast, expensive telegrams charged by the word and cheap letters assessed by weight and constrained by their material conveyance from point to point.

In light of the geographies, the time scales and the physical persistence and movement involved, an imperial letter emerges as a media object charged with the sense of material uniqueness, provenance and history that Walter Benjamin calls 'aura' – an aura boosted by the bifurcated electrico-postal media system itself.[32] In fact, the Caldigate envelope seems imbued with a dual status as both a singular item from a long way off and a routine postal article marked with the imprimatur of the system. The evidentiary issues raised by the envelope encapsulate this doubleness. Instead of bearing postmarks for both the sending and receiving post offices through which it passed, the letter has been marked only with the rubber stamp for Sydney, although the imprint of this stamp is particularly crisp and legible. Indeed, that very precision may be a puzzle as well. Like the absent postmark for Nobble, the unusually neat mark for Sydney might suggest either the everyday vicissitudes of a postal system handling millions of letters (some postmarks land neatly on letters, some letters lack one postmark or another) or fakery. Curlydown and Bagwax, the expert witnesses from the post office who testify during Caldigate's bigamy trial, question the authenticity of the postal markings but admit that even they cannot be certain.

After the conviction of John Caldigate, the original envelope is 'preserved among the sacred archives of the trial', as if in further confirmation of its aura. Yet although the document is not 'bodily confided' to him in its unique materiality, Samuel Bagwax obtains careful photographic reproductions of it – a demotion of the envelope from auratic talisman to research programme, which allows him to continue pursuing his suspicions.[33] *John Caldigate* not only features one of the earliest fictional incorporations of the forensic use of photography but also attests more broadly to the rise in the second half of the nineteenth century of the 'forensic imagination', part of what Matthew Kirschenbaum calls a 'signature discourse network of modernity at the juncture of instrumentation, inscription, and identification'.[34] A dozen years after *John Caldigate*, Arthur Conan Doyle would offer late-Victorian literature's most famous exploration of media forensics in 'A Case of Identity' (1891).[35] In that tale, Sherlock Holmes detects a phony suitor – a double and impostor – through the un-fakeable individuality of a typewriter. But Bagwax has a different goal: to place the Caldigate envelope in the context of other posted letters, to consider its material make-up in relation to a larger media system, in order to assess the story it seems to tell.

Bagwax's professional diligence and attention to detail clearly amuse and engage Trollope's narrator. As the focus of Bagwax's expertise, the postmark comes under his special scrutiny.[36] He tries to ascertain whether its crisp appearance suggests that it is indeed a careful forgery, not the hasty impression of a half-worn cancellation stamp whose impression should be blurred from the quick processing of many similar items. As John's barrister points out, 'Letters in the post-office are hurried quickly through the operation of stamping, so that one passing over the other while the stamping ink is still moist, will to some extent blot and blur that with which it has come in contact' – that is, the sharp imprint might reveal that it is indeed a unique counterfeit and not the regular product of a large-scale media system at all.[37] In that case, the missing postmark for Nobble would confirm that the envelope was never delivered there in the first place.

Not much should depend on the marks on this envelope, but somehow everything does; as Kate Thomas notes, 'it is hard to overemphasize how much of the drama of the novel is displaced onto Bagwax', a figure with whom Trollope privately admitted he identified.[38] With a self-conscious but earnest hobbyhorse obsession that the narrator seems to enjoy as much as the character, Bagwax – whose name compounds the postal repository for envelopes with a substance that can seal them – tracks down other Sydney postmarks from around the same time as the one on the Caldigate letter in order to compare them.[39] He assembles an impressive collection, but as he ruefully recognises, it's always possible that another postmark stamp had even briefly been pressed into use in Sydney in May 1873. At this point, several years later, no number of specimen envelopes can ever prove that this variantology of postal media is complete.

But at last Bagwax realises that he has been looking at the wrong kind of stamp altogether. As Trollope's narrator explains with admirable technical clarity, 'In post-office phraseology there is sometimes a confusion because the affixed effigy of her Majesty's head, which represents the postage paid, is called a stamp, and the post-marks or impressions indicating the names of towns are also called stamps.'[40] Bagwax's breakthrough comes when he focuses on not the postmark but the postage stamp, discovering that the tiny letters in its corners mean that it belongs to a series of stamps only printed after the May 1873 postmark on the envelope. Manufactured in England in 1874 or later, the postage stamp would have been further slowed by its physical transit to Australia (in real life, many stamps for the Australian colonies were printed in London).[41] Courtesy of Bagwax's high-resolution photographs and a magnifying glass, here is material media research with a vengeance, philately's own search for variants. The 'two P's in the two bottom corners' of the 'twopenny queen's-head . . . on the corner of the envelope' represent not phonemes in a human language but the coded identifier for a set of media objects.[42] Hidden in a queen's head identical to all others, the code amounts to a paratext within a paratext, metadata whose connection to the material manufacture of the stamp belies the deliberately misleading postal metadata imprinted on the envelope.

In a moment of playfulness or sexual enticement, John addressed an envelope to a woman who did not exist – at least not yet. The writing is his; the postage stamp is genuine; the cancellation stamp is real, although it must have had its date illegally set back by a confederate in the Sydney post office. The conspirators mimicked the 'unintelligible hieroglyphics' deposited during postal transmission with a postage stamp that was made too late and a backdated postmark, forging not a signature or a document but the traces of a passage through a media system.[43] Little should have hinged on whether the envelope actually made that passage, but the conspirators must have assumed, correctly, that its marks would help validate the name on the envelope as more than idle castle-building: 'a letter sent regularly by the post, – that would be real evidence'. As Curlydown somewhat hyperbolically puts it, 'Nothing has ever been considered better evidence than post-marks.'[44] With a twopenny Australian stamp and a Sydney postmark belatedly affixed, the envelope was actually intended to make a unique passage into the English legal system, not a routine passage through the colonial postal system at all.

Now the difference between a made-up name and a mocked-up postmark becomes the difference between mimesis and forgery, between fiction and fraud. The discovery of the deception by Euphemia Smith and company leads to no sudden release and exoneration for John Caldigate; rather, the narrative continues in Trollopian fashion to trace out the workings of institutions via the actions of particular agents who come with their own dispositions and characterological quirks. Again Trollopian mimesis imagines the way individual variants help map the functioning of the system. But after a sufficient delay and an imperfect resolution John Caldigate will go free and the conspirators will find themselves on trial for perjury.

From the technical details of a medium to its relationship to media systems that range from the post office to forensic photography: *John Caldigate*, like Samuel Bagwax, evinces a certain 'delight [in] showing how important to the world was a proper understanding of post-office details'.[45] The novel also helps suggest some of the possibilities for linking media archaeology to imaginative literature – and not just because Bagwax might qualify as a fictional media archaeologist *avant la lettre*. Differences between physical media orient them in media systems – and help us excavate the mediated imagination of Anthony Trollope and of nineteenth-century fiction.

Notes

1. R. H. Super, *Trollope at the Post Office* (Ann Arbor: University of Michigan Press, 1981), p. 87.
2. Henry James, 'Anthony Trollope', in *Partial Portraits* (London: Macmillan, 1888), p. 122; see David Pearson, '"The Letter Killeth": Epistolary Purposes and Techniques in *Sir Harry Hotspur of Humblethwaite*', *Nineteenth-Century Fiction*, 37 (1982): pp. 396–418, and Ellen Moody, 'Partly Told in Letters', *Trollopiana*, 48 (2000): pp. 4–31.
3. James, 'Anthony Trollope', p. 122.
4. See Coral Lansbury, *The Reasonable Man: Trollope's Legal Fiction* (Princeton: Princeton University Press, 1981).
5. See Richard Menke, *Telegraphic Realism: Victorian Fiction and Other Information Systems* (Stanford: Stanford University Press, 2008), pp. 54–66, pp. 181–7; Anthony Trollope, *An Autobiography*, ed. Michael Sadleir and Frederick Page (Oxford: Oxford University Press, 1989), ch. 12, p. 227.
6. Jean Farrugia, *The Letter Box: A History of Post Office Pillar and Wall Boxes* (Fontwell: Centaur, 1969), pp. 25–6, pp. 29–32, pp. 120–2; Super, *Trollope at the Post Office*, pp. 26–8.
7. For an analysis of this mediation in authors from Charles Dickens, George Eliot and Trollope to Henry James and Rudyard Kipling, see Menke, *Telegraphic Realism*.
8. Jussi Parikka offers a useful and wide-ranging introduction to the subject in *What Is Media Archaeology?* (Cambridge: Polity, 2012).
9. Rowland Hill, *Post Office Reform: Its Importance and Practicability* [1837], in Gavin Fryer and Clive Akerman (eds), *The Reform of the Post Office in the Victorian Era and Its Impact on Social and Economic Activity* (London: Royal Philatelic Society, 2000), vol. 1, p. 20.
10. Rowland Hill and George Birkbeck Hill, *The Life of Sir Rowland Hill and the History of the Penny Postage*, 2 vols (London: De La Rue), vol. 1, p. 395.
11. Wolfgang Ernst, *Digital Memory and the Archive*, ed. Jussi Parikka (Minneapolis: University of Minnesota Press), p. 25, p. 113.

12. Andrew Burkett has recently provided a worthy assay into the conjunction of British literature and media archaeology. He examines how the creative work of Blake, Byron, Keats and Mary Shelley not only anticipates future technical media but also lives on in them. *Romantic Mediations: Media Theory and British Romanticism* (Albany: State University of New York Press, 2016).

13. Siegfried Zielinski, *Deep Time of the Media: Toward an Archaeology of Hearing and Seeing by Technical Means*, trans. Gloria Custance (Cambridge, MA: MIT Press, 2006), p. 3, p. 7.

14. Trollope, *Autobiography*, ch. 10, p. 176, p. 177.

15. E. Cobham Brewer, *Dictionary of Phrase and Fable* (London: Cassell, 1900), p. 1154.

16. Trollope, *Autobiography*, ch. 7, p. 118, p. 119.

17. Ibid. ch. 15, p. 272.

18. Walter M. Kendrick, *The Novel-Machine: The Theory and Fiction of Anthony Trollope* (Baltimore: Johns Hopkins University Press, 1980), p. 33. Reading the *Autobiography* as a theory about the production of realistic writing, Kendrick confirms the promise of a technical approach to Trollope.

19. Anthony Trollope, *John Caldigate*, ed. N. John Hall (Oxford: Oxford University Press, 1993), ch. 42, p. 399.

20. Ibid. ch. 24, p. 225.

21. Alexander Welsh, *George Eliot and Blackmail* (Cambridge, MA: Harvard University Press, 1985), p. 33.

22. Ibid. p. 44.

23. Trollope, *John Caldigate*, ch. 1, p. 6.

24. Ibid. ch. 30, p. 280.

25. On the significance of paratexts in the context of literature and publishing, see Gérard Genette, *Paratexts: Thresholds of Interpretation*, trans. Jane E. Lewin (Cambridge: Cambridge University Press, 1997).

26. Emma Griffiths, 'Data retention laws: Tony Abbott says Government "seeking metadata", not targeting people's browsing history', *Australian Broadcasting Corporation News Online* (6 August 2014). Available at <http://www.abc.net.au/news/2014–08–06/security-laws-abbott-browsing-history-not-collected/5652364> (last accessed 23 November 2016).

27. Trollope, *John Caldigate*, ch. 30, pp. 280–1.

28. Ibid. ch. 42, pp. 401–2.

29. Anthony Trollope, Australia and New Zealand, 3 vols (Leipzig: Tauchnitz, 1987), vol. 3, p. 86.

30. Trollope, *John Caldigate*, ch. 47, p. 454.

31. Ibid. ch. 24, p. 221, p. 223.

32. See Walter Benjamin, 'The Work of Art in the Age of Its Technological Reproducibility: Second Version' [1935], in Michael W. Jennings, Brigid Doherty and Thomas Y. Levin (eds), *The Work of Art in the Age of Its Technological Reproducibility, and Other Writings on Media*, trans. Edmund Jephcott et al. (Cambridge, MA: Belknap-Harvard University Press, 2008), pp. 22–4.

33. Trollope, *John Caldigate*, ch. 24, p. 221, p. 223.

34. Matthew G. Kirschenbaum, *Mechanisms: New Media and the Forensic Imagination* (Cambridge, MA: MIT Press, 2008), p. 250.

35. A. Conan Doyle, 'A Case of Identity', *The Strand Magazine*, 2 (September 1891): pp. 248–59.

36. On postal professionalism in *John Caldigate* and the *Autobiography*, see Laura Rotunno, *Postal Plots in British Fiction, 1840–1898: Readdressing Correspondence in Victorian Culture* (Basingstoke: Palgrave Macmillan, 2013), pp. 94–118.

37. Trollope, *John Caldigate*, ch. 42, p. 402.

38. Kate Thomas, *Postal Pleasures: Sex, Scandal, and Victorian Letters* (Oxford: Oxford University Press, 2012), p. 84.

39. Bagwax, or Trollope, is ahead of his time. By one account, during the 1860s there were 'only two active devotees' in Britain who collected postmarks. R. K. Forster, *The Postmark on a Letter* (London: Chambers, 1952), p. 58.

40. Trollope, *John Caldigate*, ch. 52, p. 498.

41. See T. Todd, *Stamps of the Empire* (London: Thomas Nelson, 1938), pp. 81–4; *The Postage Stamps, Envelopes, and Post Cards of Australia and the British Colonies of Oceania* (London: Philatelic Society, 1887), p. 68.

42. Trollope, *John Caldigate*, ch. 52, p. 501, p. 498.

43. Ibid, ch. 47, p. 452.

44. Ibid. ch. 52, p. 503.

45. Ibid. ch. 47, p. 450.

16

Trollope's Living Media: Fox Hunts and Marriage Plots

Tamara Ketabgian

Trollope was at best a middling fox hunter; but what he lacked in skill he made up for in determination. 'Nothing has ever been allowed to stand in the way of hunting', he reflects in his *Autobiography* (1883), 'neither the writing of books, nor the work of the Post Office, nor other pleasures.'[1] While we may question whether Trollope's art imitated his life or his life his art, this sport pervades the logic and structure of his fiction. As Trollope concedes, 'I have dragged it into many novels – into too many, no doubt – but I have always felt myself deprived of a legitimate joy when the nature of the tale has not allowed me a hunting chapter.'[2] Critics have often dismissed such hunting chapters, viewing them either as mere action sequences or as traditional fantasies of harmonious class hierarchy. This essay, however, explores Trollope's sport from a different perspective, as a form of living media and 'mediation' – a dynamic ecology of 'organic and inorganic entities', as theorist Richard Grusin defines the term.[3]

Modern media and technology pervade Trollope's fiction; his readers and characters live, move and feel through the postal service, the telegraph, the railway and the steamship. The hunt, I argue, joins these systems as yet another site of technical and emotional mediation. This chapter explores the shifting social, narrative and ecological contours of fox-hunting for Trollope – as a strategic game, a system of conduct and a technology of both character and local resource management. Indeed, in *The Eustace Diamonds* (1871–3), *The American Senator* (1876–7) and Trollope's earlier *Hunting Sketches* (1865), the hunt reveals character *as* a mode of resource management, while supporting hybrid connections also familiar to us from social theory today. Portrayed both affectionately and ambivalently by Trollope, this sport emerges as a complex network of human and non-human actors, engaged in fluid, geographically rooted relations of status, influence and agency.

For Trollope, fox-hunting is a probabilistic social event, involving the adjustment of one's pace, place and resources to the likely actions of hounds, foxes, horses, huntsman, assistants, other riders, equipment, climate and terrain. His novels and essays analyse the struggle for privilege and proximity in the field (a place at 'the kill'), and the allied role of contingency, influence and risk management. Trollope advises a deliberate system of the long game, of constancy and restraint as a practice of character – whether in life, love, hunting or literary competition. These practices deeply mark the social networks of his fiction, which critic R. H. Hutton has likened to 'the moral "hooks and eyes" of life' – to 'the hold [people] get or fail to get over other characters, and . . . the hold they yield to other characters over them'.[4] Through Lizzie Eustace and Arabella Trefoil, the ambitious single females of *The Eustace Diamonds* and *The American Senator*, Trollope tests the limits of this pursuit, as it ramifies amid webs of influence in the marriage plot, the true realm of Trollopian blood sport. Treating agency as a complexly mediated force, these two novels view 'the theory and system of fox-hunting' as an enduring principle of human conduct and character – among animals, objects and relations that sometimes bite back.[5]

Marriage, Mediation and Blood Sport

As an 'invented tradition', mid-Victorian fox-hunting evolved from a local pastime of rural gentry and farmers into a more urban, middle-class pursuit, transformed by railway commuting, paying subscribers, intensive agriculture, exhaustive breeding, sporting journalism, and new standards of speed and agility.[6] Trollope himself was a steadfast subscription-hunter, travelling by rail from London to meets in Essex for many years.[7] In his essays for *The Pall Mall Gazette* and *Saint Pauls Magazine,* reprinted in *Hunting Sketches* and in *British Sports and Pastimes* (1868), Trollope recognises changes to the sport, but he still idealises its conservative pastoral values, staunchly defending the hunt against charges of elitism and animal cruelty. Responding to Robert Freeman, who stresses the fox's 'deadly fright' and 'physical suffering'[8] in an 1869 essay for the *Fortnightly Review*, Trollope praises the hunt's greater social value, as an egalitarian field where men of varied ranks may test their gentlemanly 'ambition, courage, and persistency'.[9] For Trollope, this pursuit captures communal English identity at its rural core, creating 'a feeling of out-of-door equality' among landowners and tenants that permeates 'all the relations of country life', and is noticeably absent 'between man and man in cities'.[10] As critics Robert Hughes and Jackson Trotter note, hunting serves a similar function in Trollope's fiction, as 'a metaphor for social harmony',[11] an image of 'society in microcosm',[12] and an expression of 'Trollope's belief in a traditional, and increasingly threatened, social hierarchy' of 'gentlemen'.[13]

Trollope was irresistibly drawn to the hunt as a fantasy of conservative social order and community, but this sport also gains a more conflicted emotional meaning for him in his literary and personal accounts. In his *Autobiography*, he admits that – for himself, at least – the hunt's appeal resists all rational inquiry: 'The cause of my delight in the amusement I have never been able to analyse to my own satisfaction.'[14] As Coral Lansbury has compellingly shown, Trollope's love of the hunt is rooted in a deep sense of ambivalence – in divided impulses of sympathy and distance toward the fox, its pursuit by hounds and the surrounding theatre of violent blood sport. According to Lansbury,

> The rules of the hunt fulfilled the part of his nature which responded to discipline, and the cruelty of the exhausted fox finally torn apart by the hounds . . . was not only permissible, it was socially approved. Nevertheless, Trollope had an instinctive sympathy for the fox, and as he cried halloo with the best of them, he could still find pity for 'the poor beast'. The raucous clamor of the hunt made him forget the disgrace of his school days, the misery of being an object of derision for a pack of bloody-minded little boys at Harrow.[15]

It is hard to resist a Freudian gloss on this sporting passion: through the hunt's 'authoritarian'[16] rules and practices, Trollope seeks to repeat, re-stage and transform his schoolboy trauma, as well as the discipline and restraint of his later work at the Post Office.

Yet, beyond expressing Trollope's ambivalence toward power, the hunt also offers him a different outlook – an intensely visceral and technically mediated way of imagining the navigation of institutional privilege. For Trollope, these elaborate networks of influence include not only schools but also clubs, the civil service and publishing.[17] Like these traditional British institutions, fox-hunting would seem to rely upon a static and intricately prescriptive code of conduct, consisting of detailed ritual, specialised jargon and highly mediated local hierarchies and relations. In Trollope's own portraits, however, the hunt is hardly so static and orderly. Certainly the sport is premised upon a number of dominance hierarchies: among dogs of the pack, among horses, among humans and domestic animals, and among the 'field', whose mounted human participants are subject to the commands both of the huntsman (who leads and supervises the hunt) and the master of fox hounds (who sponsors and maintains the pack). In theory, the hounds of the pack are the agents and servants of their human masters; these hounds are followed and urged on by riders who have trained them to chase, 'break down' and eat foxes in areas maintained to deny any shelter. But, in practice, these relations are by no means consistently obedient or deferential. Trollope's hunting scenes instead explore dynamic and unpredictable linkages, in which non-human entities – or 'actants', to invoke theorist Bruno Latour's term – occasionally push back.[18] Here, dogs, horses, foxes, climate and terrain all interact in fluid assemblages that challenge unitary accounts of human causality, thus demonstrating 'the ability of each actor to *make* other actors *do* unexpected things'.[19] Or, more briefly, humans may claim to 'go hunting', but, in truth, their actions are more complexly mediated: to hunt, they must be mounted on horses that follow dogs that, in turn, follow the scent that may lead them to a fox. Like Grusin's account of 'radical mediation', Trollope's hunt is a process where 'all bodies (whether human or non-human) are fundamentally media and life itself is a form of mediation'.[20]

In the hunting scenes of *The Eustace Diamonds* and *The American Senator*, Trollope acknowledges the dynamic action and influence of non-human things – what Latour terms the 'many metaphysical shades between full causality and sheer inexistence' in actor-network theory.[21] Both novels are punctuated by risky chases, during which unexpected human injuries, upsets and even fatalities occur. Complementing plots of romantic pursuit and reversal, these scenes pivot upon the changeable behaviour of their non-human actants: rivers swell; ground erodes; horses kick and balk; dogs lose scent and run riot; and foxes hide, change direction, disguise scent and swim rather than run. These variables all form part of the media of the hunting 'field' and terrain, showing how its forms of being shape its different ways of knowing.

In *The Eustace Diamonds,* the fox's movements and choices crucially drive the novel's Scottish chase scenes. As we learn from Lord George de Bruce Carruthers, Lizzie Eustace's potential suitor and informal hunting coach, 'a fox doesn't always choose to be evicted at the first notice. It's a chance whether he goes at all from a wood like this.'[22] In the novel's first anticlimactic hunt,[23] where the fox is prematurely 'chopped' by hounds, Lizzie simply dismisses it as a 'stupid beast': 'Why didn't he run away?' (*ED*, ch. 37, p. 379). At the same time, she also mistakes the hounds' actions as transparently those of their human masters: 'Who killed [the fox]? That man that was blowing the horn?' (*ED*, ch. 37, p. 379). Unlike Lizzie, however, Lord George

approaches the fox more analytically and probabilistically, viewing its most fleeting acts as strategic choices and openings. At Lizzie's next meet at Craigattan Gorse,
Trollope's narrator combines these two attitudes, recounting how the 'stupid fox'
crosses a river and, once upstream, goes 'back across' in a circle that ends with 'a little
spurt, . . . back toward his own home' (*ED*, ch. 38, p. 394). Dialogically blending the
voices of Lizzie, Lord George and others members of the hunt, the narrator's tone is
notably uneven: attentive, admiring, but also dismissive toward the fox's apparently
unaccountable choices, as acts central to the interest of the chase and its corresponding narrative.

Aside from the fox, Trollope's hunt scenes explore the highly charged mediation
between horse and rider. In *The Eustace Diamonds* and *The American Senator*, Trollope challenges the view that riders drive horses as passive vehicles, and instead treats
the two as a collective assemblage essential to success on the field. As many period
hunting manuals advise, horse and rider must establish a 'firm and lasting' 'partnership' and approach fences '*together* and not *separately*'.[24] For Trollope, certainly, this
unpredictable relation creates much of the suspense of the chase. At Craigattan Gorse,
for instance, Lizzie's houseguest Lucinda Roanoke roughly whips and pushes on
her horse when it follows the cues of earlier steeds and refuses to jump before a wall
(*ED*, ch. 38, p. 390). While this act arguably sets the stage for Lucinda's later fall,
Lizzie and her horse Dandy are more fortunate. They successfully negotiate several
difficult jumps, including one across a wide brook:

> To Lizzie it seemed as though the river were the blackest, and the deepest, and
> the broadest that ever ran. For a moment her heart quailed, but it was but for a
> moment. She shut her eyes, and gave the little horse his head. For a moment she
> thought that she was in the water. Her horse was almost upright on the bank,
> with his hind-feet down among the broken ground, and she was clinging to his
> neck. But she was light, and the beast made good his footing, and then she knew
> that she had done it . . . When she looked round, Lord George was already by her
> side. 'You hardly gave him powder enough', he said, 'but still he did it beautifully'.
> (*ED*, ch. 38, p. 393)

Here Trollope stresses the fluidity of the jumping subject. First, Lizzie knows '*she* had
done it', but then Lord George notes that '*he*' – the horse – was the actor and 'did it
beautifully'. Finally, Lord George's metaphor of 'powder' treats Dandy as a ballistic
projectile controlled by a human subject. In truth, both rider and horse move together
in potentially explosive tactile contact, their agency further mediated by the dynamic
terrain – the swollen river and its steep, broken bank. Or, to invoke Grusin again, we
may interpret Lizzie and Dandy's resulting partnership as a dynamic living form of
mediation, 'generat[ing] . . . affective moods or structures of feeling among assemblages of humans and nonhumans'.[25]

While Trollope celebrates successful riding as a feat of human and non-human
mediation, he paints a failed and more troubling relation in *The American Senator*,
in Major Caneback's attempt to discipline the spirited mare Jemima. Lent to Caneback during a hunt sponsored by Lord Rufford, the mare is unruly from the start
– 'kick[ing] and squeal[ing] and back[ing]' (*AS*, ch. 22, p. 147) – and the Major himself is equally stubborn, repeatedly returning to scale gates at which Jemima balks.

The Major insists that he will 'break' her and '[h]ave her like a spaniel before the day's over' (*AS*, ch. 22, p. 148). Declining to switch horses even after several hours of mercilessly brutal riding, Caneback eventually approaches a rail with a 'ha ha' ditch. Here, as Lord Rufford predicts, horse, terrain and human obstinacy all lead to Caneback's eventual fatal end: to a fall and terrible accident, as the mare 'blunder[s] out, roll[s] over him, jump[s] on to her feet, and lunging out kick[s] her rider on the head as he [is] rising' (*AS*, ch. 33, p. 151). *The American Senator* largely relays Caneback's misfortune through the opportunistic viewpoint of Arabella Trefoil, a poor aristocrat who feigns hunting zeal in order to pursue the eligible bachelor Lord Rufford. Arabella is perfectly willing to use all contingencies – including the Major's fatal accident – to attract her prey, even while she is engaged to another man. Still, as the novel proceeds, the Major's death resonates powerfully and unexpectedly with her. She dwells repeatedly on 'the sound of that horse's foot as it struck the skull of the unfortunate fallen rider' (*AS*, ch. 55, p. 378). In a work suffused by hunting imagery and debate (including that of the eponymous 'American Senator', who argues against fox-hunting as an irrational feudal tradition), Jemima's fatal kick speaks to the messy realities of the sport and its living media.

Is it any coincidence that Caneback's horse is a mare – and that (as his name suggests) he seeks so determinedly 'to break either [her] neck or her spirit' (*AS*, ch. 22, p. 150)? Certainly, as a female who is disciplined, pursued and may still lash out, Jemima casts an uneasy light on both the feminised beasts of the hunt and related fields of imagery: Trollope's frequently shifting metaphors not only of women as predators and prey but also of romantic pursuit as hunting and husbandry.[26] Thus linked and defamiliarised, Trollope's scenes of fox- and husband-hunting together expose agency as a fluid force, exerted through the pressure of non-human objects and creatures.

In *The Eustace Diamonds* and *American Senator*, Trollope portrays his single female characters with a variety of hunting metaphors and subject positions. Arabella Trefoil primarily resembles a human or canine hunter, whose tireless pursuit of wealthy aristocratic husbands is 'the game for which she live[s]' (*AS*, ch. 75, p. 518). Both she and Lord Rufford recognise their respective positions in this romantic sport: Arabella 'hunt[s] him as a fox is hunted' (*AS*, ch. 49, p. 336), and, as Rufford later reflects, this pursuit '[is] a matter of course' (*AS*, ch. 67, p. 464). Arabella even likens Rufford not only to a fox but also to a landscape obstacle – 'a sort of five-barred gate' (*AS*, ch. 37, p. 252) – that she will attempt to vault as a horse. Robert Tracy stresses this sustained metaphor of the sport as a 'great husband hunt',[27] with all of its attendant challenges. For Arabella, man is 'a heartless, cruel, slippery animal, made indeed to be caught occasionally, but in the catching of which infinite skill was wanted, and in which infinite skill might be thrown away' (*AS*, ch. 75, p. 517). Yet, in *The American Senator*, Arabella also shifts from hunter to hunted: the lack of a suitable home leads her to a nomadic life of social visits, where she has 'as many holes to run to afterwards as a four-year-old fox – though with the same probability of finding them stopped' (*AS*, ch. 20, p. 133). While Arabella's role as a fox highlights her efforts at flight, shelter and concealment, Lizzie Eustace resembles a wilder and more aggressive sort of prey – or pet – that continually threatens to turn predator. As Lucy Morris tells Lizzie's cousin Frank Greystock, 'she looks like a beautiful animal that you are afraid to caress for fear it should bite you; – an animal that would be beautiful if its eyes were not so restless, and its teeth so sharp and so white' (*ED*, ch. 12,

p. 147). With her sharp teeth and 'almost snake-like' (*ED*, ch. 2, p. 54) movements, Lady Eustace brings to mind a fox, a weasel or 'something not quite so tame as a cat' (*ED*, ch. 12, p. 147). Only later, after both her friends and the greater social world discover her lies, does Trollope no longer compare Lizzie to a clever, beautiful fox but to a wounded, hunted bird, 'terribly mauled by the fowlers' (*ED*, ch. 79, p. 758) and incapable of public flight.

Trollope treats romantic prey most vividly, however, in Lucinda Roanoke, whose turbulent engagement to Sir Griffin Tewett supports uneasy metaphors of non-human mediation and exploitation. From the start, Sir Griffin approaches Lucinda as a difficult and desirable object, whom he aims to possess through forms of violent mastery and pursuit perfected through the chase. He is a man 'in whose love a good deal of hatred is mixed; – who loves as the huntsman loves the fox, towards the killing of which he intends to use all his energies and intellects' (*ED*, ch. 41, p. 410). In fact, like her suitor, Lucinda is also a spirited hunter who likes her own way and resists being 'driven without showing something of an intractable spirit in harness' (*ED*, ch. 41, p. 414). However, with no fortune, pressure from her aunt and the bearish Griffin as her only marital option, she steels herself to accept him. As Lucinda seals the bargain with a kiss, Trollope captures her powerful revulsion with another familiar sporting metaphor: 'She would sooner have leaped at the blackest, darkest, dirtiest river in the county. "There", she said, "that will do", gently extricating herself from his arms' (*ED*, ch. 42, p. 421). Evoking Lizzie's earlier jump – and Lucinda's own fall – over the river at Craigattan Gorse, this conditional leap is not equivalent but rather preferable to any relation with her fiancé. It is followed, moreover, by Lucinda's own figurative shift from hunter to quarry. Anticipating the burdens of marriage, she resolves 'to go on and bear it all', and 'by study and due practice [to] . . . become, – as were some others, – a beast of prey, and nothing more' (*ED*, ch. 42, p. 422). Yet, becoming a 'beast of prey' is still a fraught task, and Lucinda – like the mare Jemima – also exercises the option to push and kick back. Ultimately, she refuses to behave as a kept beast by falling into madness on her wedding day. With this act, Lucinda arguably rivals the behaviour of Trollope's 'stupid foxes', unaccountable dogs and horses that balk and rear at their appointed tasks: by simply refusing to go forward, she throws off the careful stratagems and manipulations of her aunt and other interested parties. Through Lucinda, *The Eustace Diamonds* exposes the vexed texture of agency, in the shifting, non-human connections that mediate both her marriage plot and its alternate form in blood sport.

Hunting and Trollope's Middle Way

While Trollope's hunting scenes may suggest the fluidity of actor-network theory, these narratives of mediation are – unlike Latour's theory – also fixed in important ways. Much as the traditional goal of the hunt is killing the fox, so do we usually know *where* Trollope's marriage plots will end – or at least will likely end, based on a short menu of options. What matters instead for Trollope is not where but *how* plots will unfold along the way – which paths are taken and choices pursued, and in what manner, tempo and mode. In Trollope's hunting essays and fiction, these questions of character and conduct prevail before all other considerations. As both a sporting practice and a metaphor for social and romantic pursuit, the hunt thus provides Trollope with a highly technical system of behaviour, which emphasises judgement, restraint and attention to contingency.

In *Hunting Sketches* and *British Sports and Pastimes*, Trollope offers a clear overview of hunting as a strategic game, rooted in social conduct, probabilistic calculation, non-human mediation and ecological resource management. The sport's explicit aim is death, but, as Trollope stresses, the intervening chase must allow for challenge, variety and diversion – across time, space and a variety of moving parts:

> The cream of fox-hunting certainly consists in a quick run from a small covert. It should be straight, over a grass country strongly fenced, with a scent that shall enable the hounds to work on without assistance from the huntsman, in which the fox shall seek protection in no large wood, and which shall be brought to a finish by 'a kill' in the open before the horses are tired, and with no necessity for cold-hunting [hunting without a 'warm' scent] at the close. (*BSP*, p. 106)

In its ideal form, fox-hunting requires riders to start at a correct 'time and pace' (*BSP*, p. 106), to maintain an appropriate position behind the hounds, to economise the power of one's horse, to respond properly to obstacles and, finally, not just to see the kill, but to see it 'in the open' and at the right location. '[F]or those who have lived and kept their place through the heat and turmoil of the chase', Trollope stresses, seeing the kill is an exclusive distinction: '[t]hey see it, and none others do see it' (*BSP*, pp. 111–12). Yet, other pleasures exist in the hunt beyond the ritual closure of the kill. By the 1820s, the hunt increasingly stressed horsemanship and hard riding, spurring debate between those who favoured hunting to ride or riding to hunt, who privileged either the play of horses or of hounds. This conflict grants the hunt two alternate narrative satisfactions, both of which we encounter in Trollope's fiction: the final, teleological closure of the kill and the punctuated suspense of jumps and gallops in the middle.

While Trollope is drawn to the hunt's narrative pleasures, he also stresses the deeply technical aspects of the practice – the breeding of fast horses, of hounds endowed with speed and nose, of foxes preserved for sport, and of landscapes cultivated for a strategic balance of openness and cover. His essays explicitly define the sport as a science of transforming instinct, premised on human interference and design. For, as Trollope notes, inspiring a fox to run – and dogs to scent and pursue it – is a decidedly artificial task. 'Few men', he remarks, 'are aware how much of science and how much of other outward circumstances is [*sic*] added to the instinct of the dog in the ordinary hunting of the present day' (*BSP*, p. 81). Trollope is undoubtedly influenced by the 'Meynellian system' or 'Science', pioneered by Dr Hugo Meynell of Quorn (1753–1800), a breeder of hounds who transformed the hunt by emphasising scent and sound over sight. In *The Eustace Diamonds*, Lord George pointedly invokes Meynell in his account of 'the theory and system of fox-hunting' (*ED*, ch. 37, p. 378). Offering a detailed lesson to Lizzie, he

> explained the meaning of scent, was great on the difficulty of getting away, described the iniquity of heading the fox, [turning the fox back the way it came] spoke of up wind and down wind, got as far as the trouble of 'carrying', and told her that a

good ear was everything in a big wood, – when there came upon them the thrice-repeated note of an old hound's voice, and the quick scampering, and low, timid, anxious, trustful whinnying of a dozen comrade younger hounds, who recognised the sagacity of their well-known and highly-appreciated elder, – 'That's a fox', said Lord George. (*ED*, ch. 37, p. 379)

As he shows in his attention to the scent, sound and hierarchy of the pack, George is keenly attuned to the hunt's interdependent system of animals and information. He recognises that participants often must hunt by other senses and through non-human assistance. Trollope embraces this immersion into the living media of the chase; for him, 'the acme of bliss' is 'a hot scent carried breast-high by fleet hounds' (*BSP*, p. 82, p. 81).

The support of the hunt's various hounds, horses and foxes is, of course, insepa-rable from the management of its greater landscape. In the agricultural countryside of Trollope's mid-Victorian contemporaries, lords and tenant farmers typically cooper-ated to maintain the land of the hunt – whether by preserving hedgerows, by building artificial fox earths (to support their populations), by filling holes where foxes might hide, by removing wire fences (that might damage leaping horses), or by promoting fair compensation for damages (for trampled crops or poultry killed by foxes).[28] With the exception of Goarly, a disgruntled tenant who poisons a fox to protest against the chase in *The American Senator*, Trollope's fiction provides a largely idealised vision of this sport's local community, despite its transformation by railway-travelling subscrip-tion hunters and urban social pressures.

Fox-hunting supported a modern ecology of speed and shelter. As historian Donna Landry notes, the popularity of the chase encouraged ecological conservation among sporting landlords, who, beginning in the late eighteenth century, cultivated a new landscape of cover for foxes, consisting of hedges, ditches, gorse patches and shel-ter belts.[29] These conservation efforts accompanied the parliamentary Enclosure Acts, which effected a massive drainage of land and planting of hedges in the agricultural Midland shires of the South and East – what would become the new popular hunt districts. According to Raymond Carr, these transformed landscapes marked the 'end of the old-style hunting over open country where hounds could be seen at work'[30] and the growth of new faster racing and leaping. Carefully bred by Meynell and his follow-ers, these fast hounds in turn produced 'faster, straight-running foxes' in a 'technical revolution' of pace that found its match in hard riding.[31]

With its many variables – its fast terrain and animals, its limited visibility, its hard riding, its complex history and its feast for the senses – the chase is nothing if not over-whelming. To master these stimuli, Trollope advises following a consistent 'system' while hunting. He defines enjoyment of the sport as premised upon a steady pursuit of the long game. Indeed, he stresses, 'the men who don't like [hunting], have no system, and never know distinctly what is their own aim.'[32] Instead of praising hard riding and being first, Trollope upholds a figure of systematic restraint: 'The Man Who Hunts and Never Jumps'. This person 'must always remember his resolve, and be true to the conduct which he has laid down for himself' (*HS*, p. 60). Renouncing the ambitious gamble of jumping and possibly becoming trapped, this man prevails through self-control and a greater informatic grasp of the hunt's terrain, animals, equipment and social conduct. 'No one', Trollope remarks, 'knows the line they have all ridden as well as he knows it' (*HS*, p. 68).

For his own output in the literary market, Trollope repeatedly advocated careful, regular control and pacing.[33] Yet, as he suggests, even if riders *do* plan to jump, the wise course is the middle way. They should seek not to follow immediately behind the hounds and risk them losing their scent, but rather retire and 'giv[e] place to those eager men who are breaking the huntsman's heart . . . Not behind hounds but along-side with them, – if only you can achieve such position, – should be your honour' (*HS*, p. 114). As Trollope here shows, he is deeply concerned with the role of place, as a crucial site of influence, privilege and proximity, whether in the hunt or in other competitive fields and institutions. He advises the long view – restraint and economy – because these strategies will still allow an eventual position close enough to the action. The judicious horseman must foresee the probable actions of populations (human and non-human) and then map them onto a greater, systemic vision of country and terrain. Guided by 'the leading hounds' and their 'turning' (*HS*, p. 113), his status is fluid and relational: what matters is not who he is, but where he is, and in relation to whom. Keenly conscious of the rider's links to other groups and individuals, to the pack, and to the chase's non-human actants, Trollope treats the sport as a powerful statistical model for realising influence through mediation.

Trollope recognises the ambitious seductions of being first in the hunt. *The Eustace Diamonds* celebrates Frank and Lizzie's 'success' at Craigattan Gorse. Mounted on another man's particularly fine mare, which he acquires through a mixture of chance and easy humour, Frank rides at the head of the field. He, Lizzie and Lord George all realise the distinction of a place 'at the kill' – an experience with 'just enough to give something of selectness to the few who saw the fox fall, – and then he fell' (*ED*, ch. 38, p. 394). Trollope acknowledges the especially comparative pleasure of this position, where '[t]o shake your friends off and get away from them, will soon come to be your keenest delight in hunting. To be there, in the proper place alongside of the hounds, is very sweet; but to know that others are not there is sweeter' (*BSP*, p. 108). Yet, Trollope argues, it is foolhardy to define an honourable place as consistently first. He notes that the man 'who rides foremost in most runs is generally where he ought not to be' (*HS*, p. 100). These over-striving riders not only open themselves up to risk; they also lack a sense of the broader view. Through this ambitious self-seeking, Trollope claims, 'we are overdoing our Sports' (*BSP*, p. 5).

In *British Sports and Pastimes*, Trollope suggests that the true pleasures of hunting are not about keeping score or reductive outward display, but about unquantifiable experience, through which one realises and expresses character. Unlike other popular sports such as cricket, Trollope notes, 'there is no scoring of runs in hunting, no count-ing up of achievement; – and it is not the foremost rider who is the best sportsman' (*BSP*, p. 99). Instead, the true triumphs of hunting 'can hardly be weighed and mea-sured, and should ever be treasured deep in the silent bosom, – without a word, with-out a sign, on the part of him who has earned them' (*BSP*, p. 100). Beyond language or representation, these triumphs are a silent mark of distinction among those who do *not* finish in front, but conduct themselves with honour and poise within the field. For Trollope, genuine success requires understanding the hunt as a living and ultimately incalculable form of media.

Hunting, Cleverness and Keeping Score

Through Lizzie Eustace and Arabella Trefoil, Trollope explores the flip side of his 'theory and system' (*ED*, ch. 37, p. 378) of hunting and human conduct. Unlike 'The Man Who Hunts and Never Jumps', both women are swayed by excessively competitive scorekeeping, whether in the chase or in the ambitious pursuit of life's privileges. For these characters, the hunt serves as both a metaphor and medium for navigating hubs of power and influence. It is a practice of statistical risk, play and rivalry – a network, in the classic sense of a '*competitive* system . . . in which nodes fight fiercely for links'.[34] Lizzie and Arabella thus hunt to gain social capital – and husbands – in a competitive race for primacy through relations of kinship and affiliation.

In *The American Senator*, Arabella largely confines her risk-taking to the pursuit of metaphorical quarry. During her campaign to attract and marry Lord Rufford, she concedes her 'long odds' (*AS*, ch. 25, p. 166), and – in pointed contrast to Trollope's *via media* – follows an all-or-nothing strategy. 'I can hardly expect to win', she reflects to herself, 'but if I do pull it off I'm made for ever!' (*AS*, ch. 25, p. 166). The narrative at first appears to take Arabella's part, suggesting that despite her daunting task, '[i]t was quite possible that she might be able to dig such a pit for [Lord Rufford] that it would be easier for him to marry her than to get out in any other way' (*AS*, ch. 31, p. 208). Yet, risky and foolhardy, Arabella not only fails in her hunt of Rufford; she also loses her prior engagement to John Morton, the absentee squire of Bragton and Foreign Office Ambassador to United States. By the end of *The American Senator*, Arabella must retreat in ignominy, trading her ambitions for social exile and a merely adequate match with Mounser Green, a Patagonia-bound clerk in the Foreign Office.

Elsie Michie has insightfully compared Arabella's practices to the emerging capitalist 'experience of society as a network', where 'action is distributed among agents'[35] and individuals who lack social capital may instead use 'cleverness' – an array of personal stratagems and contacts – to undermine traditional hierarchies.[36] From the viewpoint of network theory, Arabella is keenly aware of place as a strategic element leveraged through 'the number of connections it commands, and how it loses its importance when losing its connections'.[37] Yet, unlike Trollope's non-jumping rider, Arabella takes social risks to pursue these connections – and later suffers for them. To cement her relationship with Lord Rufford, she remains strategically stationed by the injured Major Caneback, despite no prior acquaintance with the fallen man. After Caneback's accident, she leaps at the chance to find herself alone in a lengthy carriage ride with Rufford – again, despite questions of honesty and propriety that later return to dog her. Supported by the social and ecological media of the hunt, her 'cleverness' exploits the competitive form of *The American Senator*'s various networked hubs and relations, as they ramify in both society and sport. Even so, Arabella's actions are hardly predictable. Sometimes she navigates her social world with calculating finesse, but at others she does so more unevenly and inconsistently, recurring to earlier models of honour, custom and kinship. For instance, Arabella follows a more archaic code of honour when she makes the surprising – and highly non-strategic – choice to stop her dogged pursuit of Lord Rufford to visit the deathbed of her former fiancé Morton. Similarly, Arabella relies perhaps too blindly on patriarchal patronage and hierarchy when she asks her uncle, the Duke of Mayfair, to advocate for her engagement to Rufford.

In her play for Lord Rufford, Arabella is challenged by her world's – and the hunt's – blend of traditional hierarchies and modern capitalist networks. Defined by both lateral and vertical bonds, this social order still bears the mark of past, established institutions – such as patriarchal kinship, marital alliance, aristocratic honour, and fealty among tenants and squires.[38] In this blended system, Arabella's prospects suffer at least in part because she lacks a paternal proxy figure to support her position in the field. To husband-hunt with skill, Arabella must act not only on her own, but also through the influential mediation of a male guarantor – typically a parent or guardian serving the offices of host, patron, mentor and chaperone. Ideally, this guarantor should act as a reliable informatic hub, using his well-connected proximity to help his charges gain and sustain valuable social links and contacts. For, as network theorists note, it is through their 'extraordinarily large number of links' that hubs may create new connections and efficiencies – new 'short paths between any two nodes in the system'.[39] Of course, Arabella has no such 'hub' to facilitate her marital associations. Aside from her estranged father and hopelessly vulgar mother, she only has a distant and uninterested uncle to take her part.

To compensate for this paternal power vacuum, Arabella uses other clever technical stratagems and media, including the post, the railroad, carriages and even gambling to buy her wardrobe. In her pursuit of Rufford, she employs the logistics of the hunting field – and supporting modes of transportation – to her initial advantage. During a lengthy carriage ride after one meet, Rufford makes pronouncements of love that Arabella considers tantamount to a marriage proposal, but she cannot repeat them without damaging her propriety, and – lacking her own horses or financial means – she cannot follow Rufford when he suddenly leaves her uncle's estate later that night to join another distant hunt. While she bemoans her limited mobility, Arabella ultimately faults the Duke for her failure: 'If that heavy stupid duke would have spoken to him that night at Mistletoe, all would have been well! But now, – now there was nothing for her but weeping and gnashing of teeth' (AS, ch. 67, p. 467). Clearly, Arabella's views of patriarchal obligation differ from those of the Duke, for whom '[p]arental duty might make it necessary [to act] when a daughter had not known how to keep her position intact; – but here there was no parental duty' (AS, ch. 40, p. 273). However, the final death blow to Arabella's campaign occurs not through the absence of a paternal mediator, but rather through the acts of an inappropriate female substitute: her mother Lady Augustus, who seeks to transform Arabella's relationship with Rufford into a calculating financial transaction, through the payment of a £8,000 settlement – a 'vulgar bargain' that Arabella refuses, castigating her mother for 'ruin[ing]' her standing in The American Senator's perpetual husband hunt (AS, ch. 62, p. 432).

While Arabella hunts to gain social capital and influential proximity, Lizzie revels in the sport's opportunities for competitive risk-taking, high-flying and leaving her peers behind. Throughout the hunt, Lizzie's enjoyment is fuelled by comparison and one-upmanship. In Scotland, she rides especially competitively with her houseguests and 'friends' Lucinda Roanoke and Mrs Carbuncle. Ultimately unconcerned with dogs and foxes, 'in her heart' Lizzie views Lucinda as her 'quarry': 'If she could only pass Lucinda!' (ED, ch. 38, p. 389), she reflects during the chase. If we return again to Lizzie's jump across the river at Craigattan Gorse, this event gains an even greater impact in her memory, which casts it in explicitly comparative terms:

> How glorious it was to jump over that black, yawning stream, and then to see Lucinda fall into it! And she could remember every jump, and her feeling of ecstasy as she landed on the right side . . . It was all delightful; – and so much more delightful because Mrs Carbuncle had not gone quite so well as she liked to go, and because Lucinda had fallen into the water. (*ED*, ch. 40, p. 403)

For Lizzie, the true pleasure of hunting is 'not simply to have ridden well, but to have ridden better than others' (*ED*, ch. 38, p. 391). Socially, strategically and mathematically, nothing raises the absolute value of her position more than the misfortune of others – of Mrs Carbuncle's trouble and Lucinda's fall.

In a world that promises Lizzie few certain satisfactions, the hunt affirms her comparatively better place in the field – or so she believes. She remembers her first meet as 'the most triumphant day of her life' – more triumphant even than her marriage with Sir Florian Eustace, as 'that was only a step to something good that was to come after . . . Up to this period of her career she had hardly reached any pleasure; but this day had been very pleasant' (*ED*, ch. 40, p. 403). In the novel's early chapters, the young widow has 'not as yet quite formed a definite conclusion' as to 'what her enjoyment was to consist in' – at least beyond a general liking for 'jewels', 'admiration', 'good things to eat' and 'the power of being arrogant to those around her' (*ED*, ch. 2, pp. 50–1). However, Lizzie's turn to hunting reveals a more focused view of pleasure: as something calculable and quantifiable, designated by external signs of value and success. She seeks 'to be the possessor of the outward shows of all those things of which the inward facts are valued by the good and steadfast ones of the earth' (*ED*, ch. 10, p. 126). For Lizzie, a 'select' place 'at the kill' (*ED*, ch. 38, p. 394) is an unassailable sign of this distinction.

Lizzie's approach towards the hunt is part of a broader career of fakery, display and competitive scorekeeping. Tellingly, she misreads not only the sport itself but also the mediated experiences and relations that shape it. She does not understand the pursuit's more subtle joys, which Trollope allies with honourable conduct, character and restraint. Instead, Lizzie flattens these models of pleasure and success into a calculable and predictable script, much like the algorithms that govern artificial intelligence. As Megan Ward has shown, this resemblance between Lizzie's conduct and intelligent machinery exposes an imitative flatness at the heart of literary character and mimesis.[40] Other critics have also interpreted Lizzie's calculation as 'lived performativity',[41] emotion without content, 'signification without significance, [and] meaningfulness without meaning'.[42] Her feelings mimic the logic of capitalist exchange, reducing the 'manifoldness of things' into a measure of only 'how much'.[43] Focused on quantitative difference and display, Lizzie's pleasures are opposed to the silent, incalculable experience of Trollope's true sportsmen.

Lizzie errs not only in misreading the hunt as a scoring game, but also in overlooking its complex mediated communities. During her second meet, we learn:

> There had been nothing special in the way of sport . . . no great need for coaching, no losing of her breath, no cutting down of Lucinda, no river, no big wall – nothing, in short, very fast. They had been much in a big wood; but Lizzie, in giving an account of the day to her cousin, acknowledged that she had not quite understood what they were doing at any time. 'It was a blowing of horns, and a galloping

up and down all the day', she said; 'and then [the huntsman] got cross again and scolded all the people. But there was one nice paling, and Dandy (her horse) flew over it beautifully. Two men tumbled down, and one of them was a good deal hurt. It was very jolly; – but not at all like Wednesday'. (*ED*, ch. 41, p. 409)

As Lizzie here shows, she understands very little of the greater logic or context of the chase. '[W]hat they were doing at any time' is vague to her, as is the pace, direction and relationship of these various actions within the 'big wood' (*ED*, ch. 41, p. 409). She seeks to keep score, but she has no legible narrative or geographical markers to aid her. Trying and failing to generalise from her earlier 'triumph', she can only list decontextualised events and focus on minutiae, such as her horse's jump over 'one nice paling' (*ED*, ch. 41, p. 409). Lizzie even juxtaposes the serious injury of one rider with her own 'jolly' – and oddly disengaged – sense of the greater event.

Viewing the hunt through a narrowly individual lens, Lizzie misreads the sport both narratively and temporally. She presents a linear and diachronic view of what is actually a more synchronic network of relations, whose simultaneity resists sequential order and isolation. Despite their differences, both of her hunting accounts share this insistence on signposted narrative progress – on individually surmounting obstacles, surpassing rivals, arriving first and witnessing the kill. Yet, as we learn, Lizzie's focus on immediate wins and short-term goals is not without risk. For, in the obscure 'big wood' of the hunt, leading the pack is a relative position, subject to the evolving perspectives of the network and its various relationships. Being ahead from one viewpoint may not present an advantage from another.

In *The Eustace Diamonds,* this emphasis on short-term gain defines both Lizzie's 'cleverness' and related practices of calculation and acting. Lizzie's friends caution her 'against being clever when there is nothing to get by it' (*ED*, ch. 75, p. 724), but she is obsessed with dramatic skill, cunning and display. She is blinded by the fleeting pleasure of petty triumphs – of 'beautiful' lies (*ED*, ch. 79, p. 762), showy jumps and arriving first. At first, Lizzie's gamesmanship appears to yield dividends. She successfully uses deception, such as the display of spuriously acquired jewels, to win the heart of Sir Florian, 'but that had been but for an hour, – for a month or two' (*ED*, ch. 21, p. 230). Lizzie prizes lying as the height of cleverness and mastery – and as a source of immediate and reliable triumph: 'To lie readily and cleverly, recklessly and yet successfully, was, according to the lessons which she had learned, a necessity in woman and an added grace in man' (*ED*, ch. 79, p. 762). Yet, distracted by these short-term gains, Lizzie crucially neglects the long game – both in the hunt and in other aspects of her life, such as marriage, kinship relations and the management of property.

As *The Eustace Diamonds* never hesitates to note, Lizzie's deceptions add up in ways that she cannot anticipate, beyond the measure of her own reductive scorekeeping. Her cleverness fails most dramatically in her misreading of the property gained from her brief marriage to the late Sir Florian. She describes Portray Castle, Florian's Scottish estate, as 'her own, forever' (*ED*, ch. 2, p. 48) when it is only a temporary life interest, to be inherited by future Eustace heirs. Similarly, and even more centrally, Lizzie misrepresents the novel's eponymous diamonds, which she again defines as 'her own' (*ED*, ch. 16, p. 186). Embellishing a lie 'first fabricated . . . when she had the jewels valued', she insists that Sir Florian gifted the 'trinket' to her 'as her own peculiar property' (*ED*, ch. 16, p. 181). John Plotz has shown how diamond tales such as

Trollope's express a deep 'preoccupation with portability in the mid-Victorian period', revealed in the failure of these gems 'to turn either into pure liquidity or pure bearers of sentimental value'.[44] Certainly Lizzie experiences this same tension. In her pursuit of immediate profit and pleasure, she mistakes the diamonds as portable, calculable and easily exchangeable property – as decontextualised objects ('paraphernalia' [ED, ch. 25, p. 264]) outside of history. Thus, just as she neglects the living media of the hunt, so does Lizzie overlook these jewels' greater social and synchronic meaning, as heirlooms rooted in historical familial relations and traditions. Obsessed with the gems' theoretical exchange value (£10,000), yet never able to sell them, Lizzie disregards other more enduring forms of social capital, realised through networks of collective influence.

While based on initially clever designs, Lizzie's attachment to the diamonds deeply harms her long-term social, marital and economic goals. To keep the jewels in her possession, she swears false oaths, loses her property and alienates her friends, including her fiancé Lord Fawn and her more ambiguous suitors Frank and Lord George. In her zest to score cheap points against the Eustace family lawyer, and to own a triumphant marker of value, she 'absolutely ruin[s] herself' – and 'all . . . for nothing' (ED, ch. 71, p. 686). Her errors are both ethical and temporal: she does not realise that, despite its easy gains, deceit still yields accretive effects over time, visibly shaping the contours of character. Lizzie discovers, too late, that 'craft, let it never be so crafty, will in the long run miss its own object' (ED, ch. 21, p. 229).

Whether in the realm of blood sport or of marital intrigue, both *The Eustace Diamonds* and *The American Senator* fault their anti-heroines for their reductive focus on cleverness, primacy and quick wins. In the hunt, Lizzie and Arabella's analogue is Trollope's 'triumphant rider' who, through his showy array of habit and equipment, is 'an odious man' – an over-striver 'who sins in boasting, [and] will be presumed also to sin in lying' (BSP, p. 125). Both women learn – the hard way – that status and power are not won through individual gamesmanship, but instead result from complex, mediated relations of influence. In the end, Trollope's novels chasten these female tricksters, and instead reward other honest, unassuming women – such as *The Eustace Diamonds*'s Lucy, who realises her only simple wish: marriage to Frank Greystock. Along with her counterpart Mary Masters in *The American Senator*, Lucy serves as Trollope's 'Man Who Hunts and Never Jumps', and as a model for the play of restrained desire, trained towards more modest goals. For, while Arabella chases lofty ambitions, and Lizzie lies with beauty and alacrity, Lucy waits patiently, 'giving place' (HS, p. 114) to the speed and cunning of others in order to gain a later strategic position.

Through the final marriages of both Lucy and Mary, Trollope upholds his 'theory and system' (ED, ch. 37, p. 378) of hunting as a technology of character and self-management. Embodying Trollope's middle way, Lucy and Mary are figures of enduring honesty, consistency and restraint – and instructive contrasts to Lizzie's and Arabella's showy deceit. Even Lizzie herself 'see[s] – or half see[s] – that Lucy with her simplicity was stronger than was she with her craft . . . And a man captivated by wiles was only captivated for a time, whereas a man won by simplicity would be won for ever – if he himself were worth the winning' (ED, ch. 21, pp. 229–30). Prized for her value within a social network of shifting and opportunistic connections, Lucy is a 'treasure' (ED, ch. 3, p. 61) – a 'real stone' to Lizzie's 'paste' (ED, ch. 65, p. 628).

Moreover, both Lucy and Mary display a level of self-knowledge and social insight that Trollope's more ambitious characters lack. Poor and unassuming, these women recognise their limited objects – their faithful love for unavailable men – but they still navigate the field of marriage according to their own careful systems and values. Refusing to compromise themselves, they seek only to 'hav[e] a purpose and a use in life' (ED, ch. 3, p. 63). Like the man who never jumps, Lucy and Mary realise the most 'silent' of distinctions (BSP, p. 100): a humble, expansive and ethically scrupulous grasp of their world. They show how mediation and Trollope's *via media* are complementary practices, rooted in social and moral engagement.

In effect, Lucy and Mary follow the Quaker proverb (from Tennyson's 'Northern Farmer' of 1864) that Frank so memorably repeats and ponders: 'Doan't thou marry for munny, but goa where munny is' (ED, ch. 13, pp. 155–6). They succeed, in a relative sense, because they understand their place within a larger network, and maintain appropriate relations of proximity, distance and desire. As Lucy and Mary learn, simply sustaining one's presence in a field of influence has its own benefits. In *The Eustace Diamonds* and *The American Senator*, the hunt embodies this living media of character, community and the middle way. This sport offers compelling ways to imagine human and non-human agency and relationship, in all of their intricacy, materiality and resistance. If the 'acme of bliss' is, for Trollope, 'a hot scent carried breast-high by fleet hounds' (BSP, p. 82, p. 81), for his readers, it is the imagined sense-perception of influence itself, of entangled threads and shifting patterns that shape the chase's synchronic world of love, death, status and sport.

Notes

The author wishes to thank Gordon Bigelow, Elsie Michie, Megan Ward and Frederik Van Dam for generously sharing their work with her.
1. Anthony Trollope, *An Autobiography* (London: Trollope Society, 1999), ch. 4, p. 40.
2. Ibid. ch. 4, p. 50.
3. Richard Grusin, 'Radical Mediation', *Critical Inquiry*, 42 (Autumn 2015): p. 146.
4. Donald Smalley (ed.), *Trollope: The Critical Heritage* (London: Routledge and Kegan Paul, 1969), p. 198. I thank Elsie Michie for directing me to this reference.
5. Anthony Trollope, *The American Senator*, ed. John Halperin (Oxford: Oxford University Press, 2008), ch. 6, p. 38. Subsequent references are in the main text (AS).
6. Donna Landry, *The Invention of the Countryside: Hunting, Walking, and Ecology in English Literature, 1671–1831* (Basingstoke: Palgrave, 2001), p. 14.
7. Trollope began his hunting career in Banagher, Ireland, using his travel as a postal surveyor to support his sporting excursions. Later in England, he kept his horses at Waltham Cross in Hertfordshire, and one or two of these would have been taken to the meet by train, probably through Shoreditch Station in London. I thank David Skilton for this information.
8. Robert Freeman, 'The Morality of Field Sports', *Fortnightly Review*, 12 (October 1869): p. 372.
9. Anthony, Trollope, 'Mr Freeman and the Morality of Hunting', *Fortnightly Review*, 12 (December 1869): p. 230.
10. Anthony Trollope (ed.), *British Sports and Past-Times* (London: Virtue & Co., 1868), p. 76. Subsequent references are in the main text (BSP).
11. Robert Hughes, 'Trollope and Fox-Hunting', *Essays in Literature*, 12.1 (1985): p. 76.
12. Jackson Trotter, 'Foxhunting and English Social Order in Trollope's *The American Senator*', *Studies in the Novel*, 24.3 (1992): p. 230.

13. Hughes, 'Trollope and Fox-Hunting', p. 77. On fox-hunting as a 'symbolic form of sovereign rootedness' (41), see also Frederik Van Dam, *Anthony Trollope's Late Style: Victorian Liberalism and Literary Form* (Edinburgh: Edinburgh University Press, 2016). Van Dam explores the fox as a theatrical personification of monarchy and the hunt as a site of resurgent aristocratic barbarism in *The American Senator*.
14. Trollope, *Autobiography*, ch. 9, p. 107.
15. Coral Lansbury, *The Reasonable Man: Trollope's Legal Fiction* (Princeton: Princeton University Press, 1981), pp. 40–1.
16. Ibid. p. 40.
17. Trollope eventually belonged to several London clubs, including the Garrick Club, the Arts Club, the Civil Service Club, the Athenaeum and the Cosmopolitan.
18. Bruno Latour, *Reassembling the Social: An Introduction to Actor-Network Theory* (Oxford: Oxford University Press, 2005), p. 373.
19. Ibid. p. 129. Latour's emphasis.
20. Grusin, 'Radical Mediation', p. 132.
21. Latour, *Reassembling the Social*, p. 72.
22. Anthony Trollope, *The Eustace Diamonds* (London: Penguin Books, 2004), p. 379. Subsequent references are in the main text (*ED*).
23. During this unsatisfying hunt, three foxes are almost immediately 'chopped', a fourth hides and is 'dug out ingloriously', and a fifth is lost after riders move in front of the dogs and cause them to lose scent (*ED*, ch. 27, pp. 380–2).
24. Duke of Beaufort and Mowbray Morris, *Hunting* [1885], 3rd edn (London: Longmans, Green, and Co., 1886), p. 197.
25. Grusin, 'Radical Mediation', p. 125.
26. In Trollope's hunting narratives, however, these gender ascriptions are also remarkably fluid. Many of his wild and unruly creatures are *not* feminised (foxes, for instance).
27. Robert Tracy, *Trollope's Later Novels* (Berkeley: University of California Press, 1978), p. 222.
28. On Trollope's growing ambivalence toward the fox hunt in his last and unfinished novel, *The Landleaguers* (1883), see Gordon Bigelow, 'Trollope and Ireland', in Carolyn Dever and Lisa Niles (eds), *The Cambridge Companion to Anthony Trollope* (Cambridge: Cambridge University Press, 2010), pp. 196–209. In *The Landleaguers*, the chase is interrupted (and never to be resumed) by the peaceful protest of Irish peasants who seek Land Reform. As Bigelow notes, this novel addresses criticism of the hunt as increasingly distant from the local communities upon whose land it is pursued.
29. Donna Landry, *The Invention of the Countryside: Hunting, Walking, and Ecology in English Literature, 1671–1831* (Basingstoke: Palgrave, 2001), p. 69.
30. Raymond Carr, *English Fox Hunting: A History* (London: Weidenfeld and Nicolson, 1976), p. 70.
31. Ibid. pp. 37–8.
32. Anthony Trollope, *Hunting Sketches*, 2nd ed, (London: Chapman and Hall, 1866), pp. 2–3. Hereafter cited parenthetically as '*HS*'.
33. On Trollope's writing practices and strategies within the literary market, see Silvana Colella, 'Sweet Money: Cultural and Economic Value in Trollope's *Autobiography*', *Nineteenth-Century Contexts*, 28.1 (2006): pp. 5–20; and Walter M. Kendrick, *The Novel-Machine: The Theory and Fiction of Anthony Trollope* (Baltimore: Johns Hopkins University Press, 1980).
34. Albert-Laszlo Barábasi, *Linked: The New Science of Networks* (Cambridge: Perseus, 2002), p. 106. Barábasi's emphasis.
35. Latour, *Reassembling the Social*, p. 50; quoted in Elsie Michie, 'The Clever Son of a Clever Mother: Anthony and Frances Trollope', in Deborah Denenholz Morse, Margaret Markwick

and Mark Turner (eds), *The Routledge Research Companion to Anthony Trollope* (London: Routledge, 2017), p. 277.

36. Michie, 'The Clever Son', p. 277. Michie traces the origins of this 'cleverness' to Trollope's novelist mother, Frances Trollope, who explores the trait 'as a negative but useful talent', realised through 'the hold characters achieve over one another' (pp. 276–7).

37. Bruno Latour, 'On Actor-Network Theory: A Few Clarifications', *Soziale Welt*, 4.4 (1996): p. 373.

38. Kathy Alexis Psomiades shows how, for Trollope and other Victorians, such archaisms are popular fictions, particularly as they treat 'heterosexual exchange' as a stable, 'ancient system' predating the theoretically 'gender indifferent' world of the modern market. See 'Heterosexual Exchange and Other Victorian Fictions: *The Eustace Diamonds* and Victorian Anthropology', *Novel: A Forum on Fiction*, 33.1 (1999): pp. 98–9, p. 117.

39. Barábasi, *Linked*, p. 54, p. 64.

40. Megan Ward, 'Human Reproductions: Victorian Realist Character and Artificial Intelligence', Unpublished manuscript, 2017, p. 23.

41. Lauren M. E. Goodlad, 'The Trollopian Geopolitical Aesthetic', *Literature Compass*, 7.9 (2010): p. 868.

42. Walter M. Kendrick, '*The Eustace Diamonds*: The Truth of Trollope's Fiction', *ELH*, 46.1 (1979): p. 138.

43. Georg Simmel, *On Individuality and Social Forms* (Chicago: University of Chicago Press, 1971), p. 330.

44. John Plotz, *Portable Property: Victorian Culture on the Move* (Princeton: Princeton University Press, 2009), p. 25.

17

Lane-ism: Anthony Trollope's Irish Roads in Time and Space

Claire Connolly

THIS CHAPTER TAKES its title from the curious opening scene of Anthony Trollope's *The Macdermots of Ballycloran*, his 1847 novel concerning a tragic murder in county Leitrim. The novel locates its action at an Irish roadside inn, '72 miles W.N.W. of Dublin, on the mail-coach road to Sligo'.[1] Having dined in this county Leitrim establishment, the narrator takes a walk, 'taking two or three turns to look for signs of improvement'.[2] Rather than yielding a perspective on unfolding countryside or affording an encounter with local people or customs, however, his encounter with the west of Ireland is mediated by 'as dusty, ugly and disagreeable a road as is to be found in any county in Ireland'. Encountering 'evident signs on the part of the road of retrograding into lane-ism', the narrator follows a ramshackle route until he comes upon a dilapidated house, the history of which is told to him by the mail coach guard, and the retelling of which occupies the remainder of the novel.[3] This negatively framed connection between out-of-the-way Irish places and a neglectful transport infrastructure is repeated in the opening of *The Kellys and the O'Kellys* (1848) where Dunmore is described as being 'on no high road': 'It is a dirty, ragged little town, standing in a very poor part of the country, with nothing about it to induce the traveller to go out of his beaten track.'[4]

In the examples quoted above, roads redirect the flow of time between past, present and future. They act upon the present moment, breaking forms of spatial and temporal connection where they might be expected to build social relationships. Roads also possess a curious kind of agency. To borrow some terms from philosopher Bruno Latour, Trollope's Irish roads yield a 'type of force, causality, efficacy, and obstinacy'.[5] More than 'simply the hapless bearers of symbolic projection',[6] roads lead readers along unpredictable routes and serve as sites of 'complex repertoires of action'.[7] In what follows I suggest that, in giving the road itself a kind of agency in the wider system, Trollope's Irish novels suggest the potential of non-human actors to affect networks across time. They also bring into focus what R. F. Foster calls 'the shade as well as the light' in Trollope's account of Ireland.[8]

In Trollope, to move off the high road is also to slip backwards in time. As the narrator of *The Macdermots of Ballycloran* meanders along an unimproved road ('the county had evidently deserted it'), he meets 'donkeys carrying turf home from the bog, in double kishes on their back', 'fragments of a bridge . . . utterly fallen away from their palmy days' and a 'broken down entrance' to a boggy, grassed-over road leading to a roofless, rotting house. The fate of the house itself results not from 'poor old Time', however, but rather is the workings of his speedy modern rival, 'Ruin'.[9]

Trollope develops a curious distinction between time, with its slow and organic approach to devastation, and ruin as a rawly efficient force of change. The terms seem familiar enough at first: Trollope might be invoking Edmund Burke's account of the French revolutionaries, who to those who come after them leave 'a ruin instead of an habitation'.[10] But the passage in Trollope goes further in opposing a slow Time that is supported by nature to an image of inhuman destruction: 'Ruin works fast enough unaided.' The Romantic personification of Ruin does not disguise the speedy modern work that causes plaster to peel, coping to fall down and timbers to rot.

Roads are central to this distinction: to be off the road infrastructure is to be behind the times, trapped in the era of transport by donkey, but also to be backwards in a very modern way – to be speedily passed by, missed in the blink of an eye. Such backwardness might shape a political diagnosis, of the kind offered by Irish nationalist John Mitchel, who at once invokes and accuses a progressive modern nation when he asks of the Irish Famine: 'Are we living in the nineteenth century – amidst all the enlightenment, steam, philanthropy and power-looms of the illustrious British Empire?'[11] Or perhaps Trollope's mixed temporalities reflect the tenor of British political commentary regarding the supposedly beneficial effects achieved by the Famine in speeding up the pace of political change in Ireland. In particular, the Encumbered Estates Act of 1849 – an Act to allow 'the swift an efficient sale of heavily indebted estates' – was seen as 'potentially inaugurating a new anglicized dawn for the Irish countryside in particular and the Irish economy in general'.[12] In such a narrative, Ireland was a ruined country on course 'for a brighter future'.[13]

But that is to run ahead of the novel's own time frame, and it seems wiser to approach its discussion of ruin versus time by staying close to the narrative location on the road. Trollope's neologism is worth closer consideration. What does 'lane-ism' mean? A glance at the OED tells us that -ism as a suffix was widely used by the end of the nineteenth century, to mean theory or ideology, as in J. R. Lowell's 1864 usage: 'That class of untried social theories which are known by the name of isms.'[14] Yet the retrograding road can hardly be aligned with systems or theories: rather it seems to depart from same, leaving the official transport network for the less defined space of the lane, moving from the present into a confused past. Trollope's knowledge of this and other such twists and turns in Irish infrastructure derives from an intimate experience of state systems, known to him as part of what he described as 'continual journeys through its south, western and midland portions'.[15] This paradoxical relationship between system and local experience or between theory and practice informs my chapter and I return to it at the conclusion.

Anthony Trollope travelled extensively and routinely around Ireland and his 'comings and goings'[16] meant that he knew 'not only the map of Ireland but the surface of the roads'.[17] As an employee of the Post Office, Trollope lived in Ireland for eighteen years, domiciled in Banagher, Clonmel, Mallow, Cork, Belfast and Dublin. He wrote his first novels in Ireland, later set novels there and threaded Irish characters and Irish political issues through the tapestry of his political novels. As Gordon Bigelow shows, his Irish novels can be seen to 'draw from and refer openly to' earlier fictions by Maria Edgeworth and Lady Morgan.[18] John McCourt's 2015 study,

Writing the Frontier: Anthony Trollope Between Britain and Ireland, makes a persuasive and sympathetic case for Trollope as an honorary Irish writer who seeks to 'describe and explain the country for an English reader with a steady hand and with a sense of fairness'.[19]

There are moments, however, when Trollope's descriptions of Ireland can be strikingly official in tenor. When the narrator of *The Kellys and the O'Kellys* tells us that Kelly Court is situated in 'that corner of County Roscommon which runs up between Mayo and Galway', the description directs the reader to a map rather than a place.[20] John McCourt remarks that the opening passage of *The Macdermots of Ballycloran* 'seems more the work of a precise topographer – with all the controlling tendencies of that profession – rather than a budding novelist'. He goes on to note that Trollope 'boasted of having visited every parish and was capable of Ordnance Survey-style descriptions of the most remote places in the country'.[21] Meanwhile the action of *Castle Richmond* (1860) is located via a question which seems to hold official and local kinds of knowledge in humorous, knowing balance:

> The readability of a story should depend, one would say, on its intrinsic merit rather than the site of its adventures. No one will think that Hampshire is better for such a purpose than Cumberland, or Essex than Leicestershire. What abstract objection can there be to the county Cork?[22]

To begin to address these paradoxes of intimate experience and formal knowledge involves us not only in Anthony Trollope's professional role within the Post Office but also in the key questions that concern the historiography of the operation of the British state in nineteenth-century Ireland. Do roads represent the power of the colonial state or rather its uncertain reach? How porous were the channels through which power flowed in nineteenth-century Ireland? In *The State of Freedom*, Patrick Joyce gives an account of how the great public works projects of the nineteenth century effected a transformation in the basis of power, as local landed interests gave way to a centralising state: in the process the fiscal-military state of the eighteenth century became the nineteenth-century infrastructure state.[23] Joyce's two key examples of the operation of this infrastructure state are the roads and the Post Office: in Ireland, Trollope was closely involved with both. While in Clonmel, he got to know the stage coach entrepreneur Charles Bianconi, an Italian businessman who successfully established a comprehensive system of travel by stagecoach in Ireland in the aftermath of the Napoleonic wars. Bianconi advised Trollope on the design of postal travel routes and McCourt speculates that 'perhaps Bianconi's coachguards were of even more assistance in providing Trollope with information about the country that would be just as useful for building the postal service as it would be for constructing his novels'.[24]

The case of Trollope helps us to see that the infrastructure state operated not simply as an external set of circumstances but rather as a pervasive matrix, with social, cultural and political effects.[25] Infrastructural developments were quickly integrated into debates about Irish literature, as a metaphor that seems to come readily to hand in Victorian discussions of Irish cultural distinctiveness. Despairing of the way in which the 'real progress' of Irish literature is rendered invisible by 'the overpowering demand' of the London culture industry, Isaac Butt notes 'the business of the English press and book market is as largely carried on as the paving of London, by Irish labourers'.[26] Samuel Ferguson boasts of Irish roads and insists that:

> Great works, . . . which might normally have to wait for the development of society . . . are, by a generous anomaly, extended through our most remote and savage districts; high roads, canals, embankments, piers, and harbours, await prospective use and reproductive operation; and dormant facilities for the development . . .[27]

Ferguson's 'generous anomaly' by which Ireland has a more advanced infrastructure than that of the larger island echoes comments made by Arthur Young in the 1780s on the precocious modernity of Irish roads: 'For a country so far behind us as Ireland, to have suddenly so much the start of us in the article of roads, is a spectacle that cannot fail to strike the English traveler exceedingly.'[28] These remarks might point us towards an account of the accelerated experience of social, cultural and political change characteristic of Ireland's colonial modernity. Many of the great projects of the modernising nineteenth-century British state were first developed in Ireland, which by the 1830s had seen the introduction of the first national school system; the first national police force and the first national system of lunatic asylums. The Ordnance Survey of Ireland, Patrick Joyce reminds us, was a 'state science project of immense size, without parallel anywhere in the world'.[29]

In addition to knowing the Famine-struck years of the 1840s, Trollope was also familiar with the politics of amalgamation and conciliation that characterised the decades that followed. Trollope also spent periods of time in Ireland in the 1850s, living in Donnybrook, Dublin as Post Office Surveyor for the north of Ireland. During that decade, Ireland experienced 'a relative period of prosperity and stability'[30] while also witnessing what John Bew calls 'the fraying of the pro-Union consensus in the British governing classes'.[31] Trollope's narrative strategies seem to recognise these temporal twists and turns in the narrative of Irish modernity, and to realise them via the road network along which so many of his plots run. Roads are present in Trollope's Irish fiction in all their various forms: as avenues, paths, cuttings, lanes; as shaped by grand juries, relief works and mail companies. The word 'lane-ism' alerts us to the ironies and instabilities of infrastructure, which we can explore further via a return to the opening section of The Macdermots of Ballycloran.

The story told is framed by the recollections of the mail coach guard, whose speech is rendered for us by the narrator:

> I got up behind, for McC– the guard, was an old friend of mine; and after the usual salutations and strapping of portmanteaus and shifting down into places, as McC– knows everything, I began to ask him if he knew anything of a place called Ballycloran.
>
> 'Deed, then, Sir, and I do', said he, 'and good reason have I to know, and well I knew those that lived in it, ruined, and black, and desolate, as Ballycloran is now': and between Drumsna and Boyle, he gave me the heads of the following story.[32]

The narrator is keen to stress the steady value of such a travelling storyteller, adding: 'And, reader, if I thought it would ever be your good fortune to hear the history of Ballycloran from the guard of the Boyle coach, I would recommend you to get it from him, and shut my book forthwith.'[33] John McCourt argues that the driver in question is likely to be based on the solid reality of one of Charles Bianconi's workers, a man named McCluskie who was well known to Trollope.[34] It is perhaps not surprising that Trollope would identify a steady strength inherent in the viewpoint of the employee who pursues his work on the road. Additionally, there is more than an echo here of *Waverley* and the 'humble English post chaise' of Walter Scott's narrator, who asks readers to imagine the story as a journey taken in 'a humble English post-chaise, drawn upon four wheels, and keeping his majesty's highway': a journey that Scott asks readers to imagine in terms of 'heavy roads, steep hills, sloughs, and other terrestrial retardations'.[35]

Trollope's Irish novels, however, do not feel obliged to keep to 'his majesty's highway'. As with the coach driver of *The Macdermots of Ballycloran*, the reality represented is anchored in the kinetic experience of a mobile landscape; a reminder of what can still be the disorientations we experience in encountering Trollope's Ireland. Roads configure relationships between time and space and also operate as a kind of root metaphor in culture: think of the 'high road to ruin' invoked in *The Kellys and the O'Kellys*.[36] The interrelationship of time passing and roads travelled might be analysed in terms of Bakhtin's discussion of the road as chronotrope: 'varied and multileveled are the ways in which road is turned into a metaphor, but its fundamental pivot is the flow of time'.[37] Sometimes it seems as if the road network stands in for the past itself, as when 'the solid, slow activity' of Lord Cashel's daughter Lady Selina in *The Kellys and the O'Kellys* is compared to the movements of an aged vehicle:

> Lady Selina . . . like some old coaches which we remember – very sure, very respectable; but so tedious, so monotonous, so heavy in their motion, that a man with a spark of mercury in his composition would prefer any danger from a faster vehicle to their horrid, weary, murderous, slow security.[38]

Tedious, heavy, slow: travel on the roads does not present itself to the reader equipped with the same narrative of progress that we associate with railways. No one writes in relation to roads as Paul Fyfe has of 'the disorientation, unmeasurable expanse and uncertain social force' heralded by the railways in Britain or as Chris Morash has done on 'railway mania' in Ireland.[39] But Trollope's novels remind us to avoid 'the binary of old and new' technologies and think of rail and road together in any understanding of Irish modernity.[40] At the outset of his 1860 Irish novel *Castle Richmond*, Trollope describes Duhallow as 'in that Kanturk region through which the Mallow and Killarney railway now passes, but which some thirteen years since knew nothing of the navvy's spade, or even of the engineer's theodolite'.[41]

How can we locate roads in terms of the narratives of progress and modernity normally associated with the transport infrastructure? Here it is helpful to turn to Nitin Sinha's study of *Communication and Colonialism in Eastern India*. Complaining of 'an easy equation of communication with railways', Sinha calls for scholars to 'situate the railway-generated changes amidst the existing patterns and networks of circulation in which the role of roads and ferries was crucial'.[42] Such a historiography 'potentially threatens to flatten the rich and *changing* history of circulation that existed in the pre-railway days'.[43] Sinha comments that 'scholars who have worked on nineteenth-century transport issues related either with trade or social aspects have barely tried to situate the railway-generated changes amidst the existing patterns and networks of circulation in which the role of roads and ferries was crucial'.[44]

In the case of Ireland, the co-existence of technologies of travel is quite marked. Although histories of the nineteenth century tend to plot roads, steam and railways as separate or sequential developments, they were in fact closely interrelated across several decades. Maria Edgeworth said of her first sea-crossing on a steam-powered vessel that the 'jiggling' sensation generated by the movement of the paddles through the water reminded her of 'the shake felt in a carriage when a pig is scratching himself behind the hind wheel while waiting at an Irish inn door'.[45] Living as she did through major advances in travel technology (steam on the Irish sea, Thomas Telford's suspension bridge over the Menai Straits and the modernisation of the Holyhead Road), Edgeworth, like Trollope, is an astute observer of the speed at which technologies age. Travelling on the Royal Canal in 1804, she notes the rusting 'racks and pinnions and hinges' of the leaky sluice gates and imagines the locks as 'a sort of Castle Rackrent on the waters'.[46]

One of Trollope's most evocative accounts of the expected and familiar miseries of Irish travel appears as part of an account of a journey by canal boat. In *The Kellys and the O'Kellys*, Martin Kelly travels on the Ballinasloe canal. Describing the departure from Portobello in Dublin, Trollope vividly evokes the discomforts of the boat and suggests that the known limitations of the coach are preferable to the false promises of the canal boat:

> I hardly know why a journey in one of these boats should be much more intolerable than travelling either inside or outside a coach; for, either in or on the coach, one has less room for motion, and less opportunity of employment. I believe the misery of the canal boat chiefly consists in a pre-conceived and erroneous idea of its capabilities. One prepares oneself for occupation – an attempt is made to achieve actual comfort – and both end in disappointment; the limbs become weary with endeavouring to fix themselves in a position of repose, and the mind is fatigued more by the search after, than the want of, occupation.[47]

In a characteristic move, Trollope sets the life and experiences of his character outside this third-person narrative discourse while also using him to enhance the reader's experience of the everyday wretchedness of travel: 'Martin, however, made no complaints and felt no misery. He made great play at the eternal half-boiled leg of mutton, floating in a bloody sea of grease and gravy, which always comes on the table three hours after the departure from Portobello.'[48] Martin Kelly proves 'equally diligent at breakfast', after which he disembarks at Ballinasloe and takes Bianconi's car from there on to Tuam, from where, in turn, a hack car takes him home to Dunmore. The name Bianconi might be there simply to signal the rapid extension of the road network in the aftermath of the Napoleonic wars; a history normally narrated in terms of improvement and change rather than imagined in terms of a retrograding 'lane-ism'.[49] Yet as canal boat, stagecoach and hack car combine to get Martin Kelly from Dublin to Dunmore, Trollope again asks us to see Irish roads as part of a patched-together network that seems ever in danger of slipping backwards in technological time.

Contrary to Trollope's account, however, developments in Irish transport infrastructure up to and after the Famine have been described as "Ireland's time-space revolution".[50] Cormac Ó Gráda remarks that '[b]y 1845, when Ireland's car and coaching system was at its most extensive, it covered a greater network of routes than the railway ever would do – travel times had been cut substantially, and a regular service established between all towns of any size for about 1s.5d a mile'.[51] Ó Gráda goes on to show how 'Between 1801 and the late 1830s journey times on the main routes were cut by one-third and fares by one-half or more.' Travel times shortened considerably as part of this new network and some of the most notable changes involved 'the opening of west Connacht and the north-western and south-western regions, which had been virtually inaccessible before'.[52]

In his book on *Dickens and Public Transport*, Jonathan Grossman asks us not to neglect the cultural meanings of the road system in our rush to describe the sensational experience of speedy travel by rail. His book 'aims to recover the significance of the rise of a fast-driving, stage-coach network that systematized – before the railways – swift, circulating, round-trip inland journeying, with regular schedules, running continuously, available to ordinary passengers. The railways copied and intensified this system as a system.'[53] Dickens was interested in and aware of this older (but not outdated) road system, especially as it intersected with rail. His novels develop, argues Grossman, a 'narrative perspective . . . capable of taking in its precarious formation'.[54]

For Trollope in Ireland, quickening travel times across increasingly concentrated road networks might also serve as a spur to narrative coherence. Yet what is most striking about Trollope's Irish novels is the extent to which they imagine a strong but flawed road network whose failures, gaps and discontinuities emerge in relation to violence. In Grossman's account of the public transport known to Dickens, he asks us to think about 'the passenger transport system specifically as a system: that the here-and-now of mobile individuals is its contents, that it arrays living bodies into a network'.[55] In Trollope's 'here-and-now', we find dead or mutilated bodies alongside the living ones and a retrograde network that exists at the edges of the official one. People and events are arranged in relation to one another via this retro-grading network and, in a further paradox, it is these arrangements that propel the plots forward.

Consider some examples of the role of roads in the movement of Trollope's plot. In *Castle Richmond*, an isolated Lady Clara takes her forlorn walks along the 'little well-worth path by the roadside, not on the road itself'.[56] *The Kellys and the O'Kellys*, not least because of its ingenious double plot structure, is full of examples of characters who meet on the road or whose paths cross on their various journeys, as if to exemplify Bakhtin's argument that '[t]he road is especially . . . appropriate for portraying events governed by chance'.[57] When Martin Kelly takes Bianconi's car on from Ballinasloe to Tuam, he shares a car with Mr Daly the attorney, little knowing that their missions are bound up in the same situation and yet utterly opposed. In this case, legal and transport systems meet and interconnect. Medicine too is integrated into the plot via a meeting on the road: when Lord Ballindine drives Mr Armstrong to Tuam to catch the coach, they encounter Dr Colligan in his gig on the road. He tells them about Barry Lynch's effort to persuade the doctor to murder his sister and once more the two plots of the novel become entwined on the road.

In *The Macdermots*, when Thady is led to the hideout of the ribbonmen in the hills, he leaves the road that runs along the east side of Lough Allen to follow a 'small boreen or path' up the mountain. The 'boreen' too is left behind for another path that runs 'by the sides of the loose-built walls with which the land was subdivided' until finally they arrive 'at just the spot where the open mountain no longer showed any signs of man's handiwork'.[58] Boreen derives from *bóithrín*, meaning small road or lane, and McCourt comments on Trollope's 'impressive range of vocabulary derived directly from Irish', in particular 'diminutive nouns' such as this one.[59] Rather than just being used here to 'bolster the realism of his Irish novels',[60] however, the word 'boreen' signifies indigenous, unofficial pathways that lead to open country. Trollope's careful tracking of the journey from road to boreen to open mountain sees Thady move along a dwindling infrastructure, away from the rule of law. The final destination is a ribbonmen's hideout, a 'lifeless, desolate spot' on a mountain top that affords a view of any approaching police or military force. Yet when Thady takes his decision to leave it is because he loathes the thought of becoming himself a spectacle on the roads: 'and then at length to be taken away to the fate which he knew awaited him, and be dragged along the roads by a policeman, with handcuffs on his wrists – a show, to be gaped at by the country!'[61]

Yet more dramatically in *The Landleaguers* (1883), we see how incomplete and residual aspects of the road system facilitate murder. *The Landleaguers* is itself an unfinished work; left incomplete at the time of Trollope's death, with only forty-nine of the sixty chapters complete. Following Michael Sadleir, critics regularly remark that *The Landleaguers* is little more than a tract on the agrarian troubles in Ireland in 1879–81: 'Sad accounts of wretched actuality, in which characterization is submerged in floods of almost literal fact.'[62] Noting the way in which the novel 'moves on two tracks' and assessing the 'bitterness of the repudiation' of Ireland found in its pages, R. F. Foster identifies in *The Landleaguers* 'a deliberate representation of a fracturing society'.[63]

The plot of *The Landleaguers* concerns the murder of Florian Jones – a young boy, the son of an English landlord father, Philip Jones, who, having bought Irish land via the Encumbered Estates Act, might be just the kind of improving landowner imagined by proponents of that legislation. At the Estates Court, Jones buys two adjacent estates that 'lay to the right and left of the road which runs down from the little town of Headford to Lough Corrib'.[64] Some eighty of his acres, previously under water and yielding only rushes, are reclaimed via drains and sluices and begin to afford profitable crops and after-crops. Florian, a Catholic convert, witnesses landleaguers in the act of smashing the hinges of sluice gates that protected the reclaimed land from the lake. He first sides with the agrarian protestors by refusing to reveal the identity of the men that flooded his father's fields and then turns witness against them. The latter action brings down a boycott on the heads of the entire family (including a boycott on providing transport to any visitors to the estate, with only the railway 'beyond the power of the boycotters')[65] and eventually results in the murder of Florian. Trollope, in writing the novel, had gone 'to some trouble to find out the exact schedule of the Lough Corrib steamer' and is highly exact in his account of the journeys that can and cannot be made around the estate.[66]

The sensational story of Florian's murder unfolds via a kind of infrastructural drama. Travelling along the main road in a carriage with his son, Philip Jones sees a masked man and 'the muzzles of a double-barreled rifle presented though the hole in the wall'. The wall referred to is situated at a cutting on the road, part of the works for an unfinished famine road. (Herbert Fitzgerald has already complained about the uselessness of such famine public works in *Castle Richmond*, suggesting Trollope's awareness of the presence of these fresh ruins on the landscape).[67] And later in *The Landleaguers*, when Captain Yorke Clayton is shot at in front of his friend Frank Jones, the action is located 'at a corner of the road, from which a little boreen or lane ran up the side of the mountain between walls about three feet high'.[68] Even as the reader learns that Captain Clayton has in fact fainted from fright rather than died from a fatal injury, the narrator takes care to locate further the position of the gunman in relation to a stalled and unfinished project of improvement that runs along the 'boreen or lane': 'But here some benevolent enterprising gentleman, wishing to bring water through Lower Lough Cong to Lough Corrib, had caused the beginnings of a canal to be built, which had, however, after the expenditure of large sums of money, come to nothing.' These ruins of past improvement afford real danger in the present: 'The whole spot up and behind the corner of the road was so honeycombed by the works of the intended canal as to afford hiding-places and retreats for a score of murderers.'[69] Once more, the narrative makes use of Irish infrastructure in ways that exceed its potential as symbol. The 'honeycombed' canal works are disused but not inoperative: they exist as fixed sites of physical and material meaning whose location is time is subject to such jolts and displacements as the murder attempt described above.

For Bruno Latour, time is not conceived as a purposeful sequence of distinct periods but rather in terms of overlapping forms of movement: 'whirlpools and rapids, eddies and flows' rather than a fast-flowing river,[70] meaning that 'the past is not surpassed but revisited, repeated, surrounded, protected, recombined, reinterpreted, and reshuffled'.[71] Actor-Network Theory – with its telling acronym ANT – stays close to the ground in its tracking of 'polytemporal' actions, opting to stay 'bogged down in the territory'.[72] One of Latour's key examples of the operations of ANT is the speed bump on a road, a concrete inscription of regulatory force that signals a need to conceptualise power in ways that exceed 'meaningful human relations'. Rather than introducing 'a world of brute material relations', however, Latour uses the speed bump to signal the significance of '[d]etour, translation, delegation, inscription, and displacement' in the realm of politics. As he puts in in *Reassembling the Social*:

> it is possible to trace more sturdy relations and discover more revealing patterns by finding a way to register the links between unstable and shifting frames of reference rather than by trying to keep one frame stable.[73]

Such 'sturdy relations' are a matter of literary style as well as social history. By connecting the present to the past as well as characters with one another, roads do important work on behalf of Trollope's realism. Benedict Anderson's classic study *Imagined Communities* discusses the ways in which realist novels manage the kinds of 'temporal coincidence' that can be 'measured by clock or calendar' – or, we can add, be made possible via road network.[74] Anderson's famous description of third-person realist narration as 'a complex gloss on the word "meanwhile"'[75] helps us to see that the 'meanwhile' effects of Trollope's Irish novels cannot be produced without a reliance on the roads: those roads, in turn, both model and shape the connective tissue of Trollope's realism.

If we can imagine roads as possessing a temporal agency in Trollope, however, we must also pay attention to the ways in which the gapped and discontinuous Irish road system inflects the narrative treatment of time. Grossman says that the public transport system 'transformed walking on the intercity highways into a comparatively slow, onerous, and solitary mode of journeying and recreated it as the possibility of falling out of its network'.[76] This account does not quite work for Trollope's Irish novels, where characters choose to exit the network or are forced out of it. In *The Landleaguers* the boycotting of Castle Morony has the effect of barring the Jones family from the system of public transport. In both *The Macdermots* and *The Kellys and the O'Kellys*, walking on roads is associated with reflection and the promise of purposeful action, as with Father John in *The Macdermots*. The priest's regular recourse to such walks makes it more striking when the narrator describes how the community chooses to stay off the roads in order to avoid becoming witness to the execution of Thady Macdermot:

> Not one human form appeared before the gaol that morning. Not even a passenger crossed over the bridge from half-past seven till after eight, as from thence one might just catch a glimpse of the front of the prison. At the end of the bridge stood three or four men guarding the street, and cautioning those who came, that they could not pass by; and as their behests were obeyed, the police did not interfere with them.[77]

This powerful conclusion to Trollope's first Irish novel imagines a kind of communal identity wrought via a disciplined collective withdrawal from state systems: in doing so it arguably captures the impress of O'Connellite mobilisation, even as the narrative appears to censure same.

Castle Richmond is very different in this regard. Despite noting developments in modern travel (Herbert speeds from Castle Richmond to Euston Station and back again), the novel as a whole is careful to depict an infrastructural network marked by gaps and disconnections. When the disinherited Herbert Fitzgerald goes to inform Lady Clara of his change in fortunes, he 'did not take the direct road to Desmond Court, but went round as though he were going to Gortnaclough, and then turning away from the Gortnaclough road, made his way by a cross-lane'.[78] Crossing 'poor, bleak, damp, undrained country', he comes across a cabin 'abutting as it were on the road, not standing back upon the land, as it most customary; and it was built in an angle at a spot where the road made a turn, so that two sides of it stood close out in the wayside'.[79] This cabin is itself located amidst a patchwork landscape of subdivided land, and the uncultivated remains of a field system bisected and abandoned banks of earth.

The raw appearance of the cabin and its surroundings gives way to a painful and near pornographic rendering of the figure of a corpselike woman and her dead child – one of the ugliest scenes in all of Trollope. Noting the 'nakedness of the exterior' and

then 'the nakedness of the interior', the narrative describes how shifting light gradually reveals to Herbert the spectacle of a dying woman wearing 'some rag of clothing
which barely sufficed to cover her nakedness'.[80] Margaret Kelleher discusses this scene
in terms of the dynamics of an intrusive male gaze: '[t]he result', she argues, is an
'extensive and disturbing' 'representation of famine's effects, through the construction
of female spectacle'.[81]

Versions of the words nakedness, misery and brightness recur in this 'terrible and
intolerable'[82] scene of crude spectatorship. These passages, with their clumsy and
repeated vocabulary, recall and revisit the novel's seventh chapter, entitled 'The Famine Year'. There, the reader is introduced to the famine via the narrator's own journeys
on Irish roads: 'I was in the country, travelling always through it, during the whole
period.' The 'Famine Year' chapter of *Castle Richmond* is difficult to read: politically reprehensible because of the way in which Trollope presents the facts of famine
('the greater part of eight million people were left without food') alongside a blithely
providentialist account of the potato blight as divinely ordained; but also aesthetically
disagreeable, as the narrative moves between polemic and reportage. In both chapters,
the unbalanced prose reverberates on the rutted surface of the cross lane – or, to extend
this idea – it is as if Ireland's uneven modernity finds formal expression on the lane.

To return to the idea of lane-ism: perhaps we can think of Trollope advancing a
kind of road knowledge or proto-dromology. In *Roads: An Anthropology of Infrastructure and Expertise*, Penny Harvey and Hannah Knox argue that roads have a
powerful capacity to 'conjure a sense of the potential of enhanced connectivity'.[83]
In the passage from *The Macdermots of Ballycloran* with which I opened, it is this
'potential of enhanced connectivity' that creates the perception of the speedy workings of 'Ruin', with its showy tendency to outpace slow decay. In all of Trollope's Irish
novels, connections are developed along broken remnants of older or failed infrastructure, so that the concurrent events imagined via the horizontal ties of realist narration
depend on a dilapidated and dangerous infrastructure.

Benedict Anderson's account of the ways in which narrative time creates national
space has been much debated and revised. David Lloyd, for instance, argues that
Anderson's account misses the ways in which the novel form possesses a 'regulative
function' in postcolonial contexts.[84] Franco Moretti directs our attention away from
the novel as the singular form of nation and towards movements between and across
the internal differences of genre and geography.[85] Anderson's own account of his 'fic-
tive and selective kinship' with Ireland might further inflect these debates, suggesting
as it does the ways in which 'the ancestries of the imagination' must give way to the
material history of a felt and remembered place.[86]

A distinctly formal discussion of the impact of Anderson's theories of nationhood
is found in Jonathan Culler's essay on 'Anderson and the Novel'.[87] Culler argues that
what we encounter in Anderson and his critics is a vital tension between rich and
rewarding critical readings of individual novels as opposed to the power and attraction
of encompassing theories of the novel:

> What we seem to find is that the more interested one becomes in the way in which
> particular sorts of novels, with their plots and their imagined worlds, might
> advance, sustain, or legitimate the operations of nation-building, the richer and

more detailed one's arguments about novel and nation become, but at the cost of losing that general claim about the novelistic organization of time that was alleged to be the condition of possibility of imaging a nation.[88]

It may be strange to find Trollope on the side of theory and general claims, but his use of Irish roads to structure meetings and develop connections between past and present seems quite strictly suited to Anderson's theorisation of the operation of the function of the 'meanwhile' in the formation of national culture. Scholars of Trollope continue to debate his politics, whether those of a paternalist Englishman, a broad-minded liberal or a characteristically colonial cosmopolite, and it would be too crude in any case simply to ask what is the nation on whose behalf Trollope's realism works.[89] Instead my purpose in the chapter has been to point to roads in Trollope as markings on a map, directing our attention to the interrelationship between present and past and pointing out the urgent need to apprehend the speed and force of social and political change in Ireland. In the Irish novels and tales of E. O. Somerville and Martin Ross, to offer a counter-case, roads regularly 'melt' away into lanes, bogs and lakes as 'the wilds of Ireland' reclaim their territory.[90] Trollope's roads protrude, serving as signposts to a systematic reading of Irish society in the present. Such a reliance on the abstractions of space rather than the rich particularities of place – on theory rather than lived reality – may help to explain the unforgiveable harshness we sometimes find in Trollope's Irish novels.

Readers of Trollope's Irish novels will find real interest in Bruno Latour's argument that modernity is best theorised from the perspective of a traveller bogged down in the territory.[91] Latour's Actor-Network theory, which offers an account of critical method as slow travel on lesser-known roads where times cross and overlap, might also be visualised via the flow of letters in the postal network, their movements tracing spatial patterns that are dictated by powerful external structures but also inscribing journeys motivated by immediate, contingent and material circumstances.[92] Even as infrastructure signals the operation of a centralising state, the narratives of Trollope's Irish novels pause to notice the relationship between temporal progress and ruination and attribute agency to residual aspects of the network such as lanes and boreens. In doing so, they inscribe the 'bumpy territory'[93] of Irish modernity in compelling ways.

Notes

1. Anthony Trollope, *The Macdermots of Ballycloran*, ed. Robert Tracy (Oxford: Oxford University Press, 1982), ch. 1, p. 1.
2. Ibid. ch. 1, p. 2.
3. Ibid.
4. Antony Trollope, *The Kellys and the O'Kellys*, ed. W. J. McCormack (Oxford: Oxford University Press, 1989), ch. 4, p. 52.
5. Bruno Latour, *Reassembling the Social: An Introduction to Actor-Network-Theory* (Oxford: Oxford University Press), p. 76.
6. Ibid. p. 10.
7. Ibid. p. 55.
8. R. F. Foster, 'Stopping the Hunt: Trollope and the Memory of Ireland', *The Irish Story: Telling Tales and Making it Up in Ireland* (London: Penguin, 2001), pp. 127–47 (p. 147).

9. Trollope, *The Macdermots of Ballycloran*, ch. 1, pp. 2–5. See Gordon Bigelow for a reading of the novel in terms of a resistance to historicism and a breaking of the form of the historical novel. 'Form and Violence in Trollope's *The Macdermots of Ballycloran*', *Novel: A Forum on Fiction*, 46, 3 (2013): pp. 386–405. Bigelow cites Trollope's *Autobiography* and its account of the influence of seeing the ruins of Headfort House in County Galway.

10. Edmund Burke, *Reflections on the Revolution in France* (Harmondsworth: Penguin, 2004), p. 192.

11. [John Mitchel], 'The Civilizer!', *The Nation*, V, 248 (July 3, 1847).

12. K. Theodore Hoppen, *Governing Hibernia: British Politicians and Ireland 1800–1921* (Oxford: Oxford University Press, 2016), p. 151.

13. Ibid. pp. 152–3.

14. 'ism, n.' *OED Online* (Oxford University Press, January 2018). Available at <http://www.oed.com> (last accessed 1 March 2018).

15. Anthony Trollope, *The Examiner*, 1849; quoted in John McCourt, *Writing the Frontier: Anthony Trollope between Britain and Ireland* (Oxford: Oxford University Press, 2015), p. 52.

16. Stephen Gwynne, 'Trollope and Ireland', *Contemporary Review*, 129 (January–June 1926): p. 77; quoted in McCourt, *Writing the Frontier*, p. 97.

17. Christine Longford, 'Trollope in Ireland', *The Bell*, 5.3 (December 1952): p. 185.

18. Gordon Bigelow, 'Trollope and Ireland' in Carolyn Dever and Lisa Niles (eds), *The Cambridge Companion to Anthony Trollope* (Cambridge: Cambridge University Press, 2011), pp. 196–209 (p. 203).

19. McCourt, *Writing the Frontier*, p. 53. For a more critical view, see Gordon Bigelow, 'Irish Questions: Ireland and the Trollope Novels', in Deborah Denenholz Morse, Margaret Markwick and Mark W. Turner (eds), *The Routledge Companion to Anthony Trollope* (London and New York: Routledge, 2016), pp. 336–77.

20. Trollope, *The Kellys and the O'Kellys*, ch. 2, p. 19.

21. McCourt, *Writing the Frontier*, p. 18.

22. Anthony Trollope, *Castle Richmond*, ed. Mary Hamer (Oxford: Oxford University Press, 1989), ch. 1, p. 2.

23. Patrick Joyce, *The State of Freedom: A Social History of the British State since 1800* (Cambridge: Cambridge University Press, 2013), p. 47.

24. McCourt, *Writing the Frontier*, p. 17.

25. See Joyce, *State of Freedom*, on the 'common sense' operations of state power (p. 194).

26. Isaac Butt, 'The Present and Past State of Irish Literature', *Dublin University Magazine*, IX (1837), pp. 371–2. Butt also compares 'the slipshod newspaper prose of a modern debate' to the 'flowered carvings, on the rough but useful masonry of Kingstown pier' (p. 366).

27. Samuel Ferguson, 'Hardiman's Irish Minstrelsy – No. III' *Dublin University Magazine*, October 1834, vol. 4, p. 448.

28. Arthur Young, *A Tour in Ireland* (London, 1779), p. 869. He goes on: 'I found it perfectly practicable to travel upon wheels by a map; I will go here; I will go there; I could trace a route upon paper as wild as fancy could dictate, and every where I found beautiful roads without break or hindrance, to enable me to realize my design' (p. 871).

29. Joyce, *The State of Freedom*, p. 44.

30. John Bew, 'Ireland under the Union: 1801–1922', in Richard Bourke and Ian McBride (eds), *The Princeton History of Modern Ireland* (Princeton: Princeton University Press), pp. 74–108 (p. 90).

31. Ibid. p. 100.

32. Trollope, *Macdermots of Ballycloran*, ch. 1, p. 7.

33. Ibid.

34. McCourt, *Writing the Frontier*, p. 17.

35. Walter Scott, *Waverley*, ed. Claire Lamont (Oxford: Oxford University Press, 1986), p. 24.

36. Trollope, *The Kellys and the O'Kellys*, ch. 2, p. 27.

37. Mikhail Bakhtin, *The Dialogic Imagination: Four Essays*, trans. Caryl Emerson and Michael Holquist (Austin: University of Texas Press, 1981), p. 98.

38. Ibid. ch. 28, p. 352.

39. Paul Fyfe, *By Accident or Design: Writing the Victorian Metropolis* (Oxford: Oxford University Press, 2015), p. 175; Christopher Morash, *A History of the Media in Ireland* (Cambridge: Cambridge University Press, 2010), p. 74.

40. Nitin Sinha, *Communication and Colonialism in Eastern India: Bihar, 1760s to 1780s* (London and New York: Anthem Press, 2014). See also Jonathan H. Grossman, *Charles Dickens' Networks: Public Transport and the Novel* (Oxford: Oxford University Press, 2012), p. 91 and Ruth Livesey, *Writing the Stage Coach Nation: Locality on the Move in Nineteenth-Century British Literature* (Oxford: Oxford University Press, 2016). Wilkie Collins published an essay entitled 'The Last Stage Coachman' in 1843 *Illuminated Magazine* of August 1841.

41. Trollope, *Castle Richmond*, ch. 1, p. 2. Ernest Baker uses the same metaphor to discuss Trollope's English novels: 'But this cosmopolitanism, though constantly recurring, was only a digression. Fiction makes its conquests in other ways; its real advance is on internal lines. Trollope was beginning to deal with every aspect of English life, as methodically as if he had mapped out the ground with a theodolite.' *The History of the English Novel*, XI, 111 (1924).

42. Nitin Sinha, *Communication and Colonialism in Eastern India: Bihar, 1760s to 1780s* (London and New York: Anthem Press, 2014), pp. xx–xxi.

43. Sinha, *Communication and Colonialism in Eastern India*, p. 155.

44. Ibid. p. xxi.

45. Quoted in Augustus Hare (ed.), *The Life and Letters of Maria Edgeworth*, 2 vols (London, 1894), II, 274.

46. Maria Edgeworth to Mrs Edgeworth, Black Castle, 4 September 1804; quoted in Valerie Pakenham (ed.), *Maria Edgeworth: Letters from Ireland* (Dublin: Lilliput Press, 2017), p. 84.

47. Trollope, *The Kellys and the O'Kellys*, ch. 8, p. 97.

48. Ibid. ch. 8, p. 97.

49. Cormac Ó Gráda, 'Industry and Communications, 1801–1845', in W. E. Vaughan (ed.), *A New History of Ireland*, V (Oxford: Oxford University Press, 1989), pp. 137–57.

50. Arnold Horner, 'Ireland's time-space revolution: improvements to pre-Famine travel', *History Ireland 5* (2007). Available at <http://www.historyireland.com/18th-19th-century-history/irelands-time-space-revolution-improvements-to-pre-famine-travel/> (last accessed 1 March 2018).

51. Ó Gráda, 'Industry and Communications, 1801–1845', p. 146.

52. Oliver McDonagh 'The economy and society, 1830–45' in Vaughan (ed.) *A New History of Ireland: Ireland Under the Union, 1801–1870* (pp. 218–41), p. 229.

53. Jonathan H. Grossman, *Charles Dickens' Networks*, p. 4.

54. Ibid. p. 5.

55. Ibid. p. 71.

56. Trollope, *Castle Richmond*, ch. 16, p. 180.

57. Bakthin, *The Dialogic Imagination*, p. 244.

58. Trollope, *Macdermots of Ballycloran*, ch. 22, pp. 412–13.

59. McCourt, *Writing the Frontier*, p. 229.

60. Ibid. p. 228.

61. Trollope, *Macdermots of Ballycloran*, ch. 23, p. 427.

62. Michael Sadleir, *Trollope: A Commentary* (London: Constable & Co. Ltd, 1927), p. 144.

63. Foster, 'Stopping the Hunt', p. 129; p. 145.

64. Anthony Trollope, *The Landleaguers*, ed. Robert Lee Wolff (New York: Garland, 1979) ch. 1, I, 1.

65. Ibid. ch. 23, III, 109.

66. Foster, 'Stopping the Hunt', p. 142.

67. Trollope, *Castle Richmond*, ch. 18, p. 205.

68. Trollope, *The Landleaguers*, ch. 46, III, p. 242.

69. Ibid. ch. 23, III, 109.

70. Rita Felski, *The Limits of Critique* (Chicago: University of Chicago Press, 2015), p. 158.

71. Latour, *Reassembling the Social*, p. 23.

72. Ibid. p. 17.

73. Ibid. p. 23.

74. Benedict Anderson, *Imagined Communities: Reflections on the Origin and Spread of Nationalism* (London: Verso, 1991), p. 24.

75. Ibid. p. 25.

76. Grossman, *Charles Dickens' Networks*, p. 91

77. Trollope, *Macdermots of Ballycloran*, ch. 33, pp. 622–3.

78. Trollope, *Castle Richmond*, ch. 33, p. 367.

79. Ibid. ch. 33, pp. 367–8.

80. Ibid. ch. 33, p. 369.

81. Margaret Kelleher, 'Anthony Trollope's "Castle Richmond": Famine Narrative and "Horrid Novel"?', *Irish University Review*, vol. 25, no. 2 (Autumn–Winter, 1995): pp. 242–62 (p. 250).

82. Melissa Fegan, *Literature and the Irish Famine, 1845–1919* (Oxford: Clarendon Press, 2002), p. 126.

83. Penny Harvey and Hannah Knox, *Roads: An Anthropology of Infrastructure and Expertise* (Cornell: Cornell University Press, 2015), p. 22.

84. David Lloyd, *Anomalous States: Irish Writing and the Post-Colonial Moment* (Durham, NC: Duke University Press, 1993), p. 154.

85. Franco Moretti, *Atlas of the European Novel, 1800–1900* (London: Verso, 1999), p. 20.

86. Benedict Anderson, 'Selective Kinship', *Dublin Review*, 10 (Spring 2003): pp. 5–29 (p. 26; p. 29).

87. Jonathan Culler, 'Anderson and the Novel', *Diacritics*, Volume 29, Number 4 (Winter 1999): pp. 20–39.

88. Ibid. p. 25.

89. See Deborah Denenholz Morse, *Reforming Trollope: Race, Gender, and Englishness in the Novels of Anthony Trollope* (Aldershot: Ashgate, 2013) on Trollope as liberal; Lauren M. E. Goodlad, *The Victorian Geopolitical Aesthetic: Realism, Sovereignty, and Transnational Experience* (Oxford: Oxford University Press, 2015) on Trollope as 'a pronounced racialist and Anglo-Saxon expansionist' . . . exemplifying 'a mid-Victorian tendency to regard modernity's cosmopolitan features with ambivalence' (p. 67). See also Elaine Hadley, *Living Liberalism: Practical Citizenship in Victorian Britain* (Chicago: University of Chicago Press, 2010), which reads the place of Phineas Finn in the Palliser novels in terms of the contradictions of liberalism:

> Mainstream midcentury liberals – the parliamentary population of professionals and industrialists presumed to enter government on the coattails of suffrage reform – are dramatized through the life adventures of handsome young Irishman Phineas Finn.
>
> That liberalism, seen so jealously by history as an organic outgrowth of English Protestant liberty and the ancient constitution, should be put into action by a Catholic doctor's son from the western reaches of Ireland has been oddly minimized by most literary critics who otherwise are thinking about the political novel in this period. (p. 229)

90. See Mary Kelly, 'Landscapes of order and (dis)order in Somerville and Ross's *The Irish RM*', in Patrick J. Duffy and William Nolan (eds), *At the Anvil: Essays in Honour of William J. Smyth* (Dublin: Geography Publications, 2012), pp. 537–44 (p. 541).

91. See Latour on travel as method: '"where to travel" and "what is worth seeing there" is nothing but a way of saying in plain English what is usually said under the pompous Greek name of "method" or, even worse, "methodology". The advantage of a travel book approach over a "discourse on method" is that it cannot be confused with the territory on which it simply overlays. A guide can be put to use as well as forgotten, placed in a backpack, stained with grease and coffee, scribbled all over, its pages torn apart to light a fire under a barbecue.' Latour, *Reassembling the Social*, p. 17.

92. See Richard Menke's chapter in this volume, 'Mimesis, Media Archaeology and the Postage Stamp in *John Caldigate*'.

93. Latour, *Reassembling the Social*, p. 22.

18

IMPERIAL LOGISTICS: TROLLOPE AND THE QUESTION OF CENTRAL AMERICA

Robert D. Aguirre

TROLLOPE ARRIVED IN the West Indies late in 1858, having sailed from Southampton on a Royal Mail Steam Packet. Over the next several months he travelled throughout the Caribbean, the Spanish colony of Cuba and several independent Central American republics. He kept a journal and upon returning to London published his travel account, *The West Indies and the Spanish Main* (1859). Mixing the familiar conventions of literary travel with the inimitable ironies and social commentary associated more frequently with his novels, the work details the author's journeys across lands both well known and more remote for the typical British reader. His narrative fulfils generic expectations by providing information about far-off places while offering a witty gloss on local manners and incidents. This blend of instruction and delight was a staple of the Victorian travel narrative, and in *The West Indies and the Spanish Main* Trollope proved his mastery of it, even as he departed from the well-trodden path of emphasising the special relationship between Britain and the United States in favour of accenting emerging areas of geopolitical concern such as Central America. Yet what Trollope fails to reveal about his journey is as important as what he includes. For he went to the Americas not to write a travel narrative but more significantly to carry out a specific, logistical mission on behalf of his employer, the British Post Office, and beyond that the British state. His bosses at the Post Office, who played an important role in binding a global empire together, were eager to improve British mail service in the Caribbean and Central America, and particularly their linkages to the Pacific basin. As I demonstrate below, Trollope's analytic and administrative powers and his keen understanding of global politics made him the logical choice for this assignment, which had significant imperial potential. Turning his attention to the turbulent global South, he assessed advancing US territorial ambition in the hemisphere and measured the increasing importance of Central America as a transit point to a rapidly globalising world, in which Britain hoped to play a major role.[1]

Throughout the text, however, Trollope rather maddeningly downplays these official motivations, suggesting only that he was concerned with 'certain affairs of State' – affairs he keeps scrupulously in the dark.[2] It is not that he doesn't drop a few hints. At one point he writes 'that Jamaica should be the head-quarters of these [mail] packets', only to add that 'the question is one which will not probably be interesting to the reader of these pages' (ch. 15, p. 225). Furthermore, his identity as a Post Office employee was hardly a secret. When E. S. Dallas penned his *Times* review of *West Indies and the Spanish Main* he referred openly to the postal mission.[3] Yet in the text itself, Trollope conceals his journey's official motivations, even as they shaped his movements. This effort to disguise the work's thrust of business imperialism poses less of a problem in the reader's understanding of the Jamaican sections, which come first, than in the Spanish American chapters that follow. The Jamaican material concerns matters that had long been in the public eye: slavery and abolition in the colonies; the effects of ending protective trade tariffs; increased competition from European beet sugar; and the decline of sugar production itself, which fell from 77,300 US tons in 1824 to 26,600 US tons in 1854.[4] At least since Thomas Carlyle's notorious essay on the 'Negro Question', which informs Trollope's views, the British public had been fed a steady diet of newspaper and magazine articles about the island. Another British commentary on the island's misfortunes would not have been unusual.

By taking up the Central American question within a largely hemispheric understanding of the region, this essay seeks to complexify prevailing postcolonial readings of the text which, while illuminating Trollope's racial attitudes, have reduced a complex, transnational itinerary to a black-and-white tale about Jamaica. For although Trollope devotes only one third of his book to the West Indies, critics such as Simon Gikandi describe the work's geographical purview as the 'the West Indian space', 'the West Indies', 'the islands' and the 'Caribbean landscape'.[5] This seems in part an effect of anticipatory reading. The Morant Bay rebellion of 1865 looms over many interpretations of *The West Indies and the Spanish Main*, transforming Trollope's text, with its pro-planter stance, into an admonitory precursor of racial troubles to come.[6] Yet however much postcolonial criticism has illuminated Trollope's activities in Jamaica, it has largely ignored the ways in which Central America, and particularly Panama, was becoming a global transit zone, a funnel for diasporic movement on a grand scale, a link of empire, a source of conflict between Britain and a territorially aggressive United States, and the subject of intensive literary and pictorial representation. The 1841 publication of John Lloyd Stephens's *Incidents of Travel in Central America, Chiapas, and Yucatan* had drawn attention to the ruined Maya cities buried deep in the jungles of Honduras and Guatemala, suggesting rich fields for antiquarian discovery. William H. Prescott's *History of the Conquest of Mexico* (1843) and Fanny Calderon de la Barca's *Life in Mexico* (1843), both of which received much attention in London, spurred the growth of Hispanism as an amateur field of study, and the US war with Mexico (1846–8) focused British anxieties about a newly emboldened United States, with concerns over Central America's fate not far behind. Those fears were galvanised by the 1848 discovery of gold in California, which turned the world's gaze to the Panamanian isthmus. This narrow neck of land between the seas became a focal point when throngs of hopeful travellers crossed over Panama on the way to the California gold fields, and US entrepreneurs, led by the aforementioned Stephens, obtained a concession from the government of Nueva Granada (in present day Panama) to construct a railroad across the forty-nine miles that separated Colón on the Atlantic side from Panama (City) on the Pacific, connecting the oceans and presaging the Panama Canal.

Trollope, of course, would later explore the theme of transnational railroad schemes at greater length in *The Way We Live Now*, weaving it masterfully in a larger plot about fraudulent paper, the feverish psychology of financial speculation, and the uncertain, frequently tragic outcomes of a market-oriented world. While a consideration of Trollope's novel is beyond the scope of this chapter, there are many striking parallels between the Panama Railroad and the fictional plan to lay a line between Salt Lake City and the Mexican port city of Vera Cruz, and it is clear Trollope was thinking of Panama as he described Melmotte's North American railroad. In Chapter 22 the Panama Railroad is described, accurately, as an 'affair which had paid twenty-five percent'.[7] In Chapter 30, the language moves beyond the merely financial to capture the quasi-religious meanings that were frequently attached to such ventures during the heyday of transport enthusiasm: 'what had been the meaning of that paragraph in which the writer had declared that the work of joining one ocean to another was worthy of the nearest approach to divinity that had been granted to men?'[8] As Trollope understood from his Central American travels in the late 1850s, just four years after the completion of the Panama Railway in 1855, railways were also becoming increasingly important to a transport-oriented world. The US control of the railway unsettled British officials, who struggled to exert influence in the region even as their sway was gradually being diminished. They were particularly concerned to ensure the smooth passage of mail to their outlying territories and sought to exploit the isthmus and its already-built railroad as a shortcut to distant parts of their empire.

Trollope's remit, which dealt with establishing new mail routes in the Caribbean basin and across the isthmus to the Pacific, put him in a privileged position to comment on and shape these changes. His logistical mission to the Spanish Main did not entail the blunt exercise of military power, or even techniques of embargo or blockade, which the British frequently employed in South America, but rather a softer, informal style of influence organised around the smooth conveyance of paper letters, a matter that, according to an 1860 parliamentary committee on steam packets, involved 'our political relations, our colonial empire, the efficiency of our army and navy, and the spread of our commerce'.[9] The high importance the British government attached to such communications is reflected in the lengthy letter of instruction composed by Frederic Hill, assistant secretary in charge of the mail packets. This seven-page, twenty-seven-point memorandum directed Trollope's every move, stipulating which local officials he was to see, what he was permitted to say (and not to say), and the arrangements he was to make on behalf of the British government.[10] A displaced and imaginatively reworked representation of these instructions, Trollope's travel narrative is an important literary and political commentary on British attitudes towards the isthmus in the wake of the US railroad. Its ambivalence on matters imperial (US and British) reveals a more complicated Trollope than postcolonial readings might otherwise suggest, while its geopolitical scope suggests the necessity of joining Atlantic models of cultural analysis with hemispheric ones.

* * *

Susan Zieger has framed the Post Office's growing power to coordinate information as a 'foundational example of logistics', arguing that postal officials discovered in Trollope someone particularly skilled at this quintessentially modern form of management.[11] Indeed, Trollope's postal work in this period demonstrates his sophisticated understanding of the post *as a system*, first locally and then abroad, one that, as Patrick Joyce shows in *The State of Freedom*, involved 'a remarkable extension of [the state's] communicative powers and an equally remarkable deepening of human and non-human connectedness'.[12] He joined the Post Office at a time of unprecedented reform and growth. From 1839 to 1853 chargeable letters rose from 75.9 million to 410.8 million.[13] His work as a postal surveyor in the west of Ireland revealed his ability to grasp the complexities of large, multimodal systems. The same passion for efficiency and the mastery of time that later drove his writing habits – arising at 5.30 a.m. to write by the clock – also motivated his work as a postal surveyor, in which he analysed a vast, interlinked network of delivery that was increasingly driven by the need for speed. Rowland Hill, his superior at the Post Office, characterised the work as the application of analytical rigour to personal movement: 'The surveyor determines the length of a walk a letter carrier might reasonably make in a day, arranges the walk to include as many villages and hamlets as he can, determines whether the weekly volume of letters for those places be sufficient to pay the expense . . . [and] establishes the route.'[14] According to his biographers, Trollope walked his routes religiously; 'it was', he said, 'the ambition of my life to cover the country with rural letter carriers.'[15] After his stint in Ireland he assumed responsibility for reviewing mail service in several English counties (Gloucestershire, Herefordshire, Monmouthshire, Oxfordshire, Wiltshire, Worcestershire), the six southern Welsh counties and the Channel Islands, where he recommended the experiment of roadside letter collection.

In 1858 he extended his domain outward to the far reaches of British influence, travelling to Suez – just then in the beginning stages of canal construction – to forge an agreement for mail delivery to colonial possessions in India and Australia. With characteristic zeal, he assessed each link in the complex web, going so far as to calculate, timepiece in hand, 'the normal speed of a camel' across the desert sands.[16] The next year, having won his superiors' confidence (he was praised by name in the Post Office annual report of 1859), he sailed to the Americas to carry out a similar analytical project. Here, as in Ireland and Suez, he brought his logistical powers to the task of rationalising the post as a system. Despite Trollope's disavowals of his official purpose, his logistical inclination is evident throughout *The West Indies and the Spanish Main*. He reports, for example, that he judged the Panama route superior to a competing route across Honduras because he had measured the speed of the prevailing trade winds and calculated that a steamer from Belize to Jamaica 'is timed only at four miles an hour', while one from to Honduras 'is timed at eight miles an hour' (ch. 21, p. 322) – a piece of data analysis lifted directly from his official reports to the Post Office.[17] The letters of instruction he carried with him reinforced this mindset as an imperative of global information policy, informing him that on 'visiting Colon and Panama the experience derived from your recent mission to Egypt will aid you in examining thoroughly the arrangements connected with the transit of mails across the Isthmus'.[18] They directed him to reconceive the existing individual segments in view of strengthening the large, multi-point network that led across the Atlantic to the Caribbean, over the isthmus, and from there to cities and towns throughout the Pacific: Victoria (British Columbia), Sydney and Canton.

The prospect of a shortcut to the Pacific, whether by paved road, railway or canal, drew increasing attention in the years preceding Trollope's journey, and was perceived on both sides of the Atlantic as critical to nation-building and global empire. In 1838, the Scottish geographer James MacQueen issued *A General Plan for a Mail Communication by Steam, between Great Britain and the Eastern and Western Parts of the World*, which proposed the development of steam packets to the West Indies, the carriage of mail across the isthmus, and further service to Canton and Sydney. Identifying the analogic relationship between local and global technologies of communication, MacQueen defined steam packets as 'the mail-coaches of the ocean' and described their informational function as central to the armature of British gentle-manly capitalism:

> The rapidity and regularity with which such communications can be made, gives to every nation an influence, a command, and advantages such as scarcely anything else can give, and frequently extends even beyond the sphere of that influence and that command which the direct application of mere physical power can obtain.[19]

In 1842, one year after Trollope began his work as a surveyor in Ireland, the Post Office introduced adhesive postage stamps, began bi-weekly steam packets to the West Indies and landed its first steamer at the isthmus.[20] Three years later, Captain W. B. Liot scouted the mail route across the isthmus, which, once established in 1846, connected established Atlantic routes with new ones branching into the Pacific.[21] And in 1852, the Royal Mail initiated a line from Savannah to Chagres. Despite these advances, in the early 1850s a letter sent from London to Victoria, British Columbia took on average three months to arrive and relied on assistance from Hudson Bay ships and Native American canoes. In the year Trollope set out for the West Indies, British Columbia's colonial governor pleaded with the Colonial Office for a direct steamer line from Panama to Vancouver Island, which he represented as 'advantageous to British interests in this part of the world'.[22]

MacQueen claimed that by the cutting through the isthmus 'the valuable, but almost unknown, British territory on the west coast of North America, would be brought near, and cleared, and cultivated', and that more generally, the opening of such a passage would benefit the cultural mission of British imperialism.[23] It would do more, he wrote, 'to people, to cultivate, and civilize the world, than any other effort – than all other efforts made by the world at large, when combined and brought together'.[24] In an 1851 Post Office report on steam communication with India, Robert Lowe described the delivery of mail to outlying regions as a strategy of maintaining colonial coherence: 'if you mean to maintain those colonies, you must either absolutely abandon to them the whole of the government, or else you must shorten the distance; people cannot wait; the larger the communities become, the more impossible it is to wait.'[25] A few decades, later another British official, J. Henniker Heaton, grounded his appeal for lower-cost overseas mail by asserting that it would foster patriotism, 'cement the social and political bonds of the empire' and provide a 'formidable blow to the foreign competition with which we are threatened in colonial markets'.[26] The affective consequences of this improved sense of connection cannot be underestimated. The British Vice-Consul Bidwell, writing in 1865, captured the emotions produced by the imminent arrival of letters: 'One of the most refreshing sights to a European stationed at Panamá is, I think, the sight of the long row of mule-carts bearing towards the English consulate their goodly loads of British mail-bags.' He went on to describe Panama as the 'very St. Martin's-le-Grand' where 'all the correspondence for the whole coast of South America is distributed and despatched by Her Majesty's Consul'.[27]

The US control over the isthmus, whose emblem and embodiment was the Panama Railroad, posed a significant problem for Trollope's governmental mission, and not only for its monopoly on trans-isthmian mail service. The western hemisphere's first transcontinental line, the railroad's scale and broad effects left no doubt of the growing power of the US to integrate distant territories into its political imaginary – a power with which Britain was well acquainted in other parts of its own empire. The iron road that stretched forty-nine miles across the isthmus constituted in its day the largest outlay of US capital in both Central and South America. Relative to the US economy of its time, the $8 million dollar investment in 1858 would equal $28.5 billion dollars in 2009.[28] The railroad reshaped hemispheric and global politics, helped to modernise California and Panama, and altered Central American trade and commerce.[29] The population of the city of Panama tripled between 1840 and 1860. Along with the war against Mexico, efforts to annex Cuba, and US incursions in Central America, the railroad signalled a new era of US imperial ambition. Writing in 1849, the American oceanographer and naval official Matthew Maury crystalised the aggressive view that control over the isthmus would vault the US ahead of its rival Britain in the race for global dominance: 'Cut through this Isthmus, "Uncle Sam" will then turn the corner, and England will be distanced. Instead, then, of meeting us in India, China, and even on our own Pacific coast with the advantage of some ten days' sail, or more, the scales will be turned, and we shall have the advantage.'[30] Many US documents from this period evince similarly hawkish views.

Although the land on which the line was built lay within the sovereign territory of Nueva Granada, the overland railway path and its associated infrastructure became known as the 'Yankee Strip', a zone of commerce and culture designed to provide the goods, services and comforts demanded by foreign travellers. This represented a linguistic concession to a new, albeit contested, reality, in which throngs of US travellers crossed the isthmus but primarily enriched the expatriate community, not the locals. California gold, according to the Panamanian historian Alfredo Castillero Calvo, did as little for the local economy in the 1850s as silver in an earlier era from the mines of Potosí; the Panama Railroad and 'New York capitalists' absorbed all the transit and resulting economic benefits.[31] The British naval officer Bedford Pim noted in 1863 that since the railway bypassed the city of Panama 'all merchandise therefore passes through the country without in any way affecting the prosperity of the city'.[32] Many of the Americans were rough and ill-mannered. According to one Panamanian observer in 1857, they comprised all manner of travellers, businessmen, two-bit speculators, profiteers, gamblers, keepers of gambling houses, shoplifters, thieves and assassins who flouted the rule of law, settling disputes with 'la pistola, el rifle, el puñal [dagger], y el machete'.[33] Contemporary observers, such as the Jamaican creole Mary Seacole, noted the racially inflected quality of these interactions, which appear to have been shaped by the perception that travellers in this in-between zone were under no obligation to conform to reasonable standards of conduct. Seacole's *Wonderful Adventures* (1857) recounts the tensions that welled up on the isthmus as 'the extreme class of [US] citizens' encountered a society where blacks, who were in the majority, were not only free, but held important positions in public life. Seacole's transnational experience of travel had taught her that 'Americans (even from the Northern States) are always uncomfortable in the company of coloured people, and very often show this feeling in stronger ways than by sour looks and rude words'.[34] As she subsequently put it, the 'New Granadan's experiences of American manners have not been favourable'.[35]

In the years just prior to Trollope's arrival sweeping changes in transit and transport altered the isthmian landscape and culture. In 1848 just 335 foreign travellers made their way across the isthmus. By 1852, that number had risen to 31,826.[36] In 1848 California's population stood at 20,000. A year later it had risen to 100,000 and by

1852 had reached 225,000.[37] The isthmus became a massive throughway for wealth; from 1855 to 1867, the railroad conveyed $750 million dollars of specie (money in coin), mostly from California.[38] The communications of two empires – Great Britain and the United States – surged through as well. The *California*, the first Pacific Mail steamship to serve the Panama to San Francisco route, carried 6,000 letters in its hold on its maiden voyage in 1848–9. Within months the number had risen to 36,000.[39] In the space of twelve years, the railroad had transported 300,000 bags of mail.[40] Writing in 1869, Berthold Seemann, the naturalist who collaborated with Captain Bedford Pim on several Central American projects, commented on the centrality of the isthmus to communication, describing it as the central spot for 'obtaining information and news, and carrying on trade with the East and the West, the North and the South'.[41] Persons, currency, state communications and letters – all these moved from one ocean to another in a seemingly endless stream, first by mule and canoe, then later by rail. The isthmus became a contact zone, a place where peoples intermingled and sometimes clashed. The sizeable number of US citizens that crossed through, unusual throughout all Latin America, brought with it extra tensions, as the military and economic backing of a large and powerful nation gave an extra charge to interactions between these highly mobile foreigners and the locals, as well as between representatives of competing nations.

Trollope's stance toward the new isthmian order demonstrates the ambivalence at the heart of his critical enterprise. Like other Britons such as Mary Seacole, he took umbrage at US excesses, seeing Central America within a larger hemispheric contest for influence. He deplored the Yankee insistence that Colón (the Atlantic terminus of the railroad) be known as Aspinwall (after the US tycoon who founded the railroad), remarking that 'our friends from Yankee-land', despite the 'disgust' of the Nueva Granadians, 'like to carry things with a high hand, and to have a nomenclature of their own' (ch.16, p. 236). With his novelist's ear for the power of words, he grasped that the desire to fix the names of things and places was itself an expression of power. And he knew, of course, that Aspinwall was no mere name, but a stark reminder of how US capital had forever transformed the isthmus into a link in a global system of transport, one that in privileging the traveller's mobility increased immobility for the locals, whose livelihoods as guides across the isthmus were decimated by the arrival of industrialised machines. In this, he agreed with Panamanian critics of US expansionism such as Justo Arosemena, who in the years immediately preceding Trollope's arrival had contrasted the peaceful and religious 'raza latina' with the warlike expansionists of the north, who would cry from their New England redoubts, 'I need another world; this is mine; and I will conquer you entirely.'[42] Their mission, he writes, is to subdue, and in a compelling burst of anti-imperial rhetoric, he assembles evidence of a larger hemispheric imperialism emanating from the US. He describes US expansion across the 'deserts' of the West and the annihilation ('aniquilando') of the indigenous races that lived there.[43] Not content with Mexico's submission, the Americans, he argues, had used diplomatic means to steal California, and now they were intent on spreading their 'corruption' throughout the hemisphere. They were ultimately a distinct race: materialist, thieving, a grave threat to Latin America and the future of universal commerce itself.[44]

Trollope's position, of course, differed considerably from that of Panamanian commercial elites such as Arosemena. But we can see the deftness of his approach in his dealings with local officials who were in a position of economic dependency – a key component of Britain's informal imperialism in the Americas. His behaviour illustrates key differences between British and US tactics on the isthmus. The Post Office wanted efficiencies and lower costs, and thus his instructions included forging new, more favourable economic agreements with the government of Nueva Granada and the Panama Railroad Company, both of which levied tariffs on trans-isthmian mail. Trollope was particularly concerned about the practice of taxing *individual* letters, which he felt would discourage personal communication by post. As explained in a substantial letter to his superior Rowland Hill, he raised the matter with the US engineer George Totten of the Panama Railway Company, who advised him that the United States simply refused to pay the Nueva Granadian levy, certain of no adverse consequences.[45] Such disregard of local sovereignty typifies the larger and more aggressive US domination in the 1850s that Panamanian officials such as Arosemena decried. In 'La cuestión Americana' of 1856, Arosemena described the non-payment of taxes as an insult to national sovereignty and a sign of disrespect to Nueva Granada's laws and moral traditions. In light of the concession across the isthmus that had made the railroad possible, he felt that the refusal to pay fees and tariffs was particularly galling.[46] Great Britain was in no position to act similarly, but it is striking that rather than refuse to pay, as Totten had recommended, Trollope chose another path, negotiating the tax downward. His solution produced the required result – lowering the cost – but avoided the tensions created by a heavier-handed US approach. His skill was not, then, simply a result of logistical thinking, but a demonstration of the power of soft influence and the deft negotiation of different sovereignties – understandings that Trollope evinced both in his travel writings and his novels.

Yet if Trollope in some respects remains wary of the advancing of US power, he echoes in others the railway promoters in characterising dark-skinned locals as obstacles to the mobility of goods, persons and mail. His theme of cultural decline would have resonated with British readers accustomed to travellers' accounts representing Spanish American civilisation as inimical to modernity. Describing Nueva Granada, Trollope claims that 'civilization here is retrograding' and 'making no progress' (ch. 16, p. 231). Time itself appeared to have rolled backwards, and with it the fruits of a progressive society: 'Land that was cultivated is receding from cultivation; cities that were populous are falling into ruins; and men are going back to animals' (p. 231). Dickens's *Household Words*, similarly, had described the local population as 'poor and ignorant aboriginals and mixed races, [trapped] in a state of scarcely demi-civilisation'.[47] Even in their hyperbolic form, these characterisations mesh with conservative British opinion that Latin America would have been better served had it been colonised by Anglo-Saxons, not Spaniards. In Argentina thirty years before, young Darwin wondered 'how different would have been the aspect of this river if English colonists had by good fortune first sailed up the Plata! What noble towns would now have occupied its shores!'[48] In these accounts a critique of Spanish civilisation's failings – its bondage to Catholic superstition, its hostility to modernity – is admixed with a strong dose of regret, a recognition that Great Britain had missed a grand imperial opportunity. By the time of Trollope's writing, the realisation of having lost out to the Spanish in the sixteenth century was joined by the more pressing and present concern of losing out to the US in the nineteenth.

A committed believer in Britain's 'noble mission' to preserve the 'welfare of the coming world', Trollope finally came down on the side of viewing the local population of Central America as a hindrance to the schemes of development and increased commerce that arose from the energy and drive of the 'Anglo-Saxon race' (ch. 5, p. 83). Disparaging mestizo Costa Ricans as a 'humdrum, contented, quiet, orderly race of men' with 'no enthusiasm, no ardent desires, no aspirations', he claims that they simply 'vegetate' under the hot tropical sun (ch. 18, pp. 264–5). Like Carlyle, he links what he sees as low human productivity to an overly hot and fecund climate, arguing that '[it] seems God's will that highly fertile countries should not really pros- per' (ch. 19, p. 263). Like the railway promoters and gold rushers of the previous decade, he defines the Western traveller as the master of time and speed. Evoking the customary foil of the laggard Spaniard, he reminds the reader that in 'any coun- try that is or has been connected with Spain', 'men have no idea of time'. His mule driver's assurances – 'Yes, señor; you said twelve, and it is now only two! Well, three. The day is long, señor; there is plenty of time . . .' (ch. 16, p. 277) – only reinforce his belief that the local people lack the energy and drive necessary to succeed in the coming world of mobility, speed and transport. His own difficulties with movement across space function textually as an admonitory sign of the larger challenges facing the Spanish Main's modernisation, and suggest his view that Central America could not be left to the Central Americans.

Trollope reserves his most damning comments for Nueva Granada's black resi- dents, who in the years before Trollope's visit were the principal beneficiaries of the final abolition of slavery (1852) and the establishment of universal manhood suffrage (1853), this last the result of what Aims McGuinness has correctly called 'the most radical constitution in the world'.[49] Reverting to a Carlylean perspec- tive familiar from the Jamaican chapters, Trollope recoils at the latter develop- ment, praising abolition as a 'good deed' (ch. 16, p. 231) but criticising suffrage for allowing every man, whether an 'industrial occupier of land' or an 'idle occupier of nothing' to have an equal vote (p. 231). He argues that the prospect of all men being 'equal for all state purposes' was 'not gratifying', for universal male suffrage implied the unimaginable, that a white man might be represented by a black one. He makes clear that his reasons are explicitly racial by invoking Carlyle's ugly phrase – the 'unfortunate nigger gone masterless' – employed here to argue that black people have no 'strong ideas of the duties even of self-government, much less the government of others' (ch. 16, p. 232).[50]

To see these matters from another side, as it were, it is instructive to turn here to Seacole's *Wonderful Adventures*, which was published in London just two years before Trollope's work. Seacole's text offers an important counterweight to these disparaging views of black self-government, and since Trollope mentions having lodged in Kingston 'with a sister of good Mrs Seacole' (ch. 2, p. 23), it seems likely he had read her narrative and was familiar with her sojourn in Panama. It's also likely he disapproved of her radical opinions, especially her opposing view of sov- ereignty on the isthmus – a major preoccupation of both works. Among many other examples, Seacole's account of the arrest of an 'American by the New Granada authorities' stands out for its quite different treatment of exactly the issue to which Trollope objects above – the political and judicial power of emancipated black citizens in Nueva Granada.[51] Providing a level of eyewitness specificity that only one who has endured similar slights could offer, Seacole briskly narrates the arrest of a US citizen for 'highway robbery'. At the start of her brief account she uses an objective third-person viewpoint to describe an 'angry crowd of brother Americans' surrounding the frightened soldiers who had made the arrest, 'abusing and threat-ening the authorities in no measured terms, all of them indignant that a *nigger should presume to judge one of their countrymen*' (emphasis added). The crux of the matter, of course, is who has the authority to judge, or rather, whether a black man has the authority to judge a white one. Seacole then goes on to remark that the ruckus 'roused the sleepy alcalde', or mayor, who charges his soldiers to quell the disturbance before delivering a speech to the unruly crowd. Through Seacole's narration, we now see the incident through the attributed words of the local official. The content of the speech, like so many representations from this period, is filtered through a more literate narrator. The alcalde himself does not speak, but is spoken for, albeit by a subject who herself has known the slings and arrows of being black in Panama. Importantly, however, the speech's content corroborates other accounts we have seen of lawlessness and disrespect among the new arrivals: 'he addressed the crowd, declaring that since the Americans came the country had known no peace, that robberies and crimes of very sort had increased, and ending in his deter-mination to make strangers respect the laws of the Republic.' Notably, the alcalde reinforces the crucial idea of sovereignty by reminding the mob that they are not in the United States but in another country, whose laws they must respect. Yet to ensure that the reader grasps not only *what* was said but *who* said it, Seacole again switches perspective, voicing the thoughts of the bewildered white US citizens: 'the Americans seemed too astonished at the audacity of the black man, who dared thus to beard them, to offer any resistance.' As historians have documented, many of the local mayors or 'alcaldes' in Nueva Granada were black, a reflection of the liberal policies towards suffrage and abolition noted above. Their power – here on display both in the ability to order the soldiers and to quell a disturbance caused by white men from the US – was indisputable, giving the lie to, and perhaps the rationale for, Trollope's mistaken ideas about black self-government.[52]

It is, however, not surprising that Trollope dismissed the ability of Nueva Grana-dians to conduct their own affairs. For he had concluded that Central America could only be 'great in the world' by serving as a 'passage between other parts of the world which are in themselves great' (ch. 21, p. 339). He thus defined the region as a nodal point in a large logistical network that organised the flow of mobilities across the world. That he saw the region this way is clear from 'The Journey to Panama', one of the short stories inspired by his West Indian and Spanish American travels. His narra-tor argues that the West Indian route is great

> not on account of our poor West Indian islands which cannot at the present moment make anything great, but because it spreads itself out from thence to Mexico and Cuba, to Guiana and the republics of New Granada and Venezuela, to Central America, the Isthmus of Panamá, and from thence to California, Vancouver's Island, Peru, and Chili.[53]

Defined as a connection point for the communications of larger, more important nations, the Spanish Main and its Caribbean neighbours dissolve as places with their own inherent value. Absorbed into a global system of travel dictated from afar, they become places between; intersections. The disruptive technology that changed the landscape was the 'great fact' (ch. 16, p. 237) of the Panama Railway, which served as a technological prosthesis for larger economic and geopolitical imperatives, both for the British Empire, which Trollope represented, and the United States, the hemisphere's coming power. As a traveller along, and a colonial administrator of, this larger system, Trollope was well placed to understand and analyse its reach and power, its limitations and exclusions.

Notes

1. Asa Briggs estimates that mid-nineteenth-century British writers composed over 200 travel volumes about the United States. 'Trollope the Traveler', in *The Collected Essays of Asa Briggs*, 3 vols (Urbana: University of Illinois Press, 1985), vol. 2, pp. 89–115 (p. 90). For a nuanced account of Trollope's work on North America, see Amanda Claybaugh, 'Trollope and America', in Carolyn Dever and Lisa Niles (eds), *The Cambridge Companion to Anthony Trollope* (Cambridge: Cambridge University Press, 2011), pp. 211–13.

2. Anthony Trollope, *The West Indies and the Spanish Main* (New York: Carroll and Graf, 1999), ch. 1, p. 11. Further citations are given parenthetically (*WISM*).

3. E. S. Dallas, review of *West Indies and the Spanish Main*, by Anthony Trollope, *Times* (London: 9 January 1860, 4b and 18 January 1860, 12a). For historical overviews of Trollope's postal work, see R. H. Super, *Trollope in the Post Office* (Ann Arbor: University of Michigan Press, 1981), pp. 38–44, and N. John Hall, *Trollope, A Biography* (Oxford: Clarendon Press, 1991), pp. 171–82. For the correspondence, see Trollope, *The Letters of Anthony Trollope*, ed. N. John Hall, 2 vols (Stanford: Stanford University Press, 1983), vol. 1, pp. 78–88.

4. Jan Rogozinski, *A Brief History of the Caribbean from the Arawak and the Carib to the Present* (New York: Penguin, 1992), p. 188. Cuba's production rose from 55,400 US tons to 287,000 US tons in the same period.

5. Simon Gikandi, *Maps of Englishness: Writing Identity in the Culture of Colonialism* (New York: Columbia University Press, 1996), pp. 92–4 (p. 96, p. 109).

6. For this strain of postcolonial critique, see, for example, Catherine Hall, '"Going-a-Trolloping": Imperial Man Travels the Empire', in Clare Midgley (ed.), *Gender and Imperialism* (Manchester: Manchester University Press, 1998), pp. 180–99.

7. Anthony Trollope, *The Way We Live Now* (1874–5; New York: Barnes and Noble Classics, 2005), ch. 22, p. 180.

8. Ibid. ch. 30, p. 241.

9. As quoted in M. J. Daunton, *Royal Mail: The Post Office since 1840* (London: Athlone Press, 1985), p. 146.

10. 'Instructions issued to Anthony Trollope, Esq. for his Guidance in the Survey of the Post-Offices in the West Indies', 16 November 1858, in Post Office Records, 'Instructions to Packet Agents, Colonial Administrators, &c.', Post 44/12, pp. 95–101, British Postal Museum, London.

11. Susan Zieger, 'Affect and Logistics: Trollope's Postal Work', *Victorians Journal of Culture and Literature*, 128 (Fall 2015): p. 227.

12. Patrick Joyce, *The State of Freedom: A Social History of the British State since 1800* (Cambridge: Cambridge University Press, 2013), p. 20. Jonathan Grossman analyses the interplay between these imperatives and British literary culture in *Charles Dickens's Networks: Public Transport and the Novel* (Oxford: Oxford University Press, 2012).

13. Daunton, *Royal Mail*, p. 23.

14. Super, *Trollope*, p. 21.

15. Ibid.

16. Ibid. p. 36.

17. For another example of his meticulous calculations, see his eight-page report of 6 September 1859, written at the conclusion of his journey back, in which he justified his argument for making Jamaica, not St Thomas, the central point for mail distribution on detailed accountings of the speed of ships, with and against the prevailing winds. Post 29/93, British Postal Archive, London. See also the 22-page report of 16 July 1859 (Post 29/93).

18. 'Instructions issued to Anthony Trollope', pp. 98–9. British Postal Archive.

19. James MacQueen, *A General Plan for a Mail Communication by Steam, between Great Britain and the Eastern and Western Parts of the World* (London: B. Fellowes, 1838), p. 1. MacQueen included two charts in his plan, one of the West Indies and Central America, and a larger one, drawn by John Arrowsmith, of the entire globe, setting forth 'all the routes of both steamers and sailing-packets, to every quarter of the world that has been adverted to' (p. xi).

20. T. A. Bushell, *Royal Mail: A Centenary History of the Royal Mail Line, 1839–1939* (London: Trade and Travel Publications, 1939), p. 86.

21. W. B. Liot, *Panama, Nicaragua and Tehuantepec: or Considerations upon the Questions of Communication between the Atlantic and Pacific Oceans* (London: Simpkin and Marshall, 1849).

22. 'Copy of Despatch from Governor Douglas to the Right Hon. Sir E. B. Lytton, Nov. 5, 1858', *Correspondence and Other Papers Relating to Hudson's Bay Company, The Exploration of the Territories [Captain Palliser's Expedition], and Other Affairs in Canada, 1859* (Shannon: Irish University Press, 1971), p. 298. Indeed, as Bushell argues, Canada's western coastline might have been much longer had the lack of a trans-isthmian route not hampered trade between the west coast and Europe. *Royal Mail*, p. 87.

23. MacQueen, *General Plan*, p. 85.

24. Ibid. p. 100. See also Charles Toll Bidwell on the importance of the isthmian passage to Britain's connection with British Columbia: 'Panamá has been particularly brought under the notice of England and English travellers of late by the establishment of the colony of British Columbia, and the reports of the recent gold discoveries therein. During the year 1862 particularly, hardly a steamer arrived at the Atlantic port of the Isthmus that did not bring a hundred or two of stout young Englishmen full of life and energy, bound for the new colony.' *The Isthmus of Panamá* (London: Chapman and Hall, 1865), p. 305.

25. Daunton, *Royal Mail*, p. 146.

26. Ibid, p. 151.

27. Bidwell, *Isthmus of Panamá*, p. 288.

28. Noel Maurer and Carlos Yu, *The Big Ditch: How America Took, Built, Ran, and Ultimately Gave Away the Panama Canal* (Princeton: Princeton University Press, 2011), pp. 46–7.

29. Ralph Lee Woodward, Jr attributes the long economic decline of British Honduras, Britain's sole colony on the Spanish Main, to the railway's 1855 completion, which made it more profitable for Guatemala to route its commerce through Pacific ports, rather than through Belize, as formerly. *Rafael Carrera and the Emergence of the Republic of Guatemala, 1821–1871* (Athens, GA: University of Georgia Press, 1993), pp. 308, pp. 357–60. For a brief summary of Panama's modernisation in response to the railroad, see Alex Pérez-Venero, *Before the Five Frontiers: Panama from 1821–1900* (New York: AMS Press, 1978), pp. 35–42.

30. M. F. Maury, 'Maury's Estimate of the Resources of the Gulf of Mexico and of the Caribbean Sea, and of the Importance of Interoceanic Communication', in John T. Sullivan, *Report of Historical and Technical Information relating to the Problem of Interoceanic Communication by way of the American Isthmus* (Washington, DC: Government Printing Office, 1883), p. 158.

31. Alfredo Castillero Calvo, 'Transitismo y dependencia: El caso del istmo de Panamá', *Anuario de Estudios Centroamericanos*, 1 (1974): p. 184.

32. Bedford Pim, *The Gate of the Pacific* (London: L. Reeve, 1863), p. 208.
33. As quoted in Ernesto Castillero Reyes, *El ferrocarril de Panamá y su historia* (Panamá: Imprenta Nacional, 1932), pp. 11–12.
34. Mary Seacole, *Wonderful Adventures of Mrs Seacole in Many Lands*, The Schomburg Library of Nineteenth-Century Black Women Writers (New York: Oxford University Press, 1988), p. 14.
35. Ibid. pp. 72–3.
36. John Haskell Kemble, *The Panama Route, 1848–1869* (Berkeley: University of California Press, 1943), p. 254.
37. Doris Muscatine, *Old San Francisco: The Biography of a City from Early Days to the Earthquake* (New York: G. P. Putnam's Sons, 1975), p. 71.
38. Fessenden N. Otis, *History of the Panama Railroad; and of the Pacific Mail Steamship Company. Together with a Traveller's Guide and Business Man's Hand-Book for the Panama Railroad* (New York: Harper and Brothers, 1867), p. 49.
39. Robert J. Chandler and Stephen J. Potash, *Gold, Silk, Pioneers and Mail: The Story of the Pacific Mail Steamship Company*, Pacific Maritime History Series, no. 6 (San Francisco: Friends of the San Francisco Maritime Museum Library, 2007), p. 15.
40. Otis, *Panama Railroad*, p. 49.
41. Bedford Pim and Berthold Seemann, *Dottings on the Roadside in Panama, Nicaragua and Mosquito* (London: Chapman and Hall, 1869), p. 14.
42. Justo Arosemena, 'La cuestión Americana', in Arosemena, *Escritos de Justo Arosemena. Estudio introductorio y antología*, ed. Argella Telo Burgos (Panamá: Universidad de Panamá, 1985), p. 249.
43. Ibid. p. 250.
44. Ibid. p. 251.
45. Trollope to Rowland Hill, 8 May 1859, from Panama, Post 29/103, British Postal Archive. Trollope's letter of 25 July 1859, Post 29/103, British Postal Archive, refers to negotiations with Totten to secure an annual charge for mail to Australia.
46. Arosemena, 'Cuestión Americana', p. 255.
47. 'Short Cuts across the Globe: Panama', *Household Words* (13 April 1850), p. 66.
48. Charles Darwin, *Journal of Researches into the Natural History and Geology of the Countries Visited During the Voyage Round the H.M.S. Beagle*, 11th edn (London: John Murray, 1913), p. 390.
49. Aims McGuinness, *Path of Empire: Panama and the California Gold Rush* (Ithaca, NY: Cornell University Press, 2008), p. 86.
50. See Thomas Carlyle's *History of Friedrich II of Prussia, called Frederick the Great*, 4 vols (London: Chapman and Hall, 1858–65), vol. 1, pp. 23–4.
51. Seacole, *Wonderful Adventures*, pp. 44–5.
52. See McGuinness, *Path of Empire*, pp. 84–122 and Marixa Lasso, 'From Citizens to 'Natives': Tropical Politics of Depopulation at the Panama Canal Zone', *Environmental History*, 21.2 (2016): pp. 39–41.
53. Trollope, 'The Journey to Panama' in *The Victoria Regia: A Volume of Original Contributions in Poetry and Prose*, ed. Adelaide A. Procter (London: Emily Faithfull, 1861), p. 189. For other stories inspired by the journey, see 'Miss Sarah Jack, of Spanish Town, Jamaica', and 'Returning Home', collected in Trollope, *The Complete Short Stories*, vol. 3, *Tourists and Colonials*, ed. Betty Jane Slemp Breyer (Fort Worth: Texas Christian University Press, 1981).

Part IV

Economics

19

HIGH INTEREST AND IMPAIRED SECURITY: TROLLOPE'S WOMEN INVESTORS

Nancy Henry

In Anthony Trollope's *The Last Chronicle of Barset* (1866–7), the beautiful Clara Van Siever stands to inherit a fortune originally made by her father, a Dutch merchant who traded in the City of London. The artist Conway Dalrymple muses to Johnny Eames: 'Miss Van is to have gold by the ingot, and jewels by the bushel, and a hatful of bank shares, and a whole mine in Cornwall for her fortune.'[1] As a modern heiress, Clara's fortune would be more likely to include bank and mining shares than gold and jewels. She is a passive investor, but her widowed mother is an active investor who is increasing her wealth through unsavoury dealings in the City of London. Mrs Van Siever's business partner, the gambling, alcoholic Dobbs Broughton, is happy to take her money, but when he is unable to pay her the interest on the loans for which she has supplied the capital, he remarks: 'She had better put her dirty money into the three per cents, if she is frightened at having to wait a week or two' (*LCB*, ch. 37, p. 367). Doubting that she would withdraw her capital, he scowls, 'when she began to find that she didn't like four per cent, she'd bring it back again' (*LCB*, ch. 37, p. 368).

Dobbs is correct that Mrs Van Siever prefers the 10 or 12 per cent interest of money-lending to the 'three per cents', the consolidated government debt also known as the consols and associated with both safety and women, or to the 4 per cent mortgages favoured by the Demolines, another mother/daughter pair of investors in the novel. She holds the power in their partnership, which he resists by disparaging her. Trollope's narrator dwells on Mrs Van Siever's ugliness and associates it with her mixing in the masculine world of business and finance. We cannot say that the novel is sympathetic to her unseemly pursuit of high interest, but her expectation of receiving the interest on her investments is reasonable. Along with Mrs Proudie, who dominates her husband throughout the Chronicles of Barset, Mrs Van Siever represents an inverted order about which the novel is ambivalent, and her example illustrates how gender dynamics in Trollope's fiction are complicated by a modern context in which single and widowed women particularly embrace the legal freedom to invest their money.

This essay argues that Trollope drew on the real phenomenon of women investing in the nineteenth century – including his family members – to examine the relationship between risk and security in the overlapping financial and domestic spheres in his fictional world. Anticipating Henry James, Trollope is interested in seeing what women do with their money when they have the freedom to choose. How women investors behave becomes another way of viewing intermingled familial, romantic and business relationships. Beginning with Trollope's financial life, I examine how he treats a series of women investors, focusing specifically on the relatively neglected novel *Miss Mackenzie* (1865) in which the heroine's investing decisions are inseparable from her affective familial and romantic choices. In fiction, as in reality, decisions about what to do with excess capital are personal, even intimate, but they also have implications in the public sphere of business and finance. As more people in Victorian Britain invested, women's livelihoods connected them to local, national and global economies.

Throughout the nineteenth century, women became more numerous and influential as investors in joint-stock companies financing canals, railroads and banks, as well as in a wide range of foreign and domestic bonds and securities. George Robb writes: 'The industrial economy of the Victorian period was fundamentally different from the mercantile economy of the seventeenth and eighteenth centuries, and women could participate in it in ways that have largely gone unstudied.'[2] Until recently, we knew little about nineteenth-century women as investors, but pioneering archival work by historians such as Robb, Josephine Maltby, Janette Rutterford, Mark Freeman, Robin Pearson, James Taylor, David R. Green, Alastair Owens and others has revealed the presence, and explored the significance, of female shareholders in public and private companies.[3] Over the course of the nineteenth century, women comprised between 5 and 20 per cent of the investing public. Establishing the extent of women's involvement as shareholders, Maltby and Rutterford show that, in contrast to married women before the Married Women's Property Acts of 1870 and 1882, spinsters and widows held shares with the same rights as men: 'Indeed, although women did not gain the right to vote for governments until 1919, they were generally allowed to vote in annual general meetings.'[4] They could canvass and vote for board members and, like men, stood to profit or lose from their investments.

Investing women appear in the works of many Victorian novelists. Notable examples include: Charles Dickens's *David Copperfield* (1849–50), W. M. Thackeray's *Vanity Fair* (1847–8) and *The Newcomes* (1853–5), Charlotte Brontë's *Shirley* (1849), Elizabeth Gaskell's *Cranford* (1851–3), George Eliot's *The Mill on the Floss* (1860) and *Daniel Deronda* (1876), Charlotte Riddell's *Austin Friars* (1870), Margaret Oliphant's *Hester* (1883) and George Gissing's *The Whirlpool* (1897). While characters such as Dickens's Betsey Trotwood, Gaskell's Matty Jenkyns and Eliot's Fanny Davilow are passive investors who fall victim either to fraud or financial downturns, Trollope makes the active financial choices of his female investors central to both his characterisations and to the larger themes of his novels.

Critics have explored the complex role of women in Trollope's novels. Concentrating on the Palliser series, Deborah Denenholz Morse first made the feminist case that Trollope subverts the traditional structure of the courtship plot. Following Morse, Jane Nardin traced the origins of his concern with the condition of women in his early work (1855–65). Both critics note tensions and ambiguity in Trollope's attitude towards traditional gender roles.[5] Rutterford and Maltby, Elsie Michie and Jill Rappoport have examined the topic of women and money in his work.[6] Looking specifically at women investors, we see the mentality of investing money with the expectation of a return, whether that money is invested in the market, in efforts to gain or promote a husband or even in paid companions. In Trollope's fiction, romantic and familial relationships are rarely free from questions of the woman's money.

Trollope's Financial Life

Like Thackeray, Dickens, the Brontës, Gaskell and Eliot, Trollope invested in the stock market, and his financial life provides relevant context for his fiction. Biographer Victoria Glendinning argues that the miseries of Trollope's early life arose from lack of money so that later, '[m]oney and the efficient management of money were to be central to his feelings of security'.[7] In his mother Frances (Fanny) Trollope, Anthony had the model of a woman who took control of her family's finances. Like Riddell and Oliphant, Fanny Trollope frantically published fiction in order to pay her husband's debts. Fanny had £900 a year as well as income from rents in Somerset shared with her sister, and she bought an annuity of £250 a year for herself and her daughters.[8] This pattern of collaborating with female family members is typical of how nineteenth-century women strove to survive economically and provide stability in the midst of domestic chaos and national economic volatility. After Fanny returned from her failed attempt to establish a bazaar in Cincinnati, she succeeded with her authorship of *The Domestic Manners of the Americans* (1832) and subsequent novels. Her son Anthony's fiction represents the kinds of financial entanglements faced by women when their husbands, brothers and sons fell into debt.

Fanny had to confront the same evasive tactics for avoiding debt that were common in Anthony's novels. Glendinning writes that Fanny's husband 'was caught in a web of IOUs and "bills" which he had signed against loans – bills which could be sold on from hand to hand, the interest rising exponentially until the last in the chain attempted to collect some impossible total from the initial borrower'.[9] Anthony too experienced the escalation of interest on a loan, a traumatic lesson that was recalled in *An Autobiography* (written 1875–6 and published posthumously in 1883). As a young man, he was in debt to a moneylender who appeared at his office every morning to tell him: 'Now I wish you would be punctual.'[10] In *The Three Clerks* (1858), Mr Jabesh M'Ruen torments Charley Tudor with entreaties to be punctual. In a chapter titled 'Do Be Punctual' (ch. 21) in *Phineas Finn* (1869), Mr Clarkson pursues Phineas and repeats this phrase, which clearly caught the novelist's ear as an ominous if humorous refrain. While the inflation of interest rates on bills to fantastic proportions is a staple of Victorian financial plots, Trollope had personal experience to draw on when incorporating such scenarios in his fiction.

Trollope's wife Rose (née Heseltine) also came from a family that suffered pecuniary embarrassments. Her father spent his career working as a banker in Rotherham (South Yorkshire). After he retired in 1853, the bank's losses were discovered. He was the director of the Sheffield and Rotherham Railway during the railway share crisis of 1849 and probably used bank funds to cover his own debts. Glendinning observes: 'Mr Heseltine was one of the thousands who swindled in a small way in the shadow of George Hudson – millionaire, master-swindler and entrepreneurial genius.'[11] Hudson was central to the railway empire and speculation bubbles of the 1840s. Heseltine and his second wife fled to Le Havre, France, as the Trollopes had fled to Bruges, Belgium in 1834. Debt, financial scandal, railway speculation and bankruptcy were all part of mid-Victorian financial reality, and such scenarios appear throughout Trollope's fiction.

Upon her death in 1863, Fanny left Anthony her shares in the Joint Stock London Bank. These shares, along with Anthony's holdings in the Garrick Club and the Smyrna Railway, paid dividends that augmented his income from writing. In 1880, the publishing house of Chapman and Hall, in which Trollope's son Harry had been a partner from 1869 to 1873, became a joint-stock company. Trollope was one of the directors, and both he and Harry bought shares.[12] Upon Anthony's death, Rose inherited his shares in Chapman and Hall. In his will, Anthony gave his executors, Rose and Harry, 'discretion to keep or sell his stocks and shares as they saw fit, but new investments must not be in any companies outside the United Kingdom or its colonies and dependencies'. He stipulated that Harry could make no investments without Rose's written consent. These investments continued to pay, and Rose's investment income in 1896 was £538.[13] The widows Fanny and Rose Trollope were among the women investors whose numbers grew throughout the nineteenth century. Taking advantage of joint-stock bank and railroad companies, as well as other proliferating options, investors had new opportunities to invest their capital. Fanny looked to stocks and shares to supplement her income, and Rose made investment decisions that would affect her well-being. Furthermore, Trollope's American friend Kate Field received shares in the Bell Telephone Company in 1879, 'which increased ten-fold in a very few years, so her money problems were over'.[14]

Investing Women in Trollope

In *The Last Chronicle*, a minor character named Mr Summerkin inherits a fortune from a maiden aunt (even before she dies) enabling him to marry (*LCB*, ch. 40, p. 396). Phineas Finn is saved from financial difficulties by what the narrator calls a 'wonderful piece of luck'.[15] Miss Marian Persse, his mother's aunt and 'an eccentric old lady', dies and leaves him £3,000. The narrator remarks: 'He owed some £500, and the remainder he would, of course, invest' (*PF*, ch. 35, pp. 355–6). The casual mention of the mundane use to which Phineas will put the 'wonderful' inheritance is typical of Trollope. The fantastic nature of the coincidence is downplayed by the observation that he would 'of course' invest the lucky money.

Throughout Trollope's novels, investing is a ubiquitous middle-class practice that is registered alongside unexpected inheritances and sensational speculation plots. His speculators include: Dobbs Broughton in *The Last Chronicle*, George Vavasor in *Can You Forgive Her?* (1864–5), Ferdinand Lopez in *The Prime Minister* (1875) and Augustus Melmotte in *The Way We Now* (1876). Among his female characters, single women including Miss Dunstable, Alice Vavasor and Miss Mackenzie, as well as the widows Mrs Van Siever, Arabella Greenow, Lizzie Eustace and Madame Max Goesler, are all investors, though some take a more active role than others in managing their money.

Phineas Finn and *Phineas Redux* (1874) are remarkable for the degree to which women's money underwrites the careers of men. In addition to Miss Persse, Aspasia Fitzgibbon is 'an old maid, over forty, very plain', who unexpectedly inherited £25,000 – 'a wonderful windfall' that she uses to live independently (*PF*, ch. 4, p. 78). Though she dislikes lending to her spendthrift brother Laurence, she nonetheless buys the accommodation bill that Phineas has signed for him, negotiating with the creditors to lower the price on the loan. For a second time, the intervention of a wealthy spinster relieves Phineas of his debts. He refuses to accept money from Lady Laura, but his career is ultimately made through the wealth of Madame Max, whom he marries at the end of *Phineas Redux*. In this way, women sustain him financially and blur the boundaries between financial and domestic spheres. Trollope's novels suggest the impossibility of isolating business and finance from familial and romantic relationships.

Female characters in Trollope's novels are simultaneously denigrated for knowing too much about money and dismissed for being ignorant. Women who look after their financial interests are often characterised as bloodthirsty animals. Broughton complains that Mrs Van Siever is a 'downright leech' (*LCB*, ch. 37, p. 367). In *The Eustace Diamonds* (1872), the lawyer Mr Camperdown calls Lizzie Eustace a 'greedy, blood-sucking' harpy.[16] Trollope's narrator remarks of Lizzie: 'She knew nothing as to spending money, saving it, or investing it . . . had no idea what her money would do and what it would not' (*ED*, ch. 2, p. 17). Yet, the logic of investment permeates Lizzie's thinking about all aspects of life. She objects to her paid companion Miss Macnulty, reflecting that 'seventy pounds was a great deal of money, when so very little was given in return'. Lizzie feels cheated because Miss Macnulty cannot discuss Shelley, but Miss Macnulty can discuss 'the sorrows of the poorest heroine that ever saw her lover murdered before her eyes, and then come back to life with ten thousand pounds a year' (*ED*, ch. 27, p. 205). Talking about novels is not worth as much to Lizzie as talking about Shelley. In this way, Trollope comments ironically on the high cultural value of Romantic poetry in contrast to the stronger popular appeal of outrageously sensational plots of murder, marriage and money.

In *The Eustace Diamonds*, Lucy Morris is the antithesis of female harpies and leeches. She serves as an unpaid companion to Lady Linlithgow, who calculates her income from the widow's jointure on which she lives. When Lucy confesses that she cannot 'make two and two come to five on the one side of the sheet, and only come to three on the other', the old lady replies: 'Then you ain't worth anything to me' (*ED*, ch. 9, p. 71). Just as Lizzie judges Miss Macnulty to be worthless, Lucy is worthless to Lady Linlithgow because she cannot help the widow through fraudulent accounting. Lady Linlithgow explains her bad temper: 'I don't get much above half what I ought out of my jointure' (*ED*, ch. 9, p. 73). The interactions between these parallel pairs of women are comical but nonetheless sensitive to the financial positions of both the penniless spinsters who must work to survive and the money-obsessed widows who employ them as companions.

Miss Mackenzie

Miss Mackenzie is Trollope's most concentrated study of a woman and her money. One reviewer wrote that no other novelist 'had made the various worries connected with the want of money so prominent a feature in most of his stories'.[17] In *An Autobiography*, Trollope recalls his heroine Margaret Mackenzie as 'a very unattractive old maid, who was over-whelmed by money troubles' (*A*, ch. 10, p. 123). His narrator observes of Margaret: 'Like all other single ladies, she was very nervous about her money. She was quite alive to the beauty of a high rate of interest, but did not quite understand that high interest and impaired security should go hand in hand together.'[18] This image of beautiful high interest walking hand in hand with impaired security embodies the inseparability of money and romance in *Miss Mackenzie*. The terms interest, security and liberty are multivalent. For example, in a conversation about interest rates, one of her suitors asks, '"how can I fail to feel an interest about you?"' (*MM*, ch. 5, pp. 59–60). Miss Mackenzie has liberty to do what she pleases with her money, but her brother takes a liberty with that money, putting it at risk.

Margaret lived for years as a nurse and companion to one of her brothers, a civil servant in Somerset House whose investments have increased the £12,000 he inherited from an uncle. When he dies, he leaves this money plus a freehold estate paying £600 a year to his sister, thus initiating her new life of freedom but also of financial and romantic problems. For the first time in a dependent and dreary adult life, she begins to taste independence: 'no power of the purse had been with her – none of that power which belongs legitimately to a wife because a wife is a partner in the business' (*MM*, ch. 2, p. 25). Despite what we know about the relative power of single women to control their money, Trollope thought they remained outside the true business of marriage, which conferred the only real power in Victorian society. Without husbands to guide them, he implies, single women were inevitably overwhelmed by their financial freedom.

Miss Mackenzie is to have a little over £800 a year, that is, £600 from property and £200 on the £12,000, but her lawyers look for higher paying interest. When her surviving brother asks her for £2,400 to take a mortgage on his oil cloth factory at a rate of 5 per cent, Miss Mackenzie's first worry is that the lawyers might allow this opportunity to slip through their hands. Initially tempted to place the money in the 3 per cents, 'she had gone to work with the figures' and 'ascertained that by doing so twenty-five pounds a year would be docked off her computed income'; thus she is persuaded to lend her brother the money to buy property at a rate of 5 per cent: 'Mortgages, she knew, were good things, strong and firm, based on landed security, and very respectable' (*MM*, ch. 3, p. 37). She calculates the difference between receiving 3 per cent in the consols and 5 per cent on the mortgage, choosing the higher interest because she does not consider lending money to her brother a risk. She also rationalises the calculation in moral, gendered terms: mortgages are good, strong, firm and respectable – qualities that would be ideal in a husband. Her brother and his partner Mr Rubb assure her that she cannot do better than 5 per cent. Rutterford, Malty and Laurence contextualise this transaction: 'With the greater safety of mortgages and loans on personal bonds, the development of the capital market and fall of the interest rate, landowners borrowed on security from land. So women's income derived from land . . . was increasingly commuted into securities', and mortgages in particular were attractive to women investors.[19]

From the moment she inherits, Margaret is negotiating between proposals to invest her money and proposals of marriage. Following her brother's death and her inheritance, she receives her first proposal from a former suitor (and intimate friend of her brother), who had given up his suit when her brother objected. She rejects his offer because 'she was not prepared to sacrifice herself and her new freedom, and her new power, and her new wealth, to Mr Harry Handcock' (*MM*, ch. 1, pp. 12–13). The heroine experiencing freedom, power and wealth for the first time anticipates Henry James's Isabel Archer in *The Portrait of a Lady* (1880–1) and Gissing's Marian Yule in *New Grub Street* (1891). Like these later heroines, Miss Mackenzie's sense of freedom is complicated by pressures from the men in her family and male suitors who are attracted to that money. Trollope seems to accept and assume that women with money will be more attractive wives, and from that assumption, he moves on to explore the practical and emotional dilemmas faced by women contemplating both marriage and financial investments.

Miss Mackenzie's freedom entails a set of difficult choices. She must decide how to invest her money and which social set to join in the fictional town of Littlebath, where she has taken up residence; and she has to choose among suitors. The narrator is sympathetic: 'She was doing what we all do – endeavouring to choose her friends from the best of those who made overtures to her of friendship' (*MM*, ch. 6, p. 71). Miss Mackenzie's troubles throughout the novel involve her attempts to assess the financial advice she receives from various men and to evaluate their relative sincerity. These problems are related because, as Trollope recognises, passion for money and romantic passion are often intertwined, even in the mind of the suitor himself.

Her cousin, the widower John Ball, lost his chance of wealth when Margaret's brothers inherited the money he had expected would be his. Like Trollope's father, John Ball is a barrister who cannot make a living from his practice and whose great expectations of inheritance are disappointed. His title, estate and nine children are in peril from his inability to earn money, a calamity that he and his overbearing mother trace back to the lost inheritance. They are thus eager for him to marry Miss Mackenzie and recover thereby a diminished fortune they believe rightfully to be their own. John's father, Sir John Ball, a disappointed Baronet, at one point awkwardly blurts out: '"Women have plenty of lovers when they have plenty of money"' (*MM*, ch. 16, p. 204). John Ball the younger is attuned to percentages and share values. His constant attention to his investments 'gave him perhaps five per cent. for his capital, whereas he would have received no more than four and half had he left it alone and taken his dividends without troubling himself' (*MM*, ch. 6, pp. 74–5). Despite his own failures as an investor, John schools his cousin on the folly of investing in her brother's company:

'My dear Margaret, their word for five per cent. is no security. Five per cent. is nothing magnificent. A lady situated as you are should never part with her money without security – never: but if she does, she should have more than five per cent'. (*MM*, ch. 6, p. 78)

Her brother's partner Mr Rubb makes it especially difficult for Miss Mackenzie to keep business and romance separate because he employs financial language to seduce her: 'Five per cent. and first-class security were, she knew, matters of business', however Mr Rubb, 'winked his eye at her as he spoke of them, leaning forward in his chair and looking at her not at all as a man of business' (*MM*, ch. 5, p. 57). Later, he gets 'nearer to her on the sofa as he whispered the word money into her ear' (*MM*, ch. 8, p. 107). Mr Rubb tries seductive charm to obscure the fact that there is a problem with the mortgage. He asks for Margaret's trust, and she agrees to take her interest without asking for any security for the principal. This is a bad business decision, clouded by familial loyalty. Her brother and Mr Rubb know that their firm had 'no longer the power of providing her with the security which had been promised to her' (*MM*, ch. 6,

p. 70). She has been manipulated and betrayed by her brother and his partner. When she refuses Mr Rubb's offer of marriage, the narrator comments: 'I tremble as I look back upon her danger' (*MM*, ch. 28, p. 397). Security and danger refer to Miss Mackenzie's money and her person, both of which her suitors desire.

As a member of a landed and titled but impoverished family who tries to make money in the City, John Ball has been 'defiled by the price of stocks, and saturated with the poison of the money market' (*MM*, ch. 25, p. 332). This language of defilement and poison betrays Trollope's bias against City finance as corrupting a man who might have made an honest living. Ball is a guinea pig; that is, for two guineas per meeting, he sits on the boards of various City companies. While thinking of Miss Mackenzie at a meeting of the Abednego Life Office, Ball 'votes for accepting a doubtful life, which was urged on the board by a director, who, I hope, had no intimate personal relations with the owner of the doubtful life in question' (*MM*, ch. 19, p. 244). This commentary by the narrator about the ways in which human lives are discussed as investments on the board of a life insurance company resonates with the inseparability of Miss Mackenzie and her money in the eyes of suitors. For those taking out a policy, life insurance was a way of mitigating risk, but for investors in the company, accepting a 'doubtful life' was the epitome of risk.

Furthermore, Trollope links life insurance not only with the treatment of women on the marriage market but also with American slavery. A late scene in *Miss Mackenzie* takes place at a great charity bazaar on behalf of the 'orphan children of negro soldiers who had fallen in the American war' (*MM*, ch. 27, p. 354). Trollope says in *An Autobiography* that he wanted to express his criticism of such ways of raising money. This is apparent in the exhausted, bedraggled appearance of the women at the close of the bazaar. But the shadow of American slavery and the commodification of 'doubtful lives' in the insurance business also reinforce the conflation of Miss Mackenzie and her money.[20]

Four men court Margaret in one year: Handcock, Ball, Rubb and the greedy, squinting curate from Littlebath, Mr Maguire. The narrator remarks:

> One man had wanted her money to buy a house on mortgage, and another now asked for it to build a church, giving her, or promising to give her, the security of the pew rents. Which of the two was the worst? They were both her lovers, and she thought that he was the worst who first made his love and then tried to get her money. (*MM*, ch. 19, p. 248)

She does lose the money she invested in her brother's business, but what she loses through her loan, she regains when a railway company offers to buy property she now owns. The railway company's purchase of her land is one financial plot twist; another is the discovery of a legal technicality that causes Margaret's inheritance (which her brother had enjoyed until his death) to revert to John Ball. In this way, Trollope takes away from Miss Mackenzie what he had briefly given her: freedom, money and power. She relinquishes financial responsibility with a sense of relief and accepts her cousin's proposal. But as Nardin argues, this resolution is not unambiguously happy. Their union requires at least a brief struggle between his desire to control her and her recently aroused independent spirit. He wants her as a mother to his nine children and relishes her dependence on him and his newly acquired wealth. Without any money of her own, Miss Mackenzie has lost her independence and her freedom to take risks; she must be grateful to have the security of marriage rather than that of low-paying investments.

When Henry James reviewed *Miss Mackenzie* in the *Nation* (July 1865), he criticised its commonplace vulgarity. Elsie Michie has demonstrated the connections between Trollope's *The Prime Minister* and James's *Washington Square* (1880) and *Portrait of a Lady*.[21] But Margaret Mackenzie's inheritance and subsequent freedom to choose also has parallels with James's Isabel Archer. As Michie has shown, Isabel's hellish marriage is comparable to that of Emily Wharton in *The Prime Minister*; yet like Margaret, Isabel is a poor woman who unexpectedly inherits a fortune and must choose how to lead her life without guidance. Michie writes that James found in *The Prime Minister* the germ of his own design to 'place the center of the subject in the young woman's own consciousness'.[22] *Miss Mackenzie* is an experiment in seeing what a woman would do with her freedom to choose and in this respect it anticipates James's later novel.

Michie identifies a pattern in Trollope's novels in which 'the heroine is finally brought to marry the man her clan approves of, the man who represents endogamy as well as the conservative values embodied in the land in contrast to the radical possibilities associated with the man who believes in liquid wealth and speculation'.[23] In *Romance's Rival*, Talia Schaffer describes the familiar marriage plot in which the heroine marries a man who is either a relative, a neighbour or a close family friend.[24] The argument for marrying within the family is urged upon Lily Dale as a reason for marrying Johnny Eames in *The Last Chronicle* and on Emily Wharton as a reason to marry Arthur Fletcher in *The Prime Minister*. *Miss Mackenzie* conforms to both these types of plot when she marries her cousin and keeps the money in the family.

In contrast to contemporary critics of capitalism including Karl Marx, Thomas Carlyle, John Ruskin and Dickens, Trollope accepts that commodification is a reality of Victorian life when it comes to marriage, inheritance and other family dynamics. He reserved his anger for futures trading and company promoting. In the *Prime Minister*, Ferdinand Lopez describes the type of speculation that Trollope found absurd by explaining to his partner Sexty Parker that '"there was no need at all of real coffee or real guano"' to watch the rise and fall of prices: '"You needn't have coffee and you needn't have guano."'[25] This was a practice that Trollope perceived as corrupt and that disturbed him more than the notion of people marrying for money or children looking upon their parents as sources of inherited wealth.

Written between August 1863 and April 1864 (just before *Miss Mackenzie*), *Can You Forgive Her?* shows George Vavasor manipulating his cousin Alice Vavasor in order to pay debts and finance his speculations and political career. Bad bills of exchange begin to circulate early in the novel and return to cause problems later. In the chapter titled 'Alice Vavasor's Name gets into the Money Market' (ch. 60), George extorts four bills of exchange for £500 each from Alice only to find that no one will honour them in the City. He is told, '"bills with ladies' names on them, – ladies who are no way connected with business, – ain't just the paper people like"'. Trollope personifies the City to suggest that it had a coherent identity separate from the rest of London and operated with its own logic. 'The City, by one of its mouths, asserted plainly that ladies' bills never meant business.'[26] George particularly exploits Alice's personal feelings for him, calculating her reactions and pretending to care for her in ways that are even worse than those of Miss Mackenzie's suitors. As his mania for money begins to fragment his identity, his fantasies and his actions turn violent.

In *The Last Chronicle*, Trollope is specific about the percentages at which money is loaned. Dobbs sneeringly comments of Mrs Van Siever: '"For the last three years she's drawn close upon two thousand a year for less than eighteen thousand pounds. When a woman wants to do that, she can't have her money in her pocket every Monday morning"' (*LCB*, ch. 37, p. 368–9). Here again is the question of risk versus security and scepticism about a woman's ability to understand that 'high interest and impaired security should go hand in hand together' (*MM*, ch. 3, p. 36). Dobb's other partner, Augustus Musselboro, tells Mrs Van Siever: 'When you go in for high interest, there must be hitches here and there.' She assures him: 'I know all about it' (*LCB*, ch. 37, p. 373). If Mrs Van Siever wants over 10 per cent on her loans, she cannot have the regularity of picking up her dividends at the bank, a ceremony associated with cautious investors such as governesses, widows and wealthy wives who liked the regularity of the 3 per cents. As discussed earlier, Dobbs points out that when a woman is getting over 10 per cent in the shady, unregulated world of money lending, she cannot expect a cheque like clockwork.

Among those borrowing from Dobbs and Mrs Van Siever is Adolphus Crosbie. Dobbs explains to Crosbie that he raises money at 4 or 5 per cent, lending it at 8 or 9. But Crosbie is actually paying 12 per cent, wondering whether that was 'not more than he ought to be mulcted for the accommodation he wanted', and yet he is so desperate that he would be glad to get the money for 20 per cent (*LCB*, ch. 43, p. 428). As a point of comparison, George Vavasor is forced to borrow £200 for £40, or a rate of 20 per cent. Dobbs is unwilling to take the risk of extending credit to Crosbie. The narrator breaks in on Crosbie's struggles to renew a bill in a comment that recalls Trollope's own experience: 'I know no more uncomfortable walking than that which falls to the lot of men who go into the City to look for money, and who find none' (*LCB*, ch. 43, p. 435). Rejected by Dobbs, Crosbie is forced to borrow money from a colleague at 5 per cent.

Mrs Van Siever's behaviour suggests that women can be just as successful and just as ruthless as men at making money. In not conforming to conventional separate spheres for men and women, the businesswoman appears unnatural but perhaps no less scary than other monsters of business who populate Trollope's late novels. In *The Way We Live Now*, the frustrated Georgiana Longstaffe warns her parents that if they cannot support her way of life, she may be driven to marry 'some horrid creature from the Stock Exchange'.[27] Her comment, however, is ironic since her suitor is a respectable Jewish banker who proves too good for her and withdraws his proposal. Mrs Van Siever falls into the 'horrid creature' category, exhibiting a Jekyll and Hyde personality. By night she is a society lady ridiculously got up in false hair. In her business attire, she is old and ugly but perhaps more in her natural element.[28] Mrs Van Siever is a woman born with an aptitude for business, as other women in the Palliser series such as Lady Laura and Lady Glencora are born to politics, though social restrictions keep them from realising their innate capacities. Crossing from the West End into the City and wearing her business dress, the ugly socialite Mrs Van Siever is a physical manifestation of her leech-like behaviour. She presses Dobbs for the money he owes her and thus contributes to his financial ruin and bloody suicide when he blows his brains out in the City. It turns out, however, that Musselboro is the real villain, defrauding Mrs Van Siever as well as Dobbs. Mrs Van Siever, despite her threats, does not disinherit her daughter Clara when she marries Dalrymple.

Trollope became increasingly preoccupied with the psychological, sometimes pathological, responses to money in all its forms, even among otherwise sympathetic characters. Mr Crawley's obsession with a lost £20 cheque is at the centre of *The Last Chronicle*'s plot; Lord Brentford's senility in *Phineas Redux* is expressed through an obsession with his daughter's fortune. The madness of speculators George Vavasor and Ferdinand Lopez follows from their inability to get money, and both take out their frustrations on the women in their lives.

Risk or security is a choice faced by Trollope's heroines in marriage and in investment. Elsie Michie shows that they usually choose security, as when Glencora marries Plantagenet Palliser rather than Burgo Fitzgerald. Michie writes that the marriage is 'a matter of economics, a union of fortunes rather than hearts'.[29] But women must make similar choices when it comes to their money. Miss Mackenzie takes 5 per cent over 3 per cent and loses because her brother is untrustworthy. Mrs Van Siever takes 10 per cent over 3 per cent and also loses because of Dobbs's drinking and Musselboro's treachery. When Lady Laura resists her father's advice to invest in Indian Stock at 5 per cent or mortgages at 4 per cent, he 'proceeded to explain to her how very important an affair money is, and that persons who have got money cannot be excused for not considering what they had better do with it'.[30] But she makes her own choices, which turn out worse than those of Miss Mackenzie.

In *The Last Chronicle*, the histrionic Miss Madalina Demolines invests her money in 'a first-class mortgage on land at four per cent' because she knows that 'land can't run away' (*LCB*, ch. 25, p. 255). But she maintains a voyeuristic fascination with people who play the market and describes Dobbs Broughton and his wife as 'living in the crater of a volcano': 'The risk is everything to them' (*LCB*, ch. 39, p. 390). She also claims to have turned down a suitor who had 'two thousand a year of his own, in India stock and other securities' (*LCB*, ch. 46, p. 462). Trollope consistently presents characters with choices between safety and risk. But good characters do not always choose safety and bad characters don't always choose risk. Financial risk is often, but not always, correlated with moral choices in his novels.

In *The Prime Minister*, Lizzie Eustace, for whom love, excitement and money are so inextricably entwined in *The Eustace Diamonds*, briefly considers Ferdinand Lopez's offer to join him in speculation. Living in a small house bordering on Mayfair, 'She had given her money to no lover, had not lost it on race-courses, . . . She still liked a lover, – or perhaps two, – though she had thoroughly convinced herself that a lover may be bought too dear' (*PM* ch. 54, p. 133). Lizzie is still thinking of relationships as investments, and Lopez, like Mr Rubb in *Miss Mackenzie*, offers her both a business deal and himself. She considers his proposition, 'panting with anxiety, struggling with herself, anxious for the excitement which would come from her dealing in Bios, but still fearing to risk her money' (*PM* ch. 54, p. 136). Ultimately, Lizzie refuses the offer to purchase joint shares in Bios with Lopez and also his proposal that she run away with him to Guatemala. In doing so, she wisely chooses security, despite panting over the prospect of gain. This final rejection drives Lopez to step in front of a train at Tenway Junction. Lizzie the 'harpy', like Mrs Van Siever the 'leech', refuses to speculate and gamble and thus becomes the indirect cause of a speculator's suicide.

While it is true that land can't run away, like a guilty speculator, to the Continent or to Eternity, Trollope recognised that low-interest investments like mortgages or the consols constituted security for the growing members of the middle class without the benefit of land ownership. His characters' relationship to money is a manifestation of their temperament, moral outlook and psychological state. His female characters particularly must constantly assess the risks of their investment decisions, which symbolise their relative freedom in a modern economy. Mrs Thorne (née Dunstable), 'the richest woman in England', may have inherited a fortune made by the sale of ointment, but she redeems herself by making good use of that money; though vulgar, she is extravagantly generous (*LCB*, ch. 45, p. 454). Mrs Van Siever is the rare woman who takes the risk of high interest and impaired security. Such decisions about money provide insight into the identities of Trollope's characters.

For Miss Mackenzie, keeping her money safe is keeping herself safe. The freedom to do what she likes with her money is the freedom to do what she likes with herself. For the period of the novel's action during which she has money, Miss Mackenzie has an identity that she previously lacked, and which disappears in the end when it turns out the money never was hers. Upon marrying her cousin John Ball, she becomes Lady Ball, assuming the name of her overbearing mother-in-law, who has sought to convince her throughout the novel that the money is not hers. The happy marriage ending is in fact quite dark in its obliteration of the person named Miss Mackenzie. In this sense, *Miss Mackenzie* raises an existential problem that Trollope would treat later in different forms, especially with the speculator/suicides Melmotte and Lopez: society has become such that the loss of money amounts to an annihilation of self. In *Miss Mackenzie*, this equation of a person with his or her money is subtly echoed in the minor themes of life insurance and American slavery, two forms of monetising the value of human life.

Investing women were a reality in Trollope's life. He inherited shares from his mother and left shares to his wife. In representing the investor Miss Mackenzie, he devised a plot in which her inheritance leads, not to her ultimate independence, but to her marrying and becoming Lady Ball. But the question remains whether his equation of Miss Mackenzie and her money is evidence of his cynicism about the economic basis of society or of anxiety about what a woman might do with her freedom to choose. Either way, his fictional, psychological scenarios anticipate the works of Henry James and George Gissing, among others. We can understand his investing characters within the context of an increasingly democratised culture of investment. Business historians have observed that women were legally able to deal in the market simply because 'no one had thought to exclude them'.[31] Their money was good on the Stock Exchange, and like men, women braved the risks of financial downturns and crashes. Whether they pursued risky high-interest ventures or sought the safety of low-interest securities came down to a question of character, making the investment of capital a fitting subject for Trollope's fictional experiments.[32]

Notes

1. Anthony Trollope, *The Last Chronicle of Barset*, ed. Sophie Gilmartin (Harmondsworth: Penguin, 2002), ch. 24, p. 249. Subsequent references are in the main text (*LCB*).

2. George Robb, 'Ladies of the Ticker: Women, Investment, and Fraud in England and America, 1850–1930', in Nancy Henry and Cannon Schmitt (eds), *Victorian Investments: New Perspectives on Finance and Culture* (Bloomington: Indiana University Press, 2009), p. 120.

3. See Anne Laurence, Josephine Maltby and Janette Rutterford (eds), *Women and Their Money 1700–1950: Essays on Women and Finance* (New York: Routledge, 2009) and David R. Green, Alastair Owens, Josephine Maltby and Janette Rutterford (eds), *Men, Women, and Money: Perspectives on Gender, Wealth, and Investment 1850–1930* (Oxford: Oxford University Press, 2011).

4. Josephine Maltby and Janette Rutterford, '"She Possessed Her Own Fortune": Women Investors from the Late Nineteenth Century to the Early Twentieth Century', *Business History*, 48.2 (2006): p. 227.

5. Deborah Denenholz Morse, *Women in Trollope's Palliser Novels* (Ann Arbor: UMI Research Press, 1987) and Jane Nardin, *He Knew She Was Right: The Independent Woman in the Novels of Anthony Trollope* (Carbondale: Southern Illinois University Press, 1989).

6. See Janette Rutterford and Josephine Maltby, '"Frank Must Marry Money": Men, Women, and Property in Trollope's Novels', *Interfaces*, 33.2 (2006): pp. 169–99; Elsie Michie, *The Vulgar Question of Money: Heiresses, Materialism, and the Novel of Manners from Jane Austen to Henry James* (Baltimore: Johns Hopkins University Press, 2011) and Jill Rappoport, 'Greed, Generosity, and Other Problems with Unmarried Women's Property', *Victorian Studies*, 58.4 (Summer 2016): pp. 636–60.

7. Victoria Glendinning, *Anthony Trollope* (New York: Random House, 1993), p. 36.

8. Glendinning, *Trollope*, pp. 58–9.

9. Ibid. p. 58.

10. Anthony Trollope, *An Autobiography*, ed. David Skilton (Harmondsworth: Penguin, 1996), ch. 3, p. 36. Subsequent references are in the main text (*A*).

11. Glendinning, *Trollope*, p. 225.

12. Ibid. p. 348, p. 453, p. 483.

13. Ibid. p. 503, p. 506.

14. Ibid. p. 449.

15. Anthony Trollope, *Phineas Finn*, ed. John Sutherland (New York: Penguin, 1985), ch. 35, p. 355. Subsequent references are in the main text (*PF*).

16. Anthony Trollope, *The Eustace Diamonds*, ed. Helen Small (Oxford: Oxford University Press, 2011), ch. 2, p. 14. Subsequent references are in the main text (*ED*).

17. Donald Smalley (ed.), *Anthony Trollope: The Critical Heritage* (London: Routledge, 1969), p. 216. Criticism of *Miss Mackenzie* has been concerned with form and genre. Christopher Herbert describes the novel as shifting between literary modes to illustrate that 'comedy is a flexible form'. See *Trollope and Comic Pleasure* (Chicago: University of Chicago Press, 1987), p. 61. More attention might be given to how the financial plot influences the novel's form along the lines of Frederik Van Dam's reading of *Ayala's Angel* as intersecting with self-help narratives. See '"Getting and Spending": The Aesthetic Economist' (ch. 2) in *Anthony Trollope's Late Style: Victorian Liberalism and Literary Form* (Edinburgh: Edinburgh University Press, 2017). For the intersection of romance and financial plots in *The Prime Minister*, see Audrey Jaffe, *The Affective Life of the Average Man: The Victorian Novel and the Stock-Market Graph* (Columbus: Ohio State University Press, 2010).

18. Anthony Trollope, *Miss Mackenzie*, ed. A. O. J. Cockshut (Oxford: Oxford University Press, 1992), ch. 3, p. 36. Subsequent references are in the main text (*MM*).

19. Laurence, Maltby and Rutterford, *Women and Their Money*, p. 9
20. For Trollope's critique of West Indian and American slavery in *He Knew He Was Right* and *Doctor Wortle's School*, see Deborah Denenholtz Morse, *Reforming Trollope: Race, Gender and Englishness in the Novels of Anthony Trollope* (Burlington, VT: Ashgate, 2013).
21. Elsie Michie, 'The Odd Couple: Anthony Trollope and Henry James', *The Henry James Review*, 27.1 (2006): pp. 10–23.
22. Michie, 'Odd Couple', p. 20.
23. Michie, *Vulgar Question*, p. 122.
24. Talia Schaffer, *Romance's Rival: Familiar Marriage in Victorian Fiction* (Oxford: Oxford University Press, 2016).
25. Anthony Trollope, *The Prime Minister*, ed. Jenny Uglow (Oxford: Oxford University Press, 2008), ch. 43, p. 31. Subsequent references are in the main text (*PM*).
26. Anthony Trollope, *Can You Forgive Her?*, ed. Andrew Swarbrick (Oxford: Oxford University Press, 1982), ch. 60, p. 207; ch. 60, p. 209.
27. Anthony Trollope, *The Way We Live Now*, ed. John Sutherland (Oxford: Oxford University Press, 2016), ch. 21, p. 203.
28. On widows in Trollope's novels and the significance of their dress, see Christopher S. Noble, 'Otherwise Occupied: Masculine Widows in Trollope's Novels', in Margaret Marwick, Deborah Denenholz Morse and Regenia Gagnier (eds), *The Politics of Gender in Anthony Trollope's Novels* (Burlington, VT: Ashgate, 2009), pp. 177–92.
29. Michie, *Vulgar Question*, p. 122.
30. Anthony Trollope, *Phineas Redux*, ed. John Bowen (Oxford: Oxford University Press, 2011), ch. 52, p. 374.
31. Laurence, Maltby and Rutterford, *Women and Their Money*, p. 4.
32. I am grateful to Graham Handley, Deborah Denenholz Morse and Frederik Van Dam for their comments on earlier drafts of this article.

20

THE WAY WE LIVE NOW AND THE MEANING OF MONTAGU SQUARE

Francis O'Gorman

THE WAY WE LIVE NOW is vague about many things. Some are important matters concerning Trollope's characters. From where does Melmotte come, for instance?[1] What are his crimes prior to forging signatures? Some puzzles are more general. What *exactly* does Trollope dislike about that which he claimed, in *An Autobiography* (1883), was 'the commercial profligacy of the age'?[2] I have discussed in other essays the imprecision of Trollope's understanding of finance and financial law in an effort to explore why the novel is not reliable about the way we lived then.[3] The sustained interpretative preference since the recovery of this novel's critical fortunes in the second half of the twentieth century has been to see the text as, in Denise Lovett's symptomatic words in 2014, 'an attack on rapacious capitalist values, particularly as they manifest themselves in the market for finance capital'.[4] But *The Way We Live Now*, in fact, is remarkably misty about the workings of money – which is not untrue of many another novel on such a topic. One of the strangest features of the reception of Trollope's satire in the twentieth and twenty-first centuries is that he has been celebrated for a supposed critique of capitalism when in fact he represents finance (*understands* finance?) only in the most general and, where the legal environment is concerned, inaccurate of terms.

But *The Way We Live Now* is not vague about everything. Indeed, a curious complexity of its realism resides in the fact that Trollope offers many empirical details, particularly about London, crisply realised against an impressionistic background. This is, peculiarly and accurately, a novel of the capital city of Great Britain and Ireland in 1872.[5] Hetta Carbury, we learn, 'had studied her geography' – and so had Trollope. The speed of modern London is caught, for instance, in Hetta's journey in Chapter 91 to Islington. She 'trusted herself all alone', Trollope's narrator says, 'to the mysteries of the Marylebone underground railway, and emerged with accuracy at King's Cross.'[6] For a moment, the reader can imagine an actual journey. The Metropolitan line, running through Marylebone, opened in 1863 and was extended east in 1868. It was the world's first underground railway. Hetta walks – we can envisage her – from Welbeck Street either to Baker Street station or to Portland Road station (this became Great Portland Street in 1917), both off the Marylebone Road. She then travels either three or two stops (depending where she boarded) to King's Cross, which at this point was not the end of the line and not the current station. Hetta would have arrived on the site of what was subsequently the King's Cross Thameslink station at the top of the

Pentonville Road, which closed in 2007. It was the most convenient stop for her short walk up to Islington.[7]

The topography of London is real. We know from the novel about the City Road Music-Hall, The Angel at Islington, Mount Street, Euston Square, Lincoln's Inn Fields, Commercial Road, Grosvenor Square, Berkeley Square, Bruton Street, Welbeck Street and Goswell Road. We know where the clubs are; where all the important city characters live; and we know about the suspiciously 'small corner house' on Abchurch Lane where Melmotte conducts his business not far from the Bank of England. When Mr Fisker visits this office in Chapter 9, Trollope provides information, as befits a former civil servant at the Post Office, of the journey of Fisker's letter announcing his imminent arrival: 'The letter written at Liverpool', Trollope tells us, 'but dated from the Langham Hotel, had been posted at the Euston Square Railway Station at the moment of Fisker's arrival' (vol. 1, p. 55, ch. 9). This is strictly faithful to what could have occurred in real life. The Langham Hotel, completed only in 1865, is about four minutes' walk, as it happens, from where Lady Carbury lives in Welbeck Street.

Intriguingly, however, one detail of the novel's representation of Mayfair and Marylebone did not survive into the published book. Some of the author's notes from the early stages of planning the fiction (as well as the contract and the crucial diary that enabled Trollope to set his novel in 1872) remain in the Bodleian Library, Oxford. On the back of one sheet, Trollope has pencilled a thought: 'Melmotte's house south side of M Square'.[8] This almost certainly means 'south side of Montagu Square'. It is a name that survives in the published novel in Paul Montague, who was originally planned, according to those notes, to be called 'Montagu'.[9] The Square, between Marble Arch and Baker Street, was built between 1810 and 1815 and named after Elizabeth Montagu (1718–1800), social reformer, author and literary hostess, who had constructed Montagu House for herself in 1781, a few paces away on Portman Square.[10] If Melmotte had been real, then (and the novel set after April 1873), the Great Financier would have been able to leave his front door and, looking to the top left hand corner of his Square, see the house in which Anthony and Rose Trollope lived.

Quitting Waltham House, Waltham Cross, Trollope turned himself back into a Londoner with the purchase in February 1873 of 39 Montagu Square – a property still with a plaque declaring his residence. Trollope claimed, in a letter on 30 September 1874, that he was not fond of the move back to the capital, however much he liked the house. 'But', he added, '. . . I shall live here now till I die.'[11] It was the same phrase he used in An Autobiography, where he presented his delight in acquiring a large place in Marylebone, and the material prosperity that accompanied him. 'We returned from Australia in the winter of 1872', Trollope says:

> and early in 1873 I took a house in Montagu Square, – in which I hope to live and hope to die. Our first work in settling there was to place upon new shelves the books which I had collected round myself at Waltham. And this work, which was in itself great, entailed also the labour of a new catalogue. As all who use libraries know, a catalogue is nothing unless it show the spot on which every book is to be found, – information which every volume also ought to give as to itself. Only those who have done it know how great is the labour of moving and arranging a few

thousand volumes. At the present moment I own about 5000 volumes, and they are dearer to me even than the horses which are going, or than the wine in the cellar, which is very apt to go, and upon which I also pride myself.

When this was done, and the new furniture had got into its place, and my little book-room was settled sufficiently for work, I began a novel, to the writing of which I was instigated by what I conceived to be the commercial profligacy of the age. (*A*, ch. 20, p. 218)[12]

It is a funny moment. At the conclusion of Trollope's announcement of how pleased he is with his library, and after he has reminded his reader that he owns horses and a good private cellar, he tells us that his first fiction project in the new house was a complaint about the profligacy of the age. Trollope is not, of course, describing book, horse or wine collecting as by definition a symptom of profligacy. But the transition from pride in material possessions (note all the new furniture 'got into its place') to an objection to too many possessions produces a wry smile.

The Way We Live Now is proud of that house. And there was every good reason to be. In the novel's implicit affirmation of where Trollope was now able to afford to live, and, beyond that, the complicated implications of the text's interest in properties around Montagu Square and how (or whether) they are paid for, there is peculiarly important personal significance. This text – the reception of which has been almost overwhelmed by assertions about its handling of corrupt capitalism – was intimate with Trollope's own understanding of the good that legitimate capitalism could achieve. And in particular of what good such legitimate capitalism had done for his private sense of self and his memory of who, and what, he could have been. *The Way We Live Now* was, it may be, in the most general of terms a public rebuke to the so-named 'commercial profligacy of the age'. Yet its more exact financial meaning is private, and it is about success.

Number 39 Montagu Square – a seven-storey terrace house now divided into apartments – was paid for by writing. Trollope, of course, had left the Civil Service in 1867 to devote himself initially to politics (the failed Beverley campaign) and thereafter to writing and hunting. He had become a man of letters and a squire, both at once; an elevated personage of town and country. His social fortunes were not to be higher. Trollope's principal source of income after 1867 were the advances paid for his fiction (and it is worth remembering that Trollope shrewdly protected himself against financial loss by requiring advances rather than royalties, leaving the publisher to take the risks: he was good at the management of money).[13] Frederic Chapman, now solely in charge of Chapman and Hall and at this point Trollope's publisher,[14] was asked on 1 February to forward Trollope £1,250 to help the novelist purchase his new Marylebone property (*Letters*, vol. 2, p. 579).[15] This was the remaining half of the advance contractually agreed for *The Eustace Diamonds* (1871–3), a novel that concentrates on Warwick Square ('houses in Warwick Square were cheaper than they are now',[16] Trollope notes in Chapter 32, as if he has been recently looking). Trollope then discovered, as he half-comically told his friend, the historian G. W. Rusden (1819–1903), that as houses on the scale of 39 Montagu Square were not cheap to buy, they were not cheap to furnish either. 'We are taking, – I hope have taken', Trollope told Rusden on 3 February,

a house in London, and are going to enter into the ruinous pleasures and necessary agonies of furnishing it. I remember I used to hear Consule Planco [i.e. 'in my
youth'], that a modest man might supply himself with beds, tables and a chair to
sit on for £200. Now I am told that £1500 for the rough big things is absolutely
indispensable, and that prettiness may be supplied afterwards for a further £500.
(*Letters*, vol. 2, pp. 580–1)

Such confessions of unexpected costs are rarely neutral. Here, as in many other cases,
they amount to something like a boast. Trollope means, though faced with an unexpected bill, that his pockets are, of course, deep enough to cover it. The sum of £2,000
for prettiness was not insignificant and Rusden was meant to be impressed. In 2014
terms, it was £158,300.

This house, and the secure funds that paid for it and its decoration, mattered to
Trollope. Owning 39 Montagu Square – either the freehold or the leasehold, I cannot
determine – mattered not least because of history. The Trollope family, as the novelist knew it, had begun with the loss of a large property. Trollope's father, Thomas
Anthony Trollope (1774–1835) had grown up expecting (biographers have generally
assumed that his expectation was correct) to inherit Julians. This was (as it still is) a
country house and estate near Royston in Hertfordshire that, then, belonged to his
uncle, Adolphus Meetkerke. Anthony's brother, Thomas Adolphus (1810–92), recalled
in his autobiography, *What I Remember* (1887–9), the contrast between Julians and
the vicarage of his grandfather, the Rev. Anthony Trollope (1735–1836) of Cotten-
ham, also in Hertfordshire: 'The house and establishment at Julians were on a far more
pretentious scale than the home of the vicar', Thomas Adolphus said, 'and the mode of
life in the squire's establishment larger and freer.'[17] It was this estate that was expected
to become the future novelist's family home because Uncle Meetkerke had no children
of his own. But, unexpectedly, his wife died. And even more unexpectedly, the spritely
Uncle Meetkerke married again, and he married a young woman: 'he was as fine an
old man physically as anybody could wish to see', Thomas Adolphus remembered,
and before long, he became 'the father of six children!'[18] Thomas Anthony's expected
inheritance of Julians vanished in that exclamation mark.

The loss was commemorated, and intended to be compensated for, in a new Julians
that was not inherited but constructed, unfortunately, on hired land. The new Julians
(the name is not as pointed as it looks but probably the result of a strange coincidence:
a field nearby was locally known as Julians) was the farm that Trollope's father built
in 1818 on a plot leased from Lord Northwick's Harrow estate from October 1813.
(By an irony that might not have been lost on Anthony later in his life, this was exactly
the time that Montagu Square was being built in Marylebone.) That farm, said Anthony
in *An Autobiography*, was a disaster: it was 'the grave of all my father's hopes, ambition, and prosperity, the cause of my mother's sufferings, and of those of her children,
and perhaps the director of her destiny and of ours' (*A*, ch. 1, p. 9). This Julians was
'ruinous', he continued, and echoed what was his father's view that the fault partly
lay elsewhere: 'we all regarded the Lord Northwick of those days as a cormorant who
was eating us up' (*A*, ch. 1, p. 10). Here was a history of substantial property that was
lost and substitute property that ruined. And it was a substitute property which, as
Trollope looked back in the year *The Way We Live Now* was published in volume

form, had been at the root of the family's fate. He was not wrong. Frances Trollope's efforts to keep the family afloat had been prompted by this failing project. And her work had been simultaneous with her husband's decline into cantankerous sickness and further financial incapability. As the *Oxford Dictionary of National Biography* remarks: 'In December 1830 Trollope petitioned Lord Northwick for reduced rents on behalf of all the tenants because of the agricultural depression – in terms so offensive that all rents but his were reduced.'[19] By 1834, Thomas Anthony Trollope, who had already once moved from the new Julians (in fact moved *back*) to another cheaper farmhouse that Anthony memorialised as Orley Farm, fled to Belgium to escape his creditors. There he died in Bruges the following year. The *ODNB*'s final statement of 'Wealth at death' is a bleak summary of what he had made of his life: 'estate seized but declared under £50 so creditor (Geo. Barney) got nothing.'[20]

The Way We Live Now is interested in estates where the heir receives a lot more than nothing. Roger Carbury, owner of the ancestral Carbury Hall, hopes that he will marry Hetta Carbury and that in turn their son will inherit the Hall. But Hetta turns him down. Part of the problem, in the absence of a direct heir to Roger, is that the estate should, by rights, descend to the wretched Sir Felix Carbury. His recklessness with money, as Roger well knows, will bring it to ruin. In finally reconciling himself to Hetta's marriage to Paul Montague, Roger is also ensuring the safety of his estate ('Montagu(e)' is indeed a restorative word for Trollope). Carbury Hall will be inherited by the right person. 'Hetta's child', Roger thinks in Chapter 93,

> must take the name of Carbury, and must be to him as his heir, – as near as possible his own child. In her favour he must throw aside that law of primogeniture which to him was so sacred that he had been hitherto minded to make Sir Felix his heir in spite of the absolute unfitness of the wretched young man. All this must be changed, should he be able to persuade himself to give his consent to the marriage. (vol. 2, ch. 93, p. 271)

The matter of substantial property – an estate on which there are farm properties, like Lord Northwick's – passing to the right hands is not an innocent topic for the son of an estate-less barrister who had hoped for Julians and failed with its replacement.

The Way We Live Now is concerned with what is the optimal future for an important family property just as *Orley Farm* (1861–2) was centred on a dispute about the inheritance of an estate. The Roger Carbury plot, like that of *Orley Farm*, is one about 'who deserves to inherit a house?' The narrative rewards moral integrity (such integrity as Paul Montague has, anyway) with bricks and mortar, land and farms. But aside from this assessment of worth in terms of property, the novel is more extensively interested in property, and its 'prettiness', which cannot be afforded by those whose moral worth is as low as their credit. *The Way We Live Now* is a novel intently considering people in relation to their houses and what they do to them – inherited, bought or hired. And the first clue to the significance of this – though R. H. Super makes nothing of the same observation in his important biography of Trollope (1988) – is that they are all houses close to Montagu Square.[21]

To start simply with the matter of decorating. We know, suggestively, a lot about the preparations for Marie Melmotte's party in Chapter 4 of *The Way We Live Now*.

This is the first opulent event to take place in Melmotte's house in Grosvenor Square, then one of Mayfair's most elegant addresses, and just over half a mile south of Montagu Square. Trollope's description of those preparations is extended:

> The large house on the south side of Grosvenor Square was all ablaze by ten o'clock. The broad verandah had been turned into a conservatory, had been covered in with boards contrived to look like trellis-work, was heated with hot air and filled with exotics at some fabulous price. A covered way had been made from the door, down across the pathway, to the road, and the police had, I fear, been bribed to frighten foot passengers into a belief that they were bound to go round. The house had been so arranged that it was impossible to know where you were, when once in it. The hall was a paradise. The staircase was fairyland. The lobbies were grottoes rich with ferns. Walls had been knocked away and arches had been constructed. The leads behind had been supported and walled in, and covered and carpeted. The ball had possession of the ground floor and first floor, and the house seemed to be endless. 'It's to cost sixty thousand pounds', said the Marchioness of Auld Reekie to her old friend the Countess of Mid-Lothian. The Marchioness had come in spite of her son's misfortune when she heard that the Duchess of Stevenage was to be there. 'And worse spent money never was wasted', said the Countess. 'By all accounts it was as badly come by', said the Marchioness. (vol. 1, ch. 4, p. 23)

At this stage, no reader can be *sure* that the money is badly come by, though suspicions are being raised, not only by the Marchioness. But £60,000 of party preparation is staggering. Trollope intends his reader to gasp. The equivalent in 2014 was £4,748,000.

Trollope, as he says himself in *An Autobiography*, did not care for extravagance. He certainly did not care for what he denounced – with his usual financial vagueness – as modern dishonesty coupled with extravagance. There was, he airily declared, a 'certain class of dishonesty, dishonesty magnificent in its proportions, and climbing into high places' (*A*, ch. 20, p. 219). It is not clear whom he means or why he should have thought this a new phenomenon. But the point about the magnificent extravagance of Marie Melmotte's ball was that it rendered such dishonesty into fiction. The ball could not be paid for legitimately. We know by the end of the novel that this, like all of Melmotte's activities, has been funded by fraud: Melmotte had, as we learn in Chapter 64, been 'cheating and forging and stealing all his life' (vol. 2, ch. 64, p. 89). The 'prettiness' of the Grosvenor Square house is eye-wateringly costly – and also criminal.

This is not a theme, with all its implications, which Trollope can easily leave. He continues to plot Melmotte's life around the property he rents – the other is the house on Bruton Street in Mayfair – and decorates. Bruton Street is where the family repairs during the preparations for the visit of the Emperor of China, the great angry climax of Melmotte's efforts to establish himself in British high society. Bruton Street is also the Longestaffe home and Trollope has some things to say about their place, too. The Bruton Street residence, he remarks in Chapter 13,

> was not by any means a charming house, having but few of those luxuries and elegancies which have been added of late years to newly-built London residences. It was gloomy and inconvenient, with large drawing-rooms, bad bedrooms, and

very little accommodation for servants. But it was the old family town-house, having been inhabited by three or four generations of Longestaffes, and did not savour of that radical newness which prevails, and which was peculiarly distasteful to Mr Longestaffe. Queen's Gate and the quarters around were, according to Mr Longestaffe, devoted to opulent tradesmen. Even Belgrave Square, though its aristocratic properties must be admitted, still smelt of the mortar. Many of those living there and thereabouts had never possessed in their families real family town-houses. The old streets lying between Piccadilly and Oxford Street, with one or two well-known localities to the south and north of these boundaries, were the proper sites for these habitations. (vol. 1, ch. 13, p. 80)

Trollope saves himself from directly identifying Montagu Square as a preferable location in which to live. But he does admit the elegance of some properties north of Oxford Street, which would certainly include his Square. These lines, more plainly, record his recent activity in decorating, in adding 'luxuries and elegancies' to his new house. And they make other contrasts with the novelist's property choice too. Trollope, so different from the fictional characters he has created at Bruton Street, possesses a 'real family town-house', which did not smell of bricks and mortar and was, as *An Autobiography* confirms, far from the Longestaffes' experience of a dwelling both 'gloomy and inconvenient'.

The owner of 39 Montagu Square is, in a work of the imagination, an assessor of others' property. Trollope looks out in *The Way We Live Now* for what is commodious, elegant, well-established, or otherwise; and he looks out for how, or whether, it was funded. Carbury Hall is important in the novel's property plots in part because it imaginatively re-processes something of the lingering memory of the Trollope family's loss of both Julians, and all that meant for that family's early destiny. But it also provides the novelist with an opportunity, for a moment, to evaluate who has an admirable house that is *not* close to Montagu Square. The discrimination over Carbury Hall's advantages in comparison with those around occupies a significant portion of Chapter 14 and reveals Trollope, although away from Mayfair and Marylebone, still regarding bricks and mortar with the eye of an estate agent or a property developer:

[Carbury Hall] itself had been built in the time of Charles II., when that which we call Tudor architecture was giving way to a cheaper, less picturesque, though perhaps more useful form. But Carbury Manor House, through the whole county, had the reputation of being a Tudor building. The windows were long, and for the most part low, made with strong mullions, and still contained small, old-fashioned panes; for the squire had not as yet gone to the expense of plate glass. There was one high bow window, which belonged to the library, and which looked out on to the gravel sweep, at the left of the front door as you entered it. All the other chief rooms faced upon the garden. The house itself was built of a stone that had become buff, or almost yellow with years, and was very pretty. It was still covered with tiles, as were all the attached buildings. It was only two stories high, except at the end, where the kitchens were placed and the offices, which thus rose above the other part of the edifice. The rooms throughout were low, and for the most part long and narrow, with large wide fire-places and deep wainscotings. Taking it

altogether, one would be inclined to say, that it was picturesque rather than comfortable. Such as it was its owner was very proud of it, – with a pride of which he
never spoke to anyone, which he endeavoured studiously to conceal, but which had
made itself known to all who knew him well. The houses of the gentry around him
were superior to his in material comfort and general accommodation, but to none
of them belonged that thoroughly established look of old county position which
belonged to Carbury. Bundlesham, where the Primeros lived, was the finest house
in that part of the county, but it looked as if it had been built within the last twenty
years. It was surrounded by new shrubs and new lawns, by new walls and new
outhouses, and savoured of trade; – so at least thought Roger Carbury, though he
never said the words. Caversham was a very large mansion, built in the early part
of George III'.s reign, when men did care that things about them should be comfortable, but did not care that they should be picturesque. There was nothing at
all to recommend Caversham but its size. Eardly Park, the seat of the Hepworths,
had, as a park, some pretensions. Carbury possessed nothing that could be called a
park, the enclosures beyond the gardens being merely so many home paddocks. But
the house of Eardly was ugly and bad. The Bishop's palace was an excellent gentleman's residence, but then that too was comparatively modern, and had no peculiar
features of its own. Now Carbury Manor House was peculiar, and in the eyes of its
owner was pre-eminently beautiful. (vol. 1, ch. 14, pp. 87–8)

It would be hard to think of another mid-century novel so absorbed by comparing
what other men's houses are like.

Melmotte, as we know by the end of *The Way We Live Now*, cannot afford to buy
Pickering Park in Sussex from Mr Adolphus Longestaffe. He is obliged to forge signatures. But he certainly *seems* able, at the start, to decorate it. Pickering, like Melmotte's
place in Grosvenor Square, is transformed. '[Before] a week was over', Trollope writes
in Chapter 35, 'a London builder had collected masons and carpenters by the dozen
down at Chichester, and was at work upon the house to make it fit to be a residence
for Madame Melmotte' (vol. 1, ch. 35, p. 219). The same was going on in real life in
Montagu Square as Trollope began the novel. Only there, it had been paid for with
money that both existed and had been legitimately earned.

It is with more unaffordable, over-extended prettiness that Trollope concludes the
history of Melmotte's dishonesty as he turns his London house into a palace without
lawful resources again. This work at Grosvenor Square is undertaken in honour of the
Emperor of China.[22] We hear, over a sequence of chapters, about the gradual transformation of a rented house into somewhere fit for a – man greater than a king. In Chapter 56, for instance, the vexing priest Fr Barham (a survival from Trollope's original
plans to discuss religious doubts in the novel) arrives to rebuke Melmotte. Barham is
accidentally given admission since no one is concentrating on who should or should
not be let in. That is because the house 'was in great confusion':

The wreaths of flowers and green boughs were being suspended, last daubs of
heavy gilding were being given to the wooden capitals of mock pilasters, incense
was being burned to kill the smell of the paint, tables were being fixed and chairs
were being moved; and an enormous set of open presses were being nailed together
for the accommodation of hats and cloaks. (vol. 2, ch. 56, p. 36)

These preparations, for a dinner intended for the highest ranks of the British establishment, turn out a disappointment, since not all guests decide to attend. Ill-gotten
money has not been able to purchase everything or everyone. Pointedly at the close of
Chapter 59, Melmotte – having spent another fortune on an only partially successful
entertainment – inquires about the absences. Miles Grendall's blunt answer faces him
with the accusation that will in due course destroy him. And it is an accusation about
property. '"They say there's been something – forged. Title-deeds, I think they say"',
Grendall remarks: '"Title-deeds!"' Melmotte replies, '"that I have forged title-deeds.
Well; that's beginning well"' (vol. 2, ch. 56, p. 57). The 'Dinner' sequence, at its close,
unites the two material markers of Melmotte's deceptions: his redecorations and his
house purchase, neither of which he can rightfully afford.

Anthony Trollope, on a different scale, could afford both. Each passage narrating
Melmotte's houses, their characteristics, decorations and funding, forms a contrast
with what the novelist had just achieved a few minutes away from Grosvenor Square,
only legitimately. Having purchased a Marylebone town house and decorated it with
funds produced from hard literary labour, Trollope imaginatively constructs a counter-
figure, reminding himself of his own success as it was embodied, literally, in a building.
And he was not only reminding himself.

There are crucially absent fathers in *The Way We Live Now*. There is, for
instance, Lady Carbury's husband, the father of Sir Felix. We know from Chapter 2
that Felix 'was known to have had a fortune left to him by his father' (vol. 1, ch. 2,
p. 10), though its extent is debated. Whatever money there was, alas, is transformed
by Felix at the Beargarden into a huge debt. This violent, mean and drunken father,
the missing Sir Patrick Carbury, has left behind a crisis: a son in need of guidance
and less money to waste, and a widow in need of more money *not* to waste. And in
line with Trollope's peculiar attentiveness to the Marylebone and Mayfair property
market, her financial situation is measured, revealingly, in relation to another house
near Montagu Square. Lady Carbury's home in Welbeck Street – ten minutes' walk
from the Trollopes – is more or less satisfactory, though nothing to boast about. It
was 'a modest house enough', Trollope tells us, – 'with no pretensions to be a mansion, hardly assuming even to be a residence; but, having some money in her hands
when she first took it, she had made it pretty and pleasant, and was still proud to feel
that in spite of the hardness of her position she had comfortable belongings around
her when her literary friends came to see her on her Tuesday evenings' (vol. 1, ch. 3,
p. 14). It is not as large or as smart as the newly decorated writer's residence just a
few minutes away, with its books, shelves and wine cellar. Despite the seemingly safe
possession of Welbeck Street, however, the problem of Lady Carbury's dead husband
remains. His absence, as well as her son's recklessness with his dead father's money,
obliges her both to 'puff' her own literary achievements and to seek a wealthy man
to marry. Lady Carbury is a struggling fictional author in a modest fictional house
a little north of the real Grosvenor Square. Trollope, creating her, is a hugely successful real author in a real seven-storey town house a little north west of the same
Grosvenor Square.

A missing father causes money problems. And there is a telling oddity about
another father too: Melmotte. Who *is* Marie's father? We gather from Chapter 4
that Marie looks nothing like either apparent parent. 'There was', we read further
on, 'considerable doubt whether Marie was the daughter of that Jewish-looking

woman' (i.e. Melmotte's wife): 'Enquiries had been made, but not successfully, as to the date of the Melmotte marriage. There was an idea abroad that Melmotte had got his first money with his wife, and had gotten it not very long ago. Then other people said that Marie was not his daughter at all' (vol. 1, ch. 4, p. 23). The rumour, in this capacious novel of gossip and suspicion, confuses the reader's idea of Marie's parentage just as, in fact, we are never certain who Melmotte is or from which country he originates. Marie might pass most of the novel without her real father, or she might simply be mistreated by a violent bully who actually is her father. At the end, nevertheless, the heiress, after the suicide, is undeniably without Melmotte, whether he is her father or not.

There are dead fathers. And there is also a paternal ghost in this novel, like Hamlet's. The most important missing parent in *The Way We Live Now* is no longer alive – but, unlike in *Hamlet*, he never appears. Each time Trollope evaluates a property near Montagu Square, each time he wonders about the advantages or disadvantages of this house in London or that in Suffolk, each time he thinks of the funds required to buy or beautify an address, he is thinking of his own experience. But he is also thinking of the exceptional difference between himself and Thomas Anthony Trollope, dead those forty years. The novel makes a habit of evaluating men's houses (and most of these men, as it happens, are fathers as if they confirm somehow Trollope's covert act of paternal comparison). Lord Nidderdale, we learn, for instance, lives in a house in Berkeley Square about which we know almost nothing: it cannot be impressive (or maybe it is too impressive?). Mr Alf possesses a 'small house . . . close to Berkeley Square' (vol. 1, ch. 1, p. 6), which is certainly not a seven-storey town house *in* a Square; Lady Carbury and Hetta live modestly in Welbeck Street conscious they are without resources to improve it, let alone move; the Longestaffes inhabit that 'gloomy and inconvenient' property on Bruton Street; and Melmotte, as well we know, hires a grand abode at Grosvenor Square and another temporary house in Bruton Street, and he tries to buy Pickering Park – none of which he can afford. These properties, as Trollope enumerates them, are all unassuming, limited, unappealing, unfunded or illegitimately funded. And they are all statements to the grave. They are cryptic messages to Trollope's father, which declare that, despite it all, his novelist son has succeeded where his father did not; that the paternal legacy – or rather the utter absence of legacy – has not stifled the new generation. These scenes announce that the son had made up for the father and that he had done so in exactly the same way that had ruined Thomas Anthony: through property. In place of the seized estate of the novelist's father, Anthony Trollope's wealth at his death would in due course be recorded in the probate records of 1883 as £25,892 19s. 3d. That in 2014 terms is £2,329,000, which included money from the sale of Montagu Square in July 1880. Trollope wrote *An Autobiography*, begun at the same time as *The Way We Live Now* was published in volume form by Chapman and Hall, in part for his sons. But it was also for his missing father. And the first novel Trollope began in his newly purchased and newly decorated writing room in 39 Montagu Square, a novel with a sustained assessment of success and moral worth in relation to properties that were largely in the vicinity of that Square, had the identical ghostly audience.

It is easy to think *The Way We Live Now* a novel impatient with material success because the most dramatic manifestations of such success prove to be funded by crime. But it is also a novel deeply conscious of the significance of legitimately obtained material achievement not least as signified by the possession of property. Anthony Trollope celebrates where his novel was written, and all for which his new house stood in his own history: in relation to the legacy he never received, the legacy his father never received, and the disastrous events on Lord Northwick's estate.

There was one final, private, significance, too, which confirmed the distance that Trollope, as he sat down to start *The Way We Live Now*, had travelled. And I mean distance, literally. Between 1835 and 1837, as Trollope records in *An Autobiography*, he had lived at 22 Northumberland Street in poverty as a junior employee of the Post Office. Often powerless to afford any supper, he could not in *An Autobiography* remember any longer how he had made his daily bread. Number 22, Trollope remarked, was 'by the Marylebone Workhouse, on to the back-door of which establishment my room looked out – a most dreary abode, at which I fancy I must have almost ruined the good-natured lodging-house keeper by my constant inability to pay her what I owed' (*A*, ch. 3, p. 39).[23] Northumberland Street is now Luxborough Street, and it is half a mile on foot from Montagu Square. Buying Number 39 – exactly forty years after Trollope's father's death and his taking-up of residence near the Marylebone Workhouse – the author of *The Way We Live Now* could hardly have made a more plain statement about the difference from where he started and where he had arrived. He was still in the vicinity of the workhouse. But he was in no danger of being taken there.

The most heartfelt and privately exact meaning of this novel's title, then, is really *The Way We* (i.e. Anthony and Rose Trollope) *Live Now*. With that declaration, and the meaning of the ownership of 39 Montagu Square, the novelist could express his pleasure in the success he had made of his life. It was a life that might, after such an unpromising start with a lost paternal inheritance, the disastrous Harrow farm(s) and the lean years in rented rooms at 22 Northumberland Street, have been a failure. Augustus Melmotte, Trollope tells us, was 'magnificent in his expenditure, powerful in his doings, successful in his business, and the world around him therefore was not repelled' (vol. 1, ch. 9, p. 55). The novelist himself, picking up his new house keys sometime in or just before April 1873, had done far, far better than that because his achievement was both actual – he would, revealingly, emphasise that his fiction was also a form of property that reflected the work that went into it in *An Autobiography* – and legal.[24] The property plot of *The Way We Live Now*, the first fiction Trollope wrote in Montagu Square, celebrates that house – and all its conspicuous significance in and for his life.

Notes

I am grateful to Nicholas Shrimpton and Kate Williams for helping me think about the terms of this essay. They are not responsible for the errors or views here. Note that the original volume editions of Trollope's novels have been cited here together with chapter numbers.

1. There is a searching comment on one aspect of this in John Sutherland, 'Is Melmotte Jewish?', in *Is Heathcliff a Murderer? Puzzles in Nineteenth-Century Fiction* (Oxford: Oxford University Press, 1996), pp. 156–62.
2. Anthony Trollope, *An Autobiography*, ed. Nicholas Shrimpton (Oxford: Oxford University Press, 2014), ch. 20; p. 218. Subsequent references are in the main text (*A*).

3. See the 'Introduction' to Anthony Trollope, *The Way We Live Now*, ed. Francis O'Gorman (Oxford: Oxford University Press, 2016); Francis O'Gorman, 'Is Trollope's *The Way We Live Now* (1875) about the "commercial profligacy of the age"?', *Review of English Studies*, 67 (2016): pp. 751–63; and Francis O'Gorman, 'The Way We Didn't Live Then', *Journal of Victorian Culture*, 20 (2015): pp. 570–4.

4. Denise Lovett, 'The Socially-embedded Market and the Future of English Capitalism in Anthony Trollope's *The Way We Live Now*', *Victorian Literature and Culture*, 42 (2014): p. 691.

5. On the certainty of this date as the setting of the novel, see Appendix 2 to my edition.

6. Anthony Trollope, *The Way We Live Now*, 2 vols (London: Chapman and Hall, 1875), vol. 2, ch. 91, p. 259.

7. For more on this journey and the transport systems Trollope mentions see the note to p. 684 of my edition of *The Way We Live Now* on p. 791.

8. Bodleian Library, Oxford, MS Don c.10, fol.16.

9. For more details about the working notes, see Appendix 1 to my edition and John Sutherland's 'Trollope at Work on *The Way We Live Now*', *Nineteenth-Century Fiction*, 37 (1982): pp. 472–93.

10. Montagu House was destroyed by an incendiary bomb in 1941.

11. *The Letters of Anthony Trollope*, ed. N. John Hall with the assistance of Nina Burgis, 2 vols (Stanford: Stanford University Press, 1983), vol. 2, p. 631. This letter is to Trollope's American friend, Mrs Harriet Knower. Subsequent references are in the main text *(Letters)*.

12. Trollope's catalogue is described in Richard H. Grossman and Andrew Wright, 'Anthony Trollope's Libraries', *Nineteenth-Century Fiction*, 31 (1976): pp. 48–64.

13. This is discussed in full in my 'Is Trollope's *The Way We Live Now* (1875) about the "commercial profligacy of the age"?'

14. William Hall had died at the age of forty-six on 7 March 1847, leaving Chapman to manage the business. The official history of the company is Auberon Waugh, *A Hundred Years of Publishing. Being the Story of Chapman and Hall Ltd* (London: Chapman and Hall, 1930).

15. £1,250 is, in 2014 terms, £98,920. Equivalent values used in this essay are taken from <www.measuringworth.com>. Methodologically, I have presented equivalents calculated via comparisons of the Retail Price Index. There are problems with the RPI method, not least because consideration of labour value or of income value (if the capital were invested optimally) will give different and usually larger conversion figures. But there is, at least, simplicity about using the RPI (based on familiar commodities). Sums are nevertheless indicative, not definitive.

16. Anthony Trollope, *The Eustace Diamonds*, 3 vols (London: Chapman and Hall, 1873), vol. 2, ch. 32, p. 74.

17. Thomas Adolphus Trollope, *What I Remember*, 3 vols (London: Bentley, 1887–9), vol. 1, p. 63.

18. Ibid. p. 68.

19. Mickie Grover, 'Thomas Anthony Trollope', *ODNB*, <www.oxforddnb.com> (last accessed 26 February 2017).

20. Ibid. For details of the Trollope property and their house moves, see Nicholas Shrimpton's account in his edition of *An Autobiography*, p. 282.

21. See R. H. Super, *The Chronicler of Barsetshire: A Life of Anthony Trollope* (Ann Arbor: University of Michigan Press, 1988), p. 319.

22. Not a moment of empirical exactness: technically ruled by the Tongzhi Emperor (1856–75) in 1873, China was governed in practice by his mother, the Empress Dowager Cixi (1835–1908). Neither visited Great Britain: indeed, *The Times* on 2 September 1873, p. 7, observed

that in July of that year for the first time in nearly thirteen years foreigners (including the Ambassador of Great Britain and Ireland) had been allowed to see the Emperor.

23. What survived of the Marylebone Workhouse building was finally demolished in 1965: part of the University of Westminster now stands on the site.

24. The forms of labour and the difference between financial and aesthetic value for Trollope in the mid-1870s are well analysed in Silvana Colella, 'Sweet Money: Cultural and Economic Value in Trollope's *Autobiography*', *Nineteenth-Century Contexts*, 28 (2006): pp. 5–20.

21

'CEADE MILLE FALTHA': QUESTIONS OF HOSPITALITY IN THE IRISH TROLLOPE

John McCourt

Englishmen who have lived here [in Ireland] have imbibed something which changed and strengthened them. There is an Irish soil, an Irish climate, and an Irish atmosphere, which are a potent moulder, not alone of men's bodies, but of their minds.[1]

ALONG-TIME RESIDENTIAL guest in Ireland, Trollope made but one attempt to write in Gaelic: the single, misspelt 'ceade mille faltha' which is to be found in *The Macdermots of Ballycloran*, his first novel.[2] It occurs in an exchange between the tragic hero of the novel, Thady Macdermot, and the treacherous middleman, Pat Brady, who feigns to work on his behalf. They are arguing about the speculator, Joe Flannelly, who built their home and is now, along with his lawyer and son-in-law, Hyacinth Keegan, trying to wrestle it from them at an excessively low price:

'D – – n Flannelly!' was Brady's easy solution of the family difficulties. 'Let him take the house he built, and be d – – d to him; and if we can't build a betther one for the masthur and Miss Feemy and you, without his help, may praties choke me!'
    'By dad, if he'd take the house, and leave the ground, he's my welcome, and ceade mille faltha, Pat. But the land will stick to the house; and mark me, when ould Flannelly dies (an' the divil die along with him), Mr Keegan of Carrick will write himself, Hyacinth Keegan, Esquire, of Ballycloran'. (*MB*, ch. 2, p. 21)

The pointed 'ceade mille faltha' is employed to say that Flannelly is welcome to the house, but means, of course, quite the opposite. In using this clichéd Irish language idiom (meaning 'a hundred thousand welcomes'), Trollope is introducing notions of home, land and ownership, all of which are key issues in his Irish novels (and indeed in his output, *tout court*). The phrase suggests issues of hospitality and its ethics, which are recurring concerns in Trollope's writing. In considering the exercise of hospitality as an 'application of the broader virtue of benevolence to the specific relationship of host and guest',[3] I have in mind an ethical concern – about how best to treat a neighbour, a stranger, an 'other' within the domestic and the national home. Trollope sees this from both sides: from the point of view of hosts called upon to open their house but also to impose behavioural rules over a new arrival; that of the guest who accepts the hospitality. The host's intentions, authority, and overall behaviour are also measured.

Despite being constantly labelled as the quintessential Englishman, Trollope lived a huge portion of his life away from home as a guest: in Ireland, first, for fifteen years, and later travelling the length and breadth of Britain, Ireland and indeed the wider world on Post Office duty. The results of this experience spilled over into his fiction. Trollope came to Ireland in 1841, anxious to put behind him pretty much everything about his past life up to that point. There was little, it seemed, to salvage from a broken family life, an unhappy education and a dull, unpromising position as a junior clerk at the Post Office. Things could only get better. Arriving in the remote town of Banagher, County Offaly, he was given as good a welcome into the country as any overbearing (if then lowly) British official of the Post Office could have hoped for. As he later described it in his *Autobiography*, the Irish turned out to be unexpectedly accommodating:

> The Irish people did not murder me, nor did they even break my head. I soon found them to be good-humoured, clever – the working classes very much more intelligent than those of England – oeconomical and hospitable. We hear much of their spendthrift nature; but extravagance is not the nature of an Irishman. He will count the shillings in a pound much more accurately than an Englishman, and will with much more certainty get twelve pennyworth from each. But they are perverse, irrational and but little bound by the love of truth. I lived for many years among them – not finally leaving the country until 1859, and I had the means of studying their character.[4]

If the experience of Irish hospitality clearly impressed and even moved Trollope, it also caused him to question the more general quality of hospitality that he would come to describe and explore widely in his fiction. For good reason, then, Deborah Denenholz Morse refers to the 'core Trollopian values of duty, hospitality, and stability'.[5] To Trollope's stern eye, Ireland would have offered precious little by way of stability and too many of the Irish he would have seen as lacking in a proper sense of duty. However, he did come to enjoy hospitality in abundance in 1840s Ireland, in a country caught in political and economic turmoil and about to suffer the horrors of the Great Famine. Once settled in Ireland, Trollope's dual careers as novelist and Post Office administrator finally took off and within a decade of settling in Ireland he had emerged as a leading light in both professions. It might not have gone so well. Hospitality might not have been so automatically offered to the man James Russell Lowell described as 'a big, redfaced, rather underbred Englishman'[6] who adopted what John Pope Hennessy called an 'abrupt bow-wow way'[7] when addressing the Irish. Trollope was made to feel at home in the various corners of 1840s and '50s Ireland, a country that, despite its huge material problems, still took hospitality as a matter of pride and duty. He attested to his sense of belonging in Ireland and among the Irish at various points and with great sincerity throughout his life:

> It has been my fate to have so close an intimacy with Ireland, that when I meet an Irishman abroad I always recognise in him more of a kinsman than I do in your Englishman. I never ask an Englishman from what county he comes, or what was his town. To Irishmen I usually put such a question, and I am generally familiar with the old haunts which they name.[8]

In his travels around Ireland, Trollope never turned down the chance to sample Irish hospitality. He knew that there was always an element of exchange involved, one that could be rewarding to both the giver and the receiver. As Thackeray puts it in *Pendennis*: 'to receive small kindnesses flatters the donors very much, and . . . people must needs grow well disposed towards you as they give you their hospitality.'[9] Trollope would have learnt this first hand, when for example he visited a squire's house in County Cavan. His host on this occasion had written complaining of a poor postal service and so Trollope appeared on his doorstep to hear his problem. Once in the house, Trollope was offered hospitality that was both charming and coercive and clearly of more benefit to the giver than to the recipient:

> The Irishman turned on all his charm and sent his butler for brandy and hot water. Then he insisted that his guest must dine and spend the night. It was only after breakfast the next morning that the squire agreed to discuss business and admitted that he had no real complaint. He amused himself in his lonely abode by writing outraged letters to various government departments.[10]

Trollope was given a welcome in many parts of the country and from people positioned at various points on the social scale as if in illustration of the ancient Greek idea of individual responsibility to provide hospitality (*xenia*) which defined behavioural duties for host and guest. He was welcomed into great homes, such as Coole Park, by William Gregory, or Gurten-le Poer, on the Waterford–Tipperary border, by Count Edmond James De la Poer, to name but two. But more often than not, he would have been welcomed into homes of a far more humble nature which would have taken pride in welcoming this well-disposed and curious English official.

The application of this duty of hospitality is contained in the word '*philoxenia*' meaning love (*philia*) for the stranger (*xenos*). But hospitality is a two-edged concept. It stems from the Latin *hospes*, meaning 'host', but also 'guest', or even 'stranger', which itself is formed from *hostis*, meaning 'stranger' or 'enemy' (we think of 'hostile'). It refers to both a host and a guest who might well be a stranger or an enemy but who must accept or be accepted nonetheless. In Rachel Hollander's useful explanation, 'Hospitality concerns the arrival of the stranger, and the necessity of an ethical response to an unpredictable and not fully knowable demand.'[11] Immanuel Kant, in his essay *Towards Perpetual Peace*, defined 'universal hospitality' as

> the right of a stranger not to be treated as an enemy when he arrives in the land of another. One may refuse to receive him when this can be done without causing his destruction; but, so long as he peacefully occupies his place, one may not treat him with hostility.[12]

However, the very acceptance of a guest in one's home is never unconditional but happens through the imposition of terms and conditions, the assertion of ownership and authority, and the application and acceptance of local or house rules. A sampling of these local rules was very much part of Trollope's life in Ireland and he would then dissect them in the pages of his fiction where he makes hospitality, Irish style, a key element. He would later turn the tables and offer a conditional hospitality all of his own, to Irish characters and issues, within his 'English' fiction. The fact that he did so, against the backdrop of the Irish Famine that sent hundreds of thousands of starving

Irish across the water to Britain in search of home and succour, adds a very particular if purely implicit edge to his treatment of this theme. After an initial upsurge in sympathy and compassion for the Irish in the early period of the Famine, resentment gradually grew in Britain towards this population inflow and, as Frank Neal has shown, the 'press continually highlighted what they believed to be examples of an Irish propensity to abuse British hospitality'.[13] Trollope for the most part did not take part in any such highlighting although in his fourth letter to the *Examiner* in defence of British policy in Ireland during the Famine he does write contemptuously of 'Pat Carroll and all the little Patlings [who] must now be fed'.[14] This echoes his description of Captain Carroll in *Mr Scarborough's Family*, a posthumous work that represents the reactionary nature of the later Trollope's attitude to Ireland during the Land War. Carroll is the most negatively drawn of his Irish leeches: 'An improvident, worthless, drunken Irishman' with six daughters, he never loses an opportunity to sponge off his brother-in-law, the decent English lawyer, John Grey, who had injudiciously promised Carroll that he 'would never see his sister want'.[15] Trollope dedicates an entire chapter to describing the Grey family dreading the visit of their dysfunctional Irish cousins and shows Mr Grey capitulating, once again, to his sister's pleas and agreeing to pay off more of Carroll's debts even though he knows that he is giving money to a lost cause. This relationship of craven dependence is the later Trollope's harsh metaphor for the connection between Britain and Ireland and to what the limits of British sympathy and hospitality should be.

Irish hospitality was of course not identical with its English equivalent, as Trollope's fellow writer and friend William Makepeace Thackeray pointed out in his *Irish Sketchbook*. Irish hospitality, in his view, was somewhat rough and ready, generalised, and all too liberally dished out:

If an Irish gentleman does not give you a more hearty welcome than an Englishman, at least he has a more hearty manner of welcoming you and while the latter reserves his fun and humour (if he possess those qualities) for his particular friends, the former is ready to laugh and talk his best with all the world, and give way entirely to his mood.[16]

Thackeray philosophises about the qualities of hospitality in different nationalities before concluding that despite the Frenchman's 'wit', the German's 'sentiment' and the Englishman's 'constancy':

it is clear that for a stranger the Irish ways are the pleasantest, for here he is at once made happy and at home or at ease rather; for home is a strong word, and implies much more than any stranger can expect, or even desire to claim.[17]

Doubtless Trollope would have agreed. However, if two of his Irish short stories, 'The O'Conors of Castle Conor' (published in *Harpers* in 1860 and reprinted the following year in *Tales of All Countries*) and 'Father Giles of Ballymoy' (which initially appeared in the *Argosy* in 1866 and was later reprinted in *Lotta Schmidt and Other Stories*) are anything to go by, it took him some time to get acquainted with the ways of the Irish. Both stories turn on a kernel of misunderstanding, a naïve Englishman's misunderstanding of Irish ways. In these light-hearted tales, Trollope plays with issues of hospitality as a means to explore larger Irish–English misunderstandings. In these and other stories, such as 'The Man Who Kept His Money in a Box', he can also be seen to be transforming his personal experiences into cautionary tales that illustrate 'the chastening of Britons blundering abroad'.[18] Each of the stories also carries a political twist. Trollope later admitted the autobiographical nature of the stories in a gesture which could well be seen as a means of vouching for their authenticity:

> Some adventures I had; – two of which I told in the *Tales of All Countries* under the names of 'The O'Conors of Castle Conor', and 'Father Giles of Ballymoy'. I will not swear to every detail in these stories, but the main purport of each is true. (*A*, ch. 4, p. 66)

'The O'Conors' narrates the visit of Trollope's alter ego, Archibald Green, to Castle Conor in County Mayo. The narrator is green in name and callow in nature. Having taken enjoyable part in an Irish hunt (and we recall that it was in Ireland that Trollope began to hunt and that this became one of his life's enduring passions), he is pleasantly surprised by an invitation from the O'Conor family to spend the evening at their castle: 'I shall never forget my first introduction to country life in Ireland, my first day's hunting there, or the manner in which I passed the evening afterwards. Nor shall I ever cease to be grateful for the hospitality which I received from the O'Conors of Castle Conor.'[19] While there, however, he will learn much about the possible discomforts to be endured as a dependent guest. On arrival, he meets the two attractive older daughters of the house, one of whom he thinks might make a perfect wife for him. However, a third younger sister has every intention of spoiling his plan. When Green goes to dress he discovers the servant at the inn where he had been staying has sent his huge, heavy-nailed hunting shoes instead of the pumps for which he had asked. Knowing he cannot appear for dinner and dancing wearing these boots, Green bullies Larry, the compliant servant, into lending him his own down-at-heel shoes. Larry's subsequent strange behaviour – he falls over himself and complains about the tight and uncomfortable boots Green has forced him to wear – finally brings Green's plight of being without his proper shoes to public knowledge among the highly amused members of this Irish family, at least one of whom is determined to put a limit to the hospitality on offer to the visiting Englishman.

In the second story, the protagonist-narrator risks more than mere embarrassment. 'Father Giles of Ballymoy' offers an original illustration of what Thackeray refers to as 'the elastic hospitality of some Irish houses' when referring to an overcrowded Irish coach which 'accommodated an almost impossible number' and, 'like almost every other public vehicle I have seen in Ireland, was full to the brim and over it'.[20] The narrator, Archibald Green, arrives in Ireland as a 'stranger', a 'traveller' and a 'spectator' (*CSF*, p. 438) and he becomes the means through which Trollope can have his readers view Ireland with the detachment of an unknowing outsider whose general ignorance of customs and habits in Ireland is indispensable for the development of the narrative. Green, with a degree of self-deprecation, retrospectively makes clear his own preconceptions as he enters the town of Ballymoy:

> Ireland is not very well known now to all Englishmen, but it is much better known than it was in those days. On this my first visit into Connaught, I own that I was somewhat scared lest I should be made a victim to the wild lawlessness and general

savagery of the people, and I fancied, as in the wet, windy gloom of the night, I could see the crowd of natives standing round the doors of the inn, and just discern their naked legs and old battered hats, that Ballymoy was probably one of those places so far removed from civilisation and law, as to be an unsafe residence for an English Protestant. (*CSF*, p. 541)

In writing this, Trollope drew on his own early feelings about Ireland. He is not unaware of his mostly English readership, however, and so is also challenging provincial English attitudes and what he calls, in *West Indies and the Spanish Main*, 'dear good old thickly-prejudiced native England'.[21] The story describes Green's shock at realising that an unknown stranger is getting into his bed in Larry Kirwan's small Ballymoy hotel. Green had earlier not understood when the maid told him that he would be sharing his bed with the local priest; thus he reacts aggressively when he sees 'a tall, stout, elderly man' enter his room and then brush 'his clothes with the utmost care' (*CSF*, p. 441). When the unknown man then tries to enter his bed this causes Archibald to eject him unceremoniously before bundling him down the stairs:

So, when I got him through the aperture of the door, I gave him a push, as was most natural, I think, for me to do. Down he went backwards, – down the stairs, all in a heap, and I could hear that in his falls he had stumbled against Mrs Kirwan, who was coming up, doubtless to ascertain the cause of all the trouble above her head. (*CSF*, p. 443)

The people of Ballymoy are incensed at this attack on their beloved priest and threaten to have Green hanged. The landlady is equally indignant that such a 'born blagghuard . . . should ever have darkened my door!' (*CSF*, p. 445). Green is shown to have misunderstood, repudiated and insulted the hospitality that he was offered and now fears for his safety:

I had heard of Irish murders, and heard also of the love of the people for their priests, and I really began to doubt whether my life might not be in danger! (*CSF*, p. 445)

Green is locked up for the night for his own protection, only to be ultimately saved by Father Giles himself, who calms his defenders and invites him to breakfast the following morning so as to persuade the locals to forgive him. Victim and assailant are reconciled and become close friends in the story's happy ending which is an effective illustration of how hospitality can be tested and checked and ultimately reinforced through acquired understanding.

This story, like 'The O'Conors', is a reflection on Irish hospitality and an augury of improving English–Irish relations which carries a tinge of nostalgia for the welcome Trollope himself was pleased to receive in Ireland and which he initially found so enabling. Green's fault as a guest is that he did not pay sufficient attention to what he was told on arrival and thus had no awareness of the Irish habit of bed-sharing at an inn. In Ireland at the time, sharing was seen as a better alternative to turning a person away and Green was lucky to have been given a bed at all, even if it was a shared one, in a hostelry that was already full. Trollope avoids causing offence by noting (in the footsteps of Sir Walter Scott) that the narrated events are set twenty years since he became 'acquainted with one of the honestest fellows and best Christians whom it has ever been my good fortune to know . . . As he has now been ten years beneath the sod, I may tell the story of our first meeting' (*CSF*, p. 438).

In the light of Trollope's ongoing interest in Anglo-Irish relations, the fact that this Catholic clergyman rather than the owner of the inn is the agent of forgiveness, tolerance and reconciliation between a single Englishman and many Irishmen is significant. Alluding to the persuasive power of the Catholic Church in Ireland, the story makes it almost seem as if the only form of Home Rule that Trollope might be willing to countenance in Ireland is Rome Rule. Which, in his way of viewing things as a life-long Unionist, is to argue that the Church could play a key role in pacifying the Irish within the Union of Great Britain and Ireland. In this sense, Father Giles can be aligned with a series of older Irish priests, such as Father McGrath in *The Macdermots of Ballycloran*, Father Bernard M'Carthy in *Castle Richmond*, Father Marty in *An Eye for an Eye* and Father Giles in *The Landleaguers*, who play similar reconciliatory peacemaking roles. They are all depicted as agents of mutual accommodation. Father McGrath is 'a man of taste', of 'good family', who lives and works in one of the country's poorest parishes. Although 'always in want of money', he is liked and respected for his 'natural bonhomie, and perpetual good temper' (*MB*, ch. 5, pp. 40–1). On the exterior, his home is 'the prettiest house in his parish' but 'interiorly, it was discomfort personified'. And yet, what distinguishes him most is the manner in which his home is always a place that welcomes friends and strangers alike: a 'more hospitable man than Father McGrath never lived even in Connaught' (*MB*, ch. 5, pp. 40–1).

On a less particular note, elsewhere Trollope reflects with warm, appreciative humour on another key element in Irish hospitality – food. In his second novel, *The Kellys and the O'Kellys*, Martin Kelly travels on the 'floating prison'[22] that is the Ballinasloe Canal boat and partakes of the served lunch. Trollope describes this with singular care:

> Martin, however, made no complaints, and felt no misery. He made great play at the eternal half-boiled leg of mutton, floating in a bloody sea of grease and gravy, which always comes on the table three hours after the departure from Porto Bello. He, and others equally gifted with the *dura ilia messorum*, swallowed huge collops of the raw animal, and vast heaps of yellow turnips, till the pity with which a stranger would at first be inclined to contemplate the consumer of such unsavoury food, is transferred to the victim who has to provide the meal at two shillings a head. Neither love nor drink – and Martin had, on the previous day, been much troubled with both – had affected his appetite; and he ate out his money with the true persevering prudence of a Connaught man, who firmly determines not to be done. (*KOK*, ch. 8, p. 78)

In addition to a nod to the classics – in particular to Horace, with an evocation of the strong intestines of reapers – we are given hints of Trollope's appreciation of the Irish capacity for careful economy, but we also see his sense of humour emerging in his ironic take on the 'vast heaps' of food, on the Irish consumer who pushes the hospitality on offer to its limit as he ploughs his way through his meal. The focus then turns to the unfortunate supplier of the fare who will struggle to make a profit given his customers' appetites. Even if this passage points to excess (at a time of great material scarcity), Trollope was clearly appreciative of the generosity of the scruffy Irish kitchen which, however humble, is the heart of the house, and which he favourably compares to its neat and orderly English equivalent:

> The difference of the English and Irish character is nowhere more plainly discerned than in their respective kitchens. With the former, this apartment is probably the cleanest, and certainly the most orderly, in the house. It is rarely intruded into by those unconnected, in some way, with its business. Everything it contains is under the vigilant eye of its chief occupant, who would imagine it quite impossible to carry on her business, whether of an humble or important nature, if her apparatus was subjected to the hands of the unauthorised. An Irish kitchen is devoted to hospitality in every sense of the word. Its doors are open to almost all loungers and idlers; and the chances are that Billy Bawn, the cripple, or Judy Molloy, the deaf old hag, are more likely to know where to find the required utensil than the cook herself. (*KOK*, ch. 4, p. 43)

What might also surprise and shock the reader is that Trollope was writing this disposition on the Irish kitchen between 1847 and 1848, almost as if in denial of the calamitous realities of the Irish Famine that were taking place around him. It would not be the first nor the last time that Trollope would show such a lack of tact and understanding. Despite including some harrowing descriptions of the Famine, Trollope's controversial later novel on the subject, *Castle Richmond*, is weakened by its overwhelming desire to justify English administration of the country against all the painful evidence of its failure.

And yet, *Castle Richmond* provides much socially realistic portraiture of the Ireland of the Famine and a fine example of what can be learnt about a character from the manner in which he or she accepts the hospitality that is offered to them. The incident in question involves Mr Carter, the 'tall, thin, austere-looking'[23] High Church English Protestant clergyman who is invited by Mr Townsend to his Drumbarrow Parish to help distribute Famine relief donated by English sympathisers. Carter is possibly the last man you would want to invite to dinner because '[a]s to his eating and drinking it was, or might have been for any solicitude of his own, little more than bread and water'. Although a 'good man . . . there was about him too much of the Pharisee. He was greatly inclined to condemn other men, and to think none righteous who differed from him' (*CR*, ch. 37, p. 403). The Townsends await his arrival with trepidation and Mrs Townsend is so suspicious that 'in her heart she believed him to be a Jesuit' (p. 404). Their biggest dilemma is what to give him for dinner given that 'the larder had of late been emptied', which is not surprising in Famine Ireland, even in the house of a Protestant clergyman, as Mr Townsend explains when tendering his invitation to Mr Carter: 'the *res angusta domi*, which was always a prevailing disease, had been heightened by the circumstances of the time' (ch. 37, p. 405). After lavish apologies for 'the poorness of his table', Mr Carter is offered 'just a bit of fish I found going the road' (ch. 37, p. 406). In reality 'that day fortune had been propitious' and he had managed to procure a turbot from Mallow: 'And now they sat down to dinner, and lo and behold, to the great surprise of Mr Carter, and perhaps also to the surprise of the host, a magnificent turbot smoked upon the board' (ch. 37, p. 406). Much to the distress of the hosts, however, Mr Carter is not impressed and feels his hosts are showing off:

Mr Carter said nothing. He said not a word, but he thought much. This then was their pretended poorness of living! with all their mock humility, these false Irishmen could not resist the opportunity of showing off before the English stranger, and of putting on their table before him a dish which an English dean could afford only on gala days. (CR, ch. 37, pp. 406–7)

He self-righteously chooses to be offended by what he considers excessive hospitality and refuses to eat the fish with the result that 'the face of Mrs Townsend was one on which neither Christian nor heathen could have looked without horror and grief' (CR, ch. 37, p. 407). Only when she reveals that there was 'an uncommon take of fish yesterday at Skibbereen' and that the turbot cost but a modest price does Mr Carter finally relent and, after several moments of interminable awkwardness, say: 'If you'll allow me to change my mind, I think I will have a little bit of it' (CR, ch. 37, p. 408). All that the reader needs to know about Mr Carter has been revealed through this one scene of in which hospitality is doubted and slighted by this clergyman who, though outwardly charitable, reveals himself to be smug and heartless.

Another concern for Trollope with regard to hospitality concerns its misuse on the part of the giver rather than the receiver. Two examples will suffice. The first is relatively straightforward and is used as a black mark against a negative character, the villain Barry Lynch in *The Kellys and the O'Kellys*. He attempts to convince Dr Colligan to see to it that his ailing sister Anty does not recover so that he can take possession of the entire family farm which has been split between them. Colligan is invited to his house and Lynch almost inflicts hospitality upon him as he attempts to discuss the situation and impose his will, like his wine, on the guest. Dr Colligan has little hesitation in preserving his distance between the villain at the cost of refusing his false generosity which is simply intended (along with the bribe of a small farm) to convince him to take his side against Anty:

'Well, will you take a glass of wine?' – and Barry filled his own glass quite full.
   He drank his wine at dinner like a glutton, who had only a short time allowed him, and wished during that time to swallow as much as possible; and he tried to hurry his companion in the same manner. But the doctor didn't choose to have wine forced down his throat; he wished to enjoy himself, and remonstrated against Barry's violent hospitality. (KOK, ch. 27, p. 280)

Shortly afterwards, Dr Colligan realises Barry's vicious, indeed murderous, intent and, after a row, withdraws entirely. But the refusal of hospitality was the first sign of a rift between them.

A more generalised use of feigned hospitality and one that came under Trollope's scrutiny was 'Souperism'. The attempts to win hungry people over to Protestantism through supposed benevolence was a phenomenon that was all too common in Trollope's Ireland and one which he never failed to condemn. In *Castle Richmond*, Mr Townsend is criticised for taking advantage of the hardship caused by the Famine to try to win converts to his Church, and this is something his Catholic counterpart, Father McCarthy, is not willing to forgive: 'What he called the "souping" system of the Protestant clergyman stank in his nostrils – that system by which, as he stated, the most ignorant of men were to be induced to leave their faith by the hope of soup, or other food' (CR, ch. 10, p. 103).

Trollope shared this view and depicts the Townsends as being guilty of engaging in this practice in an attempt to win over needy Catholics:

> But neither Mr nor Mrs Townsend were content to bestow their charities without some other object than that of relieving material wants by their alms. Many infidels, Mr Townsend argued, had been made believers by the miracle of the loaves and fishes; and therefore it was permissible for him to make use of the same means for drawing over proselytes to the true church. If he could find hungry Papists and convert them into well-fed Protestants by one and the same process, he must be doing a double good, he argued; – could by no possibility be doing an evil. (*CR*, ch. 10, p. 103)

Trollope, on the other hand, has no such problems with the notion of hospitality, which necessarily involves some kind of fair exchange in which both parties benefit. An example of such a non-exploitative exchange is to be found in *The Kellys and The O'Kellys* when Mrs Kelly agrees to offer refuge to Anty after she has been attacked by her brother:

> In this manner did Mrs Kelly express the various thoughts that ran through her head, as she considered Anty's affairs; and if we could analyse the good lady's mind, we should probably find that the result of her reflections was a pleasing assurance that she could exercise the Christian virtues of charity and hospitality towards Anty, and, at the same time, secure her son's wishes and welfare, without subjecting her own name to any obloquy, or putting herself to any loss or inconvenience. She determined to put no questions to Anty, nor even to allude to her brother, unless spoken to on the subject; but, at the same time, she stoutly resolved to come to no terms with Barry, and to defy him to the utmost, should he attempt to invade her in her own territories. (*KOK*, ch. 6, p. 63)

Of course, Mrs Kelly's motives are mixed and not entirely selfless. And yet foremost among them is an acceptance of the need to provide refuge to a person who is clearly in need. That this then has the knock-on effect of helping her son's cause is a secondary if nonetheless important consideration.

The various forms and connotations of hospitality seen in in an Irish context form a thematic nexus in Trollope's writings, but similarly he was keen to explore the nature of the hospitality shown to the Irish in Britain in his more exclusively 'English' short stories and novels. Trollope's own 'English' fiction offers an unusual amount of space in which to accommodate Irish characters and Trollope clearly enjoys studying various classes of Irish men and women, seen out of context in Britain and trying to come to terms with the restrictive set of conditions to which they are subjected and which are often fuelled by prejudice. In this, Trollope's novels can be read alongside other mid-century realist classics, such as *A Tale of Two Cities* or *Middlemarch*, in their capacity to study characters who respond to the challenge of appreciating difference. Thus, for all his own wavering views about Ireland, his Irish novels and his treatment of the Irish in his English novels show an ongoing concern or engagement with what Rachel Hollander calls 'narrative hospitality' which she identifies as a 'shift in both the plot and form of the late Victorian novel, as characters and authors open themselves to that which is other, and suggest the value of recognizing rather than overcoming the limits of knowledge'.[24] Trollope's writings seem to anticipate what Hollander calls 'the particular constellation enacted by the late Victorian novel' and also, as I have argued elsewhere, to be at the forefront of what she identifies as a shift 'from sympathy to hospitality'.[25] Of particular relevance in this regard are the second and fourth Palliser novels, *Phineas Finn; The Irish Member* (1869) and *Phineas Redux* (1874), both of which have as their hero the Irishman, Phineas Finn, who, for the most part, resides in Britain and, despite intermittent difficulties, forges a career in politics there. His place in both the domestic and the political spheres, always remains somewhat unstable, and despite his considerable romantic charm and political acumen and success, he is, in a sense, forever dependent on the hospitality of others for security and survival. His precariousness is underlined by his various romances with Lady Laura Brentford (later Kennedy), daughter of the Earl of Brentford, Liberal cabinet minister and one of his early political supporters – he is the great love of her life but she does not have the courage to wed this penniless Irishman who must live on his wits; with orphan and heiress, Violet Effingham, who ultimately dismisses him and marries Lord Chiltern; and finally with the fashionable, rich and exotic Madame Max Goesler who, as a fellow outsider, is the one he will eventually marry. In the first novel, after a steady but unremarkable start in law, Phineas is offered the extraordinary opportunity to run to represent Lord Tulla's pocket Irish Loughshane constituency at Westminster. He is initially almost overwhelmed by what is essentially the gift of a safe seat for the Liberals. Once elected, however, there is a real sense that he is essentially a guest in that seat, expected to follow the will of Lord Tulla but also of his Liberal Party leaders who feel that he will understand how he should always toe the line. When the Loughshane seat is abolished, Phineas is gifted the English constituency of Loughton by the Earl of Brentford at the behest of his daughter Laura. Throughout, Phineas remains acutely aware of his lack of financial and political autonomy and of the anomaly of representing a pocket borough but knows that as long as he plays by the party rules he will be secure. Soon he is appointed as Undersecretary for the Colonies but his poverty renders his position precarious. As he tells his great sponsor and friend, Lady Laura, he is 'very poor'[26] and this, as much as his Irishness, compromises his political career and his sense of belonging. The hospitality offered by politics, unless one is born into money, is shown to be 'nothing more than a peg for their hats and a locker'[27] and this is something Phineas rapidly finds out when voting against his Party. By taking a political stand against the Liberal Party, he quickly finds that its hospitality is very limited indeed. He is exiled from the fold and sent back to Ireland to a dull but decently paid Inspectorship of Poor Houses in the County of Cork.

His somewhat precarious guest status is also underlined by his attempts in love, where he flits from one great house to the next, depending on the generosity of his English friends for invitations. And although he is an exception within the system, and a successful one, his liminal status is never fully overcome. His position is ultimately made possible only by the patronage of Lady Laura Standish first and Madame Max afterwards. Phineas's status as an outsider, however welcome, renders him an exception, and thus he embodies, to quote from Giorgio Agamben in his discussion of Alain Badiou's *Being and Event*, 'a kind of membership without inclusion'.[28] This description to some extent sums up the precarious situation in which Phineas Finn lives his life or lives in Britain. And this is certainly how he comes to see it, especially while he is forced to endure the hospitality of an English prison in *Phineas Redux*. While an inmate his outsider status becomes abundantly, overwhelmingly, clear to him. And there is no little irony in the fact that it takes the extraordinary, last-minute actions of another exceptional outsider, Madame Max, who is tolerated and partially integrated only because of her great wealth, to engineer his exoneration, his release and, more slowly, his psychological rehabilitation.

Phineas's return to politics comes after a considerable break but he does go on to enjoy a successful career, managing almost, but not quite, to belong fully within government and parliament. And yet, his vulnerability remains evident even after his rehabilitation within the British political establishment and and his fragile position as a visitor, an Irish guest, in the great houses of his political masters drives this point home. An example is to be found in the 'Phineas Finn's Success' chapter of *Phineas Redux* when he is at Matching, home of the Duke of Omnium who has been asked by Prime Minister Gresham to tell him that they hope to have his 'assistance next session'. Phineas agrees to go to London and then to return to Matching: '"Of course you will return to us, Mr Finn". Phineas said that he would return and trespass on the Duke's hospitality for yet a few days.'[29] Although this is standard, polite conversation, it highlights Phineas's awareness of his guest status – awaiting and depending on both political and domestic invitations, ultimately unable to play the host himself.

If this chapter has confined itself to examples drawn essentially from those Trollope novels with a core interest in matters Irish, it should not be assumed that hospitality is not also a major theme throughout his wider corpus. It clearly is. The seeking, offering and accepting of hospitality in the great houses is the means by which political and romantic affairs are conducted and is a vital element in Trollope's constructions of plot. Once again, the question of knowing or not knowing how to give or receive hospitality is crucial. Thus, in *The Warden*, Mr Harding is praised for his 'frank hospitality' while in *Phineas Finn*, the Earl of Brentford's 'hospitable house' stands in stark contrast with Mr Kennedy's 'dull house at Loughlinter' and Laura's initial marital troubles are signalled by Kennedy explaining 'to his wife, more than once, that though he understood the duties of hospitality and enjoyed the performance of them, he had not married with the intention of living in a whirlwind'. Elsewhere, in *Framley Parsonage*, Mrs Proudie's failure to be hospitable is a key black mark on her character. She is shown to to use hospitality in order to increase her standing (she was 'much at a loss to know by what sort of party or entertainment she would make herself famous')[30] but her rules will prove overly restrictive. She will not, for example, allow dancing because 'dancing at her house – absolutely under the shade of the bishop's apron – would be a sin and a scandal' (*FP*, ch. 17, p. 215). Driven by meanness, she backs away from organising 'suppers' because 'of all modes in which one may extend one's hospitality to a large acquaintance, they are the most costly'. The clergymen's wives to whom she says that it 'is horrid to think that we should go out among our friends for the mere sake of eating and drinking' only appear to agree. In reality,

> the elder among them would remember with regret, the unsparing, open-handed hospitality of Barchester Palace in the good old days of Bishop Grantly – God rest his soul! One old vicar's wife there was whose answer had not been so courteous – 'When we are hungry, Mrs Proudie', she had said, 'we do all have sensual propensities.' (*FP*, ch. 17, p. 215)

All of which leads Trollope into a more general discussion on the topic of hospitality in which he insists that 'as a rule in affairs of hospitality, . . . whatever extra luxury or grandeur we introduce at our tables when guests are with us, should be introduced for the advantage of the guest and not for our own'. Hospitality must never be for self-aggrandisement: 'if I decorate my sideboard and table, wishing that the eyes of my visitors may rest on that which is elegant and pleasant to the sight, I act in that matter with a becoming sense of hospitality; but if my object be to kill Mrs Jones with envy at the sight of all my silver trinkets, I am a very mean-spirited fellow' (*FP*, ch. 17, p. 218).

In Trollope's hands, the term 'hospitality' stands to indicate how individuals interact with those they encounter in the world. It is a shorthand term for all forms of human engagement, of offering and receiving, of interacting with friends and strangers alike. It is the human quality that makes the world go round. And, as Trollope shows, so much human interaction takes place within the walls of our own homes or of those that we visit, and the quality of that engagement, the quality of the 'ceade mille faltha', depends to a large degree on individuals' knowing how to behave in both private and public spheres, on their ethics of hospitality, whether they be host or guest, rich or poor, Irish or English, at home or abroad.

Notes

1. P. S. O'Hegarty quoted in Keiron *Curtis, P. S. O'Hegarty (1879–1955): Sinn Féin Fenian* (London: Anthem Press, 2009), p. 55.
2. Anthony Trollope, *The Macdermots of Ballycloran* (Oxford: Oxford University Press, 1989), ch. 2, p. 21. Subsequent references are in the main text (*MB*). Trollope would have found 'ceade mille faltha!' written in this way in John and Michael Banim's *Canvassing, A Tale* (Philadelphia: Carey, Lea & Blanchard, 1835), p. 8.
3. Nancy E. Snow, 'Hospitableness: A Neglected Virtue', in Maurice Hamington (ed.), *Feminism and Hospitality: Gender in the Host/Guest Relationship* (Plymouth: Lexington Books, 2010), p. 7.
4. Anthony Trollope, *An Autobiography* (Oxford: Oxford University Press, 1999), ch. 4, p. 65. Subsequent references are in the main text (*A*).
5. Deborah Denenholz Morse, *Reforming Trollope: Race, Gender, and Englishness in the Novels of Anthony Trollope* (Farnham: Ashgate, 2013), p. 71.
6. Quoted in Horace Elisha Scudder, *James Russell Lowell: A Biography* (Boston, MA: Houghton Mifflin, 1901), vol. 2, p. 82.
7. James Pope-Hennessy, *Anthony Trollope* (London: Phoenix Press, 1971), p. 81.
8. Anthony Trollope, *North America* (New York: Harper & Brothers, 1862), vol. 2, ch. 16, p. 599.
9. William Makepeace Thackeray, *The History of Pendennis* (New York: M. Doolady, 1867), p. 72.
10. Richard Mullen, *Anthony Trollope: A Victorian in his World* (Savannah: Frederic D. Beil, 1990), p. 121.
11. Rachel Hollander, *Narrative Hospitality in Late Victorian Fiction: Novel Ethics* (London: Routledge, 2013), p. 3.
12. Immanuel Kant, 'Perpetual Peace: A Philosophical Sketch', in L. W. Beck (ed.), *Kant: Selections* (London: Collier Macmillan, 1988), p. 439.
13. Frank Neal, *Black '47 Britain and the Famine Irish* (London: Palgrave Macmillan, 1998), p. 113.
14. Helen Garlinghouse King (ed.), 'Trollope's Letters to the *Examiner*', *The Princeton University Library Chronicle*, 26.2 (Winter 1965): p. 90.

15. Anthony Trollope, *Mr Scarborough's Family* (Hamburg: Karl Gradener & J. F. Ricter, 1883), p. 193.
16. William Makepeace Thackeray [M. A. Titmarsh], *The Irish Sketch-Book* (London: Chapman and Hall, 1845), vol. 1, p. 51.
17. Ibid. p. 52.
18. Donald D. Stone, 'Trollope as a Short Story Writer', *Nineteenth-Century Fiction*, 31.1 (June 1976): p. 33.
19. Anthony Trollope, *The Complete Shorter Fiction* (New York: Carroll & Graf Publishers, 1992), ed. Julian Thompson, p. 42. Subsequent references are given in the main text (*CSF*).
20. Thackeray, *The Irish Sketch-Book*, vol. 1, p. 158.
21. Anthony Trollope, *West Indies and the Spanish Main* (New York: Carroll and Graf Publishers, 1999), ch. 3, p. 46.
22. Anthony Trollope, *The Kellys and the O'Kellys* (London: The Folio Society, 1992), ch. 8, p. 77. Subsequent references are in the main text (*KOK*).
23. Anthony Trollope, *Castle Richmond* (London: The Folio Society, 1994), ch. 37, p. 403. Subsequent references are in the main text (*CR*).
24. Hollander, *Narrative Hospitality*, p. 4.
25. Ibid. p. 4, p. 13. Trollope seems acutely aware of the limits of sympathy both as an ethical stance and a narrative ploy. See John McCourt, *Writing the Frontier Anthony Trollope between Britain and Ireland* (Oxford: Oxford University Press, 2015), pp. 42–5.
26. Anthony Trollope, *Phineas Finn, The Irish Member* (London: Penguin, 1972), ch. 15, p. 168.
27. James McConnel, 'The Irish Parliamentary Party in Victorian and Edwardian London', in Peter Gray (ed.), *Victoria's Ireland? Irishness and Britishness, 1837–1901* (Dublin: Four Courts Press, 2004), p. 38.
28. Giorgio Agamben, *Homo Sacer: Sovereign Power and Bare Life* (Stanford: Stanford University Press, 1998), p. 25.
29. Anthony Trollope, *Phineas Redux* (Oxford: Oxford University Press, 2011), ch. 77, p. 545.
30. Anthony Trollope, *Framley Parsonage* (London: Penguin, 2004), ch. 17, p. 214. Subsequent references are in the main text (*FP*).

22

POWER IN NUMBERS: FETISHES AND FACTS BETWEEN TROLLOPE AND LAW

Anat Rosenberg

'Total Sums Received'

LET US BEGIN WITH Trollope's summation of his professional achievements in *An Autobiography*:

comfort myself by reflecting that the amount of manuscript described as a book in Varro's time was not much. Varro, too, is dead, and Voltaire ; whereas I am still living, and may add to the pile.

The following is a list of the books I have written, with the dates of publication and the sums I have received for them. The dates given are the years in which the works were published as a whole, most of them having appeared before in some serial form.

Names of Works.	Date of Publication.	Total Sums Received.
The Macdermots of Ballycloran,	1847	£48 6 9
The Kellys and the O'Kellys,	1848	123 19 5
La Vendée, .	1850	20 0 0
The Warden,	1855 }	
Barchester Towers,.	1857 }	727 11 3
The Three Clerks, .	1858	250 0 0
Doctor Thorne,	1858	400 0 0
The West Indies and the Spanish Main, .	1859	250 0 0
The Bertrams, .	1859	400 0 0
Castle Richmond, .	1860	600 0 0
Framley Parsonage,	1861	1000 0 0
Tales of All Countries—1st Series,	1861 }	
„ „ 2d „ .	1863 }	1830 0 0
„ „ 3d „ .	1870 }	
Orley Farm, .	1862	3135 0 0
North America,	1862	1250 0 0
Carry forward,		£10,034 17 5

Names of Works.	Date of Publication.	Total Sums Received.
Brought forward,		£10,034 17 5
Rachel Ray, .	1863	1645 0 0
The Small House at Allington,	1864	3000 0 0
Can You Forgive Her?	1864	3525 0 0
Miss Mackenzie,	1865	1300 0 0
The Belton Estate, .	1866	1757 0 0
The Claverings,	1867	2800 0 0
The Last Chronicle of Barset,	1867	3000 0 0
Nina Balatka,	1867	450 0 0
Linda Tressel,	1868	450 0 0
Phineas Finn,	1869	3200 0 0
He Knew He Was Right, .	1869	3200 0 0
Brown, Jones, and Robinson,	1870	600 0 0
The Vicar of Bullhampton,	1870	2500 0 0
An Editor's Tales, .	1870	378 0 0
Cæsar (Ancient Classics), .	1870[1]	0 0 0
Sir Harry Hotspur of Humblethwaite,	1871	750 0 0
Ralph the Heir,	1871	2500 0 0
The Golden Lion of Granpère,	1872	550 0 0
The Eustace Diamonds, .	1873	2500 0 0
Australia and New Zealand,	1873	1300 0 0
Phineas Redux, .	1874	2500 0 0
Harry Heathcote of Gangoil,	1874	450 0 0
Lady Anna, .	1874	1200 0 0
The Way We Live Now, .	1875	3000 0 0
The Prime Minister,	1876	2500 0 0
The American Senator,	1877	1800 0 0
Is He Popenjoy? .	1878	1600 0 0
South Africa,	1878	850 0 0
John Caldigate, .	1879	1800 0 0
Sundries, .		7800 0 0
		£68,939 17 5

[1] This was given by me as a present to my friend John Blackwood.

Figure 22.1 Trollope's earnings, from Chapter 20 of *An Autobiography* (vol. 2, Edinburgh and London: Blackwood, 1883). Courtesy of Trinity College, Cambridge.

Trollope's table posited an objectified register, just the clear facts, reduced visually to a simple structure, easy to follow: which book, when, how much, what is the total. If these facts signify nothing else, he said, they signify hard work. And hard work produced some indisputable goods:

> I have allotted myself so many pages a week. The average number has been about forty. It has been placed as low as twenty, and has risen to 112. And as a page is an ambiguous term, my page has been made to contain 250 words; and as words, if not watched, will have a tendency to straggle, I have had every word counted as I went. In the bargains I have made with publishers I have, – not, of course, with their knowledge, but in my own mind, – undertaken always to supply them with so many words, and I have never put a book out of hand short of the number by a single word. (*A*, ch. 7, p. 80)

The prices in Trollope's account are justified by counted, objective elements of his work.

In associating prices with counted pages and words, Trollope's register seems almost too precise a case of Marx's theory of commodity fetishism. According to Marx, while commodities are nothing but incorporated labour, and hence an instance of social relations, the value of commodities is perceived as a function of their qualities: 'the social character of men's labour appears to them as an objective character stamped upon the product of that labour.'[1] In this chapter I want to take a closer look at the fetishistic effect of Trollope's representation of his novels in *An Autobiography*, and read it with processes which took place in this era in consumer law. I have a number of goals in mind, involving history and theory.

First, I seek to highlight historical processes of objectification, particularly numerical objectification, in Trollope and in consumer law in the late Victorian era. Each illuminates the other in relation to deep cultural currents. Trollope's almost vulgar objectification, which I will read closely, sheds light on similar but under-explored processes in law, while developments in law, which capture broader transformations, and which I will describe in broader strokes, illuminate the resonance of Trollope's apparent idiosyncrasies. The processes I discuss involved fetishism and fact-ishism.

Theoretical and historical scholarship that examines the cultural significance of fetishes and of facts reveals a joint problematic: both are processes of objectification, which rely on an unstable distinction between the socially constructed and the real; both ultimately embody a tension between construction and reality. That problematic bears reminding at the outset; I therefore begin with a discussion of scholarship which engages with the tension. I then examine historical processes of objectification in the late Victorian era – both fetish-making and fact-making – in Trollope and law.

Second, in observing processes of objectification, I suggest that theories of false consciousness do not capture the historical occurrences at hand, which involved awareness of the sociality of evaluation. To understand these historical cases, both construction and reality need to be kept simultaneously in view: the processes of objectification I examine were conducted with acute awareness of the sociality of evaluation. At the same time, they did involve an effort to separate the real from the socially constructed, an effort which should not be downplayed, as it sometimes is.[2] Precisely the sociality of evaluation motivated the effort to isolate the real from the socially constructed; both are part of the historical experience of objectification.

Finally, the attempts I examine are narrow enough to trace particular motivations, and move beyond explanations of objectification as a response to somewhat abstract problems, such as a crisis of representation, the incomprehensibility of capitalist realities, fear of market unpredictability, or search for control. Objectification, I suggest, was responsive to a historical concern about the power of new economic actors, the working classes and women,[3] Britain's traditional outliers, to affect the processes of capitalist evaluation. Precisely because facts and commodities alike were perceived as social, an effort was made to isolate certain constructs from further social shifting, and generate, as it were, a status quo.

From Fetishes *versus* Facts to Fetishes *and* Facts

The process of fetishisation described by Marx speaks to a conceptual closure whereby commodities become detached from the human, social processes that determine their value. One manner of reaching closure is by reducing social concreteness to interchangeable units of calculation, a process that mystifies, that is, diverts attention from inequalities in the conditions of production to the object itself, by denying uniqueness.[4] Georg Lukács read Marx's concept of commodity fetishism in this manner, and observed its relation to Weber's account of rationality.[5] From such a perspective, the locus of mystification lies in the production of calculation, of numerical facts. Trollope was moving in that direction; his register, read with his reports of the countable elements of his novels, used numerical representation, the paradigmatic modern fact, as Mary Poovey describes it in *A History of the Modern Fact*.[6] He moved from the uniqueness of art, to hard facts, placing his labour at the forefront, and turning it into numbers.[7] As Andrew Miller says, Trollope's 'habits appear to locate him firmly within a buffering Weberian scheme of bureaucratised subjectivity'.[8]

The fetishistic moment in *An Autobiography*'s calculative turn is complete when value is associated with objective features of the commodity. In Trollope's account, pages and words offer not just an anchor of value but a minimal justification for it. When the stream of income stabilises in his narrative, he explicitly explains prices as a minimal return for quantity: 'From that time to this I have been paid at about that rate for my work, – £600 *for the quantity* contained in an ordinary novel-volume, – or £3000 for a long tale, published in twenty parts which is equal in length to five such volumes' (*A*, ch. 9, p. 106) (emphasis added).

The fetishistic effect is obvious in *An Autobiography* because the project of numerical rationalisation and commodity standardisation was pursued on textual art, a practice regarded as impervious to the rule of numbers. As Poovey recalls, figures of speech were the paradigmatic contrast to figures of arithmetic, as cultural value accrued to the latter. For heroes of modern factuality, fiction, hyperbole and rhetoric were damning elements; numbers were dull in comparison to textual art, but numbers were associated with 'incontrovertible facts'.[9] Trollope, in other words, was working with the material least likely to bolster the project of the modern fact. Taking issue with criticisms levelled at him, he openly insisted that artists were like artisans, favouring shoemakers as his analogues, and that artistic production could be rationalised, indeed broken down to countable units and set apart from romantic visions of artistic inspiration and from the heated question of aesthetic quality. In the concluding register of literary achievement, Trollope seemed to follow to the dot the agenda of the Statistical Society of London, which preferred 'to employ figures and tabular exhibitions . . . because facts . . . are most briefly and clearly stated in such forms'.[10]

In exercising numerical factuality on the least convincing case for it, the convergence of effects between facts and fetishes becomes clear. *An Autobiography* offers a lucid example of a hard fact functioning like a fetish, that is, a denial of the sociality of things, their openness to politics, power, convention, dispute and diversity. It leads us to Bruno Latour's analysis of the 'Factish', which posits a connection between facts and fetishes and challenges the object/subject dichotomy of modernity in terms that are illuminating for this chapter.

In *On the Modern Cult of the Factish Gods*, Latour implicitly takes issue with Marx's commodity fetishism, and more broadly with the modern tendency in theoretical thought to move between two poles: constructivism (human-made) and realism (unconstructed, real). Facts, with which critical social theory chastises fetishists (as when fetishists are told that the value of their commodities is *in fact* determined by social relations), are no less constructed than fetishes, he points out. Modern thought has simultaneously created the idea of interiority and belief, which enables the notion of fetish, and the idea of exteriority and knowledge, which enables the realm of factuality. For Latour, the important point is that fetishes and facts alike have effects in the world, and are in that sense autonomous entities – indeed, a world without intermediaries between individuals and social structures would be impossible: mediating images make attachments (Latour's term for relations) possible. But they are nonetheless constructs. Latour thus resists two extreme positions: either the subject controls the object (liberty), or the object controls the subject (alienation). Neither is tenable.

The point I want to highlight is not the controversy about the loci of political action (do objects carry political agency too?), but rather the historical convergence in modernity between commodity fetishes and facts around a single problematic: telling apart the constructed from the real. Like commodity fetishism, the treatment of factuality involves an attribution of reality to constructs, which isolates them from the human action at their basis. In both cases, there is no need to deny the power of objects in order to see that the denial of social construction is bound to reach a dead end.

While Latour speaks at a high level of abstraction, Poovey's work gives us a concrete analysis of British history supporting his insights, showing how the modern fact embodies the tension between construction and reality.[11] In Poovey's account, separating the constructed from the real was an effort to tell apart interpretation and description. This conundrum is the heart of the modern fact, and has never been surmounted; Poovey traces the fragile efforts to sustain it in sciences of wealth and society. Numbers, as noted, are particularly important in her narrative, from double-entry bookkeeping to modern statistics: they are the paradigm of the modern fact 'because they have come to seem preinterpretive or . . . noninterpretive at the same time that they have become the bedrock of systematic knowledge'.[12] The history of modernity, which leads Poovey into the first decades of the nineteenth century, was a process of problematising the confluence of interpretation and description, and then trying to separate them, and in particular to see numbers as impartial descriptions which could erase interest and politics. Poovey's history reveals how numerical factuality shared with commodity fetishism the same problematic of isolating objects, giving them the status of the unconstructed real.

This scholarship points to the shared problematic of fetishes and facts, around the tension between social contruction and reality. I start, then, by examining historical processes of objectification in the late Victorian era, fetish-making and fact-making, in Trollope and law. In both, objectifying moves were set against the sociality of evaluation. After examining these processes, I will turn to the historical motivations behind objectification.

The Sociality of Numerical Facts and Fetishes – in Trollope

Trollope's counted quantities, sold to publishers in a secret deal known only to himself, solved a two-pronged difficulty with the economic evaluation of his books: evaluation was disconnected from Trollope's idea of artistic truth, and was also wildly unpredictable, thoroughly contextualised, unanchored in factors which could provide a consistent, formally rational, account of value.

Trollope articulated an idea of artistic truth in a well-known passage in *An Autobiography*, where he distinguished between 'a confidence in facts, and a confidence in vision'. While only the former is a matter of 'information' and relies on 'a rock of fact', both are orders of truth, hence '[e]ither may be false . . . as also may either be steadfastly true' (*A*, ch. 7, pp. 86–7). This was an apology for a travel book (*The West Indies and the Spanish Main*), but Trollope located his art in the realm of vision more broadly, and developed a theory of aesthetic merit.[13] The books' economic value, meanwhile, seemed to have little to do with either order of truth, a point most obvious in Trollope's organisation of *An Autobiography* around the distinction between the books' artistic merits and their sale price.

Narrating the history of one book after another, *An Autobiography* repeats a plot of separation: Trollope reported the pecuniary results of each sale, and commented on the work's artistic quality. There is a clear disconnect. Sums are associated with power struggles with publishers, Trollope's reputational standing, and anecdotal events. His assessment of quality is fully separate from the price, as well as from subsequent market fortunes. Here is one instance, dealing with three novels published in 1858–9:

> I had then written *The Three Clerks* which, when I could not sell it to Messrs Longmans [who refused his demands], I took in the first instance to Messrs Hurst & Blackett . . . I had made an appointment with one of the firm, which however that gentleman was unable to keep. I . . . had but one day in London in which to dispose of my manuscript . . . Thence I took *The Three Clerks* to Mr Bentley and on the same afternoon succeeded in selling it to him for £250 . . . the firm have I believe, done very well with the purchase. (*A*, ch. 6, pp. 74–5)

> I received £400 from Messrs Chapman & Hall for *Doctor Thorne*, and agreed to sell them *The Bertrams* for the same sum . . . *Doctor Thorne* has, I believe, been the most popular book that I have written – if I may take the sale as a proof of comparative popularity. *The Bertrams* has had quite an opposite fortune . . . I myself think that they are of about equal merit, but that neither of them is good. They fall away very much from *The Three Clerks* . . . (*A*, ch. 7, p. 84)

The contract price of *The Three Clerks* is the lowest, when its literary value is the highest of the three novels; while the market value of *Doctor Thorne* is higher than *The Bertrams*, when they are literary equals. There is a clear misalignment of different registers of value.

The Trollope of *An Autobiography* was unable to reconcile monetary values with artistic merit, or with social processes that he was willing to defend on other grounds. Cynical about 'dealings with . . . critic[s]' (*A*, ch. 4, p. 53) and conscious of the irrationality of popularity waves, his narrative shows income coming from volatile and arbitrary occurrences that he criticised even as the wave turned in his favour and he admitted to enjoying it.

Against this dual problematic with evaluation, detached from artistic merit, and unpredictable, Trollope introduced a production-output realm of factuality, which could justify and anchor economic processes. It is worth noting that this move reconciled the two parts of the declared purpose of *An Autobiography*: 'to speak . . . of my failures and successes such as they have been, and their causes, and of the opening which a literary career offers to men and women for the earning of their bread' (*A*, ch. 1, p. 7). The numerical facts generated by labour explain bread-earning by a literary career, without committing Trollope to bend his assessment of successes and failures, thereby rescuing, rather than commodifying, as has sometimes been argued, the aesthetic meaning of his art, isolating it from the process of economic evaluation. Indeed, after the stream of income from novels is stabilised (or almost stabilised, for he admitted that fluctuations existed (*A*, ch. 9, p. 106)), Trollope stopped accounting for each sale in detail, and instead expanded on the aesthetic assessment of his art. The irrational sociality of evaluation, openly narrated in *An Autobiography*, could not be brought under full control in the narrative, but was twice delimited: it was not allowed to touch artistic merit – a move which turned a problem (the market does not evaluate artistic merit as it should) into a benefit (artistic merit does not depend on the market); then again, the socialised determination of prices was marginalised, for the bulk was captured by counted elements.

Silvana Colella, who brilliantly analyses Trollope's labour theory of value, observes that the system of his labour appears fully rational and gives the impression that the value of the novel may not be entirely arbitrary, in contrast with the unpredictable market exchanges described in *An Autobiography*.[14] The point I would emphasise is that Trollope did not gloss over or downplay the difficulties; he puts them up front. He acknowledged the sociality of economic value, and sought ways to delimit its implications. If, as Colella suggests, he was framing himself as a free agent, that effect becomes significant only in the context of a narrative of difficulties: the isolation of numerical factuality is meaningful when viewed as factish in the sense that the role of social construction and the powerful reality of facts are both present, and motivate the attempt to separate them (the separation is where the process parts ways with Latour's definition; Latour insists on inseparability). Rather than deny the significance of social processes that his numerical facts cannot explain, Gradgrind-like, Trollope was acknowledging them and hoping to fence off a realm beyond their reach.

Trollope's objectifying turn in *An Autobiography* also inflected other writings. In the next section I examine *The Way We Live Now*, and read it with Trollope's representation of his mother in *An Autobiography*, to clarify the deeper motivations for the objectifying move; those motivations were more systemic, and exceeded Trollope's frustration with individual control. It is worth observing already that this analysis complicates arguments in Trollope scholarship about a subjective turn. Anna Korn-bluh and Audrey Jaffe, for instance, each argue in different ways that concerns with the fictitiousness of economic value and the unpredictability of the market were dis-placed onto what Jaffe calls a structure of feeling, and Kornbluh a psychic economy.[15] As we have seen so far, and as I explain further below, Trollope was not embracing subjectivism; he was trying to resist a move from the (naïve or analytically exasper-ating) objective pole, to the fully subjective.[16] The middle ground was a search for anchors that keep sociality at bay without denying the constructed nature of value.

Trollope was not alone in seeking to anchor evaluation to numerical facts. In the same decades, legal actors too tried to get away from historical forms of assessment openly based on social processes. They replaced them with assessments that they perceived as asocial and objective. The connection is hardly surprising; Trollope was responding to the consumer economy from which I draw the two examples that follow.[17]

The Sociality of Numerical Facts and Fetishes – in Law

The legal regulation of household consumption is a historical example of numerical objectification in law.[18] The common law regulated credit purchases of consumer goods for the household through a setting known as the doctrine of necessaries. The doctrine allowed married women, who had extremely limited contractual capacity and prop-erty under coverture, to manage their households by buying commodities on their hus-bands' credit. Courts routinely dealt with suits of traders against husbands for unpaid purchases made by their wives, and developed frameworks for assessing the terms of liability. In the closing decades of the nineteenth century, a budgetary logic of domestic routines was introduced into the legal determination of liability. The new logic came to dominate over an older assessment which was oriented toward social processes.

The traditional doctrinal assessment proceeded through a presumptive responsibil-ity of a husband for credit given to his wife for 'necessaries' – defined as goods suitable for the husband's degree and estate – as opposed to luxuries. So long as the couple were married and lived together, a wife was not only a vicarious consumer (in the Veblenian sense of maintaining male valour in the public sphere),[19] but could also expand the implications of 'necessaries' by assuming the appearance of an upper station. 'Degrees' and 'estates', or a person's 'condition' as it was often described, as well as the implica-tions of joint life in marriage, were considered socially observable by traders, consumers, judges and juries, in a way which could be associated with appropriate quantities and qualities of goods, from meats to dresses. Evaluation, that is, the determination of the scope of liability for financial debt, was conceptually reliant on the observation and construction of class and gender statuses; it was an openly social construct.

In the second half of the nineteenth century, the traditional, socially oriented approach was decentred as a domestic budgetary logic assumed dominance in doctrinal analyses. The logic of consumption articulated through the doctrine came to be that of domestic expense administration: liability now depended on a husband's consent to the credit contract, explained as a matter of rational budget management. The logic of the budget could not be immediately perceived by observers, and was only known to those familiar *with the numbers* – somewhat like the hard if hidden numerical facts which made up Trollope's novels. Within the budgetary domain, allocated to men as heads of households, women's consumer agency too was revised in the doctrine. Women's traditional role as vicarious consumers was turned into the role of the guardian of domestic routines. The shift reflected a search for simple factuality, most easily perceived when budgets, that is, counted elements, became a standard explanatory reference, but no less present in efforts to make domestic management a technically defined endeavour set in terms of specified routine tasks, as close as possible to the factual dullness of numbers. In broad terms, courts moved from social status to budgets as the basis for contractual liability in household consumption.

A resonant trend was present in the regulation of personal consumer credit, where courts had to decide how to evaluate consumers' financial standing.[20] The background was the 1869 Debtors Act, which declared the abolition of imprisonment for debt, but in fact perpetuated it for the working classes. In the decades that followed the Act's enactment, the county courts, the main legal forum which dealt with small debts, heard thousands of suits every day and annually issued hundreds of thousands of commitment orders against working-class consumers. To issue orders, courts had to evaluate financial ability, because imprisonment was only incumbent when a debtor had been ordered to pay his debt and did not do so *even though he had means* to pay. The determination of means attracted increasing attention because of the singularity of imprisonment of the working classes. Critics of the Debtors Act did not manage to abolish imprisonment for debt until late in the twentieth century, but they did manage to launch three parliamentary investigations within forty years. Committee discussions reveal a change in the way financial ability – that is, the category of 'means to pay' – was assessed, from an outward-turned examination of social credit, to a numerical framing: a balance-sheet paradigm.

The actual practice of assessing financial means in courts spoke to evaluation as a social construct. County courts viewed consumer debtors as having means to pay not because their assets exceeded or even matched their liabilities, but rather on the assumption that they had access to credit, an assumption that we can describe as a social-credit paradigm. Courts issued imprisonment orders without collecting data on the liabilities of consumers, and yet statistics of imprisonment spoke to a huge gap between orders issued and actual imprisonments; that gap was filled by new injections of credit when imprisonment was looming. The new credit kept debtors out of prison. Trollope himself reported on this kind of experience in *An Autobiography*, when he recalled his early years of financial distress:

> The debts of course were not large, but I cannot think now how I could have lived, and sometimes have enjoyed life, with such a burden of duns as I endured. Sheriff's officers with uncanny documents, of which I never understood anything, were common attendants on me. And yet I do not remember that I was ever locked up, though I think I was twice a prisoner. In such emergencies some one paid for me. (*A*, ch. 3, pp. 37–8)

Money was somehow found, and courts knew that it would be. They knew that their orders were putting pressure on the social circulation of credit, and relied precisely on that circulation to determine that a person had means, without ever examining closely the numbers. Courts thus assessed the financial standing of consumers by dispersing value among those potentially willing to ascribe it, envisioning consumption on credit as a social process.

From a balance-sheet perspective, by contrast, if the liabilities of a person exceeded his assets he had no means to pay; the social willingness of unspecified networks to extend credit had little relevance to the evaluation. The balance-sheet perspective was gradually embraced as epistemologically correct at the close of the century by legal actors, while social credit was rejected as a way of assessing means. Increasingly, legal actors argued that 'means to pay' could not rely on social willingness to provide credit, and instead proposed a balance-sheet assessment where all *facts* would be taken into account. Debates about the Debtors Act increasingly associated balance-sheet numbers with truth and certainty, as opposed to social speculation. The language was already available from trade contexts. George Rae's celebration of the balance sheet in his treatise on banking practices not only hailed the device, but explicitly contrasted it with information on a debtor's means emerging from social perceptions, or as he described it, 'that most unreliable of authorities – everybody'.[21] Don't count on a man's referees, said Rae in a chapter entitled 'The Testimony of the Balance Sheet'; the only authentic evidence offering exact knowledge was the balance sheet. Rae's logic was increasingly embraced as the proper way to understand private consumer contexts as well. Overall, legal thinking revealed a move from the sociality of credit ascription to the numerical factuality of balance sheets.

Trollope's efforts to anchor economic value in numerical facts were resonant with legal developments in consumer credit law, which likewise embraced the formality of numerical representation. With this in mind I would like to scratch the surface and examine the anxieties motivating these processes beyond the general sense that too much of the determination of value depended on the contextual and irrational.

Why Objectify?

The causes of the shifts toward objectivity are somewhat hazy. On Marx's account, commodity fetishism was an inevitable consequence of the structures of capitalist exchange, which obscure the human agency at stake. Yet, in the realm of consumer transactions, openly social forms persisted as methods of evaluation in prominent legal contexts late into the nineteenth century. More crucially, as we have already seen, there was no failure in awareness of the sociality of evaluation, a failure that has been dominant in readings of commodity fetishism as a theory of false consciousness. And so, an argument about a misrecognition of sociality, premised on capitalist structures, does not tell us enough about the allure of objectification in Trollope and consumer law.

In Poovey's historical narrative, the search for facts isolated from social processes is a consequence of intellectual shifts; she does not so much motivate as trace them, and necessarily so for her history cuts through a period of some 250 years. Latour meanwhile relegates the separation of the real from the constructed to theory, and so does not fully acknowledge the experience of separation in history; on the contrary, he argues that people are never deluded into separating the constructed from the real in practice. Both Trollope and consumer law, however, are hard to confine to theory.

Reading together the concrete cases of Trollope and consumer law allows us to see that the historical charm of objectification was rooted in concrete cultural fears of late

Victorianism: women and the working classes were increasingly able to affect evaluation; their perceived agency prompted intuitions that evaluation needed shielding from social involvement.[22] These fears offer an explanation beyond the two dominant explanatory paradigms applied to Trollope: concerns with the capitalist market and the meaning of capitalist value which were becoming increasingly abstract, and concerns about realist writing as a human creation dependent on social convention, yet seeking to establish the real.[23] While I do not contest these explanations, I suggest that fears of mass agency, as we might call it, should be added to the historical account.[24] Let us begin this time with consumer credit law and end with Trollope. In both, the embrace of numerical objectification was responsive to concrete historical concerns with the agency of social outliers. Concerns can be traced in legal discussions of doctrinal and legislative content, while in Trollope they come into sharper view when the broader question of the market, as Trollope probed it in *The Way We Live Now*, is brought to bear on the problem of evaluation in *An Autobiography*.

Why Objectify – Law

Recall the move to budget rationality in the doctrine of necessaries. Legal debates in that context were inflected with concerns about female and working-class agency, rooted in the expansion of consumer capitalism. From the Victorian period up until World War II, the British enjoyed the highest standard of living in Europe. In the last three decades of the nineteenth century average real wages rose by 84 per cent, while the population increased from 22.7 million to 32.5 million. Significant parts of society attained means exceeding subsistence needs. Producers, meanwhile, collectively offered unprecedented ranges of consumer goods.[25] The rising wages and opportunities of the lower economic strata were entangled with processes of democratisation that were reaching the upper echelons of the working classes and making the implications of their expanding economic power culturally salient. As the lower classes gained potential economic standing, the economic role of lower-class women as manageresses of household consumption also became conspicuous. This intersection of gender with class converged with a cross-class gender anxiety. Women's agency beyond the working classes was a source of cultural drama as they gained visible leeway in struggles for autonomy: expanding rights to property and contract, advancing divorce reform and suffragist struggles. While the implications of economic changes remain contested given limited data on family dependants, and given the pervasive use of credit, these changes, coupled with other progressive reforms, certainly made the working classes and women seem less constrained by traditional social expectations. It should therefore come as no surprise that consumption was politicised and that its trivialisation by political economists was challenged as it emerged as a social force rather than epiphenomenon.[26] In adjudication of the doctrine of necessaries, this context was translated into legal responses.

The new budgetary logic was a new discipline which did not resort directly to class and gender hierarchies, increasingly unavailable in their traditional form – but fortified them nonetheless. From the perspective of women the point is easy to grasp, for the domestic budget is a familiar site of gender oppression.[27] Male budgetary control, as grounded in the new doctrinal structure, responded to fears about women, often voiced as accusations that reckless credit was extended to feeble minds. As Erika

Rappaport suggests, both husbands and shopkeepers looked to the legal system to protect their economic well-being from female consumption.[28] Women's sphere of discretion within male-determined budgets was in turn framed as a matter of daily routines, itself a delimiting impulse, as Leonore Davidoff's work on the rationalisation of household management in the nineteenth century reveals.[29]

Working-class men's place too was at stake in legal changes. As working-class women acted in their capacity as spouses, their consumer agency implicated that of their husbands, and tapped into the broader anxiety about working-class men's place in the expanding consumer economy. The language of householder virtue had a broad political resonance, in line with middle-class ideals of normative masculinity.[30] Budget rationality was part of that language, a middle-class ethic that is properly viewed as a disciplining effort.

The same point applies to the embrace of the balance sheet in discussions of liability under the Debtors Act. To be sure, preference for a balance-sheet evaluation of financial standing was often framed as a matter of helping the working classes. Historians, too, have treated the balance-sheet paradigm as a moral economy infused with equitable ideas which militated against the harsh market rule of freedom of contract.[31] It could, indeed, keep consumers out of prison despite their failure to pay legally valid debts. Yet, from a broader perspective, it is unclear that the rejected paradigm of social credit, which relied on social processes to determine liability, was a harsh market rule. The balance-sheet view contained far-reaching implications for market consciousness. It construed consumers as individualised financial entities, knowable, conceptually isolated and assuming a present-ness – in ways previously inapplicable to the expanding circles of consumption. The balance-sheet view attributed irrationality to the social-credit way of evaluating consumer finance. In doing so, it encouraged a shift in evaluation which could lower the number of imprisonment orders, but, at the same time, it framed the logic of working-class credit realities as baseless. The working classes were thus chastised while provisionally saved.

Working-class men's discipline was not merely a matter of inculcating a middle-class morality, but was also a concrete style of limitation of consumer activity which needed no explicit reference to class. This point is clear in the doctrine of necessaries: Working-class men were a social group whose small budgets meant that freedom to consume framed through the notion of budget management was often a mockery, no more liberatory than the traditional evaluation of necessaries.

Overall, I am suggesting, processes of evaluation in law which adopted numerical factuality represented a historical attempt to isolate evaluation from the discretion of women and the working classes, whose decision-making processes were framed as baseless. When budgets or balance sheets were sought, the sociality of evaluation was not overlooked but, on the contrary, was all too present to legal thinkers, its perceived faults in need of formal restriction.

Why Objectify – Trollope

Trollope's immediate concerns with evaluation appear disconnected from women or working classes; his transactions are arbitrary in a small way, having to do with rashness in dealing, individual characters, and his and the publishers' standing and reputation at any junction. However, if we examine Trollope's representations of the

market it becomes clear that the same systemic concerns with the effects of marginalised groups on processes of evaluation informed his thinking. In that light, his efforts
to isolate facts from social processes were part of a broader cultural anxiety which was
cognisant of the troubling effects associated with particular social identities.

Nowhere was Trollope more concerned with economic evaluation than in the railway plot of *The Way We Live Now*, written shortly before *An Autobiography*. In *An
Autobiography* he described the novel as a critique of the age's 'commercial profligacy'
(ch. 20, p. 107), yet profligacy turns out to be a specific social problem: irrational economic evaluation. Irrational evaluation is associated, I suggest, with the weaknesses
of femininity. The working classes appear less threatening to Trollope, partly because
of his own familiarity with material struggles, although some suggestions in *An Autobiography* speak in that direction too. Most well known is his self-definition as an
advanced conservative-liberal, who accepts both social inequality and the diminution
of inequality as matters of a divine will. For the most part, Trollope's plot in *The Way
We Live Now* keeps in place the divine organisation so that working-class processes of
evaluation do not come to bear on the railway story to begin with. The concern about
female vices, however, clarifies the consciousness I want to recover.

The railway plot turns on a contrast between socially constructed value and real
value anchored in economic facts. It begins with American rational economic plans.
Fisker claims that American/English competition would heighten share value: 'nothing encourages this kind of thing like competition. When they hear at St Louis and
Chicago that the thing is alive in London, they'll be alive there. And it's the same here,
sir. When they know that the stock is running like wildfire in America, they'll make
it run here too.'[32] The railway too is examined in economic terms: the reader learns
that there is no paid-up capital, that the railway is unnecessary and that it may never
be built, all points that carry an air of verifiability. After the clear introduction, as the
company's English presence becomes important – both in the plot and as a structural
principle pulling together the novel's plot strands – a movement toward unknowing
economic facts assumes prominence.

Melmotte grows secretive about the railway. The problematic, first elaborated
openly, is made more and more opaque, the railway progress and the share allocations
in the public company less and less clear. This movement culminates in the *Evening
Pulpit* article which is 'in nothing more remarkable than in this – that it left on the
mind of its reader no impression of any decided opinion about the railway' (*WWLN*,
ch. 30, p. 229). As Tara McGann argues, the reader is placed, like the fictional investing public, in an unsure position.[33] Critics have sometimes argued that Trollope's
representation of finance was limited, and that it failed to understand and engage
the complex questions of capitalist finance.[34] Contra such arguments, I suggest that
vagueness was itself part of the problem represented in *The Way We Live Now*, and
worked toward the conceptual separation between facts and social constructs. To see
the point, we might go along with Trollope and ask: with no decided opinion about
the railway, why and how is the public investing?

An elaborate answer is found not in the railway story, but instead in the market
for tickets for Melmotte's dinner party. The logic of the railway share trade, having
been obscured, is dislocatingly elaborated in the ticket-trade subplot, which functions
as a mock market trading in social desires. At stake is a social process of evaluation,
and here, in Georgiana Longestaffe's adventure with tickets, Trollope is concrete and

detailed. Outcast Georgiana buys her way back into a desired milieu by trading tickets for the party with her friend Julia. This little story links a market-like world of exchange with the social aspirations at its heart, and closely tracks the rise and fall of exchange value. The deal is contract-like: Julia first promises to entertain Georgiana – specifically, to chaperon Georgiana at Melmotte's party, to take her as a visitor for three days and to have one party at her house during this time – in return for dinner tickets, because 'so greatly had the Melmottes risen in general appreciation' (*WWLN*, ch. 44, p. 344); she then agrees to raise the price and entertain Georgiana's Jewish fiancé as well, because the ticket value continues to rise with Melmotte's popularity; finally Julia finds that she had given her pricey promises for nothing, because the fall in ticket value – following the fall in social faith in Melmotte – made her tickets worthless, a worthlessness concretised in the novel through Julia's failure to meet the royal guests.

The formal dislocation of railway shares onto dinner tickets explains trade in terms of a particular social logic. Investors extending credit to Melmotte are, like Julia, interested in English social capital, concretised in the dinner event: mixing with social superiors, meeting symbols of English culture and appropriating English inherited land. The movement is herd-like and explicitly uninterested in Melmotte's financials, the underlying suggestion being that Melmotte's financial rise has nothing to do with economic solidity. The ironic rendering of the Melmottian project insists on the fact/social-process opposition: 'Mr Melmotte was indeed so great a reality, such a *fact* in the commercial world of London, that it was no longer possible for such a one as Montague to refuse to *believe* in the scheme' (WWLN, ch. 10, p. 74; emphasis added). With facts present, belief is mandated in line with the basic epistemological formula, but, an ironic narrator implies, Melmotte rises on the non-factual; he is a fetish, a belief as opposed to knowledge, as Latour describes the distinction with which anti-fetishists arm themselves. Investments are driven by processes of social interaction in contrast to verifiable knowledge. This problem is an epidemic spreading through the novel.

Perhaps the clearest symbolic failure to separate economic facts from social processes occurs in Melmotte's appearance in parliament, where he wants to speak:

> Melmotte listened . . . in the course of the debate . . . a question arose about the value of money, of exchange, and of the conversion of shillings into francs and dollars. About this Melmotte really did *know* something . . . It seemed to him that a gentleman whom he knew very well in the City – and who had maliciously stayed away from his dinner – one Mr Brown . . . understood nothing at all of what he was saying . . . [A] statement had been made . . . containing, as Melmotte thought, a fundamental error in finance; and he longed to set the matter right. At any rate, he desired to show the House that Mr Brown did not know what he was talking about – because Mr Brown had not come to his dinner. (*WWLN*, ch. 69, pp. 529–30; emphasis added)

The attempt fails. Melmotte's courage slips away under the intimidating presence of statesmen and House members; when corrected on formal forms of address he loses the gist of his argument. The scene performs at a small scale the move of the novel as a whole: a question of finance is at stake, described as a matter of knowledge, and so of error. The question, however, is transformed in the social space of parliament and becomes something worth talking about because – and only because – it relates to social injuries, hierarchies and rules of conduct. The question of knowledge disappears completely, hence Melmotte is unable to pronounce it.

Trollope represented the social processes of evaluation as problematic. Lack of factual basis for investment becomes a farce in the railway's board of directors:

> At the regular meeting of the board, which never sat for above half an hour, two or three papers were read by Miles Grendall. Melmotte himself would speak a few slow words, intended to be cheery, and always indicative of triumph, and then everybody would agree to everything, somebody would sign something, and the 'board' for that day would be over. (*WWLN*, ch. 22, p. 171)

Each director understands his nomination outside the question of the railway, as opportunity for Melmotte's personal and social favours, hence the inverted commas: 'board'. Note how the minimisation of numbers – short time, few papers, few words – the opposite of a Trollope novel – intensifies the problem. The ironic rendering of board scenes turns comical as the directors' silence becomes a new form of discourse; words, which Trollope liked in large quantities, disappear: 'Lord Alfred bowed down to the table and muttered something which was intended to convey most absolute confidence. "Hear, hear", said Mr Cohenlupe' (*WWLN*, ch. 37, p. 284). The representation insists on the social process which fails to know what is evaluated – just the problem that haunts public investment.

Crucial to the critique of investment is its feminisation, visible in the declining effeminate aristocracy, and more fundamentally in the ticket mock market, which is not just a detailed explanation of the problem of evaluation, but one run by women. Feminisation is particularly telling in this instance because, as Nancy Henry notes, while Victorian women could do little else under formal law, they could be and were investors in financial markets, an activity which attracted mixed views.[35] Trollope could represent women in the stock exchange, but opted for a stereotyped scene in which women are irrational social players. The pathetic character of the exchange is nonetheless perfectly rational as a matter of internal logic: Georgiana and Julia respond correctly to social demands on them. This is a case of the 'rationalisation towards the irrational'.[36] Trollope represented a system of evaluation with an operative logic, rather than some idiosyncratic occurrence – the same concern we saw in law about social evaluation.

This concern with irrational women is clearly articulated in Trollope's complex self-modelling on his mother, Frances Trollope, in *An Autobiography*. Trollope praised her literary industriousness and the economic success that came from authorship, which saved her family from ruin time and again. Trollope's practice of writing books almost ceaselessly was modelled on Frances Trollope, as was the hidden industry which began and ended daily in early hours before others even rose. In Chapter 2 of *An Autobiography* he described his mother's literary career with the same logic as he later did his own, separating income from literary quality. Her first book, *The Domestic Manners of the Americans*, was an economic success marked by a sum, £400. But then followed a devastating gendered critique: 'No observer could have been worse adapted by nature for the task of learning whether a nation was in a way to thrive. Whatever she saw she judged, as most women do, from her own standing-point' (10). In summing up his mother's life, his last words are critical, and frame the assessment:

> She was an unselfish, affectionate and most industrious woman, with great capacity for enjoyment and high physical gifts. She was endowed too with much creative power, with considerable humour, and a genuine feeling for romance. But she was neither clear-sighted nor accurate; and in her attempts to describe morals, manners, and *even facts*, was unable to avoid the pitfalls of exaggeration. (*A*, ch. 2, p. 27; emphasis added)

The notion that economic value could attach to books like Frances Trollope's *Manners*, written by a woman who exhibits a typical inability to reason 'from causes', whose motivations begin with her love of 'society', whose politics 'were always an affair of the heart', who gets things right almost accidentally, because she is good and 'in spite of her want of logic' (*A*, ch. 2, p. 20), who, simply, does not respond to any order of truth, illuminates Trollope's search in *An Autobiography* for an anchor for the economic value of his books. Trollope was in search of an anchor which, while disconnected from the books' literary quality, does not appear fully arbitrary – but rather responsive to his minimal demand for 'facts' to ground value. *An Autobiography* answers the question left open in *The Way We Live Now*: how, concretely, to evaluate? If not by social processes, then how? The narration of Trollope's own literary career added production output as a numerical factual anchor missing from his account of Frances Trollope's work, and so narratively offered a remedy, a bracketing off of the risk of unclear sight underlying economic value.

Frances Trollope succeeded, on her son's account, by having an exceptionally perfect heart (*A*, ch. 2, p. 20), but in *The Way We Live Now* Georgiana and Julia have no redeeming qualities; they retain only Frances Trollope's faults. The difficulty of separating facts from processes of evaluation lacking in logic, motivated by a love of sociality which relies on fashion rather than critical reasoning, drives the plot of economic collapse. The feminised qualities of investment are the locus of critique and ideological construction of an ideal concept of the economy as a factually rather than socially based process. It is worth noting that this effect, of demarcating the economy, shares much with the effect of marginalist economics. While Trollope's interest in differentiating sources of desire (factually versus socially based), and his ideas of real value, might seem closer to classical political economy, and while, as a matter of description, he describes an economy inseparable from the socio-political realm, his conceptual effort to exclude social relations from the market and to deny their normative relevance for evaluation associates him with the ideological implications of the 1870s turn to marginalism.[37]

*   *   *

Every account of the constructed (subjective) v. real (objective) distinction, whether of fetishes or facts, speaks to its impossibility, yet acknowledges its dominance in modernity. Trollope's framing of his commodities, and legal framings of consumer realities, reveal that one side of the distinction drove the other. The isolation of objective things was driven by a consciousness of their constructed nature; commodity fetishism or fact-ishism first emerges *not* when the social basis of economic evaluation is misrecognised, but rather when it is clearly perceived, yet perceived as a threat. When suspected social players appeared to dominate the processes of construction, objectification was a way of placing limits on that domination, catering for the status quo. The result was an ideology of a rational consumer economy. Its allure was as great as the risk that it would assume an independent power, and become a fetish in the traditional sense. That risk was present when Trollope departed from the world with an 'adieu to all who have cared to read *any among the many words* that I have written' (A, ch. 20, p. 233; emphasis added); with these departing words, Trollope left the readers of *An Autobiography* with a sense of vagueness, a not knowing what is talked about, or why – just the fear that drove him to accumulate words in the first place.

Notes

1. Karl Marx, *Capital*, in Karl Marx and Friedrich Engels, *Collected Works*, 35 vols (Lawrence & Wishart, 1996), vol. 1, p. 83. There is another side to commodity fetishism: market processes of evaluation themselves appear to be objective and beyond control. This side too was operative in Trollope who, as I argue below, made an effort to bracket off market processes, and so inadvertently framed them as incontrollable. However, my discussion is largely interested in the reified representation of the commodity itself.
2. See discussion of Latour's relegation of objectivism to theory, as opposed to practice, below.
3. These social categories of course overlap; I separate and generalise for analytic purposes.
4. The process of fetishisation in Marx has also been read in terms of the fantastic rather than the rational. On Richard Sennett's reading, for instance, commodity fetishism is a matter of turning mass-produced products into expressions of uniqueness. To mystify, goods acquired 'a mystery, a meaning, a set of associations which had nothing to do with their use'. While utilitarians associated an object's value with direct uses or 'hard fact[s]', Marx, according to Sennett, recognised that the fetish depends on a 'psychomorphic world'. That is how commodities become 'social hieroglyphics'. Commodities were powerful hieroglyphics, and as Marx put it, 'the productions of the human brain appear as independent beings endowed with life'. Richard Sennett, *The Fall of Public Man: On the Social Psychology of Capitalism* (New York: Penguin Books, 1978), pp. 145–6; Marx, *Capital*, p. 85. I leave the fantastic for another day, because Trollope fits with the rational account of fetishisation discussed in the text.
5. Georg Lukács, *History and Class Consciousness* (Cambridge, MA: MIT Press, 1971), 83–113.
6. Mary Poovey, *A History of the Modern Fact: Problems of Knowledge in the Sciences of Wealth and Society* (Chicago: University of Chicago Press, 1998).
7. From a formal economic perspective, Trollope's association of novel-writing with labour was not ridiculous once he removed himself from 'the half-profit system' (royalties – a position which drew him closer to that of a capitalist), and instead sold the copyright in one-off deals.
8. Andrew H. Miller, *Novels Behind Glass: Commodity Culture and Victorian Narrative*, (Cambridge: Cambridge University Press, 1995), p. 159.
9. Poovey, *History of the Modern Fact*, p. 313.
10. Ibid. 311, citing from the first issue of the Society's journal.
11. Poovey saw her work as aligned with Latour's research agenda in *We Have Never Been Modern*. Ibid. p. 19.
12. Ibid. p. xii.
13. His theory of realism, widely discussed, is beyond my scope here.

14. Silvana Colella, 'Sweet Money: Cultural and Economic Value in Trollope's *Autobiography*', *Nineteenth-Century Contexts*, 28.1 (2006): pp. 5–20.

15. Audrey Jaffe, 'Trollope in the Stock Market: Irrational Exuberance and *The Prime Minister*', *Victorian Studies*, 45.1 (2002): pp. 43–64; Anna Kornbluh, *Realizing Capital: Financial and Psychic Economies in Victorian Form* (New York: Fordham University Press, 2014). The broader context of this debate is the troubled relation between signs and substances in modern capitalism, sometimes described as crisis of representation. For discussions of Trollope's concerns about capitalist realities see Patrick Brantlinger, *Fictions of State: Culture and Credit in Britain, 1694–1994* (Baltimore: Cornell University Press, 1996), p. 172; Paul Delany, *Literature, Money and the Market: From Trollope to Amis* (Basingstoke: Palgrave Macmillan, 2002), pp. 19–31. On the use of numbers in the eighteenth century in response to capitalist crisis see Jonathan Sheehan and Dror Wahrman, *Invisible Hands: Self-Organization in the Eighteenth Century* (Chicago: University of Chicago Press, 2015), pp. 115–17.

16. Kornbluh points to the difficulty of the turn when she observes Trollope's ironic conclusion. *Realizing Capital*, pp. 107–12.

17. On *An Autobiography*'s relation to the growth of financial credit see for instance Christina Crosby, '"A Taste for More": Trollope's Addictive Realism', in Martha Woodmansee and Mark Osteen (eds), *The New Economic Criticism: Studies at the Interface of Literature and Economics* (London: Taylor & Francis, 1999), pp. 293–306.

18. The account that follows is expounded in detail in Anat Rosenberg, 'Rational Households: Consumption Between Love and Hate', *Georgetown Journal of Gender and the Law*, 29.3 (2018): 499–531.

19. Thorstein Veblen, *The Theory of the Leisure Class: An Economic Study of Institutions* (New York and London: Macmillan, 1899).

20. The account that follows is expounded in detail in Anat Rosenberg, 'The Realism of the Balance Sheet: Value Assessments Between the Debtors Act and *The Picture of Dorian Gray*', *Critical Analysis of Law*, 2 (2015): pp. 363–82.

21. George Rae, *The Country Banker* (New York: Charles Scribner's Sons, 1920), p. 7.

22. These terms overlap; I use both for analytic purposes.

23. See references in note 16 above. I discuss further the question of realism in relation to the fact/sociality conundrum in *The Way We Live Now* in Anat Rosenberg, *Liberalizing Contracts: Nineteenth Century Promises Through Literature, Law and History* (Abingdon and New York: Routledge, 2018), Chapter 2.

24. David Simpson clarifies the element of social control common to facts and fetishes in discussing Dickens's *Hard Times*. Simpson says that 'fact' is itself a fetish, that is, 'an imposed constraint on the kind of phenomenological variability that might remind individuals of their capacities for creating alternatives'. David Simpson, *Fetishism and Imagination: Dickens, Melville, Conrad* (Baltimore: Johns Hopkins University Press, 1982), p. 65.

25. As Thompson says, the figures support a compelling argument about a 'consumer revolution' in this period. Noel Thompson, *Social Opulence and Private Restraint: The Consumer in British Socialist Thought Since 1800* (Oxford: Oxford University Press, 2015), pp. 43–74. For a review of debates about the implications of these changes (relief or misery), see Jan de Vries, *The Industrious Revolution: Consumer Behavior and the Household Economy, 1650 to the Present* (Cambridge: Cambridge University Press, 2008), pp. 37–9.

26. Matthew Hilton, *Consumerism in Twentieth-Century Britain: The Search for a Historical Movement* (Cambridge: Cambridge University Press, 2003), pp. 27–52.

27. Most familiar in contexts of welfare studies and home economics; classic works include Lucie White, 'Subordination, Rhetorical Survival Skills, and Sunday Shoes: Notes on the Hearing of Mrs G', *Buffalo Law Review*, 58 (1990): pp. 1–58; and Jan Pahl, 'Patterns of Money Management Within Marriage', *Journal of Social Policy*, 9.3 (1980): pp. 313–35.

28. Erika Diane Rappaport, *Shopping for Pleasure: Women in the Making of London's West End* (Princeton: Princeton University Press, 2000), p. 49.

29. Leonore Davidoff, *Worlds Between: Historical Perspectives on Gender and Class* (Cambridge: Polity Press, 1995), pp. 73–102.

30. Ben Griffin, *The Politics of Gender in Victorian Britain: Masculinity, Political Culture, and the Struggle for Women's Rights* (Cambridge: Cambridge University Press, 2014), Chapter 9.

31. Margot C. Finn, *The Character of Credit: Personal Debt in English Culture, 1740–1914* (Cambridge: Cambridge University Press, 2003), Part III and *passim*; Michael Lobban, 'Consumer Credit and Debt', in *The Oxford History of the Laws of England Volume XII* (2010), 838.

32. Anthony Trollope, *The Way We Live Now*, ed. Frank Kermode (London: Penguin Books, 1994), ch. 9, p. 72. Subsequent references are in the main text (*WWLN*).

33. Tara McGann, 'Literary Realism in the Wake of Business Cycle Theory: *The Way We Live Now* (1875)', in Francis O'Gorman (ed.), *Victorian Literature and Finance*. (Oxford: Oxford University Press, 2007), pp. 133–56.

34. See for instance recently, Francis O'Gorman, 'Is Trollope's *The Way We Live Now* (1875) about the "commercial profligacy of the age"?' *Review of English Studies*, 67.281 (2016): pp. 751–63, and further references there.

35. Nancy Henry, '"Ladies Do It?": Victorian Women Investors in Fact and Fiction', in *Victorian Literature and Finance*, pp. 111–32.

36. Karl Löwith, *Max Weber and Karl Marx* (London: Routledge, 2003), p. 68.

37. For further discussion see Rosenberg, *Liberalizing Contracts*, ch. 2. For a reading of Trollope's style in *The Way We Live Now* as a challenge to marginalism see Frederik Van Dam, *Anthony Trollope's Late Style: Victorian Liberalism and Literary Form* (Edinburgh: Edinburgh University Press, 2016).

23

SHODDY TROLLOPE

Kate Flint

SHODDY IS ONE of those substances to which we barely pay any attention: rough cloth made out of recycled woollens, or the shredded wool itself, used as stuffing for cheap mattresses or car seats. Yet the word 'shoddy' is one that we use all the time, speaking of a shoddy piece of workmanship – badly finished, and likely to fall apart, something executed without care and attention – or a flimsy, 'shoddily' constructed argument. Shoddy is highly mundane; its transformation into a trope creates a word that signifies something inferior and second-rate. This chapter builds on contemporary concerns in both literary criticism and material culture studies with the ordinary, the everyday and the overlooked. This is *stuff* – on this occasion, very shabby stuff – that one takes for granted, yet that, whether encountered at first hand or via the pages of a literary text, can be made to reveal multiple layers of cultural, political, economic and ecological history.

In turn, examining this material demands, like so many ordinary things, a highly attentive reading. I here take my cue from cultural anthropologist Daniel Miller, who in his book *Stuff* claims:

> Objects are important, not because they are evident and physically constrain or enable, but quite the opposite. It is often precisely because we do *not* see them. The less we are aware of them, the more powerfully they can determine our expectations by setting the scene and ensuring appropriate behavior, without being open to challenge. They determine what takes place to the extent that we are unconscious of their capacity to do so.[1]

Miller is describing the importance of paying attention to the overlooked when it comes to our *own* daily practices. Such recuperation can also be found in the work of those who, over the last decade, have examined the resonances of material culture's quiet presence within nineteenth-century imaginative writing. These scholars have laid bare the hidden history of material objects that is latent in references to furniture or commodities or souvenirs or cloth that lend their weight to the realist enterprise, and that allow us to imagine and place ourselves within an environment – work by, say, Elaine Freedgood, John Plotz and Clare Pettitt.[2] Trollope provides a number of possibilities for investigation along these lines, although his descriptive prose is not as rich in particularities as, say, that of Dickens or Elizabeth Gaskell or George Eliot in this respect. Even the terrible, badly made patent steel furniture in *Orley Farm*, which doesn't screw together properly, and which Mr Green characterises as 'utter trash', is something that we are invited to shudder at in its generic tastelessness, rather than being invited to see in detail.[3] Rather, Trollope tends here, as elsewhere, to let readers furnish the specifics of a room through their own imagination and their own internalised standards, building on such generic terms as 'chair', 'sofa', 'little table'. By contrast, his descriptive energies are more generously expended on the gestures, actions and details of appearance that characterise an individual, as Michael Riffaterre has usefully noted – and these details include their dress, and the quality of materials that constitute their garments.[4] Shoddy, as we shall see, signifies, for Trollope, material stuff with very explicit resonances – and his naming it is the more conspicuous coming from someone whose prose is not over-burdened with adjectives that qualify the detailed texture of the world. Our interrogative reading demands that we ask about the contemporary understanding and associations of shoddy for Trollope and his readers, that we ask about *its* history, and that we acknowledge the connections between shoddy's literal and metaphorical senses, and Trollope's own fictional practices.

More specifically, my advocacy for attentive observation does not, on this occasion, depend on going to nature, as Ruskin would bid us do when commending this practice; nor does it mean considering the material environment in terms of the objects that fill a room or a wardrobe, whether these be luxuries, or the repositories of association and sentiment, or everyday, utilitarian things. Rather, considering shoddy involves exploring the details of surplus consumerism, especially in their regional specifics. Among those who made their living from scavenging discarded things – like the Thames mudlarks, who scraped the banks of the river at low tide, looking for stuff that had been jettisoned – were the rag merchants who bought up the surplus stock of the old clothes shops. These are shops made familiar from descriptions in, for example, 'Meditations in Monmouth Street' (1836), one of Dickens's *Sketches by Boz*, and John Thomson and Adolphe Smith's *Street Life in London* (1876–7). As Smith writes, once an item of clothing becomes so worn as to be unwearable by even the poorest person, 'the hour of regeneration is near at hand'.[5] If made of cotton, these rags went off to supply the paper industry – certainly until the 1860s – and in 'one part of the window' of Krook's rag and bottle warehouse in *Bleak House*, that paper-obsessed novel, there was, Esther tells us, 'a picture of a red paper mill, at which a cart was unloading a quantity of old rags'.[6] But if made of wool – I return to Smith – 'these disgusting rags . . . constitute the "devil's dust" of the Yorkshire woollen manufacturer. The cast-off clothes of all Europe are imported to supply food for the mills' where they

> are torn into shreds by toothed wheels, animated with all the power of steam, till they are reduced to the condition of wool. They may then be mixed with a certain amount of new wool, and finally reappear as new cloth, woven according to the latest pattern, and resplendent in the dye of the most fashionable colours. Thus the cloth of our newest coat is, after all, probably made from the cast-off garment of some street beggar.[7]

This recycled cloth was known as 'shoddy', and three towns in West Yorkshire, Ossett, Batley and Dewsbury, were at the centre of this global trade. Consider Ossett's unofficial coat of arms, with shoddy mills on top, and the motto *Inutile Utile Ex Arte* – 'useless things by art made useful'.[8] Samuel Jubb, of Batley, in his 1860 *History of the Shoddy Trade*, remarked that shoddy manufacture had become 'a source of national wealth, by utilizing materials of value, which were previously almost thrown away'.[9] Peter Lund Simmonds, in *Waste Products and Undeveloped Substances* (1862), amplifies this recycling philosophy through referencing the model established by nature:

> When we perceive in nature how nothing is wasted, but that every substance is reconverted, and again made to do duty in a changed and beautified form, we have at least an example to stimulate us in economically applying the waste materials we make, or that lie around us in abundance, ready to be utilized.[10]

This concern with waste material – or rather, with *avoiding* waste – is indicative of a debate that lies at the heart of industrial modernity. Whereas a good deal of critical attention has recently been paid to the residue of industrial processes, with the pollution arising from, say, dye-filled and chemically poisoned rivers, or with the coal-fuelled smoky chimneys that significantly contributed to climate change, waste is not necessarily equivalent to pollution.[11] 'Waste can pollute', Tim Cooper tells us, but the word itself demands more nuanced consideration, since it 'carries a complex set of ethical meanings about the proper uses of resources. As a category of thought, "waste" is a concept within which ideas about the right relationship between society and nature have been contested.'[12] Drawing on John Scanlan's account in *On Garbage*, Cooper has described how, in post-Enlightenment Europe, 'enlightened propagandists of "improvement" believed that they were opening up the prospect of the progressive and universal elimination of waste'.[13] That this utopian vision failed was, as Cooper puts it, 'largely due to the fact that the emergent capitalist order itself exhibited an unparalleled capacity for waste'.[14]

Yet shoddy manufacturers, and those who promoted them, were proud of their frugal, careful attitude towards the by-products of commercial manufacture. A newspaper piece circulated in America on the eve of the Civil War drew attention to the presence of shoddy in everyday life – in woollen tablecloths and protective pianoforte covers as much as in overcoats and uniforms. Although, as the writer points out, these commodities are reconstituted from beggars' rags – 'Let us hope that the steam was hot, and the chemicals powerful, by which the rags were purged of their former iniquities' – shoddy was celebrated, in decidedly overblown terms, as an example of modern progress: progress manifested on a global stage. It was hailed as 'one of the greatest triumphs of modern art, and betokens the advance of civilisation. The utilisation of refuse, as in China and Japan, is one of the most silent features of an economical and thoughtful race, as contrasted' – the writer is strikingly uninformed – 'with the spendthrift habits of a North American Indian for instance.'[15] The pollution caused by burning the coal producing the steam that drove the machinery, and the streams and rivers that were severely contaminated by the chemicals involved in the shoddy-making process, go, however, uncommented upon in the nineteenth century. As Susan Strasser points out in *Waste and Want* (1999), '[p]ublic discourse about household trash' – and she certainly includes rags in this category – 'has until very recently stopped at the borders of the household'. This taboo was toppled in the mid-twentieth century, she notes (she is writing in a North

American context, but the same generalisation is applicable to Europe), at which point '[c]ontemporary interest in trash as part of a global environmental crisis has made household waste-disposal practices into a topic for schoolchildren's lessons, television public service announcements, and utility bill inserts'.[16] While, as we have seen, the recycling of woollen materials might be understood within a commendable culture of thriftiness, there was no comprehension of the degree to which economical recycling of one substance could also mean significant pollution to air and water. The practice was not discussed – and shoddy production was symptomatic in this respect – on such a holistic level.

For the remainder of this chapter, I will build on these approaches by examining how the material world becomes caught up within metaphorical language in ways that we barely register. We might think of metaphors, indeed, as recycled and repurposed words. Specifically, I consider how Trollope uses the word 'shoddy' to show how certain words carried a weight of meaning to which a contemporary reader would very probably have been sensible, but that have by now undergone such slippage that we're familiar only with the derivative term – as in 'a shoddy piece of work' – not with the resonances of its origins. Or, to put it differently, I'm giving voice to what Susan Stewart has termed 'the silence of the ordinary' as it inhabits figurative language.[17] Understanding the loaded implications of 'shoddy' will entail exploring its nineteenth-century production in a little more detail, and standing back from the optimistic spin given to the shoddy trade by the enthusiastic proponents of recycling.

Shoddy production began in the early nineteenth century, when certain Yorkshire manufacturers thought that there had to be more profitable uses for old woollen garments and carpets than selling them to be used for manure.[18] Local historians generally believe that shoddy was first made by Batley woollen manufacturer Benjamin Law in 1813.[19] Shoddy was one of three categories of recycled wool, made from soft or relatively loosely woven fabrics: the highest quality, made out of hard or felted cloth rags, was known as 'mungo'. Post 1860, 'extract' was also produced, derived from cotton-warped wool fabrics. The etymology of 'shoddy' itself – a word first found in print in 1832 – is uncertain, but without censorious overtones. Most probably it is related to the Old English *scádan* ('to divide'), and then first appears as a formation from the small pieces of wool 'shed' in manufacturing cloth.[20] The local lore that says that 'mungo' derives from a manufacturer telling a sceptical workman that this product 'mun go' – i.e. must go – through a needle's eye would seem to be apocryphal: the word seems semantically connected to 'mongrel', or mixed.

As a *Morning Chronicle* account of a Dewsbury shoddy mill puts it – a description itself recycled by Henry Mayhew in *London Labour and the London Poor* – mill machinery was developed for the

> tearing up, or rather the grinding, of woollen rags by means of coarse willows, called devils; the operation of which sends forth choking clouds of dry pungent dirt and floating fibres – the real and original 'devil's dust'. Having been . . . reduced to something like the original raw material, fresh wool is added to the pulp in different proportions, according to the quality of the stuff to be manufactured, and the mingled material is at length reworked in the usual way into a little serviceable cloth.[21]

This cloth was used not just in the garment trade – for men's suits, overcoats, and for military uniforms – but to make blankets. Unwoven, it was used to stuff furniture and mattresses. The uncontrollable dust that Mayhew described created undesirable working conditions, damaging the lungs, and causing 'shoddy fever', like a continual bad cold, with a 'continual acrid running from the nose' and a sore throat relieved only by drinking mint tea.[22] Moreover, as an article in *All The Year Round* in 1872 drily phrased it, 'as the rags are often of ill odour in the first instance, the dust of course does not emit a very refreshing perfume'.[23]

But it was not the conditions in the mills that excited the greatest comment in the nineteenth century, and that were responsible for creating the word's pejorative associations. Rather, shoddy was repeatedly associated with cheating and deception. It looked like broadcloth – until the shine wore off; it was often sold as such. In this *All the Year Round* article, it was discussed alongside chalk, commonly put into calico to whiten it, and 'Jonathan', the sawdust often added to various forms of barley and maize meal. Adulteration was, for Marx, a mode of capitalist 'sophistry' that demonstrated 'that everything is only appearance'.[24] Yet whereas those who adulterated their products with these two additives deliberately set out to deceive, the *All the Year Round* writer makes it clear that in the case of shoddy, 'there is nothing reprehensible in this utilizing of half-worn fibres, provided the commodity be not sold to us as "all new wool"'. Indeed, quite a bit of cheap wool cloth may well contain shoddy, and will nonetheless 'render a fair amount of useful service', so that it is 'worth what it has cost'.[25] Shoddy thus may be counted among the Victorian 'conundrums of culture', as Lara Kriegel terms it in relation to a different branch of textile manufacture, of deciding what is, and is not, the real thing.[26] Shoddy could certainly be incorporated in material that claimed, and appeared, to be made entirely of new fibres. Yet shoddy could also be sold with no pretence that it was anything other than recycled wool, and found a ready market – as itself. It allowed working-class men to buy suits that they could not have otherwise afforded.

Trollope was well aware of the original, textile-trade meaning of 'shoddy'. When he described the clothing purveyed by the wealthy breeches-maker Mr Neefit, in *Ralph the Heir* (1869), he tells us that 'he made the best of breeches, put no shoddy or cheap stitching into them, and was, upon the whole, an honest tradesman'.[27] This reference to the shoddy-free breeches shows also that Trollope not only understood the nature of the material, but its associations with the adulteration of fabrics. Elsewhere, he expects that readers will see shoddy's presence as shorthand for the grubby world of trade. In *Hunting Sketches* (1865), he contrasts the advantages of being a farmer, of whom nobody will ever complain if he takes a day off to go hunting, to the position of his shop-keeping relative, 'who never has a holiday, and does not know what to do with it when it comes to him; to whom the fresh air of heaven is a stranger; who lives among sugars and oils, and the dust of shoddy, and the size of new clothing'.[28] But more often, however, Trollope employs the word figuratively rather than literally: that which is 'shoddy' may well deceive in a general sense. 'Poor Emily Hotspur' – in *Sir Harry Hotspur of Humblethwaite* (1871) – cannot see through the facade presented by her cousin George, for 'he had gifts of simulation, which are valuable', and she 'had not yet learned the housewife's trick of passing the web through her fingers, and of finding by the touch whether the fabric were of fine wool, or of shoddy made up with craft to look like wool of the finest'.[29]

Trollope reprises the idea of the potentially false suitor three years later, in *Phineas Redux* (1874), but here Adelaide Palliser shows herself to be far more discerning when she talks to Lady Chiltern about the forthcoming visit of her fiancé Gerard Maule. Both of the two young people are, at this point in the plot, without much money – but she says that she doesn't care, and that it doesn't matter to her, either, whether 'you think him perfect or imperfect. He's just my own, – at least I hope so; – the one thing that I've got. If I wear a stuff frock' – that is, a dress made out of some woven fabric – 'I'm not going to despise it because it's not silk.' 'Mr Spooner would be the stuff frock', says Lady Chiltern, alluding to another, and decidedly unsuitable suitor. 'No', says Adelaide, making very clear that she can discriminate between worthy and unworthy forms of everyday cloth, 'Mr Spooner is shoddy, and very bad shoddy, too.'[30] Shoddy became widely synonymous, indeed, with the antithesis of fine clothing: recollect Don Alhambra, in the Gilbert and Sullivan opera *The Gondoliers*, singing of how one wearies of riches:

When you have nothing else to wear
But cloth of gold and satins rare,
For cloth of gold you cease to care –
Up goes the price of shoddy.[31]

Trollope's most sustained engagement with shoddy's associations can be found, however, not in his fiction, but in his 1867 article for *Saint Pauls Magazine*, 'An Essay on Carlylism; Containing the Very Melancholy Story of a Shoddy Maker and his Mutinous Maid-Servant'. This opens as a reflection on Thomas Carlyle's increasingly gloomy stance as a prophet of doom; his implication that everyone in England is 'void of truth and honesty . . . The manufacturers make shoddy. And the maid-servants give warning.' Trollope makes some careful distinctions in this piece. He focuses on the manufacturer, a shoddy-maker, whose business it is 'to supply certain customers with a somewhat ephemeral article made of old woollen rags, and so concocted as to have some resemblance to good cloth'. He makes his 10 or 15 per cent profit, to be sure – the same as he would if he were making broadcloth – 'But the world wants shoddy, and someone must make it.'[32] He's not trying to pass off shoddy as something *better* than shoddy – that would, indeed, be a sin in Trollope's eyes – but what he shows is that Carlyle cannot stomach the making of *any* kind of cheap and inferior material, even though people may be willing to pay for it. The same, Trollope argues, is true of cheap bricks, and cheap carpentry – for him, in this piece, the workings of the free market economy provide more of an imperative than does good quality workmanship.

Carlyle's jeremiads were to continue, and one in particular passed into very common currency. Originally formulated in a letter to the Manchester engineer and entrepreneur Sir Joseph Whitworth, it was quoted by Samuel Smiles in *Thrift* (1875) and much reprinted in periodicals. Would that all captains of industry had a soul like Whitworth's, lamented Carlyle – but by contrast, 'all England has decided that the profitablest way is to do its work ill, slurily, swiftly, and mendaciously'. He suggests that the country is offering up a heartfelt prayer to Beelzebub: 'Oh, help us, thou great Lord of Shoddy, Adulteration, and Malfeasance, to do our work with the maximum of sluriness, swiftness, profit, and mendacity, for the devil's sake. Amen.'[33] His rhetorical

heir, in this, is William Morris, who in 1892, towards the end of his life, was lament-
ing that '[i]t is a shoddy age. Shoddy is king. From the statesman to the shoemaker, all
is shoddy.'[34]

But Trollope took a more nuanced approach, and chooses the example of fiction
to make his point. Carlyle, he tells us, has started to weigh in against novel-writing,
seeing it 'on a par with, almost worse than, that unfortunate shoddy-making'.[35]
Paraphrasing the master's comment that '[f]iction, while the feigner of it knows
that he is feigning, partakes, more than we suspect, of the nature of *lying*', he
counteracts this accusation.[36] For Trollope, there is in fiction, for the most part, 'a
preponderance of truth'. He is not referring to the manipulations and coincidences
of improbable plotting, but to the kind of moral imperatives that underpin his own
novels – for today's

> fictionists do not make out virtue to be bad and vice to be good. They do not pal-
> liate ill-manners. They strive to show that the thief, the adulterer, the bad liver will
> suffer punishment; and that the honest, the pure, and the self-denying among us are
> those who shall be loved and venerated.[37]

The maker of adulterated *fabric,* one might say, will only suffer punishment, in Trollope's
scheme of things, if he is trying to pass something off as that which it is not.

I don't want to overstate Trollope's recourse to the trope of shoddy and shoddiness – there's only one more notable example of it to come. But he stands out
by contrast to other mid-nineteenth-century novelists: no mention of it, in literal or
figurative form, in Gaskell (writing on the cotton side of the Pennines) or in Dickens –
and we have to wait for Dorothy Parker's clerihew on that writer: 'Who call him spu-
rious and shoddy / Shall do it o'er my lifeless body'.[38] George Eliot invokes it late in
her career, referring in *The Impressions of Theophrastus Such* to an American writer
whose English 'could not pass for more than a syntactical shoddy of the cheapest
sort', a condemnation of linguistic deception that recalls Leslie Stephen's attack, six
years earlier, on an Anglican preacher who 'calmly retailed his lengths of theological
shoddy – old fragments of decaying systems woven into a web of the usual polish
and flimsiness'.[39] Although shoddy gave rise to its own literature, from writings in
working-class dialect almanacs to at least one novel, Arthur Wood's 1877 *'Shoddy'. A
Yorkshire Tale of Home,* it quickly passed from signifying a specific kind of material
or manufacturing industry to being broadly synonymous with deception covering up
poor quality work.[40]

Shoddy's history in America plays an essential role in that shift of meaning from
designating a specific material substance to indicating something – anything – that was
poorly made. The American context is an important one. Though very localised in its
production within the United Kingdom, shoddy featured in a global textile economy,
something made possible by the development of the railroad network and the growth
of the shipping industry. The bales of old clothes that filled the West Riding mill yards
came not just from England, but from Germany, Belgium and Denmark; the resulting
cloth had an international market, cheap enough to be imported into pre-Civil War
America at the lowest tariff rates.[41] Samuel Jubb, publishing his *History of the Shoddy
Trade* in 1860, wrote that 'the bulk of these blankets is consumed in the Slave States

of America, and . . . are designed chiefly for the use of the slaves, both as coverlets and materials for garments'.[42] By 1860, the US was annually importing over 6 million pounds of shoddy, used also for military garments and blankets. This moment of transition is made quite explicit in American Henry Morford's 1864 Civil War novel, *The Days of Shoddy: A Novel of the Great Rebellion in 1861*.

At the time of the Civil War, shoddy production increased exponentially in America. From the 1820s onwards, shoddy mills grew up in Connecticut, Rhode Island, Pennsylvania and Illinois, usually in places that were already centres of textile production, a trend that continued post-war. Both mill owners and workers frequently came from the Batley–Dewsbury–Ossett area. Domestically produced fabric rather than imported shoddy was used to make soldiers' uniforms – an industry much satirised in contemporary cartoons showing military men in rags (and for that matter in quickly disintegrating cardboard shoes).[43] The first weeks of the war, to which the term 'the days of shoddy' particularly refers, 'gave to that word, before but little known, a wide and disgraceful significance' – and Morford explains its manufacturing origins:

> It has been [from the beginning of the war], and must be in the dictionaries of all future periods, a synonym for *miserable pretence in patriotism* – a shadow without a substance. Shoddy coats, shoddy shoes, shoddy blankets, shoddy tents, shoddy horses, shoddy arms, shoddy ammunition, shoddy boats, shoddy beef and bread, shoddy bravery, shoddy liberality, shoddy patriotism, shoddy loyalty, shoddy statesmanship, shoddy personal devotion, – these and dozens of other ramifications of deception have gone to make up the application of the name.[44]

War profiteers quickly became known as 'shoddy millionaires' or members of the 'shoddy aristocracy'.[45] Bulk rag prices rose twenty-fold in 1861.[46] A *Vanity Fair* column-filler in November 1861 claims that '[w]e learn from a correspondent with Gen. STONE's column that "The 'boys' have nick-named the army-contractors in general 'Shoddies', and when any of these personages make their appearance the cry of 'Shoddy! Shoddy!' goes up from all parts of the camp!"[47] The widespread popularisation of the term would have ensured that Trollope's use of it was well understood transatlantically. And we find it invoked, in all its scathing metaphorical weight, in an obituary of Trollope in Boston's *Literary World*, urging readers to read him if they have not already done so: 'you will leave off with a larger sympathy for what is true, and fair, and square, and good, and a heartier contempt for shoddy in all of its nineteenth-century forms'.[48]

The inferior nature of shoddy products gave rise to what is, today, the term's common understanding: something of poor quality and workmanship, especially when it's mendaciously being passed off as something better. These were the terms in which shoddy was still being discussed in the United States at the end of the nineteenth century. Free-trade supporter W. B. Estell, in an extended piece on shoddy, fraud and tariff reform, wrote in 1892 that tariffs against imported woollen material had been passed in order to protect both wool-growers and manufacturers from the 'shockingly poor cloth that the wicked Batley Englishmen made', and, as he sarcastically put it, the result shows how far we can surpass Englishmen. We have succeeded in making immeasurably poorer goods than any one else has ever put together; goods so poor that they are never sold as cloth; no one could ever be fooled to buy them in that shape, but they are sold direct by the hundred pieces to ready-made clothing shops; so rotten that they are never allowed to be seen by the unfortunate customer until they are made into clothes and given somewhat of apparent consistency by being sewn together with the trimmings.[49]

Nothing could be further from Trollope's – or his critics' – understanding of ethical imperatives in general, and in particular, of the principles that underpin his own practice as a novelist. He makes his favoured characters display complete probity – especially to the content of their hearts – even when it may be hard to live up to the requisite standards. Trollope's principled hatred of any form of cheating is best articulated by the Duke of Omnium, in *The Duke's Children*, when he is speaking to Gerald, his son, about the folly of gambling. He has Gerald agree with him that it is terrible to cheat at cards, and then advances the view that 'He who plays that he may make an income, but does not cheat, has fallen nearly as low.' He asks Gerald if he understands what money *is*, and goes on to explain that 'Money is the reward of labour . . . or rather, in the shape it reaches you, it is your representation of that reward' – for, he acknowledges, the actual money that Gerald sees is likely to have been made for him by the labour of others. 'But it is a commodity of which you are bound to see that the source is not only clean but noble.'[50]

Trollope was, famously, an author who proclaimed how deeply he cared about workmanship and the degree of effort and self-regulation that went into his own writing, and I will return to this point. Yet his regularity in producing novels, let alone his travel writings and other publications, and the steady, non-flashy quality of his prose led to him being accused of writing prose that was too regular, too mechanical. The *Saturday Review* mounted a sustained attack on what they saw as this monotonous predictability and regularity. In an 1866 review of *The Belton Estate*, it compared him to an artist who year after year submits to the Royal Academy a painting of a donkey between two bundles of hay, the only difference between the pictures consisting of a slightly varied expression in the donkey's eye, a slightly different shade to the donkey's coat, a different background. How can one expect variety and inventiveness, the reviewer asks, when Trollope wrote so much?

> Such fertility is not in nature. Only why should the novelist 'do' his three novels a year? Of course, if Mr Trollope only looks upon his art as manufacture, there can be no reason why he should not take as just a pride in turning so many novels out of his brain in the twelvemonth as a machine-maker takes in turning so many locomotives or looms out of his shed . . . Unfortunately . . . [h]e loses all freshness and interest and vivacity, and grows at each repetition heavier and more mechanical.[51]

Henry James summed up Trollope's career in similar terms, writing in the *Century Magazine* after his death that '[h]e published too much; the writing of novels had ended by becoming, with him, a perceptibly mechanical process'.[52]

The *Saturday Review*'s accusation of repetition points to what has proved to be an enduring trope in the criticism of Trollope's fiction. Its very texture displays a tendency to – well, what one may accurately term recycle. This recycling takes place both at a macro level, and in the weaving of sentences. Henry James, again, reviewing *Can You Forgive Her?* (1865) in the *Nation*, claimed that if one were to 'take any one of his former tales, change the names of half the characters, leave the others standing, and transpose the incidents . . . you will have "Can You Forgive Her?"'.[53] In a similar vein, Hugh Walpole, in 1928, while noting that much of this tendency to repeat was surely the result of the exigencies of serial publication, gave the specific example of the highly similar way in which heroines hesitate to accept their suitors in four successive Barsetshire novels: 'it is not in these maidenly and exceedingly proper refusals that the repetition lies, but rather in the constant and exceedingly drawn-out reiteration of them.'[54] N. John Hall states bluntly that Trollope 'was not a man who hesitated to repeat his favourite themes, situations, formulas'.[55] In a more close-grained scrutiny, Laurie Langbauer remarks that Trollope's prose is a 'loosely proverbial' assemblage of 'colloquialisms, mottoes, maxims, platitudes, clichés and tag lines'.[56]

Yet not every treatment of Trollope's tendency to repeat himself should be seen as contributing to a portrait of the author as a tired hack, with nothing new to fall back on, endlessly rehashing phrases and plots. Elizabeth R. Epperly's *Patterns of Repetition in Trollope*, in offering an extended reading of his predilection for thematic parallels, well-used literary allusions and inter- and intra-textual echoes, sees the constancy of his style as a means of building a relationship with his readers, ensuring that he shares with them 'an accessible and sophisticated shorthand'. Moreover, the echoes serve to create powerful interconnections that allow readers to draw parallels between apparently dissimilar situations, or to spot small variations and their implications (not least, the stress that Trollope places on human differences) in what superficially looks like another version of the same. For her, 'repetition is the key to Trollope's polyphonous unity.'[57] More recently, Jonathan Farina has discussed Trollope's use of repetition in the interests of realism and ordinariness. He emphasises the novelist's use of one particular verbal tic: 'of course'.[58] This phrase may return one to a previous detail of plot or behavioural tendency; it is also a means of establishing 'common-sense' opinion, the ground he shares with his readers; it is also a way, on occasion, of introducing irony. More than this: Farina reminds us that some readers regarded – and still regard – Trollope's repetitions, and the familiarity that they engender, as a source of pleasure. Trollope's comparison of a dubious suitor to the unseen presence of recycled garments in what seems like a fine woollen garment is, indeed, just one among very many metaphorical repurposings.

Turning to one final Trollopian invocation of shoddy, we may see quite how interwoven, in fact, this controversial form of recycled fibre is with Trollope's fictional production – with, one might say, the writing of someone who doesn't use repetition as dishonest padding, but as part of the easy rhythm of his writing. In his *Autobiography*, Trollope wrote that if

> a man writes his books badly, or paints his pictures badly, because he can make his money faster in that fashion than by doing them well, and at the same time proclaims them to be the best he can do, if, in fact, he sells shoddy for broadcloth, he is dishonest, as is any other fraudulent dealer.[59]

The same would be true, he says, for a barrister who takes money he doesn't earn, or a clergyman who lives on a sinecure. A writer, he says, has a particular burden here, since it's up to him to settle 'within himself what is good work and what is bad, – when labour enough has been given, and when the task has been scamped' – but ultimately, this writer should live to a broadly applicable standard: 'he is to be governed only by the plain rules of honesty which should govern us all'.

Shoddy – like an imperfect human being, indeed – is not necessarily a bad thing in and of itself. As Samuel Jubb enthusiastically put it, 'not a single thing belonging the rag and shoddy system is valueless, or useless; there are no accumulations of mountains of debris to take up room, or disfigure the landscape; all – good, bad, and indifferent – pass on, and are beneficially appropriated.'[60] But when shoddy is being passed off as something else, as when an individual is knowingly presenting a false facade – then it's to be condemned. To this end, Trollope regularly deploys – and relies on his reader to recognise – the web of cultural reference surrounding this particular word, 'shoddy', linking literary production, the importance of maintaining standards within a profession, and probity of character. If shoddy's resonances go largely unacknowledged today, Trollope's use of the word serves as a potent example of the ease with which figurative appropriation can muffle the material history that it contains. It also, of course, proves a remarkably apt metaphor in the hands of a writer whose own prose and plots regularly recycle – on both a small and a large scale – the materials of fiction.

Notes

1. Daniel Miller, *Stuff* (Cambridge and Malden, MA: Polity Press, 2010), p. 50.
2. See Elaine Freedgood, *The Ideas in Things: Fugitive Meaning in the Victorian Novel* (Chicago: University of Chicago Press, 2008); Clare Pettitt, 'Peggotty's Work-Box: Victorian Souvenirs and Material Memory', in Kate Flint (ed.), *Materiality and Memory, Romanticism and Victorianism on the Net*, 53 (2009). Available at <http://www.erudit.org/revue/ravon/2009/v/n53/029896ar.html> (last accessed 30 October 2016); John Plotz, *Portable Property: Victorian Culture on the Move* (Princeton: Princeton University Press, 2009).
3. Anthony Trollope, *Orley Farm* (Oxford: Oxford University Press, 2008), ch. 23, p. 235.
4. Michael Riffaterre, 'Trollope's Metonymies', *Nineteenth-Century Fiction*, 37.3 (1982): pp. 272–92. See also Margaret P. Harvey, 'Trollope and Material Culture', in Deborah Denenholz Morse, Margaret Markwick and Mark W. Turner (eds), *The Routledge Research Companion to Anthony Trollope* (Abingdon: Routledge, 2017), pp. 111–19.
5. J. Thomson and Adolphe Smith, *Street Life in London* (London: Sampson Low, Marston, Searle, & Rivington, 1877), p. 43.
6. Charles Dickens, *Bleak House* (Oxford: Oxford University Press, 2008), p. 61. For rag recycling to make paper in general, see Mark Kurlansky, *Paper: Paging Through History* (New York and London: W. W. Norton, 2016), pp. 169–71; pp. 245–8; for rag recycling, paper, and *Bleak House*, see Patrick Chappell, 'Paper Routes: *Bleak House*, Rubbish Theory, and the Character Economy of Realism', *ELH*, 80 (2013): pp. 783–810.
7. Thomson and Smith, *Street Life*, p. 43.
8. See N. C. Gee, *Shoddy and Mungo Manufacture* (London: Emmott & Co., 1950), p. v.
9. Samuel Jubb, *A History of the Shoddy Trade: Its Rise, Progress, and Present Position* (London: Houlton and Wright, 1860), p. 4. Jubb was co-partner with his brother Joseph in the family firm, Joseph Jubb and Sons, of Bank Foot Mill, Batley.
10. Peter Lund Simmonds, *Waste Products and Undeveloped Substances: Or, Hints for Enterprise in Neglected Fields* (London: Robert Hardwicke, 1862), pp. 1–2. See further Timothy

Cooper, 'Peter Lund Simmonds and the Political Ecology of "Waste Utilisation" in Victorian Britain', *Technology and Culture*, 52.1 (2011): pp. 21–44.

11. See two excellent treatments (the first by an ecological historian, the second by a literary eco-critic), Andreas Malm, *Fossil Capital. The Rise of Steam Power and the Roots of Global Warming* (London and New York: Verso, 2016), and Jesse Oak Taylor, *The Sky of Our Manufacture. The London Fog in British Fiction from Dickens to Woolf* (Charlottesville and London: University of Virginia Press, 2016).

12. Tim Cooper, 'Modernity and the Politics of Waste in Britain', in Sverker Sörlin and Paul Warde (eds), *Nature's End: History and the Environment* (Basingstoke: Palgrave Macmillan, 2009), pp. 247–72 (p. 247).

13. John Scanlan, *On Garbage* (London: Reaktion Books, 2005), pp. 56–88.

14. Cooper, 'Modernity and the Politics of Waste', p. 247.

15. 'Shaddy Cloth', *Vermont Patriot* (4 February 1859). Reprinted from the *Hartford Courant*.

16. Susan Strasser, *Waste and Want. A Social History of Trash* (New York: Metropolitan Books, 1999), p. 19.

17. Susan A. Stewart, *On Longing: Narratives of the Miniature, the Gigantic, the Souvenir, the Collection* (Baltimore: Johns Hopkins University Press, 1984), p. 14.

18. For the history of the shoddy trade in Yorkshire, see in particular J. C. Malin, 'The West Riding Recovered Wool Industry, ca. 1813–1939', unpublished PhD thesis (University of York, 1979), and Hanna Rose Shell, 'Shoddy heap: a material history between waste and manufacture', *History and Technology*, 30.4 (2014): pp. 374–94.

19. For details of the controversy surrounding the attribution of the invention, see <http://www.maggieblanck.com/Land/Jubb.html> (last accessed 9 September 2015).

20. Malin cites E. Partridge, *Origins: A Short Etymological Dictionary of Modern English* (1861), p. 617 and *Chambers Encyclopedia* (1891), vol. 9, p. 414. Also see the *Oxford English Dictionary*.

21. Henry Mayhew, *London Labour and the London Poor: A Cyclopaedia of the Condition and Earnings of Those That Will Work, Those That Cannot Work, and Those That Will Not Work*, 3 vols (London: Griffin, Bohn, and Company, 1851), vol. 2, p. 30. Repurposed woollens were but one, relatively small, aspect of the West Riding wool textile industry: for the bigger picture, see Pat Hudson, *The Genesis of Industrial Capital. A Study of the West Riding wool textile industry c. 1750–1850* (Cambridge: Cambridge University Press, 1986).

22. Mayhew, *London Labour*, vol. 2, p. 35

23. Unsigned article, 'Shoddy, Chalk, and Jonathan', *All the Year Round* (27 July 1872), pp. 246–9 (p. 247).

24. Karl Marx, *Capital: A Critique of Political Economy*, ed. Friedrich Engels, revised from 4th German edition (New York: The Modern Library, 1906), p. 274.

25. 'Shoddy, Chalk, and Jonathan', p. 247.

26. Lara Kriegel, 'Culture and the Copy: Calico, Capitalism, and Copyright of Designs in Early Victorian Britain', *Journal of British Studies*, 43.2 (April 2004): pp. 233–65 (p. 235).

27. Anthony Trollope, *Ralph the Heir*, 3 vols (London: Hurst and Blackett, 1871), vol. 1, ch. 5, p. 79.

28. Anthony Trollope, 'The Hunting Farmer', *Hunting Sketches*. Reprinted from the *Pall Mall Gazette* (London: Chapman and Hall, 1865), pp. 53–4.

29. Anthony Trollope, *Sir Harry Hotspur of Humblethwaite* (London: Chapman and Hall, 1877), ch. 2, p. 20.

30. Anthony Trollope, *Phineas Redux* (Oxford: Oxford University Press, 2011), ch. 14, p. 295.

31. W. S. Gilbert, *An Entirely Original Comic Opera in Two Acts entitled The Gondoliers or the King of Barataria* (Philadelphia: John Church, 1889), p. 35. First produced 12 July 1889, Savoy Theatre, London.

32. [Anthony Trollope], 'An Essay on Carlylism; Containing the Very Melancholy Story of a Shoddy Maker and his Mutinous Maid-Servant', *Saint Pauls Magazine*, 1 (1867): pp. 296–8.
33. Samuel Smiles, *Thrift* (London: John Murray, 1875), p. 223.
34. William Morris, *Clarion* (19 November 1892), as quoted in E. P. Thompson, *William Morris: Romantic to Revolutionary* (London: Pantheon Books, 1977), p. 108.
35. Trollope, 'Essay on Carlylism', p. 304.
36. [Thomas Carlyle], 'Biography', *Fraser's Magazine*, 5 (April 1832): p. 255. One should note, however, that with characteristic ludic duplicity, Carlyle invented the Professor Gottfried Sauerteig who allegedly uttered these words: it's unclear whether Trollope was alert to Carlyle's own invention of this fictitious literary commentator.
37. Trollope, 'Essay on Carlylism', p. 305.
38. Dorothy Parker, *Dorothy Parker* (New York: The Viking Library, 1944), p. 322.
39. George Eliot, *Impressions of Theophrastus Such* (London: William Blackwood and Sons, 1879), p. 195. Sir Leslie Stephen, *Essays on Freethinking and Plainspeaking* (London: Longmans, Green, and Co., 1873), p. 156.
40. See Patrick Joyce, *Visions of the People: Industrial England and the Question of Class, c. 1848–1914* (Cambridge: Cambridge University Press, 1993), p. 260. Arthur Wood, *'Shoddy': A Yorkshire Tale of Home*, 3 vols (London: Tinsley Brothers, 1877).
41. 'Shoddy, Chalk, and Jonathan', p. 247.
42. Jubb, *History*, p. 52.
43. See Régis de Trobriand, *Four Years with the Army of the Potomac* (Boston: Tichnor and Company, 1889), pp. 134–6. The Civil War appears not to have damaged the English shoddy industry: the substantially decreased amount of cotton being imported led to a stimulation of the production of shoddy and mungo products to take its place. See O. Greeves, 'The Effects of the American Civil War on the Linen, Woollen and Worsted Industries of the UK', unpublished PhD thesis (University of Bristol, 1969).
44. Henry Morford, *The Days of Shoddy: A Novel of the Great Rebellion in 1861* (Philadelphia: T. B. Peterson & Brothers, 1863), p. 174.
45. See Gary L. Bunker and John Appel, '"Shoddy", Anti-Semitism and the Civil War', *American Jewish History*, 82.1 (1994): pp. 43–71. In addition to supplying numerous examples of how the idea of shoddy permeated American popular culture during the Civil War, Bunker and Appel argue for the anti-Semitism at play in the attacks on profiteering merchants – as with the figures of 'Shoddy the Jewish Tailor', 'Mr Shoddy', and 'Shoddy the Vulture' who could be found in the pages of Frank Leslie's *Illustrated Newspaper*. See also Myron O. Stachiw, 'For the Sake of Art and Commerce: Slavery, Antislavery, and Northern Industry', in Martin H. Blatt and David R. Roediger (eds), *The Meaning of Slavery in the North* (London: Routledge, 1999), pp. 33–44.
46. Adam D. Mendelsohn, *The Rag Race: How Jews Sewed Their Way to Success in America and the British Empire* (New York: New York University Press, 2014), p. 170.
47. Unsigned column, 'A Choke in Time', *Vanity Fair* (23 November 1861), p. 230.
48. *Literary World* (16 December 1882), p. 456.
49. W. B. Estell, 'Shoddy', *Tariff Reform* (October 1892): vol. 5.16, p. 11. The most relevant tariff was that imposed by the Morrill Tariff Act of 1861.
50. Anthony Trollope, *The Duke's Children* (Harmondsworth: Penguin, 1995), ch. 12, p. 412.
51. Unsigned review, 'The Belton Estate', *Saturday Review*, 21 (3 February 1866): p. 141. For a discussion of the *Saturday Review*'s attack on the 'mechanical' aspects of Trollope's writing, see David Skilton, *Anthony Trollope and his Contemporaries: A Study in the Theory and Conventions of Mid-Victorian Fiction* (Basingstoke: Macmillan, 1972), pp. 53–7.
52. Henry James, 'Anthony Trollope', *Century Magazine*, 26.3 (July 1883): p. 385.
53. [Henry James], *Nation* (28 September 1865): p. 409.
54. Hugh Walpole, *Anthony Trollope* (New York: The Macmillan Co., 1928), p. 53.

55. N. John Hall, 'Anthony Trollope: Honest and True', *Notes and Queries*, 217 (November 1972): p. 416.
56. Laurie Langbauer, *Novels of Everyday Life: The Series in English Fiction* (Ithaca, NY: Cornell University Press, 1999), p. 97.
57. Elizabeth R. Epperly, *Patterns of Repetition in Trollope* (Washington, DC: Catholic University of America Press, 1989), pp. 1–2.
58. Jonathan Farina, '"As a Matter of Course". Trollope's Ordinary Realism', Morse, Markwick and Turner (eds), *Routledge Research Companion*, pp. 142–53.
59. Anthony Trollope, *An Autobiography* (New York: Harper & Brothers, 1883), ch. 6, p. 97.
60. Jubb, *History*, p. 24.

INDEX

Page numbers in *italics* refer to illustrations.

EU representative:
Easy Access System Europe
Mustamäe tee 50, 10621 Tallinn, Estonia
Gpsr.requests@easproject.com

www.ingramcontent.com/pod-product-compliance
Lightning Source LLC
Chambersburg PA
CBHW081401090726
47908CB00012B/2752